D0857225

The Story of Boogie-Woogie

A Left Hand Like God

Peter J. Silvester

THE SCARECROW PRESS, INC.
Lanham, Maryland • Toronto • Plymouth, UK
2009

SCARECROW PRESS, INC.

Published in the United States of America
by Scarecrow Press, Inc.
A wholly owned subsidary of
The Rowman & Littlefield Publishing Group, Inc.
4501 Forbes Boulevard, Suite 200, Lanham, Maryland 20706
www.scarecrowpress.com

Estover Road
Plymouth PL6 7PY
United Kingdom

British Library Cataloguing in Publication Information Available

Library of Congress Cataloging-in-Publication Data

Silvester, Peter J.
  The story of boogie-woogie : a left hand like God / Peter J. Silvester. —
[2nd ed.]
    p. cm.
  Rev. ed. of: A left hand like God, [1989].
  Includes bibliographical references, discographical references, and index.
  ISBN 978-0-8108-6924-0 (hardcover : alk. paper) — ISBN 978-0-8108-6933-2
(ebook)
  1. Piano music (Boogie-woogie)—History and criticism. I. Silvester, Peter J.
Left hand like God. II. Title.
  ML747.S54 2009
  786.2'165—dc22   2009005090

Manufactured in the United States of America.

This present edition is dedicated to the memory of

Pete Johnson (1904),
Meade Lux Lewis (1905),
and
Albert Ammons (1907)

—members of the Boogie-Woogie Trio,
the centennial of whose births fell in the period 2004 to 2007.

Contents

Preface

I began writing this book in 1980 because I felt that the story of boogie-woogie, and the myriad piano players who practiced it, had never been satisfactorily written. In 1982, or thereabouts, I learned that Denis Harbinson, a professor of music at University College in Cardiff, was also preparing to write a book on the same subject. We corresponded and sent each other articles and reviews. Sadly, Denis died in 1983 and left behind research notes analyzing some of the recordings of various pianists, a detailed and well-documented chapter on the lumber industry, and the outline of another chapter on nomenclature and definition. I had already completed about seven chapters when I heard of his death. It seemed pointless to ignore the groundwork that Denis had completed, and so, with the encouragement of his widow, I read his notes and found that most of them could be adapted and incorporated into what I had already written. In doing so, I was conscious that his musical examples gave an enhanced credibility to the work, as well as adding to the unfolding story. The inspirational element in the title was also provided by Denis and was taken from a description by Eubie Blake of William Turk's piano playing, that he had a left hand like God (reported in R. Blesh and H. Janis, *They All Played Ragtime*, published by the Jazz Book Club in arrangement with Sidgwick and Jackson, London, 1960).

It would have been impossible to begin writing a book on the subject of boogie-woogie without the continuing help and support of many record collectors and pianists actively playing and recording in the boogie-woogie style. In the early stages of gathering information about the topic, invaluable help was given by three people: Dan Gunderman, a pianist and collector from Milwaukee; Richard Lindaman from Minnesota, whose intelligent and perceptive comments I came to respect and appreciate as our correspondence continued; and, from England, Bob Tomlinson, the record collector supreme, who introduced me to the work of the European pianists. All three helped to get the project under way and without their regular tapes and letters, the book would have been stillborn. They also gave moral support during those black moments when I began to doubt the wisdom of my undertaking.

I was fortunate to make contact with Tom Harris from Fort Worth, Texas, who introduced me to Ben Conroy of Austin, Texas. Both of these men were good exponents of boogie-woogie and had met pianists Albert Ammons and Pete Johnson personally. They generously shared their reminiscences with me as well as provided material and photographs from their personal collections. Through their introductions I was able to make contact with Phil Kiely and Dick Mushlitz, a founding member of the Salty Dogs Jazz Band, both of whom knew the Yanceys and made frequent visits to their apartment. Dr. John Steiner sent his taped recollections of his contacts with Albert Ammons and Jimmy Yancey. Then there were the pianists: Charles Booty, a boogie-woogie pianist and raconteur from Tennessee who shared his experiences; Bob Seeley of Detroit, a brilliant interpreter of boogie-woogie and other styles, whose long friendship with pianist Meade Lux Lewis was faithfully recalled for me; and Axel Zwingenberger, from Germany, an international artist and one of the foremost exponents of boogie-woogie today who advised me on historical and distinctive features of the genre.

Edsel Ammons, the son of Albert Ammons, gave me the essential living link with the past. Now a retired bishop in Columbus (Ohio), his wise and apposite comments enabled me to sort out the truth from the fiction surrounding famous people.

David Home, the then librarian at the University of Exeter, responded with tolerance to my early requests for access to tape recordings, transcriptions, magazines, and books held in the excellent jazz and blues section for which he was responsible.

These were the major sources of inspiration for the initial writing. I like to think that our joint endeavors sewed the seeds of a lasting friendship.

Twenty years on, I can say that the reception given to the first edition of the book by piano players, patrons, and record collectors of boogie-woogie music has been most gratifying. Newspaper and magazine reviews have been predominantly supportive of the book, not least because it was a first attempt to document the history and evolution of the piano style.

The quest for the direction in which any new writing on the subject might take was eventually decided after discarding my initial thought of a biography of Meade Lux Lewis—Pete Johnson's own story had already been produced in the admirable *Pete Johnson Story* by Hans J. Mauerer in 1965 and Albert Ammons's life revealed in *Boogie-Woogie Stomp* written by Christopher Page in 1997; or of writing about the rising phenomenon of the European boogie-woogie pianists. Reading again some of the reviews of the book convinced me that although much valuable ground had been covered by listening to many hours of live and recorded music, collating evidence from disparate visual, oral, and written sources for the historical background and personal judgments in the book, there were still gaps. In the years since the completion of the initial study, new information had become available about the lives of pianists, their movements, recordings, and the social settings in which they lived and worked; and some had not even been included in the first writing. It became clear that what was required was a review, expansion, and reordering of the original text.

Consequently, more analysis of the boogie-woogie recordings of various pianists has been included within the book in order to align them more closely with the biographical information and to place them in a temporal context. The sources of these recordings have either been vinyl long-playing records (LPs) or compact discs (CDs) in the belief that any keen collector will want to hunt them down from secondhand sources if they no longer exist in company catalogs. This has resulted in the discarding of the limited selected discography of the first edition for a more substantial and inclusive listing of recordings.

One criticism was that the parameters of the original study were too narrowly defined by not considering the influence of boogie-woogie piano playing on rhythm and blues and other musical styles. This has now been addressed by examining the growth of rhythm and blues on the West Coast of America and New Orleans and been included in a newly written chapter. Coterminous with this study of rhythm and blues, listening to the work of pianists Maceo Merriweather, Otis Spann, and others associated with urban blues bands convinced me that their deployment of boogie-woogie was critical in helping to lay down the pulsatingly electric beat of these groups; and coincidentally, to sustain the boogie-woogie style after it had peaked in the immediate post–World War II period. A new chapter on pianists in blues bands has been added that also considers the work of other, mainly blues pianists, whose piano styles have been substantially shaped by boogie-woogie. Finally, the current interest being shown in "'classical" boogie-woogie by European pianists was deserving of detailed examination and review. Pursuing this topic led me to write of the early appearances of the genre in Britain and several other European countries. The chapter on the role of the national and independent companies in recording boogie-woogie music has been rewritten and lengthened.

With an expanded text and seeking fluidity and conciseness in the writing, many of the extracts quoted directly from other sources that were included in the first edition have been removed and their gist produced in the text of this edition. The references in the chapter endnotes are, as a result, more comprehensive and greatly improved for other researchers to use. A bibliography, significant magazine articles on boogie-woogie, and useful record liner notes have been added.

I sincerely hope that both new readers and those who have read the earlier edition will find stimulation and satisfaction from these attempts to record the fascinating story of boogie-woogie. If that is so, I rest my pen happy in the knowledge that the genre continues to thrive.

Since completing the rewriting, I have to report the sad news that pianist Charlie Booty and pianist and collector Phil Kiely have both passed away. The death of Tom Harris following a long illness occurred as this edition was in preparation.

Peter J. Silvester
May 2009

Acknowledgments

Assistance with transferring the first edition onto computer in preparation for writing this edition was provided by Dr. Edward Neather and Otter Computers of Budleigh Salterton. Renée Camus of Scarecrow Press proved to be a patient editor. My grateful thanks to all three. I have been assisted in my task by the generous and unstinting support of numerous collectors who have unconditionally allowed me access to their letters, photographs, and memorabilia.

Correspondence with the author was taped recollections provided by John Bentley, Charlie Booty, Phil Kiely, Richard Lindaman, Jan Montgomery, Dr. Ray Nelson, William Russell, Dr. John Steiner, Ralph Sutton, Ernest Virgo (all deceased); and Edsel Ammons, Denise Buckner with Michel Hortig, Charlie Castner, Michel Chaigne, Ben Conroy, Mr. and Mrs. John Dawkins, Steve Dolins, Frank Giles, Dan Gunderman, Tom Harris, Dick Mushlitz, Konrad Nowakowski, Christopher Page, Michael Pointon, Bob Seeley, Bob Tomlinson, William Wagner, and Axel Zwingenberger.

My thanks for permission to use the following: extracts from interviews by Don Hill and Dave Mangurian, "Meade Lux Lewis," *Cadence* (October 1987), copyright 1987 *Cadence Jazz Magazine* (www.cadence building .com); extracts from Ronald P. Harwood, "Mighty Tight Woman: The Thomas Family and Classic Blues," *Storyville*, no. 17 (June/July 1968); letter from Estelle Yancey and photographs of Jimmy and Estelle Yancey and Clarence Lofton from William Russell's estate by agreement with William Wagner; reminiscences of Grace and Jack Dawkins on their impressions of Jimmy and Estelle Yancey; taped interviews with Rufus Perryman and Roosevelt Sykes conducted by John Bentley and photographs of Jack Dupree, Rufus Perryman, and Roosevelt Sykes from his collection bequeathed to Dick Mushlitz, by agreement with Mushlitz; advertisement for the "Apartment" at the White House Club, St. Paul, Minnesota, from Bob Seeley; advertisements for Frenchy's, Café Society clubs, other memorabilia, and a photograph of Bob Zurke from Dan Gunderman; Carnegie Hall programs dated April 23, 1941, and April 11, 1943, from Carnegie Hall Archives; covers of the sheet music "The Fives" and "Hop Scop Blues" from Performing Arts Special Collection Library, University of California, Los Angeles; selection from bass transcriptions included in Paul Oliver, *The Story of the Blues* (London, Barrie & Rockliffe, 1969) by agreement with Don Kincaid, who also prepared the basses in the appendix and the musical examples in the text; inclusion of adapted notes on recordings and the lumber industry, bass patterns, and musical examples from the late Denis Harbinson by agreement with Edna M. Harbinson; photographs of Buster Pickens (Flyright Records) and Henry Brown from Paul Oliver, *Conversation with the Blues*, 2nd edition (London, University of Cambridge Press, 1997) by agreement with Paul Oliver; photograph of Clarence Smith Jr., from Eva Henning; photograph of Jabbo Williams and Robert McCoy and sketch of Pete Johnson by Harold Lehman from Konrad Nowakowski; extract from letter sent by Charlie Castner to the author; photograph of Doug Suggs at Yanceys' apartment from Dick Mushlitz; photographs of records "Pinetop's Boogie-Woogie" and "The Rocks" from Francis Wilford Smith; record cover of *Heavy Timbre* from Steven Dolins of the Siren Record Company; photographs of Meade Lux Lewis's appearance in the film *New Orleans*, Pete Johnson, Jimmy Yancey with Charlie Spand, and the Boogie-Woogie Trio at Café Society Downtown from Duncan Scheidt; photograph of a young Albert Ammons and Café Society Downtown from Christopher Page; photograph of Robert Shaw from Ben Conroy; photograph of Martin Pyrker from Patrick Smet; photograph of Jay McShann from Andre Hobus; photograph of Pete Johnson in St. Louis from Tom Harris; photograph of Meade Lux Lewis from Denise Buckner; photograph of J. H. Shayne and letters from Estelle Yancey from Phil Kiely; photograph of Mary Lou Williams from *Jazz Journal International*; a copy of the flyer, "I Saw Pinetop Spit Blood" from *Downbeat* magazine. Agreement was sought from Jan Montgomery to re-use a photograph of her husband Little Brother Montgomery, but she is now deceased.

Census and other sources: Twelfth Census of the United States 1900; Thirteenth Census of the United States 1910; Fourteenth Census of the United States 1920; Fifteenth Census of the United States 1930 and Alabama State Assistance. Data from these concerning Clarence "Pinetop" Smith and his family were kindly provided by the Troy Public Library Service, Alabama, United States.

The information about the recordings of pianists and other musicians included in the text was obtained from or confirmed by B. Rust (compiler), *Jazz Records 1897–1942* (Chigwell, UK: Storyville Publications, 1970) and R. Dixon and J. Godrich (compilers), *Blues and Gospel Records 1902–1943* (Chigwell, UK: Storyville Publications, 1982).

The accuracy of the chapter end notes would not have been possible without the continuing assistance of Konrad Nowakowski, whose archive provided the fine detail necessary for completing the references. The majority of references have been fully completed.

A special thanks to *Downbeat* magazine for the invaluable socio-historical and musical information provided between its covers on the period circa 1935 to 1950.

Part One

THE BEGINNINGS

1

Boogie-Woogie: Early Appearances and Names by Which It Was Known

Toward the end of the nineteenth century and in the early years of the twentieth, as much as evidence will allow, American blues music spawned a noisy offspring that was eventually given the name of boogie-woogie. It was, and is, a primitive and rhythmical style of piano playing that achieved its zenith during World War II, in the early 1940s. At this time it was heard incessantly on the radio, in concerts, and on film sound tracks. Solo pianists of all shades played it, from Meade Lux Lewis, an original performer in the style; through Bob Zurke, a skilled technician who learned boogie-woogie with the Bob Crosby Band; to Jose Iturbi, a classical pianist of some repute. Most of the leaders of the top swing bands commissioned novelty boogie-woogie compositions that featured their pianists. Tommy Lineham played "Chips Boogie-Woogie" with the small group of the same name drawn from the Woody Herman Band, while Mary Lou Williams did a similar job for the Andy Kirk Band on numbers such as "Little Joe from Chicago." In its most commercial form, lyrics were added to its rhythms to produce popular songs with the endearing titles of "The Boogie-Woogie Bugle Boy of Company B" and "Scrub Me Mama with a Boogie Beat," which climbed high in the hit parade when interpreted by the Andrews Sisters, the most successful close harmony vocal group of the period. By the end of the forties, however, boogie-woogie had slipped quietly out of public favor, a victim of dilution, commercial exploitation, and overexposure.

The style, which started in the southern and midwestern states of America, is attributed to untutored black piano players who emphasized the rhythmical properties of the piano instead of the more usual melodic ones in their playing. Boogie-woogie music was fashioned from the blues, which, in turn, had its roots in the chants and field hollers of work gangs as they sang to relieve the monotony of laying rail tracks, quarrying stone, or plowing the land. The southern states were the setting for the early blues because of the high proportion of newly emancipated black slaves living in that region. They took their musical heritage with them when they eventually uprooted and moved to the cities of the Midwest and northern states in search of work—a migration that began in the early years of the twentieth century. The close lineage of boogie-woogie and the blues, its reported appearance in southern states and later Kansas, St. Louis, and Chicago is not, therefore, difficult to explain.

The traditional pattern of the blues is one of twelve bars, but less common versions of eight and sixteen bars are also played. From the earliest known days, blues were sung with a guitar accompaniment that provided a rhythmical backing and fill-in phrases between the verses. This pattern continues today, with the guitar player alternating between laying down a solid ground rhythm of short repetitive phrases (ostinato) of single notes and chords in the lower registers of the instrument, and embellishing the singer's sentiments—with extemporized runs, trills, and chords—in the medium and high registers. The blues is a simple yet effective musical form that can be played at many levels ranging from the elementary chording of the amateur musician to the complex and evocative sounds produced by the musician with superior technical skills. The lyrics are often sad, sometimes humorous or aggressively assertive, and are normally concerned with human frailties associated with love, loneliness, sex, drink, and poverty. The themes sometimes take their inspiration from catastrophes and significant events in the singer's life. The great Mississippi Delta flood and the tornado that struck St. Louis during the past century have been both commemorated in blues compositions. The blues runs the whole gamut of human emotions and experience.

At one stage removed from boogie-woogie, which is essentially a solo performance, the piano accompaniment to blues singing was a direct copy of the guitar player's technique. Treble phrases on the piano replaced the fill-in passages on the guitar, and the ostinato ground rhythm of the guitar was replicated on the piano by similar figures played deep in the bass. Another left-hand pattern that was sometimes used alternated on the beat between chords in the bass and middle registers of the piano. Known as stride bass, it was initially adapted from the syncopated stylings of ragtime pianists. (*Stride* is the term reserved for the eastern-coast school of piano playing that was centered in New York and exemplified in the works of Thomas Waller, James P. Johnson, Willie "The Lion" Smith, and Luckey Roberts.) Stride basses were not popular with unschooled pianists because of the superior technique required for playing them. Most pianists could get by when called on to play a stride bass for a blues, but they were on surer ground playing a rhythmically acceptable accompaniment in which the left hand was anchored in the bass notes as in boogie-woogie.

Boogie-woogie gradually became recognized as a distinct piano form as it evolved from its secondary function as a blues accompaniment to a solo performance. The subtle embellishments supporting the singer's lyrics were discarded and replaced in the treble by short repeated phrases, runs, sharply struck chords, repeated single notes, and trills that emphasized rhythm at the expense of melody. Where the guitar player switched between playing in the bass and treble ranges of his instrument, the pianist was able to produce a continuous series of varied and contrasting tones at the same time in both registers, each hand working independently of the other—a defining attribute of boogie-woogie playing. The left hand would endlessly repeat an ostinato bass pattern, usually of eight beats to the bar in the three blues chord positions (C, F, and G in the key of C), while the right hand supported or played across the bass rhythm, and in so doing, produced complex cross rhythms. Although dating from a later period than the embryonic stages under consideration, Delta bluesman Robert Johnson shows in his guitar playing the kind of deep ostinato rhythms that early boogie-woogie pianists copied from guitarists in numbers like "I Believe I'll Dust My Broom" (later recorded by pianist Eddie Boyd), "Kind Hearted Woman," and "Rambling on My Mind," all laid down in 1936 in San Antonio, Texas. A minority of boogie-woogie compositions are "blue" in tone and feeling—notably those of Jimmy Yancey and Montana Taylor—but the mood engendered by boogie-woogie playing is generally different from the blues. A solid rumbling tone is endemic to the music, giving it an exciting quality for both listener and player. The blues in its various moods evokes sadness; boogie-woogie at whatever tempi transmits a raw, buoyant energy. William (Bill) Russell considered it rhythmically less complex than some forms of African music but more rhythmically complex than the conventional style of jazz piano with the repetitive bass patterns constantly contrasting with the varying rhythms of the treble to produce galvanizing polyrhythms. Further, good boogie-woogie generates a distinctive swing not found in the imitators whose playing, although possessing an excellent tempo, sounds dull and ineffectual.[1]

Although the music is quintessentially rhythmical, a cause-and-effect link with African drumming and racial memory patterns brought to America by slaves transported from Africa is probably too simplistic for explaining the dynamic qualities of boogie-woogie. However, it is considered by some to be the purest musical example of African elements merging with a culturally mixed music: The result of its mainly rhythmical African heritage combined with ragtime, an American phenomenon, is music that, though not found in Africa, has all the qualities of music from that continent.[2]

While recognizing that boogie-woogie was partly formed by integrating these two cultural elements, it does not fully explain the rich and diverse process that must have occurred temporally rather than through some kind of "big bang." For a clearer understanding of how boogie-woogie finally emerged from chrysalis to unique piano style played by black Americans, we have to draw parallels with other, better documented changes that occurred in African-American culture and make considered hypotheses.

The eclectic nature of African-American culture, it has been suggested, is the result of the adaptation and reshaping of the music from one culture to meet the aesthetic requirements and social needs of African-Americans.[3] An example of this would be the introduction of syncopated rhythms (African inspired) into the piano playing and singing of (European) hymns in black churches and their later cross-currents with secular music. Similar processes occurred in other art forms when the stylized European dance steps of jigs and reels were modified and emerged, in the 1890s, as the more rhythmical cakewalk. By the 1920s, many of the regional songs of African-Americans residing in isolated turpentine and logging camps of Florida had begun to disappear and were being replaced by songs learned from the radio and records. Popular blues of the day were taken up enthusiastically in these and other black communities as people became more dependent on the ubiquitous phonograph for their entertainment. Interestingly, the original words and music were frequently modified to reflect local circumstances, so producing a new and vital form of the music. The process of acculturation is a two-way journey, however, with many European art forms benefiting from African-American initiatives—not least jazz music itself. Similarly, the uninhibited expressive qualities of the dances created by Katherine Dunham and her troupe, particularly active in New York in the 1940s, had a beneficial releasing impact on more stylized, European dance forms.

So, how does the foregoing relate to the birth and flowering of the boogie-woogie piano style? To begin with, it helps us to realize that it probably passed through several evolutionary phases. Change is multilayered, involving exposure to, and interaction with, many influences dating, in this case, probably from the end of the American Civil War (1861–1865) and the post-Reconstruction period (1865–1867) when black slaves were enfranchised. The first impact of this would have resulted in a greater freedom of expression and creativity, no longer dictated by the cultural constraints of the former white slave owners. However, the hereditary African heritage would have been continuously susceptible to modification by the predominantly European culture, albeit in a less deterministic way than previously. Within this framework, one of the social requirements for the mainly poor urban and rural communities, in which African-Americans lived, would be for a simple music with a powerful rhythm for entertainment and dancing. Whereas the guitar supported the subtleties and vocal expression of the blues singer, its role would have been modified when providing the stimulus and rhythm for dancing, even to the extent of employing two guitars: one laying down a deep and steady ostinato ground rhythm, while the second filled in over the rhythm with chords, runs, and other devices. Before amplification, this ensured that the music could be heard by the dancers. It would be a short step to replace two guitars with a piano, for producing the same effect. As dancing became increasingly popular and halls got bigger, a piano with its front cover removed could reach all corners of a noisy dance area. The potent mix of alcohol, release from grinding work, for a few hours at least, and both sexes looking for a good time meant that the musical demands on pianists were few. They had to be able to play fast numbers for dancers to "stomp" and slow drags for the more sexual "belly-rubs." Early boogie-woogie pianists who provided the music for these social activities brought an untutored approach to their playing, uncluttered by the European traditions of a learned technique or "set" compositions. Their own creativity and its expression were paramount, stimulated and sustained by the sounds and rhythms of gospel church music, guitar blues, and popular music of the day usually played by ragtime pianists or from piano rolls. All went into the melting pot that finally produced the boogie-woogie piano styles of today.

Roberts and Amouroux[4] draw attention to the similarity between the repetitive xylophone rhythms produced by native Africans and boogie-woogie basses that is more of a subtle and melodic parallel than a singular cause-and-effect relationship with the rhythms of African drumming. Indeed, boogie-woogie does have certain melodic features that are frequently omitted from its analysis. Trains provided endless themes, as it was possible to represent the haunting sound of whistles, expresses romping along on a full head of steam, wheels clattering over points, and, of course, the insistent rhythm of the driving wheels. A recording by Lemuel Fowler, "Express Train Blues" (1929), which might be expected to be one of the earliest of a train boogie, turns out not to possess any of these qualities but is a droll jazz piece complete with "real" train noises. However, examples of a kind of musical onomatopoeia can be heard on many recordings of train numbers: Clarence Lofton's "Streamline Train," Charles Davenport's "Cow Cow Blues," Wesley Wallace's "Number Twenty-Nine," and later compositions by Meade Lux Lewis such as "Honky Tonk Train Blues," "Six Wheel Chaser," and "Chicago Flyer."

Such a preoccupation with trains is seen by Alan Lomax as having important psychological benefits, raising optimism for a better life as the piano was changed by untrained African-Americans into a complex, rhythmical train that offered the prospect of a joyous independence for its listeners.[5] Whereas the guitar and piano accompaniment to blues singers provided an emotional bedrock for expressing many of the unhappy circumstances in their lives, boogie-woogie piano in its various train manifestations promised an escape to a better life further on down the line for many African-Americans.

Bugle calls were sometimes used either as choruses in the melody or as "breaks" between choruses. The best-known example is provided in Jimmy Yancey's "Yancey's Bugle Call"—a piece designed completely around a bugle call motif; other pianists who made use of them were Montana Taylor in "Lowdown Blues," Jabo Williams in "Jab's Blues," and Albert Ammons in "Reveille Boogie."

The word *"chimes"* was originally thought to be a synonym for boogie-woogie, but an examination of two numbers, "Chimes Blues" by Davenport and "Eastern Chimes Blues" by Henry Brown, suggests that this is not so. Despite the former having an occasional passage or two of walking bass, neither piece could be said to fall into a typical boogie-woogie form. In fact, the complete melodic structure of Brown's piece is built around a descending sequence of chiming chords. Chime effects were sometimes used to introduce a number, as in Ammons's "Shout for Joy" in which the softly delicate treble chimes of the introduction contrast with, and give emphasis to, the powerful bass. Ammons also employed the same effect in his recording of "Mecca Flat Blues."

In examining the evolution of boogie-woogie, we already have it on record that Chicago pianists Albert Ammons and Meade Lux Lewis learned their early pianistic skills from a player piano (see chapter 15), and there is a strong possibility that earlier exponents of the style acquired at least some of their technique from the player piano, also known as a Pianola.[6] These instruments were popular in the early 1900s and provided the only outlet for hearing "recorded" music through the variety of tunes imprinted on piano rolls, preceding the popular shellac recordings by some years. They could be found in bars, clubs, and any places where people gathered to socialize; the precursor of the jukebox, the player piano churned out ragtime, blues, and popular songs of the day. Jelly Roll Morton recalled their impact in New Orleans in about 1902, when it seemed that every household possessed one and their sounds could be heard in the city throughout the night and day.

The self-taught boogie-woogie tyros would have absorbed the tonal properties as well as the tunes emanating from the mechanical player piano. For example, in the absence of the sustaining pedal, which could not be used with a player piano, tremolos and trills brought light and shade to a performance by extending the time that chords could be held, which is still an important feature of the boogie-woogie player's technique. Another similarity is the sharp percussive tone of both. Whereas the sudden expulsion of air in the player piano causes the hammers to strike the wires sharply, the boogie-woogie player employs a firm finger technique for obtaining a richly varied rhythmical effect in his playing.

Typical of many of the early practitioners of boogie-woogie was the unrecorded and unschooled pianist William Turk from Baltimore. Probably born around 1866, he was a massive three hundred pounds in weight and nearly six feet tall. He died in about 1911. Turk had a large girth that hampered his technique to the extent that he had difficulty playing chords for ragtime in the mid-range of the keyboard, so he often introduced a walking bass much lower down. He would then play one note in the treble accompanied by four with his left hand, which was called "sixteen" but later became known as boogie-woogie. Eubie Blake was so impressed with Turk's forceful piano style that he said Turk possessed a left hand like God.[7]

From Blake's description it is clear that the style was not then called boogie-woogie. The first use of the term is claimed to be "Pinetop's Boogie-Woogie," a composition by Clarence Pinetop Smith and recorded on the Vocalion record label on December 29, 1928. Smith used the term both as a title and, in talking on the record, to infer music and dancing. The interesting question is what gave Smith the idea of naming his piece boogie-woogie? To answer this, one has to examine his background as a vaudevillian and a tap dancer. The "boogie-woogie" was a series of dance steps and the term was in use long before Pinetop's recording. Veteran dancer Joe Price is reported as saying that Rubber Legs Williams, when working with Bibby Grant's troupe of female dancers, brought it from the South in 1919 together with other "eccentric" dances, as they were called. They were all eventually adapted and used by chorus lines in the shows.[8]

Pinetop was undoubtedly familiar with the term *boogie-woogie* as it related to certain dance steps, some of which he may have used in his own dance routines in vaudeville. Having picked up the term, he enjoyed rolling it off his tongue, if interviews with his wife are to be believed, and used it for the title of his piece because it is concerned solely with telling the "little girl in the red dress" how to perform a particular kind of dance. What better term could there be than the onomatopoeic "boogie-woogie" for both the rhythmical, driving piano tune and the equally rambunctious dance? Additional evidence to support the notion that Pinetop drew on his vaudeville background comes from his use in the piece of another phrase, "shake that thing," as a direction to the dancer. A popular dance of the time, of which he would also have been aware, was named "Shake That Thing." It seems that Pinetop took the term *boogie-woogie* from one art form (dance) and applied it more generally to another art form (music). Because of the public's unfamiliarity with the expression, the name gave the appearance of originality, thereby contributing to the success of the record.

By the following year, other performers were doing the same thing and copying Smith's successful format on record. "Pitchin' Boogie" (1929) by Will Ezell similarly employed the term both as a title and, in talking on the record, to indicate dancing. His statement that "we're going to pitch the boogie right here" is possibly indicative of the term being used to mean a party. "Head Rag Hop" (1929) by Romeo Nelson used the term, in talking on record, to indicate dancing and "feeling" ("makes me feel so boogie-woogie"). In the 1929 recording of "Hastings Street," Charlie Spand (piano) and Blind Blake (guitar) inform us, through their patter, that the term *boogie-woogie* was used to mean either dancing or music in the city of Detroit. Also of interest is the reference made in three of the recordings to a girl (one of those dancing at these recorded re-creations of the barrelhouse or house rent party scene) in a colored dress. The color varies; in Pinetop's piece she wears a red dress. Clarence Smith's wife Sarah always maintained that the reference was to a red dress that she owned and that was a favorite with her husband. Romeo Nelson wishes to inspire a girl in a black dress while Will Ezell prefers his girl in a green one. A song entitled "Fat Fanny Stomp," recorded in 1930 by a little-known pianist, Jim Clarke, used several similar phrases in what appears to be a parody of Pinetop's tune. He also refers to doing the "Sally Long," a dance step not mentioned by Pinetop. The tradition established in these early recordings of associating the term with dancing continues today, so that "to boogie" means to dance. The wholesale adoption of the term for a style of piano playing may initially have been fortuitous, but it has now become accepted through common usage over the years.

Smith recorded two takes of his composition. The original, C 2726 A, was issued on Vocalion 1245 and has since been reissued many times. A second version, C 2726 B, was also released on Vocalion, and it is likely that only a small pressing was made, for, in its original form, it is still a very rare record. Apart from some different ordering in the piano choruses, the recordings can be identified by changes in Pinetop's patter. On Take A he introduces the dance choruses with the words, "Now I want all of you all to know this is Pinetop's Boogie-Woogie," whereas on Take B he says, "Now listen here all of you—this is my Pinetop strut. I want everyone dancing like I tell you." It is thus just conceivable that if Take B had been issued as the original version we should now have a different name for the boogie-woogie piano style.

A further confusing feature is the belief, held by some collectors, that the word used by Smith on Take B is *trouble* and not *strut*.[9] The first unissued recording session coupled "Pinetop's Blues" with "Pinetop's Troubles," and it has been inferred that Take B of "Pinetop's Boogie-Woogie" is really "Pinetop's Troubles." Although the evidence allows for such a conclusion, the insertion of *troubles* in the context of his patter about a dance does not make much sense. Opinions also differ about whether the word is *troubles* or *strut* on the aural evidence from the recording. Under the circumstances described, *strut* would seem to be a more appropriate word than *trouble*, denoting a dance of a particularly aggressive kind with sexual connotations, as in "strut that thing." Could it be perhaps that "Pinetop's Troubles" was an alternative take of "Pinetop's Blues"—the word suggests a blues—or a completely different blues composition that was never released?

The early boogie-woogie pianists entertained workers in the lumber, turpentine, and railroad industries situated in the southern states. Their stage was the barrelhouse, a crude building given its name from the liquor barrels supporting planks from which the rough liquor was served, with floor space for dancing, to the piano, and gambling. There is no doubt that in many instances, the barrelhouse also acted as a brothel. In less remote communities, boogie-woogie could be heard being played in roadside bars known as juke joints. When the piano players later moved to Chicago and other large conurbations in the 1920s, they provided the entertainment at house parties. As entertainers, pianists were required to give rudimentary directions to dancers as they played. As we have seen, there are several examples of piano solos on record illustrating a pattern of spoken directions that sometimes acted as "breaks" between choruses, as in "hold yourself." Breaks had two effects: They prepared the dancers for the next phase of the dance and they recharged the music by suspending the rhythm for a short time. It is in the latter capacity rather than the former that the break has been assimilated into contemporary boogie-woogie playing and has become one of its defining attributes.

The close interaction between pianists and their audiences was an essential ingredient in the growth of the boogie style and it accounted for much of the spontaneity and creativity. The dancer and the pianist each depended on the reactions and responses of the other for stimulation. Indeed, the removal of boogie from its sustaining environment may account, in part, for its gradual disappearance as a flourishing and developing art form; numbers that were first tried out and retried at rent parties in the twenties are still played today—evidence to some extent of an ossified art form. The social milieu of the house party, evoked by Romeo Nelson in "Head Rag Hop," appears to have largely disappeared by the early 1940s, coincidentally with the entrance of the United States into World

War II and the inevitable social and economic changes occurring at that time. In his strangely high-pitched voice, Nelson gives directions to the ghosts of many dancers who shuffled and gyrated together in dimly lit, smoke-filled tenement flats. Years later, Nelson said that he shaped and constructed his musical ideas at rent parties, explaining that as everyone was so drunk no one noticed if the keys were struck with fist or elbow. He would often create a new piece by improvising and working on phrases to produce a finished form while entertaining at rent parties.

The identification of 1928 as the year in which the term *boogie-woogie* was first adopted as the generic title for the piano style leads one to ponder on earlier names that it bore and of reports of its appearance in regions and cities in the United States before 1928. The boogie-woogie style was called "Dudlow Joe" in Mississippi, as reported by bass player Willie Dixon. A number actually recorded in 1929 by pianist Lee Green and given the title of "Dudlow Joe" bears a close resemblance to a piece recorded later by Little Brother Montgomery entitled "Farish Street Jive." Both pianists were active in the South during the 1920s and 1930s and their paths crossed frequently, accounting for the similarity of some of the material in their respective repertoires. Dixon described Montgomery's composition "Farish Street Jive" as a thing of beauty that in an earlier era had gone by the generic name of Dudlow.[10]

The form, structure, and repetition of musical material of "Farish Street Jive" (1936) may be shown as follows:

Chorus 1 2 3 4 5 6 7 8 9 10 11 12
      A B B C D E B C¹ B C B C (beginning only)

Comparing this with "Dudlow Joe," it is noticeable that the B material of "Farish Street Jive" (choruses 2, 3, 7, 9, and 11) corresponds with choruses 5 and 14 and to a lesser extent with choruses 8 and 12 (and possibly chorus 9 also) of "Dudlow Joe." The C material of "Farish Street Jive" (choruses 4, 8, 10, and the beginning of 12) corresponds only with chorus 7 of "Dudlow Joe." A marked similarity between the two pieces is the single-note walking bass in crotchets (i.e., four-to-the-bar) used for part of some choruses. On the other hand, while "Farish Street Jive" has twelve choruses, "Dudlow Joe" has fifteen (perhaps, an introduction followed by fourteen choruses would be a more accurate description, but for the purpose of the above comparative analysis it has not been used as such but has been designated chorus 1). Other differences are that "Dudlow Joe" uses ten-bar choruses as well as twelve-bar choruses, plus an occasional irregularity here and there; and that the ubiquitous bass figure ♩. ♪ ♫ ♩ employed in "Dudlow Joe" never appears in "Farish Street Jive." Strangely, this bass figure—which appears in very nearly every chorus of "Dudlow Joe" (and continually throughout the whole of some choruses)—although employed as an ostinato, seems somehow to lack the urgent character of a typical boogie-woogie bass. However, the use of such boogie characteristics as walking basses (eight-to-the-bar as well as four-to-the-bar) and other ostinato bass figures may be used as evidence to point to an embryonic boogie-woogie style—and to explain the reason for the first part of Willie Dixon's statement. Regarding the second part of his statement, the similarities and differences between "Dudlow Joe" and "Farish Street Jive," as we have just seen, are such that one can assume that—though they are definitely not one and the same composition—one could be a varied version of the other, or both pieces could originally derive from the same source.

Some pieces are of a boogie-woogie character but use only a four-to-the-bar crotchet accompaniment in the left hand. A fast-tempo piece by Turner Parrish entitled "Trenches" (1933) features a few bars of ♩ ♫ ♩ ♩ | in the left-hand accompaniment. "Pitchin' Boogie" (1929; piano/talking accompanied by clarinet, guitar, and tambourine) by Will Ezell uses a stomping four-to-the-bar bass, as does another recording of his "Just Can't Stay Here" (bass example 9). Other pianists who made use of this rhythm are Meade Lux Lewis in "Bear Cat Crawl" (bass example 5) and Henry Brown in "Henry Brown Blues" (1930)—but this piece also features an eight-to-the-bar walking bass for two full choruses. A further variation introduced into the bass was an eight-to-the-bar bass with an anacrusis (upbeat) beginning but which emphasized a four-to-the-bar (crotchet) rhythm. The Henry Brown piece "Deep Morgan Blues" (bass example 17) is perhaps the best example of this type of bass where it is most noticeable (and consistently) used at the beginning of the piece and for the penultimate chorus. This same type of bass also makes a brief appearance in the latter half of "Fanny Lee Blues." Although this bass has eight notes to the bar, its anacrusis beginning stressing the (four)-crotchet beat ♪♩♫♩♫♩♫♩♪ etc., and above all its nonmoving, static melodic design, results in its possessing a peculiarly non-boogie-woogie character.

The first half of Hersal Thomas's "Suitcase Blues" (bass example 15—the second half is completely non-boogie-woogie in all respects) uses a similar type of bass as regards the rhythmical accentuation and anacrusis beginning, but as it now possesses a certain amount of melodic movement, it assumes something more of a boogie-woogie character. Occasional use (a single bar and two bars consecutively in the course of a chorus) is made of this type of bass in Hersal Thomas's "Hersal Blues"—but only in some of its choruses; and apart from this, the piece mainly uses a vamping type of ragtime bass that, of course, contributes to anything but a boogie-woogie character.

Albert Ammons, in his version of Hersal Thomas's "Suitcase Blues," not surprisingly uses the same type of bass—though not the variants of Hersal's original (Albert uses only the version with eight notes to the bar). This same type of bass, namely eight-to-the-bar, with an anacrusis beginning stressing the four-crotchet beat, is again featured by Albert Ammons in a recording made in Chicago on October 17, 1939, and reissued on the Storyville LP 670183 under the title of "Monday Struggle." It is a different piece from the "Monday Struggle" recorded for Solo Art.

It is to Ferdinand "Jelly Roll" Morton that we turn for a more detailed picture of the playing of boogie-woogie in the sporting houses and honky-tonks of the Storyville District of New Orleans at the turn of the twentieth century, when he was active there. In his Library of Congress interviews, Morton reported to have heard Benny French playing boogie-woogie in Storyville in 1906. However, the main reason for involving him in the search for early examples of the style is found in the statement made by Ernest Borneman that Morton reconstructed Buddy Bertrand's "Crazy Chord Rag" during the making of his Library of Congress recordings for Alan Lomax.[11] In Borneman's estimation, it is an early example of recorded boogie-woogie. To start with, the piece referred to is not Morton's "Crazy Chords," which turns out to be a commercial and not a Library of Congress recording made in 1930. It is an instrumental jazz number that has nothing to do with boogie-woogie, Buddy Bertrand, or the "Crazy Chord Rag." What Borneman is referring to is the recording made for the Circle record label by Rudi Blesh from Morton's original Library of Congress recordings and issued as Album VII: *Everyone Had His Own Style*, JM-50: *Albert Carroll and Buddy Bertrand—The Crazy Chord*.[12]

Morton made all his Library of Congress recordings during the late spring and summer months and a final one in December 1938, but, of course, most of the music he is recreating belongs to a much earlier period—to the turn of the twentieth century. One such piece is AFS 1699A, the "Dirty Dozens," a piece warranting investigation on account of the boogie number utilizing the same title that was first recorded by Rufus "Speckled Red" Perryman in 1929 and subsequently on a number of other occasions. Morton confirms the title as the "Dirty Dozen" at the commencement of recording AFS 1669, adding that he initially heard the tune in Chicago. It is generally accepted that the "Dirty Dozen" is an insult song, and Morton's version certainly fulfils these requirements with a sexual reference in the first verse and a concluding refrain that the mother of the person being insulted wore no "drawers." After other obscene references throughout the piece, there is a recurrence of this latter refrain about the mother's underwear. There is a similarity between Morton's repeated refrain and the one found in Speckled Red's version of the number. Apart from this similarity of form, however, Morton's version is in no way related to the pieces by Speckled Red—neither textually nor musically—and it is definitely not boogie-woogie; but it does serve to demonstrate what the real text actually sung by Speckled Red, when performing in the barrelhouse or juke joint, was really like—for beyond doubt, it was certainly something cruder and more obscene than the expurgated texts of his commercial recordings of the "Dirty Dozens." Morton's Library of Congress recordings AFS 1656 A and B and AFS 1687 A and B entitled, in both cases, "The Winding Boy"—alternative titling as "(The) Winin Boy (Blues)" on the commercial issues—contain a reference to the legendary folk hero Stavin Chain. Whether this is a reference to an early boogie-woogie pianist by this name whom Richard Jones encountered (see chapter 2) remains in doubt.

Morton, it seems, was not greatly attracted to the boogie-woogie style of music. He once made an impromptu guest appearance in New York in 1939 at a place featuring boogie-woogie artists, probably Cafe Society, and favored the customers with a couple of numbers. He told Lomax of his visit and said his music had been well received. When Lomax inquired if he had matched the efforts of the boogie-woogie pianists, Morton responded by saying that he fully expected to hold his own against pianists who only had one tune in their repertoires.[13] Morton's playing of boogie-woogie for Alan Lomax needs to be set within the context of the times. In 1938 boogie-woogie was undergoing an unprecedented surge of popularity with followers of jazz and swing music. Under these circumstances, it would be apposite for Lomax to ask about boogie-woogie for the archives and for Morton to try to oblige by recreating some of the music he had heard but without himself holding much feeling for it or commitment to it. After all, Morton's musical tastes were developed by listening to Scott Joplin's ragtime tunes and he no doubt considered that his compositions were more technically complex and melodic than any boogie-woogie piece could ever be. He may even have been hoping to revive his flagging career by demonstrating that when commercial interest was high, he, the great Jelly Roll Morton, could also play boogie-woogie, and once again become the popular pianist that he had been in Chicago in the 1920s.

Touches of eight-to-the-bar motion in the left hand do appear in his playing here and there, but they are usually of brief duration. Two such instances that may be mentioned—and that are of especial interest on account of the terminology employed—occur at the endings of both "I Hate a Man Like You" and "Michigan Water Blues" (same title for all issues). In the first of these pieces, after completing the song, Morton says he had to pacify the young lady by playing some blues or, as he calls it, "some rolling stuff" and then follows with (left hand only) an eight-to-the-bar walking bass. Similarly, after completing the song in the second number, Morton plays some music using a four-to-the-bar "single running bass" that he then changes to an eight-to-the-bar walking bass that he speaks of as a "double running bass."

Possibly the best instance of Morton playing boogie-woogie, as it must have been heard in New Orleans, is in "Honky Tonk Music" (1938). The relationship of the ostinato bass, on this recording, with the treble passages suggests a greater interdependence between the two than is normally found in later boogie-woogie playing. This results in less dissonance and more melody, which may have been a general feature of the early forms of boogie-woogie emanating from New Orleans. One of the first professional engagements undertaken in the 1920s by the then young Chicago pianist Albert Ammons was as a member of a small band working on the excursion trains that took black people back to the South from Chicago for a short holiday. They were called honky-tonk trains and were fitted out with a drinks bar and a dance floor in a converted baggage car. These trips were frequently organized by the Democratic Party as political celebrations. A stop would be made at Memphis where the musicians often played a gig before traveling to New Orleans and then returning to Chicago. Ammons traveled to New Orleans on several occasions, and his playing of boogie basses was a revelation to local musicians who were familiar with their structure but not with the continuous, driving manner in which Ammons played them.

In his Library of Congress recordings, Morton often referred to boogie-woogie as honky-tonk music, a name derived from the cheap pleasure houses of the same name in New Orleans where the music was an important part of the entertainment. The association of the term *honky-tonk* with having a good time is similarly reflected in one of Meade Lux Lewis's accounts of the way in which his own train blues was given its title. In conversation with Alan Lomax when he recorded for the Library of Congress in 1938, Lewis said that he was playing the piece at a house party, possibly in 1923, shortly after he had constructed the choruses and decided on their order, when a guest inquired of him what the tune was called. Lewis told him that it was a train blues, which drew the response from the guest that as they were all together enjoying themselves at the party it ought rightfully to be called the "Honky Tonk Train Blues." This account suggests a strong link between one of the names by which the piano style, was known, and the environment in which it was succored.

The personal contribution of Jelly Roll Morton to the evolving boogie-woogie genre was not as an outstanding practitioner of the art whom others copied but, in a much more subtle way, as one composer whose rhythms and melodies provided a stimulus for embryonic boogie-woogie and blues pianists. This influence can only be hinted at as one of several that were absorbed by piano players, but there is some evidence to suggest it. Morton lived in Chicago between 1914 and 1917, having left New

Orleans, returning later in 1923 to begin recording. His tunes were all the rage, and during their heyday Morton and Tony Jackson played at all the popular bars, including the Elite, situated on State Street, in a neighborhood known as the Section. When Morton was appearing there, he would often play for hours and attract a large audience that not only filled the bar but overflowed onto the sidewalk. Entertainers were regularly seen and heard in person, before recordings and radio and cinema coverage of jazz superseded theatre and club appearances. Morton was certainly one of the most visible models for all up-and-coming pianists in the city through his personal appearances and sales of records and piano rolls. He introduced his audiences to the "Spanish Tinge," a tango or habanera rhythm that he featured in compositions such as "Mamamita" and "New Orleans Joys." It is a much more broken and staccato rhythm than the one used by Jimmy Yancey in his compositions, but it is reasonable to speculate that Yancey may have heard Morton playing and may have been influenced by the experience to the extent that he experimented with similar rhythms in his own playing. He most certainly did not pick them up from traveling to other countries, such as Cuba, or other regions in Latin America, because after his early juvenile work as an international traveling dancer he rarely left Chicago. Morton's influence is seen in one of the better known compositions of pianist Jimmy Blythe entitled "Lovin' Been Here and Gone to the Mecca Flats," which drew inspiration for its melody from a minor theme from his piece "Tom Cat Blues."

There were other regions, however, far removed from the Storyville District of New Orleans, where pianists could be heard playing boogie-woogie. One such center was Texas, where the seeds of the music grew and flourished. At the turn of the twentieth century, Texas supported crop farming and cattle rearing on its rich fertile prairies in the western counties and lumber and turpentine industries in those to the east, bordering on the state line with Louisiana. The oil industry and the burgeoning railway companies provided work as track layers for a black labor force that was still disenfranchised for all intents and purposes and dependent on menial forms of employment to eke out a living. The cities of Dallas, Shreveport, and Houston, and the port of Galveston drew in a black labor force to work in their many commercial enterprises. The majority of industries were served by a largely migrant workforce, and moving around the region with them in the 1920s and 1930s, continuing an earlier tradition dating from the beginning of the century, was a group of pianists who hitched rides on the trains of the Santa Fe Railroad Company serving the region. They provided a brash musical back-drop for the gambling, drinking, whoring, and dancing that were the popular forms of entertainment in many of the isolated communities near or within the workplaces. A more detailed consideration of the growth and decline of some of the industries in the South and the sustenance they gave to boogie-woogie piano playing is the topic of the next chapter. But it is interesting to note, in the context of identifying the names by which the piano style was known, that two of the colloquial terms prevailing in Texas—*Fast Western* and *Fast Texas*—were so called, it is said, to distinguish them from the "slow blues" of New Orleans. The "Galveston" was yet another Texan term for the piano style.[14]

Stepping back even further in time, a pianist known simply as "Birmingham" was recalled by several of Jelly Roll Morton's contemporaries and is mentioned in interviews made for the Archive of New Orleans Jazz at Tulane University. Birmingham was thought to have been one of the earliest pianists to play boogie-woogie in New Orleans; as his name suggests, his base was Birmingham, Alabama. The importance of this city as a piano center is further acknowledged in blues pianist Perry Bradford's autobiography *Born with the Blues*, in which he mentions that Jelly Roll Morton knew a Birmingham pianist named Lost John who came to Chicago playing a piano style with a rolling bass before World War I.[15]

Not all early boogie-woogie pianists emerged from Alabama, but their influence in other regions of America cannot be gainsaid. A piano style using an ostinato left hand appears to have originated from the state and to have been transplanted to the East Coast before the end of the nineteenth century. It could be heard in the family rooms of beer saloons situated in the Tenderloin District of New York. The pianists were invariably youthful African-Americans from Alabama who played alongside a banjoist or harmonica player and were reported by H. M. Kay to be playing boogie-woogie in the Tenderloin District in the period leading up to the Spanish-American War (1898).[16] The music had certainly reached the mideastern region of America, just south of the Great Lakes, before 1910, where it was heard by Garvin Bushell (born 1902), a black clarinet player living in Springfield, Ohio. He started piano lessons when he was six and remembers hearing the popular "Maple Leaf Rag" at that time as well as the "fast western," confirming its later name of boogie-woogie and its origin as Texas.[17]

The accumulated evidence points to the existence of many minor figures playing in the boogie style, each displaying personal and regional features in their playing. The fact that the evidence is anecdotal and was collected in the 1930s onwards from musicians who would only remember as far back as the late 1890s frustrates any attempt to identify an earlier date for the emergence of boogie-woogie. This was probably followed by a cross-fertilization of regional boogie-woogie styles, particularly in the South, assisted by the newly laid railroads on which many itinerant pianists traveled. What can be said with a degree of certainty is that the states of Texas and Louisiana (and probably Mississippi) and the cities of Birmingham (Alabama) and New Orleans hosted some of the earliest pianists who played a rudimentary piano style utilizing a boogie-woogie ostinato bass. The several titles by which it was known imply, initially at least, a strong regional tie particularly in the South where the piano players worked clearly defined circuits. The piano style was given the name of boogie-woogie in 1928 with the release of Pinetop's recording, and this has been adopted as the generic title ever since. The two meanings of the term *boogie-woogie* have been retained to the present day: the heavy bass style of piano playing and the good time dance.

It might prove helpful to a better understanding of the music to reflect a little on its character and status, its purpose and function, and its audiences and venues. It was not heard in the drawing-rooms and salons of the highest stratum of society, it was shunned by the respectable law-abiding and church-going element of black society, and it was not performed (even) in the highest-class bordellos and brothels of the larger towns and cities. It was primitive and unsophisticated music—music for the rough, uncultured, uneducated, and frequently illiterate workingman, for the violent and undisciplined lawbreaker and wrongdoer, and for the pimp, pander, and prostitute. It was "low-down" music—music for the backwoods and the back streets. Apropos of this, one might consider Roy Carew's observation that he heard boogie-woogie in New Orleans in about 1904, but the music was usually classed as the naughty boy of the rag(time) family who neglected to study.[18]

Not only does it confirm that such music was of the back streets, but it also forwards the opinion that such music was considered inferior as music per se. If one had some technical ability as a pianist, creative talent as a composer of melodies, plus some knowledge of harmony in addition to the tonic, subdominant, and dominant chords of the twelve-bar blues, then one could move out of the shadows and gain employment in the better establishments on the better streets in the bigger towns and cities—as did, for example, such ragtime and jazz pianists and composers as Tony Jackson and Jelly Roll Morton. If, on the other hand, one lacked these attributes, then one played the honky-tonks—containing (as Morton in his Library of Congress recordings has remarked) low-caliber clientele, usually unwashed, and frequently lousy—and pounded away in the barrelhouse and jukes, grinding out primitive and relatively simple boogie-woogies and blues. The blues was the only music suitable for the lowly barrelhouse, opined Walter Lewis.[19]

The term *boogie*, or derivations of it, appears in the titles of several tunes dating from the 1890s: "Dance of the Bogie" (1892), "The Bogie Coon" and "The Bogie Dance" (1898), "The Bogey Walk" (1900), "Boogie Boo" (1908), and "Hoogie Boogie Dance" (1909). These pieces appear as musical scores, but none has the defining attributes of boogie-woogie.[20] Although we do not comprehend the composer's intentions in using the term, there does appear to be an association between *boogie* and dancing or moving to a rhythm, possibly the cakewalk that anticipates Pinetop's composition. Finally, the earliest recorded reference to the musical term appears to be the "Boogie Man" (1880), composed by J. P. Skelly, which was published as sheet music for piano and described as a comic song and polka. The title and lyrics confirm that the reference is to the "Bogey" or "Boogie Man," an imaginary spiritlike creature whose presence was conjured up to discipline children through fear; the song's recurring chorus tells them to beware the boogie man. Clearly, these sentiments bear no relationship to boogie-woogie piano music as we understand it today.[21]

It is of interest to know that the term *boogie-woogie* has had other meanings that were used within the underground culture of black America and that also had no associations with music or dancing. *Boogie* was a term used for describing a form of secondary syphilis and sexual activity. An example of the latter can be found in a recording made by Bessie Jackson (alias Lucille Bogan) who sang of Boogie Alley in "Down in Boogie Alley" (1934; piano accompaniment by Walter Roland). *Boogie Alley* refers to "Prostitute Lane" or the "Street of Brothels." Her lyrics warn that no man is safe down there, and she is particularly worried about her own man because he frequently visits house number three. Boogie Alley's nefarious character is further emphasized by her recommendation that if returning to its precincts one should carry a razor or a .44 revolver. Incidentally, this piece is not, musically, of a boogie-woogie character. It is believed by some blues authorities, including Paul Oliver, that *booger-rooger* is a French derivative used for describing an uninhibited party and could be the parent of *boogie-woogie*. It has also been suggested by others that *boogie* is an alliteration of *bogey* as in *bogeyman* (see above), but why the connection with spirits? The dependency of pianists on train travel lends some credence to an association between *bogie*—the pair of pivoted wheels at the front of a flat truck—and *boogie*. It now remains to examine some of the industries and centers in the southern states that sustained this embryonic piano style.

NOTES

1. W. Russell, "Boogie-Woogie," in *Jazzmen*, ed. F. Ramsey and C. Smith (London: Sidgwick and Jackson, 1958), 183–205.

2. J. S. Roberts, *Black Music of Two Worlds* (New York: Praeger Publishers, 1972), 203.

3. L. W. Levine, *Black Culture and Black Consciousness* (New York: Oxford Press, 1977), 199.

4. Roberts, *Black Music*, 203; see also liner notes by Jean Paul Amouroux for *Boogie-Woogie Story*, vol. 1, Milan Jazz, CD 887795.

5. A. Lomax, *The Land Where the Blues Began* (London: Methuen, 1992), 170.

6. L. Harap, "Boogie-Woogie and the Piano Player," *Jazz Information*, March 1940, 2.

7. R. Blesh and H. Janis, *They All Played Ragtime* (London: Sedgwick and Jackson, 1958), 192. D. Harbinson's explanation of Blake's reference to "sixteen" suggests that ragtime is notated in 2/4 time, with the left hand playing the standard accompaniment of four quavers to the bar. This he interprets Blake as meaning:

That is, the left hand plays eight notes to the bar, but because of the 2/4 rotation, they are sixteenth notes (semiquavers). (Also, two of the standard walking basses use patterns consisting of sixteen actual notes—eight in the first bar walking up, and eight in the second bar walking down.

8. M. Stearns and J. Stearns, *Jazz Dance* (New York: Macmillan, 1970), 234.

9. R. Hall, liner notes, *The Barrelhouse Years*, vol. 20, *Piano Blues*, Magpie Records, PY 4420.

10. K. G. zur Heide, *Deep South Piano* (London: Studio Vista, 1970), 33.

11. E. Borneman, "Boogie-Woogie," in *Just Jazz*, ed. S. Traill and G. Lascelles (London: Peter Davies, 1957), 13.

12. This is a copy of what is cataloged by the Archive of Folk Song (now, incidentally, the Archive of Folk Culture) of the Library of Congress as AFS 1688B1, "Boogie-Woogie Blues"; B2, "Albert Carroll Blues"; and B3, "Dialogue"; and this—in both cases the B-side of a twelve-inch 78 rpm record—has in more recent times been issued on the LP record *Jelly Roll Morton* (Swaggie) S.1314, the Library of Congress Recordings, vol. 4, which is simply titled "Albert Carroll." Thus, the conclusion to be drawn is that the piece Borneman is referring to is the one that occupies the first part of AFS 1688B and that bears the title "Boogie-Woogie Blues" or the alternative title of "Crazy Chord Rag." A certain sense of disappointment is experienced, however, when one listens to this piece, as it is a stomping four-to-the-bar, over-repetitive piece that is neither strictly ragtime nor boogie-woogie—and nowhere does Morton, in speaking on the record, provide any indication as to its origin, authorship, or title except in his concluding comment that everybody went wild when Buddy Bertrand played his piano blues.

13. R. Carew, "Of This and That and Jelly Roll," *Jazz Journal* 10, no. 12 (December 1957): 10–12.

14. M. McCormick, liner notes, *Texas Barrelhouse Piano, Robert Shaw* (Almanac 10), refers to *Fast Western* as the name by which boogie-woogie was first known, with confirmatory explanation by Andrew Everett—heard in volume 1 of the set—who worked in turpentine camps at the time. He identifies different pieces that he plays on his guitar, saying that he first picked them up incidentally from hearing them being played on a piano. See also S. Charters, liner notes, *The Barrelhouse Blues of Speckled Red* (Folkways, FG 3555) who refers to boogie-woogie as originally being known as *Fast Western* or *Galveston*—the Texas seaport situated on the Gulf of Mexico.

15. K. G. zur Heide, "Spotlight on Early Boogie-Woogie: Birmingham, Alabama," *The Blues* (Japan), no. 12 (May 1975): 6.

16. H. B. Kay, "8 to the Bar: Gay Ninety Reminiscences," *The Record Changer*, May 1949, 14, 20.

17. Levine, *Black Culture*, 202.

18. R. Carew, "Of This and That," 10–12.

19. K. G. Zur Heide, *Deep South Piano*, 13.

20. E. Virgo, correspondence with the author, March, 27, 1992.

21. J. P. Skelly, "The Boogie Man, 1880," *Library of Congress Sheet Music Archives* (1870–1885).

2

Industries and Centers Supporting Boogie-Woogie in the South

Originally, much of the United States of America was covered with primeval forest: great areas in the western half and a vast area in the eastern half that stretched from around the Great Lakes south through Wisconsin, Minnesota, Missouri, and Oklahoma into Texas before curving back to meet the Gulf coast in the vicinity of the Brazos river and proceeding eastward through Florida and finally northward along the Atlantic seaboard. By 1662, when the word *lumber* first appeared in writing, there had been established a flourishing trade in the export of timber and its by-products—turpentine, pitch, and tar—to Europe. It was not until the 1830s, however, that large-scale lumbering operations commenced, and lumbering became a major industry as important as the railroad and iron industries.

By 1850, quite substantial inroads had been made into the virgin timber of the vast forest area in the eastern half of the United States, sufficient to be able to demarcate a southern portion, which still remained largely untouched. Known as the Southern Forests, it embraced parts of Georgia and Florida, and then moved westward into the states of Alabama, Mississippi, Arkansas, and Louisiana, where the prevalence of the pine tree gave the Piney Woods of Louisiana its name. From here the forested area ran into Texas and, from the point of view of this story, hosted the earliest recorded evidence of the musical style that was to become known as boogie-woogie. It was the black labor force working throughout the length and breadth of this entire region who, if not responsible for the creation of boogie-woogie, at least ensured its early appearance and survival in Texas by providing a sympathetic audience for the music.

23

There was some lumbering activity in the Southern Forest during the 1850s near Cedar Keys, Florida, and Amos Kent had established his lumber and brick company at Kentwood just south of the Mississippi/ Louisiana border, but the lumber boom did not begin in earnest in the South until after the end of the Civil War in 1865. Shortly after 1880, owing to, in part, the introduction of the crosscut saw to fell the trees, and encouraged by the planters of the Mississippi Delta[1] who were eager for more forest land to be cleared for the planting of cotton, the lumber boom commenced in the area around Memphis, Tennessee; Mississippi; and Arkansas. During the next decade, in the 1890s, large-scale lumbering operations commenced in the western Louisiana/eastern Texas area, with J. H. Kirby—nicknamed "Prince of the Pines" and eventual owner of thirteen sawmills in east Texas—forming his Kirby Lumber Company in 1901. By 1909, half of the total of the lumber production for the whole of the United States came from the Southern Forests, but 1927 saw the lead in lumber production pass from the Southern Forests to the western states. The reason, of course, was the rapid depletion, denudation, and disappearance of the virgin forest: Eighty-three million acres of timberland had been laid waste by 1933. Companies went into liquidation as a consequence of having exhausted all the lumber; and in 1943 the entire town of Weirgate, Texas—which, in its life of only twenty-five years, had managed to denude a hundred thousand acres of longleaf pine—went to a wrecking company.

By 1942 there was not a great deal left of the vast virgin forest that originally covered all the eastern part of the United States, and although the enormous demand for timber created by the Second World War caused a temporary boom, the lumber boom proper was definitely at an end—the Big Time in the Big Woods was over.

Although, in the woods of the North and the West, the majority of lumberjacks were white men, in the Southern Forest, the labor force employed in all aspects of the timber business was predominantly black. White men filled the management and supervisory posts, but it was mainly the brawn and muscle of African-Americans that swung the axe or pushed and pulled on the crosscut saw to fell the trees of the Piney Woods. The resulting timber meant that the rails and ties of the spur railroad (the "dummy line") had to be extended deep into the forest to connect the remote logging camp to the main railroad. African-Americans also sweated and strained over the massive logs in the process of getting them from the forest to the sawmill, be it by skid road, watercourse, or river, or by loaded wagon drawn by locomotive, ox, horse, or mule. It was still mainly their brawn and muscle that finally manhandled the timber into position for cutting in the sawmill. It was hard and dangerous work. Men were killed or maimed by falling trees, were crushed when loaded flatcars or wagons overturned, and had their feet and legs smashed when a log slipped and rolled back on them; and while flying chokers and hooks could gash arms and bellies, so snapping cables could lash around to mutilate and even decapitate those unfortunate enough to be in the way.[2] Inside the sawmill, men were exposed to a number of crippling injuries, and not only lost fingers, hands, and arms because of the saws but also had their lungs damaged through inhaling the timber dust from the planing and sandpapering machines. The natural conditions of the forest could also make working life unpleasant: the heat and humidity, the snakes and the insects. In some cases, black lumberjacks—often referred to as "flatheads," incidentally—had to cover their bare backs with kerosene-soaked sacks as a protection against mosquitoes, and in swamps or flooded bottomlands had to work standing in water up to their hips. Hard and dangerous work necessitated a workforce of men who were equally tough; and a certain percentage of them comprised prison escapees, men fleeing woman trouble, and fugitives from knifing or shooting incidents—the remote camp in the forest providing an ideal hideaway. Convict labor was also deployed: Some of the southern states leased out their prisoners, in chains and under an armed guard, for work in the lumber camps. Convict labor and African-Americans also dominated the labor force in the turpentine camps of Florida, Georgia, and Alabama.

In the twenty-year period from 1890 to 1910, black labor increased phenomenally throughout the industry. In broad figures, it almost quadrupled to 14,309 from a base of 3,742 for lumbermen and craftsmen; almost doubled to 24,630 from 12,034 for turpentine farmers and laborers; and increased almost sixfold to 108,811 from 17,276 for those engaged in sawing and planing in the mills.[3] The resultant shows that at least from the early 1890s until the mid to late 1930s, there existed a potentially explosive, racially mixed, and captive labor force confined in closed, cramped, and isolated communities with few opportunities for personal expression or even personal freedom. The continuing presence of the cathartic music of boogie-woogie pianists and other instrumentalists in these communities must have assisted in some small measure to alleviate this volatility.

The logging camp normally consisted of a collection of shacks: bunkhouses for accommodating between seventy-five and 150 workers, a cookhouse, a company store, and a foreman's office.[4] The camps were established along defunct railway cuttings no longer required for transporting timber. The shacks were either converted railroad boxcars or boxlike structures built on railroad flatcars. The essential point is that they were on wheels, so that as the surrounding area of forest was reduced to stump land, and as the "dummy line" of the logging railroad was then laid farther into the depths of the forest, so the whole camp could be moved to its new location. One of the shacks functioned as the barrelhouse, honky tonk, or the juke joint catering to dancing and crap games, and in some instances, provided the services of a brothel.[5] Furnished, by the lumber company, with drink and a piano, it could be a rough, tough place. Crap games that started on a Saturday afternoon would keep going until Monday morning. Fighting, often razor slashings with one of the gamblers invariably getting killed, was fairly common. Such was the cheapness of life that the gambling activity continued, according to Little Brother Montgomery, using the still warm corpse to sit or stand on while the women continued dancing on top of the piano.[6]

These kinds of entertainment provided in barrelhouses serving the logging camps were also replicated in the turpentine and sawmill camps, the latter soon turning into sawmill towns completely owned and dominated by the lumber companies.[7] Such company towns, shabby and squalid, and lacking any sanitary facilities, saw workers paid irregularly and often in the form of tokens, which were redeemable only at the company store.[8] The local sheriff and police were often in the pay of the company, and during times of union unrest and strikes, the company would hire an additional force of gunmen to intimidate and control the workers; they also set barbed wire fences around the mill and lumber yard.

The names of some of these towns are indicative of their origins: Millville, Woodville, Pineville, Oakdale, Lumberton, Electric Mills, Cedar Keys, and Kentwood. Journeying between such sawmill towns, calling in at the larger towns, following the railroads, and traveling deep into the forest to visit the logging camps and the turpentine camps were itinerant black musicians—particularly, pianists. In the absence of a visiting musician, there is no reason to doubt that the workers would have made their own entertainment and played the piano. If they did, what they played and who they were are impossible to determine with any degree of certainty. The only clue we may have in attempting to answer this is given by guitarist and blues singer Huddie Leadbetter (Leadbelly); in a conversation with Frederick Ramsey Jr., Leadbetter said that when boogie-woogie was around in 1903 and 1904, people in his hometown walked the basses without really knowing what they were doing.[9]

Leadbelly seems to imply that even the untutored could get things under way and stimulate dancing if they had learned a rudimentary walking bass pattern. The attraction of the walking bass was its rhythmical stepping movement and simple, catchy melody in progressing up and down the keyboard. This was probably the earliest form of boogie-woogie played on the piano, possibly without any treble accompaniment in its most basic form.

Little Brother Montgomery spent his early years traveling on the Santa Fe trains playing the barrelhouse circuits of the South. It is not surprising that he should do this, having spent his impressionable childhood years in Kentwood, Louisiana, where his father owned a barrelhouse in which he listened to many pianists perform there and recreated some of their numbers in his own way from about the age of five. Shortly afterward, he could pick out a single note walking bass but had to wait until his teens before he could double up the notes to play an octave bass line. The Montgomery barrelhouse served the workforce of the previously mentioned Kent's Mill. It was a popular place for weekend revelry when card games like Georgia Skin, Cotch, and Monte were played. Dice shooting was another diversion. A room containing a piano was set aside for dancing. The first piano player that Little Brother remembers hearing, when he was four years old, was Ford who came from New Orleans. Others that he heard were Tommy Jackson, cousin of Tony Jackson, the ragtime pianist from New Orleans and friend of Morton; Bob Martin whom Montgomery described as a good blues pianist; and Loomis Gibson who apparently only knew three numbers, "Twelfth Street Rag," a waltz, and the blues. Montgomery began playing professionally on the Santa Fe circuit during the First World War, before moving to Chicago in 1928. He remembers hearing many different versions of the rolling-bass style during his time in the South, recalling its name as "Dudlow Joe." Certain barrelhouse circuits became associated with other musicians: Will Ezell played in Fullerton, Oakdale, De Ridder (a stronghold of the Brotherhood of Timber workers[10]), and De Quincy; Walter Lewis in Haynesville, El Dorado, Tallulah, and Vicksburg; and Poor Joe Williams traveled around Mobile Meridian, Electric Mills, Shuqulak, and on into Alabama.[11] (See map for all these circuits.[12])

The most common method of traveling the circuits was by freight train, and the pianists sat or lay on the metal crosspieces underneath the flat trucks, if they were unable to hitch a lift in the caboose off a friendly conductor or brakeman. Riding the rods was certainly the fastest and cheapest way of getting around the countryside for them, and they seem to have accepted the dangers and discomfort with stoicism. Other, less intrepid of the brotherhood picked up a train just as it was moving out of the marshaling yard, waiting for their moment to slip past the armed guards (bulls) and dog handlers, who were employed to deter them, before running and heaving themselves into an empty truck as the train gathered speed. This was the favored mode of departure, in which timing was critical, as the train could be safely boarded after the trucks had been inspected shortly before departure. More often than not, pianists would find themselves in the company of hobos and other down-and-outs seeking fresh pastures.

One pianist, Wesley Wallace, left a detailed account of a typical train ride from Nashville to East St. Louis in a famous piece entitled "Number 29," made in 1930 for the Paramount Company and available on *Piano*

Blues, Volume 1: Paramount 1929–30 (Magpie, PY 4401). The bass plays in an unusual 6/4 time, typifying the relentless power of the engine, and is embellished by a series of chiming chords in the treble, reminiscent of a train bell. The climax of the journey is reached as the non-paying pianist shuts both eyes tightly and leaps from the train as it approaches East St. Louis. Rolling down the embankment and dusting himself down, he watches the receding train, secure in his anonymity. The wonderfully evocative recording by this little-known pianist illustrates the significance of this form of transport for pianists and how it acted as an inspiration for their music.

The Santa Fe railroad, with a main line running north from Galveston and Houston through Texas into Oklahoma, which, together with its side lines branching off to the east and the west, claimed to serve eighty-eight Texas counties. From playing in the back streets of Galveston, Houston, and Richmond, the Santa Fe group of pianists—including such men as Conish Pinetop Burks, Son Becky, Robert "Fud" Shaw, and Edwin "Buster" Pickens—traveled the numerous lines around the barrelhouse circuits to play in the various camps and towns. A splendid testimony is provided by Pickens—named the last of the itinerant barrelhouse pianists—and who was not discovered and recorded by Paul Oliver until relatively late in his career (1960). On his recording entitled *Santa Fe Train Buster Pickens* (Flyright Records, FLY 536), he describes hearing the mournful whistle of a distant Santa Fe train and likening it to a crying child. After successfully pleading for and obtaining a free and illegal ride on a freight train to Cowswitch, Pickens later meets Robertson, an aged piano player, now worn out by the incessant grind of the unpredictable and hazardous traveling. The older man invites him to take his place on the circuits, and Pickens accepts. Then Pickens reminds us of the brutal intensity of the commitment expected of the workforce in the sawmill, with the constant and relentless switching of manpower between those completing their shift and others waiting in the barrelhouse to take their place. Pickens, whose dark suit, bow tie, and contrasting quiff on an otherwise cropped head emphasized his status as a pianist and not a laborer, tells this personal tale while accompanying himself on the piano—and, it is worth noting, the music of this piano accompaniment is solid boogie-woogie.[13] A few years after making his recording, in 1964, Pickens was killed in a bar-room altercation.

The Santa Fe group displayed several distinctive features in their piano playing: a tendency to anticipate the beat, a fairly heavy touch, and the inclusion of ragtime runs and stride basses—the latter interspersed with boogie-woogie bass figures. The mixture gives their music a melodic quality compared to the cruder attempts of some pianists from other regions. Despite these common features, however, there are also certain distinctive embellishments in their style that identifies individuals with particular cities and even districts within cities. A number of popular themes were included in most repertoires, among which were "People, People"; "Piggly Wiggly Blues"—a parody on the grocery store of the same name; "The Cows"; "The Clinton"—a stopping place on the line in Oklahoma; "Hattie Green"; and "Black Gal," which became nationally known when it was recorded by Joe Pullam in his melancholic falsetto voice.

Pianists would remain at a lumber camp for as long as the mood took them before moving on to their next destination. The duration of their stay was determined partly by the reception they were accorded. To an extent, they were protected by their status as entertainers from some of the incipient violence that pervaded the camps, but it was not unknown for rough justice to be meted out if they did not perform to the satisfaction of the customers. Newcomers were regarded with suspicion, and as camp owners often resorted to the gun for maintaining order and control, it ill behooved an unknown pianist to attempt to break new ground without first being known or giving advance warning of their arrival. However, visitors to the barrelhouse were eagerly awaited for the news they brought from distant places as much as for the entertainment they provided. Many early pianists were called by exotic names: Jack the Bear, The Toothpick, Cat Eye Henry, and Papa Lord God were some who played the barrelhouses.

During their stay they were given food and a bed, but they were mainly dependent for financial payment on the unpredictable generosity of the clientele who gave tips or, more usually, supplied them with drinks because the workers were normally paid in tokens that could only be spent at the campsites—and this usually meant the barrelhouse. Some of the toughest places were the levee camps where black labor built, bolstered, and repaired the river banks—particularly along the great Mississippi River between Tennessee and Louisiana. Lomax reported that living conditions for this workforce were similar to lumber camps, and it was difficult for anyone to achieve sufficient financial independence to be able to leave them and move on.[14] There were frequently "paydays" involving no money, only an allowance that enabled the worker or his wife to draw victuals and other necessities from the commissary store. At the end of a week's labor, after the allowance had been drawn on, the worker was given what remained. Many were illiterate and innumerate and were frequently cheated of their rights by unscrupulous owners who overcharged them. Short of money, they were obliged to stay on at the camp, which served the purposes of the owners very well.

The mode of living of pianists had much in common with those for whom they played, and many succumbed to heavy drinking. It was this hazard and their method of traveling between destinations that shaped their tough existence and, in many instances, led to their premature deaths. It was also accepted that the extremes of temperature they experienced between riding the cold, merciless rods and the stifling alcohol-infected heat of the barrelhouse hastened their deaths. It was exceptional for a pianist not to be self-taught. The small amount of musical knowledge they acquired came from others in the brotherhood who shared ideas and passed on their own pieces in reciprocation for help given to them. They were proud men and engaged in fiercely competitive cutting sessions to demonstrate their mastery of the piano. The popularity of certain pianists was related to the range and variety of their repertoires, although this became less important as the weekend revelry reached its alcoholic climax. As this time approached, they pounded on their instruments and sang their songs in a high falsetto in order to be heard above the general hullabaloo. Technique was perfected in the hothouse of public performance, and each pianist became known for their unique rendition of a well-known number. Thus, Little Brother achieved fame for his playing of the "Vicksburg Blues," which he taught to Lee Green, a clothes presser from Louise, Mississippi, in 1922. Some of his own specialties were similarly reworked from versions of traditional blues that he learned from other pianists when their paths crossed. Loomis Gibson taught him a blues, which he retitled "Crescent City Blues," and from Joe Martin he learned "Joe Martin Blues" when they played the same venue in Arkansas.[15] For all its deprivations, the nomadic life offered black pianists a degree of independence and a measure of control over their destiny—an aspect of life denied to many African-Americans.

Although the work camps and towns connected with the timber and turpentine industries provided the traveling barrelhouse pianist with his main source of employment and constituted the majority of the places where he worked, he also visited and played in the juke joints of work camps and towns connected with other industries where a black labor force was employed. These included, as we have seen, the levee camps and the oil fields and the oil boom towns such as those found in the Beaumont district (see map on page 28) and in the southeastern corner of Texas (served, incidentally, by the Santa Fe railroad). In fact, one could postulate that any employment that was open to African-Americans of the South and that attracted a reasonable percentage of their labor would also attract the barrelhouse pianist.[16] Perhaps one might single out the railroad industry—the track-laying side of it—as deserving of a little more attention, for following the cessation of hostilities in 1865, the southern states not only commenced rebuilding railroads that had been destroyed by the Civil War but entered upon the construction of new railroads as well. Many thousands of miles of railroad track were to be laid down: In Texas alone the mileage increased from a paltry 711 in 1870 to 9,886 in 1900 and 16,125 in 1920, while in Louisiana it rose sixfold from 450 to 2,824 between 1870 and 1900—an expansion that was to be repeated in neighboring states.[17]

Black labor was used mainly in the southern states for track laying but not to any great extent, initially, in the North and West. In 1866, for building its railroad, the Union Pacific employed mainly Yankee ex-soldiers of the Civil War plus the recently immigrated Irish and only three hundred African-Americans; on the other hand, for its massive construction program after the end of the First World War in 1918, the Illinois Central Railroad could claim that it was completely dependent on black labor from the South.[18] As with logging, in the South, some white labor was used alongside the black labor, although, in later years, some sectors of the industry such as railroad-track maintenance were to become almost exclusively the preserve of African-Americans. Chinese labor was deployed in 1869 during the laying of the Alabama and Chattanooga Railroad—but they were working together with black laborers. There was no dearth of black brawn and muscle to swing the hammer and drive in the spike, to shoulder and carry the two-hundred-pound ties, and to manhandle the long, heavy rails into position.

The New Orleans, Mobile, and Chattanooga Railroad reached Donald-sonville, Louisiana (see map on page 28), and began to run trains to New Orleans in 1871. Some thirty years later, the Texas and Pacific Railroad was also involved in construction around Donaldsonville. The local jukes provided entertainment for the construction workers billeted in Donald-sonville, and one of them, Bully Reynolds's TP Saloon, was a particularly notorious drinking establishment. It was there in 1904 (or 1906, depending on the source)[19] that jazz pianist Richard M. Jones, as a young boy, saw and listened to Stavin Chain playing the piano. Stavin Chain was a broad-shouldered man whose dual talents were singing and playing the piano. His short life ended in a fracas over a disputed dime during a popular gambling game called "Coon Can." At the TP Saloon, Chain announced that he would play "Lazy Rags," which featured a powerful walking bass that very quickly drew a large, appreciative, and excited crowd of listen-ers who, shouting encouragement for him to keep on playing his walking basses, told him to keep them rolling for a week.[20]

The popularity of the saloon increased with Chain's regular presence there, and the construction workers were later joined by women laborers from the nearby levee who performed a kind of can-can dance to the mu-sic, the climax of which was reached by kicking a side of ham suspended from the ceiling. Another dance, recalled by Jones, was called the Pop-Open, a forerunner of the Lindy Hop and the jitterbug of the 1940s. The universal response to the boogie rhythm does not appear to have changed very much over the years.

The Vicksburg, Shreveport, and Pacific Railroad pushed westward to Shreveport, Louisiana, in 1884. Earlier, between 1872 and 1876, the Texas and Pacific Railroad had been laying track to the west of Shreveport at Marshall and to the north of Shreveport at Texarkana. In this general area, in Caddo County (see map on page 28), or in Shreveport, itself, is where Leadbelly first heard barrelhouse pianists playing boogie-woogie walking basses in 1899 (or 1901, depending on the source).[21] Leadbelly might have heard these pianists and this music in the honky-tonks of Shreveport's notorious Fannin' Street, or perhaps in the juke joints of Caddo County's lumber camps, but it is also possible that he could have heard them playing this music in the barrelhouses of railroad camps any-where in the general area.

In several southern states, pianists and guitarists provided the mu-sic for dancing and entertainment at sharecropper's farms. Cotton was picked and put in bales during the week, and this was followed by the entertainment that commenced on Friday evenings and ran until Sunday, the day of rest, when the workforce prepared itself for another tough, punishing week of physical toil. The small township of West Helena in Arkansas played host to the many farmers from the surrounding countryside who arrived each Saturday to sell their wares, usually cotton, hogs, and corn. After replenishing their animal stock and feed, the sharecroppers spent the remainder of their time enjoying the recreations offered by the town, including gambling, drinking, dancing, and whoring. The musical entertainment in these communities was provided by pianists and guitarists who hammered out boogie-woogie and the blues. Roosevelt Sykes, a member of this brotherhood in his early days, likened the expansive and riotous weekends to celebrating Christmas twice a week.[22] In Mississippi, Saturday night "fish fries" were weekend parties by another name at which similar entertainment was the staple provision. In contrast to their itinerant brothers who rode the rods, some of these pianists often remained in a locality, initially at least, before the major population movements to the North occurred—garnering a local reputation. They worked full-time at the sawmills, on farms, and at other jobs, using their music only during weekends to earn extra cash.

In the latter years of the nineteenth and early years of the twentieth centuries, very few African-Americans owned pianos, so public places such as barrelhouses, jukes, and, possibly, churches became important in providing the budding pianist with some limited opportunities for learning and practice. Acting as magnets within a community, a piano would draw together piano players of all levels, allowing them to share ideas and compare techniques. Sammy Price first heard boogie-woogie played on the guitar in Waco, Texas, in about 1917 by Blind Lemon Jefferson. He confirms the scarcity of pianos available to African-Americans in Texas, considering it to be one reason why he initially heard boogie-woogie being played on the guitar.[23] In some circles, the piano was even considered an effete instrument for men to play and would certainly have been too expensive for the average African-American family.

Boogie-woogie made inroads in the city of Memphis around the turn of the nineteenth century and that is where W. C. Handy, the composer of "St. Louis Blues" and "Memphis Blues" first heard it. However, the most consistent reports of an urban version of the style by musicians who worked there are centered on New Orleans (vide Jelly Roll Morton, etc.). A white trumpet player, Tony Calento, recalls hearing boogie-woogie on his first visit to the city in 1907—the beginning of a twenty-year association working on the Mississippi riverboats. Veteran trumpet player Bunk Johnson recalls that the piano blues was being played in the bars and barrelhouses of the same city right through the night until early in the morning, to which he added his own rugged trumpet tone, during the early years of the twentieth century.[24]

The emergence of New Orleans as a center where boogie-woogie flourished at the beginning of the twentieth century serves as a reminder that it was one of the largest cities in the Mississippi region and was positioned strategically on a bend of the river. As such, it became an important center for trade and commerce, offering work in its port and pleasures in Storyville—the red-light district of some notoriety—both to its citizens and many thousands of transients.

Alabama, particularly Birmingham and its surrounding districts, has already been identified as a region where boogie-woogie appears to have had a long and established tradition. The quality of the piano players from there who went on to make recording careers in the 1920s and 1930s suggests that they were strongly influenced by local players of exceptional talent in their formative years. Both Charles "Cow Cow" Davenport and Clarence Pinetop Smith came from similar backgrounds in rural Alabama before spending their early years working in Birmingham; Davenport was there in 1912, and Smith, as a precocious fourteen-year-old, worked at East End Park in 1918. One of the city's better-known pianists in the 1920s and 1930s was Jabo Williams, who was born in Pratt City but was later associated with St. Louis. Reputedly a difficult man, he often commandeered the piano from anyone who happened to be playing it when he arrived at a party or similar event.

Walter Roland (aka Alabama Sam), a pianist with a big local reputation, was also raised in Pratt City. He recorded prolifically in the 1930s, frequently in the company of Lucille Bogan, a blues singer who had settled in Birmingham. Some of his pieces are taken at a slow to very slow tempo, such as "Back Door Blues" (1933), with vocal and piano; his accompaniment to Lucille Bogan's singing in "Changed Ways Blues" (1934); and "Bad Dream Blues" (1935), in which he accompanies his own singing. In such pieces the left-hand bass pattern may not always adhere to an eight-to-the-bar rhythm, and four-to-the-bar ♩ ♫♩ ♩| and |♫♩ ♫♩| patterns may occur to a greater or lesser extent. Leaving aside his "Early This Morning" (1933), a vocal accompanied by piano (this is Roland's version of Charlie Spand's "Soon This Morning"—complete with the same eight-to-the-bar walking bass), two faster pieces than the three pieces mentioned show Roland in fine form as a boogie-woogie pianist. They are "House Lady Blues" (1933), vocal and piano, and his accompaniment to Lucille Bogan in "Stew Meat Blues" (1935).

A noticeable feature of Roland's piano style is his employment in the right-hand passages of rapidly repeated single notes or chords, which appear in much of his work. With the exception of "Back Door Blues," such passages occur in all the pieces mentioned and tend to be featured more in the faster than in the slower ones. They are particularly evident in "House Lady Blues" and "Stew Meat Blues," but can be described as ubiquitous and dominating in "Jookit Jookit" (1933). This piece, issued by the Jolly Jivers, is—apart from the single exhortation by Sonny Scott to "Ah! Jookit"—a piano solo by Roland. Although not particularly distinguished by its melodic invention, it is taken at a bright tempo and propelled along by the insistent passages of rapidly repeated notes exploding from Roland's right hand to make it an exciting piece of boogie-woogie.

An interesting feature of this number is its close structural similarity to "Pinetop's Boogie-Woogie," including a tremolo introduction, breaks, and an anticipatory bass rhythm, implying perhaps a common genesis in Alabama for both pieces or, at least, elements of a regional style. Such determinants are reinforced by another Roland recording, "Big Mama" (1934), which is so similar to "Fat Mama Blues" (1932), a number recorded by Jabo Williams, that it can be assumed they knew each other well or shared a common influence. The best collection of Roland's piano work can be heard on *Piano Blues, Volume 6: Walter Roland* (Magpie, PY 4406).

A contemporary of Walter Roland from North Birmingham, who claimed to have had contact with Pinetop Smith from when they were both working in Birmingham, was Robert McCoy. Not a major figure, he made only a few recordings in the 1930s and 1960s, preferring to play piano as a sideline while holding onto the security of a full-time job. He also recorded with Lucille Bogan at some point in his career. McCoy came from a musical family and learned his early skills from his two brothers who were both pianists. Later, he worked in the juke joints and bars of that city and did not venture far beyond its boundaries. His career was revitalized when he was rerecorded in the early 1960s by Pat Cather for the neophyte Birmingham company Vulcan, after being discovered working for a construction company. McCoy's style was strongly influenced by Leroy Carr's blues playing, an approach that underpins many of his interpretations. Davenport, Clarence Smith, and Jabo Williams were others who helped define his work. A degree of eclecticism in his choice of material reflects recordings from the 1930s, including the standards "Honky Tonk Train Blues," "44 Blues," and "How Long Blues."

McCoy's mature piano work employs a variety of bass patterns, including a walking bass that underpins his interpretation of Pinetop's "Jump Steady Blues," which he entitled "Bessemer Rag" after a township near Birmingham. His accompaniments are also well constructed with the spirit of Pinetop Smith's treble phrasing appearing on "Eight Avenue Blues" (1937), supporting the vocal by James Sherrill. A similar coherence between bass and treble is evident on "Silver Spades Blues" (1937) with the same singer who, apparently, using the pseudonym of Peanut the Kidnapper, was a stand-in at the recording sessions for the indisposed Lucille Bogan. Both numbers are available on *Piano Blues, Volume 10: Territory Blues 1934–1941* (Magpie, PY 4410).

So then, the region supporting the genesis and flowering of the boogie-woogie style has been defined: the Southern Forest region, which means, basically, an involvement with the southern states of Florida, Georgia,

and the Carolinas, Alabama, Tennessee, Mississippi, Louisiana, Arkansas, Texas, and Oklahoma. The period has been established: between the
end of the Civil War in 1865 to the Second World War of the 1940s, with,
perhaps, more emphasis on the period circa 1890 to 1930 (plus an ongo-
ing extension from the 1940s with markedly less emphasis). The location
has been determined: the barrelhouse, honky-tonk, or juke joint in the
various work camps and townships. What now remains to be done is to
chart the progress of boogie-woogie from this unpromising beginning by
reference to the musical influences bearing upon it and the work of some
of its early practitioners. Before doing so, however, we are reminded of
one of the functional qualities of boogie-woogie—in its early appearances
at least—by a graphic and colorful offering from Robert "Fud" Shaw that
to understand fully the impact of the music one has to imagine all the girls
on the dance floor swinging their hips (butts) to the rhythm of the music
and exciting the onlooking men.[25]

NOTES

1. The Mississippi Delta referred to is not at the mouth of the river, to the
south of New Orleans, where the Mississippi River meets the sea and flows into
the Gulf of Mexico, but the area known, geographically, as the Mississippi Delta
Region. This region borders the lower Mississippi River between a point where
the states of Missouri, Arkansas, and Tennessee tangentially come into contact
and a point about forty miles into Louisiana, south of where the Red River meets
the Mississippi River. The width of this river border known as the Mississippi
Delta Region may measure between fifteen and thirty-five miles on both sides of
the Mississippi River, with a large bulge in the middle of its length extending its
width some seventy miles eastward from the river into the state of Mississippi
and some seventy miles westward from the river into northern Louisiana and
southern Arkansas. The term *Mississippi Delta* is also sometimes used to refer to
only a part of the above area (the Mississippi Delta Region), namely, the ellipti-
cally shaped tract of country between Memphis and Vicksburg bordered by the
Mississippi and Yazoo Rivers.

2. Although essentially a male preserve, the lumber industry witnessed large
numbers of women entering its employment for the period of the First World
War. At this time, 125,000 women were employed throughout the southern states
in all the various jobs necessitated by the timber business: light tasks in the sawmills and heavier work in the forest camps; on occasion black women even swung
the axe and pushed and pulled on the crosscut saw in actually felling the tree.

3. C. H. Wesley, *Negro Labor in the United States, 1850–1925* (New York: Vanguard, 1927), 315–17.

4. C. Todes, *Labor and Lumber* (New York: International Publishers, 1931), 70.

5. S. McIlwaine, *Memphis Down in Dixie* (New York: Dutton, 1948), 25.

6. G. Oakley, *The Devil's Music* (London: BBC Publications, 1976), 79.

7. It is interesting to compare Little Brother Montgomery's description with the euphemistic description of a turpentine-camp honky-tonk given by pianist Clarence Williams, *Boogie Woogie Blues Folio* (New York: Clarence Williams Music, 1940), 11. Williams relates that he was hired to entertain at a boarding house in Oakdale, Louisiana, where turpentine workers lived. Dancing, gambling, and beautiful women, acting as hostesses, were all available. It was necessary to provide entertainment for the workers because of the isolated position of the camp and the absence of any other diversionary amusements nearby.

8. Company store tokens or, more properly, commissary checks, were popularly known as "robissary" checks. The "robbery" was committed by the company store through charging prices from 5 to 10 percent higher than normal and by subjecting its commissary checks to a discount of 10 to 20 percent if presented elsewhere. See G. T. Morgan Jr., "No Compromise—No Recognition—John Henry Kirby: The Southern Lumber Operators Association, and Unionism in the Piney Woods, 1906–1916," *Labor History* 10 (Spring/Summer 1969): 195 and footnote 7.

9. Fredrick Ramsey Jr., liner notes: *Boogie Woogie and Jump and Kansas City*, vol. 10, Folkways Jazz, FJ 2810.

10. The Brotherhood of Timber workers was an independent union (only briefly affiliated with the Industrial Workers of the World) that was first organized in late 1910. At the peak of its activity, its membership—of whom about half were black—numbered about 35,000. It is chiefly remembered for its bitter—and, at times, violent and bloody—struggle against the employers and their organizations.

11. K. G. zur Heide, *Deep South Piano* (London: Studio Vista, 1970), 12.

12. Map was produced by the author by reference to K. G. zur Heide, *Deep South Piano* and J. P. Davis, ed., *The American Negro Reference Book* (New York: Prentice Hall, 1966).

13. Edwin Buster Pickens, "Walk a While, Ride a While," in *Conversation with the Blues*, ed. Paul Oliver (London: Cassell, 1967), 73–74.

14. Alan Lomax, *The Land Where the Blues Began* (London: Methuen, 1993), 249–52.

15. Little Brother Montgomery, "Little Brother Tells His Story," *Mississippi Rag*, January 1975, 2.

16. One should not overlook the continuous importance of cotton—surely the most black-dominated of all employments. Mack McCormick's liner notes for *Robert Shaw: Texas Barrelhouse Piano*, Almanac 10, reports that the barrelhouse pianist Robert "Fud" Shaw entertained around Kingsville, South Texas, in the cotton-picking season.

17. G. H. Stover, *The Life and Decline of the American Railroad* (New York: Oxford University Press, 1970), 154–55.

18. S. D. Spero and H. L. Harris, *The Black Worker* (New York: Columbia University Press, 1931), 162.

19. E. Borneman, "Boogie-Woogie," in *Just Jazz*, ed. S. Traill and G. Lascelles (London: Peter Davis, 1957), 15. See also G. Oakley, *The Devil's Music*, 78.

20. Onah L. Spencer, "Boogie Piano Was Hot Stuff in 1904," *Downbeat*, July 1939, 22.

21. Traill and Lascelles, *Just Jazz*, 14; and P. Oliver, *The Story of the Blues* (Harmondsworth, UK: Penguin Books, 1969), 36, 86.

22. Paul Oliver, ed., *Conversation with the Blues* (London: Cassell, 1967), 67–68.

23. Dan Kochakian, liner notes, *Sam Price and His Texas Blusicians, Do You Dig My Jive*, Whiskey, Women Records, KM 704.

24. N. Shapiro and N. Hentoff, eds., *Hear Me Talkin' to Ya* (New York: Rinehart, 1955), 243, 249–51. See also Traill and Lascelles, *Just Jazz*, 17.

25. M. McCormick, liner notes, *Robert Shaw: Texas Barrelhouse Piano*, vol. 6.

3

Boogie-Woogie Eras, Musical Influences, and Significant Early Pianists

It is a commonly held belief that all boogie-woogie music sounds alike. This criticism can be quickly dispelled by listening to the approach and attack of different pianists playing the same composition. An untutored ear would not have much difficulty in distinguishing between the distinctive tones of Rufus Perryman, Clarence Lofton, or Clarence Smith rendering "Pinetop's Boogie-Woogie," which all three recorded at some time in their musical activities. Even allowing for the fact that pianists from the same geographical region displayed similarities in their selection of material, bass patterns, and the structure of choruses, an unmistakable individuality shows through in their playing. This criticism of sameness can also be challenged on the aural evidence of recordings made by pianists from different regions of America. Thus Robert Shaw from Texas shows little in his boogie-woogie interpretations that is comparable with anything produced by Charlie Spand, who is also thought to have come from Texas but lived in and worked mostly from Detroit and Chicago. Nor do Henry Brown from St. Louis and Charles Avery from Chicago share much that is common in their styles. All these men, and others who learned to play boogie-woogie before the 1920s and were recorded between 1920 and 1930, had acquired and retained a marked regional coloring in their piano playing, yet still managed to leave their own stamp on the music. What they had in common during their formative years was a minimal exposure to pianists and instrumentalists from other regions, which left their original styles largely intact.

Pianists acquired their repertoires through their own unschooled attempts to master the boogie-woogie idiom by assimilating phrases from pianists working in their home regions. Early boogie-woogie music showed its attachment to the blues tonality by retaining a melancholic quality. The pianists played a limited range of themes and possessed rudimentary keyboard techniques. When they did stray beyond state boundaries, it was normally to make recordings after their discovery by talent scouts working for the record companies. In the heyday of the recording period, between 1928 and 1930, Henry Brown traveled to Chicago from St. Louis to record "Stomp 'Em Down to the Bricks" for the Brunswick Record Company and then to Richmond to record "Henry Brown Blues" for the Paramount Record Company. Apart from one or two further recording trips from St. Louis and a sojourn in England during World War II, he spent the remainder of his years living and working in that city. Pianists could expect little financial return for their labors. With so much recording activity and a multiplicity of willing talent available, the scales were tipped in favor of the companies who paid minimum rates to recording artists. Thomas McFarland ("Barrelhouse Buck"), also from St. Louis, was tempted to make the trip to Chicago with a promise of attractive financial remuneration for his recordings. Charlie Spand trod a similar path from his base in Detroit to Richmond, Indiana, in August 1929, and two months later to Grafton, Wisconsin, in order to make his early recordings for the Paramount Company.

BOOGIE-WOOGIE ERAS

Reference has already been made to pianists who were playing a kind of boogie-woogie at the turn of the twentieth century and to pianists who incorporated elements of it into other styles, often blues and ragtime. The merging of certain of these elements is considered later. In temporal terms, some of the men from this period should be considered the first true generation of boogie-woogie pianists, but in the absence of evidence from recordings or piano rolls, it is difficult to even substantiate their work let alone assess its significance. For the purposes of clarifying the several phases the music underwent in reaching its state of perfection in the 1940s, despite this lack of early musical evidence, it gives some perspective to consider the first generation of pianists as being those who were active and recording their significant work in the period up to about 1930 and who may have had some contact with these invisible giants of the keyboard. This group includes George and Hersal Thomas, Jimmy Blythe, Clarence Smith, Charlie Spand, Will Ezell, Charles Davenport, many less-talented pianists, and others still unknown and technically crude piano players of boogie-woogie. Their impact on those who followed is now clearly recognized and accepted.

The second generation of boogie-woogie pianists carried the music forward into a new era beginning in about 1930. They worked mainly in urban areas, notably Chicago and St. Louis, but also Kansas City, and later in New York. The best were exposed to the music of other jazz and blues instrumentalists as well as pianists who accompanied artists working in vaudeville. Such a high concentration of musical talent working in a relatively small geographical location had a noticeable impact on boogie-woogie compositions. For example, in the late 1930s and early 1940s, Albert Ammons, Pete Johnson, and Meade Lux Lewis (the Boogie-Woogie Trio) arrived in New York with extensive and varied experiences. Once there, they shared the bill and occasionally played alongside jazz musicians of the highest caliber such as Frankie Newton, Sidney Bechet, Edmond Hall, and Oran "Lips" Page in New York nightspots and appeared as guests on the Camel Caravan Radio Show with the Benny Goodman Orchestra. The order and disciplined section work of these various jazz and swing outfits contributed significantly to the elegance and virtuosity of their own playing. It is hardly surprising that boogie-woogie was given richer tone coloring, more complex harmonies, and a precision of form that was not present in the work of many of the older pianists.

Pinetop Smith was an artist of the first generation, but in 1928 he was already playing in a second-generation style. It is surely indicative of the exactness of the form of "Pinetop's Boogie-Woogie" that Smith could ask Ammons to learn it; and in the fulfillment of that request for Ammons to build on the basic structure and produce the "new" up-tempo "Boogie-Woogie Stomp," while still retaining the spirit of the original. The outstanding artists from this period were Lewis, Ammons, Johnson, Jimmy Yancey, Jay McShann, Mary Lou Williams, and, to a lesser degree, Sam Price. Other influential players with a distinctive touch from this generation were Roosevelt Sykes, Clarence Lofton, and Rufus Perryman. There was also a cache of less famous pianists living and working mainly, but not exclusively, in Texas and Alabama. This period in the history of the piano style is sometimes referred to as the "Carnegie period," because it concluded with the celebrated appearances of the Boogie-Woogie Trio and Joe Turner at the Spirituals to Swing concerts in Carnegie Hall in New York in 1938 and 1939. This period launched the international craze for the music in the following decades, which included the appearance of a "pop" version of boogie-woogie that flooded the airways.

A number of changes occurred in the structure of boogie-woogie music as it evolved, extending to the music of second-generation pianists. First, where it had previously consisted of loosely extemporized treble choruses, with a blues tonality, played over a rhythmical bass, they introduced an urbanity with clearly constructed choruses set down in a particular relationship to each other, giving coherence to the music by leading it to a natural and logical climax. In some compositions, the rudiments of a melody became more apparent, as in the Lewis composition "Far Ago Blues" or the rendering by Ammons of "Mecca Flat Blues." Second, there was a change in the emotional content of the music, exemplified by a further reference to "Pinetop's Boogie-Woogie." Like so much folk music, it expressed both joy and melancholy—the latter arising from its blues roots. In the hands of Ammons, the joyful side is eloquently expressed in his recording (1936), but the melancholic, somber aspect is retained in the later version recorded by Honey Hill (1938). This could be accounted for by the vital urban milieu of Chicago in which Ammons lived and worked, which contrasted with the insular and parochial background of the lesser-known black pianist from Indianapolis. The senses are similarly affected when listening to the then unknown Meade Lux Lewis playing "Honky Tonk Train Blues" in 1927 and later in a recording made for Blue Note (1940). In the second version, the mournful tones have disappeared, having been replaced by crisply struck chords, a staccato bass, and a faster tempo that when combined, produce a sense of urgency and raw energy.

As the boogie-woogie tidal wave gathered momentum in the late 1930s and early 1940s, a number of African-American pianists came into prominence. The more talented, such as Mary Lou Williams, showed a great feeling for the form. Two other technically proficient pianists who occasionally produced exciting touches of boogie-woogie were Ken Kersey and Hazel Scott. All were to appear later in their careers at the Café Society nightclubs in New York where boogie-woogie music was featured. A slicker brand of boogie-woogie was purveyed by Maurice Rocco and Deryck Sampson. Both were noted for their ability to put boogie basses to classical themes or popular tunes of the day, but their music was often devoid of genuine boogie-woogie tone coloring. They were, nevertheless, lauded by a public ever eager for new sensations to feed its growing addiction to boogie-woogie.

A further stage in its development occurred when white pianists working with big bands attempted to take boogie-woogie beyond its severe, self-imposed structural limits of the twelve-bar blues. Their interest in the style grew, in part, from the public's demand for this type of music and the possibilities of adapting it for band section work. Despite the commercial pressures that were to lead to the excesses of later years, some interesting byways were traveled in the search for the unusual. Notable among these pianists were Joe Sullivan and Bob Zurke, both members of the Bob Crosby Orchestra; Freddy Slack and Billy Maxted of the Will Bradley Orchestra; Tommy Lineham, the pianist with the Woody Herman band; and to a lesser extent, Johnny Guarnieri who played with several of the big bands, notably those of Artie Shaw and Benny Goodman. They extended the scope of boogie-woogie in several ways. The walking bass, which dates back to the earliest recorded boogie music and ragtime, already provided them with some of the desired flexibility they sought. Joe Sullivan in his composition "Just Strollin'" carried it further in two ways: "walking" up and down more complex chords than the simple octaves of his predecessors and making more use of passing tones. Another property of boogie-woogie evidently viewed as a limitation was the twelve-bar (or eight-bar) blues form. One way to get around this was simply to adapt already existing musical forms. Sullivan again showed how this can be achieved in his beautiful rendition of "Summertime." More variety in the bass pattern was introduced by Slack in "Strange Cargo" by alternating two similar figures. Zurke went much further by freely improvising with his left hand in "Southern Exposure." Maxted adopted Zurke's ideas and added two more devices: the double walking bass (each octave repeated) in "Overnight Hop" and a bass figure much like that in conventional "white" boogie but so complex that it ran for four bars before being repeated in "Fry Me Cookie with a Can of Lard." This figure does not fit into the twelve-bar form. Many of Zurke's later solos with the Bob Crosby Orchestra, on recordings such as "Squeeze Me," contained the contrapuntal and percussive qualities of boogie-woogie but had neither a twelve-bar form nor a repeated bass figure. He often drew on traditional thematic material associated with the boogie-woogie style to achieve this effect.

MUSICAL INFLUENCES

As we have seen, the single most important influence that has shaped boogie-woogie is the twelve-bar blues. The definitive boogie-woogie style is to all intents and purposes synonymous with the blues in regard to its form and harmony, although there are two important qualifications that need to be made to this general statement. First, the present structure of the twelve-bar blues evolved from earlier forms that did not follow this pattern. The early blues singers often extended a vocal line for as long as the inclination took them. A recording by Bill Broonzy of "Joe Turner No. 2," a song dating from 1890, ran to sixteen bars; "Slow and Easy Blues," composed and played by Jimmy Yancey, is an eight-bar piano blues. These freer forms of the music were found mostly in rural areas of the United States and named the country blues. Charley Patton, Son House, and Robert Johnson were some of the guitar-playing bluesmen who used the looser framework preceding the twelve-bar blues. Country blues are at a midway point in the evolutionary process, somewhere between the informal work chants and the "classic" vaudeville-influenced blues of Ma

Rainey, Ida Cox, Bessie Smith, and sundry other female stylists who were active in the 1920s and 1930s.

The shift toward a disciplined and interesting harmonic structure in the blues was the result of a merging of the African and European traditions in the music.[1] Early country-blues singers showed little inclination to adopt the European tradition, but dating from the appearance in print of W. C. Handy's composition the "Memphis Blues" (1913), a marriage of African and European harmonies occurred; this gave rise to the accepted chord changes in the twelve-bar blues, which, in the key of G are: G G G G[7]/C C G G/D[7] D[7] G G. Some of the early boogie-woogie pianists showed a similar disregard for the standard twelve-bar blues. Although there are no recordings available of the founding fathers of the boogie style, recordings exist of pianists who extended choruses beyond twelve bars. Robert Shaw and Buster Pickens display this characteristic, and Wallace's "No. 29" is built on the tonic and subdominant chords only. From these and other examples, it can be argued that while early boogie-woogie pianists used the twelve-bar form, it would be an unfortunate oversight to neglect the work of those who did not, on the grounds that it is a necessary and sufficient condition of the genre. To do so would be a denial of the inevitable stages through which a folk art progresses.

There are close similarities between boogie-woogie music and a form of piano playing still heard in churches where fundamentalist religion is practiced. Religious services are a documented feature of black culture going back to the days of slavery long before boogie-woogie began to be heard.[2] It is reasonable to surmise that black pianists approached the playing of hymns with much the same feeling for rhythm that they showed in their blues playing, and that the off shoot boogie-woogie was fueled to some extent by an association with sacred music. The blues singer Aaron T-Bone Walker first heard a kind of boogie-woogie being played in a church in Dallas in 1913, but the link between the two forms of music, according to Borneman, can be traced to a period earlier than this.[3] He suggests that gospel train songs were adapted, and they formed the basis of train blues in the early years of the twentieth century, with "Midnight Special," "Get on Board," and other gospel songs being the immediate forerunners of blues using a rolling left-hand bass. African-American music, notably jazz and blues, is an amalgam of many influences, but has been particularly influenced by church music. The jazz pianist and vocalist Nina Simone said that her family were very religious and forbade the playing of boogie-woogie in the house but could not see the irony of allowing her to use the same boogie-woogie beat to play a gospel tune.[4]

Recorded examples of the piano music that was played in black churches in the 1920s certainly bear a close resemblance to both barrelhouse and boogie-woogie music. Church music (often called "gospel music") and barrelhouse music served a similar purpose. In the former case it produced a form of heightened spiritual ecstasy in the congregation; in the latter case it induced a more secular abandon in the customers of the barrelhouse and juke joint, assisted by freely flowing liquor. At this point, a few observations about the distinctive barrelhouse style of piano playing will be relevant to bring out some of the common features it shares with gospel music. Barrelhouse playing bridges the gap between boogie-woogie and ragtime. It combines some of the melodic properties of ragtime with the driving bass rhythms of boogie-woogie: a rhythmical momentum achieved by employing heavy striding or walking basses. A composition attributed to a little-known pianist, Blind Leroy Garnett, and entitled "Louisiana Glide" (1929) is a good example of the barrelhouse style wherein melodic treble work is combined with a thunderous, driving boogie-type bass. Little biographical information exists about Garnett who was believed to have originated from Fort Worth, Texas. His only other known recorded solo, a coupling in a similar vein, was "Chain 'Em Down," a "set" composition with little room for extemporization—a feature shared with ragtime—and available on *Piano Blues, Volume 1: Paramount 1929–30* (Magpie, PY 4401). The same potent mix of styles can be discerned on "Easy Drag" (1929), a piano solo recorded by Herve Duerson that is included on *Ragged Piano Classics 1923–43* (Origin, OJL 16). Rufus Perryman and Robert Shaw also incorporated elements of the barrelhouse style in some of their pieces.

Fortunately, recorded examples exist of the early gospel piano style showing its close affinity with the barrelhouse style, as played by Arizona Dranes (real name Juanita Dranes) for the Okeh Record Company. She was born in Texas in 1904 or 1906 and learned to play the piano in her teen years. Her early playing experience was gained at prayer meetings, which conditioned both her later piano style and the future pattern of her life. Having decided to devote herself totally to a life of religion—the money earned from recordings went to the church—she was called upon to play at many church services in the Bible Belt of the southern states. The close proximity of gospel and barrelhouse piano playing is brought out perfectly in "I'm Going Home on the Morning Train" (1926).

At the turn of twentieth century, ragtime was the most popular form of syncopated music. The search for its roots is just as complex as attempting to trace the genesis of the blues. Ragtime is essentially a piano music, although it can be played by other instruments and in orchestral form. At its heart is a syncopated rhythm, produced by placing an emphasis in the beat on certain notes in the melody that fall between the steady two- or four-beat bass rhythm of alternating single notes and chords. In one sense, ragtime shares a similarity with boogie-woogie in its constant and unvarying ground rhythm and use of cross rhythms, but it differs most noticeably from boogie-woogie in its logical melodic structure, which allows for little extemporization or license in the playing. To improvise destroys the overall patterns and balance of a ragtime composition. At least, this was the accepted form it had evolved into by 1870 when Jess Pickett, Sam Gordon, and Jack the Bear were entertaining the patrons of bordellos in New Orleans and on the riverboats of the Mississippi. Before that time, black pianists probably interpreted European tunes of the mid-nineteenth century such as "Old Dan Tucker," and the quadrilles and schottisches brought to America by early settlers, with a predominantly African conception of rhythm in view of their ancestral heritage. This technique became known as "ragging" the melody line.[5] In common with early boogie-woogie players, very few of the early African-American ragtime pianists were schooled in the European tradition of scales and sight-reading from music, which meant that their own compositions and those learned from others had to be committed to memory. Technique was acquired only when it became necessary to produce a particular effect—a pragmatism useful for resolving an immediate technical difficulty but not a sound basis for acquiring and transferring technical skills to the playing of new compositions. Consequently, the majority of untaught black ragtime pianists had a circumscribed repertoire of pieces to which they added by observing other pianists, copying their particular phrases and listening carefully to their interpretations. Many of the famous pianists from the classical era of ragtime, however, could read and score music adequately: Jelly Roll Morton possessed a firm grasp of European chord movement and harmony, and Scott Joplin, the greatest black ragtime composer of all time, had been trained to a high level of competence by a German piano teacher.

From about 1870 until the beginning of the ragtime craze in the early years of the twentieth century, Eubie Blake, Tom Turpin, Tony Jackson, and Artie Matthews were composing the collection of formal rags that are still played today. White composers of popular music began using the ragtime form for tunes such as "Alexander's Ragtime Band" from about 1911. Whereas the ragtime style became increasingly familiar to white people, albeit in a bowdlerized commercial form, the black version, largely disregarded, continued to be played by piano players who traveled across America working in railroad camps and docks in the daytime and entertaining the workforce in saloons at night. Other pianists were engaged by minstrel shows and vaudeville tent shows, which made short stays in townships and then moved on to fresh pastures. Those pianists from the top drawer could be heard in the sporting houses and upper-class bars of large cities.

The paths of ragtime, blues, and neophyte boogie-woogie pianists seem to have crossed in the later decades of the nineteenth century, arising from their high concentration in the entertainment districts of major cities—notably New Orleans, St. Louis, and Indianapolis. Although the pianists represented distinct schools of piano playing, there was some cross-fertilization of musical ideas. Jelly Roll Morton, as we have seen, made frequent reference to the presence of blues pianists in New Orleans in his Library of Congress recordings, and Roy Carew observed that their music (boogie-woogie) was never heard in the "gilded palaces" due to its crudity.[6] Despite the difference in status between the lowly blues and boogie-woogie pianists, on the one hand, and the fashionable ragtime pianists on the other, many of the latter included elements of recognizable boogie-woogie in their compositions. For example, in the 1890s, ragtime maestro Tony Jackson included the walking bass in his music, and, as observed earlier, William Turk was known to play "Sixteen." In the 1880s, ragtime players on the eastern side of America played a number known under various titles as "Bowdigers's Dream," "Digah's Dream," or just "The Dream." It was thought to have been composed by Jess Pickett, who died in 1922. Eubie Blake called it a "slow-drag with blues (and a) tango bass." Borneman also identified its distinguishing features as a slow tempo and a bass (habanera) similar to one associated with Jimmy Yancey.[7]

The rhythm alluded to by Blake is undoubtedly the habanera or tango rhythm: $|^2_4$ ♩. ♩ ♩♩ $|$ and $|^2_4$ ♫♫ ♩ ♩♩ $|$. Fats Waller, in contrast, recorded "The Digah's Stomp" as an organ solo in 1927; there is no "Spanish" or Latin American flavor in either the melody or the accompaniment, and little discernible in the way of tango or habanera rhythms. The melody varies from an even flow in straight four-to-the-bar crotchets at the opening of the piece to more syncopated passages elsewhere, while the bass plods steadily along, emphatically marking a two-beat rhythm. One might single out the third melodic idea as possessing a feature of the tango inasmuch as it gives emphasis to the first beat of every second bar.

James P. Johnson recorded his version of "The Dream" in 1944. The melodic character of some of the musical ideas might be thought to have something of a Spanish or Latin American flavor, and certain and various rhythms (which might be attributable to a South American origin—though not exclusively so) do occur in the melodic line; but there is no marked or consistent use of tango or habanera rhythms. In fact the predominant rhythm for most of the piece is the left-hand pattern of $| ♩ | ♩. ♪♩ ♩ | ♩. ♪♩ |$ etc.

It is possible to find a thematic relationship between the Waller and Johnson pieces, particularly the stepwise descending and ascending scale passages, but each has its own individual character, thus creating the impression that they are totally different pieces of music. Neither of the two versions has a direct association with the evolution of boogie-woogie, although it is important to note that these interpretations were played by pianists of the Stride School, some way removed in time from Blake's reference to the shadowy Jess Pickett, whom he recalled as being of medium size, of heavy build, and a sporting gambler.[8]

One cannot leave the question of incorporating "Spanish" rhythms in boogie-woogie styling without some reference to their appearance in the work of Jimmy Yancey. In doing so, it is evident from his date of birth, in 1898(?), that he was playing after the period when some fusion was thought to have occurred between ragtime and boogie-woogie music (although Yancey's elder brother Alonzo played ragtime and taught Jimmy the rudiments of the piano). Yancey used both ♩♪ ♩ ♩ and ♪ ♩ ♪ ♩ ♩ rhythms for his basses, but these bass-line rhythms were employed in his blues pieces ("East St. Louis Blues," "Slow and Easy Blues," "Mellow Blues," among others). His boogie-woogie basses, on the other hand, used ♩ ♫ ♩ ♫ or ♩ ♫ ♩ ♫ and ♫ ♫ ♫ ♫ rhythms ("State Street Special," "Yancey Stomp," and "The Rocks"). However, to clear up one point, he also made considerable use of the rhythm ♩ ♪♩ ♩ as a bass line, which when compared with the predominating left-hand rhythmic pattern of Johnson's "The Dream" (see above), could account for Borneman's reference to the presence of a Yancey bass in the number.

In summary, the appearance of certain features of boogie-woogie in ragtime playing leads to the supposition that the already formed ragtime style was not changed markedly by the encounter except to the extent that additional colorful embellishments were added for special effects.

EARLY SHEET MUSIC

An examination of early sheet music tends to support this notion. Blake was reported to have composed "Charleston Rag" in 1899, though it first appeared in sheet music form in 1917. Throughout the piece there are passages of descending notes used in a stepped pattern, although they are not written in the form of a typical boogie-woogie walking bass, which employs octaves. Berlin suggests that the first appearance of boogie-woogie in published form may have been the "Alabama Bound" chorus of Boone's "Rag Medley No. 2" (1909) but goes on to say that these passages were exceptional, and only about 3 percent of rags before 1912 exhibited blues characteristics such as the blues notes and repeated melodic choruses.[9] Another published composition containing a form of boogie-woogie walking bass is "Pastime Rag Number One," written by Artie Matthews. It appeared in 1913 as the first of five "Pastime Rags" and is included on *William Bolcom, Piano, Pastimes & Piano Rags: James Scott and Artie Matthews* (Nonesuch Records, H 71299).

An example of the use of the blues form is found in "One o' Them Things" (1904), which Berlin reports as beginning with a twelve-bar blues chorus. Berlin suggests that it may be the first published twelve-bar blues, predating Handy's "Memphis Blues" by eight years. These influences are to be found in the compositions of black pianists, but white ragtime pianists were also beginning to absorb blues coloring, some of which can be found in "Minstrel Man" (1911) by J. Russel Robinson. In 1917, "Perpetual Rag" was composed by two English pianists, Harry Thomas and William Eckstine, who later emigrated from Bristol to Canada. It was reproduced as a piano roll and contains two fleeting sections of walking bass in the precise staccato manner of ragtime, which makes it almost unrecognizable from the boogie-woogie interpretations of that bass.

After the publication of "Memphis Blues," the terms *ragtime* and *blues* were sometimes used synonymously by composers. By 1915, the number of published rags with a blues content or inflexion had risen to 15 percent. There was also a movement in the opposite direction, and several compositions with blues in their title were published that contained both twelve-bar (blues) and sixteen-bar (ragtime) sections. Such a piece was "A Bunch of Blues" by Paul Wyer. Some merging of boogie-woogie and ragtime elements continued into the 1920s, although the classical ragtime format was now being adapted to popular tunes of the day. Within this category, and dating from 1919, a piece entitled "Dardanelle," composed by Felix Bernard and Johnny S. Black, was published using a rocking ostinato bass built around a tenth interval, which gave the tune a marked Latin American rhythm. This composition inspired Albert Ammons to take up the piano, and it is surely no coincidence that many of the bass patterns he used in later years were built around the same configuration of notes. From the early 1920s, boogie-woogie bass figures made an appearance on some of the piano rolls and recordings of Jimmy Blythe who used them for rhythmic effect in his playing of non-boogie-woogie compositions. A prodigious performer, his other work bore a closer resemblance to the blues and boogie-woogie forms and included typical bass and treble figurations.

Jimmy Blythe was not the only pianist to see the possibilities of incorporating boogie-woogie features into otherwise standard compositions to add spice, as piano rolls and early acoustic recordings from 1920 onward reveal. Eubie Blake appears again on a piano roll (1921) playing "Arkansas Blues" with a strong rocking bass of tenths, matched only by the composer of the piece, James P. Johnson, on a piano roll version dating from the same year. Pianist Clarence Johnson's popular tune from a similar period entitled "Corn Trimmers" is interlarded with several boogie-woogie bass patterns. All are available on *Boogie-Woogie Story, Volume 1* (Milan Jazz, CD 887795). Finally, "Golden West Blues" (1923), recorded privately for Gennett by pianist Jesse Crump (included on volume 2 of the series), bears all the hallmarks of a versatile piano player choosing to build his blues composition around boogie-woogie rhythms, replete with a resonating tenths bass line and passages of walking bass. Crump worked as a piano accompanist to blues singer Ida Cox for many years—and later married her—traveling and appearing in theatres with her, all over the South and East Coast theatre circuits. Sam Price, from a later generation, freely admits his debt to Crump through listening to his recordings and copying the fingering on his piano rolls, as well as hearing him play in a Dallas theatre. Price was also a pianist and dancer in vaudeville, a fact that, together with the similar backgrounds of Clarence Smith and Charles Davenport, suggests that boogie-woogie was a piano style known to, and frequently used by, pianists working in this field.

A composition entitled "Syncophonics" (1925) was published by Axel W. Christensen and written in five parts. The significance for boogie-woogie of this work is found in *Syncophonic No. 4*, which contains the well-known treble theme of "Pinetop's Boogie-Woogie" played over a walking bass, three years before the recording was made by Smith. Born in Chicago in 1881 of Danish parents, Christensen contributed to the popular spread of ragtime by opening a number of schools for teaching the style to would-be performers. He followed this up with a series of instructional books and developed a home-study course. The "Christensen Instruction Book for Ragtime," published in 1927, was a widely used manual that evolved from his first instructional book, published in 1903, called "Ten Easy Lessons." By 1930, it had been rewritten in the nomenclature of the day and offered instruction in "Jazz Piano Playing; Keyboard Harmony; Breaks and Bass Figures; Harmonising Melodies; Boogie-woogie, Blues etc."—note how quickly the term had been adopted only two years after Pinetop's recording. By 1935, the number of registered students had increased to half a million. The Christensen method had a wide appeal for pianists who wanted to learn to play the popular styles of the day. One such player may have been Clarence Smith, who had purchased an instruction book and taught himself the rudiments of music to enable him to write down his compositions.

Any link between Christensen and Pinetop can only be surmised, but what can be said with a degree of certainty is that plagiarism was accepted among boogie-woogie pianists from the tradition of freely exchanging ideas and tunes. Listen, for example, to Hersal Thomas accompanying Sippie Wallace with Louis Armstrong on "Special Delivery Blues" (1926), issued two years before "Pinetop's Boogie-Woogie." The sequence of tremolo chords that Smith uses as an introduction in his composition is the same substantive accompaniment played by Thomas. Did Smith perhaps learn it from Thomas?

SIGNIFICANT PIANISTS

An important lead in the search for the early appearances of boogie-woogie in written and recorded form is provided by George Washington Thomas Jr. (1885–1936). He was the elder son in the Thomas family who became its patriarchal head when their father George Thomas Sr. died in New Orleans in 1918. Living with him at the time was Sippie Wallace, his sister, and Hersal Thomas, his younger brother, whose career he was to guide in later years. George spent his early years playing piano at parties known in New Orleans as chittlin struts, where he earned the nickname of "Gut Bucket George."[10] Thomas wrote tunes in the ragtime idiom: "Bull Frog Rag" and "Crawfish Rag," blues numbers such as "Muscle Shoals Blues" and "Houston Blues," and romantic songs like "I'll Give You a Chance" and "Love Will Live." He was a talented all-around musician adept on piano, cornet, and saxophone, whose heart was really in composing music rather than playing it for a living.

One of Thomas's compositions, called "New Orleans Hop Scop Blues," is thought to be the first twelve-bar blues to be written and published with a consistent boogie-woogie bass line. It was given this name because of its peculiar bass pattern, which Clarence Williams said "rolled and hopped." The piece was published in 1916 but was first recorded in 1923 by Williams for the Okeh Record Company after Thomas had sold the copyright to him.

The two men first met when they worked together in the same theatres in Houston. Williams was hired as the pianist in the pit orchestra, which usually consisted of a drummer, piano player, and occasional trombone. Thomas provided the accompaniment for silent films on the piano and entertained during intermissions. They formed a music-publishing company in New Orleans, in 1913, which entailed song plugging and door-to-door selling. Williams moved to Chicago in 1919 to open a publishing business and three music stores in the Chicago Loop district. George Thomas moved there shortly afterward and opened his own publishing house. The other members of the Thomas family followed George to Chicago, and by 1923 Sippie, her husband Matt, Hersal, and George's daughter Hociel were all living there and using it as a base from where they toured with vaudeville shows and later made their early recordings.

George appears to have had a liking for the boogie-woogie style, because elements of it appeared again in further compositions after "Hop Scop Blues" had been published. In this sense, Thomas was a pivotal figure in the evolution and dissemination of the boogie-woogie "sound." As a schooled musician and composer, he introduced elements of the exciting piano style into his own work, probably after hearing boogie-woogie being played in New Orleans and Houston, and in so doing, added a little

spice to his pieces. His compositions appeared as sheet music and on piano rolls and recordings, and could be heard being played live by various
artists and groups. Over time, their impact must have been considerable
through their gradual assimilation by a receptive public and certainly
other musicians of both a boogie and a non-boogie persuasion. Note the
number of Thomas's composition that were recorded by "popular" pianists of the day: Fats Waller, "Muscle Shoals Blues" (1922); Clarence Williams, "New Orleans Hop Scotch Blues" (1923); and Fletcher Henderson,
"Houston Blues" (1924)—all containing boogie-woogie tonality.

Two of his pieces having a direct influence on boogie-woogie piano
playing were "The Fives" and "The Rocks"; these were possibly some
of the earliest songs with a pronounced boogie-woogie rhythm heard
on Chicago's South Side. Many of the young tyros learning to play in
the style were presumably influenced by these pieces (see later). The
copyright of "The Fives" was registered in 1921, with George and Hersal Thomas credited as the joint composers. It was published in 1922 by
George's publishing company located at 428 Bowen Avenue. The lyrics
were written by George. It is a song about a train journey from Chicago
to San Francisco and the number five refers to the time of the train's arrival there.

The cover of "The Fives" has a drawing of an express train with a large
number five on the front of the engine as well as a picture of Lizzie Miles
who, it was said, "featured" the number. Player piano rolls and records
are advertised on the cover. Until fairly recently, examples of these had
not been found and a search of the recorded output of Lizzie Miles had
thrown no further light on a record made by her with this title. Lizzie
Miles was associated with both Williams and Thomas: From 1916, she
worked as a song plugger for Williams in New Orleans, Los Angeles,
and Chicago and, in 1919, sang with the George Thomas Orchestra at
the Pythian Temple Roof Gardens in New Orleans. She also recorded for
the Emerson label in 1922 with Clarence Williams and his Creole Jazz
Hounds and made records of her own for the Okeh label in 1922. She
either recorded "The Fives" but it was never released, or Williams and
Thomas traded on their relationship with her and used her photograph
on the cover of the song to improve the sales.

The existence of recordings of "The Fives" would have remained a mys-
tery but for the discovery of an early recording by an obscure white group
called the Tampa Blue Jazz Band, led by Joseph Samuels.[11] According to
the Okeh matrix (71247), the tune would have been recorded in the first
half of February 1923. As the recording follows the sheet music exactly,
George Thomas probably rehearsed the band or was directing events in
the recording studio. There is also a link with Clarence Williams, as the
Tampa Blue Jazz Band accompanied him on his first recording. The piano

is not featured in any solo boogie-woogie passages and provides a tradi-tional rhythm backing throughout until the final choruses when a barely discernible walking bass is introduced. "The Fives" was one of three tunes recorded by the band in one session. They had already recorded Thomas's "Houston Blues" six months earlier without the walking bass included in the original sheet music—unlike Fletcher Henderson's piano solo for Columbia (1924). George Thomas, it could be surmised, may have recorded a piano solo version of "The Fives" at the same time he recorded "The Rocks" as Clay Custer, but the recording may have been rejected by Okeh. The reference to "records ready" on the cover of the sheet music of "The Fives" seems to imply that Thomas knew his own and the Tampa Blue Jazz Band versions had been made or were booked to be made.

It is to "player piano rolls ready" that we have to turn to hear the defini-tive early version of "The Fives" played by younger brother Hersal (Kim-ball Piano Roll 10222), dating from 1924 and included on *Boogie-Woogie Story, Volume 2* (Milan Jazz, CD 887796). The bass pattern of "The Fives" is a varied one consisting of passages of "stride," walking bass, stepping octave chords, and other boogie-woogie basses. The treble also contains elements of typical boogie-woogie chording. George Thomas probably chose the boogie-woogie idiom to represent a train, but it seems evident from his other published work that boogie-woogie was one of several sources upon which he drew, depending on the kind of tune he was composing. A poignant postscript to the writing of "The Fives" is recalled by Axel Zwingenberger, the German pianist, who was a friend of Sippie Wallace and her accompanist at several concerts and on recordings. She told him that Thomas composed and sold "The Fives" coincidentally with the illness of his mother. Desperate to raise some cash to visit her, he used the sale money to pay for the train fare only to arrive in Houston some time after her death. The year was 1922.[12]

"The Fives" title chosen by the Thomas brothers does not immediately suggest an explanation of why certain basses used by Chicago pianists were also known by that name—that is, the exclusive, or predominant use of the first and fifth fingers as employed in a walking bass. The basses used in "The Fives" dispute this by their variation in fingering. Similarly, another bass figure called the "rocks," although bearing the same name as the piece composed by George Thomas, shows no obvious connection with the boogie bass used in that piece. But there is surely some association beyond the possibility of coincidence. Perhaps the reason why pianists used the "fives" and "rocks" as generic names for groups of similar bass patterns was that the two compositions—Thomas was publishing his material in Chicago—were some of the earliest to contain boogie-woogie basses that the pianists heard being played and saw in print. As such, the titles of the Thomas compositions may have given them ready-made names for the bass patterns they were themselves constructing in the 1920s.

Jimmy Yancey recorded piano solos that he called "The Fives" and "The Rocks," and it is to the first named that we turn to see if there is any similarity with George Thomas's composition. "The Fives" was recorded for Solo Art in 1939 and is basically the same piece as "Yancey Stomp" and "Midnight Stomp." The most obvious differences are in their length and the number of "breaks"— "The Fives" has a single "break," whereas "Yancey Stomp" has two "breaks" and "Midnight Stomp" has three. None of this material, known by its various names, bears any relationship to the Thomas composition. It is strictly Yancey material, and the titles given to it were probably concocted for the recording sessions. There is, however, a similarity between Clarence Lofton's recording of "The Fives" and the George Thomas composition. Lofton reworks some of the major choruses, but without lyrics, to a solid chorded bass. Evidently, Lofton's title looked toward the Thomas piece for inspiration and did not relate to a particular way of playing the bass.

The real significance of George and Hersal Thomas's composition "The Fives" lies in the effect that it had on Albert Ammons and Meade Lux Lewis when they were learning to play boogie-woogie. Both men were reported as saying that it was decisive in shaping the boogie-woogie of the present day.[13] Lewis also acknowledged the impact it had had on him and the excitement he and Ammons experienced when they first heard the piece, probably played by Hersal Thomas at a house rent party, saying that as long as the melody of "The Fives" was sustained in the treble it could be accompanied by a walking bass or any other kind of boogie-woogie bass pattern.[14]

The other piece written by George Thomas, and mentioned earlier, that can claim the distinction of being among the earliest known recorded works with a boogie-woogie structure is "The Rocks" (1923). It is generally held that Thomas was both the composer and the pianist who made the recording, although the pianist's name is Clay Custer. The link between Thomas and the soubriquet is to be found in the maiden name of his mother, which was said to be Custer. The number employs a bass not unlike the one favored by Albert Ammons on such numbers as "Boogie-Woogie Stomp" but is played by Thomas without the urgent rhythm of the Ammons's bass. "The Rocks" has a boogie-woogie structure and is a twelve-bar blues, though some of its choruses are more melodic in character than is usually associated with boogie-woogie. In this respect, it fits the pattern of a composition written for its novelty effect by someone who was aware of the interest that the boogie-woogie tone coloring would arouse on the race-record market.

Jimmy Blythe (1901–1931) was born in Kentucky but made Chicago his base from 1916 in a short life of thirty years. He was an all-around pianist who accompanied many singers on the Paramount label, produced scores of piano rolls, and appeared with small "spasm" bands such as the State Street Ramblers and the Midnight Rounders. He made fourteen known solo piano recordings, some accompanied by guitar or as duets with other pianists. His total output during the 1920s was extraordinary by any standards, and his influence on other pianists in the city is irrefutable but unconfirmed by research. He could play powerful boogie-woogie but did so infrequently, preferring to incorporate elements of it in his other work. Boogie-woogie basses were often inserted to add contrast or when additional impetus was needed. Variety was paramount in his music; his tunes possessed a "good time flavor" that induced a light, optimistic mood in the listener with little of the sorrowful tones associated with the blues. There was also a touch of vaudeville in their catchy melodies and risqué titles such as "Black Alley Rub" and "Can't Get Enough of That Stuff." As a stylist he drew from stride, ragtime, the blues, boogie-woogie, and the standard format of popular tunes of the day. It is clear that Albert Ammons was influenced by his music when one gives a careful listening to the work of both men: the arpeggio runs in the treble; the blues choruses used by Ammons in slower numbers such as "Chicago in Mind"; and the familiar bass pattern of "Been Here and Gone to the Mecca Flats" (1926), which Albert Ammons re-created as "Mecca Flat Blues." Albert's early training was obtained from copying piano rolls, and Jimmy Blythe's rolls were some that would have been available to him. The well-known theme of "Pinetop's Boogie-Woogie" also appears in Blythe's piano solo, "Jimmy's Blues" (1925). though, as we have seen, the enigma surrounding the origin of that piece remains to be solved.

An attractive example of Blythe's employment of boogie-woogie piano—in both hands—can be heard in his accompaniment to Sodarisa Miller (vocal) in "Sunshine Special" (1925). On this side it is used as an accompaniment to a blues vocal, but which, as such, is not restricted in the number of musical ideas it presents. In fact, it could almost be called monothematic: The opening motive presented at bar 1 of the first chorus (after the introduction) appears in every chorus, totally dominating some of them. Not so in his earlier recorded piano solo "Chicago Stomps" (1924). Here, freed from the voice, and over a striding eight-to-the-bar walking bass, Blythe presents seven choruses (there is a boogie-woogie introduction and a drawn-out, nonboogie ending) with very little repetition—the most obvious correspondences being between choruses 1 and 6 and between choruses 5 and 7—but, even here, they are not exact or complete repetitions. Several of the ideas presented in the treble one can find being used by later pianists. "Chicago Stomps" is not the greatest piece of boogie-woogie ever recorded, but it is possibly one of the earlier recordings of a piano solo (not dependent on or related to the vocal blues) that owes nothing to ragtime, New Orleans jazz, or other "foreign" elements. Neither does it intercalate nonboogie choruses (all of which are featured in the 1923 recordings of George W. Thomas's "The Rocks," "New Orleans Hop Scop Blues," and "The Fives") and thus stands, as one of the first truly genuine piece of boogie-woogie to be recorded. It was recorded four years before Smith made his much-lauded and much-imitated "Pinetop's Boogie-Woogie": It contains more musical material than does Smith's composition, but no one—then or since—made a fuss about Jimmy Blythe and "Chicago Stomps." Many of Blythe's important piano recordings including this number are contained on *South Side Blues Piano, Jimmy Blythe* (London, AL 3527).

The employment of boogie-woogie coloring by certain ragtime players has been considered, but ragtime touches also appeared in the work of pianists who were predominantly blues and boogie-woogie players. The most prominent of these pianists were Will Ezell, Little Brother Montgomery, and Charles "Cow-Cow" Davenport. All were known to have had some contact with ragtime pianists and show this either by including ragtime numbers in their repertoires (Davenport's "Atlanta Rag" [1929], Ezell's "West Coast Rag" [1927]) or, in Montgomery's case, by using elements of ragtime phrasing and construction in some of his numbers. Of the three, Davenport bears the closest scrutiny because he taught himself to play ragtime—he ragged the marches at school—and then continued employing it during his time as an accompanist in vaudeville, before eventually introducing boogie-woogie basses into his playing from about 1914, according to his own recollection of events. Some of his recorded compositions from 1929 show this amalgam of boogie-woogie and the more melodic ragtime element: "Chimes Blues," "Slum Gullion Stomp," and "Mootch Piddle" all include passages of walking bass.

The piece showing the greatest affinity with boogie-woogie is probably "Back in the Alley" (1929), which employs both single and double walking basses, that is, four- and eight-to-the-bar tempos. "Cow Cow Blues" also contains many elements of boogie-woogie, but it was originally a tune with lyrics. Oakley[15] states that its original title was "Railroad Blues," and indeed the words of the 1925 version not only make a number of references to trains—the Cannon Ball (an express train on the Louisville and Nashville [L and N]) line from Cincinnati to New Orleans—but also Dora Carr actually sings that she had those "railroad blues." Davenport, accompanied on piano by Sam Price—his absence from the keyboard was caused by arthritic hands—with bass, guitar, and flugelhorn, did in fact record a number entitled "Railroad Blues" (1938), thirteen years after the original issue of the record (Decca, 7462).

Will Ezell (1896?–) was born and raised in Shreveport, Louisiana, and spent his early piano playing career in his home state. Some distant recollections place him as the pianist in a sawmill at Haslam on the border between Texas and Louisiana and also at a white dance hall in Fullerton. Moving north, he spent time in the infamous Hastings Street area of Detroit and was known to have visited Cripple Clarence Lofton's bar, the Big Apple, in Chicago.[16] Ezell recorded for the Paramount Record Company and also acted as their house pianist and general handyman. He is said to have taken Blind Lemon Jefferson's remains to Dallas for burial. Ezell was a typical itinerant bluesman of the time.

Two of Ezell's solo compositions, "Heifer Dust" and "Barrelhouse Woman," dating from 1929, contain elements of both blues and barrelhouse in their form. They are not strictly boogie-woogie pieces, even though some of their sections feature an eight-to-the-bar walking bass. "Pitchin' Boogie" (1929), consisting of piano and talking with accompaniment by cornet, guitar, and tambourine, is boogie-woogie in style and character but makes use of a constant four-to-the-bar bass. "Barrelhouse Man" (1927) is not the same piece as "Barrelhouse Woman," although some of the musical ideas are related and the mood and style of both pieces are practically identical. "Barrelhouse Man" contains brief snatches of four-to-the-bar walking bass, and there is a single appearance (for only four bars) of an eight-to-the-bar walking bass. "Just Can't Stay Here" (1929), with piano, vocal, and instrumental accompaniment, is similar in style, though played at a slower tempo, to "Pitchin' Boogie." It employs the same stomping left-hand figure in the bass (four-to-the-bar) and similarly has a small instrumental backing and a vocal by Ezell. Another similarity between the two pieces is their melodic character as opposed to purely rhythmical ideas or figurations. "Playing the Dozens" (1929), which bears no thematic relationship to the Speckled Red recording of "The Dirty Dozens," is the only piano solo by Ezell that has a definite claim to being true, "unadulterated" boogie-woogie. For, apart from one of the choruses, it consistently uses an eight-to-the-bar walking bass. The treble ideas, too, have more of the true boogie-woogie flavor, through being more in the style of rhythmic punctuations than of the melodic character shown in his "Pitchin' Boogie" and "Just Can't Stay Here." All are available on *Will Ezell, Chicago Piano* (Paramount Recordings, 12-002).

This chapter has attempted to identify the different generations of pianists who shaped the contours of the boogie-woogie map beginning with the earliest endeavors of untutored barrelhouse pianists and those who melded ragtime and blues characteristics within their playing. Religious

music infused with the blues contributed to the defining rhythm of boogie-woogie—a syncopation quite distinctive from that of ragtime. Later,
boogie-woogie permeated African-American vaudeville theatre, which, if
not a determinant of the style, certainly helped nurture it. Finally, a metamorphosis occurred in the hands of the later urban players who gave it a
decided compositional form that reached a peak during the 1940s when
the piano pulsated to the black sounds of the Boogie-Woogie Trio. This
was followed, but rarely equaled, by the softer tones of talented white pianists from the swing-band era. The unfolding of these events and beyond,
and the personalities involved, are now considered in greater detail.

NOTES

1. James Lincoln Collier, *The Making of Jazz* (London: Macmillan, 1978),
110–11.
2. W. E. B. DuBois, *The Souls of Black Folk* (London: Longmans, 1965), 160–69.
Chapter 14 highlights the early significance of spirituals and religion in the lives
of African-Americans.
3. E. Borneman, "Boogie-Woogie," in *Just Jazz*, ed. S. Traill and G. Lascelles
(London: Peter Davies, 1957), 13–40.
4. Phil Garland, *The Sound of Soul* (Chicago: Henry Regnery, 1969), 186.
5. Collier, *The Making of Jazz*, 44.
6. Traill and Lascelles, *Just Jazz*, 17.
7. Traill and Lascelles, *Just Jazz*, 16.
8. R. Blesh and H. Janis, *They All Played Ragtime* (London: Sidgwick and Jackson, 1958), 192.
9. Edward A. Berlin, *Ragtime: A Musical and Cultural History* (Berkeley: University of California Press, 1985), 155.
10. Ronald P. Harwood, "Mighty Tight Woman: The Thomas Family and Classic Blues," *Storyville Magazine* 17 (June/July 1968): 18–21.
11. Ernest Virgo, correspondence with the author, January 20, 1992.
12. Axel Zwingenberger, correspondence with the author, February 21, 1986.
13. George and Hersal Thomas, "The Fives," in *All Star Boogie Woogie: Five
Piano Solos* (New York: Leeds Music, 1942), 2–6. Copyright granted to the Peter
Maurice Music Co. Ltd., Maurice Building, Denmark Street, London WC2.
14. "Meade Lux Lewis: A Blues Man's Story," *Downbeat*, February 1959, 16.
15. Giles Oakley, *The Devil's Music* (London: British Broadcasting Corporation,
1976), 173.
16. Bob Hall, liner notes, *Shake Your Wicked Knees: Rent Parties and Good Times:
Classic Piano Rags, Blues and Stomps 1928–1935*, Yazoo, 2035.

Part Two

THE URBAN SOUND
OF BOOGIE-WOOGIE

4

Chicago

Chicago became an important center in the steady transmutation of boogie-woogie piano from a primitive style with distinctive regional variations to a genre with a hard-edged urban sound. The late 1920s and 1930s stand out as the watershed when a more polished form began to emerge. There were several reasons for this, the most important being the concentration of black musicians in the city, their employment on the vaudeville circuits, the expanding race-record market, and the work available to pianists at rent parties.

In these times, there was a mass migration of black folk from the southern states looking for regular employment and the chance to start a new life. Racial discrimination was still practiced against them, and, if not as marked in the hustle and bustle of urban living, it was still a factor to be contended with. Although wages were low and housing conditions very poor, some satisfaction could be had from the knowledge that the shackles of the old southern order had been broken. The black quarter was on the South Side of Chicago. It was a relatively small area situated east and west of State Street, one of the main thoroughfares, and consisted predominantly of railroad property, housing, and clubs. The southern boundary extended south as far as Fifty-fifth Street and north beyond Thirty-second Street.

Among those drawn to the city were several of the boogie pianists who had learned their craft in the bars and dives of the South. They, together with the emerging school of Chicago-born pianists, took jobs as taxi drivers, hotel porters, dishwashers, and other menial occupations that coalesce in the bloodstream of urban life. Working at these occupations during the daytime, they supplemented their earnings by playing at house rent parties in the evenings and at weekends. The boogie-woogie pianists reigned supreme at these functions, and the more proficient of them found additional work at the many dives and clubs that became a part of Chicago's nightlife. For the majority of black families, low-standard housing was forced on them by their inability to afford anything better. Many lived in aging high-rise tenement blocks built over the lines of shops situated at street level, accessible by forbidding and dark stairways leading from the streets. Without doubt, the large influx of black newcomers made an immediate impact, bringing something distinctive to the locality from their own, ancient culture.

The title of one of Jimmy Blythe's compositions was "Lovin's Been Here and Gone to the Mecca Flats" (1926), and it was in this vast tenement that many of the rent parties were held. The Mecca Flats was situated on Thirty-fourth and State streets right in the heart of the South Side. Far from being a badly constructed building for housing poor black families, it started out as a model apartment block built in 1891 with modern conveniences such as central heating and refrigeration. Italian marble was brought in for the floors, and water fountains and fish ponds abounded. The Mecca Flats was originally designed for 175 family units, but a housing shortage created by the influx of black families into Chicago and the onset of the Depression combined to turn it into a huge slum dwelling. It was said that an estimated two thousand people were living there in the late 1940s.

At the time when house rent parties were at their height, in the 1920s and 1930s, the Mecca Flats had already begun its transformation from palace to slum. The thick carpeted floors and the other fittings designed to bring splendor to the building began to disappear at the end of World War I. Changes in the occupancy of the apartments also occurred from this time. The tenants consisted of a dwindling number of black professional families, poor but respectable African-Americans, petty criminals involved in South Side gambling activities such as the numbers rackets, and entertainers and musicians who worked in the cabarets and clubs flanking the Mecca Flats along State Street and the adjoining Thirty-fifth Street.

All the well-known Chicago boogie-woogie pianists played at the Mecca Flats at one time or another. Albert Ammons, in addition to recording a version of the Jimmy Blythe composition as "Mecca Flat Blues" (1939), performed regularly there. After one engagement, according to Pearlis C. Williams and Paige Von Vorst, Ammons first played and sang "Big Butter and Egg Man," then turned to Williams with an invitation to travel with him to Chicago, where he was performing at a house party in the Mecca Flats, to see his newly born son.[1] They arrived at Ammons's home, only to find that Gene had already been born, so they repaired to the Mecca flats for the party.

The segregation of blacks and whites was brought about by the economic and social conditions that maintained a marked cultural division in the city's population. Chicago was an important center for commerce and industry. It was the second largest city in America and an important railway terminal situated on Lake Michigan. Because of its position, it acted as a trade filter for cities on the east and west coasts, sitting like a huge spider at the center of a web of railroads and highways. There were fast rail connections with Kansas and St. Louis in the southwest; to Memphis, via the Illinois Central Railroad, in the south; to Louisville in the southeast; and to Baltimore, Ohio, and New York in the east. A rapid increase in the black population began in the early years of the nineteenth century, which accelerated with the arrival of southern African-Americans seeking employment in the early decades of the twentieth century. By 1970 seven million people lived in the city, of whom approximately one-third were African-Americans.

With two distinctively defined racial groups in the city, one newly arrived, there was little immediate opportunity for any form of integration. Each group retained its own cultural traditions, largely unaware of what the other was doing. The earliest fusion of musical interests began in about 1915, when jazz was first heard in the city with the arrival of the Original Creole Band at the Grand Theatre on State Street followed by several white jazz groups led by, among others, Nick La Rocca, the cornet player with the Original Dixieland Jazz Band.

Chicago was the major booking center for vaudeville acts in the northern states, serving an area between Pittsburgh and the Rocky Mountains. As such it became the nexus for dancers, musicians, and theatrical acts of all types as they passed through the city to new engagements or waited around for employment. Black artists were booked in at Chicago before going out on the road to play in theatres and tent shows for their own race. The best known of the agencies, and by all accounts known notoriously for its tight schedules and poor pay, was the Theatre Owners' Booking Agency (TOBA).

TOBA got under way as a business in 1921 following the initiative of one Sherman Dudley who wished to bring a sense of order to a somewhat chaotic booking system for black artists. (An earlier version of the agency was started in 1909 by Anselno Barrasso but faltered before being rescued by Dudley's initiative.) It had its own theatres at which a variety show of comedians, dancers, singers, and specialty acts was offered. There was a spot for the "star" who appeared at fourth place on the bill. The show normally opened and closed with the chorus—usually the whole company, involving plenty of dancing. A typical matinee show would last for about an hour; evening shows were somewhat different, lasting forty-five minutes and running three times a night. This short-lived agency closed in 1932 because of the effects of the Depression. Many of its theatres were converted to meet the needs of the emerging cinema industry.

At one time or another, TOBA had on its books many famous artists, including the blues singers Ma Rainey and Bessie Smith; the husband and wife double act Butterbeans and Susie; and a little-known pianist, Clarence "Pinetop" Smith, who provided piano accompaniments for some of their engagements. Another pianist who achieved a degree of recognition on the TOBA circuit was Charles "Cow Cow" Davenport. These two pianists, together with Jimmy Yancey and Hersal Thomas, were the important figures who defined the path that other, later pianists were to follow in Chicago.

Working in vaudeville, Smith and Davenport were required to have a wider repertoire than the run-of-the-mill pianists who performed casually at clubs if a piano was available. They were more than "one tune" pianists. Butterbeans and Susie, for example, sang sardonic duets about their parlous matrimonial state. Pianists who provided the accompaniments for such acts were expected to contribute humorous patter of their own as well as to prime the singers and contribute solo interludes. These considerable demands called for versatility and adaptability at the keyboard and helped to shape styles that ranged from the hot to the melodic. Such richness is evident in the work of both Smith and Davenport.

Charles "Cow Cow" Davenport (1894–1955) was born in Anniston, Alabama.[2] His father, Clement Davenport, was a preacher, and his mother, the exotically named Queen Victoria Jacobs, bore eight children. Charles showed an early interest in music and taught himself rudimentary keyboard skills on an organ that his mother played at the Baptist Church. He received some piano lessons when he was twelve and began to teach himself to play ragtime. This was not to his father's liking, so he arranged for Charles to attend Alabama Theological Seminary to train as a minister. Charles was not fitted to be a preacher, however, as his interests were very much centered on the piano. He wanted to play it well and to earn his living doing so. Having been expelled from college for "ragging" a march, he drifted to Birmingham, the largest city in the region where he was living.

His first break in pursuit of his objective was when he was offered work as a pianist at a club on Eighteenth Street. Unable to read music, he began to compose his own tunes and to improve his keyboard skills, but he could still play in only one key. Having acquired a larger repertoire and a sharper technique, he persisted in his task and began touring the mining towns of Alabama playing in the honky-tonks. It was at one of these establishments that he was heard by Bob Davies, a trained pianist, who ran a touring company called the "Barkroot Carnival." Davies invited Davenport to join the show as the pianist. One of the requirements was to accompany the women singers, which necessitated being able to play in several keys, so Davis took Davenport under his wing and began to teach him. His approach was a simple one, involving humming the melodies and showing Davenport the chord patterns. Davenport then had to practice these until they were mastered. Eventually, he became adept at playing in several keys and also acquired a stage presence on which he drew when he became a member of a duet and, later, a solo performer. This occurred more quickly than Charles expected. Soon after he had become established as the show's pianist, another piano player was hired. Fortunately, he was retained and given a spot in the program playing the piano, singing some of his own compositions, and doubling as a comedian.

Following the experience gained with the "Barkroot Carnival," Davenport eventually left the show to seek work as a solo act. One or two jobs followed, the longest being as a black-faced minstrel with Haeg's Circus in Macon, Georgia. At this time, in his late teens, he met a young blues singer named Dora Carr and they formed a double act called "Davenport and Co." Charles began writing material for his partner, and before long they were booked to appear on the TOBA circuit and undertook several successful tours in the South. Davenport claimed that he and Dora were the forerunners of the popular male-and-female double acts such as Butterbeans and Susie. On one of their tours, Davenport and Co. appeared in New Orleans and left the circuit to stay there for some time. Charles kept in practice by playing at one or two of the clubs in the Storyville District. He recalls hearing the pure trumpet tones of Louis Armstrong, who he says was "selling coal" at the time. Clarence Williams was also in the city attempting to start his first music-publishing business with A. J. Piron, a local bandleader.

During his stay in New Orleans, Charles was heard playing the piano by a talent scout named Peer. He received an invitation to visit New York and, with an advance of one hundred dollars in his pocket from Peer, traveled there to play some engagements. In New York he took the opportunity of making contact with a representative of the Okeh recording company. Following a successful audition, he and Dora made their first recording together, for which they were paid three hundred dollars. Clarence Williams, who had also moved to New York to start his publishing company, was asked to accompany the vocal duet of Dora and Charles on "You Might Pizen Me" (1924). Having completed the Okeh recording, Dora and Charles returned south and lived a comparatively comfortable life together until the money from their recordings ran out. A return to the South signaled the end of their vaudeville and recording act, because Dora left Charles for another man, despite his unsuccessful pleas to return with him to New York.

Davenport was now desperate for money, so he negotiated with a piano roll company called Vocal Style, to make some piano rolls of "Cow Cow Blues," his new composition. Neither Mr. Miller, the owner, nor any of the musical stores in Cincinnati, where the company was situated, would handle the piano rolls, so Cow Cow took it upon himself to travel from house to house selling them. He managed to do this successfully on an equal-share basis with the manufacturer until he had repaid the cost of cutting the rolls. As the rolls began to sell well, Miller included "Cow Cow Blues" on the company's catalog of piano rolls. Clarence Williams agreed to publish the music, and for a short time Dora Carr partnered Charles again while he was in New York recording "Cow Cow Blues." Davenport continued touring as a solo performer and eventually arrived in Florida, where he made the acquaintance of Ivy Smith, another singer. They formed an act called the Chicago Steppers, which lasted for some months, and, in 1927, the partnership began to record for the Paramount Company. Among the first sides were "Sad and Blue," "Third Alley Blues," and "Rising Sun Blues." A good cross-section of his work is on *Cow Cow Davenport: Cow Cow Blues* (Oldie Blues, OL 2811).

While in Chicago, Cow Cow was active at house parties before moving to Cleveland for a short time to open a music and record shop. The Paramount Company owed him three thousand dollars, so he used this as credit to buy a bus, and he and Ivy embarked on an extensive tour of the South with a new act called "Cow Cow's Chicago Steppers." Their tour took in the Lincoln Theatre, in Kansas City, where the manager paid him $1,300. This seemed a good omen for the future of the show, so they moved on to Tulsa, Oklahoma, and Dallas. Unfortunately, it was the worst time of the Depression, the mid-1930s, and the show was soon playing to half-empty houses. By the time they reached Mobile, there was insufficient money to pay for the artists' expenses, so Cow Cow pawned his bus to raise the money. However, he did this more than once, which was illegal in the South; the law caught up with him and he served a six-month jail sentence in Camp Kilby, near Montgomery. He was now destitute, his bus had been impounded, and the artists from the show had gone their separate ways. Cow Cow was put to work in the prison garden, but with the cold and damp climate he contracted pneumonia, which, he claimed, affected his right arm. After his release from prison he traveled to Tallahassee, Florida, and joined Haeg's Circus again as a minstrel. When the circus prepared to cross the Mason-Dixon line to tour the South, Cow Cow decided that he had had enough of the touring life, left the show, and returned to Cleveland to live in his sister's house, a broken and disillusioned troubadour.

A typical example of Davenport's boogie-woogie style can be heard in his famous number "Cow Cow Blues." The name was said to have been inspired by a section in the music where Charles was trying to use musical imagery to describe the signalman boarding the engine from the front of the train where the cow catcher was situated. During one theatre engagement shortly after he had composed the number, and while playing that section, he sang out, "Nobody rocks me like my Papa Cow Cow do." He said later that he was feeling sad after a breakup with one of his female partners. The name stuck and thereafter Charles was known to everyone as Charles "Cow Cow" Davenport. Many of his compositions were built around walking basses, and in this number it is played with a stiff precision that owes much to his early ragtime training. The version regarded as the most authoritative is the one made in 1928. In fact, the session recorded on July 16, 1928, resulted in the issue of two records—the first master, C2063A, released on Vocalion 1198, and the second master, C2063B, issued on Brunswick 80022. As these two masters are identical in all respects, it is quite acceptable to treat them as a single version. Analysis reveals that the "Cow Cow Blues" consists of two choruses (which may be lettered A and B) that are repeated throughout the piece in the following order: ABBBA^{1}BB. These two choruses may be divided into their various sections so that chorus A = introductions + a + b + c + d and chorus B = e + f + g + b + c + d. The A^1 chorus is similar to the A chorus except that the introduction is omitted. Thus, it is clear that though "Cow Cow Blues" is one of the most recognizable of tunes, it is a highly repetitive one and less representative of much vintage boogie-woogie of the period. Two earlier recordings of the number were made by Davenport: "Cow Cow Blues" (1925), in which his piano accompanies a vocal by Dora Carr, and the "New Cow Cow Blues" (1927), in which Davenport's piano is heard with the cornet of B. T. Wingfield.

In contrast to his boogie-woogie style, Davenport produced several ragtime records, of which "Atlanta Rag" has verve and sparkle. Another piece showing this side of his work to good effect is "Alabama Strut" (1928), on which he is joined by Ivy Smith who engages in patter with him. His undoubted influence on younger Chicago pianists can be surmised from a recording in the same year of "State Street Jive," another piano solo with talk by Ivy Smith. He demonstrates an amalgam of piano tricks, but at the heart of the piece is a repeated chromatic bass pattern played against three repeated chords in the treble. The number was probably heard by Albert Ammons, an impressionable young pianist of twenty-one when the recording was released. Albert's composition "Bass

Gone Crazy" (1939) is anchored in the same bass and treble configuration. Another of Davenport's numbers, "Back in the Alley" (1929), is notable for a variable tempo. It shows traces of "Cow Cow Blues" and an attractive repeated treble phrase that was used by Big Maceo Merriweather in his own "Texas Stomp" (1945). Finally, some idea of Davenport's versatility as a popular entertainer can be gleaned from "Mootch Piddle" (1929). The lyrics are explicitly sexual, but there is also a vein of humor, both honest and vulgar, in the accompanying patter in which Cow Cow asks his female companion if her husband is married, adding that if he is, she is in a "terrible fix." The number closes to the strain of "Auld Lang Syne."

The importance of Alabama is further substantiated by the recognition given to one of its sons, Clarence "Pinetop" Smith (1904–1929), for naming the boogie-woogie piano style. His parents, Sam and Mary (nee Baldwin) Smith were married on May 24, 1890, at J. F. Harman's Place, which is close to Orion, Pike County. Sam's parents may have been slaves from North Carolina where he was born in March 1843 and raised there. He is recorded as mulatto (i.e., of mixed black and white parentage) on the 1910 Census, whereas Mary is recorded as black. Clarence, like his brothers and sisters, was also recorded as mulatto.[3] It is conceivable that the family surname was taken from the slave owner—a not uncommon practice.

At least two birth dates have been proposed for Clarence: The most likely date is June 11, 1904; the midwife who helped deliver him recalled the month but not the exact day.[4] His death certificate also shows June 1904 as the month of his birth, without a date, which matches his age of 24 at the time of his death in March 1929. What is certain is that he was born in 1904, sometime after April of that year, as he was recorded as being five when the Census took place in April 1910. Therefore, the most likely date is June 11, 1904.

Clarence was the youngest child of a large family. He had four brothers—Jay, Samuel Jr., Clem, and Obie—and four sisters—Emma, Bertha, Gussie M., and Annie. At the time of the 1910 Census, the family home was at 199 Walden Street, Troy, Pike County. Jay, a sawmill worker, and Sam Jr.—who together with Emma appear to have been born before the wedding of their parents in 1890—were not living at the family home at the time of the Census. The father (Sam) was employed as a laborer/gardener, but Mary, now recorded as Mollie on the census form (or was she Sam's second wife?), who had previously worked as a laundress, was no longer in employment, presumably due to the responsibilities of caring for the large family. The Walden Street address was certainly where Clarence was raised. We can also assume that he was born there, because the Smiths were already a well-established family in Troy and lived at a previous address on Woodside or West Street before his birth, when the 1900 Census was held.

Clarence's brother Clem was a World War I veteran who was called up in the later stages of the war, reporting to Camp Dodge on March 28, 1918.[5] Later, he settled in Dale County, Midland Precinct, where he farmed and was father to a family of seven children at the time of the 1930 Census. Presumably, members of Pinetop's extended family still remain in the South and might conceivably possess information about him and the Smith family. Another brother, Obie, was still residing in the Troy area where he died in September 1975.

Smith was an enigmatic character with some reports describing him as handsome, dapper, and well dressed, while others are less flattering, but no photograph has ever been found to bear testimony to any of the given descriptions. In his research for the *Downbeat* feature articles, Sharon Pease reported, without meeting him, that Pinetop appeared to be someone who looked after his family, and had a kind and friendly personality. Davenport said of him shortly after they met that he was of short stature, good looking, "smooth," and popular with the women. He advised Pinetop to be careful of some of the places he was visiting to play piano, as his handsome features could cause envy in other men, adding that it was difficult to stay out of trouble if you "look good."[6]

Pinetop showed an interest in the piano at an early age, although there is no evidence that members of his family were particularly musical or that they owned a piano. Seth Copeland, the mayor of Troy, said that Pinetop was playing piano when he was a small boy.[7] Having mastered the rudiments, he was already performing in public at the East End Park Club in Birmingham in his early teens. He remained in that city for about two years before moving to Pittsburgh, where he sought employment as a vaudeville entertainer. This ambition was quickly realized when he was engaged to appear in a number of traveling road shows with the Raymond Brothers, the Whitman Sisters, and as a member of Matt Dorsey's Pickaninnies on the TOBA circuits. Though essentially a pianist, he was equally adept as a tap dancer, singer, and comedian—the latter two abilities being shown to good effect on several of his recordings.

His time as one of Mattie Dorsey's Pickaninnies was documented by Russell, presumably from comments made by Lewis and Ammons.[8] Clarence's name first appeared as a member of "Mattie Dorsey's Big Four" at the Grand Theatre in Memphis in 1919 when he was just fifteen. By 1920, he was being referred to as "little" Clarence Smith, when he and Mattie were performing as a duo in shows at the Standard Theatre in Philadelphia and the Lincoln Theater in New York. Pinetop received several plaudits in letters written by Mattie to the *Freeman*, one of several vaudeville trade papers, in order to publicize their work together. Later comments mentioned his "fine-looking" appearance during his third year of training and the possibility of him becoming a Mason, with the rider that it was a fine thing for a man to do. The full flavor and authentication of this period is given in an article about Dorsey's Pickaninnies.[9]

With such a thorough vaudeville training, it is not surprising that Pinetop's all-around entertainment value began to be recognized by some of the prestigious acts working for the TOBA circuit, leading to further tours across the States with Grant and Wilson, the Ma Rainey Show, and Butterbeans and Susie. However, it is debatable if his all-around abilities as a piano player were sufficient, as some observers infer, to have provided piano accompaniments for such well-known recording artistes and stars as Ma Rainey. The breadth of his repertoire, certainly from his recordings, and his technical range suggest otherwise, and he never featured on any recordings as an accompanist. Ma Rainey used Jimmy Blythe and Lovie Austin, among others. Pinetop was more likely a valued all-around theatre entertainer in his own right.

Pittsburgh was Pinetop's base between tours, and he appeared in various cabarets in that city. While appearing in a show at the Rathskeller on 1414 Wiley Avenue in 1924, he met Sarah Horton and married her on October 11, 1924, when he was twenty. His wife, who originated from Charlotte, North Carolina, said that they had a very compatible relationship.[10]

Some time after his marriage, Pinetop met Cow Cow Davenport in Pittsburgh. The meeting resulted in Pinetop taking his first steps to greater fame and eventual immortality as an influential performer of the modern boogie-woogie piano style. The events were as follows. After Cow Cow had made his first recordings, he was asked by J. Mayo Williams, the A&R man and record producer for the Vocalion label, if he would become a talent scout for them and the parent company Brunswick, to which he agreed. Williams was a college graduate known by the soubriquet "Ink" to the many musicians he worked with. He helped establish Paramount's commercial success, a company he joined in 1924, by recording major "race" artists of the caliber of "Blind" Lemon Jefferson and Ma Rainey. He was shrewd enough to identify the kind of music (blues) that the African-Americans wanted. Later, Williams started the short-lived Black Patti record label before moving on to Vocalion and, eventually, Decca.

Cow Cow was booked to appear at the Star Theatre, also situated on Wiley Avenue in Pittsburgh. His way of relaxing between shows was to visit the honky-tonks in the cities where he was appearing. He and a friend dropped in at one called Sachem Alley, a chili parlor and beer garden run by another of his friends, Herman Smith, and here they found Pinetop playing his blues and overhand piano style. After listening to him for a time, Davenport complimented him on his "mean" boogie-woogie style, though he later claimed that Pinetop had no real idea what he was playing so he attempted to assist by explaining how the choruses might be sequenced, and how the spoken directions to dancers might be fitted to the music.[11]

The events, as described by Davenport, offer a plausible explanation for the appearance of the term *boogie-woogie* in the title of Pinetop's composition. According to Pinetop's wife, he was composing "Pinetop's Boogie-Woogie" when they were living in Pittsburgh; she believed that he adopted the term *boogie-woogie* (see chapter 1) but could offer no clues as to its source. Whatever the true story, the locations and movements of Davenport and Smith point to a meeting and the germ of an idea being sown. This seems an altogether more plausible account of the origins of the composition than the one said to have been told to Albert Ammons by Pinetop: that he wrote the number at a rent party in St. Louis. The city of St. Louis was not unknown to Pinetop, however, for he played piano there in the brothels and at the rent parties, which were known as buffet flats, during the mid-twenties. James "Stump" Johnson, pianist from that city, reported to Paul Oliver that he was a friend of Pinetop back in those early years.[12] Pinetop traveled extensively, appearing as a solo pianist at house parties in Omaha, but mainly working on the TOBA vaudeville circuit, which took him to Barley's 81 Theatre in Atlanta, Georgia, the Lyric Theatre in New Orleans, the Koppins Theatre in Detroit, and to Memphis.

One important outcome of the meeting between the two pianists was a letter from Davenport to J. Mayo Williams about the younger pianist's boogie-woogie style. Whether or not he was then invited by Williams to travel to Chicago to record is not known, but he did move his family to that city in the summer of 1928 and immediately began working at the Forestville Tavern on Forty-seventh and Forestville.

Clarence Smith is often thought to be the patriarchal figure in the development of boogie-woogie, and although he had undoubted importance in providing the name for the genre, he was only a year older than Meade Lux Lewis. When he first moved to Chicago, he took up residence in the same apartment block where Ammons and Lewis were living, at 4435 Prairie Avenue on South Parkway, before moving later, with Sarah and elder son Clarence, to 1009 Larabee Street. The Ammons's family seems to have been the only one to own a piano, and the cutting sessions and sharing of ideas that must have occurred, and the beneficial results of these, can only be imagined.

After a period of acclimatization, Pinetop introduced himself to Mayo Williams and auditioned at the Brunswick Balke-Collender studios in the Furniture Mart. He recorded his eight sides over a period of several months, commencing in December 1928. These were a mixture of boogie-woogie, blues, monologues, and one standard of the day, "Nobody Knows You When You're Down and Out." Interestingly, some of his early efforts at the recording studio were made with his "Hokum Boys," probably with kazoo and jug, but they were never released; and, perhaps tantalizingly, what may have been a train boogie-woogie, "Driving Wheel Blues," was recorded at his last session in March 1929 but never issued. In an interview with Erwin Helfer in 1957, the pianist Doug Suggs, who worked the same Chicago rent parties as Pinetop, sums up the evidence we possess about this elusive man by describing him succinctly as a pleasant person and an able pianist with a good range of tunes.[13]

Pinetop was popular with the studio engineers and frequently entertained them, after cutting his masters, with tap dancing and piano renditions. He was often accompanied by his wife and son on these occasions. According to other accounts, Pinetop was an eccentric who roamed the South Side performing where the fancy took him. Reputedly coming to life in the evening and early morning, he slept off the excesses of this existence during the daytime. He often arrived at the studio for a recording session without money to pay for the cab. Despite these alleged peccadilloes, his wife, Sarah, remembered their pleasant married life and frequent visits to their home by musician friends such as Jelly Roll Morton, Tampa Red, and Earl Hines.

Pinetop led a full and eventful life, but few could have foreseen that his curiosity to enter a dance hall would lead to an early death. He left Larabee Street in the early evening of March 14, 1929. At the time he was working with Ernest Wallace, and the two men rehearsed together for most of the evening. On his way back home, Pinetop was passing the Masonic (Adams) Lodge hall at 1030 Orleans Street, on Chicago's near northwest side where a dance was in progress, sponsored by Excelsior Lodge No. 10961, Grand United Order of Odd Fellows. Attracted by the music of William Hartshall's band, and probably by now a Mason himself, he entered the hall. There were about three hundred people present, most of whom were dancing. Seeing some friends, Pinetop joined their group and was soon on the dance floor with Miss Louise Ford, the sister of a friend he knew in Cleveland. As they danced, a disturbance broke out between two guests named Floyd Stewart and William Allen, because one of them was messing around and pulling out the shirttails of the male dancers. Pinetop's dancing partner, wishing to see what the disturbance was about, suggested they should move closer. Pinetop is reported to have told her not to get too close to fights but to keep her distance from them.[14] Hearing the disturbance, David Bell, who held the sandwich concession at the Lodge, rushed forward to stop the argument before it got out of hand. As he did so he produced an automatic .32 caliber revolver from under his apron and began waving it about, because, as he later said in his court testimony, he thought he was about to be assaulted by the combatants. Ruby Bell, his daughter, and several nearby men and women scuffled with him to prevent him using the gun. It may have been Ruby Bell's action in trying to restrain her father that caused him to fire. The time was half an hour after midnight when the random bullet hit Pinetop. Putting his hand to his chest, he spat blood and walked ten or fifteen steps forward before collapsing on the floor. He was taken to the Henrotin Hospital where he died at 1:18 a.m. on March 15, having never recovered consciousness. Bell was eventually tracked down and put on trial after fleeing from the incident.

As the case unfolded, it became clear that Pinetop had been an innocent bystander to the altercation. Fifteen witnesses at the East Chicago Avenue police station described the events leading up to the shooting and all testified that Smith had not been involved in the quarrel but, unhappily, had been in the way of a bullet fired accidentally by Bell. Bell was acquitted and a verdict of accidental death recorded.

When boogie-woogie began to be featured in *Downbeat*, at the end of the 1930s, there were various references to the death of Pinetop Smith by stabbing. The full facts only became known after Sarah Smith was interviewed about her husband and the magazine had conducted some research into the background to the killing. Shortly before this, however, a letter appeared in the columns of the magazine confirming that he was shot and not stabbed. The letter writer was Miss Curtis Mae Burson, a musician of Local 208 of the musicians' union who said she was a member of the small orchestra at the dance hall; she stated that Smith arrived at 11:30 p.m. and was shot accidentally, dying as he was being transferred to the hospital.[15] The editor of *Downbeat* responded by saying that he was happy to correct the story. On the day that Smith died, Mayo Williams was waiting at the recording studio at 623 South Wabash where he was due to appear for a recording appointment at 10 a.m. At one o'clock Mrs. Smith arrived with the tragic news. He was finally buried in the Restvale Cemetery.

The "Pinetop" soubriquet was said by his wife to have been given by his mother when he and a friend used to climb pine trees and talk to each other through a telephone system made of tin cans and string. They spent so much time in the trees that she called him "Pinetop." That there were, and still are, considerable pine forests is shown on the town map where they lie to the east of Troy (Pinewood Estates and Pine Ridge Estates). The soubriquet does not refer to his height or the shape of his head, as averred by some authorities. More recently, others have proposed that "Pinetop" derived from the pinewood vats positioned over the stills used for making illicit alcohol, which gave a particular flavor to the alcohol—presumably much like the maturing of wines in oak barrels. Further credence for this, it is claimed, comes from Pinetop's many references to drink in his material: "Jump Steady" is apparently the name for home-brewed liquor. It is

Clarence "Pinetop" Smith's death certificate, 1929

further propounded that Pinetop may have been given his name through acting as a bootlegger during prohibition.[16] Certainly his travels would have allowed him contact with potential customers, but he appears to have been given his name at an earlier age, if one accepts the testimony of Mayor Seth Copeland, who knew the family when he might have been considered too young to be associated with peddling illicit liquor.

Pinetop continued to work on his piano technique throughout his career. He received some help on chord structure from other pianists he met on tour and kept a notebook in which he wrote down his compositions. The number of keys he used was considerably more than those employed by less skillful pianists. When "Pinetop's Blues"[17] was published it was written in the key of F; "Now I Ain't Got Nothing at All" was written in A flat. It is believed that "Pinetop's Boogie-Woogie" was originally composed in the key of C despite the edited version by Tiny Parham, copyrighted in 1939, appearing in the sheet music in the key of F.

As we have seen, Pinetop supplemented his earnings from clubs and recordings by working at house rent parties, where he seems to have been a popular personality with the well-developed sense of humor demonstrated in his recordings. Several of his numbers were monologues with piano backing, such as "I'm Sober Now," which describes the plight of the rent-party pianist trying to entertain with insufficient liquor available. "Big Boy They Can't Do That" comments on the ineffectual attempts of the underdog to protest about the treatment meted out during a prison sentence. Some of the imagery has an irony in its references to poor prison food and a louse the size of a mouse. This sardonic humor was also directed toward the lot of the pianist eking out a poor living from his recordings. In the opening patter in "Jump Steady Blues," his only solo boogie-woogie composition, he complains about the big money available to some pianists and wonders if he should practice the piano in the hope of receiving similar recognition. Pinetop was paid twelve and a half dollars for each of the eight sides he recorded for the Vocalion label in 1928, a total of one hundred dollars in all. In retrospect, he probably had cause to complain about the lowly amount paid to pianists. At that time, it was not unusual for recording executives to take a share of an artist's royalties. Indeed, a good proportion of their income came from this source. Charles Davenport said that Pinetop was paid off for his recordings and had pressed ten dollars into his hand for arranging his introduction to Mayo Williams.

A postscript to this tale is provided by researcher and author Christopher Page,[18] who tracked down Pinetop's elder son Clarence Jr. in Chicago where he was still living in 1999. Together with pianist Axel Zwingenberger and his partner Eva Henning, they visited Clarence Jr., who had retired after long service as a spray painter at a steel drum factory where, for several years, he had successfully organized the company's family reunion picnic. Clarence had few recollections of his father, as he was only three at the time of his death. After the *Downbeat* articles, in which he appeared in a photograph with his late brother Eugene, both boys had been placed in foster homes by their mother who was working as a domestic help before her death from cancer in 1949. Clarence Jr. was the owner of an original pressing of "Pinetop's Boogie-Woogie" and was delighted when Zwingenberger played him a version on a small organ in the basement room of his home. Reassuringly, Clarence Jr. was receiving some royalty payments from his father's recordings.

Pinetop had a light touch that makes his playing crisp and immediately recognizable. Several of his compositions used variations of the well-known treble phrases from his boogie-woogie number. Two of them, "Pinetop's Blues" and "I'm Sober Now," are built around the theme, while a third, "Jump Steady Blues," uses it sparingly. "Jump Steady Blues" is a well-constructed number that is made the more attractive by the economically concise treble passages. It is given lift by a walking bass of single notes alternated with a chorded octave, which complements the briskly executed treble. "I'm Sober Now" is not strictly a boogie composition; the treble predominates over a supporting bass line of single notes and an occasional chord. A similar pattern is used in "I Got More Sense Than That" and "Now I Ain't Got Nothing at All," which are sparse in both the treble and bass. This leads one to infer that it was Pinetop's intention to make the music support his monologues in these compositions, reasoning that his appeal would be wider if he offered the public cleverly constructed and witty monologues as well as piano pieces. He seems to have been reasonably ambitious for success as a recording artist, and this was probably one of the reasons why he left the TOBA circuits and settled his family in Chicago. An equally determining factor was the increasing closure rate of TOBA's theatres, down to just eighty nationwide in 1929.

Smith employed the tremolo sparingly and then mainly as an introduction or break. Apart from one or two in "Jump Steady Blues," the tremolo does not appear in any of his other recorded compositions. Another noticeable feature of his style is the way in which he maintains tautness and tension in the rhythm by pushing along the bass. This technique gives the impression of a slightly faster bass rhythm that anticipates the beat. He called his boogie style "overhand playing." The last of his eight recordings was "Nobody Knows You When You're Down and Out," a version of a popular song in the repertoire of many entertainers of the time. It was pressed with the record-buying public of the Depression years in mind. The complete recordings of Smith are available on *Piano Jazz: Boogie-Woogie Pianists, The Jazz Makers* (Swaggie, S 1326).

Compared with many of his contemporaries, Pinetop's recorded output was small but of a sufficiently high quality for him to attain a place as one of the most popular of the pianists in the race-recording market. Albert Ammons was one who owed him a debt. "Boogie-Woogie Stomp" was the first number that Albert recorded for the Decca Company in 1936 and was largely responsible for bringing him to the attention of a larger public. Pete Johnson also learned a great deal about the boogie style from

Smith's recordings, and his own style shows similarities in its nimble and deft touches. Johnson's treble passages are reminiscent of Smith's, notably in "Holler Stomp" (1939), which draws inspiration, in part, from "Jump Steady Blues." The ultimate seal of approval of Pinetop's work, however, certainly in terms of its commercial popularity, was when "Pinetop's Boogie-Woogie" was taken from the rent-party scene, arranged for a big band, entitled simply as "Boogie-Woogie" (1938), and given national exposure by the Tommy Dorsey Orchestra on radio broadcasts and at concerts.

We have seen what an intriguing and elusive character Pinetop was, and it is indicative of this that various myths grew around him. The circumstances of his death are now well documented, but at least two different and fanciful versions of the event have passed into the music's folklore. The first version, associated with Jack Dupree[19] and dating from his time in Chicago, has Pinetop taking the piano chair from his friend Fisher, a club owner, who had slashed a customer with a razor in an altercation. Both Fisher and Pinetop were said to be of similar build and to have red hair. Shortly afterward, the customer reappeared at the door with a gun seeking revenge and seeing a redheaded piano player, whom he assumed from behind to be Fisher, and mistakenly shot Pinetop through the back of the head.

Another tale, this time of passion and jealousy, has Pinetop playing the piano at the Naked Club in Galveston where, it was said, he had drawn inspiration for his boogie-woogie from a girl named Bessie Rose. She was said to be the "little girl with the red dress on" and Pinetop had dedicated the number to her. Thereafter, she insisted that he should always play it just for her. On this particular evening, Bessie had not shown up and Pinetop's roving eye alighted on an attractive girl who moved up to the piano and, bending close to his ear, asked him to play the number. He was agreeing to do so as Bessie Rose entered the club. Surveying the situation, the jealous girl drew a knife, approached him from the rear, and buried the blade in Pinetop's back while he sat at the piano. Every white key turned crimson with his blood.[20]

Returning to reality, Pinetop's memory was celebrated in two ways: Johnny Mercer composed and sang an innocuous song about his "life" on one of Benny Goodman's Camel Caravan radio shows in the late 1930s, on which Lewis and Ammons were featured; and more recently in 1967, a memorial by a sculptor named Claes Oldenberg was commissioned and erected in Chicago near the intersection where Smith died. In a short life of twenty-five years, being outlived by his mother, who died in Columbus in 1938, Clarence "Pinetop" Smith helped to lay the foundations of the modern boogie-woogie piano style.

The third original figure in Chicago's piano parade was James Edward Yancey (1898?– 1951), later referred to as "Papa" or Jimmy, who claimed to have been born on February 20, 1898, in Cook County, Chicago. Jimmy was one of four children born to Moses Yancey and his wife Irene, who were married in 1895 and lived at 2732 Armour Avenue. Moses was a string player and bass singer who earned his livelihood in vaudeville. For some time he was a member of the pit orchestra at the Pekin Theatre on State Street. He died in 1901. Although 1898 appears as the year of Yancey's birth in one of his letters to Bill Russell, there is still confusion about its accuracy.[21] The census of 1900 does not include Jimmy, but he does appear at age nine on the Census of 1910 with February 20, 1901, as his date of birth. Equally puzzling is his appearance on the World War I Draft Registration with a date of February 20, 1900, from when his family lived at 3146 Federal Street in Chicago. His birth date remains a complicated and unresolved riddle. Given Yancey's lack of formal education and his early theatrical background, it is not surprising that his "schooling" was obtained mainly from his time spent in the world of entertainment. By the age of ten, he was sufficiently accomplished to travel on coast-to-coast tours of America with Jeanette Adler, the Cozy Smith Troupe, and Bert Earle, and to appear in "The Man from Bam" at the Pekin Theatre and other shows as a singer and tap dancer. Another of the Yancey boys, Alonzo, was a competent ragtime player who died in 1944.

Between 1912 and 1914, Yancey worked for the Orpheum Vaudeville Circuit, which again involved touring major cities in America and Europe. In 1913, as part of the European tour, which took place in Budapest, Paris, and Berlin, he performed his dances and sang for King George V and Queen Mary at a Royal Command Show in Buckingham Palace. He was billed as an "eccentric dancer." On his return to Chicago, he quit show business at the age of sixteen or so—he had already crammed a lifetime's experience into a few years—and dedicated himself to learning to play the piano, after receiving some rudimentary instruction from Alonzo. "The Fives" was one of the early pieces he remembers hearing and playing, around 1915 or 1916. He soon became proficient enough to play at bars and rent parties, but he never sought to earn his living solely from music, although he did play short engagements at the Cabaret Moonlight Inn and the Trap Saloon. In time, he became one of the most sought-after pianists on the rent-party circuit and made good money. Unsubstantiated reports say that he played for the Chicago African-American baseball team at Comiskey Park when he was nineteen. What is certain is that he became the groundskeeper there in 1928, a position he held for more than twenty years.

Jimmy Yancey's wife Estelle (Harris) was born in Cairo, Illinois, on January 1, 1896. She moved with her family to Chicago when she was six months old and gained her early musical experience singing in a church choir. Estelle also learned to play the guitar. They were a happily married couple who provided love and companionship for each other over many years. Momma, as well as singing the blues and recording with Jimmy, helped him arrange his recording dates and concert appearances, many of which involved them both after his rediscovery in the late 1930s.

Jimmy Yancey was a quiet, introspective kind of person who preferred to let his music speak for itself rather than talk about it. He was easygoing, according to drummer Warren "Baby" Dodds, who first saw and heard him playing at a rent party in the company of Estelle. In one sense, his hidden feelings were expressed most openly in his music: no one could play with quite the same fluid economy on slow blues numbers; and his haunting and wistful melodies remain in the ear long after the turntable has stopped spinning. He is particularly remembered for his slower numbers, but he could knock out some fierce boogie-woogie.

"Yancey Stomp" (1939) deploys a drumming three-note bass pattern to drive along the rhythm. In a similar stomping vein is "State Street Special" (1939) with its heavier chorded bass and similar rhythm to the stomp. Many of Yancey's basses employed broken and suspended rhythms, which gave an indelible mark to his music (see chapter 3). Some authorities have called this the "Spanish tinge"; others have drawn parallels with the rhythms of the Charleston and the habanera, a popular dance from Cuba, imported into America at the beginning of the twentieth century. The most plausible explanation for Yancey's use of Latin American rhythms is their absorption from his days in vaudeville. The habanera preceded the tango craze that swept through the United States shortly afterward. However, some of Yancey's feeling for this rhythm may also have come from hearing Jelly Roll Morton's music (see chapter 1). It is interesting to note that blues pianists of a later generation from New Orleans, particularly William Byrd, aka Professor Longhair, have made considerable use of Latin rhythms in their pieces.

Yancey only had about twelve basic themes, which he permutated throughout his musical career. Several of them appear under different titles on his recordings, but he usually combined choruses from different themes rather than repeating one theme in its entirety. For example, "Yancey Stomp" is very similar in conception and interpretation to later recordings of "The Fives," "Midnight Stomp," "Janie's Joys," and "Yancey Limited" from 1939. Other examples are "35th and Dearborn"—the alternative take recorded in 1940 that has, musically, quite a lot in common with "Five O'Clock Blues" (1939); and without stretching the imagination too far, one could describe "Crying in My Sleep" (1940) as a vocal blues based on material from his piano solo "Tell 'Em All About Me" (1939). The only number that Yancey recorded with a consistent eight-to-the-bar bass figure (dotted quavers and semi-quavers) was "The Rocks" or, alternatively, "Jimmy's Rocks" (1943). It is in fact the same bass figure he uses for the final two choruses of "State Street Special" (1939), and perhaps it should come as no surprise to discover him actually quoting the penultimate chorus of "State Street Special" in this piece. The same chorus appears as a right-hand theme in "Yancey's Bugle Call" (1940), though here it is set—with minor variants—against the more typical Yancey boogie rhythm in the left-hand bass figure. It also occupies the position as the penultimate chorus in the second master recording of "Yancey's Bugle Call" (053438-2), but in the alternate take it occurs as the sixth chorus. Many of the numbers recorded for Victor, together with duets by Ammons and Johnson, are available on *Albert Ammons, Pete Johnson, Jimmy Yancey: Boogie-Woogie Man,* Volume 5 (RCA, 730.561).

Meade Lux Lewis was influenced in his own playing by his close contact with Yancey during his formative years in Chicago. The recording, by Lewis, of *Yancey Special* (1936)—the piece that Yancey had been playing since 1915—did much to bring the talents of the older man to the attention of the jazz public. There were recognizable similarities in the styles of the two pianists, but the tone that each produced was unique. Lewis had a full tone, whereas Yancey's was economical. There are phrases in "Six Wheel Chaser" (1940) that were borrowed and developed from "Yancey Stomp." There is also the shadow of "Five O'Clock Blues" in the Lewis number "Dupree Blues" (1955), but the reason for this may owe more to its popularity with pianists than to a conscious imitation of the older man's playing. Lewis dedicated a second composition to his mentor entitled "Yancey's Pride" (1944), in which strains of Yancey's treble work can again be discerned.

Albert Ammons was less noticeably influenced by Yancey in his style of playing. Where Yancey's tone was haunting and wistful, Ammons's tone was assertive and crisp. Even his blues numbers demonstrated a barely restrained power in their more delicate passages. The most direct musical association is in their use of tremolos employed as passing tones or rhythmical devices played over a steady ground beat. Even here the relationship may be tenuous, for Ammons was a master of the tremolo and it appears throughout his compositions, whereas Yancey used it sparingly, preferring the grace note. Ammons owed his greatest debt to Hersal Thomas in forming a personal boogie-woogie style. There are other strong influences in Albert's boogie-woogie, which can be traced to early Fats Waller and Jimmy Blythe, but the foundations came from an early association with Hersal Thomas.

Hersal Thomas (1909–1926) came to live in Chicago in the early 1920s—probably 1923. He was a child prodigy whose name was already credited as the joint composer of "The Fives," on the copyright card, when he was twelve years old. Hersal was born in Houston and under the benign influence of brother George began to show a precocious talent for playing blues on the piano. After moving to Chicago, these abilities were recognized, and he accompanied his sister Sippie Wallace on a number of recordings, some of which were made with Louis Armstrong and Joe "King" Oliver on the Okeh label. Shortly afterward in 1925, he recorded his first solo, "Suitcase Blues," followed by "Hersal Blues." Although he was only a young boy of fifteen or sixteen at this time, Hersal's technique and originality were much respected by other musicians. These two solos and the sensitive accompaniments he gave to the singing of Sippie and his niece Hociel Thomas demonstrate why he was held in such high regard. Hersal's mature talents contrasted starkly with the boylike figure who escorted his famous sister to rent parties and recording engagements. As Sippie recalled in Ronald Harwood's article about the Thomas family,

> My brother Hersal could really tickle them keys. You know he had short fingers and he wasn't nothin' but a boy. . . not in long pants yet. But whenever Hersal went anywhere they would always ask him to play. He went with me everywhere. That's when he got his pair of long pants when we went on the road together. I bought him a full dress suit to go on stage with me, and I bought him a suit to wear after the show.[22]

Both Albert Ammons and Meade Lux Lewis considered Hersal one of the most influential pianists in Chicago during the 1920s. To his early grasp of boogie-woogie basses acquired in Houston he added more complex bass patterns during his time in Chicago, greatly impressing the two young pianists in more ways than one. Russell wrote that whenever Hersal Thomas came to a party, other pianists were reluctant to play because of his outstanding interpretations, so he became unusually popular with the girls.[23]

Ammons learned from Thomas the importance of giving all notes their full value, by striking them with clarity and precision. Ammons's recording of "Suitcase Blues" (1942) compares well with the original and adds power to Thomas's more delicate rendition. Both were renowned for their strong basses, which swung their numbers in a way that few pianists have been capable of emulating.

During the period 1925–1926, Hersal was in constant demand by the record companies. He appeared on twelve titles with Hociel, and fifteen with Sippie, as well as accompanied vocalists Lillian Miller and Sodarisa Miller. It is fortunate that he recorded so extensively at this time, because he died tragically on July 3, 1926, the victim of suspected poisoning. The exact cause was never found; one story suggested that the poison had been given to Hersal by a jilted girlfriend. It was Sippie's opinion that Hersal was poisoned by eating a can of pork and beans. Whatever the reason, he was rushed to the hospital in the middle of a road tour in

Detroit and never recovered consciousness. It was a particularly painful death. Clarence Blair said that when he visited Hersal in the hospital, "the whites of his eyes and his fingernails had all turned black and he died."[24] The important recordings of members of the Thomas family, including the moving piano playing and singing of the underrated Bernice Edwards, is available on *Piano Blues, Volume 4: The Thomas Family 1925–1929* (Magpie, PY 4404).

Sippie Wallace was devastated by Hersal's death and lost any immediate desire to continue as a performing artist. She moved to Detroit to live there permanently in 1929 and became active in a Baptist church, continuing to work there into the 1970s. Sippie did reappear on the stage from time to time. In 1937 she worked with Jimmy Noone's band at the Hotel Vincennes in Chicago, shortly after another family bereavement, this time the death of elder brother George who died of bronchitis in Washington in 1936. Albert Ammons maintained contact with Sippie and they recorded "Bedroom Blues" and "Buzz Me" for the Mercury Company in 1945. Sippie, the last of the Thomas dynasty, finally came out of retirement and was featured at many blues festivals in the United States in the 1980s accompanied on piano by Bob Seeley and others. Prior to this, she had managed a tour of Europe with the American Folk Blues Festival in 1966, and one or two recording dates. The most compelling of the latter was her final date in Munich, Germany, with Axel Zwingenberger in October 1984. Here from a live recording are several old favorites, including "The Fives," "Mr. Freddie's Blues," and, for the first time, the vocal version of "Suitcase Blues," all available on *A Zwingenberger and the Friends of Boogie-Woogie, Volume 3: An Evening with Sippie Wallace* (Vagabond, LC 7148). Together with Zwingenberger's sensitive accompaniments, this petite octogenarian brings a singular poignancy to their rendition.

If Davenport, Smith, Yancey, and Thomas were the pivotal figures in the 1920s and 1930s, whose work helped to define some of the distinctive qualities of Chicago boogie-woogie, there were others who made their own lesser contributions. Doug Suggs (1894–?) was of this group and was known only as a legendary pianist until he was interviewed and recorded by Erwin Helfer for his Tone Record label in 1956 at the age of sixty-two. Suggs was born in St. Louis and moved to Chicago where he lived for the remainder of his life. Well-known on the rent-party circuit, he played alongside Ammons, Lofton, Yancey, and Smith. Like Yancey, he worked at Comiskey Park as a porter and it is surely no coincidence that his touch at the piano is similar to that of Jimmy Yancey.

Two of Suggs's recordings give some indication of his pleasant, melodic, and somewhat archaic style. The first, "Doug's Jump," is a relaxed, swinging piece of boogie-woogie, but unfortunately it has only four choruses, and chorus 4 is a repeat of chorus 3. The little there is, however, is most attractive and original. The other number recorded by Suggs is "Sweet Patootie," which he was taught to play by the composer Claude Brown, a resident of St. Louis. Brown was also a pianist of some repute in the city and an important influence on Suggs, who was a self-taught player. Suggs also came into contact with the St. Louis ragtime players Charlie Thompson and Dave Ambrose. The simple alternating chord pattern of the bass used in "Sweet Patootie" shows that it unmistakably derives from St. Louis. Interest in this tune stems from the fact that it is one of the pieces that Albert Ammons chose to record during the Library of Congress interviews and piano recordings of December 24, 1938, wherein Alan Lomax tells us that Ammons learned it from Doug Suggs about five years previously, in 1933. The Ammons's version is not the same piece as Suggs's original, but Ammons does use, in variants, ideas based on Suggs's first chorus: the left-hand ideas that Suggs uses in choruses 4 and 6 and—with very little alteration—the idea that Suggs uses for chorus 2 (and repeats for his third and eighth choruses). Additionally, there are the trills, tremolos, runs, arabesques, and other marvelous figurations that typify Ammons's style. The slow, stomping, four-to-the-bar bass pattern that Ammons employs in the left hand for a great deal of the piece is not featured by Suggs in his recording. Ammons made a second version entitled "Sweet Patootie Boogie" (1946) for the Mercury label and Yancey also recorded it for Session (1943). Yancey's "Sweet Patootie" deserves a mention if only because of the presumed close contact between the two pianists. It is an over-repetitive number based on the musical idea of Suggs's first chorus and little else. Yancey does subject this idea to some variation—but not enough to avoid the impression that one is hearing the same thing over and over again.

William Russell mentions the impact made by "Mr. Freddie Blues," which Suggs is also said to have brought to Chicago during the years of the First World War when he was in his twenties but never recorded. This number became associated with Freddie Shayne, another shadowy figure, who used it as his signature tune. Lewis recalls hearing Shayne playing it and he (Lewis) made his own recording of it for Decca in 1936. If the number of established boogie-woogie pianists who learned these two compositions that Suggs brought with him from St. Louis is any indication, then it suggests he carried more influence than he has been credited with in shaping some of the Chicago boogie-woogie styles with elements from St. Louis. It is also indicative of the roots of a folk art that he remained in apparent anonymity, working at a baseball field and filling in off-season as a porter at a Merchandise Mart in the city.

The origins of J. H. "Freddie" Shayne (real name Henry L. Shayne) are unknown, but all his working life was spent in and around Chicago. Early in his career, he was a solo pianist at the Royal Gardens during

Joe King Oliver's tenure there. After making his initial recording with Priscilla Stewart (vocal) in 1924 when they made "Mr. Freddie Blues" together—which Art Tatum, Mary Lou Williams, and even Connie Boswell were to record later—he was employed by the Paramount Company as an accompanist to singers, but his name was frequently omitted from the label. In this recording of the piece, the left hand of the piano accompaniment features a stomping four-to-the-bar bass, which is occasionally relieved by small touches of quicker note motion. In 1927, Priscilla Stewart made another recording of this number—the "new" "Mr. Freddie Blues"—this time with pianist Jimmy Blythe. This piece is not boogie-woogie—Blythe's accompaniment being more in the "stride" piano style. However, toward the end of both chorus 3 and chorus 4, Blythe introduces one and a half bars of an eight-to-the-bar boogie-woogie bass figure, and also closes the piece with the merest touch of this same bass figure. "Mr. Freddie Blues" (1935) draws closer to a purer form of boogie-woogie with J. H. Shayne's recording for Decca, a vocal accompanied by piano. In this, an eight-to-the-bar walking bass is used at bars 1 and 2 and bars 5 and 6 in all the choruses except the final (piano solo) chorus. "Lonesome Man Blues" (piano/vocal), recorded at the same session, is similar to his "Mr. Freddie Blues" in that a boogie-woogie bass (different from that of "Mr. Freddie Blues") is used in an intermittent manner, even though more extensively. Both tunes are scintillating examples of his rough-hewn boogie-woogie playing.

By 1936, Shayne was an established member of a small Chicago group that included John Lindsay (bass), Arnett Nelson (clarinet), and Lee Collins (trumpet) backing Victoria Spivey for a set of recordings in that year on the Vocalion label. These titles were "Detroit Moan," "Hollywood Stomp," "Any Kinda Man," and "I Ain't Gonna Let You See My Santa Claus." Shayne's recording career ceased after these recordings, until 1945 when Rudi Blesh asked him to record for his Circle label. The released recordings were accompaniments to Bertha "Chippie" Hill on "Charleston Blues" and "How Long Blues" plus two solos, "Mr. Freddie's Rag" and "Chestnut Street Boogie"—a "genuine" boogie that rocks steadily along (apart from its two breaks) from start to finish, with its treble ideas also furnishing proof that, even in the mid-1940s, Shayne could produce a personal and convincing piece of boogie-woogie. In the long gap between recording dates, Shayne was intermission pianist at several Chicago nightspots and appeared for some considerable time at the Garrick Stage Lounge where J. C. Higginbotham and Henry "Red" Allen were featured; other engagements saw him at the Dreamland Café and the Ponci Café. A selection of his recordings made for Circle can be heard on *Bertha "Chippie" Hill, Also Featuring Montana Taylor and Freddy Shayne* (Hot Society, 1005).

A pianist showing a distinctive style of playing with the rugged influence of the barrelhouse school of the midwestern pianists was Arthur "Montana" Taylor (1903–1954). He also displayed a sophistication in the complexity of his harmonies, in his later work, to which many from that school could never aspire. He was born in Butte, Montana, where his father ran the Silver City Club, offering a cabaret in the front and gambling upstairs. When Montana was seven the family moved to Chicago, but they were not settled for very long before moving on to Indianapolis. He taught himself to play the piano when he was sixteen. His major influences were the blues singers and pianists "Slick" and Jimmy Collins, who passed through Indianapolis. The brothers Tom and Phil Harding were two blues pianists he heard during this formative period, learning a tune from each of them. His first professional engagement in 1923 was at the Hole in the Wall on the corner of Indiana Avenue—the main thoroughfare of black Indianapolis—and Rag Alley, in Indianapolis. Sometime afterward, he was heard playing in a music store by a Mr. Guernsey, an Englishman acting as a talent scout for Vocalion, who promptly signed him up. A move to Chicago coincided with his first recordings for the company in 1929. During the Depression years, he played mainly at rent parties and music stores before finally moving in 1936 to Cleveland, Ohio.

Two fine, exuberant pieces of boogie-woogie are "Whoop and Holler Stomp" and "Hayride Stomp" (both recorded in 1929, piano and vocal with the Jazoo Boys), which drive along in a rocking, exciting manner. Musically, "Hayride Stomp" employs more in the way of different thematic material than "Whoop and Holler Stomp"—the latter being rather limited in this respect. "Indiana Avenue Stomp" (1929)—which Taylor played for a time at the Golden West Cabaret—was recorded as a piano solo. The left hand has a couple of bars in eight-to-the-bar rhythm at the beginning but also has occasional bars of only four crotchets and a predominating rhythm of ♩ ♪♪♩ ♪|. The style and playing of Taylor's "Detroit Rocks" (piano solo, 1929) tempts one to compare him with the Meade Lux Lewis of "Six Wheel Chaser" and "Chicago Flyer"; even if Taylor does not possess the technique or the inventiveness of Lewis, he is not very far behind. This is a superb piece of boogie-woogie in which the thick and heavy bass figure thunders relentlessly against ringing treble figurations.

In 1946, Taylor made several recordings for the Circle label, after being introduced to Blesh by Cow Cow Davenport. On their first meeting at Cow Cow's place in Cleveland, Blesh described Taylor's appearance as being short, but strongly muscled and dark of skin. Everything about him was quiet: his dress, his gliding way of walking, and his soft voice. His "Indiana Avenue Stomp" (1946) recording for Circle, although containing quite an amount of repetition between various choruses, is an extremely attractive piece, a fine boogie, and a good example of Taylor's evocative piano work. This is not the same piece as, nor is it related to or derived from, his "Indiana Avenue Stomp" (1929). Both the treble ideas and the bass time are different—and in this 1946 recording the bass rocks steadily along in continual eight-to-the-bar motion. Incidentally, regarding the matter of "earlier derivation," one may notice that the treble idea that serves in choruses 6 and 7 of "Indiana Avenue Stomp" (1946) has been heard before—notably toward the end of his "Whoop and Holler Stomp" (1929). "Low Down Bugle" (1946) features the bugle-call motif (it is quoted three times in all) and maintains a four-to-the-bar bass line throughout.

Two numbers made for Circle particularly suggest that Taylor was a pianist of some stature in the blues field, and they remain classics to this day. They are "Fo' Day Blues" and "In the Bottom" (both 1946). On the latter recording he accompanies his playing with whistling. Working with a hauntingly powerful technique, he logically builds up his choruses so that they complement each other. On faster numbers, usually stomps, he plays in the particularly jerky manner of the true primitive, whereas his slower pieces are introspective and mournful, giving the impression that he, like Yancey, lived his music. One of these, "I Can't Sleep" (1946), is both an original and beautiful melody, unexpected from an untutored piano player.

An example of Taylor's accompaniment work is provided by "Black Market Blues" (1946) in which he joins forces with Bertha "Chippie" Hill, whose vocal is perfectly matched by his fine boogie-woogie piano. The kazoo and washboard also blend in to assist in creating the haunting atmosphere of this little gem of a piece. Finally, Montana Taylor also gave a performance that was broadcast on the radio. The piece is given as "The Five O'Clock," the place as Chicago, and the date as 1946. It was later issued on a Library of Congress recording on which the title is given as "Piano Solo," the place as New York, and the date as June 28, 1948; further information states that the recording is an air check from the Mutual Network radio program *This Is Jazz*. "The Five O'Clock" and "Piano Solo" are, as careful listening will confirm, exactly one and the same piece, and are also one and the same recording. One difference between the two is the introduction made by the announcer, who says that this is "The Five O'Clock," which is omitted from the beginning of the "Piano Solo." The latter was also issued at a slower recording speed than the former. In both, however, the audience applause following the conclusion of Taylor's playing has been retained. This is a most stimulating piece of up-tempo boogie-woogie, especially at the faster speed of "The Five O'Clock," and possibly the most exciting composition that Taylor produced—the whole piece possessing a somewhat frenetic, explosive quality. The first three choruses are energetic enough, but the climax—consisting of choruses 4 and 5 whose flood of notes are interspersed with additional ringing choruses—as Taylor's right hand flashes up to strike the top end of the keyboard—is played with an almost ferocious intensity demanding unstinting admiration. A selection of his tunes appears on *Montana Taylor–Cripple Clarence Lofton, Archive of Jazz: Volume 15* (Low Down Piano France, BYG 529.065).

Little is known of Taylor's life after his Circle recordings, as he appears to have slipped into obscurity. He was known to have become disaffected with the music scene because of the nonpayment of royalties for his distinctive compositions. In looking back at Taylor's significance, it has to be acknowledged that he was much underrated. He was probably one of the greatest barrelhouse players: a pianist who could wring the soul from the keyboard either as anguish-ridden blues or primeval rhythms of unsurpassed intensity. One of his last reported appearances was as a guest at the Trenton Hot Club with Rudi Blesh, shortly after the Circle sides were released in 1947, where he gave a memorable recital of barrelhouse and boogie-woogie playing.[25] His planned return as an accompanist to Davenport at the Pinwheel Club in Cleveland in the 1950s never materialized.

Eurreal "Little Brother" Montgomery (1906–1985) started life in Kentwood, Louisiana, the son of Harper Montgomery. He came from a mixed ethnic background and descended from American Indians from the Creek tribe, and people who lived in the West Indies and Ireland. To complete a cosmopolitan picture, his wife Janet, whom he married in 1967, was Swedish, and she told the author that he got his name "Little Brother" from childhood. Apparently, as a boy, he was always in the company of his father Harper Montgomery, so when they'd walk to town the father's friends would hail him as "Brother Montgomery" and someone else would invariably say, "Yeah, and look who's with him, Little Brother Montgomery."[26]

Montgomery started out on the barrelhouse circuits, traveling through Louisiana and Mississippi before moving to Vicksburg, where he played at the Steamboat Exchange. His early experiences were in playing the blues and boogie-woogie, but he developed a considerable versatility at the keyboard, and by the time he was eighteen he was a member of a small band playing alongside guitar, string bass, and drums. For a period he lived and worked in Shreveport before gravitating to New Orleans where he lived on South Claiborne Street. He worked for some time as a solo pianist at Dodo and Red Bob's barrelhouse, situated on the corner of Caligo and Franklin streets. During his time in the city, Montgomery picked up useful piano techniques for playing in a band from watching and listening to the New Orleans jazz bands. He was soon on the move again, however, to Jackson, Mississippi, where he appeared at several clubs, including the Crystal Palace and the Red Castle. There he was actively sought out by bandleader Clarence Desdune to join the Joyland Revelers as pianist. The band was engaged in a six-month tour in the Midwest and had arrived in Jackson when Montgomery joined up with them; he played his first engagement with them in Yazoo City. Although he could not read music, he learned many of the piano parts by heart with the assistance of Oliver Alcorn, a member of the reed section; this enabled him to cope as a band pianist. Tiring of the life, he left the band when the tour had been completed and the band had returned to its base in Omaha, Nebraska. In 1928, Montgomery then traveled to Chicago, where he was soon a popular and active pianist at rent parties, with engagements most nights of the week. He was quoted as saying that it was impossible to get work unless a pianist could play "The Fives"—a confirmation perhaps of the importance of the George and Hersal Thomas composition.

Montgomery had a remarkable memory for events, places, and the names of pianists, and much of our knowledge of the early Chicago piano players from this time is due to his recollections. He recalled that Davenport worked in Chicago at the old Angelus Building on Thirty-fifth and Wabash, and all the well-known boogie-woogie pianists, Yancey, Ammons, Sweet Williams, Lofton, Toothpick, and Forty Five, were active at house parties while the young Hersal Thomas used to "run" with Montgomery and Charlie Spand.[27]

Rent parties, according to Montgomery, were frequently organized by the same person on a particular night each week. On the evenings when their own parties were not taking place, they and their friends attended others. During the weekdays, the parties usually terminated at about two or three o'clock in the morning, but would extend through the night on weekends to become "Blue Monday" parties. In the two years of Montgomery's first residence in Chicago, the rent parties became his main source of income. His only club engagement was at King Tut's Tomb on Forty-seventh and Michigan, which is not too surprising given the number of high-quality pianists who were available in the city at the time: Fats Waller was living out on Sixty-second Street and Michigan, and Earl Hines and Ted Weatherford were both in town. After more spells traveling in the South and an extended residency in New Orleans, Little Brother returned to Chicago in 1942, to pick up his playing at rent parties again, though it is generally accepted that they were a unique feature of the Depression years.

Little Brother made several club appearances in the years following his return to Chicago, including spells at the Brass Rail on Randolph Street, the Hollywood Show Lounge, and the Moulin Rouge. His ability at the keyboard also took him into traditional jazz, which was going through a period of revival in the 1940s and 1950s—he even appeared in 1949 at a Carnegie Hall concert as the pianist with the Kid Ory Band, but he reverted to solo playing, because, as he said of his own venture in running a band, it was too demanding of time and effort. Montgomery was very popular in the 1960s and 1970s playing at various festivals, including the Newport Jazz festival (1965), and visiting England and Europe with the American Folk Blues festival (1966). He was also featured in two British films about the blues: *Blues Like Showers of Rain* and *The Devil's Music.* This very gifted, all-around bluesman eventually succumbed to cancer, still at the pinnacle of his career. He was by Jan Montgomery's estimate "a talented, strong man."[28] It was always his wish to write popular songs and achieve further fame in this field. Several of his compositions in this vein were recorded for the Winding Ball label in the 1950s, but he never did achieve full recognition for this diversity. One of his most successful pieces was "First Time I Met the Blues."

A suitable epitaph to Little Brother would surely recognize his versatility in being able to play successfully in several different piano styles: boogie-woogie, the blues, and a ragtime-inflected stride. Within the boogie-woogie idiom, he was the master of the difficult double rhythm, as witnessed in his version of the "Forty Four Blues," which he renamed the "Vicksburg Blues" and first recorded in 1930. His technique was sure and much admired by his contemporaries. His boogie-woogie interpretations are infused with subtle, delicate melodic effects, as in "Farro Street Jive." His singing voice, though lacking the power of many recognized blues singers, is a reminder to the listener of the early barrelhouse days when to be heard through the smoke and noise required a piercing and arresting projection. These numbers and others initially recorded for Folkways in 1968 include "Pinetop's Boogie-Woogie," the somber "Lonesome Momma Blues," and the mainstream "St. Louis Blues." This fine display of Little Brother's considerable talents can be found on the reissue of the Folkways recordings, *Little Brother Montgomery: Farro Street Jive* (XTRA, 1115).

A picture of the South Side Chicago scene would be incomplete without an appreciation of the piano playing of "Cripple" Clarence Lofton (1896–1957), so called because of a congenital lameness. This did not inhibit his style, however, and in his heyday he was an all-around entertainer who sang, danced, snapped his fingers, and played the piano. Russell saw him as a three-ringed circus. He was born in Tennessee on March 28 and spent the remainder of his life in Chicago, having moved there when he was twenty-one. Lofton was a contemporary of Yancey, Smith, and Davenport and knew the younger pianists Ammons and Lewis. Lofton was an eccentric character who roamed the joints of the South Side at night looking for a piano to play. He ran his own "boogie school" at a saloon called the Big Apple, and it was here that he instructed novices in boogie-woogie techniques to ensure that the traditions of the music were passed on.[29] Lofton earned a living washing cars but came to depend increasingly on his talents as a piano player and all-around entertainer for the basic necessities of life. Though never a full-time musician, he could claim in the 1930s to have earned reasonable money at times, even making three dollars a night.[30] However, he seems to have missed out on some of the record royalties due to him and was reported to have a deep mistrust of white people, presumably because he felt cheated of his just rewards. One of his numbers, "I Don't Know," was later successfully recorded by Willie Mabon. Never one to hide his light under a bushel as a pianist, Lofton once boasted that he had brought on Pinetop, and would not hold back from offering advice to Meade Lux Lewis and Jimmy Yancey. The man's ego was affectionately put into perspective by Russell, who said that Lofton would have no qualms about taking on Rachmaninoff should he (Lofton) find himself, inappropriately, in Chicago's Orchestra Hall, on some occasion.[31]

Clarence Lofton was an eclectic performer who played in two keys, C and G. While his pounding style and interpretation were his own, he obtained inspiration from the themes of other pianists. His most compelling composition, "Streamline Train" (1939), was inspired by "Cow Cow Blues," while "Pinetop's Boogie-Woogie" (1939) was transformed into a very powerful and almost unrecognizable number. He was known as an erratic, uneven, and eccentric pianist who would often begin playing a new chorus before he had fully completed the preceding one. The twelve-bar pattern would sometimes be reduced to ten, as was the case in "I Don't Know" (1939), or eleven and a half bars in some interpretations of "Streamline Train." What he lacked in discipline, however, he more than made up for with vivacity and exuberance. In some respects he can be likened to players such as Jimmy Yancey and Montana Taylor, because their playing was largely untouched by time and their recordings accurately reflect the closed communities in which they performed. None of them was required to perform relentlessly for the public, as Johnson, Ammons, and Lewis were obliged to do when they became commercially popular.

Lofton provided a number of unattributed accompaniments for blues singers—Red Nelson, Al Miller, and Sammy Brown are among the confirmed ones. Two of his recordings with Red Nelson, in which both artists are heard at their best, are "Sweetest Thing Born" and "Cryin' Mother Blues" (both 1936)—with an unidentified guitar joining Nelson and Lofton in the former. In these, Lofton provides accompaniments that, though exhibiting some similarities, are structurally different; and in each case they perfectly complement Nelson's expressive vocals. The "Streamline Train" (1936) with Red Nelson (vocal) is the work from which Lofton's later, purely instrumental (piano solo) "Streamline Train" derives. Although the two pieces are by no means musically identical, the latter is obviously based on the former, with the use of the same melodic material at the close of each chorus being most marked and clearly identifiable in both pieces. The piano music, which is boogie-woogie, is not (in either piece) particularly related to the train's rhythm or sounds, at least not in an obvious manner (as in "Number Twenty-Nine" and the "Honky Tonk Train"). Lofton made use of the walking bass to good effect, always with the inclusion of the open fifth to give an original modal and thunderous tone to his playing. His style is also stamped with repeated single notes played in varying cross rhythms over the bass.

"Early Blues" and "The Fives" (both 1943) are two compositions consisting mainly of repetitions (with variants) of a single idea or theme. Neither of them follows the standard twelve-bar blues pattern—the former using a four-bar (varying with a four-and-a-half-bar) scheme, and the latter following mainly a ten-bar scheme. Two pieces of good boogie-woogie that do follow the standard twelve-bar pattern are "In the Mornin'" (1943) and "South End Boogie" (1939)—but even in these the occasional odd bar (and half-bar) do occur, resulting in choruses eleven, twelve and a half, and thirteen bars in length. At his best, Lofton could produce blues of a moving starkness and intensity, as in "South End Boogie" and "Had a Dream" (1943). "House Rent Struggle" (1939) is a piece of boogie-woogie similar in mood, style, and tempo (medium fast) to his "Streamline Train," which some believe is more convincing than the latter. He could be humorous as well, singing in his coarse, deep voice about the gambling rackets in "Policy Blues" (1943), played with a four-to-the-bar left hand. "I Don't Know," another vocal, contains finger-snapping but not much in the way of musical inventiveness. As "House Rent Struggle" and "Streamline Train" may be paired together as representing Lofton in a happy and boisterous party mood, so may "South End Boogie" and "Had a Dream" be paired together as showing Lofton in a sadder, introspective mood.

Russell drew a colorful picture of Lofton in full flight with stomping feet and pounding hands, half-turned from the keyboard in order to sing and yell at his audience or drummer. In the middle of a number he would stand up, hands clasped in front of him, and pivot on the piano stool, and then, out would come a vocal break from somewhere deep in his throat. A moment later, he would attack the keyboard again with flying fingers. Lofton clearly lived his music with great passion, because his actions and facial expressions were as dramatic and exciting as his music.[32]

With the gradual demise of the rent party, Clarence was musically less active thereafter—he was barred from playing at Chicago clubs because he did not hold a union membership card. One of his last club appearances was reportedly at Maxwell and Morgan streets, where he shared the bill with a saxophone band.[33] A way was found around his lack of union membership by moving concert venues from Chicago's Loop to the plusher Lake Forest area of the city beyond the union's jurisdiction. By this means, Lofton was able to appear at one of impresario Harry Lim's jazz concerts in 1941. Lofton's work appears on many collections, but in the author's view, the recording that captures his idiosyncratic style and tunes best, including "Streamline Train," "The Fives," and "Policy Blues," as well as his robust singing and which were originally made for Session in 1943, is the LP *Jazz Immortals No. 1: Cripple Clarence Lofton* (Vogue, LDE 122).

Several Chicago pianists left only a tantalizing fragment of their talents on record. One was the exotically named Turner Parrish who produced a technically superb rendition of his own composition "Trenches" (1933), notable for its eccentric and unpredictable form. Little is known of his background, but he is said to have worked in Chicago. He had already made "Western Travelers Blues" and "Wake Up in the Morning Blues" (both 1929), on which he accompanied his own singing, before recording "Trenches" and "The Fives" in 1933. Features of his piano style have been placed as having come from Indianapolis as well as Chicago; and he may have moved from the former city as Leroy Carr; the most famous pianist entertainer from there was clearly his model for "Ain't Gonna Be Your Dog No More" (1933) .

Inomeio (Romeo) Nelson (1902–1974) moved to Chicago at the age of six and worked in and around that city for the remainder of his life, playing mainly at rent parties. He was born in Springfield, Tennessee, and was buried in the Restvale Cemetery in Chicago. The justifiable reason to applaud the coming of Nelson—in the field of boogie-woogie—is his "Head Rag Hop" (1929), a piano solo with talking by Tampa Red and Frankie Jaxon. "Head Rag Hop" is one of those pieces that present the scene of the rent party (as on Pinetop Smith's "I'm Sober Now" and "Pinetop's Boogie-Woogie" and Will Ezell's "Pitchin' Boogie"), and as it was recorded nine months later than Pinetop's masterpiece, "Head Rag Hop" may have been inspired by it. However, to claim that it is closely modeled on this piece would be misleading. Admittedly, both works contain an announcement of the title of the piece and an instruction to a girl in a certain colored dress to approach the performer and eventually to "shake it" (Nelson) or to "shake that thing" (Smith). Further, the words *boogie-woogie* are stated on both records, and Pinetop's "That's What I'm talkin' 'Bout" is heard twice on Romeo's record. But that is all there is in the way of close modeling. The treble figuration in the right hand of "Head Rag Hop" is also—apart from some stomp chord passages— entirely different from that in "Pinetop's Boogie-Woogie." While Romeo's left hand does at times play a boogie-woogie bass figure that is very similar to that employed by Pinetop, this is regularly alternated with an eight-to-the-bar walking bass figure. Finally, "Head Rag Hop" (with its ebullient glissandi) is a lighthearted good-time party piece that possesses none of the underlying melancholy of "Pinetop's Boogie-Woogie." This recording is on *Piano Jazz: Boogie-Woogie Pianists* (Swaggie, S 1326).

Charles Avery was an obscure figure about whose background little is known but who was active in Chicago as a performer and recording artist in the late 1920s and the 1930s. The title of his best-known solo recording, inspired by Pinetop's classic, "Dearborn Street Breakdown" (1929), suggests an association with Chicago's South Side. Avery devoted himself entirely to working as a fine studio accompanist for Lil Johnson, Red Nelson, Freddie "Red" Nicholson, Lucille Bogan, and possibly Victoria Spivey. Among the Avery accompaniments, one of his best must surely be his recording with Lil Johnson (vocal) and Tampa Red (guitar) entitled "House Rent Scuffle" (1929), the interest lying not so much in the music as in the lyrics, which describe the rent-party scene with Lil Johnson exhorting the patrons to enjoy themselves with fried chicken, red beans and rice, soda water, and wine. No doubt responding to the later exhortation for someone to provide the pianist with a drink, Avery gives a fine, steady rocking performance, propelling the music along by using what is basically the same left-hand bass figure as that employed in his "Dearborn Street Breakdown," though here played at a slower tempo and utilizing a ♩ ♫♩ ♫ rhythm for most of the time. In "Freddie's Got the Blues" (1930), the singing of Freddie "Red" Nicholson is accompanied by the piano of Charles Avery who here displays a style—and a left-hand bass rhythm—in complete contrast to that shown in "Dearborn Street Breakdown" (bass example 16) and "House Rent Scuffle." This piece is in a subdued mood and is taken at a moderately slow tempo, with Avery using a straight or more common eight-to-the-bar boogie-woogie bass figure that constantly, and somewhat monotonously, chugs away while the right hand exhibits a simplistic style with relatively few notes. Incidentally, this piece has nothing to do with the "Mr. Freddie Blues" of Priscilla Stewart, J. H. Shayne, and Jimmy Blythe. Avery disappeared from the recording studio and reappeared later in 1935, when he again acted as accompanist for Red Nelson on "Grand Trunk Blues." All his released recordings were as an accompanist with only the one solo and a tantalizingly unissued second one, "63rd Street Stomp." A collection of his known recordings is on *Piano Blues and Boogie Woogie 1929–1935: Charles Avery, Freddie "Red" Nicholson, "Jabo" Williams* (Blues Documents, RST BD 2034).

Dan Burley (1907–1962) was born in Kentucky, the son of a slave, and grew up in Chicago where he attended Wendell High School—the same school where Nat "King" Cole was a pupil. His talents for both writing and music-making soon became evident as editor of the school newspaper and as a somewhat laid-back and precocious student who looked older than his years, playing piano at South Side rent parties. Hersal Thomas, reputedly, taught him one of his first blues pieces. Having cut his teeth as a journalist for the *Chicago Defender*, he later moved to New York, where he became an active member of the music and social scene. His ready wit and sociability made him a popular figure. In time, he became chief sports writer and, eventually, manager of the prestigious *Amsterdam News*. A move back to Chicago in the 1950s saw Burley's newspaper career continue to flourish—he was now managing editor of the *Chicago Crusader*. He also played piano when requested to do so at private parties and lived his life to the full before finally succumbing to a second heart attack and dying in his sleep at the age of fifty-seven. Though his music may not have been memorably original, he will be remembered for his legacy of a dictionary of "jive" expressions that added to an understanding of African-American culture, particularly during the "hep" 1940s. The life and recording career of Dan Burley are contained in a well-researched and informative booklet written by Konrad Nowakowski that accompanies *Dan Burley: South Side Shake 1945–1951* (Wolf, WBJ 008CD).

Burley was one of several guest pianists who worked with the Lionel Hampton band. Unlike Albert Ammons, who was appointed on a contract to act as the band pianist, Dan Burley only played on two numbers, "Ridin' on the L & N" and "Hamp's Salty Blues" (1946). His appearance as a "guest" with Hampton is not surprising, as they knew each other in Chicago. Indeed, Burley may have recommended some of the musicians and the music for Hampton's band after he had left Benny Goodman's band. Prior to this, Hampton was featuring and recording some of Burley's compositions, namely "I'm on My Way from You" and "The Munson Street Breakdown" (both in 1939)—the latter being the first arranged boogie-woogie number recorded by Hampton. Some authorities believe that Burley instigated the boogie-woogie phase of Hampton's band. Never considered solely a musician because of his other well-developed sides, he did go on to make further recordings with Albert Nicholas, "Hot Lips" Page, and Leonard Feather.

Burley played a type of good-time skiffle music, partly boogie-woogie but with leanings toward more melodic tunes as well. His style on the Circle sides for Rudi Blesh reminds one of Jimmy Yancey and Clarence Lofton and points to a Chicago influence. Burley and his Skiffle Boys recorded six pieces in New York on November 11, 1946. Burley takes the vocal in several pieces, in addition to playing the piano. Three of the six numbers, "Lakefront Blues," "Three Flights Up," and "Dusty Bottom," are of slow or medium tempo and are not boogie-woogie. Of the three remaining pieces, which are played in medium and up-tempo, "South Side Shake" has an ostinato bass and both "Big Cat Little Cat" and "Shotgun House Rag" use walking basses. Possibly, "Shotgun House Rag"—on account of its using more typical and characteristic treble ideas and because of occasional passages of eight-to-the-bar walking bass—may be considered the piece closest to boogie-woogie. All six tunes are attractive and provide quite enjoyable listening, but a certain sense of disappointment is experienced upon hearing them, due to, of course, the lack of a really solid boogie-woogie number. When Dan Burley was a rent-party pianist in Chicago, he was said to be able to play in excess of two dozen bass patterns (and could recall their geographical origin).[34] In view of the expectations aroused by these claims, these six recordings, regrettably, provide something of an anticlimax in their listening.

Other pianists were embraced by Chicago's casual house parties. A number were "one-tune" players, while some were talented but underrecorded for a variety of reasons. Among the familiar and locally known players occupying the piano seat were Frank "Sweet" Williams, Bert Mays, Georgia White, and George Noble. Noble's trademark was an incipiently foreboding heavy bass contrasting with flashing octaves in the treble to support his vocals, and on "TB Blues" (1935), realistic bouts of coughing.

Pianists could expect little financial gain from their recording engagements. Few collected royalties for their efforts and usually received a single fee for the session. This meant that the master record became the property of the company and could be reissued without any further financial responsibility toward the artist. The plethora of willing pianists and the lusty industry of the companies in selling their wares weighted the scales in favor of their profits at the expense of the artists. At the height of the recording boom, between 1927 and 1930, scores of pianists were recorded, made possible, as we have seen, by the concentration of musical talent in Chicago. Much of it was in the one small area of the city, the South Side. Here, saloons, barrelhouses, cafés, theatres, brothels, hotels, and clubs were packed tightly together, providing plenty of work for pianists. Additionally, there was the highly developed market for their talents at rent parties. Pianists listened to each other playing and engaged in friendly, but nonetheless intense cutting sessions. With these favorable conditions, the music spread and the techniques of the many involved in playing it were expanded and refined. However, such an abundance of talent available in one city meant that some of those capable of doing so would not record. Unfortunately, their chance never did come, as the economic depression hit America and the buoyant and profitable race-record market collapsed overnight.

NOTES

1. Conversation between Pearlis C. Williams and Paige Van Vorst in *The Mississippi Rag* 4, no. 9 (February 1977): 9.

2. Biographical information about Davenport can be found in Cow Cow Davenport, "Mama Don't 'Low No Music," *Jazz Record* 27 (December 1944): 6–9 and Don Haynes, "Cow Cow Davenport," *Jazz Information*, October 25, 1940, 8–10.

3. *Thirteenth Census of the United States 1910; Pike County, Alabama State*. Assistance with this and other Census data in relation to the Smith family was provided by the Troy Public Library Service, Alabama.

4. Sharon A. Pease, "I Saw Pinetop Spit Blood and Fall: The Life and Death of Clarence Pinetop Smith, Creator of Boogie-Woogie," *Downbeat* 6, no. 10 (October 1939): 18.

5. *Honoring Our Own*, World War I Pike County Veterans. Provided by the Troy County Library, Alabama.

6. Davenport, "Mama Don't 'Low No Music," 8.

7. Pease, "I Saw Pinetop," 18.

8. William Russell, "Boogie-Woogie," in *Jazzmen*, eds. F. Ramsey and C. Smith (London: Sidgwick and Jackson, 1958), 187.

9. Doug Seroff and Lynn Abbott, "Sweet Mattie Dorsey, Been Here, but She's Gone," *78 Quarterly* 8 (Fall 1993 or Spring 1994): 103–112.

10. Pease, "I Saw Pinetop," 18.

11. A. Hodes and C. Hanson, eds., *Selections from the Gutter* (Berkeley: University of California Press, 1977), 44.

12. P. Oliver, *Conversation with the Blues* (London: Cassell, 1967), 96.

13. Erwin Helfer, "Interview with Doug Suggs (22 June 1957)," *Primitive Piano*, The Sirens Records, SR 5005.

14. Pease, "I Saw Pinetop," 4.

15. "Pinetop Wasn't Stabbed—He Was Shot Dead!" letter in *Downbeat*, May 1939, 10.

16. Bob Hall, liner notes, *Shake Your Wicked Knees: Rent Parties and Good Times: Classic Piano Rags, Blues and Stomps 1928–1935*, Yazoo, 2035.

17. *Five Boogie-Woogie Piano Solos by Pinetop Smith* (New York: Leeds Music, 1941), 4. Copyright granted to the Peter Maurice Co. Ltd., Maurice Building, Denmark Street, London W/C2.

18. Christopher Page, correspondence with the author, May 1999.

19. Paul Oliver, *Blues off the Record* (New York: Hippocreme Books, 1984), 247.

20. George Hoefer, "Tales of Two Jazzmen: One True, Other False," The Hot Box: A Column for Record Collectors, *Downbeat*, April 18, 1952, 7.

21. Jane M. Bowers, "The Enigma of Jimmy Yancey's Early Years: Notes toward a Biography," *American Music* 24, no. 2 (Summer 2006): 133–71.

22. Ronald P. Harwood, "Mighty Tight Woman: The Thomas Family and Classic Blues," *Storyville Magazine*, no. 17 (June/July 1968): 22.

23. Russell, "Boogie-Woogie," 189.

24. Harwood, "Mighty Tight Woman," 22.

25. Frank Trolle, "Montana Taylor," *IAJRC* 18, no. 1 (January 1985): 1.

26. Janet Montgomery, correspondence with the author, February 6, 1989.

27. K. G. zur Heide, *Deep South Piano* (London: Studio Vista, 1970), 45.

28. J. Montgomery, correspondence with the author, February 6, 1989.

29. Russell, "Boogie-Woogie," 196.

30. William Russell, "Three Boogie-Woogie Pianists," in *The Art of Jazz*, ed. Martin T. Willliams (London: Cassell, 1962), 96.

31. Russell, "Three Boogie-Woogie Pianists," 96.

32. Russell, "Boogie-Woogie," 196.

33. "Chicago," *Jazz Information*, February 7, 1941, 6.

34. Rudi Blesh, *Shining Trumpets* (London: Cassell, 1949), 304.

5

The Depression Years

The Great Depression hit America as the roaring twenties came to an end, bringing unrelieved gloom and poverty to a once prosperous country. Industry and commerce ground to a halt, unable to make even the most modest of profits. The crash was caused by the complete collapse of the stock market on Wall Street, New York, where money was being circulated, unsupported by bullion reserves, to match the unbridled demands of speculators and consumer spending. When pressure on the economy reached a peak, it simply collapsed like a pricked balloon. Despite the implementation of Roosevelt's New Deal in the middle of the 1930s, the Depression lasted until World War II and it left its scars on the lives of millions, none more so than on the black population, who were some of the first to lose their employment when the cold wind blew. The period immediately before the crash is remembered for its fast living, wild spending, and the disappearance of many of the social mores that had been woven into the fabric of American society. Skirts were shorter, dances wilder, and liquor more plentiful; America had entered the Jazz Age.

In legislation, which was partly a response to what was seen as the nation's unbridled decadence, emanating from right-wing pressure groups, alcohol was made illegal by the government with the passing of the Volstead Act (1919–1933). Prohibition, as it was called, hit the nation overnight. Liquor was poured into the gutters by the police force and other zealots in a show of support for the newly passed legislation; and it was recorded for posterity on newsreels. In outward appearance at least, saloons, clubs, and less savory joints became dry, but the Act gave rise to more evils than the government could have foreseen. Illicit liquor-making and drinking took over and brought in their wake the racketeers, who filled the void by providing moonshine alcohol for illegal consumption. The quality of the liquor was dubious in the extreme, being made from anything that would produce alcohol: corn was one of the more acceptable materials. The racketeers were organized in gangs, and such was the competition among them for supplying liquor that gang warfare erupted on the streets. Chicago saw more of this than most places, although Kansas City, New York, and other large cities also had their mobsters. Prostitution was another cause of friction between the various groups, leading to killings and milder flare-ups between the rival factions as they contested their territorial rights.

Early on, the gangsters targeted the clubs, demanding protection money in return for allowing them to remain open. Once control had been established, proprietors were obliged to buy their moonshine liquor from them at inflated prices. It was a brave club owner who tried to resist the mobsters, and many clubs were taken over by employees of the gangsters if the owners proved uncooperative. Musicians were sucked willy-nilly into this maelstrom and often found themselves appearing at clubs where the gangsters were in control. Art Hodes had several encounters with them in South Side clubs. On one memorable occasion, Fats Waller was frightened witless when he was summoned to Cicero, a city suburb, to play for a nervous Al Capone who wanted to hear Waller but not travel to the Regal Theatre where he was appearing.

Art Hodes once described the status of the pianist in clubs as being at the "bottom of the totem pole"; he recalled being made to drink whiskey for the amusement of one mobster until he fell off the piano stool completely inebriated. Lee Collins, the New Orleans trumpet player who moved to Chicago in the 1920s, also had a brush with a mobster, as recalled by Collins in his biography. He worked at the Up and Down Club with Albert Ammons, and one evening they were playing when the place was held up by a hoodlum who ordered them to keep the music going while he collected the takings. Collins confirms the musicians' intensity of purpose in playing the music to comply with the hoodlum's demand.[1] It seems that incipient violence was always a feature of life in the gangster-driven world of Chicago clubland. Hodes provides an equally graphic description of a holdup in a Chicago club where he was working. It began with the hoodlums' assaulting the doorman to impress on the club members that they were of serious intent before ordering the musicians to lie facedown on the floor at gunpoint.[2] A musician needed an iron will to continue entertaining when gun-toting mobsters were around.

On the South Side of Chicago, the tenements in which the black families were living had their rents raised at regular intervals in a desperate attempt by landlords to maintain an income during the Depression years. As living standards were lowered through unemployment and a valueless dollar, whole families of black residents were faced with eviction. Many were only able to pay rents, which had risen threefold in some cases, by organizing rent parties. These events offered music for dancing provided by boogie-woogie pianists, plus food and bootleg liquor, for which a charge was made to offset the costs and provide the flat dwellers with a small profit for paying the rent. A successful party was one in which as many as a hundred guests crammed into a tenement flat and the entertainment went on all night with several pianists taking turns to play for the customers. The idea of the rent party came from the southern states, where it was called a "gumbo supper" or a "fish fry." It was known by other names in Chicago, vividly evoking the pleasures in store: "the gouge," "the parlor social," "the too terrible party," "the too-tight party," and "boogies" were some of the names used. Many up-and-coming pianists accepted invitations to attend parties, often unpaid in the first instance, simply to listen to, and play with, well-established piano players. As we have seen, Albert Ammons and Meade Lux Lewis were two of the younger men who served their apprenticeships in this way. The presence of Jimmy Yancey at a party guaranteed a large following of admiring youngsters hoping to emulate him. He maintained this charisma well into the 1940s, and it was not uncommon to find Ammons and Johnson attending a function where he was performing, even though both of them had by then already made their own names in the field. Warren "Baby" Dodds, who knew Yancey in Chicago, said that he made good money playing at parties in the 1920s and 1930s. The majority of pianists, however, received very little payment, somewhere between thirty-five and fifty cents a night and all the liquor they could drink.

The social circumstances in other American cities in these times were similar to those in Chicago, with rent parties, gambling dens, and illicit drinking parlors sustaining the art of the boogie-woogie player. Foremost among them were St. Louis, Kansas, and Detroit. A description of the background of the important pianists and their music associated with Chicago and Kansas takes up the remainder of the chapter, beginning with a consideration of the early years of Meade Lux Lewis, Albert Ammons, and Pete Johnson, the three boogie-woogie players who were later to form the Boogie-Woogie Trio and be instrumental in popularizing the style when they performed together in New York in the late 1930s.

Meade Anderson Lewis (1905–1964) was born in Chicago on September 4, contrary to popular belief that he originated from Louisville, Kentucky. There were five children in the family, four boys and one girl, born to George and Hattie. The family comprised two older brothers, Joseph and Millard, a younger brother Julius, and a sister Bessie. Meade was introduced to music by his father, who arranged for him to receive violin lessons. His father played the guitar and made two recordings of his own, so there was a reasonable amount of musical talent within the family to encourage Meade's interest in music. Though he learned the violin under sufferance, it helped him to gain a rudimentary knowledge of music. Meade gave up the instrument when he was sixteen, shortly after his father's death, and switched to the piano. It was reported in one of Meade's obituary notices that he learned the violin for a time under the tutelage of the jazz violinist Jimmy Anthony.

The Lewis family home was on South La Salle near the New York Central lines where Meade's father worked as a porter on the Pullman coaches. It was in this house that Meade got his early inspiration for composing the railroad blues that eventually became the "Honky Tonk Train Blues."[3] The idea came from hearing the Big Bertha locomotives that hauled their loads many times a day past the family home, shaking it to its foundations. He became friendly with Albert Ammons when they were boys together in Chicago, and both attended Webster school until Lewis transferred to South Division School in his teen years. Meade then briefly lost contact with Albert, whose family moved to different apartments at regular intervals. The nickname "Lux" was given to him by his boyhood friends. It originated from a comic strip called Gaston and Alphonse, which was featured in one of the Chicago newspapers. The characters used to say "After you Alphonse" or "No, after you Gaston." Meade was constantly imitating them while pretending to stroke an imaginary beard as part of his impersonation. His friends began calling him the Duke of Luxembourg because of these airs and graces, and the name "Lux" stayed with him throughout his life. He was also short and rotund, which earned him the additional soubriquet of "Mr. Five by Five." When Meade was living in Los Angeles and traveling to engagements throughout America in the 1940s and 1950s, he shared his home at 629 East 116th Place with his brother Julius. Dorothy, his wife, meanwhile, appears to have remained in Chicago. She was in brief communication with Ben Conroy in 1969 after the death of Lewis when inquiries were being made about the possible release of the Boogie-Woogie Trio's Library of Congress recordings from December 1938.[4] It is not known if there were any children from Meade's marriage.

Meade's childhood. seems to have passed uneventfully. As a young boy, he played softball with Albert Ammons, whom he described as being a useful left fielder or center. He also listened to King Oliver's Creole Jazz Band when it was at its zenith, playing regular concerts at Lincoln Gardens. It is said that Meade developed his trumpet style whistle from listening to Joe Oliver's cornet playing. He heard many piano players in Chicago, and it is likely that one of these would have been Jimmy Yancey, who was an early influence on Meade's emerging piano style.

Two years younger than his friend, Albert Ammons (1907–1949) had an enviable physique in his prime. He was solidly built, well muscled, and nearly six feet in height. Albert was born in Chicago on September 23, 1907, to James Wesley and Adlyde (Anna) Ammons (nee Sherman). His father hailed from Memphis, Tennessee, and was born there on May 2, 1890. Albert's mother was born in the same year in Owensboro, Kentucky. Her parents had been slaves. It is concluded that the two young people moved independently to Chicago, in the early 1900s, in search of work. They met and married, and were living at 5345 Armour Avenue when Albert was born. James worked at various jobs as a waiter, porter, and laborer before obtaining employment as a Chicago policeman. He was employed later as a meat packer, a job he held for the remainder of his working life. There was a second son of the marriage named James Edward, born in 1908, and a half-brother Maurice, resulting from a relationship between Albert's father and another woman. From 1919, after the divorce of their parents, Albert and his brothers were raised by Samella, his mother's sister.

Albert had two wives. The first, Lila Mae Sherrod, was a talented pianist and a singer. Both he and Meade were smitten with her, but it was Albert who pursued and married her. Lila bore him two sons, Edsel, born on February 17, 1924, and Gene, whose birth was on April 14, 1925. Edsel followed a distinguished career as Bishop of the Methodist Church in Columbus, Ohio. Gene, aka "Jug," developed into an outstanding tenor saxophone player with the bands of Billy Eckstine and Woody Herman before dying at the comparatively young age of forty-nine. In their early years together, Lila appears to have given shape and purpose to Albert's life through their common interest in music and their enjoyment of playing the piano for each other. She taught him some of the rudiments of music. Unfortunately, their marriage did not survive: Albert's all-consuming interest in music, combined with his travel, made him an unreliable breadwinner, and Lila preferred to consolidate her own career in the retail trade—jobs were then hard to come by—and not to accompany him on his travels. They divorced in 1937, although they remained good friends until Lila's death in 1944. Albert's domestic and musical life are recorded more fully by Christopher Page.[5]

Albert's second partner, Hattie Young, whose name was used for the composer credits on some recordings, was probably his common-law wife. She outlived Albert by about six years and was reported to be sharing an apartment in 1954 with Estelle Yancey in Calumet shortly before her death. Albert turned to her as his music with its associated travel enveloped more of his life. Hattie was, by all accounts, a beautiful, jealous, and quick-tempered creature who offered Albert the love and support he needed. Her violent temper got the better of her on several occasions, once letting off Albert's handgun at the Yanceys' apartment because something displeased her. Only the intervention of Mama Yancey with the community alderman prevented serious consequences arising from her behavior.

It was fortunate for both Albert and Meade that the Ammons's household had a piano, which allowed them to practice and begin mastering the rudiments of the boogie-woogie style. Both of Albert's parents were musical, and it was said that Albert's father used to play boogie-woogie and was heard doing so in Louisville, Kentucky, in 1910, although this has never been confirmed by other sources.[6] Albert's early attention to the boogie-woogie style seems to have arisen mainly from his friendship with Lewis but perhaps also from his father's interest in the style. During his formative years, from the age of ten, he started learning about chord structure by marking the depressed keys on the family pianola with a pencil and repeating these until they were mastered. In this way he learned to play "Dardanella" (published in 1919) and "Rose of No Mans Land." His favorite recording at this time was Hersal Thomas's "Hersal Blues" (1925). Albert never could read music at speed but he was able to transpose into several keys without too much difficulty, a skill that owed much to Lila's early training. This ability served him well when he became a band pianist. Ammons also had an early appreciation of rhythm, because at the age of ten or eleven he joined the Illinois Home Guard, during World War I, as one of fourteen drummers in the twenty-eight-piece drum-and-bugle marching band.

Albert and Meade used to frequent the apartment of a mutual friend named Toy who lived on Thirty-ninth and State, and here the three friends, together with others, practiced their piano playing. Lewis began putting together the various choruses of his train number at these sessions in about 1923. These musical events were important in laying down their individual approaches to playing boogie-woogie. Despite their close contact over many years, the sounds they produced from the keyboard were completely dissimilar. Where Albert attacked the senses with an awesome and barely containable power, Meade delighted by stringing together clusters of contrasting tone colors.

From 1924 or thereabouts, they consolidated their early practice at the Ammons's household and with friends by working at house parties in the evenings, and as taxi drivers for the Silver Taxicab Company in the daytime. There appears to have been a clique of aspiring piano players working for this company, and after delivering the fares the drivers would disappear for further piano practice. Finding difficulty in locating them on these occasions, the owner, demonstrating much foresight, eventually installed a piano in the drivers' restroom so that there would be an incentive to return to base and be on call when a taxi was booked. Events leading up to the installation of the piano are described by Lewis in an interview reported in *Cadence* magazine. The road man responsible for checking on the cabs could not understand why there were none on the streets. He asked a passerby if he could suggest a reason, and he said that it was likely that the drivers were at a Blue Monday party. Not knowing about such parties, he went in search of the drivers. Arriving at an apartment where a party was under way, the road man saw none of his drivers but could hear the sound of music coming from the third floor. Climbing the stairs and entering the room, he saw Meade and Albert and immediately informed them that he was going to report them or, in his parlance, "write them up," as they should not have been there. At this point, one of the hostesses, seeing their plight, pushed a drink into the road man's hand and invited him to join the party. Fortunately, his arrival coincided with one of Albert's sessions at the piano, so he sat by him to listen while he finished his drink. Inevitably, the impact was sensational to the extent that the transfixed road man leaned over and said that he had no intention of reporting the pianists for absence from work in the face of Albert's brilliance.[7] Another story from this period, as told by William Russell,[8] concerns a police raid on an illegal liquor party at which Ammons and Lewis were appearing. Climbing out of the window until the place had been cleared, they returned to finish off the hastily discarded drinks left by the partygoers.

In 1924 the Lewis family left Chicago for Louisville to stay with relatives from his mother's side of the family. There were long family associations with the town and the nearby township of Harrisburg where Meade's grandfather, a native American, had lived on the Cherokee reservation. Shortly afterward, the Lewis family appears to have dispersed with Meade and Bessie returning to Chicago, presumably with their parent(s), while Millard and family moved to Minneapolis and Joseph stayed in Louisville. On his return, Meade learned that Albert had joined a band in South Bend, and in his absence, had found work for him with another group in the same town. Albert, at this time, was a more confident character than Meade and was prepared to venture beyond Chicago looking for opportunities to use his now well-developed piano skills. Meade, in comparison, had not traveled much beyond Chicago and was still not very worldly-wise. Their differing temperaments and circumstances are brought out in a conversation recalled by Meade between his mother and Albert when the work was being discussed. Albert said that he had arranged a job for the young Meade, to which his mother responded: "Well that's all right Albert, but just take care of him." Albert answered in the affirmative. Meade's reaction to the conversation tends to support the dominance of Albert in their relationship: "Well I don't know whether

Albert was trying to break me in or what but he tried to help me. I know he was always helpful in a way."[9]

Although Meade possessed a quicker ear for a melody than Albert, he was obliged to leave the job after a short period because of his inability to modulate in the keys used by the band. At this time, he played only in the keys of C and G. Albert, who had a good sense of harmony and had mastered the keys, which was necessary for playing with a band, told him that he would need to extend his range. This he did and it proved useful later in Meade's career.

Two years after Meade's first attempts to play with a group, he was still living at home in Chicago, having made no further progress in his musical career. It was now 1926, and Albert had moved to Detroit to work for James Hall (known as Red Man), who ran an illegal liquor business and a club as an outlet for his wares. Hall was comparatively wealthy and always carried a roll of sixty or seventy dollar bills in his back pocket. He also ran a large new Hudson Brougham car. Walking down a street in the South Side one day, Meade saw the car coming toward him with Albert at the wheel and Hall in the passenger seat. Meade flagged down the car and was introduced to Hall. As a result of their meeting, Meade traveled back to Detroit with Hall while Albert stayed on in Chicago. Hall lived in the Black Bottom district of the city, and when they arrived at his home, Hall's wife was upset to find that Albert had not traveled with them. Turning to Meade, she told him that he would have to sleep in the car despite the heavy fall of snow outside. Fortunately, the conversation was heard by a fellow Chicagoan then living in Detroit who took Meade under his wing and invited him to stay at his house. It was a large tenement boarding house with sixteen rooms in which the owner's wife held parties for the guests and friends on Wednesday and Friday evenings. Meade played piano for these events through the winter of 1926 and managed a reasonably comfortable existence with free board and tips from his piano playing.

One evening, sitting at the piano, Meade was approached by a guest with an invitation to play for a similar dance on the other side of Detroit. He accepted, with the intention of increasing his meager income. He only went once. On that occasion, he had been at the keyboard for most of the evening when the hostess informed him that the regular pianist had arrived and his services were no longer required. She paid him off with a fifty-cent piece. Meade's only concern now was to work out how he was going to get back to the other side of the city with only fifty cents available for a cab. He wandered into the kitchen where the gambling had started, and feeling he had nothing to lose, gambled his fifty cents on the dice. An hour or so later he had increased this to thirty-eight dollars and the hostess was beginning to take an interest in him, suggesting that Meade might like to buy her a drink. At this point he excused himself from the party by saying he was going to buy cigarettes. Once outside he took a cab back to the boarding house where he appeared at the door carrying a gallon of homemade liquor. The party, which was already in progress when he arrived, continued well into the next day.

Meade met up again with Albert early in 1927 and went back with him to South Bend once again. Albert was now employed by Big Bill Boswell, who owned the Paradise Inn at 1515 West Washington Street, and a nearby brothel. He offered Meade the position of brothel keeper, which he took. This work entailed collecting the money from clients, paying all the bills, and entertaining the girls and their clients at the piano. For this he was paid between thirty-five and forty dollars a week. Meade's business sense was not to Boswell's liking, however, and he replaced him with another brothel keeper. The owner of a second brothel, whom Meade knew as Anna, heard of this setback and invited him to become the pianist at her establishment. He earned between twelve and twenty dollars in tips, using some of this money to travel back to Chicago on the South Shore railroad to visit his mother.

In July or August 1927, Meade left this employment and returned to Chicago. Shortly afterward, he made the acquaintance of a girl named Althea Robinson (nee Dickerson) who worked for Mayo Williams's Chicago Music Company and for Paramount. She was also a pianist on more recordings than discographies give her credit for—her unusual Christian name was sometimes misheard as "Leeford," which caused that name to appear in certain recordings by Big Bill Broonzy. Althea was very taken with Meade's piano playing and asked him if he would like to make a record if she could arrange it for him. The session eventually took place in the Paramount studios on Wabash Avenue in December 1927, and one of the numbers was "Honky Tonk Train Blues." Meade's account of how the piece got its name differs from that which he gave to Alan Lomax on the Library of Congress recordings and again demonstrates how unreliable the memory of musicians can be, for whatever reason, when they are recalling dates and situations. In this version, it was the recording engineer who apparently named the piece; when Meade suggested the title of "Freight Train," he replied that as it sounded like honky-tonk music it would be better to call it "Honky Tonk Train."[10] In fairness to Meade's recollection of the event, the circumstances of the naming were similar; only the situation in which it was said to have occurred differed. It was not released until 1929, although it predated "Pinetop's Boogie-Woogie." In fact it was the popularity of Pinetop's piece that was instrumental in finally getting it onto the market. An early reissue of this classic recording by Lewis, together with several of the same vintage by Garnett, Davenport, and others, is available on *Honky Tonk Train: Classic Jazz Masters* (Riverside, RLP 8806).

During the 1930s, the Depression tightened its grip on America. The Paramount Record Company eventually fell victim to it and was wound up, closing off one avenue for making money. Lewis found great difficulty in obtaining work as a pianist and spent some time on relief working on a Works Progress Administration (WPA) shovel gang. These government projects gave work to the millions of unemployed and involved them in laboring or construction work on community-service or public-service projects. Lewis also worked on relief washing cars. He obtained spasmodic employment at rent parties, but had no permanent job until he moved out of Chicago to Indiana Harbor to play piano at the South Chicago Club. A disheveled customer approached him during one of his sets and suggested that Meade might like to try his luck in Muskegon Heights, Michigan, where a well-paid job was there for the asking. It was now in the early 1930s, and work, with free board and a wage, was not easily obtainable. As Lewis remarked ironically, the soles of his shoes were so worn he could tell whether it was heads or tails if he trod on a dime.[11]

The man's unkempt appearance was the result of riding freight trains to journey from town to town, and it soon became apparent that Meade would have to be prepared to travel in similar fashion if he was going to reach Muskegon Heights, but as the man's sincerity impressed him, he agreed to join him. The journey was made hidden under a pile of straw in the corner of an open boxcar. They eventually arrived at a boarding house run by a woman who received payment from the city authorities for boarding men who were on the dole. Next door to the house was a small dance hall for the entertainment of the guests. Meade was taken on as the pianist, playing for three nights per week and filling in his spare time with his favorite pastime, fishing. Many of the unemployed guests were illiterate but were too ashamed to admit it. They would often ask Meade to read them letters from home under the pretext of having misplaced their glasses. He felt sorry for them and assisted where he could, knowing that most did not even possess a pair of glasses.

Meade was now feeling settled, living in a country district, and he began to seek his own entertainment in the nearby city of Muskegon. He traveled there regularly, hitching a ride on the slow freights that rumbled out of Muskegon Heights. His preferred nightspot was a club situated in the black section of town. One evening when his playing had attracted a large crowd, a brothel owner heard him and invited him to visit his place. So began a lucrative sideline, playing for the white farmers up from the country who used the services of the brothel. This was one of the happiest times for Meade: His music was appreciated and he continued to enjoy his passion, fishing for bass and turtle.

In 1932, Meade returned briefly to Chicago and after further sorties to Muskegon settled back there in 1934. In Chicago, he renewed his friendship with Albert Ammons, who was now living in an apartment at Forty-second and Calamut. Once again, Albert obtained work for him as a driver for a dress salesman. They traveled to major cities in America, visiting such widely dispersed cities as Dayton, Louisville, and Detroit. It was the first time that Meade had ventured much beyond the northern states of America. This work finished in 1935, and at Albert's instigation Meade joined a trio that began to get known around the South Side. Shortly afterward, Meade began playing with another trio at a club run by Doc Huggins in the forty-sixth block of Champlain.

Albert Ammons's interests encompassed both solo playing and small-group jazz. He was a member of a band that entertained on the honky-tonk excursion trains that ran from Chicago to Memphis and New Orleans in the South. Before the excursions got under way, they were advertised by the band playing from the back of a flat truck as it toured the South Side. The group to which Ammons belonged had as its members Punch Miller (trumpet), Al Wynn (trombone), and Franz Jackson (clarinet and saxophone). One venue where Ammons was known to have played with a small group was at the Dusty Bottom, a popular open-air dance spot a few blocks away from Lincoln Gardens. It was given its name because it was said that the dust billowed from the floorboards and settled on the clothes of dancers as they twirled around.

Both Meade and Albert were friendly with a Chicago bandleader named William Barbee, who played piano in the style of Earl Hines. It is likely that both men were taught how to play a swing-type bass by Barbee. Certainly, Ammons received plenty of help in perfecting this technique, and in time he became proficient enough to work for a season with the Francis Moseley Louisiana Stompers before joining Barbee and his Headquarters Orchestra (also known as the "Serenaders") as second pianist. The experience of playing with a band served him well, taking him into theatres and clubs where he was obliged to learn and employ harmonic chord sequences as a member of the rhythm section as well as taking improvised solo choruses, often in a decided "Earl Hines" style.

Following his time with Barbee, Albert joined Louis P. Banks and his Chesterfield Orchestra and stayed with them from 1931 (circa) until 1934, thus consolidating his earlier band experience with numerous engagements at clubs and cafes. The *Chicago Defender* posted the band's movements around Chicago nightspots as follows: Booster's Night Club (September 1929), the Pleasure Inn (May 1930), and Club El Rado (November 1930). Banks's group was a six-piece outfit with the leader on drums. Other personnel at the Pleasure Inn were Elbert Topp (clarinet), Bernie Fields and Herbert Wallace (saxophones), Sylvester Burch (banjo), and Ammons (piano). Albert's first recording was made as a member of this band. Singer John Oscar exhorts him to take a solo spot on *You Can't Last Long Like That* (1934) with, "Play it boy, play it . . . . Swing it Albert Ammons, swing it boy."

The completion of Albert's movements in the 1930s finds him leading the orchestra at the Paradise, 1805 State Street, in July 1932, though it is doubtful if this was his own band. He had certainly formed his own band by 1934, known as the Rythm [*sic*] Kings, reportedly his preferred spelling, and opened at Peven's 29 Club at 29 West Forty-seventh Street at the corner of Dearborn on June 8, 1935. He had already gained a reputation for being a genial and hardworking musician and was soon in demand at other clubs. One of the most prestigious was the De Lisa Club, to which Ammons transferred his burgeoning talents in July 1935.

The club, situated at 5516 South State Street, had been started in 1933, coincidentally with the opening of the World Trade Fair, by the three De Lisa brothers, Mike, Louie, and Jim Sr. They were Italian immigrants whose early business in Chicago had been making and selling moonshine liquor during Prohibition. The arrival of the Ammons's band supplied an important vitality that helped to increase the club's growing reputation. His powerful music, together with the exotic floorshows of rumbas and taps danced by a troupe of attractive black chorines, led by their captain Freddie Cole Bates, gave a distinctive tone to the club. The club was always packed with as many as five hundred patrons on a typical Saturday evening, occupying a space reserved for three hundred and fifty covers. The club was open seven nights a week with four shows a day. Many famous personalities of the time visited the club during and after the departure of Ammons, including film stars Pat O'Brien, George Raft, Bob Hope, and John Barrymore. Of the band led by Ammons, Dempsey Travis said that the outfit was the best swinging small band in the region during their engagement at the first Club De Lisa—the latter being a reference to a devastating fire in 1941 that required the rebuilding of the club.[12]

Ammons eventually left the club because of the increasingly complex musical scores that were required for the floor shows, choreographed by Earl Partello, that necessitated a knowledge of music theory and an ability to sight-read, which he did not possess. The band continued under the leadership of Del Bright, Albert's alto saxophone player. Albert was not totally devoid of talent in this respect, though his strength lay in his natural ability to carry arrangements in his head, which, according to his bass player Bill Hilliard, served him better than most sight readers.[13] Ammons moved to the It Club, in July 1937, located at 5450 South Michigan and owned by Elliot Rouse and Bill Carter, after what is believed to have been a short spell at Hills Tavern.

In the years preceding his appearance at Carnegie Hall for the "Spirituals to Swing" concert in 1938, Ammons interspersed solo piano playing with arrangements of standards and blues by his Rhythm Kings. His band gradually acquired a reputation among discerning musicians, fans, and jazz critics. On one occasion, Ammons was sought out by members of the Bob Crosby Orchestra and Sharon Pease, the piano critic for *Downbeat*. He, together with Gil Rodin, Bob Haggart, Bill Depew, and Bob Zurke visited the It Club. They heard Ammons playing with such style that the entire club was rocking to his music. At this time in Chicago there were several bands capable of playing blues of an extremely high quality, ranging from the well-known groups led by Jimmy Noone at the Apex Club, to many lesser known ones with a local reputation. These bands played mainly "head" arrangements, and if the listening patrons had difficulty in deciding who was leading the band, the musicians had no difficulty in producing disciplined ensemble playing with a minimum of effort. Although urban boogie-woogie was molded into its definitive form in Chicago, its appearance in small-band form was not fully developed until Ammons took Pinetop's classic and arranged it for his Rhythm Kings.

Albert Ammons made his first recordings with his Rhythm Kings for Decca on February 13, 1936, with a six-piece band consisting of Jimmy Hoskins (drums), Ike Perkins (guitar), Guy Kelly (trumpet), Delbert Bright (alto saxaphone), Israel Crosby (bass), and Albert on piano. The record that made the greatest impact was the aforementioned "Boogie-Woogie Stomp." It was coupled with the popular dance tune "Nagasaki," which showed Albert's mastery of the stride style with a blistering opening chorus and a solo spot. The following day, his group was in the studio again to record "Early Mornin' Blues" with its metronomic tenths bass alternating with a slow stride, backed by the jolly "Mile-or-Mo Bird Rag," featuring good jazz guitar from Ike Perkins. All of these tracks are available on *Albert Ammons and His Rhythm Kings* (Brunswick, EP OE 9325) or the later reissue, *Albert Ammons 1936–1947* (Best of Jazz: The Swing Era, CD 40 57). It was a small band that by general consensus packed more power than a fifteen-piece outfit.

Meanwhile, Meade Lux Lewis concentrated his talents on solo playing with the occasional accompaniment to singers, or he played as a member of a trio. His recording of "Honky Tonk Train Blue" demonstrated that he was technically and imaginatively at least the equal of Pinetop Smith. By 1930, Lewis was also adept at performing on the piano in a style other than boogie-woogie, as he initially demonstrated on the Paramount label in his accompaniment to Bob Robinson in "Sitting on Top of the World." He also used his trumpet style whistling to good effect for the first time on this recording. Further accompaniments in a swing-piano vein were made with George Hannah in the same year on the salacious number "The Boy in the Boat." "Freakish Man Blues" with the same singer included embryonic choruses from the yet-to-be-composed "Yancey Special." These tunes, other Paramount releases, and later recordings for Blue Note are available on *Meade Lux Lewis 1905–1964* (Oldie Blues, Ol 2805). Both Meade and Albert showed by their keyboard versatility and technique that they had outstripped their contemporaries from the rent party circuits, and that they were destined for greater recognition.

By late 1936, Ammons had lost nearly all the members of his band to larger, more prestigious outfits and had reverted to playing solo piano, but he had already done enough to make his mark with influential jazz critics. Lewis, on the other hand, was remembered vaguely by at least one jazz critic, John Hammond, as the composer and pianist who had recorded "Honky Tonk Train Blues," a factor that would have an important bearing on both their later careers.

Kansas City was recognized as a "wide open" town under the benign control of Mayor Tom Prendergast. This arrangement benefited musicians, because it increased opportunities for their employment at the many clubs in the city. The social milieu they generated was influential in the flowering of jazz and the formation of the small combos of which Pete Johnson was a member early in his career. The authority of the gangsters was unquestioned, and life could be very difficult for club performers on occasions. If they were popular, for example, they were expected to work long hours to attract customers and increase takings. If they failed to please the patrons, it was not uncommon for musicians to receive a beating at the hands of the gangsters. Working conditions were both hazardous and frenetic, but the music was good.

Pete Johnson (1904–1967) was born in that city on March 25. His early childhood was hard, and he was raised by his mother after his father deserted the family. Financial difficulties made it necessary to place Pete in an orphanage when he was three, but he became so homesick that he ran away and returned to living at home, such as it was. His first bed was a drawer taken from a bureau. By the age of twelve he was so well built that he could pass for sixteen, enabling him to seek work and ease the financial strain at home. His various occupations included working as a shoe-shiner, in a print shop, and at a packing plant. Naturally, his schooling suffered from this arrangement, and he eventually dropped out in the fifth grade.

Johnson showed an early interest in music and began following the marching bands around Kansas, frequently getting himself lost doing so. He began to play the drums, and after taking lessons from a "Professor" Charles T. Watts, he was able to earn enough money to play professionally, which he did for about four years. At the same time that he was learning to play the drums, he began to show an interest in the piano. Johnson recalled that his early piano practices occurred in a church where he was working as a water boy for a construction company. Some of his initial attempts were not always appreciated, as he found when playing an out-of-tune piano at a card gambling club on Eighteenth Street. He was asked by one of the card players, who was becoming increasingly irritated by his efforts, if he could play "The Silent Rag." Always eager to extend his repertoire, Johnson asked him how it went. The card player told him to take his foot off the pedal and then to remove his hands from the keyboard. Finally, he was told in no uncertain fashion to remove his butt from the piano stool and clear off outside.[14] Humiliated by the general laughter that greeted this advice, Johnson walked away from the piano.

The first piano lessons were given to Pete by one of his former employers, Louis "Bootie" Johnson. The reason behind the gesture was less generous than might first appear, however, because Louis was sometimes the worse for drink, and he reasoned that it would save him embarrassment if he had a substitute pianist available when these lapses occurred. Another early teacher was Johnson's uncle, Charles "Smash" Johnson. It was with the help of his uncle that Pete eventually mastered his first complete ragtime number, "Peculiar Rag." His piano style was now being shaped by his own endeavors as well as by listening to other Kansas City pianists who were active in the World War I period. Those he remembered as being influential in his early years were Myrtle Hawkins, a marvelous ragtime player; Slam Foot Brown, who taught him a fast rag, "Nickels. and Dimes"; Udall Wilson; and Stacey La Guardia, who played at a club on Twelfth and Vine. He learned some theory from Buster Smith and, later, from Bill Steven, who was known as "The Harmony King." This pianist could improvise, and Johnson acquired a concept of harmony from him. All of these experiences gave Pete Johnson a broadly based piano technique on which his boogie-woogie styling was built. In the 1920s, Johnson was also listening carefully to the early Fats Waller recordings and began to emulate the "swing bass" used by Fats, which employed tenths in the left hand. His own hand span was large, and he had no difficulty with this type of bass. Toward the end of the 1920s, Johnson's understanding of the boogie-woogie style was helped by listening to recordings by Pinetop Smith. He had a very good ear for melodies, enabling him to pick up tunes quickly and reproduce them on the piano.

Pete Johnson began playing the piano seriously at house parties and Saturday night suppers when he was eighteen or so, usually in the company of his good friend Murl Johnson (no relation), who was his drummer. His first important professional engagement after sitting in for the pianist at Curley's Place was at the Backbiter's Club, situated in the Italian district of northern Kansas. Several club engagemants followed, too distant in time to recall all of them in detail: the Spinning Wheel, where he worked for three dollars and tips through the night with one half-hour break; the Peacock Inn, where he appeared every night of the week between ten o'clock and four or five o'clock in the morning; and the Grey Goose and Yellow Front Clubs. While he was working at the Spinning Wheel as a member of Herman Walder's Rockette Swing Unit, Pete acquired the necessary skills for playing as a band member. Although the many clubs and dives in Kansas were tolerated by Mayor Prendergast, union support for musicians whose talents were being exploited, for example by over-long working hours, was nonexistent

Joe Turner had a long and profitable partnership with Pete Johnson, which began at the Backbiter's Club when Turner was about sixteen. He used to hang around the club to listen to Johnson's piano playing, but he could not get in because he was underage and would have been recognized by his brother-in-law who worked as doorman at the club. After his brother-in-law had left the post, Turner managed to gain entry by drawing a fake mustache with his mother's eyebrow pencil and getting past the doorman with his father's hat pulled well down over his eyes. He was eventually invited to sing with the band by Johnson after making several requests to do so. The instrumentalists were a saxophonist, Murl Johnson on drums, and Pete on piano. Turner made such a good impression with his vocals that he was invited by the manager to work at the club at weekends for two dollars a night. So began the long association between pianist Pete Johnson and vocalist Joe Turner.

After spending some time together at the Backbiter's Club, Pete and his group, together with Turner, moved to the Black and Tan Club, and from this time their musical association really got under way. Turner was taught the rudiments of cellar work and served drinks at the bar. From time to time during the evening and early morning, he would discard his apron and shout the blues over Johnson's pounding accompaniment. When the band toured Kansas City and the surrounding territory, Joe Turner went with them. They were soon back but this time working at the Sunset Crystal Palace, owned by Felix Payne and managed by Piney Brown, the musician's friend. Whenever a musician got into difficulties, or was short of cash, he knew he would get a sympathetic hearing as well as financial assistance from Piney Brown. He had a different attitude toward musicians from that of many club owners, whose only interest was in gambling activities, and for whom the musicians were there purely to bring customers to the club for more profitable activities than drinking and listening to music. Pete and Joe composed "Piney Brown Blues" (1940) to immortalize his name.

From about 1933 onward, the two men were very settled at the Sunset, and despite the long hours and the scarred pianos, they enjoyed their time together there. They composed many numbers, such as "Goin' Away Blues" and "Cherry Red," which drew on Turner's vast reservoir of lyrics, but the most famous of their duets was "Roll 'Em Pete." It is important to remember that Johnson played many standard tunes of the day in his sets and made a special feature of his boogie-woogie and blues playing with Joe Turner. It was usually a request from Johnson's longtime friend Ben Webster that brought on the duo to play boogie-woogie and sing. These numbers were eventually recorded for Columbia in 1939 and are available on an important historical release produced by John Hammond, *The Original Boogie Woogie Piano Giants* (Columbia, KC 82708). They are notable for the cleanly picked and highly rhythmical piano playing of Johnson in "Roll 'Em Pete"; some fine ensemble playing from a back-up group that included Oran "Hot Lips" Page (trumpet) and Abe Bolar (guitar) on "Baby Look at You"; and of course Turner's magisterial, booming vocals.

On a good night, Johnson could play as many as fifty different choruses of "Roll 'Em Pete." Sammy Price said that he would often be passing the club on his way home from an engagement and hear Johnson beating it out. When he returned to the club, as a patron, having performed his ablutions and eaten, Johnson would often be still improvising on the same theme. Price also considered Johnson the greatest of all the boogie-woogie and blues pianists and, after listening to his recording of "Dive Bomber" (1944), commented favorably on his breadth of musical ideas, his ability as an accompanist, his versatility with styles other than boogie-woogie, and wondered why he had never considered running his own band.[15]

The most exciting time at the Sunset was around three or four o'clock in the morning, when passing musicians used to drop in for a relaxed and informal session with Pete and Joe. Turner was adept at picking out a customer possessing a distinctive feature and weaving this into his vocals. It might be a "girl with a red dress on" or a similar identification. Pete and Joe kept a kitty on top of the piano, which was topped up each time a number was requested by a customer, and this caused the only known recorded friction between the two men. As Turner was the barman, he was required to serve behind the bar when he was not singing, whereas Johnson was able to wander round the tables between sets and chat to the customers. Pete always enjoyed talking with the ladies, and Joe would often see him ordering a round of drinks surrounded by admiring females. It was not until the end of an evening when the kitty was shared that it became apparent that Pete had been using it to buy drinks for his lady friends. Although Joe resented this unfair treatment by his partner, he never did challenge Pete over the matter.

The Hawaiian Gardens was another club where Pete Johnson had an extended residency. Between engagements there and at the Sunset, Johnson kept a steady income by touring with Clarence Love's band. Once again he was expected to play standards of the day such as "Mean to Me" and "There'll Be Some Changes Made" as a member of the band's rhythm section, which helped to maintain his wide repertoire of tunes.

With so many bands working in, or passing through, Kansas City, jam sessions and friendly cutting sessions were frequent and prolonged among musicians. In these hothouse surroundings on Twelfth Street, where Johnson mostly played, he was rubbing shoulders with Andy Kirk, Count Basie, Ben Moten, Cab Calloway, and the most respected of all Kansas City jazz groups, Walter Page and his Blue Devils. *Kansas City Jazz* (Coral LP, CP 39), originally released in the 1940s and reissued in 1970, captures the punchy yet relaxed qualities of Kansas City jazz with performances by groups led by these men. It provides some idea of the context and milieu in which Johnson's talents were fashioned. Among those pianists who should be singled out for particular attention because of their contact with Pete Johnson during the late 1920s and 1930s are Mary Lou Williams and Jay McShann. Both were all-around pianists who could interpret boogie-woogie and the blues with conviction and feeling. Both were trained pianists of the "swing" school, as it was known, who absorbed boogie-woogie playing into their existing piano styles—an ability not always evident in the work of other pianists with similar backgrounds.

Mary Lou Williams (1910–1981) was born in Atlanta, Georgia, and studied piano until she was fifteen before starting work as a full-time pianist with a vaudeville act. Mary first began to play the piano as a precocious three-year-old sitting on the lap of her mother, a church pianist, while she practiced. She displayed a formidable dedication to learning the instrument and put in many hours of practice, although her mother would not permit her to have a piano teacher, arguing that it would spoil her ability to play by ear. However, there were some important influences in her mastery of the piano. One of these was a boogie-woogie piano player named Jack Howard who taught her, among other things, always to play the left hand louder than the right in order to generate the correct beat and feeling. An appreciation of boogie-woogie never entirely left her playing, and snatches of the style are evident in several of her interpretations, long after she transferred her talents to bebop and other piano styles. After Mary had moved with her family to Pittsburgh, the final decision was made to pursue a career in jazz rather than as a classical pianist. She was now sufficiently proficient to be able to entertain her family with classical pieces, boogie-woogie, Irish folk tunes, and selections from the repertoire of Fats Waller that had been learned by copying the fingering from piano rolls.

With her course now set, Williams began to play with various vaudeville troupes, including the Hottentots and others on the TOBA circuit. She also organized a band in Memphis for a short period before moving to Kansas City and, at the age of twenty, married her first husband, John Williams, who played saxophone with Andy Kirk and his Twelve Clouds of Joy. Two years went by in which she acted as chauffeur, the band's dresser who repaired their uniforms, and musical arranger before her abilities were eventually recognized and she was asked to act as stand-in pianist. This was in 1931, leading to a permanent connection with the band as its pianist and arranger. Mary Lou Williams had exceptional talents and was known as "The Lady Who Swings the Band"—the title of a number dedicated to her and recorded by the band.

During the period leading up to her departure from Kirk's band in 1942, Williams consolidated her position as the foremost female jazz instrumentalist in America and as a highly respected arranger. In the late 1930s, she was arranging for the bands of Artie Shaw, Earl Hines, Louis Armstrong, Tommy Dorsey, and Benny Goodman whose big success "Roll 'Em" (1937) was an early boogie-woogie number composed and scored for a big band by Williams. Her departure from Kirk's band coincided with her divorce from Williams, but she stayed on in New York organizing, playing with, and enjoying the intimacy of several small groups, which was her real métier. By now she was at the forefront of be-bop piano playing and acted as mentor to the many tyro be-bop pianists congregating in New York. Her apartment became an important meeting place for musicians involved with this new form of jazz that was beginning to sweep through the city and beyond. Band arrangements for Dizzy Gillespie and, in 1944, Duke Ellington followed.

Mary Lou's life went through several crises; at one point she retired to write sacred music but was back performing in 1957 after a period living in England and France. Much of her jazz composing and playing from now had a marked religious content. Her most famous composition, "Black Christ of the Andes," was recorded in 1963. Following this, she appeared at several international jazz festivals and New York clubs such as the Hickory House and the Cookery, as well as lectured at Duke University after receiving a doctorate there. She finally succumbed to cancer.

From the perspective of boogie-woogie, one of her most productive phases was the time when she was a regular entertainer at one or other of the two Café Society Clubs. Her musical programs at this time looked both forward, by embracing bebop, but also to her roots where her blues and boogie touch was not far below the surface. The traditional "Mr. Freddie Blues" (1938) and originals from 1944 such as "Mary's Boogie" and "Roll 'Em" would often be presented alongside Porter's "Night and Day," "Limehouse Blues," and, perhaps, a more progressively chorded number such as "Gjon Milli Jam Session" (the latter in the company of Don Byas [tenor saxophone], Dick Vance [trumpet], Vic Dickenson [trombone], et al.). These and other tunes provide a valuable cross-section of her different styles and are on *Mary Lou Williams: First Lady of Piano* (Giants of Jazz, LPJT 20). An equally interesting recording with her trio, produced by Frank Driggs, contains several of her numbers, also from 1944, which many would say represent the most creative of her jazz periods: "Froggy Bottom," "Taurus Mood," and "Eighth Avenue Express" are three worthy examples of her style at this time and are featured on *The Mary Lou Williams Trio 1944* (Audophile, AP 80).

With such a command of the piano at her fingertips and such a wide perspective of musical ideas available to her, it would be surprising to find that Mary Lou's interpretation of boogie-woogie was not distinctive. First, as has been implied, there was the incipient influence of boogie-woogie running through her playing, to create a contrastive effect: the appearance of a rumbling bass for a few choruses, as in "Mr. Freddie Blues," or a lazy walking bass in "Little Joe from Chicago" (1938). A second feature was the particularly welcome melodic and uncluttered phrasing in the treble. Not for her were the repetitive and deadening choruses that many inferior pianists were producing in the 1940s because they had little else to say. This resulted in intriguing compositions dating from the mid-1940s such as "Waltz Boogie," "Hesitation Boogie," and "Boogie Mysterioso," all of which, Sally Placksin felt, created a deeper and more musical quality in her music.[16] Her unique approach to boogie-woogie composing is picked up by Whitney Balliett who, in referring to her somewhat teasing style of boogie-woogie, believed she offered the chance of deliverance from the mechanical repetition into which the genre had declined.[17] Suffice to say that she was a gifted, all-around musician who understood the strengths and limitations of the genre.

Mary Lou Williams was one of Pete Johnson's favorite pianists, and he particularly enjoyed her first recorded tune, the sparkling stride piece "Night Life" (1930), reportedly improvised on the spot for the recording session. He first made her acquaintance in about 1930 when he was taken by a friend to a guest house one Sunday morning to meet some friends. No one was about, so the friend suggested that Pete might play something on the piano, which he proceeded to do. The household gradually awoke, and before long an admiring group stood around the piano listening to the best pianist in Kansas City. When he had finished his short recital, the friend asked Mary Lou to play something. Johnson recalled his reaction to her playing in an interview with Jonny Simmen in which he describes the young girl—barely twenty years old and for whom he held a fairly low expectation of her talents—taking his place at the piano and astounding him with her brilliance, which he described as being rarely equaled by any other woman and very few men.[18]

Muskogee in Oklahoma was the town where Jay McShann (1916–2006) originated. He had an extraordinary ability to memorize tunes and reproduce them on the piano, a talent that first appeared when he found that he could play by ear tunes that his sister was sight-reading. He became so adept that he was able to substitute for her on the church organ by pretending to read tunes from the hymnbook. He could play in all keys before he finally accepted that his musical advancement would be curtailed by his inability to read music. This realization happened when he was working with Al Denny's band in Tulsa during the early 1930s. McShann could normally pick up the chord changes after one listening, but after being presented with an arrangement of "Rain" at a rehearsal, which required him to play the introduction accompanied by the rhythm section, his weakness was exposed. The other musicians gave help in the ensuing months, but real success came after McShann enrolled in a music course at the Southwestern College in Winfield, Kansas, where he studied musical appreciation and sight-reading. Further experience with Eddie Hill and his Bostonians and other territory bands performing in Arkansas and Oklahoma consolidated and extended his piano playing as a member of a rhythm section. This served him well when he later formed the first of several bands in 1939.

By the mid-1930s, McShann was residing in Kansas City. Initially, the move was quite fortuitous, because he was on his way to visit an uncle in Omaha by bus and there was a stopover in Kansas. With time to kill, he visited the Reno Club where he met up with some members of the band run by Ben Moten whom he had known in Tulsa. They prevailed upon him to stay, telling him that he would have no difficulty in finding work. His mind was made up when one acquaintance offered him the keys to his apartment while he moved in with a girlfriend. From the point of view of McShann's development, he could not have stopped off at a better place, a melting pot offering a wonderful choice of clubs for listening to, and playing with, other talented jazz musicians.

His first job of any significance was at the Monroe Inn on the northeastern side of the city, and this was followed by an engagement of nine months at Wolfe's Buffet on Eighteenth Street. During this time, in the mid-1930s, McShann put the finishing touches on his boogie-woogie playing by listening to Pete Johnson and Joe Turner at the Sunset Club, as well as sitting in with them on occasions. He admits to being a great admirer of Johnson for his ability to play a powerful boogie-woogie but also for being able to switch into a convincing blues mode when required, pointing out that it is not a given that pianists can master both styles. He was to recall his time in Kansas with two early recordings dating from 1941 in the boogie-woogie style called "Vine Street Boogie"—a reference to a major musical thoroughfare—and "Hootie's Blues," named after a well-known brand of potent beer drunk in Kansas City. "Hootie's Blues" very clearly brings out McShann's experience in Kansas City, with traces of Johnson,

Mary Lou Williams, and Basie showing in his playing. Both pieces display the compositional qualities of Ammons, Lewis, and Johnson, and on this evidence, and McShann's playing of them, he should be placed as an important second-generation boogie-woogie pianist, not quite their equal in creativity but close enough to be considered an important and influential pianist of the genre.

McShann had a reputation for being a gregarious character. He was certainly a man with a large frame who filled the piano stool. He also had a pleasant singing voice that expressed lyrics (usually blues) with good timing and conviction. His early years at home were spent listening to records in his father's collection, among which he particularly recalls the Bessie Smith number "Backwater Blues," accompanied by James P. Johnson. His own early efforts at the keyboard were attempts to play the blues, which, like Mary Lou Williams, never entirely left him, resulting in a very strong boogie- and blues-inflected jazz piano. His love for the blues is also evident in the choice of material for his big band. The first real successful recording that brought him to the attention of a larger public was "Confessin' the Blues" (1941), which convinced him that his future lay upon a larger stage, so he moved to New York. He recorded the number in Texas, and this might be said to have been a defining moment for his future progress. He replicated the Johnson and Turner team by inviting Walter Brown to take the vocal on the recording, partly to oblige Dave Kapp, the Decca recording engineer whose interest at the time was in recording blues numbers.

So came into being a rival duo of piano player and blues vocalist but with essential differences from the Johnson and Turner team. This new team was more collaborative in its compositions and choice of lyrics compared to the other one in which Turner selected his own material and Johnson provided the appropriate piano backing. There was also a light touch to even the most energetic of their boogie-woogie numbers, and Brown engaged in less blues shouting than Turner but was no less effective for that. These qualities provide a pleasantly melodic and contrasting texture to their work, as shown in "Hootie's Ignorant Oil" (1941). With the establishment of McShann's big band, the duo's work was now set in the context of the band's arrangements. A significant development for jazz in particular was the presence of the young Charlie Parker, who played alto sax with the band and was credited along with McShann and Brown as one of the composers of "Hootie's Blues" (1941). McShann always claimed that Parker played at his best with the band before he got involved with drugs. Certainly, his solos show a good feeling for and understanding of the blues. All these pieces can be heard on *JayMcShann and His Orchestra* (Affinity, AFS 1006) as well as on a later release that provides greater scope for displaying McShann's piano aptitude, particularly his work with vocalists Jimmy Witherspoon, Julia Lee, and others, *The Best of Jay "Hootie" McShann* (Blues Forever, CD 68035).

McShann continued to be the living link with today's boogie-woogie, dating from 1938 when, as a twenty-two-year-old emerging talent, he was interviewed by *Downbeat*'s piano critic Sharon Pease and his piano style was analyzed, to the present. In 2003, aged eighty-seven, he was still performing at jazz festivals and he appeared in *The Piano Blues*, a film directed by Clint Eastwood. Between these seminal dates, he served briefly in the American armed forces in World War II before resuming his recording career with the Mercury and Aladdin companies in the 1950s. Jimmy Witherspoon was a featured vocalist for some of these years. McShann received many awards in recognition of his outstanding contribution to jazz music, perhaps the most prestigious being his election to the Kansas City Hall of Fame in 1971. On March 3, 1979, the governor of Missouri declared by proclamation a "Jay McShann Day." The documentary film *Hootie Blues* was produced in 1978 and McShann was also featured in the film *Last of the Blue Devils*—a reunion of famous Kansas City jazzmen, Basie and Turner included. Jay McShann's legendary achievements and, equally important, his music, have inscribed an indelible chapter in the Jazz Story.

Johnson and Turner's move from Kansas to the more cosmopolitan arena of New York was precipitated by a visit from John Hammond and Willard Alexander, the manager of Benny Goodman's Orchestra, in the mid-1930s. While visiting Kansas City to audition the Count Basie band for a recording date, Hammond and Alexander called in at the Sunset to hear Pete Johnson and Joe Turner. Hammond had picked up the Basie sound on short-wave radio from Station W9XB7 and had been so impressed with what he heard that he decided to hear the band for himself. He had also been advised to seek out Johnson and Turner, probably at the instigation of Dave Dexter, a *Downbeat* writer who had already identified their talents, and those of McShann, from his reporting days in Kansas City. Hammond liked what he heard and promised to arrange work in New York for Johnson and Turner.

They were contacted in the summer of 1936, and arrangements for them to appear at the Famous Door nightspot were made. Coincidentally, this was the same time that Meade Lux Lewis was attempting to break into the New York jazz scene. Their paths did not cross, and Johnson and Turner were no more successful than Lewis on this occasion. Before returning to Kansas City, they made a guest appearance at the Apollo Theater, but they were required to use inappropriate material such as "I'm Glad for Your Sake, I'm Sorry for Mine," which did not display their talents to full advantage. Not surprisingly, they were poorly received by the Apollo's demanding audience and clapped off the stage. On their return to Kansas City, the two men were obliged to take some jibes about their unsuccessful venture to New York. They next heard from Hammond in May 1938 with an invitation to audition for, and appear on, the *Benny Goodman Camel Caravan Radio Show*. In order to reduce expenses, Hammond suggested that they should travel by Greyhound bus. Once again they returned to Kansas City after the audition for the Goodman show, but this time they had made a sufficient impact to be asked to sign up with Willard Alexander of MCA in May 1938 who wanted to include more African-American artists on MCA's books.[19] The final call from Hammond came seven months later, in December when he invited them to appear in the first "Spirituals to Swing" concert at Carnegie Hall. After this concert, Pete Johnson and Joe Turner would only return to Kansas City on their own terms.

NOTES

1. M. Collins, *Life of Lee Collin: Oh Didn't He Ramble* (Chicago: Illinois University Press, 1974), 67.

2. Art Hodes and Chadwick Hansen, *Hot Man: The Life of Art Hodes* (Chicago: Illinois University Press, 1992), 35.

3. Alan Lomax, "Interview with Meade Lux Lewis," *The Complete Library of Congress Boogie-Woogie Recordings*, Jazz Piano Record Co., JP 5003.

4. Ben Conroy, correspondence from Mrs. Dorothy Lewis, April 14, 1969, copied to author.

5. Christopher Page, *Boogie-Woogie Stomp, Albert Ammons and His Music* (Cleveland: Northeast Ohio Jazz Society, 1997).

6. E. Paul, *That Crazy Music* (New York: F. Mueller Press, 1957), 240.

7. D. Hill and D. Mangurian, "Meade Lux Lewis," *Cadence*, October 1987, 22. Copyright 1987, cadence jazz magazine, www.cadencebuilding.com.

8. William Russell, "Boogie-Woogie," in *Jazzmen*, ed. F. Ramsey and C. Smith (London: Sidgwick and Jackson, 1958), 196.

9. Hill and Mangurian, "Meade Lux Lewis," 18.

10. Hill and Mangurian, "Meade Lux Lewis," 21–22.

11. Hill and Mangurian, "Meade Lux Lewis," 23.

12. Dempsey J. Travis, *An Autobiography of Black Jazz* (Chicago: Urban Research Institute, 1983), 123–43.

13. Page, *Boogie-Woogie Stomp*, 58.

14. Marge Johnson, "My Man, Pete Johnson," *Jazz Report* 2, no. 8 (April 1962): 8.

15. H. J. Mauerer, "Pete Johnson as Viewed by His Friends and Critics," in *The Pete Johnson Story* (Bremen: Humburg, 1965), 35. A response by Sam Price to a blindfold test listening to a Pete Johnson recording of "Dive Bomber" featured in *Jazz Hot Magazine, Paris*, June 1956.

16. Sally Plaksin, *Jazzwomen: 1900 to the Present Day* (London: Pluto Press, 1985), 129.

17. Whitney Balliett, *American Musicians* (New York: Oxford University Press, 1986), 97.

18. J. Simmen, "My Life, My Music: Pete Johnson Talks to Johnny Simmen," *Jazz Journal* 12, no. 8 (1959): 9.

19. "MCA Gets Negro Bands," *Downbeat*, June 1938, 1.

6

St. Louis and Detroit

Although the left-hand bass figures characterizing boogie-woogie may have originated in the southern barrelhouse circuits down in the Piney Woods, boogie-woogie is associated with Chicago, one of the first urban centers where it lost its primary role as either a blues accompaniment or a variant section in an otherwise straightforward blues. True boogie-woogie with rolling eight-to-the bar rhythms is probably a child of that city.

The music of St. Louis is less easily adumbrated, because pianists retained elements of blues phrasing, frequently sang the blues to their own accompaniment, and introduced boogie-woogie basses into their blues, in addition to playing boogie-woogie solos in the Chicago manner. The St. Louis style of boogie-woogie is generally economical in its treble phrasing and is played with sparse chorded basses, two distinct features that can be heard in the work of Walter Davis, James "Stump" Johnson, Henry Brown, and others. Although not possessing the drive and vitality of the city of Chicago, St. Louis has an underlying sense of urgency and disquiet to its music, which is somewhat removed from the relaxed playing of pianists from the southern states.

A number of the piano players traditionally associated with St. Louis were not born there but came originally from the South. Some, such as Rufus Perryman, arrived with a fully formed piano style; others moved to St. Louis in their formative years, with only the rudiments of a piano style, to seek work in the industries around the levee and, later, as pianists in the brothels and gambling joints on Morgan Street. Walter Davis, the doyen of the St. Louis pianists, began life in Mississippi. Henry Brown

moved to the city from Tennessee at the age of twelve, and Roosevelt
Sykes lived in St. Louis for several years after first moving there with his
family from Arkansas at the age of three.

In the eighteenth century, St. Louis was a French trading post, selected
for that purpose because of its favorable position at the confluence of the
Mississippi and Missouri rivers. By the twentieth century, St. Louis had
become a straggling commercial city, with its major river industry served
by gaunt, gray warehouses stepped along the levee. The cargo boats plied
upriver from the South, bringing cotton and other raw commodities and
either berthed at St. Louis or chugged onwards turning west up the Missouri to Kansas City. By the early years of the twentieth century, St. Louis
was a busy, thriving port that relied on a large workforce to maintain its
commercial momentum. This was mainly composed of black workers
who had moved to St. Louis in the mass exodus from the South beginning
in about 1910. Cargoes were handled by black roustabouts who worked
between the dockside and the ship's hold carrying on their backs lard,
cotton bales, and other commodities destined for the warehouses, always
under the watchful eye of a white foreman who, befitting his station,
wielded a lash or bullwhip.

The downtown part of St. Louis, as recalled by Orick Johns, a lifelong
resident, was at the time of the Depression a brutal and ugly district, with
its residents living in abject poverty and surviving on a diet of Mississippi
catfish and vegetables from the welfare agency. If not entirely segregated
from city life, the downtown residents were discouraged by the police
and watchmen from visiting the city center.[1] Although St. Louis promised
a new life to African-Americans, stimulated by reports in southern newspapers, the situation was far from idyllic. The white residents resented the
newly arrived black workforce, a resentment that eventually led to some
of the worst race riots in America's turbulent race history. They occurred
in the unlovely town of East St. Louis, across the river from St. Louis, in
July 1917. In all, thirty-nine blacks and nine whites were killed, victims of
vicious mutilation and burning.

As the river industry thrived, there grew up around Chestnut and Market streets a notorious entertainment area. One of the liveliest spots was
"Deep" Morgan, peopled by gamblers, pimps, prostitutes, and bootleg-
gers. Black families were obliged to live in shared apartment buildings in
this district, paying high rents for the most basic of unsanitary accommodation. Out of this cesspool of despair arose the conditions that gave pianists their means of employment. An effective and quick way of raising
money for the constantly rising rents was to organize the aforementioned
rent parties that in St. Louis were known as "buffet flats." They were similar in form and intention to the Chicago rent parties and replicated the
milieu that fostered boogie-woogie on the South Side. Pianists provided

the music for dancers who paid a fifty-cent entrance fee and, in return, drank as much bootleg liquor as they could ingest, ate pigs' ankles, and danced the night away. Owners of brothels and gambling joints also hired ragtime and boogie-woogie pianists.

St. Louis possesses a rich musical heritage. It was an early center for ragtime music at the turn of the twentieth century, with pianists being drawn there by the many entertainment opportunities in the "sporting" district. Blues and boogie pianists, whose appearance came later, tended to play in the Chauffeur's Club on Pine Street and Compton Avenue, at Katy Red's Honky Tonk on Main and Broadway, and at the bars and brothels around Fifteenth and Morgan. Pianist James "Stump" Johnson, a St. Louis resident, recalled hanging around these districts as a youngster to ask some of the old-time boogie and blues pianists to play for him so that he could pick up their tunes. His "lesson" would commence in the early hours and continue round the clock until the next day without once leaving the building. It was in such circumstances that Johnson heard Son Long, learned from close contact with his playing style, and later claimed him to be the originator of boogie-woogie.[2]

An older pianist, Charles Thompson, one of the last of the ragtime players who won the State Ragtime Championship in St. Louis and who died there in 1964, composed "Deep Lawton," which provides a link between the city's ragtime and blues traditions and shows the fusion of boogie-woogie, barrelhouse, and ragtime styles. He went to see the young Louis Chauvin playing his delicate ragtime tunes and blues, Chauvin being a pianist who left an indelible impression on all who heard him and whose music still lives on long after his death in 1908. Other pianists recalled by Thompson were Conroy Casey, Raymond Hine, and Willie Franklin, who were all playing blues and boogie-woogie in the sporting houses and buffet flats at the turn of the twentieth century.

Walter Davis (1909–1963) was originally believed to have been born in Grenada, Mississippi, in 1912—recent evidence suggests that 1909 is a more accurate year—before running away to make his home in St. Louis. His music was appreciated beyond the city, however, and he earned an enviable reputation throughout America, possibly because his imaginative lyrics struck a chord in the hearts of many oppressed African-Americans, despite his later piano work having a degree of sameness about it. An indication of his popularity is shown by the Fisk University Survey of the most-played recordings listed on the jukeboxes in five black bars in Clarksdale, Mississippi, in September 1941 as part of the Library of Congress Study of Coahome County.[3] The artists of the time who might be expected to appear are present—Count Basie, Fats Waller, and Louis Jordan—but also there, perhaps surprisingly considering the array of talented artists whose names could have been included, were the former singing waitress Lil Green, whom Little Brother Montgomery called "a wonderful entertainer," and Walter Davies. Why should this have been? What was the attraction of Davis? Two outstanding character-istics of his work supply some of the answers: the delivery of his material and his unique piano style.

In the first place, he sang his blues with an intense sincerity that im-mediately communicated his feelings to the listener. He described how he put himself in the frame of mind to sing the blues by allowing his thoughts to wander back to the sad times he spent at the poor family settlement in Grenada as a shoeless boy.[4] At the height of his popularity, just before the Second World War and in the early years of the conflict, Davis was making a record every few weeks. He had recorded over ninety sides in total before his last recording session in 1952. The first recordings were "M and O Blues" and "My Baby's Gone" for RCA Vic-tor at their New York recording studios in 1930. Davis was too nervous at first to accompany himself on piano, and it was left to Roosevelt Sykes to provide the backing while Davis sang the lyrics. Jack Kapp, the Vic-tor agent, was sufficiently impressed with the quality of his artistry that he arranged for a photograph of Davis and a short biography to appear in the *Chicago Defender* and the *Pittsburgh Courier*. The publicity brought Davis to the attention of a wider public from the moment he first stepped into a recording studio. He was paid fifty dollars, the first of many similar payments, which eventually allowed him to fulfill his desire to own the biggest car in the Cadillac line.

Davis's blues were notable for the diversity of their lyrics. He would sometimes use traditional material such as "Santa Claus" (1935), or the ten-bar insult song "I Can Tell by the Way You Smell" (1935), but normally he sang his own blues compositions such as "Big Jack Engine Blues" (1937) or "Frisco Blues" (1941). He also acquired a reputation for double entendre lyrics in songs such as "Think You Need a Shot" (1936). The best example of his musical originality, however, is probably "Why Should I Be Blue" (1940), a plaintively sung blues introduced with a halt-ing, descending series of notes that set the mournful mood of the number. The other attractive feature of Davis's work was his sparse piano style, which had an immediate impact on the ear because of its simple harmo-nies. Only rarely did he play more than two notes with either hand, and the melody and harmony were constructed systematically and logically, allowing for little superfluousness in their playing. Chords were often suggested rather than actually played. This technique created space in his music and gave it an underlying tension. Another important element in his music was his ability to sustain interest by playing in a wide range of keys. Unlike many of his contemporaries who were often limited to playing in the major keys—usually G, F, or C interspersed with flattened tones—Davis showed equal facility in keys such as D-flat major. He embellished many of his compositions with minor and occasional discordant tonality, which became an identifying feature of his style.

In his early years, Walter Davis played in clubs in the St. Louis district. After his discovery by Jack Kapp while playing at JC's nightclub in East St. Louis, and following his successful early recordings, he was reported to have toured the South from his base in St. Louis, accompanied by a small group consisting of Henry Townsend on guitar, a saxophonist, and a drummer. They were said to have traveled extensively in Davis's large Cadillac, appearing mainly at one-night stands in Texas, Missouri, and Tennessee. Another account of events by Townsend refutes this and suggests that Davis, a retiring character, rarely played in public and certainly did not travel extensively, but relied on his record sales and work at the Calumet Hotel for his subsistence. Other miscreant entertainers, apparently attempting to cash in on his recording fame, used his name for their own touring engagements.

Shortly after his final recording in 1952, Davis experienced a spiritual reawakening after reading Psalm 23 in an open Bible laid out in a bookshop. Thereafter, he devoted his life to religion. The newly converted pianist became a preacher in the St. Louis area and also had his own church in Hannibal, Missouri. The little money he had saved from his music now had to be supplemented from other sources, so he worked as a night clerk and switchboard operator at the Calumet and Albany Hotels. Shortly after his conversion he was smitten with a stroke—an indication that his life was not to run a very long course. He eventually died in 1964. Davis was a warm-hearted, friendly man whose humanity was expressed first in the piano blues of his race and later as a messenger of God. A typical cross-section of his recordings from his first in 1930 through to 1941 can be found on *Walter Davis: "Think You Need a Shot"* (RCA INT, 1085).

Rufus G. Perryman (aka "Speckled Red"; 1890–1973) owed his rediscovery to Charles O'Brien, a special officer with the St. Louis Police Department; during the 1950s this policeman and lover of blues and boogie-woogie music decided to trace some of the long-forgotten piano players in St. Louis. The events leading to his tracing Speckled Red bear telling, if only for the thoroughness shown by the policeman in utilizing his training to locate first, Henry Brown, and, later, James Stump Johnson. He found out that Henry Brown was alive and well after reading a postcard that the owner of the Bluenote Record Shop in St. Louis had received. It said that Roosevelt Sykes had mentioned in a radio interview that Brown was still living in St. Louis at Nineteenth and O'Fallon. Following up this lead, O'Brien found Brown and was then told of the whereabouts of James Stump Johnson and Edith and Mary Johnson. In the conversation that followed their meeting, Mary Johnson mentioned that she had seen

Speckled Red in a liquor store, a few days earlier. On checking police records, O'Brien found that Speckled Red had been the victim in a brawl in a pool hall some years before. Further inquiries revealed that Red was still living at the same address and, by chance, O'Brien visited a poolroom on Sixteenth and Franklin near Red's home and found him there. After a brief conversation, which confirmed that he was speaking to Speckled Red, O'Brien took him to the Top Deck nightspot where, fueled with a shot of whiskey, Red played many of the old numbers he had recorded in the 1930s and 1940s.

Perryman was a squat, broad-shouldered troubadour. He was given his name because he was a black albino with an almost white skin, apart from dark specks around his neck. He was born on October 22 in Hampton, Georgia, and died at the age of eighty-three in St. Louis. His father, Henry Perryman, was a blacksmith by trade who fathered sixteen children. During his time there, Red acquired a rudimentary keyboard technique by practicing on a church organ and eventually playing at church services. This early training accounts for the pervasive barrelhouse strains in his music. The family moved again to live in Atlanta, and Red, who by this time had switched to the piano, was now playing at house parties at weekends. As he was only able to earn a small amount of money by this means, he and his father went to work spasmodically at the American Machine Shop, in order to support the large Perryman family. At this time, Red was involved in selling corn whiskey as a bootlegger. Perhaps as a result of the limited work opportunities in Atlanta and an increasing confidence as a piano player, Red struck out on his own and left Atlanta for Detroit in 1924. This move marked the beginning of a nomadic existence as a barrelhouse pianist. While in Detroit he was exposed to the influences of several good piano players, setting the seal on his own technique. One pianist whom he particularly remembers was Paul Seminole, a diminutive half-caste Native Indian, who possessed an amazing piano technique. One of Seminole's favorite tricks was to play a semiclassical piece straight and then to speed it up while using a rapid stride bass.

Red was employed regularly as a pianist in Detroit at venues such as Miss Fat's Goodtime House, where he cleared tables and played on an old upright. In his spare time, he frequented the good-time houses and bars along Hastings and Brady streets, where he listened to Charlie Spand, Will Ezell, James Hemingway—so fat his stomach rested on the keyboard—and Dad Fishtail who played in a similar style to Montana Taylor. Red's most prosperous years were in 1928 and 1929. He had now acquired the soubriquet of Detroit Red and said that while in that city the money he earned allowed him to run a chauffeur-driven car.[5] He left in order to travel. At the time, he was living in a district like any other in a large urban city. The sporting area of Detroit was known as the Black

Bottom. Here, prostitution, illicit drinking, and gambling rackets carried on. Red's undoubted involvement with some of the gambling activities, in addition to his piano playing, probably added to his prosperity. It was a frantic time.[6]

Speckled Red left Detroit from the apartment where he was living at 224 West North and traveled south. At a time when many pianists were drifting from the South to northern cities, Red made the journey in the opposite direction toward Texas and finished up in the sawmill camps of the Piney Woods where he played the barrelhouse circuits for some time, traveling in the boxcars of freight trains. Due to his almost blind condition, he lacked the dexterity of his traveling companions for climbing aboard the fast-moving trains. He preferred to hide away before the trains began their journeys, but unfortunately the boxcars were often searched for illicit travelers by the brakeman and guard, and he was frequently turned off. Despite being incapacitated, he could move with surprising alacrity when the brakeman's searchlight picked him out and unfriendly bullets began to fly.

While playing at the sawmill camps, Red first put together the verses of "The Dirty Dozens," which eventually became a big-selling record for the Brunswick company. He recorded it at the Peabody Hotel in Memphis on September 22, 1929. Shortly after leaving the barrelhouse circuits, Red joined the Red Rose Minstrels in Memphis, a traveling medicine show that toured the towns of Mississippi, Arkansas, and Alabama. The owner was the rotund Jim Jackson who had formed a troupe of dancers, musicians, and comedy acts and offered patent medicine and soap for sale. These placebos were sold to the gullible to cure all manner of ailments from warts to bunions.

Jackson was a respected vaudevillian who weighed in at about 235 pounds. His show was built around his own skills as a dancer, singer, comedian, guitar player, and spieler. Red's piano playing was used to support Jackson's skills, and they often appeared as a duo, alongside Georgia Tom and Tampa Red. Jackson had already recorded "Kansas City Blues" (1927) for Brunswick, and as a result of this successful recording had made others for the company and Victor. At the time, he was also acting as a talent scout for Brunswick, and in this capacity he recommended Red as a possible artist. The company was looking for another boogie-woogie player to follow Pinetop Smith's successful recordings—on their Vocalion label—so they agreed to record Red at the same time that Jackson was making his own recording in 1929. Red recorded three numbers under his own name, "The Dirty Dozens," "Wilkins Street Stomp," and "Dance House Blues," and was also featured on a two-sided Vocalion record of Jim Jackson's Jamboree playing his version of "Pinetop's Boogie-Woogie."

By the time "The Dirty Dozens" became a best seller, Red left Memphis and so did not benefit from the publicity associated with the recording. His own financial reward, despite this favorable public reaction, was small. "The Dirty Dozens" was later recorded by a number of Brunswick and Decca artists, including Tampa Red, Kokomo Arnold, and Sam Price. Another recording session for Brunswick occurred in Chicago on April 8, 1930, which produced the "Dirty Dozens No. 2." Again there was a favorable public reaction, but the other numbers, "The Right String but the Wrong Yo Yo," "Speckled Red's Blues," "Lonesome Mind Blues," and "Got to Get That Thing Fixed," were largely ignored and sold poorly. One reason may have been the price of Brunswick records, which, at seventy-five cents each, was too much for the average African-American purchaser coping with the Depression. Soon after Red's second recording session, Brunswick discontinued the 700 series and switched its major artists to the Vocalion label. If Red had made his early recording for this label, his popular appeal may have been greater and he might not have spent so many years scuffling for work as an unrecognized barrelhouse pianist.

For a brief time in the late 1930s, Perryman was in Chicago where he recorded ten sides at the RCA studios. This session was organized for him by Walter Davis, acting as talent scout for the Bluebird label, and Red was paid $125 for the recordings, which included the eccentric "St. Louis Stomp," "Doin' the Georgia," and "Early in the Morning"—possibly inspired by Charlie Spand's tune. A period of obscurity followed, but not before William Russell had analyzed his playing technique as relatively crude but his virtuosity as overwhelming.[7]

In 1941, still largely disregarded, he settled in St. Louis, which became his adopted home until his death. Jobs were not immediately forthcoming, and he took work outside music as a truck loader and a checker at the Public Produce Market. He augmented his wages by playing occasional gigs at black taverns and he was then employed as the pianist at the World's Fair Bar on Broadway and Franklin until the police closed it down during World War II. Further opportunities for piano engagements were reduced for Red and other St. Louis pianists with the closure of the Market Street District, which had contained many dance halls and taverns.

By the 1950s, a new interest in piano blues and boogie-woogie was growing among younger record collectors in St. Louis. Following O'Brien's lead, several fans, including Bob Koester, the owner of Delmar Records, took an interest in Speckled Red's career. He thus obtained more regular employment from the time of his rediscovery in 1954 with appearances at the Dixie Matinee, two St. Louis Jazz Club meetings, and as the intermission pianist at the Jacovacs nightspot, where he shared the billing with the Young Dixie Stompers. He eventually became the pianist at a club in the famous Gaslight Square, a noted St. Louis jazz club area. This was followed by a tour of Europe and Great Britain, in 1959, as part of a U.S. cultural program. Michael Pointon, trombonist with Ken Colyer, whose band was appearing with Red at the Studio 51 Club in London recalled him as a "Southern Gentleman." Dressed in a white suit with matching stetson, Red responded patiently and politely to the questions of the eager young bandsmen luxuriating in the presence of this living blues legend.[8]

In 1963, Red moved to California and shared a house with John Bentley, a talented blues and boogie pianist who received scant recognition for his own keyboard abilities, limited to two recordings for Paul Affeldt's Euphonic label. Red and Bentley played alternate sets at the Bourbon Street Club, up in Hollywood. Bentley owned an old upright piano that he kept in the garage, and every afternoon when he returned from work he would hear the sounds of a barrelhouse piano Red was playing for all the children in the neighborhood who congregated regularly in the garage to listen to him: "Like me, the kids adored Red. And the nearby parents who didn't always have much time for children, must have considered Red a godsend."[9] Bentley described Perryman as a curious mixture of "big brother" and child who needed looking after. Watching Red's hands in action, he likened it to observing two tarantulas enveloping the keyboard.

Speckled Red's recording career took off once again with sessions for the Folkways, Delmark, Euphonic, Storyville, and Tone labels. His last public appearance, after the resurgence of interest in his music when he was once again much in demand, was aboard the steamer *Admiral* as guest of the St. Louis Jazz Club, in October 1971. Almost penniless and now in poor health after three operations for cancer, he died at the home (4515 Newberry Terrace) of Mrs. Minerva Muse, who had taken the old blind man under her wing. A collection was made among jazz fans to pay for his funeral expenses.

Although generally associated with that city, Perryman's style has little in common with other pianists from St. Louis. His two early recordings of the infamous "The Dirty Dozens" in Memphis (1929) and Chicago (1930) have the same music, but the lyrics are entirely different. It is, of course, primarily a vocal piece, with the music of the first chorus serving, through repetition, as the whole of the composition. Nevertheless, it is genuine, uproarious boogie-woogie. "Wilkins Street Stomp" is not the same piece as "Saint Louis Stomp" (1938), accompanied by R. L. McCoy on guitar and W. Hatcher on mandolin, who complete the Speckled Red Trio, but it does use a number of the same musical ideas as it tears along in a rather wild and undisciplined way from start to finish.

If ever there was a pianist who epitomized the barrelhouse style of piano playing, it must be Speckled Red. He was closest to Cripple Clarence

Lofton in his all-around abilities at the keyboard and use of unpredictable chorus lengths. In short, like Lofton he was an entertainer who played energetically, shouted exhortations to his audience, sometimes jubilant often complaining, and commanded their attention. A typical performance in full flight was captured graphically by Samuel B. Charters in the broadsheet accompanying Perryman's recording for Folkways. He notes the hunched-shoulder position over the keys and the magnetic presence as Red prepares to sing to his audience, but, as William Russell found, it was his exuberance and personality that counteracted the occasional lapses in technique.[10] And always, there were the stetson hat pulled well forward on his head and a large glass of gin in hand. Speckled Red was intensely committed to his music, and although he added to his repertoire over the years, he still retained several of the numbers he learned in his early period. Comparing early and later versions of two of his recordings, "Wilkins Street Stomp" and "The Dirty Dozens," is revealing: Few changes are evident in their playing over a thirty-five-year period. In concert, there was always a reason for including a particular number in his sets, and Red introduced them with a short preamble explaining the reason for the selection and where and how he had learned the number. All this added a certain color to his performances and created a personal and intimate atmosphere for his audiences.

The source of Speckled Red's material was mainly traditional, such as this cross-section from recordings of the 1960s: "The Dirty Dozens" and "The Right String but the Wrong Yo Yo," both bawdy vaudeville-type insult songs; solo blues such as "Four O'Clock Blues" and "Milk Cow Blues"; as well as his own compositions "Red's Own Blues" and "St. Louis Stomp." But in his playing of these numbers, he brought together all the varied techniques acquired over the years: a ragged bass line that jumps between a walking bass and an embryonic stride, thumped out with a verve that underpins handfuls of cascading notes and chords in the treble. Such an impression is endorsed by Rudi Blesh on listening to a rendition of "St. Louis Stomp" in which he vividly describes the hard-edged crudeness of the stinging, tumbling treble patterns.[11] These tunes, together with others, dating from a tour to Copenhagen in the 1960s, are available on *Speckled Red: "The Dirty Dozens," Volume 4* (Storyville, SLP 117). Examples of his earlier work are included on *Jazz: Boogie-Woogie* (Folkways, FJ 2810).

In contrast to Perryman, Henry Brown (1906–1981) was a living model of the qualities most apparent in the St. Louis boogie-woogie style: an economical left hand of single notes or sparse chords for slow numbers and a commanding walking bass for faster ones. The events in his life determined that the spark of interest he showed in piano music as a youngster would ignite and develop later into a personal and capable piano style. Born in Troy, Tennessee, he moved to the Deep Morgan area of the city when he was twelve. It is not known if Brown was accompanied by his family or whether he had run away from home. It seems likely that his family moved to Deep Morgan, because Brown had two years of elementary education at the De-Lin School. The area in which he grew up, the lower end of Delmar Boulevard by the river, ensured that he would constantly hear piano music being played in the multitude of small dives and bars along that street. The piano sounds soon superseded any interest that he had in formal education, and he began to follow a pianist called "Blackmouth" who played in the clubs on Morgan, Market, and Franklin streets. Another pianist whom he learned from was Joe Cross, a regular frequenter of the bars on Twenty-third and Market Street.

When he was sixteen, Brown had mastered the piano sufficiently to be able to play at the buffet flats and was in regular demand. He earned enough money for sustenance, allowing him to sleep in the daytime and perform through the night and early morning. Times were not always so good, however, and he had to seek other work on occasions to eke out a living. Brown and his close friend and fellow musician Ike Rogers, a trombone player, worked together in a dairy during the 1920s and, later, as steam pressers in a laundry.

As the Depression bit deeper, even this lowly paid work disappeared. There were now over eleven million unemployed in America, and destitute black families in St. Louis were squatting in rolling stock owned by the Missouri-Kansas and Texas Railroad Company. Henry Brown and Ike Rogers worked on government-sponsored projects (WPA) in stone quarries or as members of a road gang. This heavy manual work was interspersed with engagements at Katy Red's Club and the 9-0-5 Club. Brown ran a small band for a time called the Biddle Street Boys (probably in the 1930s) comprising himself on piano, Earl Bridley (drums), Ike Rogers (trombone), and Henry Townsend or Lawrence "Papa Eggshell" Casey (guitar). Alice Moore, known as "Little Alice," was the vocalist. Henry Townsend provides an absorbing picture of the many capable blues pianists that he (Townsend) worked with in St. Louis, including Brown whose versatility is mentioned for the excellent backing that he and Ike Rogers give to Alice Moore's vocals, notably on "Black and Evil Blues" (1929).[12]

Brown was drafted into the army in the early 1940s where he spent some time in Texas and Florida as a member of a small band before being posted to England to entertain the troops. On his return to St. Louis, he resumed his part-time musical employment and then left the music world during the 1960s and early 1970s. Before this occurred, he was "rediscovered" by Paul Oliver who made a trip to St. Louis to find him in the late 1950s. With the help of Charlie O'Brien, Brown was located in a poolroom. Oliver recorded him on portable equipment in a small hair-dressing and beauty salon owned by Pinkey Boxx. It was soon apparent that Brown had retained his touch and was still a capable pianist with a distinctive and original tone. Oliver believed that Brown's creative talent for composing original blues had been under-recorded and that, like good wine, his playing had improved with the advancing years. At the time of their initial meeting, Oliver noted that his first impressions of truculence in his features and sadness in his eyes both changed dramatically when they started discussing his first recording sessions for the Paramount company some thirty years earlier.[13]

Henry Brown's recording career spanned forty-five years. His first recordings, made in 1929, included "Stomp 'Em Down to the Bricks," a piano solo with accompaniment by Lawrence Casey on guitar for Brunswick and "Henry Brown Blues," a piano solo for the Paramount label. Two further sides, "Deep Morgan Blues" and "Eastern Chimes Blues," were cut for the same company in February 1930. He was active again in 1934, recording for Decca but this time as piano accompanist to Mary Johnson's blues vocals. After his recording for Paul Oliver in 1960, further dates followed for the Euphonic label and shortly afterward the St. Louis based Adelphi label, and again on this label in 1974. Altogether, it was a sustained performance by a blues pianist whose music reached out to an ageless body of appreciative fans. Apart from spasmodic work in St. Louis during the 1950s, Brown kept his technique in shape on a piano installed in a warehouse by his employers, the Edwin Brothers Shoe Company on Washington Avenue. One extended engagement in the 1960s was as the pianist aboard the *Becky Thatcher* riverboat, at which time his one recording for the Euphonic label was made.

Henry Brown had about twenty numbers credited to his name, all of which appeared on his recordings at one time or another. He was not an exciting pianist in the manner of Speckled Red, nor an original like Walter Davis, but he could lay down a steady rolling rhythm, one reason why some of his most successful work was done as a member of a small group. As a solo pianist, his strength lay in his thoughtful meditative blues and boogie-woogie, little changed from the era when underprivileged blacks sought their amusement and solace in the dives near his home in Deep Morgan. As he had lived, so he died on June 28, 1981, a resident of St. Louis, following a short illness. There were no immediate descendants: His wife had died seven years previously and the marriage had been childless.

The fourth influential pianist associated with St. Louis was Roosevelt Sykes (1906–1984). He was born in Elmar, Arkansas, on January 31 and died in New Orleans on July 17. Known variously as "Keg," the "Honeydripper," and, on some recordings, as Dobby Bragg or Willie Kelly, depending on the record company, he had moved to St. Louis with his family from Helena, Arkansas, when he was three years old. His roots, however, remained in the South to where he returned seeking work as a dishwasher and waiter in his teen years. At this time, probably after his parents had died, he lived with his grandfather, a cotton sharecropper. One pianist on whom he based his own playing was the unrecorded Jesse Bell. Others whom he heard and from whom he learned in the Helena region were Joe Crump and Baby Sneed. As a youngster, Sykes stood outside the barrelhouses where these pianists were playing to listen to their music; and later during his teen years he sometimes spent a complete weekend inside the various clubs learning points of technique from them.

Sykes was essentially a self-taught pianist, but he could also play guitar and organ. Initially, he found the transition from pump organ to piano playing difficult because of the sustained finger pressure necessary for producing notes on the organ, which was not suitable for piano playing. He devised a kind of stabbing motion that enabled him to hit the notes more cleanly, and this remained a feature of his piano technique. In the early days, he was obliged to walk between two and three miles to a neighbor's house in order to practice the piano. After developing sufficient proficiency, he began working at clubs and bars in and around Helena. The clientele were laborers and migrant workers from the farms in this predominantly rural area who worked hard all week and disported themselves at weekends. In the mid-1920s he met up with another pianist, Lee Green, and together they played at the bars and barrelhouses of Lake Providence, Louisiana; they also traveled a well-worn route "riding the rods" between Helena and St. Louis where their music provided the entertainment at several bars and clubs. Sykes's first recording was of the "Forty Four Blues," which he learned from Lee Green. He used Green's piano theme to which he added his own embellishments and ominous opening phrase, saying that he had walked all night with his .44 in his hand. The recording was made in June 1929 for the Okeh company by Jesse Johnson, a local entrepreneur who owned a record store and acted as one of Okeh's talent scouts before becoming Sykes's manager. Shortly afterward, other versions of this number were recorded by James Wiggins, accompanied by Leroy Garnett on piano, and by Little Brother Montgomery who adapted it for his own "Vicksburg Blues." The "Forty Four Blues" was a popular theme in the South, and many pianists attempted but failed to master its intricately separated bass and treble rhythms. Sykes had sufficient acumen to delay his recording debut until he was fully satisfied that his piano technique was good enough to sustain a recording career: "A first impression is a lasting impression," he told Bentley. "Once a pancake, always a pancake."[14]

Late in the 1920s, Sykes returned to St. Louis to make it his permanent home where he lived on Seventeenth Street between Cole and Carr. From there he made several tours in the 1930s to Memphis, Chicago, and other cities, interspersing solo work with playing accompaniments on recordings for many blues singers such as Mary Johnson and Curtis Mosby. When Sykes returned to St. Louis, he frequently teamed up with St. Louis Jimmy (James Oden), working bars and gambling dives. They recorded one of Oden's compositions "Going Down Slow" (1932) after Sykes had introduced him to Frank Melrose, who had connections with the major companies of Decca, RCA, and Columbia. In the late 1930s the pair toured many of the major cities in the South. During his time in St. Louis, Sykes was also active musically at Jazzland, playing intermission piano for Charlie Creath's band; and at Charlie Houston's Club, working with Henry Townsend and Henry Brown. Townsend became the regular accompanying guitar player for Sykes, having first served an apprenticeship with Sykes's brother Walter "Wyle" Sykes, a less-known performer. An active and friendly coterie of pianists existed in St. Louis who were known to each other by various nicknames: Sykes was "Keg," owing to his physical appearance; Walter Davies was called "Turkey"; while Henry Brown was known as "Hog." The prize, however, must go to the little-known pianist called "Stiff-armed" Eddie who labored under the handicap of an unbendable right arm for which he had to compensate with a less-than-vertical posture at the piano and very dexterous fingering. Apart from his musical work at this time, Sykes also acted as a talent scout for the Victor and Decca labels. One of the artists whom he claims to have introduced to the major companies was Walter Davis.

Much of Sykes's mature playing was done in St. Louis, and he always said that his style was a happy fusion of all he had learned in Helena and St. Louis, recognizing these as major influences. The time spent in the company of Lee Green was not unproductive, because he learned to play a "swing" bass from him involving tenths. No doubt becoming aware that commercial opportunities were greater in Chicago, he took up residence there in the early 1940s, forming his own group and playing at the Tin Pan Alley Club and other local bars, before once again taking to the road with his group and touring the South. During the 1940s, he made further recordings for Victor and two small Chicago record companies, Bullet and Speciality. He also accompanied Memphis Minnie and Son Joe on club dates and recorded with the Jump Jackson band. For a time, in the 1950s, he worked in Chicago with Lonnie Johnson and continued touring prior to returning to St. Louis and other cities in the states of Illinois and Texas for short periods. Although he was leading a nomadic existence at this stage in his life, it appears to have been well paid.

In 1954, Sykes moved his base to New Orleans where his successful and active musical career continued as a recording artist, accompanist, and solo club performer. The tours that Sykes now undertook embraced Europe and England with appearances in several films, including one in Belgium, *Roosevelt Sykes the Honeydripper* (1961); the French film *Blues under the Skin* (1972); and a BBC television series *The Devil's Music—A History of the Blues* (1976). He retained his popularity with an ever-increasing blues audience until his death.

Roosevelt Sykes was the most extroverted and technically capable pianist who came out of St. Louis. His lightly freckled, smiling face topped a rotund figure that sat high and straight on the piano stool. With fast-moving hands and supple fingering, he seemed to envelop the instrument. He was a versatile singer who used topical and frequently risqué lyrics, and this, together with his effortless technique, maintained his popularity over the years when the vicissitudes of ill fortune forced lesser men to give up their piano playing for alternative forms of employment. He was popular with other musicians and much admired for his integrity, intelligence, and business sense, which not only served his own interests but were generously employed to bring unknown talent to the recording studios.

The fluency he displayed at the keyboard can be heard to good effect on "Big Legs Ida Blues" (1933), on which he uses a characteristic single-note running bass line that adds to the smoothness of the performance; this was repeated some eight years later on "Low as a Toad." Sykes accompanies his own somber lyrics with a slow, punctuated rock bass and vocal asides on "Poor Boy Blues" (1929). "All My Money Gone Blues" (1929) displays a nice interplay between the bass and treble parts to support his vocal, and the strongly stated guitar playing of Oscar Carter. The spirit of Henry Brown weaves through the piano playing in "Home of Your Own Blues" (1929), which creates the typical treble chording and four-to-the bar bass of the style most associated with St. Louis. Sykes recorded what appeared to be a "cover" of Pinetop's famous piece, released as "Boot That Thing" (1929), six months after Pinetop's recording, but he claimed not to know Pinetop or his recording. Interviewed by John Bentley, he said, "He was in Chicago; I was in St. Louis. When I heard him you'd think we copied after one another. Happened a lot—different pianists playing the same thing. It was one of those tunes going around at that time."[15] A comprehensive collection of Roosevelt Sykes's numbers displaying the various facets of his playing is available on *Roosevelt Sykes/Lee Green 1929–1930, Volume 18* (Magpie, PY 4418).

In his later years, Sykes's playing was sometimes lacking inspiration through overexposure. He flirted with "jump" numbers—which was not to everyone's taste, although it must be said he was particularly pleased with these efforts. It is his early work from 1929 onwards, certainly into the 1950s, that captures the real nuances of which he was capable, particularly on numbers such as "Lost All I Had" (1929) with their beautifully balanced boogie-woogie rhythms.

Leothus "Lee" Green spent time working in St. Louis and is usually associated with that city. Earlier in his career, he resided in Louisiana working as a trouser presser, but he also lived off his wits as a gambler, alongside his music making. Lee Green was a very capable pianist who could turn his hand to most styles, two of which, the blues and boogie-woogie, were becoming increasingly popular with the record companies catering to the tastes of African-Americans in the 1920s and 1930s. When Roosevelt Sykes first met him, Green was accompanying silent films on piano at Miller's Theatre.

His voice and piano are particularly compatible: the former delivered lazily from the back of the throat with a slight nasal tone and occasional vibrato; the latter lilting with a suspended, delayed rhythm. It is usually an indication of a pianist's competence when they can produce an, apparently, independent backing to their own singing and sound like two performers. Hall comments on this ability, which Green displays in "Death Alley Blues" (1930), in which his effortless vocal is supported by a single note bass and smooth treble phrasing,[16] If the extensive number of recordings (circa forty-five) made in the eight-year period between 1929 and 1937 is any measure, then Lee Green was a popular commercial artist who may also have been an influential figure helping to shape the styles of later pianists such as Little Brother (see chapter 1 comparing Green's "Dudlow Joe" and the later "Farish Street Jive") and Roosevelt Sykes.

It is to his recording "Memphis Fives" (1934), a vocal accompanied by his piano, that we turn to see if the sung text will furnish any further information about the meaning of the word *fives*. The text of the different verses does not form a narrative; in fact, the verses seem quite unrelated to one another. The first three deal with taking a woman out, seeing her in Memphis, and tooting a whistle and blowing a horn; while the last three concern themselves with an argument with her, a separation, and his departure on a train journey. Thus, as can be seen, none of the text throws very much light upon the meaning of the word *fives*. In Green's tune there does not appear to be any musical connection with time (five o'clock when the rent party began to revive) nor the rent party itself.

Similarly, the only tenuous link with the Thomas composition is related to a train journey. If there is any conclusion, it is that the word *fives* in this particular song is used as a synonym for the word *blues* when the latter is used to mean a feeling or state of mind—that is, one has "got those Memphis fives" in the same way as one has "got the St. Louis Blues."

Is the piece boogie-woogie? Well, some of it is. To be more specific, an eight-to-the-bar walking bass underpins the lyrics, usually just in the first five bars of each twelve-bar chorus, with the first two choruses seeing its additional employment at bars 7 and 8. Lee Green disappeared from the music scene after his successful recording career and was believed to have died in the mid-1940s. Examples of his work are on the aforementioned Volume 18 of the Magpie label.

There were other pianists active in St. Louis who were not as well known as these major recording artists. As lesser-known performers, they had a defined repertoire of numbers, made a few recordings, and found regular work in the buffet flats and dives around the city. Some, like Aaron Sparks and Sylvester Palmer, were the victims of underexposure compared to Sykes, Brown, Davis, and Perryman who were fortunate in reaching a wider, national audience. Sparks and Palmer, for some reason, never quite achieved the same popularity, although it is evident from recordings that they were highly competent and original performers.

Aaron "Pinetop" Sparks (1908–1935) and Marion "Lindberg" Sparks were twins who were born in Tupelo, Mississippi. They moved with their parents to St. Louis in 1920 and later formed a musical partnership with Pinetop, who had received a rudimentary music education at school, playing the accompaniments to Lindberg's singing. They made their first recordings in 1932, putting down some interesting blues laced with boogie-woogie piano. Their most notable sides were "4 × 11 = 44," a favored combination of numbers for the illegal gambling policy racket, "Louisiana Bound," and "East Chicago Blues." There are typical examples of the work of the two brothers on *Piano Blues, Volume 20: Barrelhouse Years* (Magpie, PY 4420). Pinetop is of particular interest because he developed an excellent technique, ranging from a fierce boogie-woogie to a starker blues accompaniment of chorded basses and rich treble passages that provide a supportive cushioning for his brother's plaintively high-pitched vocals. He was particularly adept with Pinetop Smith's number—hence his soubriquet—and was said by Joe Dean, another St. Louis pianist, to engage in cutting sessions with him (Dean) playing that number. Sparks often shared engagements with Dean when they would alternate sets. He was in considerable demand as a pianist at the buffet flats and was also active at the Dirty Inn and Charlie Houston's Club on Lucas, both within easy reach of his home at 3139 Franklin.

In his early years, Pinetop Sparks was frequently in trouble with the police because of illegal drinking activities, though he was said to be an even-tempered person. Lindberg had an equally unenviable police record and was, at one time, arrested for killing a man in self-defense, for which, in 1937, he served time in the city workhouse.[17] Pinetop's sole employment was his piano playing, which, by the nature of events during the

Depression, was spasmodic. Contrary to what might be expected, the twins did not always work harmoniously together, as, like other siblings, they were never in total agreement.

Pinetop provided rich accompaniments for vocalists Dorothea Trowbridge on "Bad Luck Blues" (1933) and for Elizabeth Washington on "Whiskey Blues" (1933). His last recording date was in 1935, and shortly after that he died, the victim, it was believed, of poisoning. Lindberg lived until 1963 and worked as a school porter until a heart attack killed him. As with his brother, he had mellowed and was living a respectable life at the time of his death.

Sylvester Palmer was a confrere of Henry Townsend, but they were never musically active together. Palmer learned to play piano in Alton, Illinois, a short distance to the north of St. Louis, and developed a unique piano style that was difficult to accompany. His playing has been likened to that of Wesley Wallace, another idiosyncratic pianist, also believed to have originated from Alton. One possibility is that they may have been exposed to similar influences when they were learning their craft. In an analysis of Palmer's playing, Hall and Noblett concluded that a comparison between the piano playing of Wallace and Palmer displayed a close juxtaposition in their choice of titles and keys.[18] However, as will be shown, there could be a more obvious reason for the similarities in their styles.

Wesley Wallace and Sylvester Palmer may have been one and the same person. Attempts to prove or disprove this conclusively were thwarted by the apparent disappearance of Wallace after his brilliant, seminal recording of "Number 29" (1929). In addition to aural similarities in their playing from recordings made in 1929—"Broke Man Blues" (Palmer) and "Fanny Lee Blues" (Wallace), the voices on "Do It Sloppy" (Palmer), and the spoken commentary on Wallace's train piece—there is additional evidence, relating to Paramount's L matrix series, that recordings by "Wallace" and "Palmer" were actually made by the same person in the same studio.[19] Apparently, after using the Gennett recording studios until October 1929, Paramount was loaned the Columbia/Okeh studios for recording purposes before their own studio at Grafton was completed, in April 1930. In return for this favor, they allowed Columbia the facility of issuing some of the recordings made by Paramount artists. For example, the Hokum Boys' Paramount recordings matrix L 96-100 were made at the same session as the Columbia recordings matrix 403338-43, and Stump Johnson's Paramount recordings L156/157 were made at the same time as Columbia's recordings matrix 403314-7. Sylvester Palmer was known by this name for Columbia, but became "Wesley Wallace" for Paramount. The reason why there was no trace of "Wallace," therefore, was because Palmer died on May 8, 1930.

Thomas McFarland (1903–1962; aka "Barrelhouse Buck") owed his rediscovery indirectly to Charles O'Brien. In 1961, Samuel Charters decided to make some field recordings in St. Louis and approached the policeman to ask for his help in contacting suitable blues artists to record. It transpired that O'Brien, in the course of his police duties, had recently been in contact with a person named McFarland who was the brother of Thomas "Barrelhouse Buck" McFarland, a popular St. Louis pianist of the 1930s. Coincidentally, at the time of Charter's inquiry, Thomas McFarland was in St. Louis temporarily away from Detroit, where he was living, attending to family business. After a telephone conversation, it was agreed that Charters would record McFarland, and the recording was subsequently released as *Barrelhouse Buck: Backcountry Barrelhouse* (Folkways, FG 3554). The recording was made at the home of one of Buck's friends on a poorly tuned piano, but it captures his earthy and somewhat crude-sounding piano style.

On September 16, McFarland was born in Alton, from where his family moved to St. Louis shortly before World War I. Showing a precocious interest in the piano, he was soon playing for his mother's private parties at the family home. Believing that her small son was too impressionable to watch the guests dancing Ball in the Jack and other adult dances, his mother placed the piano facing a wall so that he was unable to watch the proceedings. Unknown to her, Buck was able to see the dancing in the reflection on the front of the highly polished instrument.

Buck's rudimentary piano style matured further by watching and listening to the many itinerant pianists who passed through St. Louis. He appeared at clubs and dives all over the city but was particularly associated with Johnny Pegg's Club on Biddle Street, as Henry Townsend recalls. For a time he was a member of the fine Charlie Creath band at Jazzland on Market Street and also toured the South with the Georgia Smart Set Show. After a successful test on Twentieth Street, St. Louis, Charlie Jordan, an active talent scout in the city, arranged for him to travel to Chicago to make a recording. When Buck was asked by the producer to name the piece, he happened to be looking out of the studio window and noticed a policeman leaning against a lamp post, which gave him the ready-made title of "Lamp Post Blues" (1934). Unfortunately, he was robbed of his earnings while there, leaving him with no alternative but to record some additional tunes to pay for his return trip to St. Louis. Like many other modestly capable pianists in the city, Barrelhouse Buck was at his musical peak in the late 1920s, and as the record market diminished and clubs closed down because of the Depression, only the better-known pianists could obtain employment. Thomas McFarland then disappeared from the music scene before his rediscovery by O'Brien.

St. Louis was the most musically active and diverse of all the urban centers where boogie-woogie flourished, because it was not only pianists who provided entertainment in the dives and clubs. Many guitar players and blues vocalists had also settled there from the southern states, and with such a mixture of talent a rich tapestry of music was available. Where the Chicago pianists often worked as soloists, those in St. Louis frequently teamed up with guitar players and other instrumentalists. Henry Townsend, for example, often accompanied Henry Brown and Roosevelt Sykes with his stomping background rhythms.

Working for a time in St. Louis during the 1930s as the best-known and respected piano and guitar playing duo were Leroy Carr (1905–1935) and his guitar-playing friend Scrapper Blackwell. Carr was born in Nashville, Tennessee, but spent his formative years in Indianapolis where he acquired a rudimentary piano style practicing on the family pianola when his mother was absent, as she did not allow blues to be played in the house. He also listened to the many barrelhouse pianists working on the "West Side" of the city, the section where African-Americans lived and worked. He joined up with Blackwell in Indianapolis who, in turn, had moved there from Syracuse, North Carolina.

Their most famous recording was "How Long Blues" (1928), which became a standard number in the repertoire of several instrumentalists, including Jimmy Yancey who built a number of his own compositions around the chord sequences. Carr employed a soft piano backing to support his arrestingly original lyrics, delivered in a voice inflected with sadness, both proving germane to the lives of many of his long-suffering black audience. Blackwell provided the sharp, biting guitar rhythms that gave them contrast. The pair could be heard at Jazzland and the Booker T. Washington Theatre in St. Louis and were able to eke out a living here during the worst of the Depression when all recording activity had virtually ceased. The two are perfectly synchronized in "I Believe I'll Make a Change" (1934), with Carr exhorting Blackwell to "lay your racket boy . . . knock a hole in it." Carr puts down a solid boogie rhythm in "Take a Walk around the Corner" (1934) to provide a boisterous contrast to the more silky stride patterns of his left hand that he sometime employed. Occasionally, the two instruments change functions, with Blackwell pushing out a tangy boogie beat, as on the plaintively beautiful "Midnight Hour Blues" (1932), and underpinning Carr's mournful lyrics of unrequited love. Carr's indulgent lifestyle finally caught up with him, as his alcohol consumption increased to deaden the pain of earlier excesses. He died suddenly after attending an all-night party. The subsequent autopsy revealed the cause of death as nephritis. The overlap between blues piano and boogie-woogie was more noticeable in the work of these and other St. Louis pianists because of the opportunities to play with other instrumentalists and vocalists. As a result, the boogie-woogie piano modality associated with the city had a looser framework and a distinctive hollow sound compared to that of Chicago's pianists. Some of the wonderfully evocative duets of Carr coupled with the guitar playing of Blackwell and Josh White are available on *Leroy Carr: "Blues before Sunset"* (CBS, BPG 62206).

A number of pianists with good local reputations at parties and in the bars of Hennepin Street did not even experience the modest fame of public attention achieved by their contemporaries through regular recording dates. In general, their playing could be described as idiosyncratically primitive. James "Stump" Johnson—so named because of his short stature—was one of them. An early recording was "Bound to Be a Monkey" (1929, piano with talking). Despite his saying that he is going to play "this good ragtime," it is in fact a piece of boogie-woogie (albeit not a very distinguished piece) using an eight-to-the-bar walking bass. Jabo Williams adopted St. Louis as his base and in 1932 recorded several distinctive piano solos, among which were "Pratt City Blues" and "Jab's Blue," two forceful, eccentric, and exciting solos displaying an amalgam of embryonic traces of a striding left hand, raggedy treble figures—often matching his vocals, note for note—and persistently hammered boogie-woogie basses. Recorded in the same year and played in a sad mood at moderately slow tempo were "Polock Blues" and "Fat Man Blues." His limited but priceless collection of known recordings appears on *Piano Blues and Boogie-Woogie 1929–1935* (RST Records, BD-2034).

James Crutchfield (1912–2001) came from Baton Rouge and spent several formative years in Texas learning his trade from such pianists as the exotically named Peg Top and Dick Moore. Many of the tunes he brought with him to St. Louis have the Texas stamp: "Pearly Mae" and "Piggly-Wiggly Blues" being two of them. As a boy, he and his mother used to stay for prolonged periods at different lumber and sawmill camps in the South after his father left them. Later, he traveled widely, taking in Louisiana, where he was taught "Forty Four Blues" by Little Brother Montgomery, then moved to Mississippi before arriving in St. Louis in 1948. He was resident pianist for Miss Rosalee at Gaslight Square for many years, before the district was closed down, and then disappeared from the music scene. By 1957, he had only managed one recording session but fortunately was identified and brought out of obscurity by the ubiquitous Charles O'Brien who contacted two Dutch record producers. They issued many of Crutchfield's earlier numbers in 1983, which are on *James Crutchfield: Original Barrelhouse Blues* (Swingmaster, 2109). Their release coincided with a successful concert appearance in Holland, both providing a deserved if belated recognition for this underrated piano player. James Crutchfield has a firm and confident vocal delivery, hitting notes full-on; his piano backing is discordant but powerful, making extensive use of repeated chorded treble phrasing, as in "Forty Four Blues." Boogie-woogie basses are used sparingly, often as a contrast to more standard types of stride bass or following sections of blocked chords, as on "Bogalusa Blues."

In order to complete this broad sweep of St. Louis boogie-woogie, several other pianists are deserving of mention. Peetie Wheatstraw, aka William Bunch, was a popular musician who was adept on both piano and guitar, and also sang heavy, menacing blues, which led to his pseudonym of the Devil's Son-in-law. Wheatstraw settled in St. Louis in 1929, having arrived there from the South. His first recordings, "Tennessee Peaches Blues" and "Four O'Clock in the Morning" (both 1930), were made in Chicago, at the instigation of his guitar-playing friend Charley Jordan, who shared many recordings and composer credits with him. Peetie Wheatstraw was popular with both black and white audiences, and when he was killed in a car crash in 1941, he had one hundred and fifty recordings to his credit. Joe Dean (from Bowling Green) and James "Bat" Robinson were two other players of note working in and around St. Louis for several years. Those with established reputations were Eddie Miller whose piano playing went beyond the blues and Jimmy Oden whose significant musical period came later during a close association with Muddy Waters and the Chicago blues bands. Fortunately, several of these lesser-known pianists were also captured on record and have since had their work reevaluated and reissued by the Yazoo record company, drawing from the collection of Frances Wilford Smith. Together with the better-known players, they help identify the subtlety and variety to be found in the playing of pianists from this city. Examples of the work of Johnson, Crutchfield, Brown, and other less-known piano players are available on *Barrelhouse: Blues and Stomps, Volume 4* (Euphonic Piano Series, ESR 1205).

Although the left-hand bass figures that characterize boogie-woogie may have originated in the South, and became fully formed in Chicago, it is with the St. Louis pianists that the first emergence of boogie-woogie as a style and form capable of existing as a piano solo begins to show. In the evolution of the style, St. Louis appears to have been a musical staging post between the softer and more melodic variants of boogie-woogie—used in the South as an accompaniment for vocal blues or as a section in an otherwise straightforward piano blues solo—and the constant repetitive rhythms associated with Chicago. The evidence provided on recordings of the piano solos of Henry Brown, Roosevelt Sykes, and more especially the cruder, more primitive piano solos of Wesley Wallace and Jabo Williams, show right hand as well as left hand—the true beginnings of an instrumental style divorced from the vocal medium and more or less consistently applied that was to become recognized as boogie-woogie piano. The explanation may lie simply in the geographical position of St. Louis, which is situated on a direct line between Chicago and the southern cities of Dallas, Vicksburg, New Orleans, and Memphis. It would have been the first large city to attract black workers, including pianists, on their way to a better life in the North and, as such, would have witnessed the earliest modification to southern styles of boogie-woogie.

Tracking the appearance of boogie-woogie in the nightspots and clubs of Detroit is more complex for two reasons. In the first place, pianists of note such as Charles Spand and Will Ezell could not be said to be full-time residents of the Motor City. Spand moved between Detroit and Chicago; Will Ezell, Charles Davenport, and Pinetop Smith passed through; and Speckled Red enjoyed an extended stay there before leaving for St. Louis. Second, many of Detroit's indigenous pianists held down full-time jobs in the daytime and supplemented their income by working as part-time musicians. As many never recorded, it becomes difficult to identify particular and distinctive features of the Detroit boogie-woogie piano style.

In seeking to identify the significance of Detroit, which later became associated with the more "muscular" forms of urban blues bands, the question is why that city more than any other? The appearance of a music scene stems from the time when African-Americans moved there in large numbers at the beginning of the twentieth century as part of the exodus from the South to work in the newly established car factories and other heavy industries. Although it was grindingly, heavy physical labor, the new arrivals had money in their pockets. Entertainment was available in the somber Black Bottom area of Detroit through which Hastings Street ran like a brightly colored ribbon. It offered the punters "blind pig" dives—so named because of the illicit liquor available there during Prohibition—and bars and brothels to cater for all tastes, with the music of guitar and piano players to provide a backdrop for the adventurers.

Charlie Spand was to be inspired in Detroit to compose and record his well-known number "Hastings Street" (1929) with his longtime friend Blind Blake, a talented and experienced guitar player. It is a riotous, good-time piece driven along by Spand's forceful piano and Blake's chorded guitar accompaniment by frequent spoken references to Brady Street: "always telling me about Brady Street"—possibly the location of a brothel or lively juke. Spand was a technically good pianist who played in a range of keys, some—B-flat major and E-flat major—possibly selected for group playing with brass or woodwind instrumentalists. He made regular use of a heavy rolling walking bass, which was coaxed from the piano with his long slender fingers, but he also deployed a barrelhouse style using cleanly executed and precise stride basses. He was successful from the start with his most famous vocal and piano blues "Soon This Morning" (1929), on which he was again accompanied by Blind Blake. This composition has become a "standard" blues regularly featured by other performers, its catchy melody and poetic lyrics lifting it to the top bracket of blues compositions.

Little Brother worked with Spand and Blake at Chicago rent parties from about 1928 to 1930, for which they were paid between three and five dollars a night. They appeared regularly at 4048 S. Indiana for Roberta McGee's all-night parties, and at weekends for a Miss Loretta Jones at 5758 S. State. Montgomery lost touch with Spand during the Depression years, and it may have been a period when he had moved his base to Detroit. There is no further information about his whereabouts except to note that he made one or two recordings for Okeh in the early 1940s. It was rumored that he was working as a taxi driver on the West Coast by this time.

Spand was an established recording artist who made twenty-three sides for Paramount between 1929 and 1931. For whatever reason, his true talents have never been posthumously recognized, though his consistent and regular recordings indicate that Paramount was aware of his commercial potential; otherwise, they would certainly not have recorded him so intensively in the two years of their association. He will be remembered best for his thoughtfully constructed blues and the delivery of their lyrics in his distinctive high-pitched voice. A typical selection of his work is offered on *Piano Blues, Volume 16: Charlie Spand 1929–1931* (Magpie, PY 4416).

Another who stayed in Detroit for an extended period before leaving for the Windy City was Big Maceo Merriweather, whose impact is covered in a later chapter but whose powerful boogie-woogie piano style on numbers such as "Chicago Breakdown" (1945) probably best epitomizes the industrial strength of Detroit. One truly indigenous pianist is Vernon Harrison, known as Piano Red for an albino skin condition similar to Speckled Red's.

Hastings Street was destroyed in the 1950s to make way for the Walter C. Chrysler Expressway. The final death blow to that section of Detroit as an entertainment district occurred after the horrific race riots of 1967, which destroyed the informal club ambience where it had been possible to drop in for a beer and listen to the blues. After the riots, many customers felt uneasy in the district and their support fell away, leaving no choice for club owners but to close down. Over time, many of the African-American players moved over to rhythm-and-blues groups or took over the piano benches of the amplified blues bands. Bob Seeley and Mark Braun, the two pianists who, ironically, have remained true to the boogie-woogie piano tradition of Detroit, are white Americans.

NOTES

1. O. Johns, *Times of Our Lives* (New York: Farrar, Straus and Giroux, 1973), 98.

2. P. Oliver, *Conversation with the Blues* (London: Cassell and Company, 1967), 95–96.

3. John Morthland, "Lost Delta Found," *eMusic Magazine*, October 25, 2005, www.emusic.com/features/spotlight/292_200510.html (accessed March 20, 2009).

4. Oliver, *Conversation with the Blues*, 108.

5. Bob Koester, "The Saga of Speckled Red," *Jazz Report* 2, no. 5 (January 1962): 14.

6. Koester, "The Saga of Speckled Red," 14.

7. W. Russell, "Boogie-Woogie," in *Jazzmen*, ed. F. Ramsey and C. E. Smith (London: Sidgwick and Jackson, 1958), 200.

8. Michael Pointon, correspondence with the author, February 24, 2003.

9. John Bentley, correspondence with the author, July 11, 1991.

10. Samuel B. Charters, liner notes, *The Barrelhouse Blues of Speckled Red*, Folkways, FG 3555.

11. R. Blesh, *Shining Trumpets* (London: Cassell, 1949), 299.

12. Charles O'Brien and Mike Rowe, "St. Louis Had to Get Credit" (composite interviews with Henry Townsend), *Blues Unlimited* 133 (January/February 1979): 4–10.

13. Paul Oliver, liner notes, *Henry Brown Blues*, 77 Records, 77-LA-12-5.

14. John Bentley, taped interview with Roosevelt Sykes, 1977, sent to the author.

15. John Bentley, taped interview with Roosevelt Sykes, 1977.

16. Bob Hall, liner notes, *The Way I Feel: The Best of Roosevelt Sykes and Lee Green*, Yazoo Piano Blues, Yazoo 2066.

17. Mike Rowe and Charlie O'Brien, "Well Them Two Sparks Brothers They Been Here and Gone," *Blues Unlimited* 144 (Spring 1983): 9–14. For a more general background of St. Louis and its blues music, see Henry Townsend and Bill Greensmith, *A Blues Life* (Champaign: University of Illinois Press, 1999).

18. Bob Hall and Richard Noblett, "A Handful of Keys," *Blues Unlimited* 112 (March 1975): 18.

19. Ernest Virgo, correspondence with the author, March 31, 1992.

Part Three

THE CARNEGIE PERIOD

7

The Spirituals to
Swing Concerts

In 1938 and 1939 three events occurred that took boogie-woogie music
from the barrelhouse and bars of the black sections of Chicago, Kansas
City, and St. Louis and into the cosmopolitan and sophisticated jazz clubs
of New York and beyond. They were the two Spirituals to Swing concerts
and the opening of the first of the Café Society nightclubs. John Hammond was the guiding force behind all three.

The concerts were held at the prestigious Carnegie Hall and featured
boogie-woogie music by including Ammons, Lewis, and Johnson in the
program. After the first concert, the three men, with Joe Turner, went on
to become popular attractions at the Café Society. The piano style and its
three foremost exponents subsequently received wide exposure, through
feature articles in newspapers and magazines, record reviews, and coast-
to-coast radio shows, beaming their music across America.

The circumstances leading to this rapid transformation began in 1935
with the rediscovery of Meade Lux Lewis by John Hammond. Hammond had been a devotee of jazz music since his youth and had particularly enjoyed listening to boogie-woogie from the moment he first heard
Pinetop Smith's recording of "Pinetop's Boogie-Woogie." The initial
favorable impression was later confirmed when he happened to hear a
recording on the Paramount label of Meade Lux Lewis playing "Honky
Tonk Train Blues." He managed to obtain a well-used copy of this recording in 1931 and began to search for Lewis in order to persuade him
to re-record the piece.

Of the many who have been associated with jazz music, Hammond is
one of the few who could claim with some justification to have helped

in shaping its path and writing its history. Born in 1910, he was the only son of wealthy parents and well placed in American society. His mother came from the rich and powerful Vanderbilt family, providing Hammond with a certain social cachet but also resulting in his being stereotyped initially as a dilettante and playboy. This all changed when his intentions as a serious critic and record producer became evident and his views on the music began to be taken seriously. After a sound private education, he went to Yale University, but withdrew to pursue his musical interests, first as a record producer with the Columbia Record Company and then as a writer and critic. Early in his new career with the record company, he showed a flair for seeking out latent talent. He helped, for example, to bring the Count Basie Orchestra to prominence after hearing it on his car radio. The Basie band was subsequently engaged to appear in New York and given a recording contract with Columbia.

Another protégé of John Hammond was jazz singer Billie Holiday, whose unique talents he first heard when she acted as stand-in for another vocalist whom Hammond had gone to audition. The outcome of their first meeting was a recording contract for Billie, leading to a successful, if tempestuous, career as the foremost singer of her time. Hammond also contributed to the success of the Benny Goodman Orchestra by his encouraging the leader to employ Fletcher Henderson—one-time leader of a respected black orchestra—as his arranger. This astute move gave Goodman access to some of Henderson's original arrangements, including two of his best, "King Porter Stomp" (1935) and "Big John Special" (1937). These and similar arrangements helped to raise the profile of the Goodman Orchestra to a preeminent position in the swing era.

In an unsuccessful attempt to revive Bessie Smith's flagging career as a blues singer, Hammond arranged what proved to be her last recording date by paying most of the expenses from his own pocket because of the reluctance of the Columbia Company to record what they believed to be an uncommercial artist at the end of her career. Shortly after making some outstandingly good sides in 1933, which included "Gimme a Pigfoot and a Bottle of Beer" and "Take Me for a Buggy Ride," Bessie Smith was tragically killed in an automobile accident.

Not content with discovering new black talent, Hammond showed an equal determination to integrate the best of black and white jazz musicians in the same orchestra, believing that the mix would produce good-quality music. He was to be proved right. In due course, and very much against the climate of the times, Teddy Wilson played the piano and Lionel Hampton the vibraphone as members of the small units within the Benny Goodman Orchestra. Some time later, Charlie Christian, an avant-garde guitar player, was successfully introduced into Goodman's rhythm section; his presence transformed it by giving lift and drive where before it had been somewhat pedestrian and leaden. In a crowded musical career, cut short by his death from tuberculosis, Christian bridged the gap between the swing era and the emerging be-bop bands that were experimenting with new rhythms and harmonies at Minton's Club in New York.

It was already becoming clear, through these and other actions, that Hammond had a distaste for all forms of racial discrimination that were being practiced against black musicians. It is difficult at this distance in time to comprehend the nature and extent of racial discrimination in America during the 1930s and 1940s. It was a commonly held belief that blacks were inferior to whites in most human attributes. They were thought to be less intelligent and were allowed only a restricted involvement in American society. The situation survived as long as it did because of state legislation that upheld discriminatory practices designed to maintain a relationship of inequality between the races—the watershed being reached with the civil-rights marches led by Martin Luther King Jr. in the 1960s.

The distinguished black writer Richard Wright spoke for many of his race who lived before and after when he wrote about the complexities of being an African-American in Chicago during the late 1920s. He concluded that the standing of black Americans relative to white Americans was defined by "color hate," and the black American, knowing of this difference and having the same dreams as his white counterpart, attempted to forget the difference; otherwise he became isolated through loneliness and fear. As he was hated by whites within their shared culture, the black American turned his hatred inward to despise those features of himself that the white American hated. However, his pride would make him hide this self-hate, because he would not wish whites to know that his behavior was really conditioned by their attitude to him. In doing so, his hatred was turned on whites who were responsible for his own self-hate. The life of an African-American, according to Wright, was governed by a continuous adjustment to this everyday reality.[1]

In popular forms of entertainment, notably the films of the 1930s and 1940s, the black person was often portrayed as an eye-rolling simpleton or, at the very most, the faithful servant of the white, Protestant family. Such crude parodies were accepted despite the ample contrary evidence presented by the talents of black Americans during the Harlem Renaissance period. By 1936, Jessie Owens had already made his statement for African-Americans on the athletics track by winning four gold medals at the Berlin Olympic Games, much to the chagrin of Adolf Hitler, who had wanted to use the games as a vehicle for demonstrating the indisputable superiority of the Aryan race. Paul Robeson, already an established international singer and actor in the 1930s, courted disfavor among whites by his open displays of sympathy both for the less well-off members of society and for the Communist ideology. Joe Louis, the "Brown Bomber," was poised to become one of the most respected and loved world heavyweight boxing champions of all time.

In the absence of serious and scholarly comment, jazz was still considered by the majority to be a novel, discordant music of little consequence and in no sense a creative force in American culture. Those black jazz artists who had established themselves in American society of the 1930s and 1940s did so by presenting themselves and their music in a manner that often confirmed commonly held racial stereotypes. This was not always from their own choice but as a reaction to the strictures placed upon them. Thus, Louis Armstrong appeared in a leopard skin as the King of the Zulus, and Cab Calloway sang gobbledygook scat vocals against a background of jungle music. At the Cotton Club when Duke Ellington's Orchestra was in residence, light-skinned African-American dancers entered the premises by the back door and then provided the floor show for appreciative white audiences. Everyday living conditions were no better, and jazz performers were obliged to live with blatant discrimination if they were going to gain access to the more lucrative white clubs and hotels where their music was being promoted. One story that highlights this state of affairs concerns Billie Holiday's engagement as the first black singer to appear with the Artie Shaw Orchestra. When the band appeared at the fashionable Blue Room of the Lincoln Hotel in New York, she was asked to use the service entrance and the freight elevator to reach her room, so that her presence in the foyer would not cause embarrassment to the hotel guests. She eventually terminated her contract because of the pressure placed on Shaw by the hotel management to employ a white vocalist.

Through his close contact with jazz musicians, Hammond was able to see firsthand some of the discriminatory methods being used to exploit black musicians. Before he became established as a writer for *Downbeat* magazine, he began to expose some of the more unsavory incidents that he came across, by writing in the columns of *New Masses*, a Marxist magazine. Using the pseudonym Henry Johnson, he revealed the under-scale contract that Count Basie had been obliged to sign for his first recording engagement with the Decca Recording Company. A legal case was prevented only when the parent company in England intervened and refused to allow the name of the company to appear in the American courts. In a further exposé, Hammond challenged the State Street Publishing Company's attempt to copyright the term *boogie-woogie* for the purpose of obtaining royalties after they had purchased the copyright to "Pinetop's Boogie-Woogie." These incidents give an indication of the sense of injustice borne by Hammond in his personal crusade against racial discrimination and the extent to which he was prepared to go in his fight for the cause of black musicians.[2] It was in this barren ground that the seeds of the Spirituals to Swing concerts germinated and bore fruit.

The reappearance of Meade Lux Lewis after several years of anonymity is now part of jazz mythology, but the events leading to his reemergence are worth recalling. Hammond's autobiography records his fascination with Clarence Pinetop Smith's original recording of his boogie-woogie piece, which he felt had never been sufficiently recognized by white audiences. On hearing Lewis's recording of "Honky Tonk Train Blues" in 1931, Hammond knew that he had found the greatest performer of boogie-woogie. His search for Lewis proved fruitless until, some years afterward, he happened to inquire of Lewis's whereabouts during a casual meeting with Albert Ammons in Chicago, and Ammons told him that Lewis was working in a car wash.[3] The course of Lewis's life changed from that moment.

Hammond asked Lewis if he would record his famous train solo again, to which he agreed, and after rehearsing the piece he made the recording for the English Parlophone Record Company on November 21, 1935. The Columbia Company was not prepared to take the risk of recording Lewis, believing that it would prove to be an uncommercial release, so Hammond approached the Parlophone Company, thinking the record would be well received in England. Any publicity that Lewis might have had from playing this version on the air, in his own country, was denied him, and it was 1941 before this version was issued as part of *Gems of Jazz, Volume 1* (Decca Album, 200). The English Parlophone "Train" was backed by an original composition by Jess Stacey entitled "Barrelhouse."

In May 1936, Benny Goodman appeared at the Congress Hotel in Chicago at a concert arranged by the Chicago Rhythm Club. Hammond, who was arranging a similar concert in New York, accompanied Goodman in order to see how the Chicago concert had been organized. While in the city, the two men and Johnny Mercer, the band vocalist, went to hear Lewis, who was again musically active and employed at a place run by Doc Huggins who dabbled in "beauty parlors, ward politics, and trucking." The music was supplied by "Lux and His Chips," a group consisting of Meade on piano and two veteran musicians playing trumpet and drums. The occasion was reported by Hammond in *Downbeat* with the observation that the first blues underpinned with a Jimmy Yancey bass ran for more than forty minutes, slightly longer than the thirty minutes it took him to play "Honky Tonk Train Blues." To conclude his set, Lewis produced a piano accompaniment to his own whistling of a blues piece, which impressed Goodman to the extent that he approached Victor to arrange for him to be offered a contract.[4]

The two unnamed pieces were probably "Yancey Special" and "Whistlin' Blues," which Lewis would record later in his career. In March 1936, he eventually recorded "Honky Tonk Train Blues" for Victor, backed by "Whistlin' Blues." This was released in England as number 136 in the 1937 "Swing Music" series. This coupling, together with the Victor duets of Ammons and Johnson, and Yancey's ten numbers are available on *Barrelhouse Boogie* (RCA ND, 88334). In May 1936, Meade traveled to New York to appear in the "First Swing Concert" at the Imperial Theatre, the concert that Hammond had been planning when he visited Chicago. Meade was not in top form and made little impact on the audience, partly, it has been suggested, because of having to use a new grand piano. He returned to Chicago and continued his search for work, undertaking an engagement at Bratton's Rendezvous on Vincennes early in 1936, but this was short-lived, for that particular job had already finished when Bill Russell went looking for him in the summer of that year. The next year, 1937, began promisingly with an appearance at a "Rhythm Concert" held at the Blackhawk Hotel in Chicago in January.

After the release of his recordings of "Honky Tonk Train Blues," both the man and his music began to be appreciated by a discerning but small number of jazz fans, and on the strength of this Meade once again returned to New York, with Hammond's encouragement, to appear at Nick's Old Basement, a jazz club in Greenwich Village. The timing seems to have been inopportune, because his arrival in New York coincided with a very hot summer. Audiences were poor, and many had left the humidity of the city in search of the cooler interior regions. After a short run of six weeks, Meade made the inevitable journey back to Chicago, no doubt wondering what he had to do in order for his talents to be appreciated.

The disappointing public response to his personal appearances was in marked contrast to the recognition that was beginning to occur from his recordings, which were added to in 1936 with "Yancey Special" and "Celeste Blues" on Decca, and "Mr. Freddie Blues" and "I'm in the Mood for Love" on Brunswick. An English jazz reviewer, John Goldman, writing about Lewis's recordings, described him as one of the most interesting jazz musicians of his time, and beyond. A most prophetic assessment, it was probably colored by the fact that this was the reviewer's first contact with the boogie-woogie piano style. In observing the predominance of the left hand, he wrote that he had never encountered this feature in jazz.[5]

Lewis now disappeared from the music scene for a period, unable to get regular work. Early in 1938, representatives of the Shapiro-Bernstein Music Company attempted to locate him following the release on Decca of "Yancey Special" by the Bob Crosby Orchestra. This record had received wide acclaim, largely as a result of a mention in Walter Winchell's nationally syndicated newspaper column. The music company was eager to take out a contract on the number, and although they were aware that Lewis was the composer, they found it impossible to make contact with him. After a number of abortive visits to clubs and various nightspots by the company's representative and the publication of advertisements in the *Chicago Defender* requesting him to contact the company, Lewis was finally tracked down in a suburb of the city where he was living with his brother in semi-retirement from music. A contract was eventually agreed to the satisfaction of both parties. There was a sequel to the agreement in the late 1940s when Shapiro-Bernstein were involved in a legal case over the copyright of the "Yancey Special."

The uncertain employment opportunities Lewis experienced were similar to those of Albert Ammons, although he did manage to hold down more regular club engagements. To some extent, his recognition began sooner than Lewis's, because he already had four recordings to his credit by February 1936. Before considering his movements in detail, however, a digression is needed to examine the part played by jazz writers of the period in shaping public taste toward a recognition and acceptance of the boogie-woogie style.

None were more supportive than the writers of *Downbeat*. The magazine combined a gossipy style of presentation with sound musical comment. By the late 1930s, most of the swing bands had either recorded, or were about to record, orchestrated versions of boogie-woogie when it became obvious that the style had a novelty value and was popular with the public. The *Downbeat* writers sensed that public acclaim would be reserved for the high-profile swing bands at the expense of the lesser-known boogie-woogie pianists. Furthermore, the bands were not only orchestrating the boogie-woogie piano style but were often using the compositions of the pianists to work from. In order to redress this situation, a number of feature articles were planned to publicize the works of the major black pianists. Hammond may have lent his support to this policy, for he was now a full-time writer with *Downbeat*. He had already reviewed Ammons's appearance at Club De Lisa, commenting that although the band was unknown, their music had a staggering impact on him.[6] This initial impetus was maintained with a feature article about Ammons and his piano style written in 1937 by Sharon Pease, the magazine's accepted authority on piano jazz,[7] and a second one on Lewis this time by William Russell for the *Record Review* magazine of the Victor Record Company.[8]

A later article about the roots of boogie-woogie was surprisingly informative about the topic: The writer explained how the appearance of "The Fives" had launched the boogie-woogie school of piano playing on the South Side of Chicago and then went on to list some of the more obscure artists who had recorded boogie-woogie solos, including Wesley Wallace, Henry Brown, and Montana Taylor. The article affirmed that with the current interest being shown in the piano style, popular and better-known pianists such as Teddy Wilson and Bob Zurke would be able to cash in on its popularity.[9] A concert given by the Bob Crosby Orchestra at Orchestra Hall in Chicago, in aid of tubercular and incapacitated musicians and underwritten by *Downbeat*, was headlined in October with the news that boogie-woogie music and the blues would be featured.[10] Meade Lux Lewis was also billed to appear. In the same issue, Hammond reviewed the appearance of Albert Ammons at Hills Tavern at 3972 Vincennes in Chicago, comparing his powerful piano playing very favorably with the bands of Jimmy Dorsey and Bob Crosby, which were both appearing in the city at the same time. His conclusion, summarizing his own and the pianists' frustrations, was directed at what he saw as an indifferent public who, with the exception of a small coterie of discerning fans, appeared to be neglecting Lewis, Ammons, and Johnson for the more exhibitionist performances of "commercial," and by definition, less talented players of boogie-woogie.

One of the best-researched features appearing in *Downbeat* concerned the life of the enigmatic Clarence "Pinetop" Smith, whose talents had been aborted by his violent and unforeseen death ten years earlier. It appeared in two parts—*Downbeat* was published twice monthly at this time—in the October editions of 1939[11] and filled in many of the gaps in his early life by using interview material with his wife and Mayo Williams, the record producer at the Brunswick-Balke-Collender Studios where Pinetop had recorded. Photographs were published of his wife and two children but, tantalizingly, not of Pinetop—none has ever been found, although it is difficult to imagine that one never existed. An account of a visit to find Pinetop's grave in the Restvale Cemetery in Chicago by Sharon Pease, Jack Teagarden, and Woody Herman concluded the feature. It was eventually found under a simple wooden cross with nothing to identify the dapper genius of the boogie-woogie style.

John Hammond's first article about Albert Ammons at Club De Lisa was read with interest by members of the Milwaukee Rhythm Club, Local Number 7,[12] a group consisting of jazz enthusiasts who, from time to time, pooled their resources for the purpose of bringing well-known musicians to the city. Shortly after reading the article, the president approached Ammons and extended an invitation for him to bring his Rhythm Kings for a concert on September 20, 1937. The personnel of the band at the time was Albert Ammons (piano and leader), Delbert Bright (clarinet and saxophone), Robert Hicks (trumpet), Jimmy Hoskins (drums), Lawrence Simms (bass), and Ike Perkins (guitar). The band played a varied program of standards and jazz numbers, beginning with their theme song "Delta Bound." This was followed by "Star Dust," "Blue Heaven," "Tea for Two," some original numbers composed by members of the band with intriguing titles such as "Ikey" by Perkins and "What's the Answer?" by Hicks, and, of course, boogie-woogie piano solos by Ammons, one of which was inevitably "Boogie-Woogie Stomp." The concert must have been something of a marathon, with fifteen numbers played before the interval and eleven afterward.

John Steiner was an active member of the Rhythm Club. Until his death in June 2000 at age ninety-one, he lived in his hometown of Milwaukee in retirement from his position as professor of chemistry at the University of Illinois. He was involved in the recording industry for some time with Hugh Davis, a business associate. They formed a company, known as SD Records, and later purchased the Paramount Record Company in the 1950s. Jimmy Yancey and Clarence Lofton both appeared on their label toward the end of their active recording careers, as did the Duke Ellington Orchestra, Baby Dodds, and Art Hodes. Steiner was also well known as a perceptive jazz commentator in the 1940s, and his name was linked with several jazz magazines. Unfortunately, he had to miss the concert given by Ammons in Milwaukee but was determined to hear him at the next available opportunity. During one trip to Chicago, he tracked Ammons down to the It Club attached to the Michigan Hotel at 5450 South Michigan near Garfield Boulevard. Albert had by now disbanded the Rhythm Kings and had been released from his engagement at the De Lisa.

The It Club was housed in a long basement partitioned halfway along its length by an archway. On one side of the archway were tables and chairs for diners and a small kitchen; on the other side, a bar ran down the length of the long wall. Each area had its own entrance. The unifying feature in the club was the piano positioned underneath the archway where it could be seen and heard by both sets of customers. Ammons began his set shortly after midnight and played intermittently for about six hours. His pattern of work at this time was to job during the week and earn most of his money at weekends. Arranging with the manager of the It Club to begin playing at midnight allowed him to fit in other work during the day as and when it was offered. After the show, Steiner and Ammons ate breakfast together and talked. While Steiner drank coffee with his food, Ammons sipped a large tumbler of whiskey—a portent, perhaps, of forthcoming tragedy. Ammons moved later to Hills Tavern, where he appeared three nights a week supported by Johnny Lewis on drums. He also spent short periods at the Beehive and the Commodore clubs.[13]

Before the first Spirituals to Swing concert held in December 1938, both Lewis and Ammons gave a foretaste of the music they would play at a reunion of the Chicago Rhythm Club held at Franklin Lyon's Schiller Studio, which was reported in the *Chicago Herald*.[14] Several prominent Chicagoans attended, among whom were Francis Stanton, Charles H.G. Kimball, Mr. and Mrs. Strother Cary, Jack Howe and his new bride Mary Louise Wilson, and William Russell of the Hot Record Society. Events got under way with Ammons introducing Lewis, who rendered a blues-tinged version of "Yancey Special." Lewis then introduced Ammons, who demonstrated his mastery of stride with a powerful version of "Three Little Words," a popular tune of the day. Presumably to give the piece atmosphere, it was accompanied by some wild Fats Waller–inspired scat and jive comments from Lewis, which may have inspired the reporter's reference to Lewis talking out of this world about music. Returning to the piano, Meade improvised on "Bearcat Shuffle," a precursor of his later Vocalion recording "Bearcat Crawl." Albert then stunned the gathering with an electrifying rendition of "Boogie-Woogie Stomp." Thus far, events were recorded and have now been commercially released on *Albert Ammons: Boogie-Woogie Stomp* (Delmark, 705-D). Piano duets and comments attributed to the pianists about boogie-woogie were also reported to have taken place, but, to date, no recordings of these have ever been discovered. It is reasonable to deduce from such a gathering of influential people that a serious interest was now being taken in the boogie-woogie form. That this should have occurred shortly before the first concert suggests that the pianists were now becoming known, and the tide of recognition was moving in their favor. About this time, in 1938, William Russell wrote the first of several scholarly analyses of boogie-woogie, which was published in *Jazzmen*.[15]

The initiative behind the Spirituals to Swing concerts came from John Hammond, who had wanted to present a major concert of jazz music for some years: a panorama of sound that would demonstrate its roots in blues and gospel songs and in more developed forms played by jazz and swing bands. There had been earlier concerts featuring the talents of black performers, so the idea was not entirely original. In 1912, Jim Europe's Clef Club Orchestra had been the first black band to play at Carnegie Hall, and sixteen years later a program of black American music had been performed there to commemorate the compositions of W. C. Handy.

Before detailed planning of the concert could begin, Hammond had to find a sponsor to underwrite the venture. Initially, he had great difficulty in raising the capital. After exhausting his usual contacts, he approached Eric Bernay, the editor of *New Masses*, who agreed to give support and cover the costs involved in publicizing the concert and Hammond's own traveling costs in search of talent. Prior to agreement on the form of the concert and the selection of artists, Hammond requested that the Communist magazine should not make obtrusive political capital from the concerts, a request to which Bernay agreed, even to the extent of not having any Communist literature displayed, or for sale. Although of different political persuasions, both men were adopting a similar liberal stance in wishing to provide a showcase for the best black musicians to play jazz before an appreciative audience, and in so doing, to publicize the underprivileged position of African-Americans. Using as evidence the social and financial privations of the artists appearing in the concert, the program's notes were full of telling comment about their exploitation.

With December 23 agreed as the date and Carnegie Hall the venue, Hammond started out on his search for talent, traveling across the southern states in his distinctive Terraplane convertible accompanied by Goddard Lieberson, a friend and kindred musical spirit. The full story of the trip appears in Hammond's autobiography: of his discovery of blues harmonica player Sonny Terry living next door to Blind Boy Fuller who, at the time of Hammond's visit, was languishing in jail awaiting trial on a charge of attempting to shoot his wife; and of tracking down the four Mitchell Christian Singers to a squalid wooden shack without running water or electricity. The saddest tale of all, certainly for posterity, was finding that Robert Johnson, the revered blues singer and later influence to Bob Dylan, the Rolling Stones, and Eric Clapton, had been poisoned days before the journey was made. However, Bill Broonzy provided a more than able substitute.

The content and running order of the program were finally agreed to by Hammond, who was acting as the producer, and Charles Friedman, the director of the concert. Examples of tribal music were provided by members of a recently returned expedition from the west coast of Africa and less secular rhythms by the spirituals and hot gospel hymns of the Mitchell Christian Singers and Rosetta Tharpe. Sidney Bechet and the New Orleans Feetwarmers were present to remind the audience of the sounds of early jazz. He was joined on piano by James P. Johnson, the acknowledged master of the New York Stride School of playing, who also accompanied the blues singing of Ruth Smith, the niece of Bessie Smith. "Soft" swing was the province of members of the Count Basie Orchestra, who played together in smaller units called Basie's Blues Five and the Kansas City Six. The vocals were provided by Jimmy Rushing and Helen Humes. The rural blues were represented by Big Bill Broonzy on guitar and Sonny Terry on harmonica.

The piano was Hammond's favorite instrument, and it was to be expected that it would feature somewhere in the program. In addition to Basie and James P. Johnson, both stride players (though by this time Basie had adopted a more economical piano style with his band), Hammond had the inspiration to feature boogie-woogie music played by three of its best practitioners—Albert Ammons, Pete Johnson, and Meade Lux Lewis—with Joe Turner shouting the blues over Johnson's pounding piano. It was the first occasion that the four men had met in preparation for the concert, and they immediately took a liking to each other. They were installed in the Woodside Hotel on Seventh Street and were advised by Hammond to enjoy themselves with the money he gave them for that purpose. These events were to provide a poignant contrast to their impecunious arrangements for traveling to the concert. It was the time of the Depression, and even the popular Greyhound bus service from Chicago to New York was costly for most people to use—the railroad was even more expensive. There was a cheaper bus service that Bill Russell told Ammons and Lewis about, but it proved a nail-biting alternative because it broke down in the mountains traveling through Pennsylvania and they were obliged to stay overnight there. Russell felt some responsibility for their plight, but was relieved to hear that their only privation was a delay of several hours.[16]

The concert was dedicated to the memory of Bessie Smith, whose death had been mourned in the jazz world some fourteen months previously. Very detailed program notes were written, which challenged the detractors of jazz for not recognizing and accepting the music as an original feature of American culture, and the role of black Americans in its origins. A link was drawn between this neglect and their low status in their own country, with an added broadside at Jim Crow unions and unscrupulous nightclub proprietors that had prevented black musicians being paid a living wage and receiving recognition for their talents. Furthermore, the program notes reminded the audience, no black musicians were employed in the house bands of radio stations, and despite white and black musicians playing in the same bands on recordings, this practice still continued.[17]

Short potted biographies of the artists were included—some of the information not entirely accurate—that were sufficient in detail to indicate the lowly circumstances of most of them. Of particular interest, in the light of Ammons's later success as a major recording artist, was the reference to his earnings of nine dollars per week for his piano playing. Lewis, working in a garage, was earning about ten dollars a week. As the authors of the notes went on to record, the artists appearing were, paradoxically, idols of their musical worlds but also extremely poor. In an anecdote that emphasizes their lowly status and general unworldliness, Big Bill Broonzy was seen by Lieberson backstage sitting by himself looking sad. Lieberson went over to him to cheer him up, saying, "Big Bill, how do you like it here?" to which Bill replied, "Oh, I like it fine. I always did like Chicago." Broonzy was not even aware that he was in New York, for he had never been there before and thought he was in Chicago. Most likely, he was sent a ticket and just traveled to the concert.

The first concert opened to a packed and expectant audience who paid between half a dollar and three dollars and thirty cents entrance fee. So great was the demand for seats that an overflow area had to be provided onstage. In an attempt to create the right climate in which the artists could perform, the audience was asked in the program notes to forget they were in Carnegie Hall. That this was achieved is revealed in recordings of the concert, which demonstrate that the performance was received by an attentive and good-natured crowd. The three boogie-woogie pianists and Joe Turner were certainly apprehensive about the thought of appearing before such a large audience, because their previous experience had been in small, intimate clubs. Despite their nervousness, they all experienced a sense of elation at appearing in Carnegie Hall. They visited the hall on the afternoon of the day on which the concert was held to familiarize themselves with the layout and found the hall and the stage to be dauntingly large.

Recollections of the concert vary according to the raconteur. Joe Turner said that the program had been arranged for them to go on separately, with Pete Johnson and himself appearing together at one point, but as they were all so nervous a decision was taken to allow them all to perform onstage together, early in the program. Whether this is entirely accurate remains in doubt on the evidence of recordings on which the three pianists play solo, in duets, and as a trio. Joe Turner sang with Pete Johnson, but it is not apparent that all four artists performed together. Permission was granted for another piano to be onstage so that each pianist could have one to play in a trio. This was discovered in a nearby hotel and manhandled by the pianists into the hall, almost dropping it into the orchestra pit on its journey to the stage. With the adrenaline now flowing, nerves were quickly forgotten as the boogie-woogie rhythms got under way and the audience responded to the beat.[18]

Meade Lux was badly positioned onstage behind the other two pianists during the trio's performance, making it difficult to fully appreciate his contribution. As the music built to a crescendo, the audience became enraptured by the boogie-woogie rhythms. The first set closed, and bedlam broke out as people stood up and clapped and shouted for an encore. Hammond declined to give an encore, his mind set on keeping the program running on schedule, and he was roundly booed for his perversity.

John Hammond had a particular enthusiasm for the old-fashioned kind of boardinghouse piano with a drum attachment and a third pedal that caused a jangle effect by engaging a banjo or mandolin attachment when it was depressed. His interest in this kind of instrument dated from his youth when he was on a family holiday in Utah, and his mother had inadvertently played a classical piece on a piano of this kind with the attachment engaged. The young Hammond had been intrigued by the tone produced, but not so his mother, who refused to use the third pedal. Hammond managed to obtain a similar boardinghouse piano, a Wing upright, for one of the pianos. Unlike Turner's recall of events, Hammond said that only two pianos were available: a Steinway for Lewis and Johnson to play and the Wing for Ammons. The three pianists opened the show, followed by big Joe Turner's arrival to sing with Johnson.[19]

The second Spirituals to Swing concert took place on December 24, 1939, and was equally successful, without having quite the impact of the first. One reporter probably spoke for many in his assessment that the delirium of the first concert had subsided to approval for the second.[20] This was to be expected to some extent, as the artists were becoming known to an increasingly wider public who were by now more familiar with the styles of music presented at the second concert. But, the second concert, however good, could only be an anticlimax after the massive success of the first one. What the second concert did achieve was to consolidate the message that the community of jazz was drawn from all races. Some years after the event, jazz writer Whitney Balliett assessed their beneficial long-term impact on the discriminatory work practices used against African-American jazz musicians that had prevented their appearances at major concert venues.[21]

Though no official record exists of the numbers played by the three pianists or of Joe Turner's vocals at the two concerts, it is possible to be fairly certain by reference to the original acetates, aural evidence from the voices of the two masters of ceremony (Hammond fulfilled this role at the first concert, while Sterling A. Brown, a professor and poet from Howard University, did so at the second one), and a review of the second concert in *Jazz Information*.[22] Using these sources, a balanced program emerges for each concert. The numbers played in 1938 were "Yancey Special" and "Honky Tonk Train Blues" by Lewis, "Pinetop's Boogie-Woogie" by Ammons, "It's All Right Baby" (later titled "Roll 'Em Pete") by Johnson and Turner, and a version of "Twos and Fews" entitled "Double Up Blues" by Ammons and Lewis. All three joined forces for "Cavalcade of Boogie," with Johnson leading off the number on the Wing upright. Albert Ammons also accompanied Big Bill Broonzy, somewhat tentatively, on "Louise, Louise," "I Had a Dream," and "Done Got Wise," as well as Sister Rosetta Tharpe. Blues accompaniment was not Albert's forte.

The program for the second concert gave the pianists more time. Included were another rendition of "Honky Tonk Train Blues" by Lewis and "Boogie-Woogie Stomp" by Ammons, previously entitled "Pinetop's Boogie-Woogie." All three joined forces for "Jumping Blues," and Johnson played and Turner sang "Low Down Dog" and "Roll 'Em Pete." Both these numbers were included in the *Jazz Information* review of the 1939 concert, but discographers, in their attempts to identify at which concert "Low Down Dog" was played, may have been confused by the title of the backing on the song's original acetate, "It's All Right Baby," which was performed at the 1938 concert. The 1939 acetate was probably incorrectly titled "It's All Right Baby"—the original name for "Roll 'Em Pete." Finally, Johnson joined Basie and Sullivan for an extended jam session on the theme of "Lady Be Good" with members of the Basie and Goodman bands. Big Bill Broonzy repeated his three tunes, again accompanied by Ammons. Several recordings together provide an overall picture of the boogie-woogie music played at the two Spirituals to Swing concerts. The first, *John Hammond's "Spirituals to Swing" Carnegie Hall Concerts of 1938/9* (Vogue, VJD 550-1 and 550-2), is a two-set LP and includes other artists as well as the three pianists, and the second, *Piano Blues, Volume 21: Unissued Boogie 1938–1945* (Magpie, PY 4421), features just the pianists and Turner. Following the concerts, all four artists received maximum publicity in the press. A *Downbeat* account of the first concert suggested that Lewis had drawn the heaviest applause of the three pianists, though he actually fluffed his opening solo number "Yancey Special," by making a slip in playing the introductory bass passage, whereas Ammons was, in reality, in top form.[23] Such comparisons were really unnecessary and reflected an occasional tendency of the magazine to use eye-catching headlines.

The measured *New York Times* report by renowned reviewer Howard Taubman summarized the content as offering something for everyone's tastes and plenty of swing. Ironic comments were made about John Hammond whose twitching responses were taken by Taubman to indicate that he was enjoying the music. There then followed a sensitive appraisal of the harmonica playing of Sonny Terry and appreciative comments about the vitality and warmth of emotion shown by the Mitchell Singers in their rendition of "The Lord's Prayer" and the traditional air "We Rise Up." Nor were the contributions of the Boogie-Woogie Trio missed by Taubman's observation that the visual spectacle was equally as important as listening to the music. He concluded that the pianists had difficulty containing themselves while they were demonstrating such amazing endurance at the piano.[24]

The writer for the *New York Herald Tribune*, in coming to terms with the "new" sound, for the first time commented that it would be too hasty for a reviewer to attempt a description of boogie-woogie without more knowledge, but there was an initial impression of perpetual motion.[25] The reviewer for the *Daily News* reacted humorously to the assertive rhythm of the boogie-woogie bass and the improvisational right hand wandering about the keyboard, which, as he saw it, frightened the life out of the notes. However, he praised the enterprise of the organizers in gathering together a group of black entertainers who were playing for the first time before a white audience.[26] A more reflective perspective, perhaps more in line with Hammond's intensity of purpose in mounting the concert, was taken by the *New York Sun* whose reporter praised the very interesting program of music and went on to recognize the impact of the Trio's piano playing both as soloists and together in friendly rivalry.[27] Immediately after the concert, the *New Yorker* ran a short feature explaining the origins of boogie-woogie to its readers with an emphatic quote from Hammond that formal music study could only destroy the naturalness of boogie-woogie music.[28] By any definition, the concerts were a triumph and an important benchmark in the recognition of jazz and black folk art in which boogie-woogie piano playing had a singular place.

This newly established tradition of celebrating America's musical heritage was continued in 1941 and 1943 with two further concerts but this time presented by Barney Josephson, proprietor of the Café Society night-clubs (see chapter 8). Each was given the title of "Café Society Concert," which was more an accurate reflection of the talented musicians flowing through his clubs than a representative cross-section of jazz styles as featured in the first two concerts. Ammons and Johnson opened the concert of April 23, 1941, with their respective compositions "Boogie-Woogie Stomp" and "Roll 'Em Pete" before joining forces for a duet of "Boogie-Woogie in Prayer" (note the slight change of title). Others on the bill were Lena Horne, Art Tatum, Henry "Red" Allen, Eddie South, John Kirby and his Orchestra, the Golden Gate Quartet, and Hazel Scott. The most noticeable emphasis in the program of this concert was the juxtaposition of classical music and jazz. Hazel Scott had built her reputation on jazzing the classics, and on this occasion she produced "The Hungarian Rhapsody" and "The Ritual Fire Dance" alongside Tatum's "Humoresque" and Kirby's version of "Clare de Lune." By the time of the concert of April 11, 1943, when America was heavily embroiled in World War II, Ammons and Johnson were now household names at the forefront of the boogie-woogie "craze" and no longer required the platform of an ethnic concert to advertise their talents. Indeed, the purpose of this second concert was to raise emergency aid for the deprived and suffering population of the Soviet Union. As the opening act, the two pianists quickened many pulses with their superlative duet "Sixth Avenue Express," which was followed by Johnson's "Minuet in Boogie." A solo from Ammons, "Timoshenko Torch," was named in honor of the Russian marshal responsible for defending Moscow against the German siege. Teddy Wilson's band shared the bill with, among others, the Ellis Larkins Trio featuring Bill Coleman on trumpet. Once again, the program veered between recognized jazz material and that usually associated with the classics: the march from "The Love for Three Oranges" (Prokofiev) played by the Larkins Trio and "In the Silence of Night" (Rachmaninoff) sung by Kenneth Spencer—in both cases a gesture toward the Russian theme of the concert. Perhaps it also signified the need to offer some "highbrow" material in order to attract sufficient financial patronage to support the cause.[29]

Immediately after the first Spirituals to Swing concert, the three pianists were interviewed and recorded by Alan Lomax for the Library of Congress archives on December 24, 1938, producing an unusual combination of their talents: Ammons sang "Dying Mother Blues," accompanied

CARNEGIE HALL PROGRAM

SEASON 1942-1943

Sunday Evening, April 11th, at 8:30

Benefit

THE AMBIJAN COMMITTEE

For Emergency Aid to

THE SOVIET UNION

•

BARNEY JOSEPHSON

presents

CAFE SOCIETY CONCERT

CLIFTON FADIMAN, *Master of Ceremonies*

Program

ALBERT AMMONS and PETE JOHNSON

Boogie-Woogie Pianists

Minuet in Boogie — Pete Johnson
Timoshenko Torch — Albert Ammons
Sixth Avenue Express — Ammons & Johnson

Program Continued on Second Page Following

CARNEGIE HALL   1941
Wednesday Evening, April 23rd, at 8:30

BARNEY JOSEPHSON

presents

Cafe Society Concert

LEONARD LIEBLING, *Master of Ceremonies*

BOOGIE WOOGIE PIANISTS

Roll 'em Pete ....*Pete Johnson*

Boogie Woogie Stomp ....*Albert Ammons*

Boogie Woogie In Prayer....................*Johnson and Ammons*

HELENA HORNE

Embraceable You ....*Gershwin*

There'll Be Some Changes Made.............*Higgins-Overstreet*

Summertime ....*Gershwin*

•

Steinway Pianos Used

Program Continued on Second Page Following

Carnegie Hall concerts, 1941–1943. Acknowledgment: Carnegie Hall Archives.

by Pete Johnson on piano. Lewis played several choruses of "Honky Tonk Train Blues" interspersed with a commentary about his early life in Chicago and the inspiration for the composition provided by the "Big Bertha" locomotives. He also recorded "Whistlin' Blues" and sang a short untitled blues, best described as a piano player's lament at the slow supply of liquor at a rent party. Johnson recorded "Four O'Clock Blues"—a mood piece usually played after an all-night party. All these recordings are available on *The Complete Library of Congress Boogie-Woogie Recordings* (The Jazz Piano, JP 5003).

The Boogie-Woogie Trio was officially born, as far as the general public was concerned, with Columbia's release of the two-part "Boogie-Woogie Prayer" on December 30, 1938. To this day it remains a masterful statement of the genre played by three of its greatest exponents. All three members possessed a rich and varied musical background on which to draw for their combined playing. The compatibility between the styles of Albert Ammons and Pete Johnson was more noticeable in their duet work than when either of them joined forces with Meade Lux Lewis. When they did perform as a trio, however, they achieved an appropriate balance between virtuoso performance and supportive keyboard work that built tension and allowed the dynamism of each to be appreciated. Ammons's and Johnson's experiences as members of various bands may have contributed to the development of the symbiosis between them. Lewis, on the other hand, had pursued a single-minded, almost introverted concern, in his formative years, for teasing new tone colors from the piano that could only be fully appreciated in solo performance. His interpretations, as a result, were different and almost too ornate to be heard alongside any other pianist. Joe Turner brought the extra dimension of exciting and powerful blues shouting, totally in keeping with the powerhouse piano sounds of the Trio. It can be said with some authority that, by 1940, boogie-woogie had finally arrived on the world stage.

NOTES

1. R. Wright, *American Hunger* (London: Lowe and Bydone Printers, 1969), 6.
2. J. Hammond with Irving Townsend, *John Hammond on Record* (London: Penguin Books, 1981), 187.
3. Hammond, *John Hammond on Record*, 164.
4. John Hammond, "Plenty of 'Swing' Talent Hidden in Chicago—Meade Lux and His Chips," *Downbeat*, May 1936.
5. John Goldman, "Meade Lux Lewis," *Swing Music Magazine*, 1936, 62.
6. John Hammond, "Plenty of 'Swing' Talent Hidden in Chicago—Albert Ammons Orch. Plays Best Swing in Chicago," *Downbeat*, May 1936.

7. Sharon Pease, "'Pinetop' Smith Influenced Early Piano Style of Swingin' Ammons," *Downbeat*, July 1937, 28.

8. William Russell, "Boogie-Woogie," *Victor Record Review* 2, no. 1 (May 1939): 10, 11.

9. Sidney Martin, "How the Boogie-Woogie was Born," *Downbeat*, July 1938, 5.

10. "Crosby to Swing in Orchestra Hall!!" *Downbeat*, October 1938, 2.

11. Sharon Pease, "I Saw Pinetop Spit Blood and Fall: The Life and Death of Clarence Smith, Creator of Boogie-Woogie," *Downbeat* 6, no. 10 (October 1, 1939), 4 and Sharon Pease, "Will Pinetop's Sons Be Great Like Their Dad?" *Downbeat*, October 15, 1939, 8.

12. John Steiner, concert program of the Milwaukee Rhythm Club, Local No. 7, dated September 20, 1937, sent to Ben Conroy; copy sent to the author.

13. John Steiner, taped recollections (one involving Dan Gunderman as interviewee) and correspondence sent to the author, January 30 through March 1985.

14. Mrs. R. Bach (nee Jean Engineer), "Out of This World," *Chicago Herald*, December 12, 1938.

15. William Russell, "Boogie-Woogie," in *Jazzmen*, ed. F. Ramsey and C. E. Smith (London: Sidgwick and Jackson, 1958), 183–205.

16. William Russell, taped recollections, correspondence, and memorabilia sent to the author, February 2, 1991.

17. J. Dugan and J. Hammond, "The Music Nobody Knows," *New Masses' Spirituals to Swing Concert Programme*, 2.

18. Bruce Baker, "Been to Kansas City," *Jazz Quarterly* 2, no. 4 (Summer 1945): 14–17.

19. J. Hammond with Irving Townsend, *John Hammond on Record* (Harmondsworth, UK: Penguin Books, 1981), 203.

20. J. D. Smith, "From Spirituals to Swing," *Jazz Information*, December 29, 1939, 2.

21. W. Balliett, *Dinosaurs in the Morning* (London: Phoenix House, 1965), 52.

22. Smith, "From Spirituals to Swing," 2.

23. "Lux Lewis Steals Show in Carnegie Hall Concert," *Downbeat*, January 1939, 1.

24. H. Howard Taubman, "Negro Music Given at Carnegie Hall," *New York Times*, December 24, 1938.

25. "Swing Rhythms Sway Audience at Carnegie Hall," *New York Herald Tribune*, December 24, 1938.

26. John Chapman, "Carnegie Goes Right Out of This World," *Daily News*, December 24, 1938.

27. Irving Kolodin, "Negro Concert in Carnegie Hall: Music of the Race Heard in Many Phases," *New York Sun*, December 24, 1938.

28. "Boogie-Woogie," *New Yorker*, December 31, 1938.

29. Michael Chaigne, information about two Carnegie Hall concerts and correspondence, sent to the author, February 8, 2003.

8

Café Society Days

The publicity given to the first Spirituals to Swing concert and the opening of Café Society Downtown allowed for a sustained public interest
in boogie-woogie music. The nightspot offered the opportunity to dine,
dance, and be entertained by high-quality jazz artists such as the Boogie-
Woogie Trio and Joe Turner, who were engaged to appear there from
opening night.

The proprietor was Barney Josephson, a shoe salesman from New Jersey, and the club was launched on a sixteen-thousand-dollar float. The
site chosen was a basement at Number Two Sheridan Square in Greenwich Village. Josephson found a strong ally in John Hammond: He became more than a token supporter in the early days of the venture when
most of Josephson's money had been spent creating the right ambience.
The walls were decorated with satirical murals by contemporary artists
Adolph Dehn, Syd Hoff, and Anton Refregier. John Hammond, Benny
Goodman, and Willard Alexander each invested five thousand dollars to
assist Josephson with the launch, and they were soon repaid in full as the
nightspot established its reputation and became the most successful in
the city. It offered high-quality entertainment by black and white artists
who performed before racially mixed audiences. What was not known
by many of the public who patronized it was that the club was originally
started to raise money for the American Communist Party.[1] Neither, it is
certain, were many of the employees aware of the political affiliation.

The period in world history when the club was opened coincided with
the emergence of both fascist and communist ideologies on the international stage. One serious conflict between the two ideologies was manifest

in the Spanish Civil War of the 1930s involving the Nationalists (fascists) battling the Republicans who were supported by the International Brigade (communists) drawn from liberal idealists in many countries. It was not unexceptional to find politically committed intellectuals and people of a radical persuasion who were card-carrying members of the Communist Party in countries throughout the world. Many saw their membership as the best safeguard against the insidious spread of fascism. The American Communist Party, under the leadership of Earl Browder, floated the idea of the nightclub to help counteract what was seen as the penetration of fascist ideals into American society. The *New Masses* magazine was involved with the launch of the nightclub as it had been in providing financial backing for the earlier Spirituals to Swing concert.

One of the intentions of the management in establishing the club was to satirize the values held by those New York citizens who saw themselves as trendsetters. As a result of a magazine article explaining the club's policy, the very people who were having the finger of scorn pointed at them were initially inquisitive and later attracted to the club in order to see for themselves what was on offer. The management also wished to challenge the discrimination against African-American and Jewish entertainers, allegedly practiced by several high-class establishments in the city, that the talented Mildred Bailey and Imogene Coca, among others, had experienced. The Café Society club was said to have been given its name by Clare Booth Luce, a prominent member of New York's fashionable society, but some of the credit was also claimed by Helen Lawrenson, an employee responsible for the public relations. The traditional recipe for success at other nightspots in the city was to put on a floor show, usually with a fair sprinkling of nudes, sell poor-quality liquor, and invite celebrities to wine and dine free of charge. The management of Café Society eschewed these practices and offered first-class entertainment, good liquor, free meal tickets, and neither nudes nor celebrities to be stared at by the customers.

Sheridan Square, where the club was located, was actually triangular in shape and was reached from the West Side subway. The basement room of number two had previously housed the Four Trees Club, well known to drinkers in the prohibition years. The basement was of an irregular shape, with large square pillars intruding into the body of the room, impeding the view of anyone unfortunate enough to be seated behind one of them. The orchestra sat on a raised ledge running along the length of one wall. Unfortunately, the musicians could be heard but not seen very well by customers occupying seats either by the wall or at the rear of the room. There were, however, a few good tables around the small dance floor. When the Trio performed, the pianos were wheeled onto the floor for their sets, and most of the customers who had come to hear boogie-woogie left their seats and moved closer to them or took up a position near the bar, which gave them a good vantage point for watching the floor show. Despite these shortcomings in the accommodation, the successful launch allowed the management to charge patrons slightly more than was customary at other New York nightclubs. For example, a typical evening out in 1943 cost about ten dollars. This covered the minimum entrance charge of two dollars in the week, and two dollars and fifty cents at weekends and holiday periods, plus drinks.

The Trio and Joe Turner were now able to concentrate on their musical careers without the need for supplementary employment to eke out a living. Ammons must have remembered his days driving taxis and Lewis his many years in the wilderness washing cars and on relief. The contrast provided by secure employment and a substantial income must also have been apparent to Johnson. When he was working in Kansas City, it had not been uncommon for him to receive three dollars for a twelve-hour day that began at six o'clock in the evening and extended through the night, with a break of half an hour at midnight until dawn the following day, every weekday including holidays. He had also been dependent on the generosity of customers for tips to make his labors profitable. Initially he was paid forty dollars a week at Café Society. His working day began at seven in the evening and finished at four in the morning with rest periods between sets. At the peak of his popularity he was being paid two hundred and fifty dollars a week.

The emergence of the Trio as a commercial group, other than a purely fortuitous musical alliance, owed a great deal to the guiding hand of the ubiquitous Hammond, for it was he who suggested to Josephson that they should be employed at the club. After their storming success at the concert, Ammons, Lewis, and Turner were hired by Josephson to appear at Café Society while Johnson was offered work at the Famous Door, a rival jazz club of long-standing reputation situated on Fifty-second Street. During rehearsals for the opening night at Café Society, Johnson was asked by Hammond if he would join the others to show Albert the keys used by Joe Turner in his numbers. It was at this rehearsal that Hammond asked Johnson if he would also like to work with the others. He was receptive to the idea, because he had enjoyed working at the concert with the other two pianists and his friendship with Joe Turner was a close one. Having made the offer and received an acceptance, Hammond was left with some hard talking to convince Josephson that it was wise and commercially sound to employ three boogie-woogie pianists and a blues shouter on the same bill. This is Johnson's version of the events leading to the formation of the partnership. This version differs from that of Josephson, who recalls hiring Ammons and Lewis and was then informed by Hammond that a third pianist was available who really belonged at Café

Society with the other two. After agreeing to take Johnson, he was then told, in a parting shot by Hammond, that there was also a singer named Turner who would have to come with Johnson. It seems unlikely, in retrospect, that Hammond would have referred to Johnson and Turner in this way, unless Josephson had been completely unfamiliar with their work; however, as he had attended the Carnegie Hall concert looking for talent for his new venture, he must have known of them. A more plausible explanation is that the conversation between Josephson and Hammond occurred some time before the concert and the opening of the club when the two men were considering acts for the club. Josephson's interpretation implies a last-minute change in the arrangements to bring in Johnson and Turner, but the decision to ask Johnson to join the others had probably already been taken and Hammond's approach to Johnson was more likely a formal confirmation of this decision.

Final preparations for the opening of the club were hampered by a number of unforeseen hitches, and even when the date, January 4, 1939, had been finally agreed on, the issue of the obligatory cabaret license was delayed and it was midnight before the entertainment could officially begin. Billie Holiday, one of the star attractions, recalled in her autobiography that the first night was an outstanding success, with each of the boogie-woogie pianists and Turner storming through their numbers and making a big impression on the enthusiastic customers.[2] From the day of its opening, the club was completely integrated with black and white artists playing to similar racially mixed audiences. It was the first New York nightspot to practice such a liberal policy and must have been a great source of satisfaction to John Hammond in his continuing campaign to improve the civil rights of black artists.

This policy was not to the liking of all customers, and there were occasions when indignant exits were made by those who objected to the presence of African-Americans and the politically slanted monologues and songs of the satirist and comedian Zero Mostel. Others were unsettled and visibly moved by the sentiments of "Strange Fruit," as a single spotlight lit up Billie Holiday on a darkened stage to sing this stark number about the lynching of an African-American in the South. One evening, a party was asked to leave the club abruptly when they complained about Paul Robeson dancing with John Hammond's wife and were required to pay for their unfinished meal before leaving, with a firm reminder of the club's policy on racial integration ringing in their ears. Robeson was again involved in another difficult situation when a drunken Southerner called out to him that his name was also Robeson, and that Robeson's father was probably one of his father's slaves, adding that Robeson probably belonged to him. The response to such a slur was predictable, and a potentially ugly scene was avoided only by the intervention of

Josephson.[3] Other incidents in the early days of the club's existence served to emphasize the management's brave and distinctive stance toward racial inequality. Josh White, who was a regular entertainer over a period of five years, did not shirk confrontation when it arose. He was set upon by a group of southern servicemen in the Village after completing his act and leaving for a party. On a separate occasion, he briefly returned to the club, leaving a taxi he was sharing with Mary Lou Williams that was to take them home, in order to retrieve his watch from the club only to reappear with a black eye. One reason for this animosity was to be found in the sentiments of his songs about racial equality. Cynthia Gooding believed that Josh White was stepping on dangerous ground by singing songs about equality to a white audience in the 1940s and 1950s. In this sense, he was before his time and never received due credit for such bravery.[4]

The first house band was led by Frankie Newton, with Teddy Wilson on piano. Jack Gilford, a talented comedian, held the show together as the master of ceremonies. The club's appeal lay in the ability of the management to select the right balance of acts later likened by one critic as an "informal repertory company." Among those who graced the shows were the folksinger Burl Ives; comedians Imogene Coca and Zero Mostel; pianists James P. Johnson, Teddy Wilson, Sammy Price, Mary Lou Williams, and Hazel Scott; jazz instrumentalists Edmond Hall and Henry "Red" Allen; and female vocalists of the caliber of Billie Holiday, Lena Horne, and Mildred Bailey. The mixture consisted of musicians, magicians, comics, ventriloquists, and fortune–tellers, but the outstanding attraction for most patrons was the Boogie-Woogie Trio. Café Society became synonymous with boogie-woogie piano playing and as its mecca drew audiences to hear for themselves the fresh and exciting playing of Ammons, Lewis, and Johnson and the blues shouting of Turner. In their early days together, the three pianists often worked on three pianos; sometimes the changes were rung and Lewis and Ammons performed together on a grand with Johnson at an oak upright. The upright usually had the front removed so that the audience could not only hear the music but could also watch the hammers being depressed by flying fingers in a nightly show of pyrotechnics. The Boogie-Woogie Trio's act consisted of solos, duets, and the trio playing together on three pianos. It remains a curious fact that the only recorded number on which the trio and Joe Turner appeared together was "Café Society Rag," an innocuous piece of advertising remembered more for its stride bass patterns and Turner's reference to Donald Duck, an aside directed at Lewis's physique. When the handsome Turner was onstage, he moved around a lot and his posturing found favor with several of the female members of the audience. This unsought popularity almost cost him his job, following one amorous encounter with the wife of a respected customer who got to hear of it and demanded that Turner be dismissed for his indiscretion. Josephson was adamant that he would have to go, until representations by the staff and artists enabled him to be reinstated.

When members of the Trio and Turner were onstage, the audience listened to their music with rapt attention. The small dance area was rarely used during their sets. Ammons often began his sessions with "Boogie-Woogie Stomp," Lewis with "Honky Tonk Train Blues," and Johnson with "Roll 'Em Pete," accompanied by Turner. Each man, playing within the confines of the twelve-bar blues, stamped it with his own distinctive touch and coloration. They mildly complained later that they were only encouraged to play fast boogies, which provided little opportunity for displaying their versatility in other styles. For two years, three shows a day were offered at the club and four on Sundays. Their impact did not go unnoticed, and the success of the newly opened Café Society owed a great deal to their presence, now that boogie-woogie was viewed as an important and popular form of entertainment.[5]

Even after two years of regular performances, the quality of their playing was untainted by fatigue or staleness as witnessed by a newspaper clipping of the period, which drew attention to the longevity of their association, implying that to be entering a third year as a successful unit was an unusual occurrence. The time spent together socially at the Café Society was remembered with affection by Pete Johnson, who considered it one of the happiest periods of his life. Turner remembered the dominating effect of the Trio's combined power and how they generated their own rhythm, never requiring any assistance in that quarter from a band or even a rhythm section.[6]

Although the three men were receiving accolades for their boogie-woogie playing, their wider musical development may have been retarded to some extent by the requirement to play boogie-woogie all the time, although, paradoxically, this narrow musical range permitted them to explore fully the possibilities within it and they were able to carve a deep but narrow furrow across the landscape of American music. It is interesting to speculate whether the high-quality performances achieved individually and collectively could have been sustained if they had not been working in a team with the attendant advantage of being able to stimulate one another. There was certainly no loss of individuality in their playing, and it seems to have been a beneficial experience in which each player introduced phrases from the others into his own solo work but gave them an unmistakable personal stamp. The metamorphosis took place through a gradual absorption of chords, runs, trills, and breaks arising from their close and harmonious working relationship rather than through any conscious attempt to copy from each other. The subjugation of some of their individuality for the collective demands of duets and playing as a trio led to a heightened awareness of the possibilities of ensemble playing in compositions such as "Twos and Fews" (1939), the Ammons and Lewis duet recorded for Blue Note; the "Boogie-Woogie Prayer," the Trio's tour de force for the Columbia label; and the excellent Victor duets by Ammons and Johnson with Jimmy Hoskins on drums.

Their music gradually became known to a wider public through the regular broadcasts that were made from Café Society on the NBW radio show. By November 1939, transmissions were going out on Mondays and Thursdays, at eleven o'clock in the evening, and on Fridays at one o'clock in the morning. All four artists were featured at various times performing their well-known numbers as well as some that have never been commercially recorded. On the broadcast of January 17, Billie Holiday sang "I'm Going to Lock My Heart and Throw Away the Key" with the Frankie Newton Orchestra. This was followed by a duet from Ammons and Lewis, along the lines of "Twos and Fews," entitled "Fast Blues." The number contained passages of stride bass interspersed with boogie basses and a tremolo ride-out chorus from Ammons. An interesting melodic strain was revealed in their playing on this broadcast that was less noticeable in their recorded duets.

In another show on January 18, Lewis produced a relaxed version of "Yancey Special" that preceded a rendition, by Newton's Orchestra, of "On the Sunny Side of the Street." Meade repeated this solo on the broadcast of the February 3. Two further transmissions on February 4 and 9 produced versions of "Boogie-Woogie Stomp" and "Bear Cat Crawl" by Ammons and Lewis, respectively. They were introduced to the listening public on February 11 with the announcement: "twenty synchronized fingers at two pianos, the boys say everything in boogie-woogie with 'Blues Incorporated.'" This thoughtfully constructed duet contained both contrasting and supportive extemporization. The same show featured Johnson and Turner, who produced well-integrated interpretations of "Rising Sun Blues" and "Oh, Wee Baby Blues." Equally successful was the transmission made sometime in January or February, which contained an economical and inspired "Closing Time Blues" from Lewis and a tranquil "Early Morning Blues" from Turner and Johnson. In addition to the high-quality boogie-woogie piano playing and blues singing, this particular broadcast was memorable for the animated and encouraging comments given to the soloists in Frankie Newton's Orchestra during the playing of "Honeysuckle Rose." Knowing of Ammons's penchant for Fats Waller, both the man and his music, it would come as no surprise to discover that the anonymously shouted "Boogie-woogie, are you with me?" and other jive phrases, similar to those used by Fats Waller, came from him. Fortunately, these air shots are commercially available, and with the aid of the late John R. T. Davies's technical skills have been remastered to an acceptable level for appreciating the music. They are available on *Rare Live Cuts: Café Society Airchecks (1939) and Milwaukee (1943)* (Document, DOCD 1003).

In listening to the recorded radio transmissions some forty years or so after the event, the vitality and freshness of the boogie-woogie music is apparent. If the genre lost some of its drive and impetus after it had been removed from the rent party, its spirit was restored at the Café Society, a unique environment that encouraged constructive extemporization. Café Society audiences, like those at the rent party, were in intimate contact with the players, which produce the required empathy; and for many the music was now being played in unbelievably glamorous surroundings. Paul Bacon, a sometime record label designer for Blue Note, spoke of the feeling of excitement and well-being as he entered this unique establishment. America had not yet committed to World War II, and though still surfacing from the Depression years he was aware of entering a glamorous and privileged world of high society.[7] These young fans were also familiar with the best sounds of boogie-woogie, and they were quick to show their appreciation when it was played by the masters (witness the response of the audience to Albert Ammons's playing "Boogie-Woogie Stomp" on recordings from the first Spirituals to Swing Concert). If their fans did not recognize a tune, the ever-obliging Ammons or Johnson would supply the answer with "big Buddha smiles" before taking a drink and starting their next tune. The receptive audiences, the cooperation among the players, and the proximity of other high-quality swing and jazz instrumentalists brought the music to a state of perfection, giving it a form and subtlety that was barely present before it arrived in New York.

The three pianists were now looked upon as entertainers. They introduced audiences to the visual spectacle of boogie-woogie being played as a solo performance, in duets, and by a trio. The potential for creating exciting polyrhythm was increased by using two different treble improvisations over a common bass. But if two pianos created a rich texture, three were more likely to cause undue dissonance, and so this was overcome by employing a common bass pattern with each man introducing solo treble passages in sequence. The Trio were not initially enamored of the idea of recording "The Boogie-Woogie Prayer" for this reason, but they did so at the insistence of the recording company and it turned out to be a success.

The response of jazz writers to the management's request for the pianists to develop their talents beyond the keyboard and to become entertainers in a broader sense was both sympathetic but sometimes censorious toward the policy. When Meade Lux Lewis began to include a comic dance routine in his act, it was noticed with regret. Introduced by Willie Bryant and bolstered by the piano movers, Lewis strutted around

the small floor under the glare of the spotlights performing his dance burlesque to the accompaniment of loud stage asides from his helpers about
his small stature and heavy weight. Lewis was philosophical about the
burlesque, realizing that it raised a few quick laughs. His willingness to
widen his appeal certainly helped keep him in employment.[8]

Toward the end of the first year of the club's existence, in November
1939, the resident band was led by Joe Sullivan. The jazz press noted that
it was a racially mixed unit with only Sullivan and one other side man
who were white. Sullivan was reported as saying about the introduction
of Ed Hall and others into his band that color lines meant nothing to him.
Joe Marsala and his band deputized for Sullivan's band on its rest day.
The arrival of Sullivan coincided with the return of the boogie-woogie
players to the Café Society for a second term after a successful appearance
at the Panther Room of the Hotel Sherman in Chicago. The engagement
commenced in the first week of November, initially without Lewis, who
had been delayed in Chicago.

The Café Society was now being advertised as the "rendezvous of
celebs, debs, and plebs," a reaffirmation of its liberal policy. The conser-
vatively inclined *New York Times* took a dispassionately ironic view of
the club's political stance, which was immediately evident on passing
through the entrance door where to the left a monkey-like caricature of
Hitler hung from the ceiling.[9] At this time, many American citizens, not
unreasonably, viewed World War II as being played out on a European
stage, believing that America should retain its neutrality. Extreme right-
wing views, sympathetic to the fascist regimes in Europe, were openly
expressed by Seward Collins, writing in his periodical, the *American Review*. These attitudes changed dramatically after the Japanese attack on
the American fleet at Pearl Harbor.

In December 1939, "jam" sessions were introduced at the club in the afternoons using a pick-up group under the leadership of James P. Johnson.
Among those taking part were Roy Eldridge, Zutty Singleton, Don Byas,
"Hop Lips" Page, and Vic Dickenson. This policy was followed throughout December and extended into the New Year. The third week of December also witnessed the reemergence of Ida Cox, whom many believed
to have been the greatest of all the classic blues singers, from obscurity
to begin an engagement at the club. Big Bill Broonzy and Sonny Terry
were booked to appear on the same bill, and the now complete trio was
supplemented on drums by Jimmy Hoskins. Sullivan's band remained
in residence until June 1940. The high-caliber musicians had combined
well and produced some inspired relaxed jazz during their tenancy. The
members included Ed Hall (clarinet), Benny Morton (trombone), Andy
Anderson (trumpet), Billy Taylor (bass), Yank Porter (drums), and leader
Joe Sullivan on piano. Joe Turner sang with the group on several occa-

sions and recorded "I Can't Give You Anything but Love" and "It's a Low Down Dirty Shame" (1940) with them for the Vocalion label.

Jack Gilford honed his talents as a comedian and provided a seamless patter as master of ceremonies. These abilities were never more in evidence than during a final early morning show. Apparently the Boogie-Woogie Trio and Billie Holiday were away doing a benefit and Joe Turner had not turned up, so only the band and Gilford were available. Gilford was told to go out and entertain the sparse late-night audience. After introducing the band for their production number, he said that he would now like to introduce Albert Ammons. As he was not there, Gilford sat down at the piano himself and did an accurate mime of Ammons complete with mobile face and rolls of fat on the back of his neck. This was followed by a wicked impersonation of Meade Lux Lewis's penchant for falling asleep at the piano, gently swaying, eyes closed. Billie, Pete Johnson, and Joe Turner were all subjected to the same treatment before Gilford finally performed his own act.[10] The next day, Josephson had a telephone call from an impresario who was putting on a review called "We the People" and who had been in the audience. He wanted Gilford for his show, and from that time, his Broadway career was never in doubt.

The success of the Café Society encouraged the management to open a second club in October 1940. The circumstances, however, were strange. Josephson, whose experience of running a nightclub was limited, found that he was out-of-pocket to the tune of twenty-eight thousand dollars at the end of the first year. He began looking for an uptown site for his club, believing that a more prestigious area of town would bring in the missing customers. His press agent sent out a release saying that the first club had been so successful that Josephson would be opening a second, uptown club. What had seemed a potential disaster became a self-fulfilling prophecy with the press release. People read about the new club and immediately began attending the downtown club. Within a very short time, the number of customers had doubled downtown and Josephson began making good money, to the extent that he could soon pay off all his loans. The clubs were known as Café Society Downtown, in Sheridan Square, and Café Society Uptown, on East Fifty-eighth Street, off Madison Avenue. *Time* magazine reported the opening with a reminder that there were few nightclubs in Manhattan for jazz connoisseurs and that Josephson's endeavors were fulfilling an important gap in the city's entertainment with Ammons and Lewis pounding out their boogie-woogie on two pianos.[11]

Such a substantial mention in this prestigious magazine reflected the extent to which boogie-woogie had now become acceptable and fashionable among the more liberal New York socialites. Playwright Eugene O'Neill frequently spent evenings at one or other of the clubs in the company of artist Harold Lehman. O'Neill's passion was to sit and listen to the duet playing of Ammons and Johnson. Lehman, meanwhile, was capturing their performance, and that of other entertainers, in pencil caricatures, producing a collection in 1941 that included Johnson at the piano, Joe Turner in full voice, and Dan Burley with microphone in hand. O'Neill's passion for the boogie-woogie rhythm also took him to other venues where it was being featured. His companion, the cartoonist Al Hirschfeld, sketched him on four or five occasions while visiting the Onyx Club (Fifty-second Street) to listen to Ammons and Johnson perform. O'Neill only drank a small amount on these occasions, but Hirschfeld said that when necessary he could certainly hold his liquor.

Even more significant in the dovetailing of one art form with another, was the regular attendance of the Dutch artist Piet Mondrian at the clubs. He had moved to New York as an emigrant in 1940, after a two-year so-journ in London, joining the important group of artists already there in exile from Europe's war-torn lands. This group included Marc Chagall and Max Ernst.

Mondrian loved jazz and the rhythms of boogie-woogie in particular. They were known to have been the stimulus for much of his later artwork, including probably his most famous painting, *Broadway Boogie-Woogie*, which hangs in the Museum of Modern Art in New York. He was in-troduced to the piano style on his first day in New York, and its impact remained with him. When members of the trio began to play, he would intimate to his dancing partner that they should sit down as he could "hear a melody." Mondrian's artistic perspective was one of simplification. He reduced the world to its most basic pattern of vertical and horizontal lines, which, when etched with primary colors and white, produced pictures of balanced rectangles and grids. The blocks of vivid contrasting colors run-ning along the capillary-like lines in *Broadway Boogie-Woogie* produce their own restless and staccato rhythms, drawing directly from boogie-woogie. The painting encapsulates the essence of New York life: yellow cabs, street lights, intersections with blocks of busy traffic, and subway trains speed-ing between stops. One could easily insinuate the Ammons and Johnson duet "Sixth Avenue Express" (1941) into the picture, because Mondrian was forceful in promoting such analogies. He considered boogie-woogie and his painting as having a common purpose wherein the removal of the melody in the former was reflected in the removal of natural appearance and construction in the latter, with both being dependent for their form on dynamic rhythm.[12]

Despite the acclamation of art critics, Mondrian was said not to be entirely satisfied with *Broadway Boogie-Woogie* and commenced a second work in 1943, pursuing the same theme, this time entitled *Victory Boogie-Woogie*, anticipating the end of World War II. Here Mondrian purveys a deep sense of unrest by concentrating on densely colored linear grids that accentuate the dynamic and rhythmical qualities of the composition. Sadly, the picture was never completed due to his death from pneumonia in February 1944. A fuller account of the life and work of Mondrian can be found in Susanne Deicher's comprehensive study, including plates of the two boogie-woogie paintings.[13]

The newly opened uptown club created an atmosphere similar to that of its parent club, with the work of modern American artists adorning its walls and the lack of a cover charge. Nor was the entertainment it provided any less satisfying. In June 1943, Teddy Wilson and his orchestra were in residence, featuring Edmond Hall on clarinet and "Big Sid" Catlett on drums. The floor show offered the spectacle of East Indian dancers, close harmony singing by the Golden Gate Quartet, and humor from comic Jimmy Savo. Hazel Scott supplied the boogie-woogie music together with Albert Ammons and Pete Johnson. Meanwhile at the downtown club, Joe Sullivan's orchestra had been reengaged, with the remainder of the bill involving Sister Rosetta Tharpe, Billie Holiday, Art Tatum, and Meade Lux Lewis. Tatum and Lewis became close friends and thereafter contrived to work together on the same bill.

A new show commenced in the downtown club at the end of November 1940. Out went the Joe Sullivan Orchestra to be replaced by the Henry Red Allen Orchestra. Billie Holiday and Rosetta Tharpe moved on, and their spots were taken by Ida Cox and Josh White. Art Tatum was retained. By mid-December, further changes occurred, leaving Lewis and Tatum as pianists, Rosetta Tharpe and Josh White as singers, and the Red Allen Orchestra. The pianists appearing at the uptown versions were Ammons, Johnson, and Hazel Scott; the band was led by Teddy Wilson with Eddie South taking solo spots on violin. The deployment of these artists continued throughout the next few months with one or two minor alterations.

Several changes occurred in the bands appearing at Café Society Uptown in February 1941. Teddy Wilson's outfit was replaced by the Bobby Burnett Orchestra, which stayed until March when it was itself replaced by the John Kirby Orchestra. In March, a new program of jam sessions was inaugurated on Sundays at the downtown club between four and seven o'clock. Those involved were musicians appearing at the Café Society clubs who took their places alongside Mugsy Spanier, Woody Herman, Nick Caiazza, Walter Yoder, Frank Carlson, and others who were playing at New York nightclubs. Those billed to appear on March 23 were Benny Carter (tenor sax), Red Norvo (vibraphone), J. C. Higginbottom (trombone), Henry Red Allen (trumpet), and the youthful band pianist Ken Kersey, who had already started to be featured on specialist boogie-woogie numbers. These jam sessions were arranged by jazz writers Leonard Feather and George Simon.

The pattern of moving artists between the two Café Society clubs became a standard procedure because of the necessity to offer high-quality shows at both of them. This meant that members of the Trio appeared together less frequently than when there was only one club, although there were other reasons as well, concerning their ambitions. The Trio ceased to function as an effective unit from the time the second club was opened. By March 1943, when Ammons and Johnson were together as the intermission pianists at Café Society Downtown and sharing the bill with the Georgia James Orchestra, Lewis was already well established on the West Coast.

Ken Kersey (1916–1983) was born in Ontario, Canada. His father played cello and his mother played and taught piano and organ. When the family moved to Detroit, Kersey began studying music seriously at the Detroit Institute. He appears to have been a precocious talent, for he was the pianist in a trio playing at a Detroit theatre when he was only thirteen, before eventually moving to New York in 1936, seeking better opportunities for his piano playing. A short apprenticeship working in Harlem, until 1937, preceded work with the Lucky Millender band as a replacement for Billy Kyle and was followed by a spell with the Frankie Newton orchestra. Ken Kersey eventually joined the Henry Red Allen band and was greatly influenced in his playing by the presence of Tatum on the same bill at the Café Society, particularly in the interpretation of slower, moody tunes. His interest in the boogie-woogie style was first stimulated by listening to Lewis and later to Johnson and Ammons. He remained with Red Allen as the band's pianist and featured soloist until 1942 when he left to join the Cootie Williams band. After war service and spells with Andy Kirk, Kersey undertook several tours with "Jazz at the Philharmonic" in the late 1940s. By this time he had given up playing boogie-woogie for a more mainstream piano style, which found its outlet with the bands of Roy Eldridge and Buck Clayton. A serious illness in the 1950s caused his retirement from full-time musicianship. Kersey had fast fingers, which are used to good effect in up-tempo numbers such as his own composition "Boogie-Woogie Cocktail" (1941). Although possessing an excellent technique and timing, he made no distinctive contribution to the development of the genre.

The atmosphere at the downtown club, as it was in 1943, is remembered by Ben (Bud) Conroy, a retired cable-television executive and himself an excellent interpreter of boogie-woogie and ragtime music with several recordings to his name.[14] Ammons and Johnson, he recalls, were often featured as the finale of the floor show and played five or six numbers selected from their recorded material. They were capable of building up such an emotional tension, as their set progressed, that the audience was left quite limp as the final notes rang out. They achieved this without appearing to put much conscious effort into their playing, seldom missing a beat, and very rarely looking at one another while at the keyboards. The only evidence of the energy being expended could be seen in their supple, fast-moving fingers. An apocryphal story about the upright posture of Albert Ammons was that he could have balanced a glass of bourbon on his head without spilling a drop. Franz Jackson, one of Albert's sidemen, said that he was a serious and intense musician whose metronomic timing and strutty, forceful playing would rock the piano.[15] The apparent nonchalance that Ammons and Johnson brought to their duet playing, however, masked an intense concentration, for they were always wet with perspiration as they acknowledged the applause at the completion of a set. When food was being served, one or other of the pianists would supply background music of a more subdued kind. Favorites from the Ammons's repertoire were "Corrine, Corrine" or "Mecca Flat Blues," while Johnson's numbers were drawn from popular tunes of the day or the blues. Another pianist who shared the intermission spot with them was Cliff Jackson, who specialized in playing stride numbers.

None of their material at the Café Society was played in exactly the same way it had appeared on recordings. One or two embellishments or new choruses were introduced to prevent predictability from creeping into their work. This sometimes caused embarrassment when customers requested particular favorites played as they had been recorded. Pete Johnson often had difficulty in remembering his well-known pieces note for note, and on one occasion a customer, much to his amusement, joined him at the piano to play a faultless rendition of "Kaycee on My Mind."

The admiration that Albert Ammons had for Fats Waller even extended to a facial similarity emphasized by his slicked-down hairstyle and fashionable Clarke Gable mustache of the period. There were other similarities with Waller: the "jive" talk and their appreciation of alcohol. Albert would often humorously indicate his two-finger measure of Bourbon by showing the barman his first and fourth fingers instead of the customary first and second. Albert's drinking capacity was an in-joke shared with the other musicians at the Café Society, who, on one occasion, produced a newspaper sales banner of the *New York Star* with the front page headline: "Albert Ammons Goes on Water Waggon. 300 N.Y. Bars Close." The most important similarity between Waller and Ammons, though, was their dominant left hand, which both employed to good effect in their powerful bass playing.

Ben Conroy was privileged to learn a great deal about the interpretation of boogie-woogie from watching and talking to Ammons and Johnson. They were tolerant toward his youthful enthusiasm and often took time to show him how to play a particular bass or treble phrase. When Ammons invited Conroy to play the piano for him, and having done so to the delight of Ammons and the listening Barney Josephson, Albert turned to Ben and said, "Bud, always be proud of this music. Not many people can play it and play it right. It's great music." During one conversation with Conroy, Ammons referred to some recordings said to have been made with Frankie "Half Pint" Jaxon, but a search of Jaxon's released material sheds no light on this claim, although several recordings were made with an unnamed pianist. Similarly, recordings have come to light in recent years of Amos Easton (Bumble Bee Slim) accompanied by an unknown pianist on the Vocalion label. Blues authority M. Chaigne and others believe the pianist to be Albert Ammons, using a slightly different tone coloring in his playing to avoid detection by the Decca Company, to whom he was contracted in 1937.

Johnson and Ammons were good friends: Albert spoke about his "brother" Pete Johnson, surely a reference to "brothers of the race" and their close affinity at the piano. Temperamentally, however, they were different; Albert was the more laidback of the two, while Pete was sometimes edgy about dates and payments. The partnership between Johnson and Turner continued successfully from their days together in Kansas City. The management of the Café Society publicized them as "Big Joe from Kansas City" and "Roll 'Em Johnson." They stayed together as partners until 1941, when Turner left amicably at about the time Lewis departed to pursue his solo career. Johnson and Turner were reunited on recording dates several times, after their partnership finished. Pete Johnson's contract with the Café Society clubs was the longest, extending over seven years, some of this time partnered by Ammons. The two of them were on the bill of Café Society Uptown in March 1943. Johnson also took part in a Sunday jam session held at the Bradford Hotel on the twenty-first of the same month. He was still around in June 1946 at Café Society Downtown, sharing the bill with the J. C. Heard Orchestra, Sarah Vaughan, Cliff Jackson, and comedian Timmy Rogers. The jazz world's flirtation with boogie-woogie was already coming under some strain, perhaps reflected in *Downbeat*'s observation that although top man in his craft, Pete Johnson should widen his repertoire.[16]

A succession of pianists passed through the doors of the clubs to maintain the tradition for boogie-woogie music after the Trio had disbanded. Most were not solely boogie-woogie specialists, but they were all expected to have a capability in this field in addition to any other talents they possessed. The most popular of them, with a genuine feeling for eight-beat music, were Sam Price, Mary Lou Williams, Eddie Haywood Jr., and the glamorous Hazel Scott (1920–1981), who contributed in no small measure to the ethos of the two clubs. She was featured as a singer and pianist and also acted as the master of ceremonies for some of the shows.

Her association with the Café Society clubs extended over a period of six or seven years, comparable with Pete Johnson's residencies.

Hazel Scott's first audition was in 1939, but this proved to be unsuccessful, so she returned to a small bar in Harlem to continue playing the piano and singing. Some time later, Jack Gilford happened to call in there and caught her act. He was sufficiently impressed with her talents to the extent that he arranged for Barney Josephson to join him on a second visit, and Hazel Scott was eventually engaged for sixty-five dollars per week. Her training as a classical musician in her native Trinidad did not initially assist her early attempts to master the rhythm and feel of boogie-woogie. John Hammond was one who was unmoved by her playing, and in her early performances was seen reading his newspaper, a disconcerting habit he displayed whenever the work of an artist was not to his liking.

One advantage of being classically trained, however, was shown in her ability to build boogie-woogie solos around "classical" themes, notably pieces by Bach and Percy Grainger's *In a Country Garden*—a unique facility that proved popular with the patrons. She was a willing learner and spent many hours sitting by the piano when Albert Ammons performed, absorbing the resonant basses and watching his technique. Although Hazel Scott's playing of boogie-woogie was never entirely convincing, her artistic talents were never in doubt and were made the more compelling by her beauty and graceful bearing.

Several recordings were made for Decca, but they often lacked sparkle and that elusive stamp of originality that marks the work of masters of the boogie-woogie genre. One recording, "Hazel's Boogie-Woogie" (1942), demonstrates both her brilliant technique and the debt she owed to the compositions of the Trio in her boogie-woogie interpretations. Hazel Scott went on to make a successful film career, appearing in many Hollywood musicals of the time. She married congressman Adam Clayton Powell, who was, in his own right, a successful politician and magazine editor. Unfortunately, after several separations, their marriage ended in divorce. Hazel Scott was the first black artist to have her own radio show in the late 1940s until she was accused of being a communist sympathizer during the McCarthy era of show business purges (see below). As a consequence, her radio show was canceled. Earlier in her career, she had made her own contribution toward better racial integration by refusing to undertake engagements before segregated audiences.

Both Café Society clubs continued to be profitable for Josephson throughout the 1940s and into the 1950s, although the unique ambience of the first was never entirely replicated in the second. Regular patrons at Café Society Downtown in the early years were, in addition to Paul Robeson, humorist and writer S. J. Perelman, world heavyweight champion boxer Joe Louis, and Eleanor Roosevelt, who frequently attended with her son Elliot. A story circulating at the time, perhaps apocryphal, was that President Roosevelt learned more about liberal attitudes in America from his wife's regular association with radicals at the club than from any other source. Toward the end of the 1940s, in the cold war period between America and Russia, an unrelieved antipathy to individuals or institutions holding sympathetic inclinations toward the Soviet Union or the communist ideology gripped America. This was a dramatic reversal of the sympathetic generosity extended to that country through the many benefit concerts and financial donations made during the war years. It was an early manifestation of the power politics that these two great nations would engage in over the next forty years. The House Un-American Activities Committee presided over by Senator Joseph McCarthy was established, which attempted to collect evidence about communist sympathizers often from informants who were themselves under pressure to confess. Those who had been identified were then "tried" at a form of public inquisition over which the senator presided. Many lives were destroyed and careers ruined by this unrelenting witch hunt.

Among the famous subpoenaed to testify before the committee were several Hollywood film stars, including Charles Chaplin, Larry Parkes, and Orson Welles. The committee's proceedings were extensively reported in film newsreels, newspapers, and on the radio. At one point the Café Society clubs came under close surveillance for allegedly harboring "reds." Josephson's brother was both a lawyer and an admitted communist. His presence in the clubs and his relationship to Barney were noted in the press and he was duly asked to appear before the committee. He at first refused on the grounds that it was illegal and was given a ten-month prison sentence for contempt. The adverse publicity arising from the incident for Barney Josephson precipitated the sale of the clubs in 1950. Business had already fallen by nearly one-half at the Uptown club immediately after his brother's court appearance. This signaled the end of a period in which boogie-woogie music had traveled from barroom to select nightclub. The closure also coincided with a cooling of interest in the craze for eight-to-the-bar music by a public that had become satiated with diluted versions such as "Chopsticks Boogie" and "The Booglie-Wooglie Piggy."

Happily, the contribution made by Josephson in safeguarding the interests of jazz and boogie-woogie did not pass without recognition. The organizers of the Newport Jazz Festival arranged a Salute to Café Society Concert in 1973 at which Josephson was presented with a plaque to commemorate the many musicians whom he had fostered and encouraged in his clubs. Without in any way detracting from Josephson's eminence, it is open to conjecture whether he or Hammond deserved it more. It was, after all, the latter's skilful perception that brought so much embryonic talent to the fore and helped establish the reputation of the clubs. The late Frank Trolle, a record collector and jazz enthusiast, spent many happy hours at the clubs, and in reflecting on the importance of Josephson's visionary concept, spoke for many in his belief that the Café Society clubs were landmarks that raised and supported the profile of jazz in New York City.[17]

NOTES

1. H. Lawrenson, "Black and White and Red All Over," *New York Magazine*, August 21, 1978, 36–43.

2. Billie Holiday with William Dufty, *Lady Sings the Blues* (London: Penguin, 1984), 83, 84.

3. Martin Duberman, *Paul Robeson: A Biography* (New York: New Press, 1989), 177, 284.

4. Dorothy Schainman Siegel, *The Glory Road: The Story of Josh White* (White Hall, VA: Shoe Tree Press, 1991), 81–82.

5. Danny Baxter, "Boogie-Woogie Comes to Life Once Again," *Downbeat*, March 1939, 14.

6. Valerie Wilmer, "The Boss of the Blues," *Downbeat*, November 1965, 42.

7. C. Page, "Boogie-Woogie Stomp," in *Albert Ammons and His Music* (Cleveland: Northeast Ohio Jazz Society, 1997), 81.

8. "Charmed Carnegie Crowd; Now Gets Laughs Hoofing," *Downbeat*, March 1940, 4.

9. "Review of Café Society," *New York Times*, January 8, 1939.

10. W. Balliett, *Ecstasy at the Onion* (Indianapolis, IN: Bobbs-Merrill, 1971), 258–59.

11. "Uptown Boogie-Woogie," *Time*, October 21, 1940, 54, 55.

12. The Museum of Modern Art website: MoMA, Piet Mondrian, *Broadway Boogie-Woogie*, 1942-43, www.moma.org/collection/browse (accessed March 21, 2009).

13. Susanne Deicher, *Mondrian* (London: Tescher, 1999), 88–89, 91.

14. Ben Conroy, taped recollections sent to the author, July 1985.

15. C. Page, "Boogie-Woogie Stomp," 99.

16. "Downtown Café Society Floor Show Offers Value," *Downbeat*, August 1946, 3.

17. Frank H. Trolle, "Café Society," *International Association of Record Collectors Magazine*, 1987, 18.

9

The Post–Café
Society Period

The public euphoria following the Carnegie Hall Concert and the open-ing of Café Society Downtown confirmed the arrival of boogie-woogie in New York and the reputations of the Boogie-Woogie Trio and Joe Turner. The early months of 1939 were a period of intense activity for them as they capitalized on their success with recording engagements, personal appearances, and radio broadcasts, all fitted around their daily work at the Café Society. They were soon one of the most respected and sought-after outfits in New York.

On January 3, immediately following the opening of the Club, Ammons and Lewis made a guest appearance on the Camel Caravan Show, which featured the Benny Goodman Orchestra. Lewis took a solo spot and pleased the audience with an up-tempo rendition of "Honky Tonk Train Blues." He then joined Ammons for a duet on two pianos on the band's closing number "Roll 'Em." An invitation was extended to Pete Johnson to appear on the show on January 31. He joined forces with Jack Teagarden to play "Roll 'Em Pete." Lewis and Ammons were back again on April 4 for a two-piano rendition of "Pinetop's Boogie-Woogie" with the addi-tion of some innocuous lyrics about "Mr. Pinetop," composed and sung by Johnny Mercer. A solo spot was then given to Lewis on the Columbia Broadcasting Company's radio show *Saturday Night Club* of February 3. He played "Yancey Special." Johnson starred on the same company's show *We the People*—a Sunday evening swing program. Feature articles were written about them in the *New York Times* and *Look* magazine.

With a six-month residency at the Café behind them, they moved to the Panther Room of the Sherman Hotel in Chicago for a two-month engagement and opened there on August 12. Sharing the bill with Fats Waller, and the resident band led by Muggsy Spanier, their arrival in the city was announced by one newspaper, with a rider that boogie-woogie was an amusing variant of swing and that it would be the first occasion that boogie-woogie had been introduced to Chicago's music fans.[1] The tone of the preview was an apt reminder of the ignorance of the popular media about the piano style that had flourished among the African-American community in the city during the 1920s and 1930s. This kind of half-digested knowledge was to be repeated on several occasions with the trio's emergence into the "show biz" arena alongside cult bandleaders such as Goodman, Shaw, and the Dorsey Brothers.

One of the indisputable attractions for the public was the visual spec-tacle of the three men in action. Their ample girths were barely contained by their smart tuxedos, which gave a spurious "respectability" to the electrifying music that was hammered out by enormous hands, the size of hams. The incongruity between their physical presence onstage and their agile music was one reason for the public's continuing fascination with them as entertainers. One typical engagement took place at the Stratford Theatre in New York on November 5. The trio and Joe Turner entertained in the intermission of a feature film called *Two Bright Boys* starring Jackie Cooper and Freddie Bartholomew, and a matinee performance of chap-ters 4 and 5 of the Dick Tracey serial. Their billing as the "Boogie-woogies, the newest and hottest swing kings" demonstrates the extent to which they and their music were entering the American psyche.

The Harry James Orchestra with new vocalist Frank Sinatra appeared at the Hotel Sherman during the Trio's engagement there. Johnson and Ammons had already made a recording with a quartet drawn from the band in February 1939. These sides, issued by the Brunswick Company, were "Boo Woo" coupled with "Home James" featuring Johnson on piano, and "Woo Woo" and "Jesse" with Ammons. The records were commercially successful and introduced the new generation of swing fans to the exciting possibilities of small-group boogie-woogie in the capable hands of musicians who were sensitive to the genre. They are some of the better examples of James's hot trumpet style, which he later forsook for a much sweeter commercial tone.

The Sherman Hotel was situated in Chicago's Loop section, and many concerts and broadcasts took place in the Panther Room. John Steiner was a frequent visitor, and he recalls an occasion when he renewed his ac-quaintance there with Albert Ammons.[2] Although not an intimate of the piano man—they had breakfasted together at the It Club—they were on friendly terms. It was a natural courtesy for Steiner to smile as he walked by Ammons on his way to his table. Ammons, ever avuncular, nodded his head in recognition as Steiner took his seat with the other expectant patrons. The show began with the Harry James Orchestra executing their sharp, brassy arrangements, and then the lights dimmed for the appearance of the Boogie-Woogie Trio. Two pianos were rolled out to the center of the floor and a third was pushed out from the bandstand: one small grand and two oak uprights. The trio hit the keys, and the Panther Room was soon throbbing to the arcane rhythms of boogie-woogie. As the notes cascaded from their fingers in the closing chorus, the audience, now totally captivated by the compelling rhythms, rose to its feet and shouted for an encore.

In one of several broadcasts made by the trio from the Sherman, Johnson sat at one piano and Lewis and Ammons shared another. They faced each other, with the microphone occupying the space between the two pianos. The engineer counted off the seconds and gave them the signal to begin playing. Johnson glanced over the top of his piano to receive the cue from his partners only to see Lewis sitting quite still, eyes closed, recovering from the excesses of a large plate of ribs that he had devoured shortly before the broadcast. Fortunately, Ammons came in on cue to bring Lewis out of his slumber. The poor condition of the pianos at the Sherman gave rise to critical comments in *Downbeat*. Recordings of some of the broadcasts that have since become available confirm that the broadside was justified; several missing notes were evident, a factor that, fortunately, detracts only marginally from the playing. The broadcasts allowed the pianists to dig into their repertoire of tunes to play old favorites as well as newer ones, previously unheard. Thus, on recordings from the broadcasts Lewis produces a brooding "Closing Time" and an excitingly layered "Bear Cat Crawl," a piece dependent on short treble phrasing for its inexorable progress; Ammons gives a powerfully controlled version of "Shout for Joy," that climaxes with a cascading walking bass, and the melodic folk song "Has Anyone Here Seen Corrine?"; while Johnson plays two somber blues, "G Flat Blues" and "Pete's Blues." The full complement of solos, duets, and trios can be enjoyed on two recordings: *Boogie Woogie Trio: Broadcasts from 1939* (Storyville, SLP 184) and *Boogie Woogie Kings: Volume 9* (Euphonic Piano Series, ESR- 1209).

Another Chicago venue for jazz and swing music was the Blackhawk Restaurant. A popular band appearing there in the late 1930s was the Bob Crosby Orchestra. The band's pianist was Bob Zurke, who captivated audiences with his inimitable style, incorporating many boogie-woogie influences. John Steiner's initial meeting with Zurke had been the result of an introduction from "Squirrel" Ashcraft, a Chicago attorney, who not only enjoyed listening to jazz but arranged recitals at his home from time to time. For a period of time, Zurke was a guest at Ashcraft's home when he was in the depths of one of his personal crises. Zurke frequented many of the small Chicago clubs to listen to other pianists in the early hours when the Crosby Orchestra had finished their show. He was, on these occasions, unable to resist the temptation to take a turn at the keyboard if he was recognized and invited to do so. If no invitation was extended he would approach the pianist in his most courteous manner and compliment the pianist on the interpretation. A little more flattery would allow him to slide onto the stool by the side of the pianist and pick up the tune. The performance then began in earnest, with Zurke transposing the number through several key changes and back to the original key before returning to his seat.

When the trio's engagement at the Hotel Sherman was finished, they returned to the Café Society and, using this as their base, undertook concert engagements and recording sessions. In their off-duty moments they were frequent participants in the impromptu jam sessions that were a feature of the New York jazz scene. Max Kaminsky remembers many Sunday sessions being enlivened by the presence of Ammons and Lewis. Johnson and Turner often patronized a small club in Harlem where they relaxed by performing many of the numbers that had brought them fame at the Café Society. By 1941, Lewis had left the trio and moved to Los Angeles to take up permanent residence there. Whether his break from the others was precipitated by an ambition to appear in films or a wish to capitalize on his recent fame as a solo performer can only remain as conjecture, but both reasons seem to fit events. Pete Johnson implied that the split was partly due to Lewis's dissatisfaction with the pay scale at the nightspot. A hint of his impending departure and the breakup of the Trio was forecast barely ten months after the formation of the Trio with the suggestion in October 1939 that Lewis would be breaking away from the others by the middle of that month.[3]

Initially, Lewis and Joe Turner, accompanied by Willie Bryant, one of the masters of ceremonies at the club, left for a theatre tour of the West Coast, but Lewis decided to stay on after its completion. On August 19 he commenced a long engagement at the unpretentious but intimate Los Angeles nightspot called the Swanee Inn. Before making his permanent home in Los Angeles's South Side, he moved into temporary accommodation in Riverside. The arrangements for Lewis's move were handled by Charles Kossi of the C. Phillips Agency. Part of the deal was that Lewis would either appear or be heard on the sound track of the RKO film *Syncopation*, but this never materialized. The boogie-woogie piano playing supposedly emanating from the childish hands of the classically trained daughter of a well-to-do family, smitten by "darkie" music, was played by Stan Wrightsman, sometime pianist with Ben Pollack and Bob Crosby, who carried out much freelance work in films and on radio during the 1940s. Lewis stayed at the Swanee Inn throughout the remainder of 1941 into 1942. Joe Turner sang with him in December 1941, and they sent their joint Christmas greetings to the public through the advertisement columns of *Downbeat*.

At the time of Lewis's break with the Café Society, he also applied to the Association of Song Composers and Publishers (ASCAP) for a union card, which was initially refused by the union secretary. His cause was taken up by *Downbeat* beginning with a denouncement of the decision to refuse Lewis's application at their meeting of October 30. Meanwhile, as the magazine reminded its readers, Lewis carried on performing and composing high-quality numbers, which ASCAP was not prepared to acknowledge with a pin for the lapel of his worn-out suit.[4] The report even led to the publication of a letter from a reader complaining about the magazine's over-sentimentalized portrayal of Lewis's poverty. A second article drew in Louis Bernstein, president of Shapiro, Bernstein, and Company and an officer of ASCAP—ironically, the company responsible for publishing some of Lewis's compositions. Bernstein knew nothing of the refusal of membership but promised to investigate the matter. *Downbeat* printed the details of Lewis's application, listed his compositions, noting that "Yancey Special" and "Honky Tonk Train Blues" were commercial successes with sales of over five hundred thousand records and that he had had several compositions published in folio form by the Leeds Music Corporation.[5] Fortunately, Bernstein's intervention on behalf of Lewis proved successful, allowing *Downbeat* to report the successful outcome of their cause.

The reasons for the initial refusal of Lewis's membership were never given, and it can only be surmised that it was either a latent form of racial discrimination or a misguided view that boogie-woogie compositions were not considered serious music. The pleasing result of the campaign was that he received a permanent financial return on the copyright of many of his compositions.

The Leeds Music Company, which had published Meade's compositions, was a leader in the campaign for just treatment for black artists, and in this respect was at the forefront of New York music publishers. The sympathetic policy stemmed from the owner, Lou Levy, who had appeared as a dancer with the Jimmy Lunceford Orchestra in Harlem. The company was one of the first to realize the commercial potential of boogie-woogie music and led the field with several albums by Ammons, Johnson, McShann, Price, and Williams. It also had successes with a number of pseudo-boogie tunes written by white composers. These included "Mr. Five by Five" by Don Raye and Gene De Paul, successfully recorded by Freddy Slack for the Capitol Record Company in 1942, and the renowned "pop" boogie tune "Beat Me Daddy Eight to the Bar," which proved an unqualified hit for the Will Bradley Orchestra featuring Freddy Slack on piano.

With public interest in boogie-woogie still at its height in the early 1940s, Lewis continued to be invited to broadcast on the subject. One such event occurred on the CBS program *What's on Your Mind*; he was joined by Bob Laine, a pianist with the Ben Pollack Orchestra, to discuss the earliest appearances of boogie-woogie bass figures in music. The debate was really a non sequitur that demonstrated the innocent and frequently ignorant endeavors to give boogie-woogie a "respectable" lineage with the European classical tradition. Two further broadcasts of note were made by Lewis on the *Jubilee Shows* for the American armed forces, with appearances on show number forty-one playing "Honky Tonk Train Blues" and "Six Wheel Chaser" (1943); and on show number eighty-seven (1944), he gave a rendition of "Boogie Tidal."

Boogie-woogie music was all-pervasive as it reached the proportions of a national craze. The dance of the period was the Lindy hop, later renamed the jitterbug because its adherents produced ever wilder versions with lots of air gymnastics involving lifts, spins, and jumps. Boogie-woogie, with its driving rhythms, was an ideal vehicle for the dance performance, and the two became synonymous in the minds of custodians of public morality who saw them as ill-conceived excesses of the young, predominantly white youth of America. It was condemned for giving rise to juvenile delinquency and defended from this attack by Frank Sinatra. However, no such concern was shown for the moral welfare of the younger members of the American armed forces (GIs), who nightly danced the jitterbug to the rhythms of boogie-woogie and the music of swing bands. Disinterested observers might have said that such an explosive combination contributed mightily to the morale of the armed forces and at least could have had some cathartic value. Fats Waller claimed to dislike boogie-woogie to the extent that he refused requests to play it on concert engagements, describing it to his friend Joey Nash as "thirty-two bars of nothing." Fats was asked for his personal opinion about boogie-woogie by Eddie "Rochester" Anderson on a *Jack Benny Show* broadcast from the West Coast. Waller replied that he had been talking to a fellow only that afternoon who told him that he had recently composed a boogie-woogie number. When asked what it was called, the fellow said: "What does the termite say to the bartender? '"Beat Me Daddy, I Just Ate the Bar.'"

Given such jocularity and evident displeasure about boogie-woogie, it is strange that one of Waller's earliest recordings of the George Thomas tune "Muscle Shoals Blues" dating from 1922 employs a rocking ostinato bass of tenths. Similarly, his very popular recording of "Alligator Crawl" (1934) was given immediate impact with a powerful walking bass introduction; and a piano album of boogie-woogie numbers appeared posthumously under the collective title of "Fats Waller's Boogie-Woogie Suite"

(1945). Waller died in December 1943 but not before he had recorded an inconsequentially short boogie number in September for Victor entitled "Waller Jive" (1943), lasting just over one minute, an indication perhaps that he ran out of ideas or found the task too objectionable. Clearly, he was ambivalent toward boogie-woogie, perhaps reacting to the excessive exposure it was receiving, and it must be admitted there was some dire piano music being played at the time. Every barroom with a piano, particularly in the armed forces, seemed to attract tyro boogie-woogie pianists, many of whom could barely match a bass to a few treble chords, but then, the music was only returning to its roots by replicating the endeavors of early African-American pianists trying to make music without the necessary piano technique.

Popular classical pianists Jose Iturbi and Oscar Levant had at least one novelty boogie-woogie composition to their credit and could be seen performing their variants of the style in Hollywood musicals. The much revered piano maestro Yonty Solomon produced a passable version of "Honky Tonk Train Blues" while Sylvia Marlowe, an internationally respected harpsichord player, recorded several boogie-woogie numbers, including "Pinetop's Boogie-Woogie," which was transcribed for her from Tommy Dorsey's recording arranged by Dean Kincaide, even down to the trombone passage in the final chorus. A long friendship between Marlowe and John Hammond probably led to this venture. Whatever the technical merits of the numerous renditions of boogie-woogie by classical pianists might have been, the various performances left no doubt in the minds of discerning listeners that the link between an ability to play convincing boogie-woogie and classical music was extremely tenuous.

The boogie-woogie bandwagon continued to roll and infiltrate the fabric of American life when the "hep" and the "high hat" joined forces at the University of Minnesota campus in a March 1941 concert to welcome Dimitri Mitropoulos, the newly appointed conductor of that city's fine symphony orchestra. It was arranged by the Boogie-Woogie Club at the university, organized and well supported by the students. A leading light and amateur boogie-woogie player, Ken Green, composed and played a semi-satirical number "Beat Me Dimitri" in honor of the great man who, though appearing somewhat bemused by the tune (and the music), was very appreciative of the reception given to him by the audience of three thousand people. Meanwhile, war continued apace in Europe with German bombers attacking London and the south coast and northeastern region of Britain. The contrast between these lighthearted and life-threatening events was brought into sharp relief by the close juxtaposition of their reportage in the *Minneapolis Morning Tribune*.

Boogie-woogie spawned several entertainers who built their acts around it, one of whom was Harry "The Hipster" Gibson, a white pianist and singer who had worked around the clubs of New York for several years doing fill-in work for the main acts. He sprang to instant fame when he was asked to stand in for the absent Billie Holiday at the Three Deuces nightclub where he was undertaking the intermission work. The audience was successfully entertained by an act of pounding boogie-woogie, hep talk, and song, soon to be followed with a recording contract for Gibson with the Musicraft label. His highly original material included "Get Your Juices at the Deuces" and the unforgettable "Who Put the Benzedrine in Mrs. Murphy's Ovaltine." These themes were not to everyone's taste, and his records were banned in Los Angeles. He later toured with Mae West's show before moving to California where he appears to have lived the life of a recluse before dying there in 1991.

There is no reason to suppose that the breakup of the Trio after two years was in any way attributable to incompatible relationships. Indeed, the friendships formed seem to have been very amicable and enduring, as revealed by later events when Pete Johnson and Meade Lux Lewis teamed up in 1952 for the Piano Parade concerts. As has been intimated, money, or lack of it, may have been one of the reasons for Meade's departure. It was always apparent that Lewis was best in solo performance and that Ammons and Johnson were a better combination as a musical duet. Between 1939 and 1941 Lewis made a number of recordings with groups led by Frankie Newton, Edmond Hall, and Sidney Bechet for the Bluenote Company, but he frequently underplayed his part in comparison to the rich tones he was capable of producing in his solos. When he did feel the need to extend his musical range, it was not done in the company of fellow musicians but by experimenting with the celeste, an instrument with unknown qualities for playing boogie. He composed at least two original compositions for the instrument, "Celeste Blues" (1936) for Decca and "Doll House Boogie" (1943) as a V Disc. On the latter recording he alternated between the piano and the celeste. There were also the excursions with the harpsichord for Blue Note with a two-record set entitled *Variations on a Theme* (1941). Despite what had already been said about the limited impact of his ensemble work, examples of his more imaginative celeste playing can be heard on the sides made with the "Edmond Hall Celeste Quartet." Lewis was a peerless soloist, and even when supported by a drummer, the presence of the additional instrument marred rather than added to the music by muffling the rich tone coloring.

After completing his engagement at the Swanee Inn, Lewis moved to another West Coast club, the Streets of Paris, in September 1942, sharing the bill with Wingy Mannone and his band and alternating with Art Tatum at the piano. His appearance at the club was reported in *Jazz Quarterly*: "We saw a small dark figure slightly reminiscent of a man and more like that of a medicine ball, waddle up to the bandstand, adjust the seat for about twenty seconds, sound out the piano and his position with a few licks and then go into the finest boogie-woogie and blues in these United States, and that means, of course, the world."[6]

Beginning his set with well-known numbers such as "Honky Tonk Train Blues" and "Yancey Special," Lewis then produced his own version of "Cow Cow Blues" with solid walking bass and beautifully chorded breaks. He could claim with some justification to play only his own compositions at this time in his musical career, because in his hands the Davenport composition became something new and invigorating.

A second, unattributed review written about Lewis's piano style captures the amazing impact that the man and his music could have on an unprepared listener during a live performance, possibly at the Streets of Paris again. On this occasion, the originality of his improvisations and their orchestral concept are flagged, presumably due to their rich tone colors, with a final opinion that Meade Lux Lewis was capable of drawing more music from the piano than the reviewer had ever heard one man produce. There is no doubt that Lewis was at the peak of his career in the 1940s. He was physically powerful and brimming with incompleted musical ideas that were yet to be framed within new compositions.

Another productive engagement began for him in the mid-1940s at Randini's Club on Hollywood Boulevard. The club was acknowledged to be the best public place to hear the music on the West Coast, and Meade increased his already large following during his residency there. Some of his most devoted followers were members of the film fraternity led by Orson Welles, who sent him a good-luck telegram on one of his opening nights out of town. His playing was always received in respectful silence in an atmosphere that was more akin to that of a seminar than a nightspot. On one occasion, the mood was shattered by a loud drunk exclaiming, "Best God-damned pianah player in the whole damn world." He was quietly shown the door.

The next important stage in Lewis's musical progress came when he began recording for the Asch label, coinciding with his engagement at Randini's Club. The receptiveness of audiences at the nightclub was instrumental in taking his conception of boogie-woogie forward to a higher level of originality. The record company was owned by Moses Asch, who was born in Poland on December 2, 1905. His family moved to the United States at the outbreak of World War I. Moses became interested in short-wave radio broadcasting as a hobby, but it soon became an absorbing interest that he developed by studying electronics at the Bingen Hochschule back in Germany. On his return to America, he began collecting recordings of ethnic folk music and recording his own material when radio station WEVD was given a license to broadcast shows in various foreign languages for the ethnic groups living in New York. After building the electrical equipment, Asch was asked to assist with finding artists and recording them for the shows. One of the first to record for him was Huddie Leadbetter, who made some sides of children's songs. The ban on studio recordings between 1942 and 1944 allowed Asch the opportunity of recording some of the outstanding jazz pianists of the period. The first was James P. Johnson, who approached Asch to make new recordings of his best-selling number "Snowy Morning Blues," but he was quickly followed by Art Tatum, Teddy Wilson, Errol Garner, Willie "The Lion" Smith, Mary Lou Williams, and, of course, Meade Lux Lewis.

Whereas the Blue Note releases from Meade's time at the Café Society showed his creativity and originality in playing traditional forms of boogie-woogie, his recorded work from the period spent at Randini's Club marked the achievement of another but different kind of peak. Six records were initially released on the Asch label in August 1944 entitled "Denapas Parade," "Glendale Glide," "Lux Boogie," "Randini's Boogie," "Boogie Tidal," and "Yancey's Pride." The most noticeable shift from his earlier work was to be found in his employment of more open basses on several of these numbers instead of the traditional repetitive ones normally associated with boogie-woogie. This switched the emphasis in the music from the bass to the treble, resulting in a quieter, but still rhythmical left hand, supporting an assertive and more melodic right hand. The sides showing the change most clearly are the dedication to Jimmy Yancey entitled "Yancey's Pride," "Denapas Parade," and "Boogie Tidal," the last mentioned reverting to a more recognizable bass of repeated descending fifth chords after several choruses of an open bass. Lewis had already served notice of his intention to experiment with flexible basses in his brooding five-part composition "The Blues" (1939) issued by Blue Note. The Asch recordings, together with numbers by Johnson and Ammons, can be heard on *The Boogie-Woogie Greats* (Jazz Piano, JP 5008).

The Asch releases indicated that these early experiments with more open basses had now come to fruition. *Downbeat* gave the recordings an enthusiastic approbation, calling them superlative piano music that provided an answer to anyone claiming that boogie was monotonous. While the new sounds were well received, it was noticeable that two of the pieces were played at breakneck speed. "Randini's Boogie," which owed a debt to the earlier "Chicago Flyer," and "Lux Boogie" had rapid, stumbling basses and short, repeated rifflike choruses in the treble. They were a portent of things to come, leading critic Martin Williams to opine in a later review of Lewis's achievements that his playing was becoming slicker, his tone heavier, and his tempo faster.[7] Two additional sides, "Honky Tonk Train Blues" and "Medium Blues," were recorded at the same time but were not released until 1974, on the Folkways label.

Lewis returned to the Hotel Sherman as a soloist in November 1944 to appear at the College Inn, a bar annex in the hotel. Located in the eastern half of the basement of the hotel, the Inn comprised a restaurant, main dining and dance room, plus a piano lounge. The dining area eventually became the Panther Room, so called because of the artificial panther skins used for the upholstery. On the evening his act was reviewed in *Jazz Session* magazine, the organ of the Chicago Hot Club, he played "Honky Tonk Train Blues," "Yancey Special," and "Bear Trap Stomp." Lewis was interviewed by two of the magazine reviewers, Marshall Turoff and John Below, shortly before starting his final set of the evening.[8] Their comments reiterated Williams's observations about the increased tempo and power of the "Train" and the "Special," finding that they had difficulty tapping out the rhythms with their feet. When questioned about his favorite jazz musicians, Lewis named pianist Billy Kyle, trumpeter Frankie Newton, and saxophonist Johnny Hodges. His favorite band was reported to be Benny Carter's, and the tunes that pleased him most were the "Song of India" and "Buck Jumpin'" by Fats Waller. Lewis returned to the Sherman on September 21, 1945, to share the piano spot with Joe Sullivan. Before that, however, an earlier appearance in Chicago in May 1945 saw him appearing at the Civic Opera Theatre alongside Lester Young, Helen Humes, and Coleman Hawkins. Lewis was now following a new pattern of work. In order to reach a wider public, he was prepared to appear at prestigious venues such as the Sherman as well as lesser-known ones like those situated in towns of the Midwest of America. It was more lucrative for him to do this rather than rely solely on getting engagements on the West Coast; but it did necessitate endlessly long car journeys to reach the right sort of appreciative public.

In the early days when he was making his mark, Meade was remembered by friends and associates for his genial nature and cheerful, sunny disposition. Sharon Pease admired his integrity and devotion to principles, and for a long time commercial pressures that might compromise his own musical standards were resisted until he was put under pressure by unpredictable financial circumstances. Even as late as 1958, he was able to say in a feature article that he would welcome the opportunity of traveling to Europe, providing the financial return was satisfactory, but until such an invitation was extended, he would continue traveling nearly one hundred miles a day to a gig in Costa Mesa that allowed him to play the way he wanted to play.[9] Life on the road could be a lonely experience, and he felt strongly about the lot of black Americans, expressing some bitterness toward the exploitation practiced by the more unscrupulous agents with whom he was obliged to negotiate for work. It is possible that such feelings resulted in him becoming more guarded and wary in his relationships with people who were not intimates. The point is illustrated by John Bentley's account of his various meetings with Meade Lux Lewis, which demonstrate the complex undercurrents beneath the apparently genial exterior.

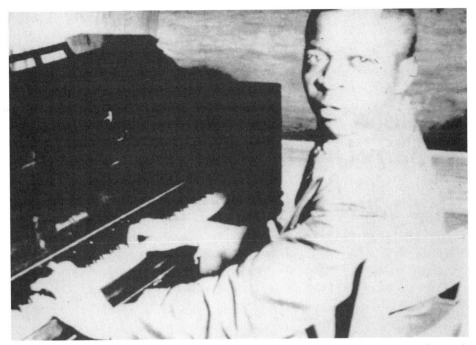

Buster Pickens: last of the barrelhouse pianists in the 1960s. Paul Oliver/Flyright Records.

The Alabama pianists, Robert McCoy (far left), Jabbo Williams (rear), unknown (front right), probably 1920s. Konrad Nowakowski.

Meade Lux Lewis takes a bow, 1950s. Denise Buckner.

A young Albert Ammons, probably Chicago in the 1920s. Christopher Page.

Pete Johnson: early career in the 1920s, probably in Kansas City. Duncan Scheidt.

Clarence Lofton at home on State Street, Chicago, November 1938. William Russell/William Wagner.

Rufus Perryman aboard the Becky Thatcher *boat, St. Louis, 1971. John Bentley/Dick Mushlitz.*

Henry Brown, St. Louis, 1960. Paul Oliver.

Roosevelt Sykes at home in New Orleans, 1971. John Bentley/Dick Mushlitz.

Mary Lou Williams, whose four-year residency at Café Society Downtown began in 1944. Jazz Journal International.

Jimmy Yancey (left) listens to Charlie Spand (foreground), possibly Chicago, early 1940s. Duncan Scheidt.

Little Brother Montgomery prior to appearing in concert with the Kid Ory band, Chicago, 1948. Jan Montgomery.

Pete Johnson sketch by Harold Lehman,
Café Society Club, New York, 1941.
Konrad Nowakowski.

J. H. Shayne (left) with Dick Mushlitz
(right). Beehive Tavern on Fifty-fifth and
Harper, Chicago, December 31, 1950.
Phil Kiely.

Café Society Downtown, Sheridan Square, New York, circa 1999. Christopher Page.

Café Society Downtown, New York, 1940s. Left to right: Meade Lux Lewis, Joe Turner (background), Albert Ammons, and Pete Johnson. Duncan Scheidt.

Bob Zurke plays piano for Bob Crosby, 1940s. Dan Gunderman.

Entertaining at the Yanceys' apartment. Doug Suggs (left foreground) and the host Jimmy Yancey (right), December 1948. Dick Mushlitz.

Robert Shaw, one of the last of the Santa Fe pianists, playing at Ben Conroy's home in Austin, Texas, 1971. Ben Conroy.

Jimmy and Estelle Yancey at home on 11 W. Thirty-fifth Street, Chicago, 1951. William Wagner/William Russell.

Champion Jack Dupree at New Orleans Jazz and Heritage Festival, 1992. John Bentley/Dick Mushlitz.

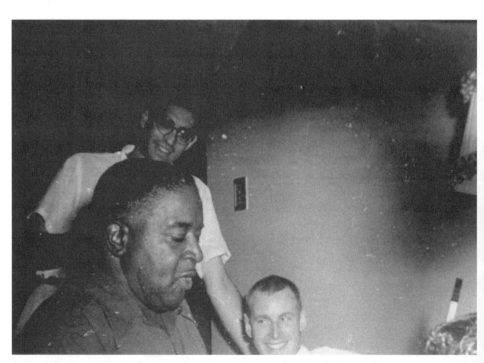

Pete Johnson plays for Tom Harris (standing) and Charlie Castner. St. Louis party, 1954. Tom Harris.

Martin Pyrker of Austria playing at the Les Nuits Jazz et Boogie Piano, Paris, 1990. Patrick Smet.

Jay McShann playing at a festival in Kansas City, July 2000. Andre Hobus.

Pinetop's son Clarence Smith Jr. (center) flanked by Christopher Page (left) and Axel Zwingenberger (right), Chicago, 1999. Eva Henning.

Bob Seeley (at piano) plays for Jean Paul Amouroux (left) and Bernard Matthieu (right) in Paris, 1994. Peter Silvester.

The Sirens label. Chicago pianists, 1976. Left to right: sitting at front, Jimmy Walker and John Davis. Standing at rear, Willie Mabon, Sunnyland Slim, and Erwin Helfer. Steven Dolins.

Meade Lux Lewis as the house painter in the film New Orleans, *1947. Duncan Scheidt.*

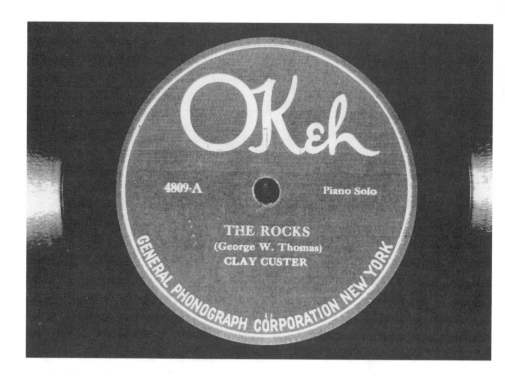

Early recordings of boogie-woogie: "The Rocks," 1923; "Pinetop's Boogie-Woogie," 1928. Francis Wilford Smith.

Two of George Thomas's early compositions showing a boogie-woogie influence. UCLA Digital Library.

Downbeat *advertisement, 1939*. Downbeat.

Café Society, one of the venues where the Boogie-Woogie Trio played in the 1940s. Dan Gunderman.

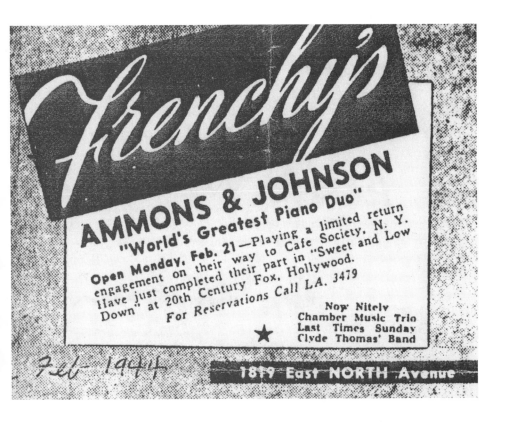

Some of the venues where the Boogie-Woogie Trio played in the 1940s. Dan Gunderman.

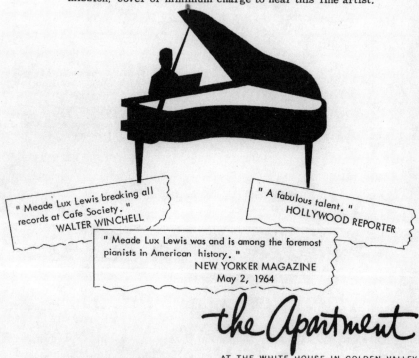

OPENING MAY 18th
the fabulous
MEADE LUX LEWIS

Meade will perform in the APARTMENT only and not be available to the public.

Consistent with our policy, there will be no admission, cover or minimum charge to hear this fine artist.

" Meade Lux Lewis breaking all records at Cafe Society. "
WALTER WINCHELL

" A fabulous talent. "
HOLLYWOOD REPORTER

" Meade Lux Lewis was and is among the foremost pianists in American history. "
NEW YORKER MAGAZINE
May 2, 1964

the Apartment

AT THE WHITE HOUSE IN GOLDEN VALLEY

P.S. Watch for sensational announcement regarding free garden parties for members only!

The venue for Meade Lux Lewis's last engagement, May 1964. Bob Seeley.

John Bentley first met Meade in the mid-1940s when he was appearing at a record promotion at Glendale (California) where he was growing up. They spoke briefly, and Meade was responsive, showing warmth and generosity with the time he had available for his fans. As Bentley was too young at this time to attend the clubs where Meade was playing, he was unable to see him in person until a few years later, after spending time in the U.S. Air Force. This occasion was at a nightspot located near the Pacific Ocean, probably Huntington Beach. During a break from his set, they talked about Meade's early Paramount recordings made with George Hannah and Rob (Meade insisted on calling him "Bob") Robinson. By then Bentley had become a record collector, but was not yet involved in researching or writing about the musicians he knew or had met. He recalls mentioning that Meade was playing exclusively boogie-woogie, although he was capable of a wider range of styles to which Meade responded with his famous cherubic smile. From that point on, Bentley heard him at various venues over the years, as opportunity allowed. Somewhere along the way, Bentley casually mentioned Lewis's ever-increasing tempos, and the decreasing opportunities to improvise freely within those meters.

With each successive meeting, their relationship appeared to grow more distant. The last time Bentley saw him was during April 1964 at a meeting of the Jazz Club of Southern California before Meade traveled east (to Minneapolis), because within a matter of weeks he was dead. A short time later (after Meade's death) at the jazz club, the master of ceremonies, Bill Bacon, offered a eulogy to his friend Meade Lux Lewis, extolling his virtues and listing his accomplishments. Bentley played piano behind Bacon's offering and then took off on a solo that was well received. As he played, the occasion affected him and he wept. One of the keys of the old upright piano, loosened by Meade the month before, broke off and embedded itself in his thumb, causing him to bleed all over the keyboard. Bentley later said, "If Meade was looking to avenge himself for some of my criticisms, wherever he was, he did it well. For me, I felt I had lost one of the people that had excited me into playing boogie piano, generally a gentle gentleman who had become a victim of many circumstances, and a fellow I genuinely admired and respected in spite of our later coolness towards one another."[10]

Bill Bacon first met Meade when, as an eighteen-year-old, he saw him performing at Lindsay's Sky Bar—a club with sparkling stars covering the ceiling—and later took a few piano lessons from him. They made contact again after several years, in the early 1960s, at the Harbor Inn (believed to be on the West Coast). Bacon later helped form the New Orleans Jazz Club in California and invited Lewis to appear there, which he did with a band in February and as a soloist in April 1964, which is the date to which Bentley refers. Both engagements followed a period of hospitalization for Lewis in December 1963. Tapes that have survived from these two meetings suggest that Lewis had regained his strength and was back in top form performing a frantic amalgam of "fast" boogie-woogie playing mingled with a couple of standards. It is probably from about this time, or even earlier, that Lewis began to cut out the heavy drinking and moderated his eating by sensible dieting. His weight of just below three hundred pounds and height of five feet six inches justified the wisdom of these measures.

Using the Café Society as their base, Albert Ammons and Pete Johnson embarked on a series of concert and club appearances of their own after the break with Lewis and Turner. Among their engagements were performances at a Boston Pops Concert on May 15, 1940, together with Joe Turner and Elliot Paul, a classical pianist and novelist who later became a pupil of Albert Ammons; at the Turkish Embassy in New York; and a concert for the New York Beethoven Society. Radio broadcasts were made for NBC by the two men, under the aegis of the fictitious Chamber Music Society of Lower Basin Street, which devoted itself each Sunday to the three "Bs," namely "barrelhouse, boogie-woogie, and the blues." One broadcast on August 18, 1941, featured Johnson and Turner performing "Goin' Away Blues" and "Roll 'Em Pete." A second broadcast on November 4 had Ammons giving a brief taster of his style with a few bars of "Shout for Joy." The chimed introduction and initial choruses followed the original Columbia recording but then broke away into a chorded walking bass and free extemporization. The pseudo-serious nature of these occasions was reflected in the pretentious continuity remark of chairman Milton Cross, the NBC announcer: "Thank you Professor Ammons until later." "Later" produced a faithful version of "Boogie-Woogie Stomp." The tempo, however, was markedly reduced when compared with earlier versions, perhaps an indication that the ill-health that was to plague Ammons throughout the remainder of his life was starting.

On one of their club engagements, Ammons and Johnson appeared at Rumbolos, a Philadelphia nightspot. At each performance a young blind man sat listening intently to their music. They were later informed that it was pianist George Shearing, who began playing boogie-woogie early in his illustrious career.

An important concert tour was made with the Count Basie Orchestra in 1941, which took place in the State Theatre of New York. It was a particularly joyous reunion for Pete Johnson, who had known Bill Basie from their time together in Kansas City. Basie revered Johnson's piano work and regularly visited the Sunset Crystal Club when Johnson was there. Basie often sat in with Johnson's small group. Their friendship had continued when Basie brought his band to New York to appear at the Famous Door. The tour with Basie lasted for sixteen days and helped to consolidate publicly the initial impact of their powerful, elemental piano style, to the extent that at least one reviewer believed they were the star attractions of the traveling package, reflecting on their superb symbiosis at the keyboard that left their audience shouting for more.[11]

Well suited as a musical team, Ammons and Johnson were also close friends. On one engagement they had to catch a train from Pennsylvania Station in New York to take them to St. Louis. As they were running late for their connection, Johnson shouted to Ammons to pick up the overcoats while he paid the cab driver. A dash along the station platform enabled them to catch the train, and as it drew out of the station they sank into their seats. The train picked up speed on a bitterly cold winter evening, and then Johnson noticed to his consternation that Ammons had picked up his own coat in the rush and left Johnson's in the cab. Such shared adventures with their attendant humor cemented their friendship. The maturing friendship was also nurtured by their complementary personalities. Sharon Pease described Johnson as a modest man who appreciated a joke; he especially enjoyed joking with Fats Waller, who drew from his endless fund of entertaining stories when he and Johnson appeared on the same bill in Los Angeles. Johnson was generous in his praise of other musicians and said that the music of Mary Lou Williams, Fats Waller, and Duke Ellington had been among his most memorable musical experiences.

Albert Ammons's personality appears to have been the antithesis of his noisy rocking piano music. He had a tranquil temperament, and family life was important to him. After recording sessions, at which he eased the strain for other musicians by playing through his own part first, he would return to his Chicago base. That his temperament did not always reflect his extroverted music is indicated by his succumbing to a nervous breakdown, probably resulting from his heavy work schedule, which required a period of recuperation in an Illinois sanatorium for thirty days. Mentioning that Albert was helping to finance his son (Edsel) through college, *Downbeat* reported that Ammons was expected back in New York immediately after Christmas. Coinciding with the absence of Ammons, Pete Johnson also had to take time off because of an injury to one of his hands.[12]

The Ammons and Johnson partnership really came to international notice with a series of very fine recordings for Victor in 1941 on which they were accompanied on drums by Jimmy Hoskins. Outstanding are the slow-paced "Barrelhouse Boogie," the frantic "Boogie-Woogie Man," and the catchy "Sixth Avenue Express"—their New York avenue of destiny connecting Carnegie Hall and the Café Society. In this last number, Ammons supplies the infectious ground rhythm for Johnson's tuneful treble phrases. Despite the undoubted success of the Victor series, which set the benchmark to which others might aspire, the two men recorded no more major duets until May 1944 when the MacGregor Radio Company issued sixteen-inch electrical transcriptions of their work. Included in this series were "Lady Be Good," "Boogie-Woogie Man," and the pop tunes "Pistol Packing Momma" and "Rhumboogie." Both the Victor and MacGregor recordings are available on *Boogie-Woogie Boys 1938–1947* (Magpie, PYCD 21).

The two men continued working as a duet, interspersing solo appearances, throughout the mid-1940s. One typical tour took in a Wisconsin nightspot called Frenchy's in October 1943 and later in February 1944. Their appearance was delayed for a week on the second occasion, because Ammons had received his induction papers for the armed services. The program drew on their repertoire of fast and medium numbers, including "Sixth Avenue Express" and "Pine Creek Boogie"—a moderately paced version—plus a duet of "Roll 'Em Pete." The young singer accompanying Ammons and Johnson was Joe Williams, a man yet to make his name with Count Basie's Orchestra, who toured with them for six weeks and, for the first time, earned one hundred and fifty dollars a week. He sang a passable version of "Roll 'Em Pete," but, not unexpectedly, without the authority that Joe Turner gave to this very personal number when it was being performed with Johnson. "Roll 'Em Pete" begins with solo choruses by Johnson but is soon extended into a duet, with Ammons joining in on the middle register of the piano with chorded accompaniment, which, in turn, allows Johnson to move higher up the keyboard. This unlikely backing for Williams restricted the piece from developing its full rhythmical potential, but it was nevertheless well received by an appreciative audience. Fortunately, John Steiner had the foresight to record the show, and the numbers have since become available on the Document label *Rare Live Cuts, Café Society* (1939) and *Airchecks, Milwaukee* (1943) (Document, DOCD-1003). During their stay at Frenchy's, the duo were also hired to perform for a private gathering by John Schaum, publisher of a boogie-woogie instruction folio and, for about fifty years, owner of a piano school on 2019 East North Avenue, some two blocks away from Frenchy's. The performers were paid twenty-five dollars each, playing on two grand pianos in the recital hall before an audience of fifty or so students and friends.[13]

Their first engagement was reported in the Green Sheet of the *Milwaukee Journal*, which also included an interview with Ammons and Johnson for the layperson on the origins of boogie-woogie and their own contributions to its development.[14] Not having a piano available in the rooming house on West Reservoir Avenue, where the two pianists were staying, made for difficulties in explaining boogie-woogie in musical terms. At one stage in the interview, Ammons rolled his fingers along the back of a davenport to demonstrate some of the bass patterns to the reporter. Speaking slowly and thoughtfully, he said that the real story of boogie-woogie lay in the importance of the left hand. At this point in the interview, Ammons left the room to fetch Johnson from a nearby restaurant where he was enjoying a meal of pork chops and fried potatoes. Johnson was more forthright in his views than Ammons, saying that it was difficult to explain boogie-woogie, which required an inherent ability to play and could not be taught. Warming to his theme, he did offer some further comments for the hard-pressed reporter, likening the bass rhythm to jungle tom-toms and the boogie-woogie style to a blues fugue, using counterpoint in the manner of Bach.

When they were due to make their second Milwaukee appearance in February 1944, a newspaper advertisement reported that they had recently completed their part in a Hollywood film *Sweet and Low Down*, a Twentieth Century Production featuring the Benny Goodman Orchestra. However, their contributions either ended up on the cutting room floor, as they do not make an appearance, or the statement was designed to stimulate publicity for their visit.

The year 1944 was a busy and productive one involving much travel. It commenced with an appearance at Symphony Hall in Evansville, Indiana, as part of a ten-day tour with the Andrews Sisters, followed by a two-day engagement at Lindsay's Sky Bar in Cleveland and a "piano battle" on four pianos in Kansas City against Julia Lee and Joshua Johnson. Local radio covered this show with fifty minutes of airtime. Both men also generously gave their time to good causes, often for minimum expenses or none at all. Many of these appearances were associated with raising money for the war effort: On December 7 they played at a War Bond Rally organized by the St. Louis Depot of the Armed Services Ordnance Department.

Descriptions of Ammons and Johnson performing at two pianos that really get inside the psyche of the two men are not readily available. One of the best was produced by Dr. S. Hayakawa following their several appearances at the Cabin in the Sky, a Chicago nightspot.[15] They were positioned at two small grand pianos, placed back-to-back, allowing them to face each other as they tore into "Jivin' the Blues," "Boogie-Woogie Prayer," and the ubiquitous "Sixth Avenue Express" to display their perfectly coordinated routine. Hayakawa observed: "Sometimes one embellishes what the other is doing. Sometimes the two pianos argue with each other . . . like brilliant but slightly demented conversationalists growing wittier and wittier as they respond to each other's brilliance. Sometimes the two pianos turn on their entire power and ganging up on the audience, mow 'em down." Throughout their performance, neither paid much attention to the other; both smiled at friends in the audience with barely a signal passing between them. The only sign of a response to the music could be seen in Ammons's blissful smile and Johnson's moving lips as if conversing with himself.

Ammons and Johnson made several trips to the West Coast for engagements at the Streets of Paris Nightclub in Hollywood Boulevard in 1943, 1944, and 1947. At the time of their first visit, Lewis was playing at Randini's, and Bob Zurke, now a solo performer, was installed at the Hangover Club in San Francisco. The shift by boogie-woogie players and other musicians from the East to the West Coast was at least in part due to the perceived opportunities to appear in films during the years when Hollywood musicals and the boogie-woogie craze coincided. Lewis played the part of a genial house decorator in the film *New Orleans*, released in 1947, a film purporting to tell the history of jazz. He ripped off "Honky Tonk Train Blues" on an old upright piano and engaged in some banter with Louis Armstrong about his "Chicago style" piano playing. None of the other two members of the trio featured in major films, and their appearances were limited to cartoons or short films such as *The Boogie-Woogie Dream*.

Much of the background information and meticulously detailed research on the making of this film was undertaken by Dr. Konrad Nowakowski in preparation for the liner notes for a record that includes the soundtrack, entitled *Pete Johnson Radio Broadcasts, Film Soundtracks, Alternate Takes (1939–c.1947)* (Document, DOCD 1009). The film was originally believed to have been made at one of the Café Society clubs, in September 1941, although Blanche Marvin, the wife of the late Mark Marvin, the film's producer, said that the filming took place at the Astoria Studios on Long Island where her husband was employed. In its complete form it runs for thirteen minutes, though it has been disassembled to make three shorter films. The four main luminaries involved in its production all had left-wing leanings and were sympathetic to the racist issues confronting African-Americans at the time. The *New Masses* magazine was also associated with financing it, as it had been involved with the Spirituals to Swing concerts. The film, directed by Hans Burger, was finally sold to the Goldberg brothers in 1944. The trade paper *Film Daily* remarked on the powerful piano work that Ammons and Johnson produced, predicting that it would be responsible for demented jitterbugs attacking the leatherette on their seats.[16] It could be seen in New York at the Metropolitan Theatre on Forty-seventh Street and as an additional attraction to the main feature film at the South Parkway Theatre Chicago starring Errol Flynn. It was mainly shown in theatres with mixed or black audiences; in December 1945, it surfaced in Harlem supporting a John Wayne film. *The Boogie-Woogie Dream* was eventually purchased by Official Films, who specialized in "soundies" (see below) and made the 16-mm film available for home-movie entertainment.

The film features Ammons and Johnson together with the Teddy Wilson Orchestra and Lena Horne. The first piece played by the duo occurs before the "dream" sequence takes place—a reference to their wish to play boogie-woogie to an audience of "highbrows"—and has Ammons clad in the white boilersuit of the painter and decorator he is pretending to be. Johnson commences this piece and Ammons goes over to another piano and joins in with him. Regrettably, they play only two choruses of this unnamed piece, which is in the manner and style of their "Foot Pedal Boogie," "Pine Creek," and "Cutting the Boogie" duets. The other number they play, announced by Lena Horne as the "Boogie-Woogie Dream," takes place during the dream part of the film and has both men in dress suits seated at their respective pianos. Ammons plays the introduction, and then both men go into action in this up-tempo, driving piece of boogie-woogie, which is a very similar sort of piece to their "Boogie-Woogie Man." Regrettably, a film editor has seen fit to excise part of the middle of this composition, and the cut and join-up has been done rather clumsily, mismatching the bar numbers (of the joined choruses) and the two different boogie bass figures, resulting in a quite audible jolt. The final choruses of "Boogie-Woogie Man" are also heard again as background music for the ending of the film. A number of the scenes from *The Boogie-Woogie Dream* were amalgamated in two short films, "My New Dress" and "Unlucky Woman," featuring Johnson, Ammons, Lena Horne, and the Teddy Wilson Orchestra.

An intriguing and potentially fertile source of music by the boogie masters has been found on the sound tracks of a series of cartoons that were made in the forties by the Walter Lanze Studios. These cartoons entitled, "Swing Symphonies," began in 1941 after the studio had made several one-shot cartoons based on popular songs such as "The Boogie-Woogie Bugle Boy of Company B" with boogie-woogie used as background music. Lanze always employed jazz musicians to make his sound tracks, among whom were Nat Cole, Jack Teagarden, and Meade Lux Lewis. Musicians were often invited to play by the firm's musical director, Darrell Calker, when they were going through a lean spell and were short of money. Bob Zurke played on the sound track of a cartoon called "Jungle Jive" in 1943 and may have been featured on other yet undiscovered sound tracks; Lewis provided sound-track music for another Lanze cartoon, "Cow Cow Boogie," in the same year. Other promising titles about which little is still known are "Boogie-Woogie Sioux" made in November 1942 and "Boogie-Woogie Man" completed in September 1943. The cartoon film "Boogie Doodle" made by Canadian director Norman McLaren used

Albert Ammons's "Boogie-Woogie Stomp" on the sound track alongside Henry "Red" Allen and J. C. Higginbotham. Cartoon sound tracks would surely continue to reward examination by enterprising researchers.

Short-lived novel entertainment in bars and diners in the 1930s and 1940s was provided by "soundies," which were short musical items played on visual jukeboxes. They permitted a film of the artist, projected on a screen, to be viewed while the music played. The Mills Novelty Company introduced the soundie jukebox, and the films were made by several companies, among which were Talkytone and RCM—this company being owned by President Roosevelt's son. Fortunately, many jazz artists were filmed before the demise of soundies in the mid-1940s when the recording companies closed down this side of their business to concentrate on the war effort.

Lewis made at least four soundies. The first, in 1942, was entitled "Spirit of Boogie-Woogie" and consisted of an accompaniment to Katherine Dunham and her dancers. The piano solo is a finely constructed, very rhythmical fast boogie-woogie. In fact there is a similarity in the style and character of the piano work of his other three soundies from 1944: "Roll 'Em," "Ain't Gonna Be Your Low Down Dog No More," and "Boogie-Woogie." Joe Turner sings the lyrics on the first two but for some reason does not make an appearance on film. Comedy is provided by Dudley Dickerson, who also mimes Turner's vocals. Other than Dunham's dancers, the visual content of the other three is negligible, consisting of a group of men and women acting and miming or dancing and shaking, which adds little to the artistic merit of Lewis's piano work. No doubt, it was intended to provide an added visual supplement to the music.

Two events conspired to prevent any further recordings being made for the national companies between 1942 and 1944. The three pianists were no less fortunate than other musicians in their loss of potential income from the recording ban imposed by J. Petrillo, president of the American Federation of Musicians. It came into force as the American government also imposed a restriction on the making of records, because the shellac was required for the war effort. Fortunately, both mandates ran concurrently. Petrillo's embargo arose from his concern for the livelihood of musicians, which he considered threatened by the spread of canned music being played on jukeboxes.

Neither Ammons nor Johnson recorded again until 1944 when normality returned. Albert resumed his recording activities with the independent Commodore Company in February. Two solos, "Boogie Rocks" and "Albert's Special Boogie," were released, and these, together with other solos, "Blues on My Mind," "Bugle Boogie" (two takes), and "Reveille Boogie," were issued in 1980. Accompanying the solos were tracks by the Rhythm Kings. Other recordings from these sessions were eventually released for the first time on the Mosaic label some forty years after they were made.

The owner of the Commodore record label was Milt Gabler. He became involved with jazz at the family business, the Commodore Music Shop, in the mid-1920s where he developed an interest in Chicago-style jazz—an up-tempo version of the original New Orleans jazz played by white musicians such as Eddie Condon (banjo), Joe Sullivan (piano), and Muggsy Spanier (cornet). His first venture into the recording field was stimulated by his business acumen. Realizing that several customers visiting the shop were asking for recordings no longer available in the record companies' catalogs, he began to reissue some of them beginning with "Pinetop's Boogie-Woogie." This initial venture, however, nearly proved costly. When he approached the owners of the recording, Vocalion, for copies, he was told that the record was no longer available but that he could order a minimum of three hundred copies for sale at sixteen cents each and sell them on his own label. He went ahead and ordered them, believing that it was a terrific record, but when they arrived from the dealer they had the Vocalion and not the Commodore label on them. To compound his difficulties, Gabler was also told by a customer that he had recently purchased a Vocalion record of the tune at a store in Times Square. When Gabler questioned the Vocalion representative how this could have occurred, he was told that as he (Gabler) had ordered three hundred copies, they reckoned it must be a good record, so they had pressed up to fifty new copies for their own dealers; a shop in Times Square had, for example, taken ten copies, leaving Gabler to cover the heavy costs of the additional records he had been obliged to purchase.

Johnson reappeared on the newly formed Capitol Company's label as pianist with a jazz group accompanying the young Peggy Lee on her first recording date. Two sides were made in January, entitled "Sugar" and "Ain't Goin' No Place" (1944). The combination of seasoned musicians Barney Bigard, Eddie Miller, and Pete Johnson in the backing group ensured a successful first recording for Peggy Lee. Lewis returned with the aforementioned selection of new compositions for the Asch label in August followed by a two-part unissued "V" Disc recording, with the title of "V" "Disc Stomp" and "Doll House Boogie." Zwingenberger in his liner notes considers part 2 of the "V" disc to represent of some of Meade's best boogie-woogie playing. "V" discs were initially issued for the entertainment of the armed forces under an arrangement with the musicians' union whereby it was agreed to destroy the masters after hostilities had ceased, in order to safeguard the royalty rights of the artists. However, a number of these "illicit" recordings have found their way onto the record market in recent years. The "V" discs, together with his soundies, cartoon sound tracks, and appearances at one of Norman Granz's Jazz at the

Philharmonic concerts and Jubilee radio shows for the American armed forces in World war II are contained in a superb collection of unusual recordings: *Meade Lux Lewis, Alternate Takes, Live Performances, Soundies, etc., 1939 to late 1940s* (Document, DOCD 5561).

By the middle of the 1940s, the three pianists were still maintaining their preeminent place as the foremost exponents of boogie-woogie piano, but they were no longer the exciting cult figures of earlier years when they made their initial assault on New York. They had now become respected entertainers who demonstrated in their piano playing that boogie-woogie was a serious and unique part of jazz music.

NOTES

1. Unattributed, "Fats Waller to Open Here on Saturday," Chicago newspaper (unknown), July 30, 1939. See also Ted Toll, "Boogie-Woogie Boys Due at Chi's Sherman with Waller," *Downbeat*, August 1939, 26.

2. John Steiner taped recollections sent to Peter Silvester circa January 30 through March 1985.

3. Ted Toll, "Chicago Gates Gripe; Boogie Trio to Split," *Downbeat*, October 1939, 21.

4. Dave Dexter Jr., "ASCAP Moguls Fluff off Lux Lewis' Bid for a Card," *Downbeat*, December 1941, 1, 21.

5. Dave Dexter Jr., "Big ASCAP Official to Bat for Meade Lux; Applied Last April," *Downbeat*, January 1942, 1, 22.

6. Jo Westheimer, "Meade Lux Lewis," *Jazz Quarterly*, Fall 1942, 11.

7. Martin T. Williams, "Lux's Boogie: On the Recording Career of Meade Lux Lewis," *Record Changer*, April 1953, 3.

8. M. Turof and J. Below, "Meade Lux Lewis—A Jazz Great," pt. 2, *Jazz Session*, November 1944, 6. This review was in two parts with the first part appearing in the October issue.

9. "Meade Lux Lewis: A Bluesman's Story," *Downbeat*, February 19, 1958, 17.

10. John Bentley, correspondence with the author, June 7, 1991.

11. H. J. Mauerer, "Boogie-Woogie Boys Steal Basie Programme," in *The Pete Johnson Story* (Bremen: Humburg, 1965), 28.

12. "Albert Ammons in Breakdown," *Downbeat*, December 1941, 1.

13. John Steiner, taped recollections and correspondence sent to the author, January 30 through March 1985.

14. Doyle K. Getter, "What Is Boogie-Woogie? Two Artists Try to Tell," *Milwaukee Journal Green Sheet*, October 11, 1943.

15. Dr. S. I. Hayakawa, "Reflections on the History of Jazz" (paper presented at the Poetry Magazine Modern Arts Series at the Arts Club of Chicago, March 17, 1945), 6.

16. K. Nowakowski, liner notes, *Pete Johnson, Radio Broadcasts, Film Soundtracks, Alternate Takes, 1939–c. 1947* (Document Records, DOCD-1009) refers to "Review of New Films: Boogie-Woogie Dream," *Film Daily*, July 7, 1944.

10

On the Crest of the Wave

In 1939, Jimmy Yancey was beginning to be known to the record-buying public. His name first came to notice when two recordings of "Yancey Special" were made by Meade Lux Lewis in 1936 and the Bob Crosby Orchestra in 1938. The Crosby recording was a novelty arrangement for the band, featuring Bob Zurke on piano. Requests for the number to be played at Crosby's engagements centered on the public's curiosity about Yancey the man, as much as an interest in the music, probably fueled by a review of "Yancey Special" in Walt Winchell's nationally syndicated newspaper column. One of the people responsible for bringing Yancey's music to the fore was the writer and musicologist William Russell (1905–1992) who, with the assistance of Meade Lux Lewis, tracked him down to his apartment at 3525 South Dearborn Street, close to Comiskey Park, the White Sox baseball field, where Yancey worked.

Bill Russell's contributions to jazz history—including his discovery and re-recording of Bunk Johnson, the New Orleans veteran trumpet player, and his definitive tome about Jelly Roll Morton—serve to remind us of the debt owed him by jazz enthusiasts. Russell's dedication in searching for the frequently obscured truths underlying the myths and his perceptive analysis of the evidence resulted in the production of several scholarly articles in early jazz literature. He first became aware of the impact of jazz music in 1929 when, as a music teacher, he listened to some of the records that his students had been playing during their lunch breaks. One particularly memorable record was the Jelly Roll Morton number "Shoe Shiner's Drag." Russell was captivated and became hooked on jazz. He was not unaware of the music, subliminally at least, as he had heard it being played on the riverboats where he lived in his home city of New Orleans. However, his violin teacher, fearing that the music might contaminate his tone, like some highly infectious disease, advised him not to listen to it. Following this revelatory experience, Russell began to collect jazz records avidly from secondhand stores and Salvation Army stalls; he even took to knocking on people's doors wherever his touring took him as a musician member of the Red Gate Players. He continued with his own musical education by studying and composing music for percussion as well as spending a period of time under Arnold Schoenberg at the University College of Los Angeles (UCLA). In 1935, he met Steve Smith, an artist, and together they started the Hot Record Exchange, which sustained his interest through buying and selling mainly vintage jazz recordings.[1]

In the period 1938–1940, Russell's brother, William Wagner, also became interested in all forms of jazz music largely through this influence. Wagner was based in Chicago studying for his master's degree and took several photographs of Jimmy Yancey, at his brother's behest, for the notes accompanying the Victor recordings of 1939. Prior to this, Russell had met many jazzmen, including Meade Lux Lewis and Albert Ammons. He had particularly enjoyed listening to the newly recorded version of "Honky Tonk Train Blues" released on Parlophone and determined to meet Lewis, but unfortunately missed him at Bratton's nightspot where Lewis had just completed an engagement there. Fortunately, he managed to catch up with him at his home where he took several photographs of Lewis and Ammons. By now, Russell had collected recordings of a number of the major boogie-woogie pianists such as Romeo Nelson and Pinetop Smith, and he had also read Hammond's articles written in the mid-1930s for *Downbeat* about Ammons and Johnson. He was similarly affected by the indifferent response of the public to their unique talents, so he decided to write an article about boogie-woogie for the European market where a growing enthusiasm for jazz had been identified. The article was sent to Hugh Panassie, editor of the French magazine *Le Jazz Hot*, and was the forerunner of the now esteemed chapter Russell wrote for the book *Jazzmen*.[2]

Early contact with Jimmy Yancey was made by letter, leading to follow-up visits by both brothers. The purpose of the correspondence was to obtain biographical information for the Victor recordings. (Jimmy had recorded for Solo Art a month before, but all but one of these recordings were issued much later.) In responding to Russell's questions on behalf of her semiliterate husband, Estelle Yancey wrote in February 18, 1940:

Dear Friend,
     I am replying to yours of the 16th and am willing to do what I can. Yes, I played in house parties. The house parties they sing and dance all kinds

of dancing and I played at the traps [Traps nightspot], the Moonlight Inn but most of all house parties. Yes I was born in Chicago and my age is 42. my parents come from Kentucky. Yes my father was a [bass?] singer and he played string music and he traveled with [a] quartet. My brother Alonzo is older than I. I developed my playing just by myself. No Bill, I just pick my own stuff for my music. Yes, every tune I play is my own. The Victor Company did not name any. They are all my own. Yes, I remember when I first started to [play]. It was about 1913—yes I have traveled from coast to coast over in England the year of 1915 when I left there at that time I was on the Orpheum Circuit. Sang and danced for the king and queen of England in Buckingham Palace. I was working on the stage when I was 10 years old. At that time I worked with "The Man From Bam" at the old Pekin theatre. I have never been south any farther than Kentucky. I have worked all in the east and west. No, I never was on any bill with Bessie Smith or Ma Rainey but was with the Cocks [Cox?] and Triffin Sisters. I met Pinetop about 1915, Cow Cow about the same time. I met Jelly Roll Morton here and on the road too. I know Albert and Lux since they were kids. I met Cripple Clarence at house parties, [indecipherable name], Stringbeans, Lotta Grady. Those were blues singers. And I am having a birthday Tuesday February 20th. Will be 42 years old. [i.e., year of birth 1898]. Mrs. Yancey sends regards. I will be here if you need a picture and your brother can get it.

Will [be] expecting an early reply.

Yours truly,

James Yancey
3525 Dearborn Street

While the tenor of the letter is probably correct, some of its contents may be inaccurate. For example, could Yancey have met Pinetop in 1915 when the latter was eleven years old? Yancey appears to have claimed 1898 as his birth date for the first time when he married Estelle in 1925, perhaps to make the four-year difference in their ages more acceptable, and he persisted with this date thereafter. Although his death certificate repeats the date, as reported by Jane Bowers,[3] she has also produced evidence of conflicting dates of birth (see chapter 4). Working from a limited information base, Bowers provides a commendable outline of Jimmy's early years in vaudeville. What is unquestionable is that Yancey proved to be a talented dancer and, like Clarence Smith, appeared in shows as a piccaninny in acts organized by Jeanette Adler. Later, in 1913, as his application to the American Embassy in London for an emergency passport shows, he was due to appear in several cities in Europe with Burt Earl, whose name also appears as Yancey's employer on his draft registration for World War I.

Russell received a further letter from the Yanceys on March 1, 1940, in response to his second letter, which had attempted to elicit more details of Jimmy's background. In it, Yancey named the cities visited on his European tour with the troupe led by Jean Adler. He also said that his father sang in shows and traveled a lot and that "Tell 'Em All about Me" was the oldest tune in his repertoire. (Recent enquiries by the author to the Royal Archives at Windsor Castle, England, and a subsequent search by one of the archivists, have revealed no additional information about the entertainment provided for the King and Queen by Bert Earl's troupe led by Jean Adler circa 1915, of which Jimmy Yancy was a member.)

The discovery of Jimmy Yancey was first mentioned in *Downbeat*[4] in a short feature article. Claiming Albert Ammons and Meade Lux Lewis as his pupils, Jimmy then stressed his longevity as a pianist of almost thirty years and opined that he would still be around in another thirty. The article presaged Yancey's recording debut on the short-lived Solo Art label with "Jimmy's Stuff" and "The Fives." The Solo Art Masters and Company files were eventually acquired by the Riverside Record Company who later issued sides that Yancey had cut for Solo Art but that had never been released. before. Further recordings were made by Yancey for the Vocalion and, as we have seen, the Victor companies in 1939—the latter being among the most absorbing sides that he ever made, with their clean technique and original ideas. No further recordings were made until 1943 when he cut several solos and accompanied Estelle's vocals on the Session label. Outstanding among these recordings are the reflectively slow-paced "At the Window" and "Eternal Blues," a previously unheard number with the Yancey stamp. The person responsible for undertaking these recordings was Phil Feathergill, who had assumed the management of the Session Record Shop in Chicago after its owner, David Bell, had been drafted into the army. Cripple Clarence Lofton and Alonzo Yancey, Jimmy's brother, were recorded at the same time, but after a considerable output of high-quality recordings, the venture was found to be too expensive and so was discontinued. The recordings of all three pianists have been preserved on *The Yancey-Lofton Sessions, Storyville, Volume 1* (SLP, 238) and *Volume 2* (SLP, 239).

It is a strange fact about Jimmy Yancey's musical career that despite his popularity as a rent-party pianist in the 1920s and 1930s, he never entered a studio during this period when sales of "race" records were at their height. It may have been his reluctance to reenter the world of professional entertainment after his early years as a dancer and his reticence that kept him out of the recording studio. Even after his deserved recognition, he still practiced on his sister's piano for a time because he did not own one.

Cow Cow Davenport came out of retirement as an entertainer on the club and concert circuits in the early 1940s. He also made several new recordings. Pianist Art Hodes was responsible for bringing his talents to the public's attention by publicizing some of Davenport's earlier achievements and a potted biography in *Jazz Record* magazine, for which he was editor. In one edition, Cow Cow claimed to have named the piano style boogie-woogie. His recollections of the period around 1917, in the same article, tend to confirm that boogie-woogie was essentially played as dance music. Several dances were fashionable at this time: "Ball in the Jack," "Walkin' the Dog," and "Jazz Dance," which Cow Cow likened to the rumba and scraunch dances of the 1940s, and to which he said he had given the collective name of boogie-woogie.[5]

Cow Cow's days as a traveling entertainer were more or less over by the mid-1930s when he moved to Cleveland to live with his sister Martha. Having now recuperated from the illness brought about by his time in prison, he began to get some movement back in his right hand again and play a little piano. He visited a show at the Grand Central Theatre on Central Avenue and was captivated by one of the artistes, Peggy Taylor (Montez), who performed a dance act with snakes. Never far from the variety halls in spirit, Davenport introduced himself to the dancer and was soon installed as her partner both in marriage and in the act. One of their first engagements together was at an Elk Convention in Cleveland. With Cow Cow wearing a cowboy hat and acting as spieler, they quickly made twenty dollars, which encouraged him to approach an agent for further bookings.

An appearance at the Cotton Club in Cincinnati was the first of several successful bookings that followed. Events did not always go smoothly, however, and the police were called out several times by anxious boarding-house owners when it was found that the snakes were being housed in a trailer in their backyard. As Cow Cow's health began to improve, he began to show an interest in music again. His first step was to contact Mayo Williams and send him some new songs. Then, in 1938, he made an appointment to visit the Decca Studios in New York where he obtained a recording contract. While in the city he met Sammy Price at the Woodside Hotel and asked him to play piano for his vocals, as he had not yet fully recovered the necessary dexterity in his fingers. Price agreed and they made a number of sides together. Among them were "I Ain't No Ice Man," "Don't You Loudmouth Me," and "The Mess Is Here" with Joe Bishop (flugel horn), Teddy Bunn (guitar), and Richard Fulbright (bass), and Price's interpretation of "Cow Cow Blues" given the title of "Railroad Blues." Cow Cow sang effectively, displaying good timing with Price's piano accompaniment. These four tunes were later released on an extended play (EP) record: *Cow Cow Davenport: This Is the Blues, Volume Six* (Brunswick, 10356).

Davenport undertook an engagement at the Plantation Club in Nashville, but this was aborted at the end of the first week of an intended four-week run, as his music was not well received; he returned to Cleveland once again. The entertainer was putting himself under considerable strain in his attempt to return to the music he loved, and in 1938 he suffered a life-threatening stroke. With careful medication, he gradually recovered, but his right hand was again affected. The initial damage had been done during the long, cold days spent as a gardener in Camp Kilby Prison. Arthritis set in, and he was never able to play the piano as effectively as he had done in his earlier years. His few club and record appearances in the 1940s were as a singer, usually accompanied by a pianist, but very occasionally he managed to produce an adequate performance using his rolling left hand and displaying his humor and showmanship. He made a guest appearance in 1940 at the Cleveland Hot Club, where he entertained an appreciative audience with "Cow Cow Blues" and "I'll Be Glad When You're Dead You Rascal You."

In 1940, at the age of forty-six, Davenport was trying unsuccessfully to gain membership of ASCAP so that he could collect copyright fees for his many published songs. His case was finally taken up by *Downbeat*, as the magazine had done for Lewis. It cited the low prices paid by publishing companies and the contracts that signed away the rights of his and other artists' compositions as evidence of the unfair treatment to which they were being subjected.[6] The feature went on to claim that several of Davenport's tunes such as "Low Down Man Blues" and "Mama Don't Allow No Easy Riders Here" had been purchased from him but were then sold on to other publishers at a profit if they showed signs of becoming popular. Other instances cited where Davenport had missed out on royalties, although given composer's credits, were his 1928 recordings of "Cow Cow Blues" and "State Street Jive," which were reissued in the 1940s in the Brunswick Collector's Series Boogie-Woogie Album. The *Downbeat* campaign was finally successful, and he was admitted to ASCAP, giving him a modest income for the remainder of his life.

Davenport was unsuccessful throughout 1942 in obtaining any form of musical employment and finished the year working as a washroom attendant at the Onyx Club on Fifty-second Street in New York. He made four sides in 1944 for Comet, the independent record company. The titles were "Run into Me" backed by "Hobson Street Rag" and "Gin Mill Stomp" with "Cow Cow's Stomp" on the reverse side. The records were favorably reviewed in *Downbeat*, which emphasized the forceful piano playing and Davenport's sincere interpretations, which was one reviewer's attempt to bring Davenport to the attention of the record-buying public. Radio appearances on the Art Hodes Show were followed by an interview with Hodes, who described him as a light-skinned African-American of short stature (5'6") with a pleasant smile.[7]

His next concert appearance was at Webster Hall in New York in December 1945, organized by Art Hodes, where he appeared on the same bill with Sidney De Paris and Albert Nicholas. He was also given a spot at the Blue Note Concert in the town hall during the same month, on this occasion with Sidney Bechet and Sid Catlett, members of the Art Hodes' Hot Seven. Cow Cow's contribution was limited to singing "That Aint Right." One reviewer asserted that he was capable of making the toughest statement in the gentlest manner. It would appear that he had now obtained effective control of his right hand for piano playing by the time of this concert but was prevented from doing so because he was not a member of the musicians' union. In June 1946, he assisted Rudi Blesh to locate Montana Taylor in Cleveland, resulting in Taylor's making his illustrious sides for the Circle label. In the same year, Cow Cow joined forces with Sonny Terry to record "Back Water Blues" and "Cake Walkin' Babies" for the JR label with the Art Hodes Stuyvesant Casino Band. Shortly after these recordings, he finally retired and returned to Cleveland where he took employment at Thompson Products, a defense plant, and remained in their employment until his death in December 1955. So came to an end a gloriously varied musical career that had spanned the ragtime era, vaudeville engagements, and, of course, boogie-woogie.

In Chicago, the South Side legacy was carried on by pianists of all shades. Everyone had one or two boogie-woogie numbers in their repertoire. Like Earl Hines, who performed "Boogie-Woogie on St. Louis Blues," they were content with a token item when a request came along. Those remembered by John Steiner were Max Miller, Floyd Bean, Jimmy Flowers, Cass Simpson, and Bob Crum—who was credited with the two soundies "Adventure in Boogie Woogie" and "Our Waltz." On the north side of Chicago, Mel Henke was reputed to be the fastest technically and, musically, the best educated pianist who based his style on that of Bob Zurke. Henke developed boogie-woogie into a production number by introducing variants of it into an otherwise straight jazz number. Another pianist with a forceful piano style was Tut Soper, who employed boogie-woogie with fluency. His interpretations were mainly of the walking-bass variety with short, punctuated treble figures. When Harry James was carrying Albert Ammons and Pete Johnson as part of his touring show, the pianist with the James Orchestra was Jack Gardner. Not surprisingly, his approach to boogie-woogie was modeled on Pete Johnson, using simple bass figures and limited movement in the treble half of the keyboard. The best acknowledged white pianist who played boogie-woogie and the blues with the touch of an African-American, however, was Art Hodes who left Chicago for New York in 1938 before returning in 1950.

Clarence Lofton was still active in his Halstead Street haunts in 1940. His recovery after a period of hospitalization was noted in George Hoefer's column in *Downbeat*.[8] Lofton was also reported as complaining that Big Bill Broonzy had stolen his blues. This was a reference to recordings by Broonzy, now a popular Vocalion artist, which Lofton averred had been taken from his 1935 recordings when Broonzy had accompanied him on such numbers as "Monkey Man Blues" and "Brown Skin Gals." It was also revealed that Lofton had at one time been employed as a shipping clerk for the CB and Q Railway Company when he first arrived in Chicago in 1917 but had played piano regularly at Schiller's Café for the last twenty-five years. George Hoefer would report to John Steiner, "Clarence has a new tune this year," and they would go and search him out to hear it. Clarence's repertoire had never been large, and by 1940 he had rearranged and given new titles to certain of his numbers, presumably in an attempt to maintain public interest: "Strut That Thing" was now "I Don't Know" with added lyrics, and "Policy Blues" and "Baby I'm Going to Take You on Out to the Outskirts of Town" were also revamped.

After the Second World War, Lofton played strictly for his own entertainment and for friends. He was not in regular employment and got by on tips and handouts. Dick Mushlitz, a self-confessed jazz addict, left Evansville in his late teens and traveled to Chicago in search of the music he loved. The year was 1946, and Mushlitz wandered round the South Side carrying a washboard. As he was passing a run-down bar near Forty-seventh and South Side Street, the sounds of boogie-woogie came from within. He entered the bar to find he was the only white person present and listened to the "Crippled One" playing his tunes. The arrival of Mushlitz had stopped the conversation, but without further consideration Mushlitz sat down by the piano and began accompanying on his washboard. No introductions were necessary; the music provided the bond. Mushlitz remembers the unusual rhythms and irregular bar lengths that made it difficult for him to provide a suitable backing on the washboard. Though in contact with Lofton over the next four or so years, Mushlitz never was able to get to know him well enough other than as a casual acquaintance.[9]

Bill Russell kept in touch with Lofton for several years, having first heard him at the Big Apple Tavern. Meade Lux Lewis had advised him to visit there in order to meet the "Lame One," as he was affectionately known. Clarence was then living at 4726 South State Street. William Wagner also visited the tavern and recalls Lofton having two drummers in attendance so that he would always have an accompaniment if one of them became too drunk to play. Wagner reiterates Russell's description of Clarence in full flight, holding his hands above his head, while circling the piano stool and picking up on the beat with snapping fingers. Wagner thought Lofton was a natural extrovert, outgoing with a very interesting personality. What you saw and heard was the real Clarence Lofton.[10]

One thing was certain: Lofton could be very unpredictable and idiosyncratic, but this only added to his charm. Sometime in 1952, Russell took two of his female students to hear him play at a summer fair in a west-side Chicago suburb. Clarence introduced all his own numbers and provided the audience with a very effective historical background of their genesis. After talking about one tune that he was about to play, Clarence announced some sort of folksy aphorism that everyone was familiar with, and just before striking the keys, grunted "Shakespeare." Naturally, this brought the house down. As Russell remarked: "We were astonished because we didn't think he would ever have heard of Shakespeare, but he wasn't really as uneducated as people thought."[11]

It is indicative of the obscure life he led that two conflicting years were initially mentioned for Lofton's death. Originally the year was thought to be 1961, but Erwin Helfer, a pianist friend and mentee of Lofton, provided the accurate date of January 8, 1957, and the place as Cook County Hospital in Chicago, following the receipt of a letter from Lofton's wife Estelle from her home at 4750 South Drexel.[12] With his death a gifted and original entertainer vacated the Chicago music scene.

Two accolades came to Albert Ammons in 1945, both from unexpected sources. The first was an invitation to give a recital to members of the music department and students at Harvard and Columbia universities. The seal of approval was given to his work after the recital at Columbia when he was awarded an honorary doctorate. The other invitation must have been equally pleasurable, because no less a personage than the newly elected president, Harry S. Truman—a devotee of the piano—requested Albert's attendance at his presidential inauguration party in Washington in 1949. Albert was joined at the piano on several numbers by Elliot Paul, a capable classical pianist. It was with justification that Ammons had "Albert C. Ammons—King of Boogie-Woogie" emblazoned on his business card.

The final years of the 1940s were spent by Ammons working around Chicago and making recordings. He reduced his touring commitments, and one of the last of these, in the West Coast, was probably at the Streets of Paris in 1947. In 1948, he appeared in a major concert at the Civic Opera Theatre in Chicago, sharing the bill with Jimmy Yancey. Tom Harris, who attended the concert, carried in his memory the picture of Albert's diamond ring dancing in the spotlight as he played his basses. One of Ammons's last club engagements in Chicago was at the Beehive Club, situated on the South Side. He and Yancey shared the intermission piano spots, which they alternated with the house band consisting of Miff Mole (leader and trombone), Darnel Howard (clarinet), Booker Washington (drums), and Don Ewell (piano). Both men had played the Beehive on earlier occasions. Jimmy sometimes replaced Albert and would remain for a month at a time. He made at least one guest appearance on the broadcasts of the Sunday jam sessions from the club. During this time, stride pianist Don Ewell began to show an interest in the boogie-woogie style for perhaps the first time, although he told Charlie Booty, a contemporary boogie-woogie pianist, that he only ever played it when he was drunk. Ewell soon developed a fine, sensitive version of the "Yancey Special."

Albert's pace of life certainly slowed down, perhaps mellowing as he got older. His interests were very family-centered at this time. Edsel Ammons's relationship with his father deepened, and they were able to share many confidences. Albert also spoke with muted pride to John Steiner about his younger son Gene's brilliance as a saxophonist while expressing a father's concern at his growing dependence on drugs. He also regretted disturbing his family as they slept, because musical ideas frequently came to him at night, necessitating him trying them out on the piano. Naturally, with Albert at the keyboard very few people slept.

As the decade drew to a close, Ammons found himself in the strange position of being a talented international artist in receipt of intermittent payment from recordings and appearances at prestigious concerts and clubs, but who was, nevertheless, obliged to seek work in lesser establishments or by other means in order to remain financially solvent, between these events. These circumstances were exacerbated by the worldwide diminishing popularity of boogie-woogie, which upset him greatly, and his reluctance, or inability, to travel beyond Chicago for work. Tom Harris and friends, all in their teens, arranged for Ammons to play for them privately. A fee was agreed and he was taken to play on a Steinway piano at the home of one of the group. Harris describes Ammons as a "stomper" who played so powerfully that the neighbors complained of the noise to the extent that it became necessary to place a pillow under his foot.[13] Between engagements, Albert worked as a private detective and was known to carry a gun. Whether this was to support the detective work is not known, but he was not averse to waving it lightheartedly at friends and family with misplaced humor. He claimed to have learned how to carry out detective work by listening to *Dragnet*, the radio series about a private sleuth.[14]

Ammons's career took an upward turn in 1945. At the beginning of that year he recorded for the Mercury Company a mixture of popular songs that included "Margie" and "In a Little Spanish Town," as well as the original compositions "The Clipper," "Rhythm Boogie," and "The Bear Den Boogie." In excess of thirty numbers were laid down in the three years to 1948 by Ammons and the Rhythm Kings, with the sessions producing a heady mix of strong basses and cleanly executed treble work for which he was renowned. He was reunited with two stalwarts from his earlier group, Ike Perkins (clarinet) and Israel Crosby (bass)—who wore protective gloves when playing his instrument. All his Mercury recordings have been made available on what has become a rare set of seven CDs: *The 1940s Mercury Sessions* (Verve, 525 609-2). A more accessible cross-section of fifteen of the popular and original numbers can be found on *Back Beat, The Rhythm of the Blues, Volume 2: Albert Ammons* (Mercury, 510 286-2). Of particular merit are the pared-down "Suitcase Blues," the delicately poignant World War I tune "The Roses of Picardy," the strong unison playing of the band on "Ammons's Stomp," and the powerfully rocking "Tuxedo Boogie." Several of these sides offer a firm pointer to the rhythm and blues conception toward which boogie-woogie music was moving. With the exception of "Baltimore Breakdown," the only missing feature in the instrumental balance is a lyrical and strident tenor saxophone lead. In the middle of this productive Mercury period, Ammons appeared on the National and Savoy labels in 1946, sharing the piano spot with Pete Johnson and others, as a member of a group backing Joe Turner. These are available on a two-record set, *Roots of Rock and Roll: Big Joe Turner* (Savoy, SJL 2223).

Ammons then became staff pianist with the Lionel Hampton Orchestra in 1949 and was featured on the studio recordings of that year. It is not certain if it was originally intended for him to fill the piano chair vacated by Milt Buckner, who left Hampton's band in September 1948 to form his own sextet but, after Ammons had died, rejoined it in 1950. Ammons played piano on seven numbers with Hampton, the best being "Chicken Shack Boogie," with his piano leading the band in dynamic fashion. On other tracks, "New Central Avenue Breakdown" and "Benson's Boogie," Ammons and Hampton inspire each other with a series of call-and-response duets between vibraphone and piano. A selection can be found on *The Most Important Recordings of Lionel Hampton* (Official Records, CD 83059 [1] and [2]).

Ammons was at the top of his creative powers in all these recordings. There was no falling away in his expression or of the inventiveness of his ideas, all the more tragic because of his death at the end of 1949 on December 5. His death came quickly. Only four days earlier, he had been listening to Jimmy Yancey and Don Ewell in Yancey's apartment, but it was evident that his health was failing because he was only capable of playing one number, having recently regained the use in his hands after a temporary paralysis. Before his demise, he had been working at a piano bar on East Forty-seventh Street dressed as ever in one of his fashionable pinstriped suits. After playing a few numbers, he was clearly very sick and had to return home abruptly with Dorsey, his valet. As he lay on the couch, he looked at Samella Ellis, his niece, complaining that he did not feel too good. An ambulance was called, but it was too late because Albert was already dead. A fuller account of these events appears in Christopher Page's book on Ammons.[15]

Albert's death was reported in the *New York Times*,[16] and an obituary was written by George Hoefer in *Downbeat* in which Albert's esteemed position as a top jazz pianist was registered. It is Hoefer's final thoughts, however, that truly reflect the public's joyous appreciation of the boogie-woogie legacy that Albert left them in his music, and the long service he gave to the cause of jazz.[17]

In the year after Albert Ammons's death, there was an important court case involving several boogie-woogie pianists who were called as witnesses to testify in a copyright dispute over the habanera bass pattern used by Meade Lux Lewis in his composition "Yancey Special," and generally attributed to the influence of Jimmy Yancey. Bill Russell became involved as an expert defense witness for the record company, at the request of Momma Yancey. Shortly before his death in 1992, Russell set down his personal recollections of the case for this author. Though some of the detail differs from a report of the trial in *Billboard*, the essence is common to both versions.[18]

In 1949, the Miracle Record Company released a record of "Tenderly," a popular hit that sold many copies. As it was the very first record of the tune, it became a sort of regular standard for jazz musicians. The backing was a boogie-woogie number called "Long Gone," which used the same bass (but only the bass) as that of "Yancey Special" that is found in Meade Lux Lewis's 1936 recording with Decca. The Shapiro Publishing Company, the publishers of the "Yancey Special," decided that they were entitled to collect a royalty fee of two cents for each copy of the record, so they sued the Miracle Record Company and had Meade Lux Lewis as their star witness. They also retained the services of Dave Peyton, the music editor of the *Chicago Defender* newspaper as a witness. Miracle was a very small company in Chicago that just happened to get that one good, popular record. They hired Jimmy and Momma Yancey and Bill Russell as their defense witnesses and rounded up all the pianists they could find who could confirm that they had heard Jimmy Yancey playing the bass in question over many years.

The court case began in November 1949 with a deposition at a lawyer's office in Chicago, where both sides were required to make sworn statements that were taped as evidence. It was one of the last appearances made by Ammons, who, after giving his evidence, died shortly afterward. The trial finally got under way in 1950 and involved Russell in making three trips to Chicago. Among the pianists asked to give evidence by the Yanceys were Lofton and Suggs.

Meade Lux Lewis recorded "Yancey Special" for Decca in 1936 and several years before in 1930 had used some of the "Yancey Special" material,

including the bass, to accompany George Hannah's vocal on his recording of "Freakish Man Blues" for Paramount. It was not copyrighted on
either of these occasions. Subsequently, Bob Crosby's band recorded the
"Yancey Special" for Decca in 1938, and Shapiro became interested to the
extent that they purchased it from Lewis and copyrighted it themselves.
However, by that time it was already too late, as Russell explains: "There
is a technicality, in this country at least, that if a phonograph record is
issued before a tune is copyrighted, it is automatically thrown into the
public domain and that's what happened to the 'Yancey Special.'"

None of the lawyers appeared to appreciate this until Russell mentioned
at the deposition that he owned a copy of Lewis's recording of "Yancey
Special" and produced the Decca catalog that dated it as June 1936. The
catalog and his copy of the record were used later as exhibits in the
trial. On the basis of this temporal sequence, the bass pattern of "Yancey
Special" was certainly in the public domain, but there was another factor
that swung the decision in favor of Miracle. This same bass pattern had
appeared in some of the choruses of "Hamp's Boogie Woogie" (1944), a
recording also released by Decca some years before the trial, but Shapiro
had not sued that record company for its use. Their case could not therefore be upheld in law because all parties using the bass should rightfully
have been sued.

The case proceeded with the pianist witnesses listening to various
tunes in order to identify the basses they had heard Jimmy Yancey or
some other pianist playing, a ritual that was repeated each time a new
witness arrived, much to the apparent disgust of the judge who Russell
felt did not appear to enjoy the music very much anyway.

Clarence Lofton proved to be a very good witness for the defense. As he
was an eccentric and always very flamboyant in his speech, nobody could
predict what he would say. When the time came for him to take the stand,
he was asked when he had first heard the bass and who had written it.
He was very positive and said, "I wrote that." He was so effective in his
confirmation of ownership and his claim that he had heard just about everybody else playing it that he supported the defense case a great deal.

Although Meade Lux Lewis was on the opposite side to all the other
pianists, they seemed to get along all right and would meet before and
after the day's events. Meade said in court that the "Yancey Special" just
referred to some name that he had picked out of "the clear." He just happened to think of a name and used it. Russell was obliged to dispute this
interpretation, as he had originally believed that the "Yancey Special"
was another train piece, similar to the "Honky Tonk Train Blues." He
had asked Meade what it meant when he first met him and been told that
it referred to Jimmy Yancey. Shortly afterward, having told Russell that
he had known Jimmy when he was a young boy, he took him to meet

Yancey. Russell took no expenses for his court appearances, proving to be a man of impeccable character to the end.

Judgment was finally given in favor of the Miracle Company in March 1950, with the judge's clinical summing-up that the bass figure in both "Yancey Special" and "Long Gone" was "old in musical art and trite," calling it "an exercise of mechanical skill and not of creative musical composition." He judged that the treble portion of both numbers contained the melody.[19] The court case was a certain reminder of how far this primitive piano form, with its "folksy" roots, had entered the commercial world of legal and financial strictures.

NOTES

1. William Russell, taped recollections sent to the author, February 2, 1991.

2. W. Russell, "Boogie-Woogie," in *Jazzmen*, ed. F. Ramsay and C. E. Smith (London: Sidgwick and Jackson, 1958), 183–205.

3. Jane M. Bowers, "The Enigma of Jimmy Yancey's Early Years: Notes toward a Biography," *American Music* 24, no. 2 (Summer 2006): 133–71.

4. "Jimmy Yancey Still Pounding Keys," *Downbeat*, October 13, 1939, 5.

5. Cow Cow Davenport, "Cow Cow and the Boogie-Woogie," *Jazz Record*, no. 5 (April 15, 1943): 3.

6. Carlton Brown, "Cow Cow Odyssey Colorful but Tragic," *Downbeat*, December 1945, 14–15.

7. Art Hodes, "Cow Cow Davenport," *Music Memories and Jazz Report* 4, no. 1 (Spring 1964): 15.

8. George Hoefer Jr., The Hot Box: A Column for Record Collectors, *Downbeat*, July 15, 1940, 15.

9. Dick Mushlitz, written and taped recollections sent to the author, January 11, 1986.

10. W. Wagner, taped recollections sent to the author, December 5, 1999.

11. William Russell, taped recollections sent to the author, 1991.

12. Letter from Estelle Lofton to Erwin Helfer, February 14, 1957.

13. Tom Harris, taped recollections sent to the author circa June 1985.

14. C. Page, *Boogie Woogie Stomp: Albert Ammons and His Music* (Cleveland: North Ohio Jazz Society, 1997), 159, 161.

15. Page, *Boogie-Woogie Stomp*, 189–90.

16. "Albert C. Ammons, 42, Jazz Pianist, Is Dead," *New York Times*, December 4, 1949.

17. George Hoefer, "Albert Ammons Left Jazz Big Legacy, Says Hoefer," The Hot Box: A Column for Record Collectors, *Downbeat*, February 13, 1950, 11.

18. Galen Gart, *First Pressings: The History of Rhythm and Blues: Special 1950 Volume* (Milford, NH: Big Nickel Publications, 1993), 4, 29, 46.

19. Gart, *First Pressings*, 29, 46.

11

The Parting of the Ways:
Rhythm and Blues
and Big-Band Boogie

It will be recalled that one of the sources from which boogie-woogie developed was the piano accompaniments to blues vocalists, but in progressing from jukes and lumber camps in the southwestern territories to clubs and dives in the Midwest and North, piano players sometimes joined other musicians to make music. Small bands frequently provided music for dancing and were known as hokum, skiffle, or spasm bands, which suggests the type of freely improvised music they played. These were more often blues, but it was not unusual for their programs to include one or two strictly instrumental numbers with a pronounced boogie beat, in sound at least if not in name. Instruments were homemade from anything that could be struck, plucked, or blown, including suitcases substituting for drums or washboards providing a staccato rhythm when played with thimbles on the fingers. A distinctive resonant sound could be achieved by blowing across a large jug and a more melodic noise produced from a kazoo and a trumpet mouthpiece held in cupped hands. By the time groups were being recorded for the race series in the late 1920s and 1930s, many of the improvised instruments had been discarded and replaced by traditional ones. Small bands were particularly active in the cities of the southern states. Dallas, Texas, for example, supported several in the late twenties. A central figure was Billiken Johnson, rotund and clownlike, who was featured on many of the records of the period. He was a colorful and amusing singer who could also contribute various vocal effects on records. His whistle can be heard on a train blues entitled "Sun Beam Blues" (1927) together with the piano playing of Willie Tyson, the bass accompaniment of Octave Gaspard, and the singing of Fred

Adams. Another group active in the Atlanta region of Georgia, known as the Blue Harmony Boys, recorded a number called "Holy Roll" (1931) on which Rufus Quillian plays a gospel-inflected piano accompaniment to his own singing and the background harmonies of his brothers Ben and James McCary. These are but two examples of the many small groups that entertained at dances and made records in the American territories.

More recent recordings by small groups with a pronounced boogie-woogie rhythm date from 1946 for the Circle Record Company made by Montana Taylor and Chippie Hill, who sings the vocals on "Mistreatin' Mr. Dupree" and "Jailhouse." These numbers serve as marvelous reminders of the tightly knit group sound that could be produced by talented musicians. The driving piano playing and animated singing are admirably supported by unknown washboard and kazoo players. Chippie Hill also appears on "Charleston Blues" in the company of J. H. (Mr. Freddie) Shayne on piano and an unknown cornet player.

An early example of supportive ensemble playing using traditional instruments can be heard on "Pitchin' Boogie" (1929), made by the popular Will Ezell for the Paramount Company for whom Ezell worked as house pianist. The title is a colloquialism for a rent party and was probably chosen to capitalize on the success of Clarence Smith's recording made for the Vocalion Company and released some eight months earlier. It is a fast piece with lyrics sung by Ezell about a wild party (a boogie-woogie) replete with moonshine and beer. There is even a thinly veiled reference to "a little girl with a green dress on." Behind his vocal choruses, Ezell beats out an insistent rhythm and some unusually melodious right-hand phrases. The most interesting feature about this record and another one entitled "Just Can't Stay Here" made at the same session is the way in which the cornet, guitar, and tambourine provide the ground rhythm to the featured piano by repeating simple phrases or riffs. The riff was a technique used by the blues-playing bands of Count Basie and others in Kansas for building up tension. It later became a feature of white swing bands and was used in many of their standard and boogie-woogie numbers for the same purpose. Ezell's compositions were certainly not the first to make use of riffs, but, as early examples on record, they point to the beginnings of section work as a support to boogie-woogie piano playing.

At this point in time, the mid-thirties, boogie-woogie ensemble playing bifurcated and proceeded along one of two main directions. The first route maintained contact with the blues and led, finally, into rhythm and blues, rock and roll, and the electric guitar playing of blues bands in Chicago and other centers during the 1950s and 1960s. The second route gradually removed boogie from the blues and transposed it into an orchestral form that many of the swing bands adopted. While the former route provided nourishment, the latter one, apart from one or two inter-esting flurries, took boogie-woogie into a commercial cul-de-sac where it finally perished, the victim of exploitation and overexposure. Events are never as clear-cut as this, however, and cross-fertilization across these two major directions did occur. For example, Albert Ammons worked as the house pianist with the Lionel Hampton band in the late 1940s; both Ammons and Johnson recorded with Harry James; and, as we have seen, all three members of the Trio were guests on the Caravan Show, subsequently released as recordings featuring the Benny Goodman band. Similarly, Louis Jordan was able to bring the precision of big-band section work, learned with the Chick Webb band, to the rhythm-and-blues play-ing of his Tympany Five.

All three of the accepted exponents of boogie piano, Ammons, Johnson, and Lewis, did most of their ensemble work in the company of musicians who had a feeling for the blues. Not surprisingly, Ammons and Johnson made more recordings as members of bands than did Lewis, who held fast to his conviction that he was, in the main, a solo performer. Ammons and Johnson never strayed too far from the blues and probably made important contributions, in their separate ways, to the rise of rhythm-and-blues music. There were few better models for the aspiring rhythm-and-blues musician than the hypnotic and insistent piano playing of Pete Johnson underlying Joe Turner's vibrant blues shouting on "Roll 'Em Pete" or Ammons's stamp marking the piano playing of "Fats" Domino on his cover version of Albert's "Swanee River Boogie." Lewis lost his way to some extent in a plethora of commercial recordings far removed from his real talents—but that is a story yet to be told.

Small-band boogie-woogie was already being brought to a sophisti-cated level by Ammons and his Rhythm Kings in the mid- and late 1930s. At Hills Tavern on Vincennes, Chicago, he was featured in a small back room on a piano with the mandolin attachment and supported by Johnny Lewis on drums. He commanded an increasingly discerning coterie who draped themselves over the tubular bar stools to listen to his playing in the basement of the It Club on Fifty-fifth and Michigan. His years of experience finally paid off at Club De Lisa where he appeared with his five-piece band. Some of Ammons's best-recorded ensemble work was made for the Commodore Company in 1944 with Oran Page (trumpet), Don Byas (tenor sax), Vic Dickenson (trombone), Sid Catlett (drums), and Israel Crosby (bass). The outcome is a series of animated tracks that express the deeply ingrained feeling that they all possessed for the blues as a medium for both sensitive ensemble work and hot, self-indulgent solos. The numbers range from the slow and deeply felt "Blues in the Groove" to "Jammin' the Boogie," an up-tempo number driven along by the masterful Catlett accents and Ammons's piano. His solo passages in this latter piece vary between fast-fingered basses and thunderous sections of walking bass that underpin cleanly executed arpeggios and fast trills in the treble. These numbers are probably some of the best that Ammons ever made with a group and they remove any lingering doubts that boogie-woogie cannot be successfully interpreted by small groups of talented musicians, and the genre enhanced in the process. The most important of these recordings are available on *Boogie Woogie and the Blues: Albert Ammons Rhythm Kings and Piano Solos* (Commodore XFL 15357). Equally good are his recordings made for the National Company with Joe Turner in 1946. Two tracks, "Miss Brown Blues" and "Sally Zu Zazz," are comparable with the best that Turner recorded with Johnson. There were occasions, however, when even the magic of Ammons was sorely tested to rescue some of the more inconsequential ventures undertaken for the Mercury label, which were probably designed to pay the rent. Even though they are not the most stimulating sides recorded by Ammons, they have a historical significance and demonstrate that even the most talented of boogie pianists had to play popular numbers with a boogie beat in order to stay in the public eye at a time when every pianist was trying his hand at it. One of the redeeming features of the Mercury recordings is the skillful way in which Ammons retains his boogie-woogie credibility within the medium of popular tunes by stating the melody in a tasteful introduction before moving into one of his typical improvisations and closing with the melody at the end of the recording. At about this time in his career, Ammons composed a number that was recorded for the Mercury label and given the title of "Mr. Bell's Boogie," giving, perhaps, an unintended immortality, in music at least, to the name of the man who shot Pinetop Smith.

There is little argument that Pete Johnson's most interesting ensemble playing was done in the company of Joe Turner on their recordings for the National label in 1945. Johnson's versatility at the piano is clearly demonstrated in a selection of sides that he did for this company. His accompaniment behind Turner on "S. K. Blues" is flowing and lyrical in the manner of Teddy Wilson. Frankie Newton (trumpet) and Don Byas (tenor sax) contribute sparkling solos as well. In January 1946, he made further sides on the Savoy label with varied personnel that included Oran Page (trumpet), Clyde Bernhardt (trombone), Don Stovall (alto), and Budd Johnson (tenor). On "1280 Stomp," Johnson produces some rolling eight to the bar, which pushes the other musicians hard. This side is really a vehicle for Johnson's walking bass and high treble work, and apart from two brief solos on alto and tenor, the other members of the band are content to give support by riffing behind the piano. At a further session later in that month, he joined forces with Oran Page (trumpet), J. C. Higginbotham (trombone), Albert Nicholas (clarinet), Ben Webster (tenor), and J. C. Heard (drums). This unusual series depicted a housewarming at Johnson's house. The personnel was gradually increased on each record from the solo piano and drums on "Mr. Drum Meets Mr. Piano" to the full group on "Pete's Housewarming." On all tracks Johnson displays a sure touch, effortless swing, and metronomic tempo, features of his craft that made him so popular with other musicians. In 1947, he recorded "Minuet Boogie," "66 Stomp," and "Pete Kay Boogie" accompanied by bass, drums, and guitar for the Apollo label in Hollywood. Johnson was known to be fond of "66 Stomp," which is executed in a fast stride. The piece is also tinged with boppish tones, reflecting the emergence of this style during this period. Overall, these sides have less musical content than those made for the National label and in comparison sound somewhat sterile. The full collection of Savoy recordings are included on *All Star Swing Groups: Pete Johnson, Cozy Cole* (Savoy, SJL 2218).

Pete Johnson played, and made recordings with, more small groups and orchestras than it would be possible to review in this chapter. He recorded with the Jo Jones Orchestra, Jimmy Rushing, and Crown Prince Waterford. He worked with Turner on the West Coast between 1947 and 1950, leading bands with a marked Kansas City sound. He flirted with pop boogie, making a record for the Capitol Company with Ella Mae Morse entitled "Early in the Morning," but it was never released. Two titles of numbers recorded in 1947 suggest that he was anticipating rhythm and blues and developments in rock music by a few years. These titles are "Rock and Roll Boogie" and, in the company of Joe Turner (alias Big Vernon), a two-part version of "Around the Clock." This latter number and earlier ones with Turner can be found on *Joe Turner: Boogie Woogie and More* (Official, 6028). Without doubt, Johnson was the most experienced band musician of the three boogie stylists. He was comfortable in the company of other musicians and was stimulated by them. His versatility, as we have seen, permitted him to submerge his piano in the rhythm section when it was necessary to do so and to ride out in solo passages when the opportunities presented themselves.

Meade Lewis made no significant contribution to ensemble boogie as a piano player, but his compositions, as we shall see, were highly influential in shaping the style and sound of swing bands in the late 1930s and 1940s. Lewis made his most important contribution to small-group jazz on a series of recordings for the Blue Note label as a member of the Edmond Hall Celeste Quartet. He was credited as the composer of the five issued sides that were not boogie-woogie and can best be described as "chamber jazz." In their way they are classics. The group was modeled on the successful Goodman Quartet with Edmond Hall on clarinet, schooled in the New Orleans tradition, and still playing an old Albert system instrument. The guitarist is Charlie Christian, more commonly associated with the new school of bop players and, on these recordings, using an acoustic guitar. The keyboard player is Lewis who is heard only on celeste, producing from that instrument a uniquely chattering and melodious tone, which helps to give the music such an interesting texture. The group is completed by the ubiquitous Israel Crosby as the bassist who, like Lewis, was a veteran of the Chicago South Side blues and boogie scene. The group produces high levels of sustained improvisation, which, given the apparently ill-assorted members, was something of a revelation to those critics who praised the results. The success of the recordings owe everything to the superlative handling of the blues form and the relaxed manner of the four men. They were made in New York in February 1941, and the set comprises five numbers: "Jammin' in Four," "Edmond Hall Blues," "Profoundly Blue," "Profoundly Blue No. 2," and the appropriately named "Celestial Express." Before making these sides, Lewis had already ventured beyond boogie-woogie to appear successfully with Sidney Bechet on a recording of "Summertime" made for Blue Note in 1939. Four of these small-group numbers and a selection of Lewis's early recordings, from the Blue Note series, are available on *Meade "Lux" Lewis: Boogies and Blues* (Topaz, TPZ 1069).

Sammy Price (1908–1990) confirmed his reputation for playing good boogie-woogie in the 1940s when he was engaged to appear at Café Society Downtown. Constant requests to play in the style honed his existing technique to the point where he became a recognized practitioner of the art. In addition to his solo work, he led several successful small bands during the decade. His background was atypical of many of the boogie-woogie pianists in that he could read music well and was an all-around musician. He never made quite the impact with the public that his solo work deserved, in this period of his career, until he took up extended residencies in France and Switzerland where he built up a big following both as a soloist and leader of the "Bluesicians" (1955) and as pianist in bands led by Mezz Mezzrow (1948) and Sidney Bechet, who were already domiciled in France.

Price spent his formative years in Dallas to where his family relocated in 1917 when he was nine years old. In addition to early musical training on alto, trumpet, and piano, Price was adept at dancing and, like Clarence Smith and Jimmy Yancey before him, joined vaudeville shows as a pianist and dancer after winning the Texas State Charleston competition in 1923. One early experience was as dancer with the territory band of Alphonso Trent. Returning to Dallas, Price formed the first of his bands and made his initial recording there. A move to Kansas City in 1930 proved significant in that Count Basie, Pete Johnson, Mary Lou Williams, and others added to his understanding of jazz piano. He later moved to New York in 1938, believing his opportunities would be greater there.

Price played with several small combinations, including groups run by Oran Page and Stuff Smith before moving to the Café Society nightspot. At the same time, he was employed by the Decca Record Company as one of their house pianists to accompany blues singers on the company's Sepia label. Some he recorded with were Georgia White, Johnny Temple, and Bea Booze, the girl who in the opinion of many critics recorded the definitive version of "See See Rider." Later, he gave superlative gospel piano support on many recordings by Sister Rosetta Tharpe and Marie Knight. Because he was under contract to Decca, some of his recordings were made under the pseudonym Jimmy Blythe Jr., which served to hide his identity but not his talents from a wider public.

When he was at Café Society, Sammy Price was to some extent in the shadow of the three giants, but he did compose some numbers that were issued in a piano album by the Leeds Music Company. However, it is with his Bluesicians, from the early 1940s, in recordings made for Decca that Sammy Price put down early markers for the evolving rhythm-and-blues style. Among these recordings is "Frantic" (1942), led by Price's highly percussive but relatively simple boogie piano style. It is a fast piece with trumpet, alto, and tenor saxophones in unison picking up the riffed melody from his piano before stretching out on their own in fine blues solos. "Boogie-Woogie Moan" (1941) features Price playing a taut bass on piano that acts as a ground rhythm for some pleasing muted trumpet playing and restrained solos on the tenor. The section work on this record is cleanly executed, giving the piece a particularly interesting tension and sense of foreboding through its sensuous, rather dreamy blues tonality. In contrast to these boogie-woogie pieces, Price demonstrates his wide-ranging piano skills with a nod toward Teddy Wilson on "It's All Right Jack" and to Basie on the sparsely economical "I Know How to Do It." He offers his own send-up of the Will Bradley success with "Lead Me Daddy Straight to the Bar." Sammy Price wrote a boogie primer for intending players of the style, but his more significant writing was reserved for his autobiography "What Do They Want?" released shortly before his death. A selection of Price's early work is on *Sam Price and His Texas Bluesicians* ("Whiskey, Woman and . . ." Record Company, KM 704).

Other groups in the 1940s were also producing a bluesy tone, often drawing on boogie-woogie rhythms to create this effect. Most comprised African-American musicians, and in time the fusion of swing, jazz, and blues elements crystallized into a form known as rhythm and blues, with its epicenter in Los Angeles (LA) and extending along the West Coast of America. The generic title for the music seems to have come from *Billboard*, the music trade paper, which overnight changed the title of its music chart for African-American popular music from the pejorative "race" chart to the more acceptable Rhythm and Blues (R& B) chart. One of the forerunners of this style was the Louis Jordan band, which achieved success playing popular tunes of the day as well as standard blues and boogie numbers. A typical selection of titles recorded by Jordan and his Tympany Five demonstrates the diverse sources of his material. Beginning with the pop boogie number "Choo Choo Ch'boogie" (1946)—his biggest hit, which won him one of several gold discs—the titles range through "Pompton Turnpike" (1940), "Sax Woogie" (1941), "Is You Is or Is You Ain't (My Baby?)" (1943), and "Caldonia Boogie" (1945). Jordan was sufficiently astute to keep a foot in both camps and was able to please serious jazz lovers and the popular record-buying public who simply wanted catchy numbers with amusing jive lyrics and a solid rhythm. The difference in sound between, for example, the band led by Jordan and the one led by Ammons was in the emphasis given in the former to the guitar and saxophone as the featured instruments, with the piano playing a subjugated role within the rhythm section. Jordan and his band have appeared on numerous compilations, but the one release capturing his early hits in the late 1930s is *Louis Jordan: The Early Years 1937–1939* (JSP Records, CD330).

This same instrumental lineup was used extensively by other rhythm-and-blues groups in the 1940s and 1950s, which gave a distinctly raw edge to their music, invariably with the tenor saxophone blowing hard and taking the lead. The piano was not entirely discarded as a solo instrument within this framework, however, and it was given greater prominence in some bands. One of them was led by Merrill E. Moore, who played a rocking kind of piano style with a marked use of boogie basses. Moore recorded several popular hits for the Capitol Company in 1952, including "House of Blue Lights" (the resurrected Freddy Slack and Ella Mae Morse number), "Rock Rockola," and his biggest success, "Bell Bottom Boogie." Moore was influential, together with Bill Haley and Elvis Presley, in transmuting the rhythm-and-blues sound into rock-and-roll, its more commercial and popular form. Although Moore had considerable success on the West Coast, he never received the accolade that others were given in the palmy days when the new rock and roll offshoot was born. Pianists Jerry Lee Lewis and Fats Domino were two piano-playing leaders and featured soloists who made many more recordings and achieved considerable international fame compared to Moore.

There were demographic reasons why the West Coast became the center for rhythm and blues. In the mid-1940s, America and her allies were making a final push to end the war with intensive bombing campaigns, culminating in the two atomic bomb drops on Japan. Aircraft construction and munitions industries proliferated on the West Coast to supply this wartime need, and, as with earlier migrations to the North, the black labor force was largely drawn from Texas and other southern states to sunny California, where a decent living was possible. They brought with them remnants of their culture, among which were the piano and guitar blues. Some of the migrants were instrumentalists such as pianists Lloyd Glenn, Willie Littlefield, and guitarist Aaron "T-Bone" Walker, and they were employed in the breakfast bars and clubs that opened in Watts, Oakland, and other districts of Los Angeles (LA) and San Francisco. Their pulsating rhythms provided a permanent backdrop to social intercourse. The piano was now subservient to the smooth-toned and honking saxophones of the talented duo Maxwell Davies and Don Wilkerson. An active record industry grew up alongside the many clubs, with several small independent labels—Aladdin, Exclusive, and Modern Records among them—recording the more talented. Their tunes were played regularly on radio by Al Jarvis, a white disc jockey with his show *Make Believe Ballroom* and Hunter Hancock's *Harlem Matinee*, which broadcast every afternoon at four o'clock on Radio KFVD. Jukeboxes helped to spread the new sounds, but also became a cheap substitute for employing live artists. For a time, in 1947 and 1948, both Pete Johnson and Joe Turner were featured in a small-band setting playing largely "jump" blues at the Memo Cocktail lounge on South Central in LA and at the Supper Club on Fillmore in San Francisco. Some of their later numbers recorded in LA from 1948 to 1949 can be heard on *Joe Turner with Pete Johnson's Orchestra: Jumpin' the Blues* (Arhoolie, R2004).

Lesser-known pianists working in the region made eminently forgettable recordings—sometimes one-shot tunes that rose and fell quicker than it took a DJ to replace a record stylus. Of more substance was Hadda Brooks, who to an extent took on the mantle of Hazel Scott and whose specialty of setting classical tunes to a boogie-woogie rhythm was repeated in "Humoresque Boogie." But she was capable of producing more substantial work, drawing on Pinetop's masterpiece for "Nightmare Boogie" (1945). Her style bears the strong influence of Pete Johnson in the light-fingered treble phrasing. The classics would not be denied their place and surfaced again in the repertoire of some artists: the showstopper "Barcarolle Boogie" (1949) is pounded out by Lucky Henry, preceded in time by Poison Gardener's "Rhapsody Boogie" (1947). The spirit of Amos Milburn appears in "Down in the Groovy" (1949), an uncanny takeoff by Lonny Lyons of Milburn's "Chicken Shack Boogie" both in voice intonation and rocking piano. Poison Gardener gives a frenetic keyboard display in "Tornado" (1947), on which his clattering piano competes for attention with an anguished tenor saxophone. Robert T. Smith sings a somewhat stylized vocal over moody section work from the saxophones, in combination with his own powerhouse piano playing on "Freeway Boogie" (1949). There are marked jazz influences in the conception of "Boogie in My Flat" (1944) by Al Killian backed by a band similar in tone to many of Lionel Hampton's outfits, including relaxed boppish trumpet playing. The talents of some of these relatively minor pianists are captured on *Uptown Boogie: The Great Unheard Performances* (Catfish, KAT CD132). The liner notes alone are well worth the record price for their information.

More-established artists also worked in California during the 1950s, including the aforementioned Lloyd Glenn and Little Willie Littlefield, both of whom moved there from Texas. Glenn's deft keyboard finesse added a marked and welcome modern tone to the heavier "down home" sound of the group accompanying guitarist Lowell Fulsom, another migrant from Texas. Glenn was in steady demand at recording sessions. Littlefield moved to San Francisco when he was seventeen and cut twenty-three sides for the Modern Label between 1949 and 1951. His best-known hit, "It's Midnight" (1950), remained in the rhythm-and-blues chart for thirteen weeks. As well as his romantic blues, Littlefield recorded some hot boogie numbers of which his later version of "Little Willie's Boogie" (1980) compares in sheer speed if not conception with some of Meade Lux Lewis's later extravaganzas. Littlefield, although claiming to be retired from the blues scene, was persuaded to appear at a boogie-woogie festival in Holland in 2005, where he now resides.

In these early days of rhythm and blues, Amos Milburn (1927–1980) was the doyen of the piano-playing and singing rhythm-and-blues artists, many of whom sought to emulate him. Originally from Houston, Texas, he did most of his recordings for Aladdin in LA, after initially being rejected by Jules Bihari, owner of Modern records. His piano playing began at the age of fifteen by drawing on the tradition of the Boogie-Woogie Trio. Taking them as models, he added dynamic blues vocals about the universal concerns of love, drink, and money—or lack of it in most cases. During the war, he served in the navy as a steward aboard American warships engaged in the Pacific conflict where he gained a fine reputation, honing his piano and vocal skills, as an entertainer in the officers' mess. Returning to Houston at the cessation of activities, he formed his own band, playing local clubs before being spotted by Mrs. Cullum, a female entrepreneur and later his manager, who took him and guitarist Lightnin' Hopkins to LA for their recording auditions. Once established, Amos Milburn headed the rhythm-and-blues chart with four of his recordings. The most successful, "Chicken Shack Boogie" (1947), remained there in 1948 for twenty weeks, followed closely by "Bad Bad Whisky" (1950), which stayed for eighteen weeks. His other alcohol-inspired numbers were "Thinking and Drinking" (1952) and "One Scotch, One Bourbon, One Beer" (1953).

The popularity of Amos Milburn was sustained throughout the late 1940s and early 1950s before waning, at which time he returned to Houston to play in local clubs, before finally retiring and turning to religion. On the majority of his recordings, Milburn plays a hard-hitting boogie-woogie piano using an incessant driving beat supported by tenor saxophone, guitar, bass, and drums. He could also produce a more melodic form of blues, much softer than the music and sentiments of the traditional country blues. In comparing the two, purists might argue that the music and lyrics of such numbers from the 1960s as "Bewildered" and "Empty Arms Blues" had become too effete, but, realistically, this was only one more manifestation of the blues and the direction it was now taking. A similar form of smoother cocktail blues tonality could be heard in the work of other pianists and singers such as Charles Brown, whose proficient piano playing supported more sophisticated ballads, clearly influenced by Nat King Cole. Indeed, Milburn and Brown, who initially trained as a chemistry teacher in Texas, worked together for some time on the West Coast, sharing the same accommodation. Milburn's own vocalizing on slower numbers began to sound uncannily like the influential Brown. He offered a thinly disguised cover of one of Brown's hits with "Let's Make Christmas Merry Baby" (1948). Ray Charles was eventually to become the heir to this branch of music, which made the blues, both in voice and piano, more accessible to the general public. Milburn's more important recordings can be found on *Amos Milburn: Greatest Hits* (Official, 6018).

In 1944, Cecil Gant set the marker in defining the direction of rhythm and blues with a first recording of a highly successful coupling: a slow, sentimental ballad entitled "I Wonder," delivered in a pleasant crooning manner, and the equally popular and contrasting "Cecil's Boogie." Gant had literally become an overnight sensation earlier in that year when he appeared in army uniform at a rally in LA organized by the Treasury Department to raise war bonds. Private Gant proceeded to stun the assembly with his thumping piano and singing to the extent that he was immediately signed up for Gilt-Edge Records. Thereafter he was billed as "Private Gant the GI Sing-Sation." He had a short life, dying at the age of thirty-two. Pianist and writer John Bentley, then growing up on the West Coast, was a friend of Gant who used to visit the family in Glendale when he could. He later observed:

> Generally, though, it was to "kidnap" his young white protégé (Bentley) and drag the latter off to the underworld section of LA. But, there were a couple of times when my father was also "kidnapped." After Cecil and I had met at the war bond rally in downtown LA and he had come to visit in Glendale, he and dad became quite friendly. Gant almost always had a bottle with him, and my dad was known to take a pull at a jug. Dad also enjoyed music, albeit mostly country-type sounds. My father was never one to put restraints on me, and excursions with Gant met with approval . . . so long as I got home at a reasonable hour.[1]

Gant's most convincing performance in boogie-woogie is undoubtedly the roughly hewn Hogan's Alley (1947), which gives the illusion of a juke joint, late in the evening, with Gant's spoken comments heard over a rolling bass played on a slightly off-key piano.

If one were to draw any conclusions about the contribution of this later wave of boogie-woogie pianists to the evolving rhythm-and-blues genre, it would be to note initially the paucity of some of the musical ideas made manifest in the title of a recording from 1947 by Betty Hall Jones: "Same Old Boogie" (1947). Without doubt, much of the creativity and originality of earlier boogie-woogie pianists were missing, to be replaced by insistent, repetitive, and rapid treble chording played over similarly hypnotic basses. But this would be an unwarranted dismissal of events, because the piano, as has already been noted, was only one feature of early rhythm and blues, a style that depended equally on the contributions of the tenor saxophone, rhythm guitar, and strong vocals, in order to interpret the newly found lyricism of the blues. Indeed, the music became even more eclectic as the big-band era closed, allowing many of the unemployed musicians to add further color and density to the blues from their ordered brass and reed section playing, invariably laced with bebop influences.

Much of the aforementioned musical activity had been regional and initially confined to the West Coast, but this began to change in 1945 when a recording on the Exclusive label entered the national Billboard charts devoted to the "Most Played Race Juke Box Chart." Entitled "The Honeydripper" (1945), it was composed and played by Joe Liggins and His Honeydrippers, a small combo comprising three saxophones, guitar, bass, and drums with Liggins singing the vocal over a boogie-woogie piano. By December of that year, Liggins occupied first place in the charts together with two other West Coast recordings tying for third place. These were Ivory Joe Hunter's "Blues at Sunrise" and "Left a Good Deal in Mobile," sung by Herb Jefferson (late of Duke Ellington's band) accompanied by the Honeydrippers. From this time, other regions of the United States were made aware of the rhythm-and-blues phenomenon, but its popularity had gradually eroded by the early 1950s as public taste changed toward its raw energy, wanting the softer and melodic music of quartet singing groups, modeled on the earlier Mills Brothers and Delta Rhythm Boys. In time, this too would be modified and become the "doo wop" and "Motown" sounds of the 1960s, together with the disappearance of assertive piano and saxophone combinations. Fortunately, the boogie-woogie piano tradition was maintained throughout the rock-and-roll years by Jerry Lee Lewis and Little Richard, two major performers.

New Orleans was another burgeoning center for rhythm and blues in the immediate post-war years. Here the famous and colorful piano traditions of the Crescent City, remembered through legends such as Jelly

Roll Morton, Tony Jackson, Champion Jack Dupree, and unrecorded boogie-woogie pianists Burnell Santiago and Stack-O-Lee—both of whom entertained at Saturday-night fish fries—were extended in a way that maintained a close affinity with piano blues. One distinctive feature of rhythm-and-blues music in the city was the accented rhythms that gave a Latin American lilt to the piano interpretations of its exponents.

Foremost among the city's pianists was Henry Roeland Byrd (1918–1980), known by the pseudonym "Professor" Longhair. His family moved to New Orleans where Byrd found work as a youngster assisting a snake oil salesman by acting as a planted customer on his pitch. He became a street tap dancer and then began teaching himself piano after discarding the guitar because the strings cut his fingers. Fellow pianists realized that Byrd had talent. Jack Dupree gave him lessons on playing the blues, but his greatest influence became Tuts Washington, who introduced him to the elemental features of the New Orleans piano tradition that Byrd assimilated alongside others. Wartime experience in the army was a blip in an otherwise single-minded determination to become an entertainer, which was successfully achieved in 1949 when Byrd and his band, The Midriffs, landed a job at the Caledonia, a prestigious black nightspot. It was here that he was given the name of Professor (piano professor) Longhair (excessively long hair). His recording debut was made in 1949 on the Star Talent label; the following year, he hit the jackpot with "Bald Head" (1950) on the Mercury label, which reached number five in the R&B chart. He continued to record successfully for the Atlantic and other labels, but despite his revered position in New Orleans, his fame in extending much beyond Louisiana was only achieved slowly.

Events caught up with him in the 1960s; music was not paying him well enough, so he took work as a janitor before becoming a card player, in the best New Orleans tradition. Returning to music after several years of poverty, he was an instant success at the second New Orleans Jazz and Heritage Festival in 1971. Thereafter, he consolidated his career through recordings and tours of Europe, including the Montreux Jazz Festival. His music was now becoming known and enjoyed by an appreciative white audience. Finally, he became the established act at Tipitina's, a club established like Preservation Hall, to showcase aspects of New Orleans music, and named after one of his numbers. Byrd's first album, *Crawfish Fiesta*, was completed for Alligator Records and delivered to stores for release on January 31, 1980, posthumously as it turned out, for he died in his sleep the day before.

Whereas Roy Byrd maintained a degree of naiveté in his piano playing that linked his work with earlier boogie-woogie pianists quite evidently, he also colored his numbers with rumba rhythms, achieved by adding rhythmical treble configurations between the beats of the suspended bass patterns he employed. The latter owed much to Jimmy Yancey's conception of the swinging habanera bass. Although an influence on Fats Domino's piano style, Byrd's piano conception of the blues was totally dissimilar to that of Fats.

Antoine "Fats" Domino (1928–) owed a good part of his early success to trumpeter Dave Bartholomew, who cowrote and produced Domino's best-loved tunes for Imperial Records. The first of these in 1949 was "The Fat Man" (1949), drawing inspiration from Jack Dupree's "Junkers Blues" and Dot Rice's earlier recording of "Texas Stomp." This was something new, with Domino stomping out a static bass pattern to generate a head of steam under a double time melody while declaiming in his opening vocal salvo that he was called the Fat Man; all this was cushioned by a seamless backing of riffing trumpet and four saxophones. This established the Domino upbeat sound to which were occasionally added strings without detracting from the vibrancy of the music. Domino was very much part of the rock-and-roll period and stood with Presley as one of its important innovators, translating the raw piano rhythms of boogie-woogie and the emotions of the blues into huge commercial hits such as "Blueberry Hill" (1956) and "Ain't That a Shame" (1955). If one were to compare Domino with any other pianist, it would surely be Albert Ammons in his powerful keyboard mastery, sense of dynamism, and control of rhythm. He repeated Ammons's success with his own cover version of "Swanee River" and has been quoted as liking Ammons's piano style. Both pianists led tightly knit backing groups, underscoring the melodic impact of the other instruments with powerful rolling piano rhythms before stepping into the spotlight to take their own solos. They differ in that Domino has the added entertainment advantage of a captivating singing voice, with a slight French intonation that makes him a true international star. An appropriate selection of Domino's hit recordings is included on *Fats Domino: Twenty Greatest Hits, United Artists Records* (UAS 29967).

Other pianists of note have sustained the New Orleans piano lineage, some more schooled and sophisticated than others. A contemporary of Domino, Huey "Piano" Smith (1928–), adopted a similar basic approach to interpreting rhythm and blues. He is best known for his strangely titled hit number "Rockin' Pneumonia and the Boogie-Woogie Flu," which showcases his solid piano work. Few of the others could be considered solely rhythm-and-blues pianists, but all have come within its ambit and used elements of boogie-woogie in their interpretations. Of these, the technically brilliant James Booker would have to be among the foremost, followed by, but in no way superior to, Alan Toussaint and Mac Rebennack, alias "Dr. John."

A lesser-known piano player who made few recordings but was eminently influential to Domino, Booker, and others was Isadore "Tuts"

Washington (1907–1984). His repertoire married boogie-woogie numbers with well-known standards. Compared to Domino and others, he might be thought old-fashioned, but Tuts played this way because he was first and foremost a club entertainer who had to reach out to a wide audience in establishments such as the Fairmount Court and leave them feeling happy at the end of his set. The catholicity of his program and his well-developed piano technique were a source of great pride, and he could be critical of contemporaries whom he considered too reliant on the backing of a band for their success. His recorded material from 1983 is invariably melodic, such as the classic James P. Johnson's "Arkansas Blues" or "Mr. Freddie's Blues" played in a stride style with passages of boogie-woogie bass; a straight stride throughout as on "Georgia on My Mind"; or the traditional "Frankie and Johnnie," played throughout with a lilting tango bass. Recordings by Washington are rare; the best selection is on *Tuts Washington: New Orleans Piano Professor* (Rounder Records, 2041).

Mention should be made here of Joe Turner, whose close links with the blues and boogie sounds of the thirties and forties are well documented but who made the successful transition from this era to the new rhythm-and-blues sounds of the 1950s. In doing so, he contributed to the shaping of the new music and provided a model for other singers beginning with his early recording "Roll 'Em Pete" with Pete Johnson, an irresistible combination of talents that also produced "Goin' Away Blues" and "Cherry Red," all recorded in 1938 for the Vocalion label. After his success at the Café Society, a lean period followed in the late 1940s before Turner made his reappearance on the music scene with "Chains of Love" (1951) for the Atlantic label followed by the equally hard-hitting "Shake, Rattle and Roll" (1954), which became a standard rock-and-roll number. With these successes behind him, Turner's career gradually took off again. Younger singers began to listen to his phrasing, and his style influenced Wynonie Harris, Eddie "Cleanhead" Vinson, Clarence "Gatemouth" Brown, and significant others in their later work. This period was recalled by Turner as one when he and Helen Humes became stars of rock and roll, and as he said to Balliett, what he was now doing was what he had always been doing, the only difference was that it now had a new name.[2]

During the early years of the thirties, the general public was largely unaware of boogie-woogie music unless they happened to hear a recording by an African-American piano player on one of the "race" series. One or two discerning individuals, notably William Russell and John Hammond, were beginning to visit the bars and joints in Chicago and Kansas to listen to the recognized exponents. Many white musicians also went to hear them play when they themselves were appearing in cities where boogie-woogie was played. Among them were pianists Bob Zurke, who often caught performances by Ammons and his Rhythm Kings, and

Freddy Slack, who was known to have visited clubs where Johnson was appearing. Both men were later to become the leading white exponents of boogie-woogie. Public interest in the style was generally at a low level and would probably have remained so if a piano solo by Cleo Brown, a popular African-American entertainer of the period, had not been issued by the Decca label in March 1935. The recording was an interpretation of Pinetop's famous solo entitled "Boogie-Woogie" when it was first released. It was subsequently reissued as part of the Decca album of boogie-woogie in 1939 and given its full title. The first recording, probably due to its novelty value, was given sufficient airtime for it to be heard by a large radio audience, and it stirred an interest in the style. Several leaders of the popular swing bands became curious and started to consider how boogie-woogie could be incorporated into their band books.

Cleo Brown (1909–1993) was born in Meridian, Missouri, the daughter of a Baptist minister. After receiving a sound musical education, including piano lessons from Nettie Reese at the Meridian Baptist Seminary, she began playing the piano for her father's choir and at various social functions in the neighborhood where she lived. Her family moved to Chicago in 1919 and while there she began to experiment on the piano with dance music. One of the incentives was her brother Everett's ability to earn twenty-five dollars a week playing this music compared to her own weekly earnings of six dollars playing piano at her father's church. By the time she was in her teens, she was sufficiently well versed in modern piano playing to strike out on her own as a professional pianist, claiming to be a better pianist than her brother Everett. But to do so, she had to run away and marry because her parents forbade her to play the music she loved (boogie-woogie).[3] Her first engagement was with an orchestra touring Canada, and on her return to Chicago she decided to make that city her base. For a time she was the resident pianist at the Kelshore Tea Room and, later, at the Lake Villa before moving in 1932 to the Three Deuces, a popular nightspot. The next year, she appeared at the World's Fair with Texas Guinan. Further work came as a member of a group led by violinist Eddie South, and for a time she replaced Fats Waller in New York as pianist on CBS radio.

It was toward the end of a residency at the Three Deuces that she recorded "Boogie-Woogie" for Decca, one of five numbers, with Gene Krupa (drums) appearing on some of them. This was backed by the fast-striding "Pelican Stomp," recorded later in May of that year, and released as a single. As a sequel to the public interest in the boogie side, she made numerous radio and supper club appearances in New York, Chicago, and Hollywood, including several guest appearances on *Kraft Music Hall*, Bing Crosby's prestigious radio show. Returning to the Three Deuces in 1939, Brown shared the bill with Johnny Dodds and his band. During this engagement she continued to enhance her reputation as a versatile pianist capable of playing boogie and other styles, in an original way. She made further recordings in LA in 1936 and, finding the climate to her liking, settled there. Despite a period of debilitating illness from which she recovered, Cleo Brown was in demand at the many clubs and theatres on the West Coast. Her style of piano playing underwent a metamorphosis in 1949 when she experienced some kind of religious conversion while entertaining in a San Francisco nightclub—not surprising given her family background. Brown now withdrew from the clubs and began playing religious music, after qualifying for, and devoting herself to, nursing in Colorado State Hospital. She eventually entered the Seventh Day Adventist Church, in 1953, as Sister Brown where she remained until her death, but not before Marion McPartland had been able to coax her out of retirement to appear on her radio show *Piano Jazz* in 1985.

The significance of Cleo Brown as an entertainer and pianist of exceptional skill goes beyond her one important recording of "Boogie-Woogie." She composed other eight-beat tunes such as "Roll That Boogie" and "Hole in the Wall"—the perennial theme of the little-known joint where one could hear unsurpassed boogie-woogie piano being played. Her pleasant, sexy vocal style draws full meaning from the lyrics of songs composed by Waller, Gilbert, Charles, and others, ranging from the romantic "When" (1935) to the more dubiously titled "The Stuff Is Here and It's Mellow" (1935). Cleo Brown was the first of the female "chee chee" singers, predating a group comprising Rose Murphy, Nellie Lutcher, and, later, Blossom Deary. Jazz pianists Dave Brubeck and Marion McPartland freely admit their debt to her influence on their own playing, and Brubeck acted as her understudy for a time when he was a university student. What is interesting from the point of view of the further development of boogie-woogie piano playing is that it was now included in the repertoire of a well-schooled popular pianist who obviously enjoyed it for what it was. It suited her muscular style of bouncy piano playing replete with its infectious rhythms. It was said that Cleo's interest in boogie-woogie was stimulated by her brother's friendship with Clarence Smith, who was living in Chicago in 1928. Cleo Brown's version of Pinetop's solo differs in many respects from the original. To begin with, it is written in the key of F and uses a walking bass throughout, although the treble phrases and the spoken commentary are retained. A selection of her work is available on *The Legendary Cleo Brown* (President Records, PLCD 548).

The Decca Company appeared to grasp the commercial potential of boogie-woogie before the other major companies. The year following Cleo Brown's recording, they released "Yancey Special" (1936), played by the composer Meade Lux Lewis. When it was issued, it was described as one of his more artistic compositions, whatever that was meant to imply. The features that attracted notice and stimulated further public interest were the eight-measure bass solos played in a "tango" rhythm that opened and closed the number. A second version of the piece was released by Decca in March 1938, but this was an orchestral rendition by the Bob Crosby Orchestra from an arrangement by Dean Kincaide. The Crosby version is both tasteful and catchy. The piano part is played by Bob Zurke. The distinctive feature of the arrangement is that it involves sections of the band playing the bass and treble parts of the composition simulating, in effect, the piano for which the number had originally been written. This was a singularly important record that took boogie-woogie one more step along its evolutionary path from a solo piano style to an orchestral form.

The success of this formula, measured by the number of records sold, and the frequent requests for "Yancey Special" when the band was appearing at concerts, indicated that Crosby had hit a rich vein. Not surprisingly, he recorded a version of another of Lewis's compositions, "Honky Tonk Train," and gave it the same treatment. The record was released in October 1938 and "Blues" was dropped from the title. This arrangement was done by Matty Matlock, who wrote the instrumental parts from the original piano solo, rearranging them slightly to accommodate the two-fisted piano playing of Bob Zurke. The band was appearing at the Black Hawk Restaurant in Chicago when the recording was made. Gene Pairan, a student of Zurke's, recalls that the band saw their parts for the first time at an afternoon rehearsal and Meade Lux Lewis was asked to join them in case advice on the rendition was needed. However, Zurke was an excellent sight reader and played it through correctly the first time.[4] Both of these important band boogies and other jazz standards such as "Royal Garden Blues" and "South Rampart Street Parade" can be heard on *Bob Crosby and His Orchestra* (MCA Records, MCFM 2578).

The featured pianist with Crosby was Boguslaw Albert Zukowski (1912–1944) or Bob Zurke, as he was known. He achieved a reputation as an eccentric, hard-living member of the Crosby band. His popularity as a pianist grew and continued unabated with Crosby until he decided it was time to leave and form his own band in May 1939.

Zurke's hometown was Detroit, where he was born to parents of Polish extraction. His father was an accordionist and his mother a concert singer. Zurke was introduced to music as a very young child and was taking piano lessons at the same time that he was learning to walk. He was considered something of a child prodigy and gave his first public concert at the Detroit Sompolski Auditorium in the presence of Ignace Paderewski by the time he was five years of age. At fourteen he was considered good enough to join the NBC orchestra in New York. Before this, however, Zurke had played his first professional engagement in a pit orchestra in a Detroit theatre, which fitted him well for his move to Oliver Naylor's Dance Band in 1928. From then until 1936, he gained further experience, including his first baptism of real jazz, with the bands of Thelma Terry, Hank Biagani, Seymour Simons, Milk Falk, and Joe Venuti. In 1936, he returned to Detroit and was working in Smokey's, a well-known club, where he was heard by Eddie Miller and Matty Matlock, who were visiting Detroit with the Crosby band. Gil Rodin, the music director, was persuaded to engage him on the recommendation of the other two men. Details were completed by June, in time for Zurke to make his first recordings for the band accompanying a youthful Judy Garland.

For a period Crosby had two outstanding pianists on his payroll, for in addition to Zurke there was Joe Sullivan. The ensemble work was initially played by Zurke, while Sullivan was featured as a soloist and intermission pianist. Zurke's big chance came when Sullivan went down with tuberculosis just before a benefit concert in 1937, and he was required to cover all the piano parts, including many of Sullivan's own compositions such as "Little Rock Getaway," "Gin Mill Blues," and "Just Strolling." It is indicative of his amazing talent that he could follow Sullivan onto the piano chair and substitute so brilliantly for him. Sullivan was, after all, respected as one of the best American white jazz pianists. That Zurke met the challenge there is no doubt, and he was considered by some, Bob Crosby included, to have surpassed Sullivan in his playing. By 1940, he had won the *Downbeat* piano poll, six places ahead of Sullivan and well in front of Ammons, Johnson, and Lewis who occupied, respectively, thirteenth, fifteenth, and twenty-third places.

The Delta Rhythm Band was formed on his release from jail, where he had been residing for nonpayment of maintenance to his wife. He was fortunate in having Fud Livingstone as his arranger, and between them they composed and arranged several original compositions as well as standards, employing a tight precision in the brass and reed section work, which became a recognizable feature in the arrangements of many swing bands of the era. The Delta Rhythm Band was never quite a top band despite the talents of the leader, and it sometimes sounded stiff and unrelaxed with generally wayward vocalists. Due to Zurke's immense following as a solo pianist, many of the thirty-two recordings made for Victor tended to be showcase numbers featuring his piano playing, a complaint made in the *Downbeat* review of his first coupling of "Hobson Street Blues" (1939) and an innocuous pop number, "Each Time You Say Goodbye." The band was a short-lived venture, and his personal problems probably hastened its demise in 1940, one year after its formation. The most stable period appears to have been the summer season of 1939 spent in St. Louis in preparation for a move to New York, which never took place. After this setback, Zurke was hired as a solo pianist at the

Pump Room of the Ambassador East Hotel and the Panther Room at the Hotel Sherman in Chicago. From this moment he began the slippery slope into obscurity, earning a meager living with pick-up groups and studio bands before finally moving to the Hangover Club in San Francisco in 1941 or 1942 where he remained until his death at the age of thirty-three from pneumonia in February 1944.

An account of Zurke's solo appearance at the Hangover Club says all there is to say about this able man and his sad decline: sitting in a restricted space, the piano top strewn with rubbish and drinks, he played with his usual panache memorable tunes such as "Honky Tonk Train," "Gin Mill Blues," and others that he would forever be associated with—sometimes playing them better than the composers. The writer reflected on the demise of Zurke from the time when his star had shone brilliantly during the Crosby years to his rapid fall into obscurity.[5] It remains a poignant obituary of a unique keyboard talent.

Art Hodes spent two years learning his craft in the joints on Chicago's South Side before leaving there for New York. The year was 1938, and he recalls one jazz session he attended at Liberty Inn when Bob Zurke breezed in and took over the piano stool. He played so much boogie-woogie that even Hodes found it too much to take and he had to leave. Zurke did play a lot of boogie-woogie, which helped to keep him in the public's eye at a time when it was the only kind of music they wanted to listen to—two and a half thousand fans clamored for more and more encores of his boogie-woogie playing when he entertained them at Sylvan Beech in Houston in 1940. Even his numbers that were not credited as boogie-woogie compositions had a flavor of the eight beat about them because of his very contrapuntal piano style, which set the bass and treble walking across each other in a feast of dissonance and cross rhythms.

In the short time that Zurke ran a band, it did manage to make some pleasing and distinctive recordings helped by the skillful arrangements of Fud Livingstone. The section work was crisp, and, supported by a bouncy rhythm section, the scene was set for the inevitable Zurke solo, which was always worth listening to, if predictable in its appearance. A bluesy piano passage introduces "Tom Cat on the Keys" (1939) before opening out into a boogie-woogie solo with a heavy "rocks" bass. Trumpet and trombone solos are taken, adding garnish to the featured piano. The band's theme tune was "Hobson Street Blues," which was paired with "I've Found a New Baby" for its release in Britain in 1940. The "New Baby" side is notable for eight totally unexpected bars of barrelhouse piano at the end of the recording. One of Zurke's most distinctive performances on record was on "Tea for Two" (1938) with the Crosby band. The melody is sketched with some pleasing chords, which are played against a bass line of repeated descending phrases of single notes. This became his hallmark and accounted for the elements of counterpoint in his work. There were other numbers that Zurke featured with Crosby in which boogie-woogie passages were included. One of these was the Sullivan composition "Just Strolling" (1937), which began with a brooding boogie introduction. He also played, and later recorded, another of Sullivan's originals, "Gin Mill Blues" (1937), using a walking bass in several of its choruses.

By the time the Delta Rhythm Band had been formed, boogie-woogie was already proving to be a commercial success for the big bands. Zurke capitalized on his ability as an outstandingly good and original interpreter and recorded several straight boogie-woogie numbers, including "Cuban Boogie-Woogie" (1939), "Rhumboogie" (1940), "Cow Cow Blues" (1940), and the astonishingly fast "Honky Tonk Train" (1939). Some of these sides, notably "Honky Tonk Train," continued in the pattern established by the early Bob Crosby recordings of simulating the piano treble and bass parts with the reeds and brass. One of Zurke's original pieces that to my knowledge has only ever been featured by one other pianist, the late Ralph Sutton, is "Southern Exposure" (1939), a slow-burning piece that commences with a walking tenths bass on piano, calling to and receiving a response from the brass section. Piano, reeds, and brass then work in unison to produce a tight melodic section, as the climax of the piece, before concluding with an altogether lighter and relaxed section. In all, four different piano bass patterns are used. Other recordings featured Zurke as a soloist, with the band simply there to provide the backing for his piano. This marked another type of orchestrated boogie-woogie that other leaders were to use, featuring a solo spot for their pianists in original boogie-woogie compositions commissioned especially for their bands. Mary Lou Williams and Ken Kersey did this with the Andy Kirk band, playing, respectively, "Little Joe from Chicago" (1938) and "Boogie-Woogie Cocktail" (1942). In Zurke's band, however, it became the rule rather than the exception. A substantial collection of twenty-eight of Zurke's Delta Rhythm band recordings is on *Bob Zurke: Honky Tonk Train Blues, The 1000 Series* (Hep, CD 1074).

Zurke possessed a quite superb technique, which was built on his very thorough early training, as well as owing something to the influence of Sullivan and Hines. He was quoted as being influenced by the veteran pianist Art Schutt, whose playing he greatly admired. His ability to produce complex counter-melodies was, in his own view, attributable to his fondness for Bach, a claim supported by British pianist and jazz critic Steve Race, who identifies him as the first jazz pianist to use counterpoint as effortlessly as one might find in classical music. "Jelly Roll" Morton, in an unusual show of generosity toward another pianist, referred to him on his Library of Congress recordings as the only modern pianist "with any idea." Besides being an excellent sight reader and an experienced band pianist, Zurke distinguished himself with his fast-moving bass pattern, which produced a truly two-handed piano style that has rarely been copied or equaled. His music was never less than rhythmical despite its complexity and denseness on occasions.

The one remaining enigma about Zurke's successful and popular piano interpretations is his deployment and obvious enjoyment of the closed and rigid patterns of boogie-woogie basses, which contrasted with the flowing openness of his two-handed style of playing. Fortunately, he was equally assured playing both boogie-woogie and in a style that gave the bass line greater freedom, drawing inspiration from the pattern already set by Earl Hines. In this respect, he rejected the straight two-and-four beat rhythm of the predominant stride style as exemplified in the piano playing of the popular duo Teddy Wilson and Jess Stacey.

A widely circulated story appeared in the American musical press in the autumn of 1940 that criticized the unseemly manner in which a little-known band had suddenly achieved national fame. The band's agent was criticized for using high-pressure publicity methods that had led to bookings at prestigious hotels and theatres as well as a top-selling record within months of the formation of the Will Bradley Band. It came into being in June 1939, when trombonist Will Bradley and drummer Ray McKinley joined forces at the instigation of Willard Alexander. Alexander had noted the commercial success of Tommy Dorsey and Gene Krupa and was convinced that a band featuring two similar instrumentalists would prove to be equally popular. In any event, he was correct, for the band did distinguish itself, despite the earlier criticism, during its short existence of three years. It built a reputation on two planks: by playing original boogie-woogie numbers at the height of the public craze for the eight beat and doing so with outstandingly good musicianship. In short, they cornered the market in commercial boogie-woogie.

The early demise of the band was partly due to conflicting views held by the joint leaders on the best musical policy to follow. McKinley wanted to play more up-tempo boogie, whereas Bradley's ideal was to feature more ballads. In 1942, they finally split without rancor when it was obvious that their wishes were irreconcilable. Will Bradley was, by general agreement among musicians, an outstanding trombone player who could play hot or sweet equally well. He was a member of the brass section alongside Glen Miller in the Ray Noble Orchestra for a year before returning to the CBS Orchestra, where he was playing when the band was formed with McKinley. He already knew McKinley, for they had both been members of Milt Shaw and his Detroiters in the early thirties. When the partnership between them was conceived, McKinley was with the Jimmy Dorsey Orchestra, having been an original member of the Dorsey Brothers Orchestra since 1934. One of the most significant events that occurred—and which was partly responsible for the band's success—was the arrival of pianist Freddie Slack from Dorsey's Orchestra at the same time. It was around these three figures that the initial boogie-woogie policy was built.

Frederick Charles Slack (1910–1965) was born in La Crosse, Wisconsin, and began studying the piano at about twelve years of age. He lacked application at first until he began to experiment with dance music. His interest and technique developed quickly after this to the point where he decided to make a career in music. He moved with his family to Chicago and enrolled at the American Conservatory of Music when he was eighteen and studied the classics under Tomford Harris. The family moved again to Los Angeles, and Slack started his professional career with the Hank Halstead Orchestra before moving to the piano chair in the Ben Pollack Orchestra for three years. Other members of the same band were Harry James, Dave Matthews, and Bruce Squires. One significant engagement for Slack was when the band played in Kansas City and he was able to hear Pete Johnson at the Sunset. His own interest in boogie began in earnest from this time. He was so impressed with what was for him a different and unusual piano style that he determined to master the technique for himself. About this time he was also listening to the recordings of Pinetop Smith. He was to incorporate a superlative version of "Pinetop's Boogie-Woogie" on one of his later recordings entitled "That Place Down the Road a Piece" (1941) for Decca. In 1936, Slack left Pollack to join Dorsey, where he was both pianist and arranger. The Jimmy Dorsey Orchestra was the featured band on Bing Crosby's *Kraft Music Hall* radio program, and during a rehearsal Slack played a few choruses of boogie that he had recently worked out. This impressed Crosby, Dorsey, and McKinley, which encouraged Slack to persevere with the style. Thereafter he used it on most of his recordings with Bradley and, later, with his own band, which he launched in 1941. The remainder of his life was spent on the West Coast where he appeared in several films in the mid-1940s, including *Reveille with Beverly*, *The Sky's the Limit*, *Babes on Swing Street*, and *Follow the Boys*.

Slack made many recordings for the new Capitol Record Company, which was started by songwriter and vocalist Johnny Mercer. Two were particularly successful in the "pop" boogie field and helped to establish the fledgling company and, in so doing, repaid Mercer for the effort he had spent helping Slack to establish his own band on the West Coast.

The first of these was "Cow Cow Boogie," recorded in Los Angeles on May 21, 1942, which brought fame to his vocalist Ella Mae Morse. Freddie had heard Ella Mae when she spent a few weeks singing with Jimmy Dorsey's band. As she was only in her early teens, Dorsey released her saying she was too young. Some years later, Slack heard her singing in a Houston nightspot—she was born in Texas—and immediately signed the now mature voiced Ella as vocalist with his band. The other success, "House of Blue Lights" (1946), attempted to recreate the atmosphere of a rent party. The exaggerated "hip" vocal on this recording was done by Don Raye, who composed this number in addition to many other very popular boogie-woogie pieces while following a career as a vaudeville dancer. Freddie Slack was a pleasant if rather vague man who was overtaken by events not of his own making. In the early 1950s, he had had enough of one-nighters, having been on the road for several years with Pollack and Dorsey as well as his own band. He disbanded and sometimes played with a trio or as a member of a piano duo in clubs and lounges around Nevada and the San Fernando Valley. There he remained until his death. After his considerable success with boogie-woogie during his days with Bradley, he never did get completely out of this mold to extend his musical range despite his considerable abilities as a pianist and arranger. He built his career around boogie-woogie but had an ambivalent attitude toward it, saying on one occasion that he preferred writing ballads. John Bentley saw and heard Slack in performance on several occasions and speaks well of his boogie interpretations, rooted as they were in the music of African-Americans:

> Even before he had met Pete Johnson, Freddie was a Pinetop advocate. There is no doubt in my own mind that, before leaving Chicago for California, Freddie had also heard Ammons. Since Meade was playing sporadically then, Freddie could have missed him. But I personally think that most of what Slack played in the boogie style was fashioned after his admiration for Pinetop. A couple of his bass configurations probably came from Ammons.
>
> He was a character, to be sure, but one helluva player on top of it all. He sat at the piano generally looking somewhat distracted, which he generally was, but in the several years that I knew him, I never knew him to play a wrong note.[6]

The Will Bradley and Ray McKinley band got under way with a tour of New England. One of the stops in their itinerary was at the Ritz-Carlton Hotel in Boston. While there in 1939, they made some of their first recordings for Columbia. Included among them are "Love Nest" and "Memphis Blues," which both feature Slack's piano and Bradley's trombone. On October 12, 1939, the band made further recordings, including an excellent arrangement by Leonard Whitney of "I'm Coming Virginia." Again, Slack and Bradley are to the fore. On this date and the earlier one when "Memphis Blues" was made, Slack gave a foretaste of his future piano direction by playing two tasteful boogie breaks. In January 1940, the band was engaged to appear at the Hotel New Yorker, which coincided with the release of two highly original compositions entitled "Celery Stalks at Midnight" and a boogie number, originally given the title of "Boogie-Woogie Nocturne" by Slack, but released as "Strange Cargo." The number later became the band's closing theme and was one of Slack's most satisfying compositions in the genre. It has a brooding quality, achieved by introducing a few bars of boogie piano over a melody line played by the reed section and then fading the piano into the ground rhythm. Further aural interest is provided by Slack's use of an alternating bass pattern.

On the completion of the New Yorker engagement, the band moved to the Famous Door on Fifty-second Street where the boogie policy really got under way. The first in the series was "Rhumboogie" (1940), a number written by Don Raye featuring a vocal by McKinley supported by Slack's piano. McKinley was the driving force behind the move away from dixieland to boogie-woogie, and he ensured that there were always one or two boogie arrangements at rehearsals as well as the popular tunes of the day. It appears that McKinley, Slack, and arranger Whitney began to consider how the boogie rhythms of Ammons, Johnson, and Lewis might be adapted for a big band at about the time that the Boogie-Woogie Trio was pulling in the crowds at the Café Society. They experimented initially with one or two numbers that had a pronounced boogie beat and were playing one of them at the Famous Door when two songwriters, Don Raye and Hughie Prince, were in the audience. At one point in the proceedings there was a drum break and McKinley held back with his sticks and instead shouted out, "Oh Beat Me Daddy Eight to the Bar." When the set had been completed, Hughie Prince said they would like to compose a tune (with lyrics) using McKinley's break and offered him a share after he agreed to them using it.[7]

The arrangement for "Beat Me Daddy Eight to the Bar" (1940) was written by Whitney, who followed the pattern set by Ross for his arrangement of "Rhumboogie." Slack introduces the record with some authentic bars of boogie piano with the band chanting in unison, leading into McKinley's solo and more piano with interjections from the brass section. Several riffed choruses by the brass and reeds are followed by tasteful solos from lead trumpet and Bradley's trombone before a flourish from Slack on piano closes the number. The tune was issued on both sides of an American Columbia 78 record, and within the first month of its release, one million copies had been sold. Without doubt, this was the band's most commercially successful recording. It was initially thought that the reference in the lyrics to the imaginary pianist from Texas was none other than Peck Kelly, an enigmatic jazz pianist who refused all offers to leave that state for the bright lights of New York. The stories about him were legendary and seemed to grow stronger the more he resisted overtures to move north. However, it was wrongly assumed that Peck had been the model, and McKinley said so shortly after the story began to circulate, even though Peck had personally thanked him for the compliment. Indeed, it would have been a pointless gesture on McKinley's part, for although Peck was a very fine jazz pianist who played with musicians of the caliber of Jack Teagarden, he was never regarded as a boogie-woogie stylist. The strengths of the swinging Will Bradley band during their boogie-woogie period with Slack on piano can be fully appreciated on *Best of Big Bands: Bradley/McKinley* (CBS, 46691 2).

Freddie Slack has never fully received credit for his contribution to the evolution of boogie-woogie by those purists who dismiss him as a successful white copyist of the Boogie-Woogie Trio. Many of his recordings are decidedly commercial, and the most generous of his fans would be hard pressed to find much jazz feeling in numbers such as "Riffette" (1942) and "Kitten on the Keys" (1945). Both numbers are recorded with a big band and are an attempt to use boogie-woogie styling on standard popular tunes. Similarly, the "Doll Dance" (1942) is Slack's version of the "Wedding of the Painted Doll," with some honest swing style piano work in the middle choruses. "Your Conscience Tells You So" (1946), a popular tune sung by Ella Mae Morse, is embellished by a boogie bass with a delayed beat. Other songs, such as "A Cat's Ninth Life" (1945), unsuccessfully attempt to integrate boogie-woogie and the sweet tones of popular music. These were commercial novelties, often popular with the public, but with little intrinsic value for the boogie advocate. He comes closer to his jazz roots with "Pig Foot Pete" (1941), in which solid boogie-woogie playing is combined with original lyrics in a thinly disguised song about Pete Johnson with its reference to a left hand like a "cannon" and a right hand like a "rifle."

Other jazz-inflected works include "Southpaw Serenade" (1941), with its fast, effortless boogie-woogie choruses and the original version of "Down the Road a Piece" (1940). Both tunes were recorded by members of small groups drawn from Will Bradley's band. Much of Slack's early work with the Bradley band had a strong jazz basis. Over the years, Slack rerecorded several new versions of his early successes, including "Down the Road a Piece"—choruses of which appear in "Cuban Sugar Mill," "Pig Foot Pete," and "Beat Me Daddy." From the point of view of this book, much of Slack's seminal piano work in the boogie-woogie field was completed during the years spent with Bradley, but his continuing exploration of the boogie-woogie genre, dating from 1941, deserves acknowledgment, from when he first ventured to become a solo artist, arranger, and bandleader in his own right. Two successful new pieces from this period, "Cow Cow Boogie" (1942) and "Two Left Hands" (1947), were produced in collaboration with Benny Carter. A move to the West Coast saw him teaming up with Joe Turner, who had also moved his base there, on four sides for Decca. They built on the Johnson and Turner creations, supported by guitar and bass. Of these, "Blues on Central Avenue" (1941) is a superlative combination of their talents, with Slack's broken boogie bass driving along Turner's animated vocal. By 1948, Slack was running a fine seven-piece group, which had an extended run at the College Inn in the Hotel Sherman in Chicago.

In the main, Freddie Slack's piano playing became the focus in his band, partly because of his earlier success with Bradley but also because his fans expected to see and hear him hammering out the "eight beat." To give his talents their full due, one needs to embrace both his work as band pianist with Bradley and the later recordings with his own band. Of this latter work, the best with a significant swing band content is on a reissue, *Freddie Slack: Boogie-Woogie on the Eighty Eight* (Official, 12 000), while his more commercial "pop" material for Capitol is available on *Hits of Freddie Slack & Ella Mae Morse* (Capitol, 1553041).

Freddie Slack should be credited with introducing several new ideas into his boogie-woogie interpretations and his arrangements of orchestrated boogie-woogie pieces. He frequently captures attention by opening his numbers with a complex bass pattern supported by a few chords in the treble before reverting to a more traditional kind of bass and treble configuration. Interest and suspense are also maintained by switching between basses as a piece progresses and, uniquely, by using two alternating basses patterned in single notes. His efforts probably helped make boogie-woogie acceptable to a wider audience by removing much of the elemental treble dissonance and introducing in its place catchy melodies that could be whistled or hummed and lyrics that were in keeping with the "hep cat" attitudes of popular American culture of the 1940s. His piano interpretations always have the credibility of the jazzman who has elected to pursue this direction, placing him on the jazz side of the big band sounds of the day rather than leaning toward the ultra commercial "pop" vocalizing of the Andrews Sisters on their various boogie-woogie inspired tunes.

When Slack left Will Bradley in 1941, his place was taken by Bob Holt. Personal differences between Slack and the two coleaders were said to have contributed to the break. In a very short period of time, Slack's piano work and McKinley's singing had put the Bradley group in the top rankings of the name bands of the period. Holt was leading a band in Worcester, Massachusetts, when the call came from Bradley. Before that, he had spent 1940 working in New York attempting to gain recognition for his piano playing. A friendship with Art Hodes assisted with the mastery of the boogie-woogie style, which he played with conviction. Bob Holt stayed with Bradley for less than two months.

Holt's rapid departure was reported in *Downbeat*[8] alongside the news that he was to be replaced on piano by Billie Maxted, who joined the band from Red Nichols in time for its opening night at the Hotel Astor in Times Square. Like Slack, Maxted came from Wisconsin, having been born and raised in Racine. His piano style was heavily influenced by Zurke and Cleo Brown, and it was hearing the former's bass work that first got him interested in the boogie-woogie idiom. More than any other white pianists playing boogie at this time, Holt experimented with playing new and complex basses. The effect was a highly original and contrapuntal form of boogie. Maxted appears on "Basin Street Boogie" (1941), which was given a seal of approval by Dave Dexter's review in *Downbeat*, and on his own composition "Fry Me Cookie with a Can of Lard" (1941). Although Bradley was beginning to have doubts about the band's boogie-woogie policy, he was still conscious of its importance as a commercial gimmick. In its pursuance, he made some drastic changes to the band's personnel and began by sacking the saxophone section. Maxted's arrival was heralded with a strong endorsement from Bradley that he would be featured a great deal, particularly in boogie-woogie numbers because of his fast left hand.[9] In 1941, Bradley made public his views about the band's boogie-woogie policy, saying that he did not want to be known as the "King of Boogie-Woogie," particularly as boogie-woogie was being misapplied to any music associated with jitterbugs.[10] How prophetic Bradley's statement was to become in the ensuing years, when boogie-woogie was accused of contributing to most forms of juvenile delinquency in America.

Further changes of personnel took place, the most significant being the replacement of McKinley on drums by the youthful Shelly Manne. These changes coincided with Bradley's decision to finish with the boogie-woogie policy and to pursue one that gave the band a sound not dissimilar to Jimmie Lunceford's band. When the band finally arrived in Denver for an engagement in June 1942 minus six men who had been drafted into the armed forces, one of whom was Maxted, there was no way that Bradley could keep his band together, so he disbanded there and then.

Whereas Bob Crosby's arrangers orchestrated such pieces as "Yancey Special" by assigning various parts to sections of the orchestra (left hand to bass, drums, and trombone; right hand to reeds), Bradley's arrangers did so much more. They did not merely force boogie-woogie piano solos onto a procrustean bed of orchestra; they produced real orchestral arrangements that had the flavor of boogie-woogie. For example, Bradley's "I Boogied When I Should Have Woogied" (1940) is a boogie-woogie flavored piece written for the band, whereas Crosby's "Yancey Special" is essentially a piano solo. Replacing "I Boogied" with a solo piano version thereof would be a loss; replacing Crosby's "Yancey Special" with the piano-solo version is a great gain.

Ray McKinley's vocals have "personality," but, more seriously, they are musical: any liberties taken with the tune are usually minor, tasteful, and in accord with the composer's interest. Despite Bradley's frequently expressed reservations about boogie-woogie, his trombone solos make a great contribution to the boogie-woogie character of his orchestra. He plays in a unique way on these recordings. For example, his trombone obbligato in "Shadows in the Night" (1941) is quite beautiful, but only in such pieces as "Strange Cargo" (1939) and "Rock-a-Bye the Boogie" (1941) does that singular quality appear.

Another soloist contributing to the special "boogie" character of the orchestra is trumpeter Joe Weidman who left the Bradley band at the same time as Freddy Slack when it was achieving the peak of its success. He employs a staccato, hot-inflected tone in his solo work, which fits perfectly the rhythms of the eight beat. Nowhere is this heard better than on "Scrub Me Mama with a Boogie Beat" (1940), "Rock-a-Bye the Boogie," and "Three-Ring Ragout" (1941). Like Bradley himself, Weidman developed a way of playing that captured and reinforced the "boogie" character of the orchestra. If ever here was a boogie-woogie bugle boy it was Weidman. After the disbandment in 1942, Bradley turned to the studio where his immense talent was avidly sought. In addition to an impeccable pedigree as leader of, and soloist in, one of the best sounding swing bands, he had begun to take an interest in contemporary classical music. In 1948, he performed his own composition, "Arithmetical for Trombone and Piano," at a concert for the League of Composers at the Museum of Modern Art in New York. During this period he formed a progressive sounding band that received much critical acclaim. In his later years, until his death in 1978, Bradley's time was taken with making jewelry, and true to his previous high standards in music, he proved equally adept in this field.

The interest shown in boogie-woogie by leaders of the more prestigious big bands began in the mid-1930s. Benny Goodman was one of the first white leaders, commissioning a number called "Roll Em" from Mary Lou Williams in 1937. It was said that her inspiration came from listening to Pete Johnson, and there is an obvious reference to him in the choice of title. The number has been recorded on several occasions with different personnel: an interesting version featuring Lewis and Ammons as guests with Goodman's band, taken from a radio broadcast of January 3, 1939, can be heard on *The Benny Goodman Caravans* (MCPS, GO1-1030), with an added bonus of Lewis playing "Honky Tonk Train Blues." In 1936, the Count Basie Orchestra produced an economical "Boogie-Woogie" built around Pinetop Smith's well-known treble phrases, but it was 1938 before the full orchestrated treatment of Pinetop's generic piece was heard. This was an arrangement by Deane Kincaide for the Tommy Dorsey Orchestra on the Victor label and was entitled "Boogie-Woogie." It follows Smith's original fairly closely with added sections of walking bass by the brass, which were in Cleo Brown's piano version but not in Smith's solo. The piano choruses are played by Howard Smith. Kinkaide's arrangement was adapted from Tiny Parham's "Original Boogie-Woogie," which he had edited for the Melrose Brothers' Music Company in 1938. Walter Melrose, then head of the company, had purchased the rights to "Pinetop's Boogie-Woogie" from Mayo Williams in the autumn of 1937. Dorsey's version of "Boogie-Woogie" has been one of the best sellers of all time, with pressings running beyond four million at the last count. It remains a beacon recording of band boogie-woogie. A four-record set of varied boogie-woogie players and band boogie, including Dorsey's masterpiece, was released on *Boogie-Woogie, Black and White Productions* (RCA, PM 42395).

There were other band leaders who commissioned boogie-woogie compositions. One of the most exciting was "Back Beat Boogie" (1939) by the Harry James Orchestra featuring Jack Gardener on piano. In the early 1940s, Teddy Powell gathered together a well-integrated unit pushed along by a relaxed driving rhythm section. Numbers made before the recording ban took effect were "Teddy Bear Boogie" (1939), "Jungle Boogie" (1941), "Bluebird Boogie" (1941) (drawing heavily on Ammons's "Boogie-Woogie Stomp"), and the best-known number, "In Pinetop's Footsteps" (1941). All were aimed at the commercial market and in this sense achieved their purpose without pretensions, or treading new ground. The piano playing is crisply executed with perhaps an undue reliance on Clarence Smith's boogie-woogie theme in several of the compositions. Other solos are taken by clarinet, tenor saxophone, trumpet, and trombone while the brass section riffs in response to the reeds' more melodic phrasing. There is already an element of sterility in these pieces, which presages the way orchestrated boogie-woogie would eventually go. Gene Krupa was prominent in his take-up of the style, recording a version of "Rhumboogie" (1941) before attempting to combine his own drumming prowess on "Drum Boogie" (1941) with a vocal by Irene Day. He used a similar approach on "Thanks for the Boogie Ride" (1941) with Anita O'Day as vocalist. Both pieces are pleasant novelties but add little to the canon of orchestral boogie.

The Woody Herman Orchestra came into prominence in the late 1930s as the band that played the blues, a policy that in retrospect could not have been sustained commercially for any length of time. Nevertheless, the band recorded some interesting and original big-band numbers with a boogie-woogie inspired flavor. They hit the charts with several blockbusters in 1939, including "Blues Upstairs" and its sequel "Blues Downstairs, Indian Boogie-Woogie" and the band's greatest hit of the year, "At the Woodchopper's Ball," which was built around riffs played over a walking bass. The band really explored the boogie-woogie genre in its smaller version, Woody Herman's "Four Chips," and recorded one notable piece,

"Chips Boogie-Woogie" (1940). These records owed their success to the piano playing of Herman's young pianist, Tommy Lineham, and the empathetic clarinet accompaniments by Herman in the duet sections with the piano. The last of these numbers with others by Bradley, Hampton, and Pete Johnson is included on *Rhythm and Blues and Boogie-woogie, Volume 3* (Swing House, SWH 43).

Herman's pianist, Tommy Lineham (1912–?) joined the band in 1936 and stayed until 1942. He began taking piano lessons when he was five. As his outstanding talent became obvious, a career on the concert platform was planned for him before he showed an interest in dance music when he was fourteen. His abilities in this field were nurtured in local bands in his hometown of North Adams, Massachusetts, before spells in Bermuda and Connecticut led him to New York. He was a member of Earl Bailey's Society band and, later, Charley Boulanger's Orchestra before joining Herman. Lineham's interest in boogie-woogie began after listening to the recordings of Pinetop Smith. He was a fluent interpreter of boogie-woogie and brought a distinctive individuality to his playing of it on Herman's recordings.

Another notable white American pianist who played boogie-woogie convincingly was Johnny Guarnieri (1917–1985), although he had no great affection for the style. His main source of employment in the early 1940s was with the bands of Benny Goodman, Artie Shaw, and Jimmy Dorsey. Guarnieri was an outstanding musician and arranger who used these abilities to freelance in recording studios throughout the mid-1940s. The best examples of his piano playing in the boogie-woogie style can be heard on a 1959 record that recreated many of the big-band hit versions of boogie-woogie. Will Bradley, the coleader of the band, also recreates some of his unique trombone solos on "Beat Me Daddy Eight to the Bar" and "Back Beat Boogie." These together with many others are on *The Will Bradley Johnny Guarnieri Band: Big Band Boogie* (RCA, LSA 3214).

Guarnieri first served notice that he could play boogie-woogie on the Artie Shaw recording of the two-part "Concerto for Clarinet" (1940), which Shaw made with his newly formed orchestra when he returned from a long sojourn in Mexico after becoming disaffected with leading a swing band. The number is in a symphonic style. Guarnieri's boogie-woogie contribution can be heard in a solo passage, using a rocks bass accompanied by Nick Fatool on cymbals, shortly after Shaw's introductory passage on clarinet. The piano work is both rhythmical and melodic. This strong solo gradually fades to provide an insistent rhythmical background on piano for additional solos from Shaw's clarinet and the tenor saxophone of Bus Bassey. "Concerto for Clarinet" was arranged by Lennie Hayton who used the boogie-woogie piano style in a particularly skillful way to produce a solid and rhythmical ground rhythm for some of the solos and ensemble passages, which contrasts well with the more melodic passages in the composition.

At the time when white band leaders were exploring the possibilities of boogie-woogie in orchestrated form, fewer African-American bands were following suit. Count Basie, as we have seen, was the exception. He had always drawn on the blues for material for his band, and it is surprising that he did not sustain his earlier entrance into the boogie-woogie arena with more band pieces in the early 1940s when the craze was at its height. When he did record numbers such as "Basie Boogie" (1944) and "Red Bank Boogie" (1946), the initial impetus for band boogie had largely passed. A selection of these numbers can be found on *Count Basie: Basie Boogie* (CBS, 21063).

An important recording by a black band that demonstrates all the finer points of orchestrated boogie-woogie is "After Hours" (1940), made by Erskine Hawkins and his Orchestra (1940) and featuring Avery Parrish at the piano. This was Parrish's finest piece, but shortly after making the recording, he suffered brain damage in a bar-room brawl and never again captured that haunting quality in his playing that had made "After Hours" such a success. The melancholic atmosphere is achieved by coupling passages of single notes with bell-like chords low on the keyboard, over slow boogie-woogie bass lines. Despite the success of this recording, Parrish, who was not essentially a boogie-woogie pianist, left no legacy of his further piano playing in the genre. This tune, though poorly reproduced, is available in a set of Hawkins's band recordings, *Erskine Hawkins and His Orchestra 1938–1945* (Bluebird, ND90363).

Of all the African-American band leaders who took up the boogie mantle, none did so with more enthusiasm or style than Lionel Hampton, a talented multi-instrumentalist adept on the vibraphone, the drums, and piano using a unique two-finger style. After early experiences with several bands in his adopted city of Chicago and in California, he joined Benny Goodman as an important member of his small units. International exposure on recordings during the four years with Goodman encouraged him to form his own band in 1940. It appears that rent-party pianist and journalist Dan Burley, whom Hampton knew from their days together in Chicago, probably helped him to choose the personnel for this venture. Certainly one of the first band boogies played by Hampton, "The Munson Street Breakdown" (1939), is credited by Nowakowski to Burley.[11] Hampton was a successful purveyor of a unique brand of boogie that leaned toward rhythm and blues in which the tenor saxophone of the hard blowing Illinois Jacquet is featured, riding on a piano, drum, guitar, and vibraphone backing. His best results were always achieved with a septet or octet producing a light spacious tone, permitting the soloists to be heard and properly appreciated. "Central Avenue Breakdown" (1940) was made with Nat "King" Cole on piano playing a foreshortened walking bass throughout. The same year, using a similar backing to underscore the number, "Pig Foot Sonata" was recorded but this time with St. Charles Thompson at the keyboard. This was not a twelve-bar format, but the end result was a pleasing amalgam of empathetic and intertwining vibraphone and piano tones. Another band boogie, "Three Quarters Boogie," was released in 1941. Lionel Hampton's most famous composition in the genre was undoubtedly "Hamp's Boogie-Woogie" (1944) with the diminutive Teddy Buckner pushing the number along from the piano stool. The piece involves the whole band and is interspersed throughout with breaks followed by changes in the piano basses. The final section contains a noisy rideout by the full band. Hampton's bands are recognized for the quality of the jazz produced by talented sidemen, but there are times when the music almost descends to the ill-disciplined and indulgent. Mention should also be made of Hampton's band cover of "Pinetop's Boogie-Woogie" (1946) with Bing Crosby, who reproduces Pinetop's patter fairly accurately with the occasional phrase of poetic license. A typical collection of Hampton's band boogies is available on *Lionel Hampton and His Big Band 1942–1949* (Jazz Portraits, CD 14565 AAD).

Albert Ammons was the featured piano player with Hampton (referred to in chapter 10), but a complete picture of Hampton's involvement with orchestrated boogie-woogie would be incomplete without marking a similar but later collaboration with German pianist Axel Zwingenberger. In 1982, they combined to record ten tunes that covered a range of boogie-woogie numbers from the early "Mr. Freddie Blues," through "Central Avenue Breakdown" to "Jivin' in Jazzland," reflecting Zwingenberger's earlier appearance at the club of that name in Vienna. This piece demonstrates one of Zwingenberger's most relaxed and fluent keyboard interpretations, touched by the ghost of Pete Johnson. His walking bass and sharp treble phrasing combine perfectly with animated riffing choruses from the band to lift the number and provide a platform for responsive solos from Arnett Cobb (tenor saxophone) and John Walker (trumpet). Of equal merit are the piano pyrotechnics on "The Sheik of Araby Boogie." The outline is similar to the version by Ammons recorded for Mercury. Zwingenberger's ideas flow effortlessly to bring a new dimension to the original. Their combined efforts can be found on *Lionel Hampton/Axel Zwingenberger: The Boogie-Woogie Album* (Telefunken, Gorilla, 6.25427 AS).

The introduction of lyrics into boogie-woogie compositions was probably the chief factor for its emergence into the popular music field. While many big bands maintained an acceptable "hot" quality in their boogie-woogie numbers, the appearance of lyrics transferred attention away from the subtleties of the music. The words of some of the "pop" boogie numbers recorded by Will Bradley's band, despite their banality, were acceptable when the musicianship of the players was so good, but jazz feeling, in its broadest sense, had gone when the Andrews Sisters and others sang their versions of "Scrub Me Mamma with a Boogie Beat" and "Beat Me Daddy Eight to the Bar." This is not to say that these pieces were not catchy or intrinsically well produced. Indeed, they were quite endearing, and the three sisters, Patty, LaVerne, and Maxine, had a combined vocal impact (two sopranos and a resonant contralto) that wrested full clarity and effect from the rhythm and words. Their most famous number, "The Boogie-Woogie Bugle Boy from Company B" (1941), is still sung and recorded by artists of today like Bette Midler. For an illustration of how the rawness of boogie-woogie was translated into vocal ditties, it is worth listening to the Andrews Sisters, Ella Fitzgerald, and other vocalists on *The Great Vocalists Meet Boogie-Woogie, Volume 5* (Joker, SM 4085). Placing "The Boogie-Woogie Bugle Boy" and similar tunes into the context of their time, it is possible to see how these much requested tunes helped to raise and sustain morale among the allied fighting forces and the populations of those countries involved in World War II. However, serious lovers of boogie-woogie departed at this point, leaving a musical form that had been compromised by commercial interests.

NOTES

1. John Bentley, correspondence with the author, July 11, 1991.
2. W. Balliett, *New Yorker Magazine*, November 29, 1976, 96.
3. D. Antoinette Handy, *Black Women in American Bands and Orchestras* (Lanham, MD: Scarecrow Press, 1981), 172.
4. Dan Gunderman, taped recollections sent to the author, circa March 1985.
5. "Bob Zurke Dead at 33," *Metronome*, March 1944, 10.
6. John Bentley, correspondence with the author, July 11, 1991.
7. George T. Simon, *The Big Bands* (New York: Schirmer Books, 1981), 95.
8. "Holt Leaves Bradley," *Downbeat*, July 15, 1941, 22.
9. "Bill Maxted Joins Bradley," *Downbeat*, August 1, 1941, 1.
10. "Don't Call Me Boogie King Says Bradley," Downbeat, November 15, 1941, 7. For a full account of the short-lived orchestra, see also Ian Crosbie, "The Will Bradley-Ray McKinley Orchestra," *Jazz Journal* 26, no. 2 (February 1973): 14–17.
11. Konrad Nowakowski, booklet accompanying *Dan Burley, South Side Shake 1945–1951*, Wolf Records, WBJ 008 CD, 18.

Part Four

THE FINAL CURTAIN

12

The End of an Era

Public interest in boogie-woogie music began to wane toward the close of the 1940s and then took a sharp downward spiral during the 1950s as pseudo-dixieland music and rock and roll took its place. This turn of events affected sales of boogie-woogie recordings other than to specialist collectors. It also reduced opportunities for regular club engagements for Lewis and Johnson, the two surviving members of the Boogie-Woogie Trio. Furthermore, with the demise of the big swing bands under way, the platform they had provided for the two men to make guest appearances at concerts and radio broadcasts also disappeared. Unfortunately, Johnson and Lewis were hoisted with their own petard. No one believed they could play in a style other than boogie-woogie, and they had to face the harsh economic reality of making a regular living from a music that the general public had now discarded. One of the last recordings of pure boogie-woogie by Lewis from this period was a four-track set from Clef in 1946, made at a Jazz at the Philharmonic (JATP) concert, which produced "Medium Boogie," "Yancey Special" with an ornate introduction, "Fast and Slow Boogies," plus "Honky Tonk Train Blues." These are all contained on the album referred to earlier: *Meade Lux Lewis: 1939 to Late 1940s* (Document, DOCD-5561).

Survival required certain adjustments to be made by both piano players. Lewis responded by extending his repertoire of tunes so that he would appeal to a wider audience. As the 1950s progressed, he began to play more standard tunes at his jazz-club appearances, as his regular broadcasts from the Hangover Club in San Francisco testify. On many Saturday evenings in 1953 and 1954 he went out on the air playing the standards "Up a Lazy River," "Deed I Do," "Dark Eyes," and so on, finishing his sets with his customary "Hey Momma, Thank You."

At this point in his career, many jazz critics were dismissive of his attempts to broaden his scope. The question remains to be asked whether they were really listening to what he was trying to do and judging the results on its merits as well as its weaknesses, of which, by normal standards of piano playing, there were several. He adopted two main techniques for coping with standard tunes: a stride bass pattern that moved from deep in the bass to well above the middle of the keyboard with the melody, which was constructed in chords and played toward the top of the treble range (he employed few single-note sequences in laying out the melody); alternatively, a single-note bass pattern played on the beat as a ground rhythm for the melody. The left and right hands were not always compatible, a result of having to adapt from a boogie-woogie background. The bass and treble parts were conceptualized independently, neither providing much harmonic support for the other. However, he brought a tremendous attack, swing, and pronounced rhythm to whatever he played, and this is sometimes overlooked when normal criteria are being applied and shortcomings found in his interpretations. In a rendition of "Coquette" from the Hangover in the 1950s, he produced a ground rhythm of single notes that "walked" on the beat to support the melody played high in the treble, with Meade's familiar growling accompaniment when he was "digging" into a tune. Another broadcast of the same period from the Hangover showed he had assimilated some slight boppish influences in playing his own composition "Round the Clock." This was, in its form, very much like the Dizzie Gillespie composition "Salt Peanuts."

The extent to which he moved from playing boogie-woogie to standards is recalled by Frank Gillis, a noted Detroit pianist and a former member of the Dixie Five and Doc Evans's bands.[1] In 1949, Gillis was appearing at a club on Northwestern Highway in Detroit where Lewis was engaged to play in the intermission. Having held a great admiration for Lewis over many years, Gillis spent his break listening to him instead of resting in the band room. One complete set was taken up with a rendition of "Honky Tonk Train Blues," which went on for half an hour or more with a series of crescendos and climaxes. It was a marathon performance in which the rhythm rolled relentlessly and the dynamic qualities of the piece were sustained throughout. Gillis went to see Lewis again in 1959, this time playing in a bar on Hennepin Street in the same city. Lewis, positioned on a small bandstand high above the bar, did two sets without once playing a note of boogie-woogie. Most of his program consisted of standard thirty-two-bar tunes, two of which Gillis recalls were "Someday Sweetheart" and "Sweet Lorraine."

The transformation was all the more remarkable because Lewis could not read music very well and did not begin taking formal piano lessons until the 1950s. He had a very good ear for a melody, extemporizing and ad-libbing constantly, and he used these abilities when playing standard tunes. He has been quoted as saying, when asked if he read music, that it looked like Chinese to him, but if he could hum the tune, he was away. Meade's playing of boogie-woogie at this time seems to have been limited to a few of his more famous compositions such as "Honky Tonk Train Blues," "Yancey Special," "Boogie Tidal," and "Six Wheel Chaser." They were frequently dressed up to make them more appealing and dramatic. "The Train," which had been getting faster in the 1940s, reached break-neck speed in the 1950s, so much so that the bass line had to be played as quarter notes in order to accommodate the clattering torrent in the treble. The original introductory tremolo to the piece was now contrasted with a meandering symphonic-type melody of a few bars length that preceded it; a similar effect was introduced at the beginning of "Yancey Special." The public still expected some boogie-woogie playing from Meade, however, and this was often presented to them as a show-stopper played at a furious pace. All of his fast boogies from the Blue Note and Asch recordings seemed to meld together, so that what audiences heard was a medley of choruses taken from "Chicago Flyer," "Lux's Boogie," "Meade's Boogie," and "Randini's Boogie." Although some of these efforts became a parody of his real talents, sometimes cliché-ridden, occasionally flashy and full of riffy choruses, at their root still lay the brilliance and originality of a masterful performer.

In 1951, Lewis recorded a collection of sides for the Atlantic label under the title *Meade Lux Lewis Interprets the Great Boogie-Woogie Masters* (Atlantic, 113). The numbers are "Yancey Special," which shows, in the appearance of several new choruses, that his creative spark was not yet extinguished; "Pinetop's Boogie-Woogie," when, after the tremolo introduction, there follows a series of strongly hit riffed choruses showing minimal dependence on Pinetop's original conception; "Mr. Freddy's Blues," a powerful solo leavened by phrases reminiscent of Jimmy Yancey; and "Jumping for Pete," in which some of Pete Johnson's influence can be detected, overlain by the Lewis touch. He also demonstrates his control of the stride style on "C Jam Blues." The most exciting piece is Meade's masterful interpretation of "Cow Cow Blues," with its rumbling walking bass and sharply phrased stop choruses. Without a doubt, this was a clever interpretation of Davenport's classic to which Lewis brought something new and original, and it became his new show stopper to rival "The Train." This recording session could not in any way be considered representative of Lewis's best work, but it did show that he could still interpret boogie-woogie with conviction. The change that had taken place between his earlier work and the Atlantic recordings was in the sustained aggression now permeating his playing. It had the effect of removing the contrastive elements in the music, leaving it devoid of much of its subtlety.

Two further recordings show Lewis's expanding style. They are the albums *Cat House Piano*, made for Verve in 1955, and the *Riverside* album of 1961. Both include a mixture of standard tunes and new boogie-woogie numbers and reinforce the aforementioned trend that Lewis was now moving beyond boogie-woogie into new areas for economic reasons as much as for a desire to extend his range beyond the confines of the twelve-bar blues. This view is reinforced in Chris Albertson's liner notes on the *Riverside* recording, in which Meade is quoted as expressing a strong preference for recording new material. Fortunately, on this recording, Meade never forsakes his impeccable sense of rhythm and timing. Occasionally, they are combined with flashes of real inspiration as on "Hammer Shatter," which is reminiscent of "Bear Cat Crawl" with its single-note bass; the fast "Bear Cat Stomp" with its sustained treble inventiveness; and, another original, the deeply felt "Rough Seas"—a reminder to Meade of "rough but beautiful days." True enjoyment of the boogie-woogie on the *Riverside* album comes from a sustained listening in which one is consistently impressed by the range of ideas and their singular interpretation. Ten numbers, with Lewis playing either piano or celeste, are included on *The Blues Piano Artistry of Meade Lux Lewis* (Riverside, OJCCD-1759-2).

The influence of musical fashions of the period can be clearly discerned in Meade's playing of both boogie-woogie and standard material on the *Cat House Piano* album on the Verve label from 1955, where bop-inflected single-note choruses, often delayed behind the beat, appear on "Torpedo Juice" alongside full-chorded choruses reminiscent of Erroll Garner; in comes the latest popular Latin American rhythm on "Meade's Mambo," producing an innocuous number of little form or melody. One unfortunate consequence of these wider ventures was a reduction in its contrapuntal and percussive elements of the music that had contributed so much to its greatness. Meade is on familiar ground with the traditionally styled "Joe Prein's Boogie" (named after a friend), a rocking fast number with breaks that rises and falls in intensity, pushed along by Jo Jones (drums) and Red Callender (bass). Similarly, "620 Boogie" has an insistent and menacing bass pattern that leaves a powerful aural impression of a particularly hard, urban stimulus for the piece. In fact, its genesis was from the Watts region of Los Angeles where Meade lived. This latter album was produced by Norman Granz, the promoter of JATP.

In the previous year (1954), Lewis had also recorded another set for Norman Granz's Clef label, partnered by a young Louie Belson who provided a sensitive drum backing with brushes. This album was later released on the Downhome Record label with the title "Yancey's Last

Ride." Several of these pieces found Lewis in an unusually subdued and reflective mood, using his open basses on numbers such as "Yancey's Last Ride" and "Shooboody," on which he builds climactic choruses of repetitive struck chords interspersed among passages of melodic blues. The six plus minutes of "Hangover Boogie" bring together all the unique features of Meade's technique: rumbling bass, sustained attack at the keyboard, speed of execution, and new configurations of treble phrases and dissonant chords rolling unfettered from his fingers. This is Lewis at his greatest, and is one of the best of his later recordings. The numbers on "Cat House Piano" and those on "Yancey's Last Ride," initially released on vinyl, have been combined and reissued on a CD as *Cat House Piano: Meade Lux Lewis* (Verve, 314 557098-2).

Popular commercial music has always been subjected to fads, some lasting longer than others. In the years before World War I and immediately afterward, ragtime was the favored style; swing and boogie-woogie held sway during the 1940s. By the time the fifties were under way, dixieland jazz was being pumped out on the radio—a diluted version of an earlier traditional-jazz revival. Shortly afterward and associated with it, came a short commercial ragtime revival played on doctored pianos. In England, Joe "Fingers" Carr and Winifred Atwell were two of the better-known performers, and in the United States "Crazy" Otto held sway. It could be posited that the earlier contrapuntal tones of Bob Zurke's unique piano technique were in part responsible for the popularity of the "jangle" piano. Its attraction was short-lived for young people, however, who were captivated more by the music of Chuck Berry, Elvis Presley, and Bill Haley and now danced to the beat of rock and roll. Joining the ragtime fashion, Meade began to include jazz numbers from the 1920s in his choice of tunes and even made recordings of them on Barrelhouse Piano (Tops) recorded in 1956 and reissued as *Meade Lux Lewis: Barrelhouse Piano* (Jasmine, JASMCD 2536). Jazz tunes were interspersed with boogie-woogie numbers and blues tunes. He produced passable versions of "Jada," "Someday Sweetheart," and "Darktown Strutter's Ball" on a doctored piano accompanied by guitar, bass, and drums. Though catchy and pleasant sounding, there was little jazz content in any of these numbers, which were quite definitely aimed at the commercial market. A similar pattern could be discerned in his final recording session from 1961, *Meade Lux Lewis's House Party* (Phillips, 200), which, in the choice of numbers, reverted to some of his well-known boogie-woogie numbers, "Yancey Special," "Glendale Glide," and others modified for popular consumption, alongside the traditional tunes "At a Georgia Camp Meeting" and "When Johnny Comes Marching Home."

It would be unfair to judge Lewis's ability as a boogie-woogie pianist solely on the evidence of his recordings of the 1950s and 1960s, though, as mentioned, there were several new and original compositions. The truth was that he lived by his music and was obliged to sell records and continue an endless round of club engagements to make enough money for his everyday needs. He should, rather, be admired for his tenacity and adaptability in adjusting to changing musical fads, enabling him to survive as a revered and original musician long after some of his music had forsaken its roots.

Meade's physical size frequently caused a ripple of whispers from the audience when he stepped onto the stage. Whatever he felt about this, he always ignored the audience reaction, bore it stoically, and silenced further comment with his wild boogie-woogie. Such was the power of his attack that some club owners were reported to have complained that he scarred the woodwork of their pianos with his fingernails. He would rub his left elbow ruefully when requested to play "Honky Tonk Train Blues," because by this time the bass had to be played at a fast rhythm to accommodate the ever-increasing speed of the treble choruses.

He appears to have given true friendship at this time to only a few close intimates with whom he had regular contact. Joe Sullivan from the Café Society days and the Hangover Club, and Art Tatum from their time together at Café Society and West Coast clubs, were the two he knew most closely, and with whom he shared his deeper feelings. Both pianists respected his keyboard ability, particularly in the playing of boogie-woogie; both played in the style and featured it within their own broad selections. Meade, for his part, had a high regard for the work of both men and no doubt saw in their playing something that he would have liked to have done himself in his later years. Of passing interest in this respect is Ralph Gleason's obituary of Lewis;[2] he believed that Meade regretted not being able to expand his horizons to include other forms of jazz piano and in his latter years felt imprisoned by the blues.

Someone who knew Meade very well is Bob Seeley, an outstandingly good interpreter of Meade's style of playing whose home city is Detroit.[3] The friendship began initially through Lewis's acknowledgment that Seeley was a fine pianist in his own right, but it flourished over the years beyond this common bond into a genuine relationship built on trust. A study of aspects of the friendship throws some additional light on Meade Lux Lewis the man. Seeley's background was typical of that of many white boys raised in a comfortable city home in the 1940s. He began piano lessons at about the age of nine and was introduced to boogie-woogie in his teens when an older brother brought some sheet music home. Finding his attempts thwarted to play from the music, Seeley listened to records by members of the Trio and was immediately captivated by the genre. The recordings by Lewis left an especially deep impression.

The first opportunity Seeley had of seeing Lewis performing in person was at the Hotel Sherman in the early 1950s. Bobby Sherwood's band was featured with Meade as the intermission pianist. As Seeley was too young to be admitted to the Panther Room where Meade was appearing, he was obliged to stay in the hotel lounge with a friend and watch through a window. He was able to pick out the fingering of "Honky Tonk Train Blues" and "Yancey Special" before Meade blended with the band to take part in a jam session.

Seeley next saw Lewis when he and some high-school friends went to see the JATP concert at the Masonic Temple Auditorium in Detroit. After the show, they waited outside for Lewis to appear to collect his autograph. Meade said he was going to a party at 421 East Warren and suggested they might like to join him there if they had nothing else to do. Excited at the prospect of hearing more of Meade's piano playing, Seeley and friends arrived at the house well before Meade. The surprised host admitted them after they had explained their unexpected invitation. Helen Humes, who was with the Count Basie band, was already there and after talking with her the young Seeley was prevailed upon to play the piano. He was well into "Chicago Flyer" before Lewis eventually appeared. It was clear from his confused expression that Meade could not quite work out who was playing one of his most technically difficult pieces so well. Without passing comment, he took the piano stool himself and began playing a very rhythmical rendition of "The Gypsy," building up the choruses with his familiar vocalizing and growling accompaniment. After Lewis had played several other numbers, he left the party and Seeley and friends remained to talk with Helen Humes well into the night.

Four years after this initial meeting, Seeley went with friends to hear Lewis again at the State Show Bar on James Couzens Highway in Detroit. Their arrival coincided with Meade playing "Cow Cow Blues," and as they passed by the piano he raised an eyebrow in recognition. Los Angeles is twenty-five hundred miles from Detroit, and Meade had driven nonstop for the engagement in his large Chrysler New Yorker. The long, tiring journey, together with the alcohol consumed during the evening, had their effects, and he fell asleep around midnight sitting at the piano. This was a typical way of traveling for Meade, which, although taxing, was preferable because segregation made it difficult to find suitable hotel accommodation serving African-Americans. Those that existed were often located in rundown areas and were not always pleasant or even clean places. Seeley attended every show during that week's engagement and was invited by Meade to play in the intermission. Meade clearly enjoyed Seeley's piano playing and on one occasion sat in a chair, eyes closed, swaying gently to the rhythm of "Boogie Tidal," a contented man. Their real friendship dated from this encounter and continued until Meade's death.

Opportunities for regular employment were uncertain and, as mentioned, Lewis would travel long distances and go anywhere to maintain a regular income. One week would see him at Hanratty's Bar in New York or a similar high-class piano bar; the next week he would be providing the background music at some nondescript bar, unannounced and largely unknown. On one occasion at the State Show Bar, Seeley remarked to Meade that it must be wonderful to travel widely and perform in so many different bars. Meade turned to the bartender and with a cynical laugh said, "Hey, tell this kid." The possibility of a steady income and less traveling were simply not available to him. The chance to earn money was in clubs, bars, and through occasional recordings—and then the return was not that good for the time and effort involved.

At this time, Meade's permanent home was in the Watts district of Los Angeles where he lived in a modest house in a well-kept neighborhood at 629 East 116th Place. Whenever Seeley was in the Los Angeles area, he would visit Meade's home to see him. In 1958, Lewis was increasing the number of standard tunes in his program, indicating that economic necessity had brought about the change of emphasis in his selection of material. Although Meade still composed and recorded boogie-woogie, he had been delighted to listen to the Paramount album *Roaring Twenties*—consisting of tunes from this period—on a reel-to-reel tape recorder that Bob Seeley had installed under the backseat of his Volkswagen. Lewis admitted to some anguish, however, at the disappointing review it received in *Downbeat*. Similarly, a review in *Jazz Journal* was equally lukewarm, suggesting that he was struggling with the material and should stick to boogie-woogie. On the other hand, he told Seeley, he had been hurt by criticisms that he could play only boogie-woogie, so how was he expected to rationalize these opposing views? Another reviewer identified the paradox of the mixed selection of tunes but came out strongly in favor of two boogie-woogie numbers, "Meade's Deed" and "Lux Flakes," believing they were a proper reflection of his talents and compared well with his brilliance of the late 1930s. Unfortunately, poor reviews meant less income, as well as hurt pride.

One indulgence that Lewis had was for large cars, and he spent many hours cleaning and polishing them. He normally drove the largest model in the Chrysler range. Seeley particularly remembers one occasion when he was asked to reverse one of Meade's cars, newly polished and with gleaming chrome over-riders, down the narrow drive leading from his house, with the diminutive Meade directing operations from behind the car. Knowing of the intense pleasure Meade obtained from his car and being unsure of the reaction of his idol if he were to scrape it, Seeley found the experience more nerve-racking than performing one of Meade's compositions in front of his mentor.

Despite the privations of his long hours spent on the road, and in indifferent bars and clubs, Lewis was still sufficiently in demand to be engaged for the "Piano Parade" package tour organized by the Gale Organization in 1952, together with Pete Johnson, Art Tatum, and Erroll Garner. The tour traveled to Chicago, Detroit, Kansas City, Minneapolis, Pittsburgh, and Toronto. An enthusiastic audience at this concert made so much noise that the pianists were unable to hear themselves playing. The program welcomed the presence of the two pianists with a reminder that they were not museum pieces but would start feet tapping with their modern melodies and rhythms. Immediately after this event, Johnson and Lewis teamed up to appear at Birdland in New York for two weeks, followed by their appearance at the Flame Show Bar and the Black and Tan Club in Detroit. There was talk while there that Meade might accompany Olive Brown, a local blues singer, on a series of club and recording engagements, but nothing concrete emerged from these discussions.

Another engagement for Lewis, interspersed between "jobbing" on the West Coast, was at the Blue Note Club in Chicago in 1954. Reporting on Lewis's appearance, Tom Harris remarked on the sparse audience, perhaps indicative of the public's growing disenchantment with the piano style.[4] Fortunately, more consistently responsive customers were drawn to the Hangover Club on Bush Street in San Francisco in 1953 and 1954. The club was situated in the Bay Area, and anyone in search of good jazz could not fail to miss the premises, which were announced by a vivid neon sign. One of Lewis's engagements there was shared with Ralph Sutton, who represented a contrasting piano style. In this most cosmopolitan of cities, they played to capacity audiences who filled the room, sitting near the bandstand and nestling behind the long bar. Plenty of liquor was consumed, fueling the audience's appreciation of the frantic boogie-woogie playing with which Lewis usually completed his intermission set. Ralph Sutton recalls that they had a good time together at the Hangover Club where Lewis was the intermission pianist and Sutton the band pianist. After Lewis finished his engagement there, Sutton never saw him again.[5] Live recordings from the Hangover Club from these years were issued on vinyl; they featured Meade playing well-known tunes such as "Glendale Glide" and "Six Wheel Chaser," accompanied by "Smokey" Stover on drums and other resident jazzmen.

Television offered Meade the chance to diversify his talents into a small speaking and piano-playing role with the making of the *Roaring Twenties* series featuring Dorothy Provine. Meade made several appearances as "Jelly," the proprietor of a bar where some of the action took place. The various episodes were filmed in the late 1950s and early 1960s. A guest appearance on the popular Steve Allen talk show in 1960 saw him performing a potpourri of boogie-woogie choruses drawn mainly from "Six Wheel Chaser" and then joining Steve Allen for a boogie-woogie duet on two pianos. NBC produced a two-part TV special entitled *Chicago and All*

That Jazz and invited Meade to appear on it, for which he was reported to have received one thousand dollars. Shortly before he recorded his contribution, he was visited by a friend at home who found him assiduously practicing "Honky Tonk Train Blues." The friend was surprised that Lewis would consider it necessary to practice such a familiar piece, but it indicates the perfection that he sought in his technique and the importance of the event for him, perhaps believing that it would provide impetus for his now inconsistent career.[6] Opportunities for film work were spasmodic: cameo appearances were made in *It's a Wonderful Life*, starring James Stewart, and *Nightmare*, a thriller from 1956. The setting for this film is New Orleans and Lewis plays the piano in a club sequence. He has one line of dialogue before the scene fades, leaving the sound of his piano continuing off-camera.

In the early 1960s, it was the mixture as before: an appearance at Embers, a nightspot in New York in 1962; various guest spots at West Coast jazz clubs, including a weekend appearance in 1964 at the Society for the Preservation of New Orleans Jazz in Los Angeles; the Chateau de Paris in the Dyckman Hotel in Minneapolis in the same year; and always, on returning home to Los Angeles, regular participation at the monthly conventions of the Los Angeles Pianists' Club situated on Sunset Boulevard. He was increasingly reported as being "at liberty" in the club's broadsheet.

It had become apparent to Meade as early as the *Downbeat* interview of 1959 that there was more work for him on the eastern side of the country. Offers from here were usually accompanied by better rates than on the West Coast. He was particularly fond of Minneapolis and St. Paul, where Mrs. James Buckner, a widowed niece, lived, and he returned to the city as often as he could, even contemplating moving his home there permanently. The recollections of these times by Denise Buckner, a grand-niece of Meade, reveal a loving and intimate family picture.[7] Denise was age seven or eight and remembers looking forward to his visits as someone special in the family. When he visited, family and friends gathered to greet him, although they were not aware of his background as one of the most famous boogie-woogie pianists, only that he was an entertainer who made a reasonable living and had a home in Los Angeles. This, she feels, must have been very significant, because at this time there were few African-American entertainers who lived in this style. Folks would take photographs and joke with him, sometimes throughout the night. At Christmastime, he always sent the family a large parcel packed with toys and food. Denise describes him as a generous and popular man who was "loved by everybody of the Minneapolis family when I was a kid" and who perhaps found his surrogate family at her mother's home.

When Meade went downtown to buy food and drink, Denise used to hide under the dashboard of his large car. He only ever drank beer, although her grandfather, who lived in the same house and with whom Meade had a good rapport, produced his own "moonshine." Meade stuck to beer and astonished the family with his ability to down a bottle at one go. At mealtimes, a handkerchief appeared that was whisked over his mouth with practiced skill. Denise found out later from her mother that this ritual was because he had false teeth and the handkerchief hid their removal and return before and after eating. He had always enjoyed food and was particularly fond of the meals prepared by Denise's mother, who observed that he was very particular about drinking and eating the right kind of food, of which fish was a major element. He maintained his passion for fishing, taking every opportunity of partaking and talking animatedly about the successes and failures with friends during his stays.

One venue in Minneapolis where he appeared annually was the White House Restaurant, a superior roadhouse situated in suburban Golden Valley. He began a three-week engagement there in the middle of May 1964, which proved to be as successful as his previous appearances. In the early hours of Sunday, June 7, at about two o'clock, Meade, having completed his engagement, climbed into his Chrysler Imperial and drove out of the parking lot turning east onto the Olsen Memorial Highway. As he did so, a car driven by Ronald Bates, estimated to be traveling in excess of eighty miles per hour, hit him from the rear. His car was shunted across the road for four hundred feet before smashing into a tree with enormous impact. He was pinned between the car and the tree and died instantly. A passenger in the other car died in the hospital the following day. On June 8, Bob Seeley picked up his mail at home in Detroit and read a letter from Meade with a St. Paul postmark dated June 6, 1964. It contained details of the White House engagement. On the same day some hours later, Seeley opened his newspaper to read of Meade's death. The letter was probably the last one Meade ever wrote.

Reports of his death and obituaries quickly appeared in the major newspapers. The *New York Herald Tribune*[8] headline got right to the point with its announcement that Meade Lux Lewis, the jazz pianist, had been killed after his car had been rammed by a speeder; while the *New York Times*[9] informed its readers that one of the leaders of boogie-woogie had been killed in Minnesota at the age of fifty-eight. The *Los Angeles Times*,[10] in an obituary written for the man who had made that city his home, acknowledged his important role in establishing boogie-woogie as an indigenous American musical style; and the local Minneapolis paper, the *Morning Tribune*,[11] announced that he had been an unfortunate victim of a crash, adding that he had been considering settling in the Twin Cities.

Denise Buckner remembers the devastating impact of Meade's death on the family and how her mother was distraught. Denise visited the room in their house where he used to stay and where there was still the lingering perfume of Old Spice aftershave. She and her mother undertook a two-day rail journey to attend the funeral in Los Angeles, but her only recollections, as a young child at the time, are of wreaths of red and white flowers. Some years later, she was delighted to be invited to attend a tribute concert arranged at the Riverview Supper Club in Minneapolis on October 11, 1992, at which Bob Seeley and others paid their respects to his originality and genius at the keyboard; and she was proud to be identified and introduced to the audience as one of Meade's last living relatives.

What can be said as a requiem to Meade Lux Lewis? His career had peaks and troughs; at the time of his death he was beginning to rise again. A new public in Europe could have been available to him with a scheduled appearance planned at a major jazz festival in Berlin in 1965. Perhaps he would have been an inspiring mentor to the coterie of boogie-woogie pianists who have been active in Germany, France, Austria, Holland, and Great Britain since the 1970s. He will be remembered as the genius of boogie-woogie; a professional musician through and through who was punctual and reliable; a man who was generous in his praise of fellow pianists, reflected in a quote made to Bob Seeley: "Everybody's got something; nobody's got it all." The private Meade loved golf and big cars, and he played a little self-taught Chopin to himself. To the public Meade displayed an awesome talent for composing original and exciting boogie-woogie numbers that brought great pleasure to thousands of people from all walks of life. The last word is given to the late Richard Lindaman, a perceptive analyst of the boogie-woogie art, pianist, and long-term collector of Lewis's recordings, who described the impact made on him by Lewis at Randini's Club in the mid-1940s: "He was still a striking genius and on the other hand I talked to him a couple of times and he didn't seem anything special, but one was just utterly astounded and it seemed like he must have been the tool of some higher power—a whole folk ethos was bubbling through him. Somehow, it didn't seem like that man could be responsible for all that wonderful stuff and yet it is interesting the extent to which he was."[12]

Pete Johnson spent the last years of the 1940s working on the West Coast. In 1947, he joined Albert Ammons at the Streets of Paris nightspot and then, in 1948, he teamed up once again with Joe Turner to play at the Memo Cocktail Lounge and at Harold Blackshear's Supper Club, both San Francisco venues. This work was followed by an engagement at the Hotel Ambassador in Santa Monica. An appearance at The Just Jazz concert took place in Pasadena in 1947 where he was introduced, to rapturous applause, to play "Yancey Special," "St. Louis Boogie," "J. J. Boogie," and "Swanee River Boogie," all released on *Gene Norman Presents "Just Jazz": Pete Johnson in Concert* (Vogue, EPV 1039). He saw the decade out, still able to obtain employment fairly comfortably. At this time, in 1949, he met and married his second wife Marge. He already had a daughter, Margaret Lucille, born in 1937, by a previous marriage. By 1952, Margaret was a more than competent pianist with five town-hall recitals in New York to her credit, not, it should be added, playing boogie-woogie. In the year of his second marriage, he and his new wife took the significant decision to move from the West Coast to the eastern side of America, settling in Buffalo on the Great Lakes. Buffalo was at that time an important port, the flour-milling capital of America. A cosmopolitan population of Irish, Germans, Poles, and African-Americans lived and worked there. Although it was centrally positioned for Johnson to travel east and west for engagements—that was one of the reasons he chose it—it was not foreseen by the Johnsons that the city and its immediate environs would be a musical desert, providing few opportunities for regular club work.

Pete and his wife rented a three-room apartment reached by a flight of steep steps in the middle of the black district. It was a warm and clean home, in distinct contrast to the neighborhood in which it was situated, where a barbershop, a drug store, and a multitude of other shops nestled together with apartments over them. Almost immediately, the decline began for Johnson and he was obliged to look for other work outside music, starting as a receiving-clerk porter, hanging and carrying meat. For this work he received forty dollars per week, but he also contracted pneumonia from working in the large refrigerators; arthritis also began to affect his joints.

In 1952, life took a turn for the better with a renewal of his partnership with Meade Lux Lewis. The high spot was the Piano Parade tour and their subsequent duet work at the Celebrity Club in Rhode Island, the Sportsman's Club in Newport, and the Flame Show Bar in Detroit, for a two-week spot. Meade stayed over with the Johnsons in Buffalo, because they both expected that an agent would find them additional work. Unfortunately, this did not materialize, so Meade returned to Los Angeles. Johnson obtained more work in August with appearances at the Boulevard Room in Kansas City and was a regular feature for two nights a week at Otey's Club, a rundown spot in Niagara Falls. He joined up with Prince Waterford for this engagement. Another venue was the Del Monica bar in Binghamton, New York, where Ray Nelson, a young lecturer working as a mathematician at IBM, made his acquaintance in 1952. He wandered into the bar and chatted with Johnson over a few drinks at the bar while the pianist took his break between sets. Prior to this, Johnson had been showing film of himself and Ammons playing at Carnegie Hall. Telling Johnson of his own interest in boogie-woogie and his ability as a player—he could play most of the Ammons and Johnson duets—he was surprised and flattered to hear Johnson announce at an intermission that he (Nelson) would play the next set. Bolstered by the atmosphere and the beers, he entertained with "Yancey Special" and Lewis's earliest recording of "Honky Tonk Train Blues." Everyone appeared to be impressed with the performance, particularly Johnson, who expressed his delight. At this point, the proprietor was asked by Johnson to provide another piano, and the evening was concluded with both of them improvising two piano boogie-woogies drawn from the Ammons and Johnson duets. Nelson left the club a very happy young man.[13]

An unfortunate accident occurred toward the end of 1952 after Johnson attended a concert at the Memorial Auditorium in Buffalo to hear his old friend Bill Basie. On the return journey, his car broke down. Hailing a passing motorist, they fixed a tow rope to the immobile car, and as the rope took the strain, one of Johnson's fingers became trapped in the rope and the end was sliced off. His financial circumstances did not allow him to take the required rest for a full recovery. A pianist from Buffalo, Hank Roberts, substituted for him at Otey's for a short period, but Johnson was soon forced back to playing the piano, in some pain, with the damaged finger heavily bandaged.

The decline continued throughout 1953, with very few opportunities for work. Between January and October he was employed by an ice-cream company washing trucks and added to this modest income money earned as a member of a trio that performed at weekends in the Bamboo Room in Buffalo. The working hours at the ice-cream company were from 3:00 p.m. until 11:00 p.m., clashing with the weekend bookings, which started at 10:00 p.m. A considerate manager, sympathetic to Pete's circumstances, allowed him to leave early in order to make the engagement on time. There were other jobs around Buffalo, but they were intermittent. Despite his earlier fame, Johnson was expected to audition for many of these low-level clubs. Audition time was often arranged at night, when customers were present, so that he often found himself providing free entertainment for them while he went through the motions of an audition.

In the following year, 1954, Johnson was once again obliged to seek employment outside music, and he washed cars at a mortuary for twenty-five dollars per week. In July, however, a prestigious job came his way at the St. Louis Forest Park Hotel, where he stayed for six weeks as resident pianist at the Circus Lounge. He and Albert had performed there together as a duo in 1943. Some broadcasts were made on Saturday afternoons from the KMOX radio station in a program entitled *Saturday at the Chase*, on which he was featured as a soloist and a member of the Bourbon Street Six, a traditional-jazz group.

It was during this engagement that an acquaintance was made with two young white pianists, Tom Harris and Charlie Castner, who had established something of a reputation for themselves as a boogie-woogie duet playing in the style of Ammons and Johnson. They already had one record album to their credit, *Powerhouse Piano*, which John Steiner had issued on his Paramount label. The two pianists and Johnson played at two weekend house parties arranged at the homes of John Phillips, a well-known figure in St. Louis jazz circles, and Bill Atkinson, a caterer and close friend of Johnson. Steiner took along some recording equipment, and private tapes were made of these very happy occasions. Apart from the improvised duets, trios, and vocal blues, the recordings display Johnson's versatility in playing standard tunes—a skill normally denied him on his recordings for national recording companies. Harris recalled the generous nature of Johnson, who spent many hours showing him various chord sequences as they sat together at the piano. Some of the recorded material has since been issued on *The St. Louis Parties 1954* (Document, DOCD 1017). The St. Louis engagement was followed by one in the autumn playing at weekends at the Ebony Room in Buffalo as a member of a small group consisting of piano, saxophone, drums, and guitar. This was probably the lowest point of Johnson's musical career since his Café Society days.

There was little work of any consequence for him during the next four years, except for three appearances in 1955 at the Berkshire Music Barn in Lennox, Massachusetts, accompanying Joe Turner and Jimmy Rushing separately at the first and second engagements and appearing as a soloist at the third one. The year 1958, however, saw an upturn in his fortunes, and it looked as though his talents, so long neglected, were once again to be recognized. He was invited to join the Norman Granz package tour, "Jazz at the Philharmonic," and although not feeling well, he accepted the invitation. This was the peak of a lifetime's ambition. A tour of Europe included visits to Brussels, Amsterdam, Munich, and other major continental cities together with Joe Turner, Stan Getz, and Dizzie Gillespie. They played to capacity houses and enthusiastic fans. When Stan Getz was brought on before the audience had heard enough of Dizzie Gillespie in Rome, the show was stopped because of the hullabaloo. The artists were given a police escort back to their hotels. Johnson even contemplated staying on in France, following suggestions from Charles Delaunay and Sam Price, who were living there, that there would be plenty of club work for him, but the uncertainty of obtaining engagements led to him turning down this opportunity. While on tour, another invitation came to him from George Wein to appear at the Newport Jazz Festival, which he accepted, as accompanist to Joe Turner, Big Maybelle, and Chuck Berry.

Returning to Buffalo, and work at Johnny Ellicott's Grill, the feeling of unease about his state of health finally led him to undergo a medical examination in August, which revealed that he had developed a heart condition and diabetes. Several strokes followed, with a loss in hand coordination that affected his piano playing.

Johnson's livelihood was now taken from him, and he had great difficulty in supporting himself financially. Four years after the strokes, he was still disabled and was also beginning to lose his eyesight. The church was beginning to mean more to him at this time in his life than at any other and he was confirmed in 1961. There were also his many friends, both in America and in Europe, with whom he maintained a regular if, at times, difficult correspondence compounded by his health problems. Pete Johnson's cause was eventually taken up by the magazine *Jazz Report*[14] with a series of articles about his life story written by Marge Johnson. Later editions attempted a discography. Auctions of records donated by its readers also raised money for him. Some of this was used to pay medical expenses for operations on his bladder and for a ruptured hernia. By this time, Pete and Marge had moved to an apartment at 76 Dodge Street, a rear ground-floor apartment in a large family house. Despite the privations, they maintained an open house for friends who rallied around, visited them, and tried to raise more money. The editor of *Jazz Report* also castigated the local union officials for not doing more to help Johnson. Ben Conroy was one who empathized with Johnson's plight early on and assisted with a gift of much-needed money. Conroy corresponded with him, through Marge who, due to his medical condition, acted as his writing intermediary. He enjoyed receiving correspondence from his fans, as Marge's letter from their earlier address at 141 Broadway indicates, with a request for Conroy to write another letter to Pete if he had the time. She also asked if he would mention a particular incident that occurred at the Café Society to jog Pete's memory of Conroy. The letter closed with their grateful thanks for Conroy's gift.[15]

In 1964, Hans Mauerer, one of his longtime correspondents from Germany, published a book entitled *The Pete Johnson Story*, with accompanying discography, and gave the money from its sale to its subject. The only other income that Johnson had at this time was seventy-nine dollars per month from Social Services, of which sixty-five was taken in rent. No regular royalty payments from recordings were received. James Wertheim reported that Johnson was experiencing difficulty in obtaining royalty payments other than from Blue Note and Victor, even after friends had written to record companies on his behalf.[16] Belatedly, in June, Johnson was accepted as a member of ASCAP, which ensured that he received at least some of his dues on a more regular basis. The close of 1964 and the early months of 1965 was a period of hospitalization for an operation on his leg, complicated by his diabetic condition.

In the last two years of his life, Pete Johnson began to regain a little more of his coordination. He even played one-handed piano with pianist Ray Bryant at a party after a concert given on his behalf by the Buffalo Philharmonic Orchestra. There was also a recital of his recordings arranged by a member of his church, which was played to a capacity audience in the church hall. Johnson's last public appearance was made at the Spirituals to Swing concert at Carnegie Hall in 1967. He had made eight appearances at these concerts in his lifetime, and it was fitting that the first and last significant musical occasions should have been on this particular platform. The climax of the concert came when Joe Turner joined the Café Society Band to sing "I'm Going Away to Wear You off My Mind." The scene was set with Joe's powerful singing and Ray Bryant's blues piano for Pete Johnson's last appearance for the most moving moment of the concert. Goddard Lieberson (the master of ceremonies) introduced the frail Johnson to the audience and reminded them that he had been one of the participants at the first concert in 1938. Turner and Johnson held hands as they stood together onstage to take the appreciative applause before the shuffling pianist joined Ray Bryant at the treble end of the piano to play "Roll 'Em Pete," with Bryant playing the bass. After a hesitant start, the number built to its usual intense climax. This was a happy event for both Pete and Marge Johnson, who was in the audience. Pete died on March 23, 1967, on the eve of his sixty-third birthday. His last years were encapsulated in a moving statement to a friend quoted in *The Pete Johnson Story* in which he acknowledged that he was now bearing the cost of his youthful excesses.[17]

Johnson was the most underrated of the three colossi who bestrode the boogie-woogie platform at the height of the music's popularity. Where Albert and Meade made an instant and immediate impact on the listener with their heavy basses, technical facility, and urgent rhythms, it was necessary to listen carefully to appreciate Pete Johnson's worth as pianist. His music was more subtle and at its best had a swing and clarity in the treble phrases that neither of the other two men ever achieved. These qualities were not easily picked out in duet and trio performances, and it is to his records that one should turn to confirm their presence in his solo piano playing. One can discern a growing confidence in Johnson's solo work as his prolonged experience and exposure helped develop his creativity, making him a consummate, all-around, modern-sounding blues and boogie-woogie pianist. His playing developed a richness and subtlety that flowered in the mid-1940s. The first recordings displaying these deeper qualities were made for Brunswick in 1944. They include a lilting stride version of "Mr. Freddy Blues" and an equally fine original "Lights Out Mood" in the same vein. Both contrast well with the compelling drumlike bass line of the medium-paced "Zero Hour," the melodic, downward spiraling bass line of "Rock It Boogie," and the supercharged "Answer to the Boogie" with its fast, hypnotic walking bass and breaks. This last number is much inspired by the earlier recorded "Holler Stomp." The full selection of these recording showing Johnson's diverse talents are available on *Pete Johnson 1940–1956, Jazz Museum, Volume 6* (MCA Coral, 0052.046).

Any postscript to Pete Johnson's musical legacy would begin by stating that he had never been given his due recognition as a jazz pianist and that he had been defined solely by boogie-woogie and the blues, whereas he possessed a wonderful technique that dispensed with virtuosity and harmonic tricks for their own sake; and this was fully demonstrated in the musical ideas he purveyed.

Following his death, Johnson drew plaudits from many quarters. Of particular poignancy was the obituary notice appearing in Canadian jazz magazine *Coda* written by John Norris, who had been in contact with the Johnsons over the ten-year period of their most difficult times, visiting to their different homes on a number of occasions in the process of cementing their friendship. He considered Johnson's endowment to jazz to be considerable, with his recordings providing a constant reminder of his greatness. His death, recorded in the *San Francisco Chronicle*, mentioned his place as a revered pianist from the boogie-woogie years of the 1940s.[18]

Jimmy Yancey's lifestyle was only marginally affected by the jazz public's discovery of his keyboard talents. In the mid- and late 1940s until his death in 1951, he rarely left Chicago, where he followed a regular routine working as groundskeeper at Comiskey Park, some eight blocks from his home, and playing the piano as a relaxation for himself and his friends. There were three important stabilizing elements in his life that no amount of public attention was allowed to disturb. They were his wife, Estelle, his piano, and the White Sox baseball team. His intention to remain apart from the professional musicians' circuit of regular club engagements notwithstanding, he did make one or two appearances at major concerts and at selected clubs. The latter engagements were featured spots, normally published in advance, when Estelle and he would play through a program of their numbers. Then there were the times he would appear unannounced at the Apex and other clubs late at night to play the piano, because he did not wish to disturb the neighbors in the tenement house where he lived. One of the clubs where the Yanceys gave several Sunday afternoon concerts was the College of Complexes, a small dingy place with a bandstand at one end and walls covered in blackboards for people to leave messages or simply to indulge their taste for graffiti. Other venues were the Hunt Club on Roosevelt Road and the popular Beehive club, which hosted many jazz groups, notably those featuring Miff Mole (trombone) supported by Warren "Baby" Dodds (drums) steering along the rhythm. It was a small, unpretentious club situated on Fifty-fifth Street near Harper. A bar ran along its length on the right-hand wall, and behind this was the bandstand, with piano, raised to the same height as the bar so that customers could see as well as hear the musicians.

As to the concerts, the most significant was an appearance at Carnegie Hall on April 30, 1948, playing solo piano and accompanying Estelle's vocals. He shared the billing with Kid Ory and his Creole Jazz Band and Lonnie Johnson. Numbers included in the Yancey contribution were "How Long," "See See Rider," and "Make Me a Pallet on the Floor." In the same year, he and Albert Ammons appeared together at Orchestra Hall in Chicago and, later, he and Estelle were together at a concert in Minneapolis, but he was unable to sing at this engagement because he had recently had some false teeth fitted.

John Steiner maintained regular contact with Jimmy Yancey in the late years of the 1940s, a relationship that culminated in a recording session for Steiner's own Paramount label—he and a friend had purchased all their masters in 1950. In 1950, Jimmy made six sides issued on a red vinyl LP: "Yancey Special," "Jimmy's Goodnight Blues," "Keep a Knocking," "Assembly Call Boogie," "Everlasting Blues," and "Barber Shop Rag," which are all on *"Yancey Special": Six Piano Numbers by Jimmy Yancey* (Paramount, CJS 101). Before this event, Steiner had been to see Yancey at his favorite Chicago haunts and also visited him at his apartment to hear him playing in the intimacy of his own home. Jimmy paid two visits to Steiner's house to play for his friends who were passing through Chicago. After the first recital, Steiner gave Jimmy a screwdriver and asked him to scratch his name on the piano lid, where there were already many distinguished signatures etched into the woodwork. Steiner collected over thirty names on the piano, which was eventually destroyed in a house fire, including those of Bob Zurke, Joe Sullivan, and Billy Kyle. Jimmy obliged but misspelled his first name by omitting a letter *m*.[19] This mistake may have been caused through embarrassment at being asked to desecrate the instrument, but a more likely reason may have been his limited literacy as witnessed by Estelle's writing most of the letters and handling the contractual side of his recording work.

It has always been assumed that Jimmy Yancey could play only blues and boogie-woogie. As this was the style in which the public was interested when he was discovered, Yancey only ever played his particular brand of boogie-woogie on recordings and at public appearances. To have made his mark on these occasions as a pianist playing in any other style would have required him to have been at least the equal, in technique and creative ability, of the top piano players of the day such as Zurke, Mary Lou Williams, Hines, Waller, Sullivan, and Henke. Clearly, his untutored background was not equal to this, although possessing the rudiments of a formal technique gleaned from his brother Alonzo. The limited evidence that does exist suggests that Jimmy could play in other styles as well as boogie-woogie but that he never put any of this music on record. On his second visit to Steiner's house, a friend remarked that he had never heard the tune "Margie" played as a piano solo. Some fifteen minutes or so later, after cogitating on this remark and picking out the melody, Jimmy produced a good straight version of the tune without any boogie-woogie influence. A private tape exists of one of the Yancey's house parties (owned by Dick Mushlitz and Phil Kiely) and since issued on *The Unissued 1951 Yancey Wire Recordings* (Document, DOCD 1007) containing many of the well-known Yancey tunes, but there are also tantalizing snatches of him playing a few ragtime choruses. Not much needs to be made of the other side of Yancey's piano playing, except to add that his recordings do not fully reflect his full range at the keyboard.

The Yanceys lived in a wood-clad frame house on Eleventh West and Thirty-fifth Street, off State Street, situated next to an alley. The wood, which had once been painted white, was now gray and peeling. A flight of stairs led from the ground floor directly into the dining room of their second-floor apartment. An archway at the end of this room opened into a lounge of modest size, some fourteen by sixteen feet in its dimensions. A window on the far wall overlooked Thirty-fifth Street and against the same wall was Jimmy's piano, scarred by numerous whiskey glasses and smoldering cigarettes—Jimmy was an inveterate cigarette smoker. He had been without a piano for some years, but after his discovery he had been presented with one by a group calling themselves the Friends of Jazz, who were, in reality, members of the White Sox baseball team. A brass commemoration plaque attached to the front of the piano testified to their generosity. After Albert's death, Jimmy inherited his piano. It was an unusual one, rather like a spinet in shape, with a mirror set above the keys for reflecting the pianist's hands. The lounge was furnished comfortably with easy chairs and a sofa, and it was here that the Yanceys played host to their many friends and admirers who came to pay their homage. They maintained open house for anyone who called to see them at any hour of the day or night, providing good music and convivial company for friends or anyone who simply wished to hear the great man playing his soft blues or accompanying Estelle's singing. These occasions were not parties in the accepted sense with food and drink being provided. Participants took along their own drinks and normally presented Jimmy with a bottle of Hill and Hill, his favorite bourbon whiskey. In truth, the impecunious Yanceys were probably glad of this generosity.

Two white American boys who were frequent visitors to their home were Phil Kiely and Dick Mushlitz. The former, until his recent death, was a retired attorney from Evansville and the latter, until a few years ago, was a leader of the Salty Dogs Jazz band. In 1949, the Salty Dogs were invited to play at the University of Chicago, and after their show, Dick Mushlitz joined members of the Cakewalking Babies, the jazz group from the university, to visit Yancey's apartment. They arrived there at about one o'clock in the morning and played through the night until six o'clock. Some time after the first meeting, Mushlitz and a musician friend from the Salty Dogs were again in Chicago as guests of George Brunies at the 11-11 Club. When this engagement had been completed, Mushlitz and his companion made another visit to the Yancey's apartment, where he accompanied the assembled musicians on tenor banjo. Many visits were subsequently made, and he recalls one occasion with particular affection. Following an all-night session, Jimmy and Estelle invited him and a companion back to join them at a private party. They duly arrived and found themselves the only white people present at the monthly meeting of the Thirty-fifth Street Social Club, a close circle of friends. They all ate fried chicken and coleslaw, helped down with a generous supply of beer and whiskey, and spent the evening playing whist, talking, and making music. It was a most convivial occasion. When the time came to leave, Jimmy took his two young guests to one side and told them that they were the first and only white members of the Thirty-fifth Street Social Club—a singularly generous gesture from this very private man.[20]

One of the regular guests at the apartment was Cripple Clarence Lofton, who would take a turn at the piano and go through his familiar singing and piano-playing routine. Jimmy and Clarence sometimes played duets together, but it was rarely a successful four-handed performance, because of the incompatibility of their piano styles: Jimmy's was smooth and liquid, and Clarence's was jerky and abrasive. Clarence normally played high in the treble over Jimmy's two-handed improvisations.

Mushlitz remembers Jimmy Yancey as a quiet, personable man who said very little. He was slightly built, short, standing at about five feet three inches in height, with a round-shouldered posture. When he was moved to speak, it was sometimes in the middle of one of his piano extemporizations. Looking up from the keyboard as the languorous tones dripped from his fingers, he would arch an eyebrow and say, "No one can play like this. No one can play Jimmy's stuff." And he was right.

Estelle was just over five feet in height, frail in appearance, and the possessor of a surprisingly powerful singing voice for one so small. Her personality was the antithesis of Jimmy's. She, too, was slightly bent and she had one bad eye, the result of an accident in her youth. Mushlitz said that the couple were nice, unassuming people who always welcomed friends into their house to listen to good music. There was a photograph of Albert Ammons above the mantelpiece in the lounge, and he once asked Estelle why it was there in such a prominent position. She responded that Ammons was a relative, which surprised him. The remark was not qualified in any way, but it is clear from subsequent correspondence between the author and Albert's son Edsel that the relationship was one of deep friendship only. However, to add further unresolved intrigue, one of the reported surviving relatives at Jimmy's funeral was Hattie Ammons, who was described as a foster daughter.

Albert came to the Yanceys' apartment shortly before his death. He sat down at the piano and played for the assembled company. No one said anything; no one played anything. Everyone sat and listened with rapt attention. Mushlitz considered him to be the most awe-inspiring pianist that he had ever heard.

William Russell managed to visit the Yanceys several times in the early 1950s but, by his own admission, not as frequently as he would have wished. He later wrote:

> Yancey lived on Dearborn near 35th Street when I first met him then he moved around the corner on 35th Street between State and Dearborn on the south side of the street up on the second or third floor. They had regular Saturday night parties, almost every Saturday night. I didn't move to Chicago until 1950, about a year before Jimmy died so I didn't get in on very many of those parties. I didn't go down as often as I would have liked or should have but I never heard many different pianists there. People like Little Brother Montgomery would be there.[21]

Evidently, the Yanceys and their friends were involved in the illegal Numbers game because on some of Russell's visits their house would be packed with people counting the tickets. The lottery involved the gambler making a daily selection of a sequence of numbers, and if the last three figures matched those appearing on the New York stock market report, indicating how much money had changed hands at the end of the day, the gambler stood to make quite a bit of money. The Yanceys would often have someone guarding the door looking out for a police visitation while the friends sitting round a table recorded the lottery figures. Jimmy's contribution to these events was to entertain the gathering with music while it was left to Estelle to organize the helpers for checking the numbers.

The recollections of two university students, Grace and Jack Dawkins, who were guests at the Yancey's apartment in the late 1940s, also helps set the climate of the times when their open-house hospitality was freely available to young, white, middle-class people:

> Jimmy and Momma sat side by side on the piano bench, Mama nearer to us, the plainness of her slight figure emphasized by a cotton home dress; Jimmy, his clothes completely nondescript, appeared willing to let her have the foreground. Both of them looked straight ahead, as if more interested in the brown designs on the upright piano than in us white college kids. Jimmy was quiet, we don't remember that he said a word. Mama spoke and sang, her harsh voice supported by her stoic presence: straight back, undaunted voice, the disturbing jellied blue of her one blind eye a symbol of—surely—everything in their past. We thought she sang just fine; here, if ever, was really the

blues (we weren't aware of it, but her effectiveness was due in part—perhaps as it should be—to her presence).

It was to see and hear the unbelievably iconic piano man and to absorb the atmosphere that attracted them and many other young people:

> Unlike Mama, Jimmy hunched up at the keyboard. His hands, of course, were not what they once were. He had to play slow stuff, even slow boogie. But his touch, as far as we were concerned, was still sensitive, gentle, true. . . . Of course, we'd had a few beers, but he was no doubt playing at the level that can be heard on the 1951 recordings [for Atlantic].
>
> As for their personalities, their quiet manner suggested they tolerated us white kids who, "liberal" though we perhaps were, had no understanding of the lives these two had, of course, endured.[22]

There were other reported occasions, going back to 1938, when Jimmy and Estelle entertained their many friends with music and hospitality. One close friend was George Hoefer, a writer from *Downbeat*, who described one memorable meeting with them when several friends had gathered at the Yancey apartment one Sunday afternoon to talk with them. The conversation turned to baseball, and Jimmy at once showed an unusual animation and gave them his preseason analysis of the prospects for the White Sox team. As frequently happened on these occasions, the friends also wanted to hear Jimmy play the piano. As he had no piano of his own at this time, Jimmy suggested that they should collect some drinks and go to his sister's apartment on Dearborn Street. There, after several rounds of drinks, Jimmy picked up his glass and wandered to the piano where he began fingering the piano and coaxing out the blues. As his playing mellowed, he seemed to bring together the wide store of melodies that he carried in his mind and they somehow seemed to slot into just the right place.[23]

Yancey's newfound fame after the release of recordings briefly took him to New York for several personal appearances, one of which was the radio show *We the People* in 1941. Afterward he was taken to the Ross Tavern, one of the recognized piano clubs in the city. One of those present was Ralph Gleason, who was intrigued to see and hear Yancey's first appearance in New York. Recalling the sad smile and bent posture, he listened to Yancey entertaining a few old friends and Meade Lux Lewis who had dropped by. The beaten-up piano, as befitted the small dive below Sixth Avenue, was adequate for rolling out his elemental, moving, and inspirational blues.[24]

Jimmy had the first of two strokes in the mid-1940s after his initial burst of popularity had subsided. Fortunately for posterity, he had by then recorded the best examples of his work for the Solo Art, Victor, and Session companies. For a period of time after the stroke, he was unable to play the piano and was not seen in public. The stroke affected the coordination of his left hand, but in 1948 he had recovered sufficiently from its effects to take on some club work. One such reported engagement captures the atmosphere of a typical appearance as an intermission pianist. As Doc Evans' Jazz Band left the stand for a break, Yancey, eyes hooded and with a stooping gait, slid onto the piano stool behind the chromium bar and began rolling out one of his swinging soft basses, cushioning the intense velvet blues covered by his right hand. His soft, gentle music, very personal to the man at the keyboard, announced to the South Side audience that he was back again out of retirement. This was his first job for thirty years, for which he received eighty-one dollars and fifty cents a week—an increase of thirty dollars on his days playing at the Beartrap, some thirty years previously. Jimmy was a month from his fiftieth birthday and affirmed that he was happy to play as long as they wanted him.[25]

It was observed earlier in the chapter that Meade Lux Lewis and Pete Johnson never received adequate financial recompense in their lifetime for their recordings and concert appearances. The position today would probably be different, with a large jazz public in America, Europe, and Asia seeking out their recordings. The sheer magnitude of reissued material, albeit much of it now out of copyright, bears testimony to their continuing popularity. The financial circumstances of Jimmy and Estelle Yancey were no better. They existed on a meager income from record royalties, occasional club and concert appearances, and Jimmy's employment as a groundskeeper. By 1951, these sources were gradually disappearing. In a letter to Phil Kiely, at the time serving in the airborne division of the United States Army, Estelle reported that Jimmy was no longer working at the Beehive and had no other club engagements in the offing, which was making life difficult for them.[26] Like other good friends of the Yanceys, Kiely regularly sent small sums of money to help them out. It was a particularly appropriate gesture to make in February when her letter was written, because they needed the money to heat their apartment against the severe winter temperature in Chicago, which had fallen to between five and twelve degrees below zero. Shortly after sending the letter, Estelle mailed two of Jimmy's Paramount recordings to Kiely, which had been made on December 23, 1950. Unfortunately, they were broken in transit, which a second letter dated April 27 acknowledged.[27] After expressing her sympathy for the breakages, she thanked Kiely for his generous financial contribution to their welfare, adding that Jimmy would be pleased to give him some assistance with his piano technique should he be able to visit them again. Jimmy was not yet working, as times were increasingly difficult in this respect. She concluded her letter by sending Jimmy's best wishes to Phil. The address was 11-W-35 St. Chicago.

Jimmy's final recording session was made for the Atlantic label on July 18, 1951, and he was already a sick man when the recordings were pressed. These are not some of his best efforts because of his deteriorating health, but they remain an important legacy of his continuing contribution to boogie-woogie piano saved for posterity by Ahmet Ertegun, the young owner of the Atlantic company whose early inspiration for making records was the blues. Several old favorites are included: "Yancey Special," "Yancey's Bugle Call," searing vocals from Estelle on "Make Me a Pallet on the Floor," and "Santa Fe Blues," the last two songs cushioned by Jimmy's soft piano playing and Crosby's thrumming bass. The session is captured on *Jimmy and Mama Yancey: Chicago Piano, Volume 1* (Atlantic, 823682). By September 6, Estelle was able to write to Kiely that Jimmy was making some improvement after an eight-week convalescence, but was not yet well enough to play the piano at one of their parties held on the Saturday before the letter had been written, which Dick Mushlitz and his father attended. The letter closed with Estelle's usual spirited good wishes. The single signature at the end of the letter was perhaps a premonition that Estelle had of Jimmy's death; the other letter had closed with both their names.

Jimmy died on September 18, 1951. He was, according to the generally accepted date of his birth, fifty-three years of age. His death was mourned in Chicago, where he had become an institution—the self-taught boogie-woogie and blues pianist from the South Side who made contact with people through his music. When Jimmy played the piano, everyone knew what he was saying. His death came shortly after breakfast. He rose from his chair and collapsed in front of Estelle, the victim of a stroke. Diabetes was found to have been a contributory cause of death. Details of his family, including Estelle and son Jimmy Jr. and of his long-serving post at Comiskey Park were reported in the *Chicago Tribune*, which noted that the funeral service would be held in the chapel at 3800 S. Michigan Avenue.[28] Jimmy had expressed a wish to Estelle sometime before his death that he would like to have a traditional New Orleans funeral when his time came. News of the wish became known, and twenty-six jazzmen called at the apartment and offered to play at the funeral. Al Jenkins (trombone), Jimmy Ille (trumpet), and Jimmy Granato (clarinet) led the cortege as it drove from the chapel to the cemetery.

Prior to his final journey, Jimmy had been laid to rest in an orchid casket covered with a rose blanket. Fading pink flowers in the yard were beginning to drop, but Momma felt they were appropriate for the occasion. She was in no rush to bury him and delayed the event by eight days; she finally capitulated, saying that she had wanted to keep him with her as long as she could, a defining statement of their mortal love.[29] The service was held at the Charles Jackson Funeral Home and led by Reverend Paul

Turner, pastor of the First Youth Community Church. Jazzmen from all quarters of Chicago and beyond came to pay their last respects, and an estimated congregation of five hundred people attended. The *Chicago Sun Times* described this gathering of loving friends as being like one of the Yancey's Saturday night parties. The cortege left the chapel to the accompanying mournful sound of the jazz band rendering "Nearer My God to Thee," followed by a few of his favorite tunes.[30] Art Hodes, who was present as one of the mourners, recorded the event in his own inimitable style, describing the full church, with its mixed, desegregated congregation and the musicians, who usually jammed with Jimmy, now respectfully standing as they played him out with hymns and other mellow tunes.[31] The service was completed, and a melancholy group of friends and admirers moved to Lincoln Cemetery for the final farewell to Jimmy. As the casket was lowered into the ground, the strains of a defiant "High Society" rang out. Yancey lies there to this day with a simple headstone: "Jimmy Yancey Pianist 1897–1951"—yet another confusing date of birth—some twenty-five feet away from the grave of Albert Ammons.

In retrospect, it is quite astonishing that such a "lowly" folk artist as Jimmy Yancey, living close to the breadline, in poor health and dependent to an extent on the generosity of his fans for survival, should receive such fulsome newspaper headlines referring to him as the father of boogie-woogie and as a jazz great. His genius shone through life's perversities, and his simple yet effective piano style reached out to so many hearts to bring happiness and joy. Jimmy was a very special person and everyone knew it. As recently as 1999, a BBC program of music and interviews set against the evocative sounds of Chicago's trains was broadcast about the pianist, taking its title from one of his most soulful recordings "At the Window." There is no more fitting tribute to his true place in the history of the piano style than the confirmatory two-column obituary he was afforded in the *New York Times*, in which he was alluded to as one of the founding fathers of the boogie-woogie style of piano playing.[32]

There is little that can be added to what has already been said about Jimmy Yancey's music in earlier chapters, in trying to assess the importance of his later recordings made for the Paramount and Atlantic labels. Most, if not all the content on both, are drawn from earlier recordings. It is possible that Yancey "composed" his numbers for recording dates by selecting the most appropriate choruses from the many he carried in his head. Thus, a blues number would bring together permutations of one group of blues choruses and a stomp would draw from another group of faster choruses. The similarity between certain numbers that was produced defies any attempt to associate a particular tune with a single title. A consideration of one of his themes will make the point. One tune he recorded in the Atlantic set was "Salute to Pinetop." On other labels this was called "Lucille's Lament" (Riverside), "Sweet Patootie" (Session), "Jimmy's Goodnight Blues" (Paramount), "Bear Trap Blues" (Vocalion), "Jimmy's Stuff" (Solo Art), and "Mellow Blues" (Victor). It is also possible that the titles of several tunes were concocted by the studio. This was certainly so when Riverside put out the unissued pieces they had purchased from Solo Art. The feature of his music that is always present and that identifies Yancey like nothing else is his "touch," giving his blues statements a poetic quality. The deceptive intricacies of their apparent simplicity came from his perfect timing.

There have always been seminal pianists throughout the history of blues and boogie piano whose influence is clearly discernible in the work of others. It is therefore appropriate that this chapter should be concluded with a consideration of one of them, Big Maceo Merriweather (1905–1953), whose wonderful and expanding talents as pianist and singer were cut short in their prime from illness and an early death. Merriweather's inclusion at this juncture also identifies another direction that boogie-woogie was to take by a closer association with the blues. Some of those who were inspired by Merriweather's playing were Otis Spann, Johnny Jones, and Henry Gray, pianists who graced the piano seats of the blues bands that proliferated in the mainly urban areas of Chicago, Memphis, and Detroit.

Merriweather was born in Atlanta, Georgia, one of a family of eleven children, and was raised in Fulton County on the farm run by his father Christopher "Kit" Merriweather. He began teaching himself to play the piano from the age of fifteen and appears to have had a facility for the instrument, as he was soon sufficiently adept to be able to entertain at parties in the Atlanta area between 1920 and 1924. By the end of this period, Maceo had honed his piano playing to the point where he could consider searching for more lucrative work, and so, like many before him, he moved north to Detroit, spending fifteen years there working outside music but taking occasional dates at house parties and clubs such as Brown's Bar and the Post Club. His move to Chicago in 1941 saw him consolidate his musical reputation at club dates supporting guitarists Big Bill Broonzy and later Hudson Whittaker (Tampa Red). He was now able to work as a full-time musician. He made his recording debut for Bluebird in 1941 as a blues vocalist backed by his own piano playing and Tampa Red on guitar, under the guidance of producer Lester Melrose. They cut six sides, and it was immediately apparent, as revealed on "County Jail" (1941), that the compatibility between the two instrumentalists predicated a happy and productive partnership. It was also apparent that Merriweather possessed superb blues intonation and impeccable phrasing in his vocals.

Big Maceo was now considered to be one of the foremost blues and boogie-woogie pianists in Chicago. He made further recordings with Big Bill Broonzy for Columbia (1945) and with John Lee "Sonny Boy" Williamson (the first performer to use that name) for Victor in the same year. Unfortunately, in the following year, he succumbed to a stroke and was left partially paralyzed in his left hand but manfully continued singing and accompanying himself on piano using his right hand. He recorded again for Victor in 1947, with Eddie Boyd taking the piano stool and then for the Speciality label with Tampa Red. A representative cover of Maceo's talents on record with Tampa Red between 1941 and 1947, including the substitute piano playing of Eddie Boyd, is available on the LP album *Big Maceo* (RCA, 730.577). An appearance was made on the Studs Terkel television show *I Come for to Sing*. With his health failing, Maceo returned to Detroit in 1950 following a successful tour of Kentucky, Louisiana, and Tennessee[33] and died from a heart attack three years later.

Merriweather's preference was to record to the accompaniment of drums and guitar—with the guitar usually being played by Tampa Red. He is known particularly for his famous "Chicago Breakdown" (1945), which exhibits his so-called "thunderous" boogie style. What impresses, in addition to the energy and drive of his forceful playing, are the streams of rapid-note ideas, which, being repetitive and played loudly, tend to create a stimulating and exciting sound for many listeners and which contribute to a solid and intense rhythm. In contrast, others see it as no more than facile finger dexterity and empty virtuosity, which has little in common with true blues/jazz spirit and feeling. Such "virtuoso" passages are identified by Harbinson as choruses 3 and 9 and also, perhaps, certain features of choruses 4 and 8 in "Chicago Breakdown."

His "Texas Stomp" (1945) is an energetic and lively piece, largely monothematic, whose hypnotic effect is relieved by the spoken dialogue between Big Maceo and Tampa Red and by the "solo" choruses for the guitar and drums. This is not the same work as the more rugged "Texas Stomp" (1936) by Dot Rice, which also features an accompanying guitar—played by Frankie Black (Scrapper Blackwell)—though here the guitar is thoroughly subordinate to the piano. There is also a certain amount of repetition, but the style and musical ideas plus the interpretation of Dot Rice place this piece firmly in the tradition of authentic and genuine barrelhouse boogie-woogie from an earlier era.

Big Maceo's "Detroit Jump" (1945), another piece with accompaniment of drums and Tampa Red's guitar, relies heavily on a simple (detached-chord) accompaniment marking out a basic rhythm for a great deal of the time. There are also three choruses, all employing rapidly repeated notes on chords, and that is very nearly all there is to this boogie number, making it one of his less interesting or imaginative compositions. What may be of some interest, however, is the occurrence in "Detroit Jump" of a passage that also appears in both "Texas Stomp" and "Chicago Breakdown." This passage—which may be designated as a "quasi-break" rather than a true "break"—is where Big Maceo's left hand stops playing the ostinato bass pattern and ascends to a higher register—still playing eight notes to the bar, however, while his right hand punctuates with chords—and then descends again to resume the ostinato bass pattern. None of the four instances of this passage, the one in "Detroit Jump," the one in "Texas Stomp," and the two in "Chicago Breakdown," is identical to any of the others, but they do use the same musical figures (arranged in varying order) and are thus related, sound very similar, and are recognizable as a Merriweather trademark. The fact that it also has talking on the record about the pleasures of going back to Detroit may cause some to feel that it was inspired by the earlier "Hastings Street" (1929), recorded by the piano and guitar combination Charlie Spand and Blind Blake.

In his blues piano playing, Merriweather produces several scintillating performances, presaging the "feel" and direction of later blues bands. "Anytime for You" (1942) offers a feast of aural sensations: He deploys contrasting rhythms, mixes short stop chords behind husky, stabbing lyrics, and changes the bass lines from stride, through stomp to walking bass. Similarly, Maceo's "32/20" (1945) draws heavily on the legacy of Sykes and Montgomery's "Vicksburg Blues" with its delayed and varied bass pattern grumbling up and down the keyboard—an unsettling support for the ominous lyrics but both perfectly meshed.

Maceo's legacy to those pianists who followed him was his "industrial strength" piano playing. He gave equal power to both hands, pared down the more elaborate arpeggios and ornamental phrasing in the treble that some contemporaries such as Memphis Slim employed, and substituted fast, repetitive chording with a blues tone and equally fast single-note phrasing. Underpinning this infectiously rhythmical treble work was a sonorous, foot-tapping bass, usually a walking bass—the groundwork that pianists in rhythm and blues groups and others in urban blues would eventually build upon. A good example for appreciating this and illustrating how it impacted on another pianist is to compare Merriweather's tour de force "Chicago Breakdown" with Otis Spann's own "Great Northern Stomp." Both are mighty beacons of modern boogie-woogie piano playing.

So ended an era that had seen boogie-woogie's assault on New York and the deserved success of its most famous practitioners. This was followed by a steady decline in their fortunes to the point where their former greatness was known only to those who held a deep affection for the men and their creative music. With their deaths, boogie-woogie music in its classic form almost died but was revived, in at least a different form, by a return to its roots, the blues.

NOTES

1. John Steiner, taped recollections, including those of Frank Gillis, sent to the author circa January 30 through March 1985.
2. Ralph Gleason, "A Glance Back at a Boogie Boy," *San Francisco Sunday Chronicle*, June 14, 1964.
3. Bob Seeley, taped recollections sent to the author, October 28, 1985.
4. Tom Harris, "Chicago Breakdown," *Jazz Report* 1, no. 11 (November 1954): 6.
5. Ralph Sutton, correspondence with the author, January 27, 1988.
6. Dave Mangurian, "The Last One-Third of Boogie," *Music Memories and Jazz Report* 3 (1964): 13–15.
7. Michael Hortig, summary of interview with Denise Buckner sent to the author in 2002.
8. "Meade Lux Lewis, Jazz Pianist Killed as Speeder Rams His Car," *New York Herald Tribune*, June 8, 1964.
9. "Meade Lux Lewis, Pianist, Is Killed," *New York Times*, June 8, 1964.
10. "Jazzman Meade Lewis Killed in Auto Crash," *Los Angeles Times*, June 8, 1964.
11. "Meade Lewis Is Crash Victim," *Minneapolis Morning Tribune*, June 8, 1964.
12. Richard Lindaman, extract included in a collection of taped reminiscences and thoughts about boogie-woogie sent to the author between 1981 and 1990.
13. Dr. Ray Nelson, correspondence with the author, July 21, 1992.
14. Marge Johnson, "My Man . . . Pete Johnson," pt. 1, *Jazz Report* 2, no. 8 (April 1962): 7–8; pt. 2, *Jazz Report* 2, no. 9 (May 1962): 7–8; conclusion, *Jazz Report* 2, no. 10 (June 1962): 5.
15. Ben Conroy, letter received from Marge Johnson December 28, 1959, and copied to the author.
16. James Wertheim, "Pete Johnson Today," *Blues Unlimited*, 1964, 9.
17. H. J. Mauerer, *The Pete Johnson Story* (Bremen: Humburg, 1965), 52.
18. "Boogie Great Pete Johnson," *San Francisco Chronicle*, June 23, 1967.
19. John Steiner, taped recollections sent to the author, January 30 through March 1985.
20. Dick Mushlitz, written and taped recollections sent to the author, January, 11, 1986.
21. William Russell, taped recollections sent to the author, February 2, 1991.
22. Mr. and Mrs. John Dawkins, written recollections sent to the author, September 9, 1992.
23. George Hoefer, liner notes, *Yancey's Mixture: 24 Minutes with Jimmy Yancey*, Pax 6011.

24. Ralph Gleason, liner notes, *Pure Blues: Jimmy and Mama Yancey*, Atlantic 1283.

25. "As Long as They Want Me," *Time*, February 9, 1948, 48, 49.

26. Phil Kiely, letter from Estelle Yancey, April 27, 1951.

27. Phil Kiely, letter from Estelle Yancey, September 6, 1951.

28. "Jimmy Yancey," *Chicago Tribune*, September 19, 1951.

29. "Jam for Jimmy," *Time*, October 1, 1951, 44.

30. "Rites Held for Jimmy Yancey," *Chicago Sun Times*, September 26, 1951.

31. Art Hodes, liner notes, *Pure Blues: Jimmy and Mama Yancey*, Atlantic 1283.

32. "Jimmy Yancey," *New York Times*, September 19, 1951.

33. Sheldon Harris, *Blues Who's Who* (New York: Da Capo, 1979), 370.

13

Many Shades of Blue

The death of Pete Johnson in 1967 signaled the departure of one of the colossi of the second generation of boogie-woogie pianists. Fortunately, Memphis Slim, Champion Jack Dupree, and others had been musically active at the same time as the second-generation players, without quite achieving their fame or public adulation as virtuoso performers. These men, together with younger pianists such as Otis Spann, carried the torch for the next phase of the music's rejuvenation. If not solely boogie-woogie players, they were certainly heirs to the title of third-generation pianists utilizing the style who inspired many younger European pianists later in their careers. For ease of definition and to aid clarification, a third generation may be said to comprise those pianists, some of whom are now dead, who were active post 1960. Inevitably, this choice of date invites a criticism of arbitrariness, but boogie-woogie was by then an established feature of rhythm and blues, urban blues bands, and rock and roll. From about 1970 onward, a more traditional form of solo and duet boogie-woogie music—inspired by the music of the Trio—was also surfacing and gaining momentum in America and Europe. For the sake of historical continuity, a review of third-generation players begins with those whose music overlapped with their second-generation predecessors—assessments of two of them, Sammy Price and Jay McShann, are included in earlier chapters because of their signal contributions to the evolution of boogie-woogie. The remainder considered in this chapter are, or were, significant blues pianists in their own right, frequently the mainstay of the rhythm sections of the urban blues bands of Chicago, Memphis, and

Detroit but with an additional capability of being able to produce their own distinctive brands of boogie-woogie.

William Thomas "Champion" Jack Dupree (1910–1992) was noted for his blues singing backed by a sparse piano style not unlike that of Walter Davies in its economy of expression. Although essentially a solo performer and all-around entertainer similar to Clarence Lofton, in certain respects, he did appear on piano with some groups. Dupree came from New Orleans and was from a more ancient lineage than those who formed that city's rhythm-and-blues "school" and therefore sits more comfortably in the blues pianist category by age and traditional style of expression. He was raised in the Colored Waif's Home for Boys after his parents' grocery store was accidentally set alight by an exploding oil container, used for fueling kerosene lamps. Both parents were killed in the accident by a falling roof, leaving him orphaned before he was one year old. He began playing piano at the age of six and later received his initial instruction in piano blues from a local pianist named Willie "Drive 'Em Down" Hall but also by watching and listening to other pianists such as "Red" Toots. Life in the waif's home was hard and Jack suffered many privations. He received no Christmas presents for several years until a kindly warden took sympathy on him and gave him money for candy. It was a lonely existence despite the presence in the city of four older, uncaring siblings. He eventually left the home when he was fourteen and to all intents and purposes became a street urchin, sleeping on the streets of the French Quarter, stealing what food he could, begging and relying on tips in order to survive. His real "home" was provided by a street friend, Richard, who, with his mother's agreement, invited him to live with them. Jack was always grateful for her compassionate generosity and recognized her as his surrogate mother.[1] Most of Jack's tips were received for singing outside the dives on Rampart Street. In time, despite being underage, Dupree was allowed inside these low-down joints, which served as an apprenticeship and enabled him to become an entertainer. It was here that he learned his blues vocals and picked up his piano skills. He recalls that the various piano players and blues singers were good models, although none of them was ever recorded: It was from the rugged "Drive 'Em Down" that he learned "Stackolee."

This was a low-life subculture where prostitutes served the needs of the visiting longshoremen and pimps rubbed shoulders with hoodlums and local tearaways. Survival was an important consideration when physical danger and intimidation were never far away. Partly to equip himself for either of these eventualities, the diminutive Jack became a professional boxer and represented the Kid Green Boxing School in many bouts both in the French Quarter and beyond the state boundary of Louisiana. This was now his source of income, although he only earned sufficient money from boxing to keep the wolf from the door. In lean times, he hoboed his way around America and gravitated toward the joints where his type of music could be found. He traveled to Chicago as a seventeen-year-old, making use of the Illinois Central Line to get him there. He had many brushes with the railroad "bulls" getting on and off freight trains. On one occasion, he gave himself up to one of them who had cornered him with a dog, and he and his companion were given sixty days in jail by the judge, which took care of their immediate needs.

Jack Dupree arrived in Indianapolis in the early 1940s, having retired from a successful boxing career in which he was only knocked out twice in 107 bouts. Dupree knew the famous Leroy Carr and was soon established at C. Ferguson's Cotton Club where Carr had been the pianist before him. Dupree's aptitude as an entertainer flowered in this city, and he was soon getting enthusiastic notices in the local newspaper as a popular singer, dancer, and comedian, and as an artist who could direct a good floor show. One of his specialties was a double act with Ophelia Hoy, a well-endowed comedienne, in which they sang risqué lyrics, engaged in patter, and generally clowned about in the style of Butterbeans and Susie. Much the same work pattern was followed in the next few years, interspersed with recording dates, until World War II when Jack enlisted in the navy and served in the Pacific theater, where he saw very heavy action at Guam before being taken as a prisoner of war by the Japanese. His first wife Ruth (known as the "Jitterbug Queen"), who had joined him in many of his show appearances in Indianapolis, unfortunately died while he was away in the war. Not wishing to return to Indianapolis because of this sad event and the associated memories, Jack made for New York. He was reasonably successful here recording and filling in as relief pianist at the Ringside Ball club. He remarried in 1948 and produced a family of five children with his new wife, Lucille Dalton. However, this marriage was not to last.

Champion Jack made his first visit to Europe when he came to England in 1959 for a series of concerts and jazz club appearances touring with the Chris Barber Jazz band. They played, among other venues, Bournemouth (November 7) and Islington (November 23). At one of his performances, the audience experienced two sides of his nature: the outrageous entertainer with a gaudy sense of dress and an amazing piano technique deploying the back of his hand, elbows, and knuckles to support his bawdy lyrics, as well as his serious, thoughtful responses to questions from the audience about events and people in his full and varied life that inspired his piano playing.[2]

His reception in England was overwhelming, and he was lionized because very few blues lovers had yet had the chance to see and hear a genuine entertainer of this caliber. Dupree decided to stay, living for several years with an English wife in Halifax, which provided a stable base from which to tour widely in Britain and Europe. An apocryphal tale suggests that Dupree decided to move to England after a uniformed customs officer addressed him as "sir." When this marriage broke up, he departed for the continent and lived nomadically in Switzerland (Zurich) and Denmark (Copenhagen) for extended periods, and then in Sweden before finally settling in Hanover, Germany toward the end of his career. Before these events, back in Britain, he had been an inspirational influence to a younger set of bluesmen such as Eric Clapton, the emerging John Mayall's Blues Breakers; he had also shared the stage with the Beatles and the Rolling Stones at concerts and rock venues. During his sojourn in Germany, Jack made club appearances and in 1988 recorded with Axel Zwingenberger and the Mojo Blues Band on *Axel Zwingenberger and the Friends of Boogie-Woogie, Volume 5* (Vagabond, VRLP 8.88014)—a singularly happy marriage of talents.

In Champion Jack's final years, ill health was never far away, and he underwent major surgery in 1989 from which he appeared to recover in time to celebrate his eightieth birthday well into the following day. Shortly before his death, he fulfilled one of his last engagements at the Chicago Blues Festival (June 1991), which was viewed as a life-enhancing experience with the octogenarian hammering the keyboard and warning the audience, with the slyest of grins, of the vexation awaiting anyone who became involved with "jail bait."[3] The *Independent* newspaper's obituary notice of this colorful troubadour includes the observation that this larger-than-life character wore a piratical earring and seven rings, with the gold matched only by the fillings in his teeth. He had a half-finished tattoo on one arm, started by a fellow prisoner when Jack was serving a prison sentence in the Indianapolis Penitentiary, but still incomplete as the artist was executed before finishing the task.[4]

Jack Dupree made his first eight recordings of traditional blues material for Okeh in 1940. He was accompanied on "Gambling Man" and "Cabbage Greens" by Bill Gaither (Scrapper Blackwell), Leroy Carr's former guitar player. Jack was back in the studios in 1941 to record sides for Columbia. One of these, "Dupree's Shake Dance," is a thinly disguised takeoff of "Pinetop's Boogie-Woogie," the patter backed by his unusually pared down, slightly discordant piano. A similar pattern emerges on the later "Strollin'" (1958) included on the Atlantic album *Blues from the Gutter*, and one has to accept that, like Jimmy Yancey, Dupree's style of presentation and piano backing display certain similarities between numbers. That apart, there is an unmistakable uniqueness to his work. His singing is both sonorous and sorrowful and is effectively contrasted with his speaking of certain choruses, giving an unexpected and appealing range to the emotional content of his lyrics. Another distinctive feature lies in the wide range of social topics covered by his blues. Narcotics are the theme of "Junker Blues" (1941), "Misery Blues" touches on his racist experiences in the South, and "Mother-in-Law Blues" (1961) reflects, self evidently, on some impressionable experiences with at least one of these relatives by marriage.

Immediately after World War II, Dupree recorded for the small Joe Davis label. Of these recordings, "Gin Mill Sal" (1945) is outstanding. By the 1950s, he could be heard giving the piano accompaniment on the Apollo label to the team of Sonny Terry (harmonica) and Brownie McGhee (guitar). He sings on the very successful and popular "I'm Gonna Find You Some Day," leaving the piano backing to Wilbert "Big Chief" Ellis. His arrival in Europe coincided with an upsurge in his recording career, and he quickly made three Atlantic LPs: the aforementioned *Blues from the Gutter* (1958), *Champion Jack's Natural and Soulful Blues* (1961), and *Champion of the Blues* (1961). Some of his earlier single releases for the King label were repackaged and released as the Audio album *Two Shades of Blue* (1965). Dupree claimed never to be able to understand how he learned to master the piano, seeing his own archaic endeavors to be more of a God-given gift than a skill: primitive, occasionally discordant, replete with spaces that hold attention by their stillness, and repetitively chorded in some treble passages but, above all, movingly effective in its simplicity.

The exodus of black families from the South to the industrial towns of the North and to the West Coast, in the 1950s, continued unabated as they searched for better living standards and a place if not free from racial prejudice, then one where prejudice was less overtly practiced. Work could be found in the factories and other commercial outlets, guaranteeing a living wage and some financial control over their lives. Many who migrated were also musicians whose talents supplemented those of older musicians who had made the same journey many years earlier. The newcomers often sought stable employment first and used their music as a supplementary income. Only the very talented could afford to make a living from their music.

Memphis was a bustling, lively center at this time, which encouraged musicians to delay their journey to Chicago or Detroit or even to remain there permanently. The city supported a vibrant recording industry with Sun Records its epicenter. The blues were popular, giving rise to several small independent record labels that fed the public's appetite for the music. Significant artists such as B.B. King, Howling Wolf, Elmore James, and Sonny Boy Williamson No. 2 (Willie Rice Miller) worked and recorded here. But there was also an exchange of talent that saw white performers Elvis Presley, Carl Perkins, and Jerry Lee Lewis also active in the clubs and the Sun recording studios. Station KFFA from Helena,

Arkansas, beamed out a daily blues program on the *King Biscuit Show*, devoted to advertising cornmeal and flour, which was hosted by harmonica player Sonny Boy Williamson. His group comprised guitars, piano, drums, and harmonica, a new combination of instruments that laid down a heavy amplified blues beat and helped to establish the pattern for other blues bands, initially introduced to Chicago by Muddy Waters (McKinley Morganfield), Buddy Guy, and others in the early 1950s.

The outlet for their talents was the Chicago-based Chess record label. All the blues bands had a piano player, a high proportion of whom had been born and raised in the South and learned to play their instruments there, with its long tradition of boogie-woogie and blues played by Little Brother Montgomery, Friday Ford, Roosevelt Sykes, and others. The pianist for many years with Sonny Boy's band was Willie Love, who was raised in Mississippi. Eddie Boyd, Otis Spann, and Albert Luandrew ("Sunnyland Slim")—whose early years were spent as accompanist to blues singer Peter "Doc" Clayton—all came from the same state. The appearance of boogie-woogie within this broader framework of the blues band was assured, and it became an important extension of a pianist's normal keyboard armory.

Pete Chapman (Memphis Slim) (1915—1988) became a permanent resident in France until his death, which ensured that the primal sounds of boogie-woogie and the blues were regularly heard in Paris nightspots. Slim was an international artist of some repute who, in a lifetime dedicated to the music, made many recordings. Although his final home was Paris, he originated from Memphis where he was born into a musical family. His father, also named Pete Chapman, was an accomplished pianist, guitar player, and blues singer, providing the right kind of musical stimulus for Slim's early experimentation with the piano. During his adolescence, he visited tonks in and around Memphis and listened to many local piano players, but he was always impressed by Speckled Red, Roosevelt Sykes, and Little Brother Montgomery when they were playing in the area. His interest in piano music was broader than that of many boogie-woogie pianists, seen in the wide choice of titles in his recordings. In his formative years, the popular artists of the day were Clarence Williams and Leroy Carr, and listening to their recordings helped to widen his conception of the blues and boogie-woogie. His roots, though essentially in the southern tradition of blues and boogie-woogie piano, were nurtured by the more sophisticated harmonies of popular stylists.

Memphis Slim attended Lester High School, where he established an early reputation at thirteen as a competent interpreter of boogie and blues. Like many another pianist, he began to realize as he got older, that the center for his music was moving away from the South to Chicago and other urban centers. In 1939, at the age of twenty-four, he moved to

Chicago to further his musical ambitions. Slim's first recording on string
bass was with his own group, Pete Chapman and His Washboard Band.
His first best seller was made with Washboard Sam and was called "Beer
Drinking Woman" (1940), released on the Bluebird label. These recordings led to regular work on the South Side, where he consolidated his
reputation as a pianist, vocalist, and composer. Slim's real opportunity for
gaining national recognition came when he was asked by Big Bill Broonzy
to take the piano chair alongside him after Joshua Altheimer, his pianist
of many years, died in 1940. The musical partnership grew into a personal
friendship, and their many good times are documented in *Big Bill Blues*,
Broonzy's biography.

Now established as one of the fastest technicians in Chicago, second
only to Pete Johnson, Memphis Slim became a member of several Chicago
blues groups, playing alongside Willie Dixon (bass) and Sunny Boy Williamson (harmonica). As a singer and instrumentalist, he was recognized
as being on a par with Muddy Waters and Lightnin' Hopkins, although
present-day assessments of the former's importance in leading the direction that Chicago blues bands took in the 1950s and 1960s might conflict
with such a generous assessment. After several European tours in the
1960s, Memphis Slim took the decision to emigrate to France in 1962,
where he joined other exiled pianists in Europe, including at various
times Sam Price, Curtis Jones, Eddie Boyd, Little Willie Littlefield, and
Champion Jack Dupree. An unending supply of work through concerts
and club appearances, and an appreciative public, so often denied them in
America, were the main incentives for moving to Europe. In due course,
Slim ran his own club in Paris and opened a second one in Tel Aviv.

After leaving Big Bill Broonzy at the end of World War II and going
solo, Slim's record output was massive. Initially recorded with Bill on the
Okeh and Bluebird labels, during the war, he moved in fairly quick succession to HY-Tone Records, the Miracle label where he recorded his hits
"Lend Me Your Love" and "Rockin' the House," and then the Peacock
and Premium labels. Other companies were flirted with before he finally
settled with Vee-Jay Records. His piano style has been called "progressive" by French jazz commentator Jacques Demetre mainly, one sup-
poses, because of the clusters of arpeggios and rapidly hit tone clusters
that color his treble work. Such adeptness does not hide his feeling for the
traditions of boogie-woogie, however, evident in his choice of material on
one of his earlier recordings from 1959, *The Real Boogie-Woogie: Memphis
Slim Piano Solos* (Folkways, FG 3524).

Slim remains close to the original playing "Cow Cow Blues" with
chorded breaks and a clean treble line. There is a nod of recognition to
Roosevelt Sykes and other pianists who played "44 Blues," with its contrasting rhythms in the bass and treble parts. Memphis Slim's own talents

as a composer are spelled out in the excellent vocal blues "Everyday," composed when he worked with Joe Williams, who later introduced the number into the repertoire of the Count Basie Orchestra. His biggest hit, "Everyday" received international coverage through additional cover versions by guitarists B.B. King and Lowell Fulson under the title "Everyday I Have the Blues." The tradition of the rural folk blues can be heard in "Crowing Rooster," adapted by Slim from an earlier version of the number recorded by Lonnie Johnson in 1928. The lyrics are sung in his strong, burnished, expressive voice, giving an added poignancy to the story of forsaken love.

The international esteem with which the Muddy Waters Band was held was not due solely to its position as the first of the Chicago blues bands or to the impact of its leader's aggressive guitar-led blues vocals. Over a period of several years, he established a band glistening with talented sidemen, any one of whom could have led their own groups or recorded independently—indeed, some did both later in their careers. The list includes many of the greatest names in the blues field: Willie Dixon (bass and composer), Jimmy Rogers (second guitar), Little Walter (harmonica), and Freddy Bellow (drums). For a time, the piano stool was occupied by "Sunnyland Slim," who was followed by Maceo Merriweather and Otis Spann, the longest-serving member who remained with the band more or less permanently from 1953 until his death.

Otis Spann (1930–1970) was a major figure warranting a high place in the pantheon of players. He was a consistently able pianist who had already made his mark with Muddy Waters in the 1950s and would have undoubtedly exceeded his already brilliant interpretations but for a premature death at the age of forty. He was born in Jackson, Mississippi, to musical parents—some sources say that his mother was a blues guitar player who had appeared with Memphis Minnie—and a father who was a preacher and pianist. He began picking out tunes on the piano in his father's church from about the age of seven but received no formal instruction in technique. Two early influences have been suggested, although with his father's background help from this quarter cannot be discounted. These were Friday Ford, a barrelhouse pianist from Belzoni, Mississippi, and Cose Davis, a local blues pianist who recorded for Bluebird in the 1930s. He also owed a debt to Maceo Merriweather's forceful piano playing. Spann achieved first place in a blues competition at the Alamo Theatre in Jackson toward the end of the 1930s, marking his entry into the local music scene as a pianist playing at parties and clubs in the area. One source reports that Spann became a Golden Gloves boxer in the mid-forties before serving in the army at the end of hostilities (19461951), although he would have been very young to have done so.[5]

Spann moved to Chicago permanently in the late 1940s to be with his father who had moved there after the death of Spann's mother. He formed a small band and began working as a full-time musician at the Tic Toc Lounge. Muddy Waters heard of his arrival and, knowing of his keyboard talents, auditioned him for his band in 1952. From this time, Spann appeared with Muddy Waters at all his engagements and on his recordings for Chess. He also acted as the company's house pianist accompanying Bo Diddley, Howling Wolf, Chuck Berry, and Jimmy Rogers. Spann made a great impact at the 1960 Newport Jazz Festival. The event was due to close two days early because of the antisocial behavior of a large group of young people who had been denied entrance to the park but who were determined to get in. After the final number given by the Waters band, the compere Langston Hughes announced the cessation of events and passed a hurriedly composed farewell blues to Spann. After a moment's thought, he played a brief introduction and sang a brilliantly spontaneous blues while the other artists, who were still onstage, improvised around his singing and playing to bring the festival to a satisfactory and moving close.

Muddy Waters' band made its first tour of England in 1958 with Otis Spann as its pianist. He was back again, touring Europe in 1963, as a member of the American Folk and Blues Festival and returned once again to England in the following year. From this time he began to record extensively in his own right. Unfortunately, just as his career as a significant blues soloist was beginning to flower, he was incapacitated by a number of debilitating illnesses leading to a premature death from cancer in Cooke County Hospital in Chicago. His outstanding work as piano player and composer was recognized at the 1972 Ann Arbor Blues and Jazz Festival when his widow was presented with a plaque by Muddy Waters with the inscription: "The people of Ann Arbor Michigan in recognition of the talent, the genius of the late Otis Spann, sweet giant of the blues, formally dedicate the Ann Arbor Blues and Jazz festival, 1972, in the grounds upon which it stands to the memory of this great artist."

Spann's singing and piano playing are more often than not to be found accompanied by a full instrumental ensemble (trumpet, saxophones, guitars, bass, and drums). Quite a high percentage of Spann's keyboard interpretations drive or rock along (depending on tempo) with an eight-to-the-bar boogie-woogie bass (played on guitar or piano), but the rest of the music—the band's style and idioms, and the piano's right-hand figurations—has, on the whole, little or nothing in common with traditional boogie-woogie. A piece in which links with the older boogie-woogie traditions are more apparent is "Mr. Highway Man" (1964), piano with vocal plus band, in which Spann's right hand presents rhythmically punctuated ideas and entirely avoids the decorative runs and ornamental figuration common to much of his work. His "Crack Your Head" (1964), piano with vocal and band, is the same in mood and style and contains similar (but not the same) music as his outstanding piano solo "This Is the Blues" (1960). This latter number is an impressive tour de force, using a variety of boogie-woogie bass figures against a dazzling display in the right hand, which relies heavily on repeated chords played with crashing force. Some may regard this piece—not without just foundation—as the ultimate development of the boogie-woogie piano; others may consider that the "modernity" of its musical language and style place it beyond the confines of the boogie-woogie idiom. It is, perhaps, a peripheral work analogous to George Thomas's "The Rocks"—both pieces standing just outside the sphere of traditional boogie-woogie—the one piece at the end and the other at the beginning of the history of this piano style.

"It Must Have Been the Devil" (1960) was Otis Spann's first solo recording. It is primarily a vocal piece, but the rocking boogie-woogie piano accompaniment Spann provides to his own singing is a fine one that could almost stand as a boogie-woogie piano solo in its own right. "Otis Blues" (1960) provides an impressive illustration of Spann's boogie-woogie blues style. The left hand relentlessly grinds out eight notes to the bar (though there are omissions and changes of bass pattern), setting a medium to slow basic tempo, above which the right hand flashes and crashes with astounding speed and energy. Rapidly repeated notes and chords, fast figuration, tremolos, and glissandi constitute most of the piece, but simpler and more subdued ideas are also featured in some choruses. This number is a thoroughly representative example of Spann at his best. Possibly his most successful essay, for piano solo, in traditional boogie-woogie is his "Spann's Boogie-Woogie" (1965), a solo with musical ideas that are more characteristic of the previous generation of boogie pianists. It also includes, incidentally, nicely veiled references to the figuration of Clarence Smith's "Pinetop's Boogie-Woogie," although, of course, this could have occurred quite unintentionally. Relatively short, with only eight choruses, it is, nevertheless, a rewarding piece.

Possibly in response to the Chess label ignoring their home-grown talent, Spann made an impressive series of recordings in 1960 for the small independent label Candid, *Otis Spann Is the Blues* (Candid, LP 9001), on which he is featured with Robert Lockwood Jr. (guitar). Both men play and sing the blues individually. The most dramatic of Spann's tracks is the modified and thunderous "Cow Cow Blues," which appears as "Great Northern Stomp." This was the first release on the neophyte record label owned by jazz critic and author Nat Hentoff, with Spann as one of only two bluesmen to appear on it (Lightnin' Hopkins was the other). The record became extremely rare with the demise of the company after two years but was reissued together with other gems, including the definitive

LP of Spann's blues playing, as *Walking the Blues,* after CBS purchased the Candid masters. Among the tracks is "Going Down Slow," the tune identified with the veteran bluesman Jimmie "St. Louis" Oden on which Spann perfectly matches the emotional tone of his piano and voice.

In 1967, Spann was continually active in the recording studios of Prestige, Vanguard, Testament, and Bluesway, accompanied by his wife Lucille, prior to attending his final recording session for Blue Horizon where he was supported by the Fleetwood Mack Rhythm and Blues group. The Bluesway LP contains a posthumous hit, the very relaxed "Hungry Country Girl." Some twelve months before, in what appeared to be a significant move toward embracing a solo career, Otis Spann had finally vacated the piano chair in the Muddy Waters Band to the capable Pinetops Perkins. The marriage of his keyboard talents and his smoky blues vocals achieve a state of musical perfection that together with the sparkling piano pyrotechnics produce a cornucopia of musical ideas.

One pianist who could be described as a reluctant talent was John Henry Davis (1913–1985)—generally known as "Blind" John Davis— because his all-around piano abilities on recordings and as the house pianist for the Lester Melrose Wabash Music Company, in the years preceding World War II, went largely unnoticed in both America and Europe. In the final decade of his life, after several trips to Europe and an increasing stash of recordings, his stature rose within the blues world. This neglect was due in part to Davis's own desire to play the lounges and clubs of Chicago where he made a steady living entertaining both white and black clientele with their catholic musical tastes, as well as his wish not to be typecast solely as a blues and boogie-woogie player.[6]

Davis was a Chicagoan by adoption, having moved there with his family from Hattiesburg, Mississippi, at the age of three. His father, John Wesley Davis, was something of an entrepreneur and while employed in a foundry making wheels, he opened up two clubs or speakeasies in Chicago where illicit alcohol, music, and, no doubt, other visceral entertainments were available to the African-American clientele. At the age of nine, John lost his sight from an infection received by stepping on a rusty nail. Always intrigued by music and hearing it being played on the piano in his father's clubs and on the radio, he recognized an opportunity to earn some money, so he set about teaching himself to play on the family piano, inevitably without sight, relying on an acute sense of hearing that enabled him to remember and recall notes. By his mid-teens, he was sufficiently adept to appear in his father's clubs and receive payment for it. In 1933, he formed his first band and undertook engagements at clubs and speakeasies in the environs of Chicago.

Much of the period in the late 1930s and in the early years of the war was taken up with a prodigious number of recordings as an accompanist.

Particularly notable was his backup on many of Tampa Red's record-ings beginning with those for the Chicago Five dating from 1937. Other recording dates were fulfilled with, among others, the guitar-playing vocalists Lonnie Johnson, Memphis Minnie, and Big Bill Broonzy. It was with Broonzy that he made his first trip to Europe in 1952—one of the first bluesmen to do so. The Johnny Davis Rhythm Boys came into being at the commencement of World War II, and they successfully toured across the Midwest and the western states of America. Later, his group was to be named the John Davis Trio with George Barnes (guitar) and Ransom Knowling (bass). They were popular with white audiences because of their broad repertoire of tunes, which might include a blues such as "The St. Louis Blues" but rarely the rawer type of heartfelt blues that were still significant for many African-Americans.

Davis made his solo recording debut in 1938 for Vocalion with "Jersey Cow Blues" backed by "Booze Drinking Benny." Two further sessions fol-lowed in the same year, resulting in four issued sides, but then there was a large gap of several years before he made any more solo tracks. Several sides were cut with his trio in the late 1940s and early 1950s, but Davis disbanded and thereafter played mainly as a solo pianist in and around Chicago with excursions to the Newport Folk Festival (1964), blues festi-vals in Canada, and further trips to Europe beginning in 1973. Additional recordings were made for his home-based Sirens company (1976) and in Europe for the Oldie Blues label in Holland (1974), the German record company L&R (1983), and back in Chicago for the Red Beans label (1985) shortly before his death.

John Davis played excellent piano blues and boogie-woogie but would intersperse these in his sets with standards such as "I Wish I Could Shimmy Like My Sister Kate" and "Kansas City Here I Come." He was a relaxed, good natured, and friendly man, traits that percolate in his musical interpretations from 1976 on *Heavy Timbre: Chicago Boogie-Woo-gie Piano* (Sirens, SR 5002). His composition "I Almost Lost My Mind" demonstrates the poignancy and expressive qualities of his high-pitched voice. An extensive use of keyboard grace notes gives shadowy emphasis to the emotional content of these lyrics; at times, his voice is unerringly matched note for note by the keyboard. His bass lines are either a stac-cato walking bass, as on the boogie-woogie number "Davis Boogie," or more generally a rumbling background of notes climbing up and down the keyboard with subtle shifts of rhythmical emphasis in their move-ment, as on "A Little Every Day." He frequently contrasts this bass line with double-tempo treble phrases, but there is always motion of some kind—and few pauses. John Davis was certainly an unknown force wait-ing to be discovered; posterity will no doubt place him correctly at the forefront of blues pianists.

Another pupil of the Mississippi piano school, Albert Luandrew, or "Sunnyland" Slim (1907–1995), did his early training on a pump organ. Born and raised on a farm in the small town of Vance, he displayed an early interest in music. The fact that his father was a preacher gave him access to the church organ. He played piano at local parties but tired of this and ran away from home on several occasions, citing poor relations with his stepmother as one reason. Using his piano skills, he toured the South as a hobo making his way by playing at parties and even, for a time, worked in a cinema accompanying silent films at Lambert, Mississippi, in 1924.[7] In the mid-1920s, he settled in Memphis and soloed at the Panama Club and the Hole in the Wall Club, which he described as being a tough joint, before touring with Ma Rainey and her show the Arkansas Swift Foot Review. A significant move was linking with Sonny Boy Williamson as pianist to his group during the early 1930s, setting him on a track for his later success with the Muddy Waters Blues Band and the Chicago Sound.

Sunnyland Slim was a powerfully built man who took his pseudonym from one of his numbers "Sunnyland Train," an equally powerful locomotive running between Memphis and St. Louis. He moved to Chicago at the commencement of World War II to work initially outside music but he was soon entertaining at the Flame Club, in 1943, and shortly afterward became accompanist to Tampa Red and Doc Clayton. Now well established at the 21 Club and others, and as a member of the Jump Jackson Band, Sunnyland invited Muddy Waters to play at one of his recording sessions in 1947. This helped establish the future path of the Chicago Sound, because the talents of Waters as vocalist and guitar player were brought to the attention of the Chess brothers at the recording session, and thereafter the Muddy Waters Band was a fixture on their label. Many recordings were made by Slim from 1948 to 1956 for labels as varied and exotically named as Blue Lake, Regal, and Tempo Tone. His most exciting tracks are, by general agreement, those from his first album for Bluesville in 1960, *Slim's Shout*, on which he was joined by King Curtis (tenor saxophone). "Brownskin Woman" and "Shake It" are particularly worth listening to as definitive examples of his blues interpretations. He ran his own label, Airway Records, for a while and used it to bring on young new talent. His final decade was spent performing mainly in and around Chicago where he was a regular fixture at the B.L.U.E.S. Club situated on Chicago's north side. In 1988, he received a National Heritage Fellowship from the National Endowment for the Arts, his final accolade as an outstanding blues artist. His death in 1995 arose from complications following a fall.

The recordings made by Sunnyland Slim are blessed with confident and clearly stated piano chording, both varied in its use of rocks basses, fast arpeggios, and tremolos, as they appear on "She's Got a Thing Going On" featured on his Sirens recording (see above), and forcefully strident vocals—packaged within a dazzling infectious rhythm. "Canadian Walk" is a boogie-woogie piece built around an extended habanera bass. Voice and piano come together well on "Gotta See My Lawyer," in which woman trouble provides the theme. Two impressions remain of Sunnyland entertaining at the piano, possibly endemic to Chicago, and these are the versatility of his piano playing, which owes something to Little Brother Montgomery's influence in its breadth of ideas and style—both were active at the same time in the city and earlier in the South—and in his assured singing, cleverly deploying intonation, pitch, and timing that draw comparisons with Champion Jack Dupree. But given all these eclectic influences, Sunnyland Slim stands out as a strong individual who could hold his own with any of his contemporaries at the keyboard.

Joe Willie "Pinetop" Perkins (1913–) hailed from Belzoni, Mississippi, and was still active at the age of ninety-one. In February 2005 he flew from his home in La Porte, Texas, to attend the 47th Annual Grammy Awards where he was due to receive the Recording Academy Lifetime Achievement Award together with Led Zeppelin, Jerry Lee Lewis, and the much lamented Janis Joplin.[8] Success came to Perkins late in life after he had left the Legendary Blues Band in the early 1980s to perform as a solo act. Prior to that time he was known as a sideman who graced the piano stools of many blues legends.

An early interest in the blues was initially expressed on the guitar, but an altercation with the knife-wielding wife of a club owner in Helena, Arkansas, led to sustained injuries to his arm and hand, prohibiting further guitar playing, so he turned to the piano. His early piano experiences were at juke joints and bars in the small townships of Indianola and Tukwila, Mississippi. In the 1930s, he became a worthy keyboard man for Sonny Boy Williamson on the *King Biscuit Show*. He then toured with Robert Nighthawk and backed that slide guitar player on an early Chess recording. Later tours followed in which he backed B.B. King (guitar) and Earl Hooker before being offered the piano stool in the Muddy Waters Band, after the death of Otis Spann in 1970, a position he held for twelve very productive years. This experience certainly added to and consolidated the range of his stock of blues numbers and prepared the way for Perkins and other members of Waters' band to leave en masse to form the Legendary Blues Band. Perkins toured England with Muddy Waters in 1972 and 1976; the latter tour combined with appearances in Europe. He was also active at various blues festivals in the 1970s, notably Ann Arbor (1972), Newport (1973), and Nice (1978). Becoming a solo performer has given Perkins a new and rewarding lease on life as a "legendary" blues pianist whose story spans the years from the Great Depression to current times. With this new if belated recognition has come a quickening in the pace of work, which he obviously relishes.

Pinetop Perkins claims to have some contact with Clarence "Pinetop" Smith to the extent that he adopted his soubriquet out of respect for Smith, though his piano style owes little to Clarence Smith's light running phrases. Perkins employs a heavy rocks boogie-woogie bass interspersed with a Yancey-style habanera bass on "How Much More," and his treble ideas are largely confined to block chords in the mid-range with occasional sorties to the top end of the keyboard. He is heard at his best singing "How Long Blues," on which he supports the melancholy sentiments with an appropriately subdued background harmony. Both numbers are featured on a recording from 2001, *Eight Hands on 88 Keys* (Sirens, SR 5003).

A review of the blues pianists covered in this chapter so far shows their overwhelming presence in Chicago, wherever they may have begun life. Post 1960, the city was an important magnet for urban blues and boogie-woogie piano as much as it was in the days of Hersal Thomas, Jimmy Blythe, and Albert Ammons. Other talented piano players were drawn to the city in the knowledge that opportunities for work and recording contracts would be enhanced by the journey. Among them were Eddie Boyd and Willie Mabon.

Eddie Boyd (1914–1994), known as "Little Eddie," was another émigré to Europe, finishing his years in Finland. He had moved to Chicago in 1941 looking for the chance to record but had to wait another six years before he was eventually signed by Victor. Born and raised on a plantation at Stovall, near Clarksdale, Mississippi, he showed an interest in music during his teens and learned to play the piano and the guitar—the latter from his father who also played this instrument. Like others before him, Boyd ran away from home to travel around the states of Arkansas, Mississippi, and Tennessee, working outside music but listening and watching other pianists before he too could offer his services as an entertainer at parties and country dances. He was finally drawn to Memphis, where his skills were deployed in various clubs such as the Big Four Club on Beale Street.

When he moved to Chicago, Boyd joined the bands of Sonny Boy Williamson (Rice Miller) and Muddy Waters and also played alongside Memphis Slim in clubs on the South Side. At one point, he provided the recorded piano accompaniments for Maceo Merriweather's vocals after a stroke paralyzed Maceo's arms. Boyd can be heard adding the piano part for Merriweather, accompanying William "Jazz" Gillum on "Gonna Take My Rap" (1947), and providing the piano backing to the vocal by Sonny Boy Williamson on "Elevator Woman" (1939). Sonny Boy's vocal and harmonica playing tend to overpower everything else, but the piano—and the mandolin—do break through at times. Boyd's left hand provides a steady, eight-to-the-bar boogie-woogie bass throughout, and while his right hand is generally unadventurous, it does have some forceful passages of rapidly repeated chords. These tunes are available on *Alexis Korner Presents: King of the Blues*, Volume 2 (RCA, RCX 203).

Many of Boyd's recordings were made with small groups, and in most, besides singing, he is also at the piano with his left hand playing a boogie-woogie bass. The right-hand treble ideas, however, are not always particularly idiomatic to the authentic boogie-woogie style. Of his first recordings for RCA Victor, his "Eddie's Blues" (1947) already reflects to some extent the trend away from the traditional boogie style toward a more commercial swing idiom. One tends to associate it more with, say, Lionel Hampton than with Meade Lux Lewis. It relies a great deal on repeated-note passages and tremolos, and uses the bass figure made popular by Freddy Slack's "Cow Cow Boogie" (namely, ♫♩ ♫♫ ♫♩ ♫♫). After he left Victor in 1949, Boyd joined Chess. He wrote and recorded "Five Long Years" (1952), which was to become a standard blues number, subsequently covered by many blues artists. Such sharply expressed lyrics are a distinctive feature of successful compositions with which many can identify. In his 1967 recordings for English Decca, Boyd is still playing much in the same vein. Of his original compositions, perhaps "Save Her, Doctor" and "The Big Bell" may be cited as examples of Boyd at his best. Of his reworkings of other men's music, his version of "Pinetop's Boogie-Woogie" is recognizably related to the original, and the solo piano of Boyd has additional interest provided by the harmonica of John Mayall. His version of Elmore James's "Dust My Broom" (1967), featuring Tony McPhee on guitar, rocks along to the consistent use of a boogie-woogie bass figure throughout—as does, of course, the Elmore James original—but although there are a few similarities in the guitar figuration, really the musical relationship between Boyd's version and James's original of 1953 is rather tenuous.

At a mid-point in his career, Eddie Boyd was involved in a bad car crash that laid him up in the hospital for several months, occurring at a time when his popularity in America was beginning to wane. After a long convalescence, he joined the American Folk Blues Festival, which visited Europe in 1965, and clearly enjoyed the adulation he received. This was followed by visits to England for a concert tour with the John Mayall Bluesbreakers and to Holland and Switzerland. Further recordings were undertaken for Phillips and smaller labels. Not surprisingly, Boyd decided in 1965 to make his home in Europe, initially in France, before marrying a Finnish national and moving there to live permanently. He died of heart failure in his adopted country.

In terms of his piano style, many would agree that "Little Eddie" was a consummate rhythm pianist for the blues bands in which he appeared or led; unspectacular with few showy features to his playing, he was never-theless very popular in the 1950s. A fair resume of his talents was written by Jim O'Neal, who praised his powerful vocals, solid piano playing, abilities as a versatile songwriter, and leader of a talented blues group.[9]

Originally from Hollywood, Tennessee Willie Mabon (1925–1986) is generally considered to be more within the rhythm-and-blues school, achieving his greatest recognition in this field with the Clarence Lofton song "I Don't Know" (number 1 in the R&B chart in 1952) and "Poison Ivy" (number 10 in the R&B chart in 1954). Both numbers were recorded for Chess. His recordings reveal a pleasant singing voice, urbane and silky, reminiscent of Charles Brown, and an arresting piano style that immediately demands attention with its earthy, basic touch. He spent his later years in France where he proved to be a popular entertainer—more so than in his native America after his star had waned there. Several solos and duets were recorded with French pianist Jean Paul Amouroux. One of the more interesting numbers for the sheer rhythm generated and the empathy shown by the two players and bassist Gilles Chevaucherie ap-pears on the French issue *Boogie-Woogie for two Pianos: Willie Mabon & Jean Paul Amouroux* (ADDA, 590119). These tunes were recorded at two concerts in 1975 and 1979. The attractive "Klickety Klock," an original composition in a minor key, but plagued by poor amplification, demon-strates the successful union of the talents of the two pianists, but equally meritorious is "Boogie-Woogie Time," with both pianists building on and extending each other's improvisations.

No known piano solos were recorded by Joshua Altheimer, who died in 1940; his date of birth is unknown. In any case, his reputation rests on his work as an accompanist for Sonny Boy Williamson's vocals and harmonica in "I Been Dealing with the Devil" (1940) with an eight-to-the-bar boogie-woogie bass—that is, when one can actually hear the left hand of the piano due to the combined efforts of the drummer and the sound recording engineer. Prior to this recording, he appeared with Jazz Gillum (vocal/harmonica) in "Got to Reap What You Sow" (1939), using a bass figure in a ♪ ♩ ♩♩ ♩ ♩♩♩ rhythm until just before the end when he changes to an eight-to-the-bar walking bass. In both pieces there is additional accompaniment—drums in the former, and guitar (Big Bill Broonzy) and saxophone in the latter—and in both pieces Altheimer's right hand plays what could be termed "ornamental blues" rather than boogie-woogie; that is to say, the treble parts are rather overladen with tremolos, arabesques, and other decorative figuration.

The younger brother of Speckled Red, William L. Perryman (1913–1985), spent much of his working life in and around Atlanta, Georgia. He began learning his trade at house parties in the 1930s and later played at the Hole in the Wall and other clubs but did not start recording his own material until after 1950, from which period we have his "name piece," "Red's Boogie" (1951) recorded with the Piano Red Trio. He was still recording it as a piano solo as late as 1974, and though some differences are apparent across the twenty years, it is still basically the same number. Both versions use the same eight-bar chorus and have a boogie-woogie bass accompaniment over which the same tune is repeated with and without variations, which tends toward repetition and also raises the question as to whether such a procedure limits it from being classified as a powerful boogie-woogie piece. The most notable differences between the two versions are that the earlier one has an introduction that the later one omits, the earlier version has a continuous boogie-woogie bass throughout (except for bars 7 and 8) while the later version maintains a boogie-woogie bass only for the first half of each eight-bar chorus, and only the later version contains three whole choruses, which are completely without a boogie-woogie bass accompaniment.

Among his 1974 recordings are a couple of boogie-woogie numbers that are noteworthy. "Pinetop's Boogie" is a piano solo, with a little talking in which the relationship to the original is clearly apparent—as are the additions to the original provided by Perryman himself—but which, of all the many versions by different artists of this piece, is far from being the worst. He gives a crisp, pleasant, and creditable performance. "Sloppy Drunk" (vocal/piano), although departing now and again from the strict twelve-bar blues pattern, is an easily acceptable piece of boogie-woogie with a stomping eight-to-the-bar bass and fluent and quite convincing ideas in the treble. This is one of his finer pieces, showing him at his best. A comprehensive collection of his tunes is present on the album *Piano Red, Dr. Feelgood All Alone with His Piano* (Arhoolie, 1064).

From 1954, Red appeared on a daily radio program on WAOK in Atlanta, which gave him exposure. He and his small rocking band were in big demand, leading to tours to Texas and the East Coast, even appearing at the Apollo Theater in New York. His barrelhouse piano—a stomping octave left hand—and plaintive, raucous singing, led to his emergence as a rhythm-and-blues artist, with the release of "Dr. Feelgood," another hit recording from the early 1960s. He was kept in productive employment thereafter until his death in the 1990s.

It is appropriate that the final selection of African-American blues and boogie-woogie pianists included in this edifice of significant artists should come from the southern states where an embryonic piano style first emerged as a phenomenon in black culture. All three came from Texas, but whereas Alex Moore rarely moved from Dallas, the other two traveled around the state and beyond. Katie Webster lived and worked in and around Louisiana, while Robert Shaw visited Missouri and Oklahoma.

Alexander Herman Moore, or "Whistling Alex Moore" (1899–1989), was born in Dallas and spent his musical life in and around that city, with occasional sorties to Austin and Houston. His active musical career spanned seven decades. Leaving school after his twelfth birthday, shortly after his father died, he worked at a grocery store as a delivery boy. In his late teens he became interested in music and began teaching himself to play the harmonica and piano; he was able to practice some of his newly acquired techniques on pianos owned by indulgent white folk to whom he was delivering. Shortly afterward, in 1916, he enlisted in the American armed forces and served in World War I. Returning to Dallas, he began to build a career there in the 1920s and from about 1924 onward began playing in its many clubs and bars, places such as the Misty Lounge and the Brown Derby. He recalled the cacophony of piano music there and the tunes he absorbed as he walked around.[10] Playing the piano became an abiding passion, and he would frequently sit at the keyboard for nine or ten hours at a time, to the point where he would be asked to "move on" by those who found his dedication too much. There is no doubt that Moore possessed a gift for learning to play by watching and remembering the sequence of notes used by other pianists. This, coupled with a good ear, enabled him to develop sufficient technique to make his first six recordings for Columbia in 1929 at the age of thirty. They were recorded in Chicago but achieved little commercial success. Additional recording dates for Decca followed in 1937, resulting in four numbers, with Blind Horace McHenry (guitar) on two of them, and again in 1947 for a small Texas record company. No marked recognition accrued from them, although they were frequently played on local radio.

Dallas was an important railway town, hosting termini for many famous railroads with transport links throughout the mid- and southwest of America: The Rock Island line, Colorado and Santa Fe, and the Gulf were some. The area known as Central Tracks was where many African-Americans lived, while the notorious districts of Froggy Bottom and Elm Street succored the blues in their clubs. Perhaps it is the city's position at the "end of the line" that determines the nature of its music, for there is no doubt that it has a uniqueness born of insularity, leaving it noticeably unaffected by outside influences. Its songs are about urban life there, captured with a lyricism that is distanced from other regional blues. As Oliver points out, the blues from Dallas tell a story and the sentiments should be listened to if they are to be fully appreciated.[11] Similarly, the piano accompaniments, at least as reflected in Moore's playing and those of his contemporaries Willie Tyson and Texas Bill Day, are definitely subjugated to the words, certainly in early recordings. The instrument becomes an additional vehicle for giving greater emotional impact to the meaning of the lyrics.

During the 1930s and 1940s, Alex Moore continued to make a steady living playing at local clubs and chock houses, interspersing this with driving a hack around the city. This was the period of Prohibition, and Moore evocatively and vividly describes the frequent visits of two local policemen to one of the chock houses where he played and their enthusiastic physical attacks on the barrels of illegal moonshine liquor.[12] In the 1950s, Moore took a job as a dishwasher at the Southern Steakhouse where he eventually became an entertainer in the restaurant lounge, after the owner had heard of Moore's talents at the piano. He enjoyed a productive stay there before transferring to a second restaurant in Houston for a period of five months. With the death of a family member, he returned for good to Dallas and did not play again for some time—until record producer Chris Strachwitz, with the cooperation of Paul Oliver, finally got him to record for his Arhoolie label in 1960. This recording, which brought him acclaim and a wider audience beyond Texas, was also released in England as *Whistling Alexander Moore* (77 Records, 77-LA-12-7). Before his retirement in 1965—he always followed the maxim of never giving up the day job—he worked as a janitor and a hotel porter.

Two of Moore's rare excursions outside Dallas occurred in 1969 when he visited England as a member of the American Folk and Blues Festival, culminating in an appearance at the Albert Hall in London; on his return, he undertook a successful weeklong engagement at the Stephen F. Austin Hotel toward the end of the 1970s. His talents were recognized by the state of Texas in 1987 when he was awarded a Lifetime Achievement Award from the National Endowment of the Arts. His eighty-ninth birthday, November 22, 1988, was celebrated by the state as Alex Moore Day. In both instances, Alex Moore was the first black Texan to be thus honored. The former award brought a typical pragmatic response from the octogenarian, who said that he played for "real folks" and not for proclamations.[13]

Alex Moore's piano style evolved over the years, and this can be seen most markedly by comparing his first recordings, from 1929, with those made in 1960. Considering the earlier recordings first, "Heart Wrecked Blues" is a quiet, medium-paced blues sung in a husky vocal accompanied by a stride piano. The piece is enlivened by a piercing whistle that replaces the vocal at some stage and frequently overwhelms the piano. Similarly, "Blue Bloomer Blues" relates an encounter with a girl of questionable morals, or a prostitute, with the listener's attention being drawn to the erotic words away from Moore's own somewhat basic, some would say tentative, piano accompaniment. However, on the vinyl recordings made in 1960, there is a marked change in the contribution of the piano playing, which in no way reduces the impact of the lyrics. It is now louder and more varied in its technique using delayed rhythms and double time. Additional coloration is provided by cascading runs and chopped chords, which are sketched and slashed across the keyboard. Strong boogie-woogie patterns now permeate the bass between passages of stride—both heavy rocks basses and walking basses appear in "Alex Moore's Blues." On "Black Eyed Peas," comparisons with Speckled Red are inevitable in the wildly hit, unpredictable treble chording, powerful walking bass, and roaring, husky voice. Delayed and double-time beats are the basic ingredients of "Boogie in the Barrel," while "Going Back to Froggy Bottom" is a slower blues, deploying a horse-clopping bass more usually associated with Western Swing music.

Moore's vocal abilities have been likened to a stream of consciousness allowing him to improvise a blues at will. This is certainly a unique feature, as is the piercing whistle that he deploys, trumpet-style, to bring variety to his music. Whistling features in the blues of other Dallas singers (Billiken Johnson, et al.), who frequently enhance their lyrics with train whistles, mule noises, and supportive melodic whistling, another indication, perhaps, of the naiveté and folksy nature of a Dallas style untouched by more "sophisticated" influences. Alex Moore made his final recordings in 1988, twelve months before his death from heart failure, which were released under the title *Alex Moore Wiggle Tail*.

Texas has maintained its early tradition as a vital center for piano blues. Katie Webster (1936–1999) was born in Houston, where she received piano lessons as a child. Both parents were very religious and forbade her to play the blues and R&B music that attracted her and to which she listened illicitly on a bedside radio, with the volume turned down. During these formative years, her parents moved to California, leaving Katie with less strict relatives in Louisiana, who allowed her to pursue her interest in the music she loved. She became an excellent interpreter of blues, barrelhouse, boogie-woogie, and that special brand of mixed southern soul and gospel music known as the "swamp" sound.

For a time, in 1957, Katie Webster was employed at Club Vegas in Dallas, owned by the infamous Jack Ruby, a small-time bit player in the President Kennedy saga who killed his assassin Lee Harvey Oswald. Further engagements followed in Dallas and Houston nightspots before she moved in 1959 to Lake Charles as a member of the Ashton Savoy Combo. Very soon, she had established a reputation as a studio musician and was used as their house pianist by Excello, Goldband, and other small record companies in Louisiana. In this capacity, she backed Lonesome Sundown, Slim Harpo, Lightnin' Slim, and accordionist Clifton Chenier, the zydeco wizard. In the mid-1960s, Otis Redding happened to be in town and caught her act. He was immediately taken with her talents and asked her to join his show, which she did, traveling with him throughout the South. Fortunately, she was not with Redding at the time of the plane crash that killed him.

Katie Webster went on to became a popular and featured soloist at major blues festivals in New Orleans, Chicago, and San Francisco, winning over audiences with her compelling blend of hard-hitting boogie-woogie and blues piano, and sensuously expressed singing. A significant move leading to her increased fame occurred in 1988 when she was signed by the Alligator record company. After these recordings had been released, her abilities became known to a much wider and discerning international public. Nominations for the WC Handy Awards—a Grammy for blues artists—followed as well as television appearances (NBC) and international tours to Europe. Unfortunately, she suffered a stroke while touring Greece; although she maintained her concert and club appearances by singing with a little right hand work on the piano, she died relatively young at age sixty-three.

Robert "Fud" Shaw (1908–1986) was a pianist and singer who played an archaic sounding kind of blues and boogie-woogie that seemed trapped in a time warp. He was born and raised in Stafford, Fort Bend County, Texas, on his father's cattle ranch and began learning to play the piano in his teens. So keen was he to master the instrument that he took piano lessons, paid for by himself. Music was an early influence in his life, with his mother and sisters all playing piano. However, it was not his mother's kind of music that attracted Robert Shaw but the music played by pianists serving the clubs and joints of Houston during the Prohibition years. As a young man, he was particularly impressed with the effusive accolades given by the dancing girls to pianists, throwing their arms around them and hugging them with requests to play "Put Me in the Alley"—a popular tune of the period requiring the pianist to play low down, funky blues that would excite the listeners. Robert saw how happy the piano players made the girls and felt he would also like to be a part of it. Early experiences saw him entertaining at local parties in and around Stafford before traveling as an itinerant pianist to work in the barrelhouses, juke joints, and brothels of Richmond, Houston, Galveston, and Kansas, mixing this with a little card and dice gambling in the back room. He was one of the last members of the Santa Fe (serving eighty-eight Texas counties) group of pianists who used the railroad for reaching their destinations.

Believing himself to be a superior pianist—which was accurate, given the speed that a crowd would gather when he began to play anywhere—gave him the confidence to strike a hard bargain over his hourly rate. If a club owner was miserly and only offered him two hours' work, then Shaw would ask for, and eventually get, two dollars an hour, but this would be reduced to a rate of a dollar and a half if the owner offered a longer period of eight or so hours. Such an entrepreneurial streak in his character fitted him well for his final venture, which occurred in the mid-1930s when he had already moved permanently to Austin to become a runner for a numbers policy racket. A brush with the law convinced him after ten years on the road to look elsewhere for developing his business interests, so he opened an ice house, eventually extending this into selling barbecued ribs and finally to a successful grocery business (Shaw's Food Market) otherwise known as "Stop and Swat." In 1962, he was awarded the title of "Texas Outstanding Businessman," and his store served the interests of both white and black Texans. Fortunately for posterity, he kept his piano skills well honed by playing for customers in his store, entertaining friends, and playing at private functions. This is the reason his style is so distinctive, having effectively been protected from outside influence for several decades. In his later years, Shaw toured with the Festival of American Folk Life, visiting Washington D.C., Montreal, as well as performing at festivals in Germany (Berlin 1974) and Switzerland (Montreux 1975).

Robert Shaw's piano style is an eclectic mix of tuneful melodies, blues, and boogie-woogie. To be accurate, it probably sits more easily in the barrelhouse school of playing than any other. He claims to have been influenced by several pianists, among whom Harold Holliday, Pig Willy, and Joe Coleman were paramount. Shaw's versatility is shown in the number of keys he used (C, F, E, E-flat, G, A, and B-flat), and, by his own estimation, he was proficient as an entertainer in his late teens, four years after he commenced playing seriously. Shaw did not have an extensive recording career. Perhaps his most productive period began in 1963 for the Houston-based Almanac label under the guidance of Mack McCormick, who also produced the well-researched and informative liner notes. These recordings were later issued under the Arhoolie label entitled *Texas Barrelhouse Piano: Robert Shaw, Piano and Vocals* (Arhoolie, F1010). They are like a bee trapped in amber, providing a wonderful unspoilt collection of Santa Fe railroad music as it must have sounded in the several chock houses where Robert Shaw played.

The next significant recordings occurred in 1971 when Robert Shaw entertained at a party given by Ben Conroy at his home in Austin. A selection of these tunes was eventually released in 1988 on *Robert Shaw: The 1971 Party Tape* (Document, DOCD1014) with liner notes by Conroy. He describes how he made his initial contact with Shaw, after hearing his work on the Arhoolie record, and followed this up with visits to his home. On one occasion when visiting with friends, Shaw's wife Martha sat in her rocking chair drinking her soda and reading the Bible while Robert entertained his guests. Shaw is at his most relaxed on these party numbers, exuding a benign mellowness in such receptive and convivial company. All the well-known tunes from his stock are included, as well as two associated with Pinetop Smith. Shaw's version of "Jump Steady Blues" contains verses from "Pinetop's Blues," and just to add a degree of eclecticism to "Pinetop's Boogie-Woogie," a verse or so from "I'm So-ber Now" are added. He was recorded again by Austrian blues collector Michael Hort in 1981 and the numbers released on the Wolf label. Further recordings made by Strachwitz at Shaw's home, in 1973 and 1977, appear on *Robert Shaw: The Ma Grinder* (Arhoolie, CD 377). This is the significant recorded output of Robert Shaw with the addition of two radio broad-casts for the local radio station KUT-FM dating from 1976 and 1984, now in the hands of private collectors.

Arhoolie Records celebrated twenty-one years of recording under the guidance of Chris Strachwitz in 1981 with a party in San Francisco. A good selection of their artists attended, including Robert Shaw, then in his seventy-third year. He had boarded a Greyhound bus in Austin and trav-eled to California and immediately after the event had retraced his jour-ney back to Austin, a round trip of thirty-five hundred miles, at his own expense. When someone queried the distance of the marathon journey, Shaw replied that it was the least he could do for the person responsible for his late recording success.[14]

Many of Shaw's pieces take their topics from the localities in which he traveled. Thus, "The Ma Grinder" (1963) became a test piece, similar to James P. Johnson's "Carolina Shout," to measure the technical capabil-ity of a pianist. When a new man arrived in town looking for work, he would be asked by a club owner to play this tune as an accompaniment for a solo dance, a modified cake-walking strut, performed by males. Shaw's version shows his technique well with its several improvised variations on the melody. "Hattie Green" (1971) is a tune about a popu-lar brothel madam from Abilene, while "Piggly Wiggly" (1971) refers to a well-known grocery chain in the area. There is a similarity in the melodies of at least two tunes, "Put Me in the Alley" and "The Cows" (both 1963) if not in their speeds, but, as McCormick observes, dancers only ever needed a fast or a slow rhythm.[15] The first of theses pieces has a bass of ascending and descending stepped octaves, suggesting a sketchy walking bass. "The Clinton" (1963) derives its name from a stopping place on the Santa Fe line in Oklahoma. This number is pure boogie-woogie, containing discordant treble chording, reminiscent of driving wheels and train bells. Snatches of a rumba rhythm are heard in "Ma Grinder," perhaps a Louisiana influence here. On "People People" (1963), Shaw accompanies his vocal with the trace of a full boogie-woogie bass. There is inspiration from Leroy Carr's number "How Long Blues" in the medium-paced "Hattie Green" with its solid, laid-down rocks bass. The theme of "Whores Is Funky" (1971) requires no elaboration and includes breaks and a roisterous walking bass. There is a nicely judged call and response between the bass and treble parts on the slow "Black Gal" (1971) and a strained, almost shouted vocal from Shaw—this is now

a standard blues number featured later by Pinetop Burks and Joe Pul-
lum, the man who was really responsible for bringing it to the attention
of a larger public. All the music on this Arhoolie record is fresh, colorful,
tuneful, and reminiscent of an earlier age in the South. Listening to it is
both a vital and intense experience.

As we have identified in earlier chapters, recognized jazz pianists
such as Earl Hines ("Boogie-Woogie on St. Louis Blues" [1940]) used
the boogie-woogie framework to perform "show stoppers" within their
otherwise orthodox jazz piano styles. Joe Sullivan in "Summertime"
(1941) and in other interpretations introduces boogie-woogie feeling and
phrases into pieces to give them a distinctive and different coloring; and
even Art Tatum and Oscar Peterson were known to have a fondness for
the style. Art Hodes (1904–1993) falls within this purview but remained
much closer to the roots of piano blues and boogie-woogie in conception
and integrity.

Hodes was born in Nikolaev, Russia, and came to America with his im-
migrant parents looking for a new life in the promised land. Art was six
months old. The family settled in a tough Italian neighborhood on Roosevelt Street on the west side of Chicago. His parents purchased a piano
on the installment plan, and Art began lessons at the age of six. As part of
the deal, he also had to take singing lessons, which helped to develop his
ear for later jazz improvisation. His proficiency allowed him to earn cash
as a member of small groups entertaining at weddings and similar neighborhood functions. As pianist in one group, he was introduced to jazz by
Earl Murphy, the banjo player, who had a comprehensive collection of
records. Hodes was smitten with the music and spent many hours listening to Louis Armstrong as well as absorbing the "white" tones of fellow
Chicagoans. At this time, in his early twenties, he met Wingy Mannone
(trumpet), and for a time they shared the same accommodation while
they both absorbed as much jazz as they could. Part of their education
was to meet up with Louis Armstrong, who shepherded them around the
black dives on the South Side to hear many obscure African-American
blues pianists. Art was immediately captivated and revisited them to listen and absorb the feel and tone of their music. One pianist called simply
Jackson taught him much, but he was also strongly influenced by Little
Brother Montgomery to the extent that he later received the ultimate compliment from him that his playing sounded more African-American than
many African-Americans. Art was gradually finding his way through a
maze of jazz and defining his own world of music; he freely admits this
was a slow process, recalling the humiliation of being laughed off the
piano stool when he first tried to play the blues in the South Side dives.
His style shows influences from significant blues piano players such as
Carr, Smith, and Montgomery, but it also has the open interconnected-

ness between the bass and treble of Earl Hines, rejecting the predominant stride style of the day as the sole way of interpreting jazz and blues. There are also traces of Lil Hardin's influence, the mainstay of the rhythm section for Armstrong's Hot Five. Gradually, he began to make a mark as a competent jazz band pianist, usually with his favored small groups—trios or quintets—until he was leading his own groups at McGovern's Liberty Inn, which he considered the one remaining "bucket-of-blood joint." If there were no fights, the customers felt cheated.[16] Where the gangsters were in control of the clubs, the status of the pianist, according to Hodes, lay somewhere between the barman and the washroom attendant.

Surmising that the opportunities were better in New York, Art moved there in 1938 where his decision was vindicated with work, recordings, and reviews in *Downbeat* and similar specialist magazines. Prior to this move, he had attended only one recording date in 1928 with Wingy Mannone's Club Royale Orchestra in Chicago, barely heard on a "bluesy" piano break on "Trying to Stop My Crying." His second recording opportunity was in New York as a soloist on Dan Qualey's Solo Art label. Although posterity does not recognize Art as the writer of any exceptional boogie-woogie compositions, he quickly built a deserved reputation as the foremost white exponent of blues piano music in America, with the release by Dan Qualey on Solo Art, of "Ross Tavern Boogie" backed by "South Side Shuffle" (1939). The record was highly acclaimed by Ralph Gleason, who said that Hodes was a "real old timer" (he was in his thirties) and the only white pianist capable of playing boogie-woogie in such an unpretentious and natural style.[17] In a feature article from 1939, *Downbeat* endorsed this view, considering him to be the most talented blues pianist around at the time.[18] Hodes was resident pianist at Ross's Tavern, the scruffy basement room with a piano and flowing beer that drew visiting pianists to listen and play mainly for each other. It was here that Art first heard Meade Lux Lewis and George Zack.

As a result of favorable record reviews and the feature article in *Downbeat*, Hodes was able to move for more lucrative work to New York, where he was variously employed at the Pirate's Den, Nick's Tavern, and Jimmy Ryan's. He eventually returned to Chicago in 1950 to raise his family there, but not before he had made a substantial contribution to publicizing the life and work of jazz musicians both as a radio presenter of a popular jazz program on the public radio station WNYC and as editor of *Jazz Record*, one of several specialist jazz magazines available in New York in the 1940s. Charles Davenport and Arthur Montana Taylor were two who benefited from the sympathetic publicity given to them by Art in this magazine.

The career of Hodes blossomed after his move back to Chicago. He had found his niche in jazz and was busy fulfilling club, recording, and concert engagements for the next few years. By 1949 he no longer drank alcohol, which blighted many jazzmen of the time. In 1980, he lost his first wife Thelma to cancer but was fortunate to make a second happy marriage to Jan. Increasingly, Art found his greatest satisfaction in touring Europe. He first went to Denmark in 1970 and followed that with many tours to England, Germany, Australia, New Zealand, and other countries. He was always appreciative of the response of European audiences, their knowledgeable background of jazz and blues, and their support at his concerts. Art's material was drawn from traditional sources to which he gave an unmistakable blues tonality. In addition to interpreting the well-known blues standards "Apex Blues" and "Chimes Blues" on the LP *Legendary Art* (Audiophile Records, AP 54 1) from 1957, he used gospel sources such as "Just a Closer Walk with Thee" and "Swing Low Sweet Chariot" on the LP *Gospel According to Art* (Jazzology, JCE- 93) from 1984 and many of Jelly Roll Morton's tunes, such as "The Pearls" and "Buddy Bolden's Blues" on *Pagin' Mr. Jelly* (Candid, 1937) dating from 1988. Increasingly, as he got older, Art appeared as a revered solo performer who could recharge the blues battery of many of his older followers but could, increasingly, spark an interest in younger listeners as well. He became an admirable ambassador for the music of which he was an unsurpassed master. His message was aided by hosting a TV series called *Jazz Alley* and teaching at the Park Forest (Illinois) Conservatory and various other schools and colleges. He retained his skills, hardly dimmed, and a wry sense of humor until his death at the age of eighty-nine.

The excursions into pure boogie-woogie numbers were actually few, but there was never any doubt that its influence was bubbling beneath the surface. On "Yellow Dog Blues" (1944) for Blue Note, Hodes was in the company of Max Kaminsky, Bobby Haggart, and others, taking a raw-sounding, edgy solo with a strong boogie rhythm underlying his clustered tremolos and rapidly hammered grace notes. A month later with his Backroom Boys, he composed and recorded "Jug Head Boogie," underpinning Kaminsky's expressive trumpet and Sandy Williams's growling trombone with a barely contained ground rhythm of boogie-woogie that threatens to spark into life and take over. These recordings, together with his earlier Solo Art pieces, show a deep understanding and feeling for boogie-woogie that gives them authenticity. A direct comparison with an African-American pianist would place him closest to Pinetop Smith, although as we have seen, his influences went beyond this. In his playing of "Ross Tavern Boogie," Hodes exhibits a similar delicate touch to Pinetop: The bass is executed with precision and the piece is propelled by a similar light, driving swing.

Erwin Helfer (1936–) is a white Chicagoan who has been playing the clubs there for several years. Helfer has had a sustained interest in boogie-woogie and the blues over many years. He is the one pianist still living and working in Chicago who provides the important temporal link between the present-day players in the city such as Chuck Goering, who performs under the name of "Barrelhouse" Chuck, and second-generation Chicago pianists Clarence Lofton and Little Brother Montgomery. His musical background emanates from his father, a jeweler by profession, who loved jazz music and took his young son to hear Louis Armstrong and other performers appearing in Chicago. Helfer received formal piano training, but by his own admission, was initially more interested in playing by ear and putting his own interpretation on tunes to the extent that his sight-reading suffered. At this time, he was more interested in classical music and was only vaguely aware of boogie-woogie as background music on the radio. During his teen years at high school, he was increasingly drawn toward New Orleans revivalist jazz, piano blues, and boogie-woogie. But it was not solely the music that he enjoyed: He also found himself attracted to the lifestyle of the musicians. When the family moved out of the city to live in Glencoe, Helfer would travel back to the center so that he could join Montgomery, Lofton, and Davis in order to be in their company and listen to their music. From them. he learned not to be identified solely as a bluesman but to absorb other styles, of particular importance when an expectant audience with a range of musical interests is waiting to be entertained. At this time, Little Brother, who had the greatest influence on Helfer's approach to boogie-woogie and blues, was appearing at the Hollywood Show Lounge on Randolph Street and John Davis was at a club in West Madison Street.[19]

William Russell was living in Chicago while Helfer was still at high school, and they first met at a party where their common interest in revivalist jazz and boogie-woogie provided a bond between them. Russell introduced Helfer to many of the older New Orleans musicians residing in the city such as Baby Dodds (drums) and Natty Dominique (clarinet); gospel singer Mahalia Jackson, then a beautician, was a friend for some time. Helfer eventually left Chicago to study psychology at Tulane University in New Orleans, where he resumed his contact with Russell who was back in the city supported by a Ford scholarship. Helfer never did graduate from Tulane—he took a master's degree later in life—finding the attractions of jazz and blues too overwhelming. He began seeking out musicians such as Punch Miller (trumpet), Emile Barnes (clarinet), and Billie Pearce, sometime pianist with Bessie Smith, but he also recommenced piano lessons from Professor Manuel Manetta, formerly a pianist with the King Oliver band. To reach his house involved a weekly ferry boat crossing the river to Algiers, Louisiana. Record collectors are thankful for the foresight and initiative shown by the young Helfer who, in pursuit of his own perfection, sought out several long-forgotten pianists during his travels in the South. Armed with a Concertone tape recorder, he recorded Speckled Red and passed the results to Bob Koester for issue on the Delmark label. In a later recording session, back in Chicago, he captured two pieces by Doug Suggs (three plus an interview under the reissue arrangement with Sirens), which are the only recordings ever made by that pianist. These were initially issued on Tone, his own label, together with tunes by Speckled Red, James "Bat the Hummingbird" Robinson, and Billie Pierce.

In the mid-1960s, after Helfer had forsaken boogie-woogie and blues to concentrate on his study of classical music, he was introduced to Jimmy Walker, a janitor and former rent-party pianist, who played a primitive type of boogie-woogie piano. They became friends, formed a piano duo, and began taking on engagements around Chicago, including two recording dates, one of which produced the LP *Rough and Ready*. Helfer's main occupation at this time was teaching aspects of both classical and boogie-woogie playing. Some time was spent in England, where he worked several gigs in 1972, combining this with travel in Europe. On returning to Chicago in 1973, Helfer established himself as an act, commencing with a weekly blues show at Orphans, a restaurant on Lincoln Avenue. He was joined by S. P. Leary, a one-time drummer with Howling Wolf. Later, in the company of Jimmy Walker and others, he helped through the popularity of his music, to establish the famous B.L.U.E.S. club, also on Lincoln. After this, he renewed his acquaintance with Mama Yancey and undertook concerts and a recording date with her. For a period of time, Sunnyland Slim also became a musical partner and was a long-standing friend.

Through a process of evolution, and after a long apprenticeship, Erwin Helfer's own niche in the panoply of jazz and blues gradually began to emerge, reflecting his own catholic and eclectic tastes. There is a decided vaudevillian flavor to some of his material, notably in songs performed with singers such as Katherine Davis. However, for Helfer the vocal blues is never far away, nor is boogie-woogie as a solo show stopper or jazz standards such as "Nobody Knows You When You're Down and Out," often sharing solo spots with clarinet and drums. Duke Ellington's compositions make an appearance in his repertoire as do those of bop pianist Thelonious Monk. Helfer is now an established figure in Chicago's entertainment world with a burgeoning international reputation that has taken him on several European tours.

Erwin Helfer's progress as a boogie-woogie and blues pianist is best illustrated by comparing his work on two recordings: the album *Rough and Ready* in the company of Jimmy Walker (piano) and Willie Dixon (bass) from the early 1970s and *I'm Not Hungry but I Like to Eat the Blues* (Sirens, 5001), released in 2001, with John Brumbach (tenor saxophone) featured on several numbers. The first of these recordings was made shortly after he had committed himself again to serious and public piano playing. "Give Me Five Cents Worth of Love" shows a good appreciation of composition and is stimulated by the melody of "Basin Street Blues" for several of its choruses, but their improvisational potential is not completely explored. It is also absent in the clean and catchy phrasing of "Sneaky Pete." Helfer takes off on Jimmy Yancey on "Four O'Clock Blues," a slower piece that allows him time for extending his ideas with greater surety. Moving on almost thirty years to the second recording reveals a fully formed keyboard technique garnered by experience and conviction. He improvises very successfully on his covers of the Ammons's numbers "Swanee River" and "The Sheik of Araby." On the former, he adds his own phrasing over the driving bass of Ammons and on the second number, he combines well with John Brumbach's breathy saxophone to produce a rich tone, as well as stretching out with some original improvisations on the melody. An appreciation of certain features of Johnson's style can be heard on "Homage to Pete Johnson," with its running bass and nimble treble, together creating vivid contrapuntal effects. Finally, a highly expressive and rhythmical interpretation of "See See Rider" is produced in which the melody is broken and underscored with varied bass patterns: a repeated single note and walking and rocks basses. Little Brother Montgomery finally sealed Helfer's status when he acknowledged him to be "a good little piano player."[20]

The group of pianists selected for consideration in this chapter found their métier in playing the blues but within this framework integrated the rumbling tones and rhythms of boogie-woogie. In doing so, their keyboard work bears an extraordinary richness, variety, and suspense that lifts it beyond the mundane.

NOTES

1. Paul Oliver, "A Rollin, Mind, Jack Dupree," *Blues off the Record* (New York: Da Capo, 1989), 246.

2. Oliver, *Blues off the Record*, 251–52.

3. "Jack Dupree," *Independent*, February 22, 1992, and an appreciation by Robert Bruce, *Independent*, February 24, 1992.

4. "Jack Dupree," *Independent*, February 22, 1992.

5. Sheldon Harris, *Blues Who's Who* (New York: Da Capo, 1979), 478.

6. David Whiteis, review of *Heavy Timbre: Chicago Piano* (Sirens, SR-5002), *Living Blues*, May/June 2002, 50.

7. Paul Oliver, *Conversation with the Blues* (London: Cassell, 1967), 86.

8. Daniel Przybla, "Big Day Coming Up for Pinetop Perkins," *La Porte County Herald Argus*, February 11, 2005.

9. Jim O'Neal, "The Eddie Boyd Interview," pt. 1, *Living Blues*, no. 35 (November/December 1977): 11–15. The remainder appeared in *Living Blues* no. 36 (January/February 1978) and no. 37 (March/April 1978).

10. Michael Point, "Plinking the Keys Keeps Pianist Young," *Austin American Statesman* 22 (November 1988): C8.

11. Paul Oliver, liner notes, *Piano Blues, vol. 15: Dallas*, Magpie, PY 4415.

12. Oliver, *Conversation with the Blues*, 53–54.

13. Point, "Plinking the Keys," C8.

14. Paul Vernon, obituary, source unknown.

15. Mack McCormick, liner notes, *Texas Barrelhouse Piano*, Arhoolie, 1010, 4.

16. Art Hodes and Chadwick Hansen, *Hot Man* (Chicago: University of Illinois Press, 1992), 38.

17. Ralph Gleason, *Columbia University* newspaper, 1939.

18. George M. Avakian, "Move Over, Stacey and Sullivan—Let Hodes In!" *Downbeat*, December 1, 1939, 7, 20.

19. "The Apprenticeship of Erwin Helfer," *Reader: Chicago's Free Weekly* 12, no. 16 (January 21, 1983), 16.

20. "The Apprenticeship of Erwin Helfer," 31.

14

The Contemporary Picture

One of the endearing qualities of present-day boogie-woogie music is that it crosses all boundaries of class, race, sex, and age. Although it no longer has the popular exposure it did in the 1940s, it is still played by pianists, some professionally, others as gifted amateurs. As a solo art form it is usually heard in jazz clubs, and at blues festivals and concerts. Many of today's foremost practioners are white, having studied the genre in order to keep the music alive, partly from a sense of respect for the traditions of the black music but also because of the satisfaction the music provides as an all-consuming interest.

If the genre claims any place in the mainstream of popular music, it is perhaps in modified form either as background music in television advertisements or, for example, as the signature tune for popular television series of the 1960s such as Neil Hefti's theme tune for *Batman* or *The Man from U.N.C.L.E.* Exceptionally, the Humphrey Lyttleton band had a huge success in the commercial record charts of 1956 with "Bad Penny Blues" (Parlophone), a boogie-woogie-inspired number featuring Johnny Parker (piano) and Lyttleton (trumpet) that drew inspiration from the earlier Harry James and Ammons and Johnson combinations; and the Beatles used a similar kind of piano backing for their hit recording "Lady Madonna" in 1968.

World War II had a cataclysmic impact on any cultural interchange between nations. With much of Europe oppressed under the Nazi jackboot, little jazz was available. Exceptionally, the music of the Hot Club of Paris, with Django Reinhardt (guitar) and Stephan Grappelli (violin) as its significant members, was heard in Paris nightspots during the early occupation, but jazz music, including boogie-woogie, was considered decadent by the Nazi regime: Its practitioners risked imprisonment at the very least. Such privations may partly account for the take-up and flowering of boogie-woogie by later generations of European piano players. Privations were less so in Great Britain, where American culture was influential through the medium of film and the high number of American armed forces stationed there who brought their musical tastes with them. In the cause of maintaining morale, these tastes were accommodated by their senior officers—hence the visit and sojourn of Glenn Miller's band, pianist Mel Powell, and many other jazzmen. Edsel Ammons, serving as a GI in England, recalled his pride in seeing his father's music advertised in British music shops.[1] The likes of pianist Maurice Rocco entertained in British cinemas with appearances in Hollywood musicals, playing a technically slick brand of boogie-woogie.

Another influence in keeping Britain in touch with American jazz music were the radio broadcasts of the American Forces Network (AFN) channel, which beamed out big-band swing and boogie-woogie in certain of its shows. Several British dance bands followed suit with recordings of their own. The Squadronaires, an RAF band modeled on the Bob Crosby outfit, recorded "Cow Cow Boogie" (1943), trumpeter Nat Gonella's band produced a spirited "Thanks for the Boogie Ride" (1945), and drummer Joe Daniel's jazzy group, the Hot Shots, were early leaders in the field with "Beat Me Daddy Eight to the Bar" and "Southern Fried" (1941) made for Parlophone. One of the better-known flag bearers for piano boogie-woogie in Britain during this period was the young blind pianist George Shearing, who made use of the style extensively in public performances and recordings, such as in his own composition "Jump for Joy" (1942), replete with an Ammons bass. An early original, "Stomp in F" (1939), including a walking bass, was followed by a catchy version of "Beat Me Daddy Eight to the Bar" (1941) for Decca.

After the various commercial recording debacles of the late 1940s and 1950s, which saw such flawed combinations as boogie-woogie and bebop thrown together (Freddie Slack's "Be-Bop Boogie"), so-called classical pieces set to a boogie-woogie rhythm (Jack Fina's "Saber Dance Boogie"), and other attempts to wring the genre dry, public taste became jaded and there was a wearied rejection in Britain and America of these hybrids. However, the Phoenix began to rise from the ashes for boogie-woogie music in particular and other forms of jazz in the late 1960s and early 1970s.

Events in Europe after World War II saw a spark of interest in boogie-woogie piano in Germany. Leopold Von Knoblesdorf was an early pianist who commenced playing it in the late 1940s. He was an important influence on, and model for, the younger generation of German pianists who followed in the 1970s. The genre is now well established in German culture and that country has some of the most talented contemporary players. Knoblesdorf produced good interpretations of many of the standard boogie-woogie numbers. His later work undertaken with the Boogie-Woogie Company, a group consisting of electric guitar, bass, drums, and piano, was featured extensively on television and radio in Germany.

In France, a link with the second generation of boogie-woogie players was established by Jean Garvanoff, an early exponent who maintained a regular correspondence with Pete Johnson during his final years. Garvanoff could produce a convincing form of blues and boogie-woogie piano without perhaps capturing the embellishments and nuances in his playing of later European players. Certainly a strong sense of rhythm is apparent in his pared-down versions of "Suitcase Blues" and "Boogie No. 29"—the latter based on Wesley Wallace's piece.

From these early stirrings in Europe, boogie-woogie has gradually reestablished itself again as a serious and expressive solo art form in that continent and, increasingly, in America, with today's pianists falling into one of two broad groups. The first group is composed of professional pianists, most of whom specialize in playing boogie-woogie whatever other talents they might possess and who appear regularly at concerts and festivals, undertake club engagements, and supplement their income from recordings frequently sold at these events. The European pianists benefited in their early years from the inspirational legacy of older American pianists living in Europe (Memphis Slim, Sam Price, etc.) and the continuous exchange of musical ideas from working together at festivals and on recording dates. The second group of pianists, though serious students of the genre, are not, or have not been, full-time musicians. They have the piano skills to record in their own right and continue to do so. Many comprising this group are older American practitioners who had direct contact with, or were influenced by, live performances and the recordings of second-generation pianists such as Ammons, Lewis, Johnson, Hodes, Shaw, and Yancey in their younger days. Pianists in both groups recreate music from an earlier period with accuracy and a distinctive technical merit. The work of the best has the stamp of individuality, sincerity, and talent, while a few gifted ones occasionally rise above the unique benchmarks of creativity set by the Boogie-Woogie Trio and others from earlier generations.

The city of Detroit has many historical associations with boogie-woogie, and today there is one white American pianist who maintains this tradition with distinction. Arguably the best interpreter of boogie-woogie today, both in America and abroad as an international leader in the field for many years, is Bob Seeley (1928–), an excellent all-around pianist whose interests and repertoire span piano music from the turn of the twentieth century to the present day, embracing Jerome Kern,

George Gershwin, and Claude Debussy as well as the standard works of ragtime, stride and, of course, boogie-woogie and the blues. After taking piano lessons, Seeley learned how to play boogie-woogie from listening to recordings, including the Leeds boogie-woogie piano albums. A fruitful and long-standing friendship with Meade Lux Lewis in the 1950s and 1960s (see chapter 12) influenced his piano playing and resulted in a very rhythmical form of boogie-woogie. At an earlier stage, before this friendship, Seeley and friends haunted the "blind pig" dives of Hastings Street, listening to the music of the jazz musicians who played together after hours and saw in the dawn. With an evolving boogie-woogie style now in hand, Seeley was sufficiently confident to sit in at several Detroit nightspots, including the Flame Show Bar and the Alamo. Although he includes many of the standard boogie-woogie compositions in his repertoire, he rarely produces an exact copy of any of them in performance. By studying the pioneers and adding his own arrangements, he achieves a driving "swing" with a buildup of excitement and intensity. His solos are notable for their coherence and progression, which propel them to a satisfying climax. Of all the contemporary pianists, Seeley reproduces the sound and spirit of Meade Lux Lewis with the most conviction and sometimes even surpasses the master's brilliance. There are three outstandingly consistent features to his playing: a tremendous rhythm, a deep emotional range, and a freshness in his interpretation of familiar material that bring something new and different to each performance.

Before his retirement in 2005, Bob Seeley appeared nightly at Charley's Crab, a superior restaurant in Troy, Michigan. His piano playing has been a magnet there in excess of thirty years, drawing such celebrities as Bob Hope, Tony Bennett, the Everley Brothers, Pamela Anderson, and Chuck Leavell, pianist with the Rolling Stones, who likened Seeley's impact on his audience to the detonation of an H bomb as his powerful bass began to roll.[2]

Bob Seeley first came to the notice of jazz and blues followers as an outstanding boogie-woogie player in the mid-1970s when he was one of seven pianists who played at the Rags to Riches concert at C. W. Post College of Long Island University in New York. The other pianists were better known than Seeley, but it was he who received the plaudits over well-respected men such as Dick Wellstood, Dick Hyman, Neville Dickie, Joe "Fingers" Carr, Trebor Tichenor, and Dave Jasen. He received praise for his abilities in both the boogie-woogie and stride styles and the high octane power of his playing compared with the other pianists. Seeley's early appearances were at concerts in Detroit and Toronto and the St. Louis Ragtime Festival, and he was accompanist to Sippie Wallace at the Detroit and Chicago Blues Festivals in 1984 and 1985, respectively. He has also performed on television. Since these early appearances, he has become increasingly known and respected in his own country, making several concert appearances at Carnegie Hall. Europe appreciates his talents, too, and during the 1990s he played to packed houses at Les Nuits de Jazz et Boogie-Woogie, an annual boogie-woogie festival held in Paris. Other tours have taken him to Germany, Austria, and France, where he has performed with local pianists. In 1992, Bob Seeley entertained at a tribute concert for Meade Lux Lewis in St. Paul-Minneapolis, the city where Lewis had so many family memories and where he tragically died. He still continues to tour extensively in the United States and Europe, often teaming up with Jim Baldori, one-time pianist with rock and roller Chuck Berry. They also appeared together in Russia in July 2008.

It is difficult to comprehend why this talented man made no recordings for several years, but fortunately this has now been rectified with, among others, an excellent CD *Boogie-Woogie and Blues Piano—Industrial Strength* (1997), which showcases his many keyboard attributes. "Amazing Grace," a firm favorite of his, offers gospel-inflected rhythms underpinned with an urgent walking bass. His original "Industrial Strength Boogie," composed in the studio, captures the essence of the Motor City with its unremitting energy. An acknowledgment to Lewis's train composition "Chicago Flyer" is given in "Chuck Muer's Boogie," with its similar bass configuration. The ghosts of Ammons and Johnson appear in two contrasting pieces: the fast "Foot Pedal Boogie" and the medium-paced "Cuttin' the Boogie," which faithfully reproduce the musical patterns of the two masters with a refreshing verve and individuality. It remains for jazz pianist Dick Hyman to sum up Bob Seeley's abilities, calling him a "force of nature . . . the best boogie-woogie player on the planet!"

Another pianist from Detroit is Mark Lincoln Braun, who has developed a very personal style of playing boogie-woogie from his early journeys across America to meet such old-time performers as Blind John Davis, Little Brother Montgomery, and "Champion" Jack Dupree. A noticeable blues inflection in his playing can be savored on an LP from 1984 entitled, *Mr. B. Detroit Special* (Oldie Blues, OL 8010). Since that time, he has been a regular and popular pianist at jazz festivals, mainly in America.

In January 1986, the *South Bank Show*, guided by Melvyn (now Lord) Bragg, arranged for four boogie-woogie pianists to visit their television studios in London to assist in the making of a boogie-woogie spectacular that, under the experienced hand of director John Jeremy (*Blues Fell Like Falling Rain* and *The Long Night of Lady Day*), traced the history of the piano style from its early beginnings in the southern states to the present. The pianists who performed were George Green and Bob Hall of England, Axel Zwingenberger from Germany, and the African-American pianist Joe Duskin, whose presence marked a long association with boogie-woogie music dating from the 1940s.

"Big" Joe Duskin (1921–2007) hailed from Birmingham, Alabama, but to all intents and purposes his home had been in Cincinnati since his teens. Duskin's father was a Baptist minister who encouraged him to pick out hymns on the family piano but showed his displeasure when he began to play around with boogie-woogie and blues, calling them the devil's music. Through surreptitious practice, when his father was not within hearing, Joe built up a useful stock of numbers by listening to local pianists in the West End district of Cincinnati and the recordings of Roosevelt Sykes. He was offered work in several nightspots on Central Avenue, including the Bucket of Blood and the Armory Café, which he took. He also worked in the bars around Newport in Kentucky before being drafted into the armed forces. Further opportunities were made available to him here as an entertainer for troops at various camps in the United States. After a period spent in Europe, Duskin was discharged and prepared to begin his career again, but seeing the anguish this action was likely to cause his ailing father, now in his eighties, Joe promised to forsake boogie-woogie music for the remainder of his father's lifetime. A gap of over twenty years occurred in his playing career, however, because his father lived to be 104. Duskin was musically active again in the early 1970s playing at Dollar Bill's Saloon, Chapter 13, and other local bars in Cincinnati, but increasingly, from the 1980s onward, he toured Great Britain and Europe where he established an enthusiastic following.

Joe Duskin's style and tunes are drawn from the "classical" period of boogie-woogie as can be heard on *Big Joe Duskin Cincinnati Stomp* (Arhoolie, 1080; 1977). "The Tribute" is a number reminiscent of the Boogie-Woogie Trio and, as its name implies, is dedicated to their memory. In the same vein, Duskin produces rousing performances of "Roll 'Em Pete" and "Honky Tonk Train Blues." The best of his solo work is heard on two standard "pop" boogie-woogie pieces, "Down the Road a Piece" and "Beat Me Daddy Eight to the Bar." These are exceptionally good on two counts. First, Duskin sings the lyrics in a deep bass voice on both and actually responds to his own questions in recreating the McKinley and Slack dialogue on "Down the Road a Piece." Second, he builds both pieces into a tour de force with his driving basses and exciting treble choruses—the latter brought to greater clarity on "Beat Me Daddy" than the original orchestrated version by the Will Bradley Orchestra from the early 1940s.

The other feature of Joe Duskin's work is his blues playing, demonstrated passionately on "Mean Old Frisco," the Arthur Crudup number. He is equally convincing on "Little Red Rooster" and "Tender Hearted Woman," supported by Bob Margolin (guitar), Truck Parham (bass), and S. P. Leary (drums). On these sides he forsakes boogie-woogie styling and produces piano work that draws inspiration from the Chicago blues bands of Muddy Waters and others.

Ten years after his first recording, he made a second one in 1988, *Big Joe Duskin: Don't Mess with the Boogie Man* (Special Delivery, SPD 1017), during a tour of Great Britain. His book had broadened to take in a fast version of the Slack masterpiece "Strange Cargo," an Ammons-inspired "Low Down Dog," and a bouncy "See See Rider" taken at medium tempo. He is backed by a riffing rhythm-and-blues group led by Dave Peabody (guitar); empathy between the group and Duskin's confident piano playing is good, but his vocals are occasionally strained. Joe Duskin helped to keep alive the traditional features of boogie-woogie between bouts of ill-health. In doing so he incorporated the dynamism of an Albert Ammons into his own interpretations of the style. Not noted as a composer of original numbers, Duskin nevertheless revisited old favorites with freshness and vitality, making them accessible to a younger generation. He continued to appear at events, notably the Cincinnati Blues Festival in his home city, shortly before his death.

The 1970s was certainly significant for four white American devotees of boogie-woogie, a time when their collective talents were brought together for the first time. Two of them, Tom Harris and Charlie Castner, had met at college in the late 1940s but knew nothing of the other two: Ben Conroy and Charlie Booty. Events began when Conroy, a keen devotee of steam trains, was leafing through an enthusiast's magazine and saw an article written by Castner. Recognizing the name as of one of the pianists on a Paramount boogie-woogie recording from 1955, he telephoned Castner and his hunch was confirmed. The two men met up and later made contact with Tom Harris who was still in touch with his old college friend. Charlie Booty and Ben Conroy already knew each other from their meeting at the St. Louis Ragtime Festival in 1970. The quartet eventually recorded a radio program from Castner's home in Louisville where they talked about their early influences and illustrated their piano styles, playing solo and duets. They remained in regular contact, meeting up regularly at house parties and pursuing their own interests on recording dates and other engagements. Their significance as a group in sustaining the presence of boogie-woogie as a piano art form in America during the bleak period of the early 1970s and beyond should be recognized.

Tom Harris (1930–2009) and Charlie Castner, who come from similar middle-class backgrounds, formed a musical partnership closely modeled on the Ammons and Johnson team at Washington and Lee University in Virginia, in the 1940s. Not only did they recreate the content and spirit of their better-known piano duets with precocious flair, they went on later to extend their own improvisational skills to a new level with compositions such as "Big Steady Roller" and others that were recorded for John Steiner's Paramount label in 1954.

Charlie Castner, now a retired public-relations executive for a railway company in Louisville, first heard boogie-woogie being played on the family's piano by a workman who had come to paint the family home. From that time he began to experiment on his own with the boogie-woogie style, learning from recordings and the Leeds Music Company's series of folios, eventually taking lessons on jazz composition from Louisville composer Don Murray and the late John W. Parker, a jazz pianist and teacher at the Wesleyan College he attended in Owensboro. Castner's broad spectrum of interest includes jazz, ragtime, musicals, and boogie-woogie. Apart from his music, his other major interest is studying and writing about railroads. Nowadays, he accompanies various vocal groups at Rotary, for charity. From 1973 until 1991, the Castners hosted an annual piano party at their home to bring together members of the group.

On one occasion, Castner and Harris, with another friend, spent an evening in Chicago in March 1949 in the company of Albert Ammons who played for them and commented on their piano playing. He was particularly impressed by Castner's interpretations of his (Albert's) numbers. Another meeting with Albert in June of that year took them to Yancey's apartment for an all-night session. Charlie Castner recalls Ammons as an affable, outgoing person, more so than Meade Lux Lewis, who seemed less forthcoming when approached in New York in 1948 and later at the Hangover Club in the early 1950s. In Castner's opinion, the Boogie-Woogie Trio had a very special quality: "I like to think though, that they added a sense of drama, taking ideas as they did, expanding on them or working toward a climax, one chorus being more exciting than the one which preceded it. Of course, this wasn't done on every tune—a Lux blues could have many moods, and Pete could work through a blues or slow boogie with as much grace and finesse as what might be found in Mozart or Haydn."[3]

Tom Harris was born in Chicago and lived in a white suburb far removed from the South Side where he was to find a lifelong inspiration in the music fostered by that depressed area. During his adolescence he became interested in the recordings of Albert Ammons and Meade Lux Lewis. He was taught the rudiments of the boogie-woogie style by Buddy Charles, a noted Chicago pianist, but always considered his interest to be a solitary one until he enrolled as a student at university. Very soon after commencing his studies, Harris was attracted by the sound of boogie-woogie being played on the piano in the Students' Union room and found Charlie Castner, also a freshman, interpreting one of Albert Ammons's numbers. So began a musical partnership that lasted over ten years and that has grown into a lasting friendship. After suitable practice together, Harris and Castner began to play boogie-woogie duets at college fraternity parties. They perfected a cross-hands style of playing on one piano; this involved the pianist sitting at the bass end placing his right hand under the left hand of his partner in order to play on the treble keys above middle C, while his partner's left hand played a bass just below this position and his right hand played improvisations using the uppermost treble keys. In time, their proficiency resulted in the Paramount recording for John Steiner, *Powerhouse Boogie, Tom Harris and Charlie Castner* (Paramount 112), which contains six boogie-woogie duets, some original, others patterned on those of Ammons and Johnson. A later release dating from 2002, *The Boogie Woogie Boys Revisited: Charlie Castner and Tom Harris* (Piano Joys, PJ012), gives a wider spectrum of their joint talents from recordings made between 1949 and 1952.

The similarity between the duets of Ammons and Johnson and their own is so close that their numbers are recognized to this day as some of the best recreations. Shortly after the release of their recording, Harris and Castner traveled with John Steiner to meet up with Pete Johnson and other pianists at a St. Louis party where many informal recordings were made. A commercial recording of this event is available as *Pete Johnson: The St. Louis Parties 1954* (Document, DOCD-1017).

Tom Harris lived in Fort Worth, Texas, where he worked before retirement as an executive for an international company making recording equipment. One of the most important annual events on the international boogie-woogie calendar has been the house party that his wife Lynne and he arranged, to which American, British, and European pianists were invited to attend, so strengthening the bonds between the younger and older piano traditions. A past party featured in the local newspaper espoused the preservation of the boogie-woogie traditions. Dick Mushlitz perceptively observed that much of America's musical heritage would disappear if events such as the Fort Worth party were not held regularly to remind people that this "vital form of music" has an important place in American culture.[4] Similar ventures have taken place in Evansville organized by Kylie, Mushlitz, and Booty. Fortunately, Charlie Booty had the foresight to collect together recordings made at these various parties and issue them commercially on his record label "Piano Joys."

The third pianist, Ben Conroy (1925), with a lifelong interest in recreating early piano styles, particularly boogie-woogie and ragtime, lives in retirement in Austin, Texas. Conroy received an early musical training on trumpet and piano and started showing an interest in boogie-woogie at about the time that Lewis, Ammons, and Johnson were appearing at the Café Society clubs. In those days, his family lived near New York City. Initially, he was unable to see and hear them in person because he was under the age allowed in nightclubs. Knowing of his son's interest in the music, his father on one occasion telephoned him from Café Society where he had met some business acquaintances. "Who do you think this is on the piano?" he asked his son over the telephone. It was Albert Ammons, and the next morning Conroy's father presented him with a short note from Ammons containing greetings and a personal invitation for Ben to visit the nightclub. The visit was duly made with his father and Conroy recalls the event: "I can still remember the state of excitement I was in that evening hearing Albert and Pete plus meeting and talking with them. From that evening on, I went over there as often as possible."[5]

Conroy has a good grasp of the work of the Trio, playing it with great accuracy and conviction but has also spread his wings and widened his repertoire by including such tunes as Spand's "Soon This Morning" and some of the lesser-known ragtime pieces of S. Brunson Campbell. Conroy continued playing boogie-woogie as a student engineer at the Polytechnic Institute of Brooklyn and gave several recitals before being drafted into the United States Navy in 1943 where he served his country with distinction as a commander in the Pacific operations. After leaving the navy in the 1950s, he concentrated on building up his business in cable television. In 1970, he attended the St. Louis Ragtime Festival aboard the *Golden Rod* paddle steamer and was delighted to hear boogie-woogie being played in one of the intermissions by Charlie Booty. Such was his enthusiasm that he went straight to the piano and joined Booty for several duets. The two men subsequently took the opportunity of playing together whenever time and inclination permitted and have recorded singly and together. Conroy has continued to play boogie-woogie over the years by giving various recitals, with commentary, drawn from his extensive background. He has been an active and important researcher of the genre through contacts with the late Texas pianists Robert Shaw and Alex Moore.

Charlie Booty (1928–2008) hailed from a small sawmill town in rural Louisiana. Initially a self-taught pianist, in later life he acquired some formal background from various musicians with whom he came into contact. He first heard boogie-woogie on local radio shows as a youngster of nine or ten, but it was after a period of illness, when he was bedridden, that he listened intently to the music on an old-fashioned wind-up record player. He admitted to an obsession in mastering the art from this time. Booty was given his first piano lesson by a soldier stationed near his hometown, in 1943, who visited the family home on several occasions and showed him the rudiments of chord construction and the twelve-bar blues form. Intensive practice copying recordings throughout the summer vacation in 1944 produced a handful of several boogie-woogie numbers.

After graduation, Booty continued his practice in the music department of his college and was shown further technique by music students in return for advice on playing boogie-woogie. The arrangement came to an abrupt end when the dean of the music school banned Booty from the college after hearing him play boogie-woogie. Additional experience was gained playing with small jazz groups in Memphis, as a member of his father-in-law's country and western band, and from a ten-year spell as pianist on the *Delta Queen* steamboat, which plied up and down the Mississippi calling at St. Paul, Cincinnati, and St. Louis. This varied experience helped Booty to acquire a good all-around command of the keyboard, and his interpretations often display an interesting amalgam of country and western music, jazz, ragtime, and boogie-woogie, giving his playing a distinctive and eclectic coloring. This can be appreciated on his Solo Art release from 1994, *After Hours with Charlie Booty* (Solo Art, SACD 108), which offers a pleasing mix of original tunes. The forcefully fast "Buck Boogie" contrasts well with the attractive slow melody of "Euro Blues," created from a haunting melody that Booty heard being played by a European pianist. "Jazzman Special" rocks along using a selection of boogie-woogie basses and achieves an archaic tonality from an earlier age of piano playing. Booty demonstrates the full range of his talents with a drum attachment on the piano pushing along a wistful version of the jazz standard "Clarinet Marmalade."

In a full life, Booty met and played with Don Ewell—he claimed not to be a boogie-woogie pianist but Booty avered otherwise—and Art Hodes, who was influential in developing the piano style of Booty's elder son Larry. However, as with all original artists, Charlie Booty's music carries its own identifiable mark. Such was his continuing dedication that it could be said that music was Charlie Booty's life force. Two serious illnesses, one of which arose from a traumatic crash in his own airplane after someone had tampered with the fuel, did not deter him from teaching himself to play the piano again after the onset of amnesia following the crash. His last appearances were centered around festivals, private functions, and recordings. Booty was an inveterate international traveler, taking in Les Nuits de Jazz et Boogie-Woogie in Paris; joining Axel Zwingenberger in Germany on the "88 Connection"; with Zwingenberg and newer generation Europeans Joja Wendt and Joe Bohnsack (2000) in Hamburg; on "The Boogie-Woogie Express" (2001), a steam train excursion; and one of his last appearances at the Jazzland club in Austria with Martin Pyrker. He retired from public performances in 2007 and died shortly afterward.

Conroy and Booty made two LP duet recordings in the 1980s, *Ben Conroy, Charlie Booty: Barrelhouse Boogie* (Dirty Shame, DSR 1239) and *Charlie Booty and Ben Conroy, Boogie-Woogie 8-to-the-Bar* (Jazzology, JCE-88). The compatibility of their piano styles has produced several original pieces. A particular feature of their duet playing is the combining of the Jimmy Yancey and Montana Taylor styles on numbers such as "Reminiscing with Jimmy Yancey and Montana Taylor." Although their work draws, collectively and singly, on boogie-woogie, they display their broad interest in the genre with recordings of Hersal Thomas's "Suitcase Blues," early ragtime tunes, and more modern composers such as the Freddie Slack number "Down the Road a Piece."

The popularity of the boogie-woogie style in Europe at the present time is a subject that sociologists might find of interest. The appearance in Germany, Holland, Switzerland, Austria, and France of several young, talented interpreters of the style since the 1970s has been more of a birth than a renaissance. It would be easy to dismiss this phenomenon as a passing fad for a music far removed from its roots and environment, but such has been the serious intent of these piano players since the movement started that it requires to be recognized as an important and sustainable branch of the boogie-woogie trunk. In general terms, boogie-woogie music has great potential in the hands of these young, dedicated enthusiasts who have the technical capability to reproduce the work of many of the old masters with a breathtaking facility, but thereby hangs a tale. To fulfill their potential and to realize fully the further growth of the genre, they will need to move beyond accurate representation of the classical pieces and adapt what they have learned from this process by adding their own creative powers to produce music that bears their stamp of originality. At this stage in the evolutionary process, there is sometimes too much emphasis on the heavy bass and power boogie-woogie, producing a clever pastiche of the genre, with less attention given to its more emotional and subtler aspects.

The pivotal figure in the emerging boogie-woogie scene of the 1970s, in Germany, was Hans-George Moeller (1944–c.1980s), an influential and forward-thinking mentor of the group of young players. He was a fast-living young entrepreneur who made his money early in life as the owner of a canned-fish company before retiring at the age of thirty-five. Moeller devoted his retirement to driving powerful motor cars and was the possessor of two motorcycles capable of speeds in excess of 130 miles per hour (circa 209 km.). He was unable to play the piano for a period in the mid-seventies after an inevitable motorcycle crash in which he broke both arms. Unfortunately, his obsession finally took his life after he crashed his motorcycle again in the early 1980s.

George Moeller was a temperamental man who, it is said, had to be in the correct frame of mind to play boogie-woogie, but when circumstances were right he could produce exciting and melodic interpretations of the standard numbers as well as innovative original numbers. It is evident from listening to "Gesprach mit dem Piano" (Talk with the Piano) that here is someone who brings an individuality and a unique approach to interpreting boogie-woogie. It is a romantically inspired tune combining piano, meditative lyrics, and a piercing trumpet-style whistle for leading some of the choruses. The blues-based piano backing rocks along with occasional forays into a walking bass. This tune can be heard on the recordings from the Boogie-Woogie Festival held in Vienna in 1976, *Boogie-Woogie Session '76: Live in Vienna* (EMI Austria, CDP 566). On the same CD, he also infuses a long-forgotten vitality into "Pinetop's Boogie-Woogie," bringing the concert audience to its feet, clapping and stamping, with his seemingly never-ending series of stop-time choruses that build the piece into a controlled tour de force. One could postulate that Moeller was an individualist in many aspects of his life, and this appears in his piano playing with its simple and quite melodic chording and underlying playfulness and whimsicality. He made no further commercial recordings, so we shall never be in a position to know just how far his talents might have developed. Appearing on the same bill with Moeller in Vienna were two young German pianists, Axel Zwingenberger and Vince Weber, and an Austrian pianist, Martin Pyrker, all of whom have since gained substantial reputations for their boogie-woogie playing.

The present doyen of the German boogie-woogie players is undoubtedly Axel Zwingenberger (1955–). Having now toured in thirty or so countries, his influence on other pianists has been spectacular. He was born in Hamburg and received eleven years of formal piano tuition. Zwingenberger was becoming disenchanted with playing the classics and was on the point of giving up his studies when, as a seventeen-year-old, he discovered boogie-woogie by chance after listening to some old 78 recordings of Pete Johnson and Lionel Hampton belonging to the father of one of his friends. He was intrigued by the boogie-woogie tonality to the extent that he did not want to do anything else but learn to play it. With his interest in the piano rekindled, he started to finger out some of the numbers for himself.

Real progress in mastering the style came after he met George Moeller and Vince Weber. The three men used to practice together at a series of musical seminars in Hamburg where they lived. Fortunately, Hamburg has many jazz and blues clubs, which provided them with the opportunity for solo and duet playing. The Logo Club became their favorite rendezvous, but sorties were also made to the ill-reputed Reeperbahn district and here their music could be heard at the Blauer Hahn (Blue Cock) by the few drunks and revelers still around in the early morning.

Boogie-woogie music was given the seal of approval by the German establishment in 1976 when these three pianists and Martin Pyrker played at the exclusive Deutcher Theater ball. Dressed in formal black tuxedos, in the presence of German socialites, they were given a rapturous reception. Shortly after this event, the pianists were engaged as the main attraction at a boogie-woogie ball, at the same theatre, playing three sets each of one hour's duration. Since that time, Zwingenberger, Weber, and Pyrker have, individually and collectively, recorded and toured extensively.

Zwingenberger's early recordings show his ability to reproduce the work of the trio at will. He has studied the works of Ammons, Lewis, and Johnson with meticulous care and is particularly adept at reproducing Lewis's open bass style of playing; on slower boogie-woogie numbers he can barely be distinguished from Albert Ammons at his most powerfully restrained. His recent interpretations incorporate more melodic strains, allowing him to use his considerable technique underpinned by driving bass rhythms. Searching for perfection and authenticity in his early career, he toured and recorded with the Lionel Hampton band, made two further recordings with the late Joe Turner—one of which was awarded a Grammy in Germany (1981)—and two recordings with Sippie Wallace (1983) before her death in 1986. Equally successful duets were made with Champion Jack Dupree, as accompanist to Estelle Yancey and with Jay McShann.

During one of his stays with Joe Turner, Zwingenberger inquired if Lloyd Glenn would be interested in recording some piano duets. Glenn was not enthusiastic about the idea and said it was pointless to attempt to recreate the successes of Ammons and Johnson. Zwingenberger attempted to explain that their duets would be different, but Glenn was still unconvinced and made it plain that he considered all boogie-woogie music sounded the same. In order to prove that it was possible to recognize a pianist's individual style of boogie-woogie, Zwingenberger played one of Turner's Savoy recordings of "Howling Winds" for him, which the liner notes said included an unknown pianist who sounded like Meade Lux Lewis. It was, of course, Glenn who had made the recording, which was confirmed when Zwingenberger suggested it was him. Now convinced that individuality could be recognized when pianists played boogie-woogie, Glenn agreed to record with Zwingenberger (1981). Such was his enthusiasm at the subsequent recording session, that Zwingenberger was obliged to call a halt to the proceedings after six numbers had been made because he had insufficient money to pay Glenn for more.

By 1998, Axel Zwingenberger had twenty-two recordings credited to his name, which augured well for a long and active recording career. Most have been produced by Frank Dostal for the Vagabond Record Company. An early venture was the publication of a book of his own favorite compositions in 1986 taken from a live recording session, and appropriately titled, *Boogie-Woogie Live.*[6] It is an indication of the growing popularity of the style, that in excess of seven thousand copies had been sold by the end of that same year.

By single-minded determination, talent, and love for boogie-woogie, Axel Zwingenberger has brought the music to the attention of a new generation of boogie-woogie followers and, more particularly, has stimulated interest among young German pianists of whom there are now a considerable number. His personal appearances on radio and television and at concerts and festivals continue unabated: the 1996 tour of West and Central Africa for the Goethe Institute with his brother Torsten (drums), more than ten appearances at the boogie-woogie festival Les Nuits de Jazz et Boogie-Woogie in the 1990s, several performances on the German NDR TV, and many more recent concerts and festivals in Europe too numerous to catalog.

Zwingenberger brings a distinctive keyboard touch and a wide emotional range to his boogie-woogie playing. On faster, heavy timbre pieces such as "Steel Dragon," he coaxes a powerful primeval ring in the bass from the Bosendorfer piano such as might be achieved by striking hollowed metal with stone. The resultant is a controlled power that contrasts markedly, at the opposite end of the expressive spectrum, with the feathery stillness of "The Snow Flake Dance." Both appear on *Axel Zwingenberger: Boogie Back to New York City* (Vagabond, VRCD 8.96022) from 1996. Both tunes are his own creations, a singular feature of his personal odyssey to move boogie-woogie onward and not simply to repeat the standard numbers of the accepted masters, which he still does with consummate brilliance. An understated entry in a jazz directory describing him as an empathetic kind of blues accompanist and master piano player implies correctly that there is yet more to come from him.[7]

Vince Weber (1955–) had an initial success with the vinyl album *The Boogie Man*, which was awarded a prize in West Germany (as it then was) and the European Music Cup. Another, maintaining the strong showing of the first, "Vince the Prince," illustrates well his commanding technique and powerfully infectious rhythms. Weber's material is broadly based, as can be heard on the 1987 recording *Vince Weber: Boogie on a Blue Song* (EMI, IC 0162; 1987). The recording includes Eddie Boyd's "The Blues Is Here to Stay," rhythm-and-blues numbers such as Jordan's "Saturday Night Fish Fry," the popular boogie-woogie tune "Beat Me Daddy Eight to the Bar," and original compositions. Such catholicity makes him accessible to a wide audience. If one were to identify significant influences in his playing, they would probably be the New Orleans pianist James Booker for the complexity of his rhythms and Otis Spann for the raw power and energy of his music. In the early years of the emerging German school, in the mid-1970s, Weber was the best known of the pianists, making regular and early appearances at the Fabrik and Carnegie Hall clubs in Hamburg. Weber's dedication to the music has been total, to the extent that he discontinued his university studies to concentrate on becoming a full-time musician. He has since made numerous concert, media, and festival appearances in Germany and in Paris at Les Nuits de Jazz et Boogie-Woogie.

The next "generation" of German players is represented by Frank Muschalle, a brilliant keyboard player, who captures the sound of Ammons convincingly on the well-seasoned "Boogie-Woogie Stomp." He tears into "Meade's Boogie," but like Lewis's original version, the speed is so fast that the rhythm becomes muddied in places. Nevertheless, it is a marathon performance in stamina—a machismo test piece for a "young pretender" to demonstrate his skills. Muschalle has an excellent, all-around feeling for several different boogie masters from the past; on "Tokyo Boogie" he successfully modifies Pete Johnson's chording with additional personal flourishes in the treble, while Freddie Slack is recalled in "Fantasies" with overtones of "Strange Cargo" and a certain mystical quality, reminiscent of much "symphonic" boogie-woogie dating from the 1940s. All can be heard on *Great Boogie-Woogie News* (Document, DOCD 7001).

A young German pianist who made an early impression for his feel for the genre and his mature creativity for one so young is Frederick Zur Heide, born in Bremen in 1987. One of his family members, Kurt Zur Heide, is recognized for his boogie-woogie research as the author of *Deep South Piano*. It was the stimulus of his father's record collection that started Frederick playing boogie-woogie at the age of eleven. He can be heard performing at the first Le Rocquebrou Festival in France, playing the original-sounding "Naptown in the Morning" on a recording released as *1st Festival of Boogie-Woogie of La Rocquebrou* (Sacem, B.W. 151500) from 1999. There are clear influences of Zwingenberger and Booker in his style, but on these recordings he already has a clear perception of how he wants his own boogie-woogie playing to sound.

Other versatile performers from Germany are Joe Bohnsack, a convincing blues vocalist and pianist, and the very able Joja Wendt who performs with effortless facility in the blues, ragtime, stride, and boogie-woogie genres. Now an experienced pianist in his forties, he shared a stage earlier in his career with Memphis Slim and Champion Jack Dupree and made a big impression in 1997 at the Montreux Jazz Festival. Michael Pewney and Martin Schmitt from Munich, who also demonstrate mastery in several piano genres, complete the canon of German pianists. There are other up-and-coming young German pianists who have yet to record and gain recognition. Such a panoply of talent backed by an enthusiastic, supportive public infers that boogie-woogie has an established reputation in that country's culture.

The acknowledged leading boogie-woogie pianist in Austria is Martin Pyrker (1954–), who has an equal standing with the first wave of German pianists. He has been both a pioneer in popularizing the music in Europe and a role model for the newer players. He was born in Vienna where he studied classical violin for several years and learned to play the drums as a teenager. His academic studies were completed in that city, culminating in a doctorate in law. In 1978, Pyrker moved to Wels where he has raised his family—one of his three daughters, Sabine, frequently accompanies him on drums at his engagements. By careful planning he has been able to marry a successful business career with an equally fruitful piano playing career.

Pyrker discovered boogie-woogie music from a radio program and began to teach himself the style by listening carefully to the works of Jimmy Yancey and Montana Taylor. Many of his compositions are strongly imbued with their qualities. As a result, his blues interpretations possess the decided melancholic and archaic tones of an earlier age. This identifiable stamp to his work notwithstanding, Pyrker is also the composer of several melodic tunes that sustain interest through their logically constructed treble extemporizations and lightly moving basses. Notable among these are the fast "Boogie-Woogie Drive" and "Gettin' Up Again" on *Martin Pyrker: Return to Blues* (EMI Austria, 33244) dating from 1980. There are other original, joyful compositions included plus beautiful interpretations of "I Can't Sleep" and "Indiana Avenue Stomp," composed by Montana Taylor, and Yancey's "Jimmy's Rocks" and the haunting "Blues for Albert," composed shortly after the death of Ammons. Martin Pyrker's development as a pianist was further enhanced through contact with visiting African-American players Roosevelt Sykes, Blind John Davis, and Memphis Slim with whom he shared the stage at numerous engagements in Europe (one thousand concerts at the last count).

Martin Pyrker has proved to be a sensitive accompanist and shows a well-developed empathy in his choice of treble phrasing, which is pitched to complement those of the singer. A particularly good combination is achieved on a 1977 tape recording, *Martin Pyrker Meets Jo-Ann Kelly: It's a Whoopee* (EMI Austria, 12C 258-33 206), where the talents of Pyrker and the late (British born) Jo-Ann Kelly successfully gel to produce some outstanding contemporary blues and boogie-woogie numbers such as the throbbing "Low Down Dog" and the slowly expressive "B. D. Woman." Both bring to this recording their deep appreciation of tasteful blues singing and piano boogie-woogie. This tape has now been reissued on CD together with Pyrker's *Return to Blues* (EMICD, 798 361 2). Pyrker is also featured on the aforementioned 1976 recording *Boogie-Woogie Session*, together with Moeller and Zwingenberg. They are ably supported by Torsten Zwingenberger, who shows a proper appreciation of the piano style in his drumming. Although this was Pyrker's first meeting with the other pianists, he was in no way overshadowed by their presence and contributed significantly to some dynamic six-handed piano work. A recording capturing his more recent work on which he appears in the company of fellow Austrians Daniel Gugolz and Tibor Grasser together with German pianist Frank Muschalle is *Great Boogie-Woogie News* (see Document, DOCD 7001 above).

Standing in a class of his own, in terms of his elegant keyboard technique, is Gunther Straub (1957). Born in Vienna, Straub started classical piano training at the age of seven. He was impressed by a Claude Bolling boogie-woogie recording during his late teens to the extent that it determined his future direction at the piano. From this early beginning, his talents have blossomed, and he has since appeared at clubs and festivals in his own country as well as in France and Germany. He manages to combine these commitments with a busy professional life as a surgeon specializing, appropriately, in hand surgery. He is probably underrecorded, given his talents, but does appear on the recording entitled *1st Festival De Boogie-Woogie De La Rocquebrou–1999* (Sacem, B.W. 15150) in which he gives a sustained powerhouse performance on Zwingenberger's composition "Boogie-Woogie Be with Me."

Many of the younger players have come to boogie-woogie with several years of formal piano tuition behind them. Tibor Grasser (1970–) is one such Austrian pianist who turned to the piano style after hearing one of Axel Zwingenberger's early recordings, "Boogie-Woogie Session." He played his first concert in 1990 and, although well qualified academically with a doctorate in electrical engineering, has pursued a dedicated interest in boogie-woogie. Grasser is a formidable technician at the keyboard. He captures the sound and spirit of Jay McShann in "Confessin' the Blues," a high-speed version of Ammons's interpretation of "Pinetop's Blues"; though technically accurate, he misses out on the embellishments and subtleties of the original. On the other hand, in "Swinging the Boogie," Grasser captures and interprets the inspiration of Pete Johnson's style extremely accurately. All recordings are included on the aforementioned *Great Boogie Woogie News*. Recognition should also be given to Michael Pewney, a capable and experienced interpreter of boogie-woogie who has recorded several CDs. Additionally, there are three Austrian pianists centered in Salzburg who appear collectively as the "Boogie Gang" as well as performing solo. They are Clemens Volger, employed as an animator by Walt Disney; Markus Brandl, whose forte is interpreting standard tunes with a boogie-woogie rhythm, in the conception of the Ammons Mercury recordings; and Richie Loidl, whose continuous inspiration is Vince Weber.

Equally talented young players have emerged from other European countries, and together with those already mentioned, should probably be considered a fourth generation of boogie-woogie players. Silvan Zingg from Switzerland, whose early interests were also stimulated by hearing French pianist Claude Bolling on the radio, offers a powerful, muscular attack at the keyboard and an interesting mix of influences in a repertoire that is played with a joyful, foot-tapping swing. "Silvan's Night Train Trip," featured on *2nd Festival de Boogie-Woogie De La Rocquebrou–2001* (Sacem, B.W. 15151), is an adventurous variant of the original "Night Train." Zingg has recorded several CD albums as a soloist and duets with

Dutch pianist Martijn Schok. One of these dating from 2000 and recorded in Switzerland is *Boogie-Woogie Duets Live in Concert: Sylvan Zingg and Martijn Schok*. Several of their pieces are played at a fast tempo as crowd pleasers, but there are also numbers that benefit from an unusual and pleasing treatment such as "The Fives," "Suitcase Blues," and "Thing Ain't What They Used to Be." Silvan Zingg has been in the forefront in promoting boogie-woogie in Switzerland and continues to mount several successful festivals of boogie-woogie there. His background, major recordings, and festival details are contained on his website.

The pianist who has helped to establish boogie-woogie in Holland is Rob Agerbeek (1937), who moved to that country with his family from Indonesia at the age of seventeen. His background is musical—his mother is an established concert pianist—which ensured that Rob would receive piano lessons as a boy. One of his earliest boogie-woogie experiences was hearing Albert Ammons's "Swanee River" recording shortly after arriving in Holland, which immediately sparked an interest in the style. Within two years he was sufficiently proficient to win an amateur contest and take the crown of Holland's "King of Boogie-Woogie." Agerbeek is not confined to playing in this style, however, and is recognized as a good all-around pianist who has accompanied saxophonist Dexter Gordon and other visiting American jazzmen to his country. He recently occupied the piano seat of the famous Dutch Swing College band—a revivalist jazz group of international renown. In his interpretation of boogie-woogie, Agerbeek still leans toward Ammons for inspiration and plays many of that master's compositions with distinction. He produced a particularly fine rendition of "Sweet Patootie Boogie" at the inaugural Rocquebrou Festival in 1999 (see above). An inherent toughness in Agerbeek's piano technique allows him to interpret the more physically demanding boogie-woogie pieces with sustained attack. At the last count, he had made seven recordings, in addition to those from various festivals and with the Dutch Swing College band. The boogie-woogie mantle has also been picked up by the younger Martijn Schok (1974), who plays a cleanly picked and rhythmical form of boogie-woogie. He has shown commendable initiative in mounting a series of annual (May) International festivals of the music in Holland, and his website contains information about them.

In neighboring Belgium, the boogie-woogie banner is carried by the capable Renaud Patigny, who was instrumental in establishing the first successful Festival of Blues and Boogie-Woogie in Brussels. Patigny, who has at least six recordings to his name, possesses a wide repertoire and frequently favors more reflective numbers with unusual coloration such as his piece "Boogie for Alain & Daniele" heard on *3rd. Festival De Boogie-Woogie De La Rocquebrou–2001* (Sacem, B.W. 15152).

With such pivotal blues and boogie-woogie figures as the late Memphis Slim and Sam Price resident in France for so long, they have been influential to many of the neophyte boogie-woogie pianists. Jean Paul Amouroux (1943), the elder statesman of French boogie-woogie at this time in his career, was one who benefited from an early contact. He recorded several duets with Slim that are found in *Boogie-Woogie Duos: Jazz A La Huchette* (EMI France Jazztime, 253-619-2) from 1984 and *Boogie-Woogie for two Pianos* (ADDA, 590118) from 1985. Successful collaborations were also undertaken with Willie Mabon, Sammy Price, and Jay McShann. Amouroux has had a long and productive recording career working as a soloist, in duets, in trios, and with his own group—reflecting the spirit if not the instrumental lineup of Ammons's original Rhythm Kings. This venture has resulted in a series of particularly good tracks with one of his albums from 1990, *Orchestral Boogie-Woogie, Volume 1* (Jazz Trade, SL-CD-5032) being awarded the prestigious Grand Prix Du Hot Club De France. Over the years, Amouroux has strengthened the link between second- and third-generation pianists in France by maintaining and extending the musical traditions of pianists such as Price, Slim, and Mabon.

Jean Paul received an early musical training on the piano and won first prize in a competition at the Concours National du Royaume de la Musique when he was ten years of age. By fourteen he had become interested in boogie-woogie music and was popular at school with his renditions of the standard numbers. After a spell of ten years working in an advertising agency, he forsook the security of this work and became a professional musician, in 1973, with the formation of his band the Walking Bass. He is now an established entertainer in Paris, with regular appearances at the Cambridge, Jardin de Beauborg, and other well-known clubs plus many appearances at French and international boogie-woogie festivals. Amouroux is both an original performer of boogie-woogie as well as an informed student of the genre, whose opinions have been sought on French television, radio, and print media. Three major influences are apparent in his work: Memphis Slim, Pete Johnson, and the more melodic recordings of Albert Ammons from his Mercury period. But Amouroux is his own man at the piano and brings his distinctive individualism to playing boogie-woogie: brief, punchy treble phrases interspersed between more brooding choruses, and a mélange of colorful runs, trills, and chords, all of which are anchored by an uncompromising rock–steady bass.

Amouroux produces a particularly fine version of Pete Johnson's "Rock It Boogie," which suits his style well with its running single-note bass line and nimble treble phrasing that together create exciting contrapuntal tones. Amouroux and fellow countryman Jean Pierre Bertrand recorded a series of duets from an appearance together in 1993 at Latitudes Jazz Club in Paris, released on *Boogie-Woogie for Two Pianos* (Honky Tonk Productions, HT 103), to remind us of the early Café Society period, with titles such as "Café Society Boogie" and "Carnegie Hall Boogie." Their talents are effectively combined to produce a well-balanced, full tone, each taking turns to lead the improvisations. "Panther Room Boogie" draws from the Ammons and Johnson piece "Cuttin' the Boogie," with additional choruses inspired by the original. A hard-driving rhythm is maintained on "St. Benoit Street Boogie," which is funky in sound and more reminiscent of rhythm and blues than a traditional boogie-woogie duet. In recent years, Jean Paul Amouroux has been the instigator and guiding hand behind the popular international boogie-woogie festival held annually in August at Le Rocquebrou in southwest France, which now appears to have superseded the earlier, successful Les Nuits De Jazz et Boogie Festival in Paris (see below).

An equally popular French boogie-woogie player, Jean Pierre Bertrand, (1955–), was born in St. Germain en Laye. He possesses a good technical background, having been a student in his teen years at the Academy of Music where he won one of their coveted prizes in 1968. Once again, the ubiquitous influence of Memphis Slim, heard on a recording, captured the interest of the young piano player who proceeded to study the genre in detail from recordings of the masters. He made Amouroux's acquaintance in 1977 and was encouraged by him to consider a professional career. Bertrand also has an entrepreneurial side that saw him opening a restaurant and jazz club, Le Harmonie, in St. Germain, Paris, which, in the four-year period of its existence from 1984, hosted appearances by Memphis Slim, Jean Garvanoff, and others. It was the first Paris venue to introduce Axel Zwingenberger to that city's knowledgeable jazz and blues audience. Notwithstanding his own increasing popularity with French jazz aficionados, from 1989 he innovated and produced a series of important sponsored piano concerts, Les Nuits Jazz et Boogie Woogie, at the Lutetia Hotel in Paris—famous for its Art Deco furnishings and as the headquarters of the occupying German Gestapo in the Second World War. The concerts have provided an international platform for the best boogie-woogie pianists to meet, play together, and entertain a receptive public. The importance of this initiative and also that of Amouroux in helping to sustain the genre cannot be underestimated. Bertrand continues to play as well as direct his own business, "Swing Organization," which plans and organizes shows and concerts of all varieties.

As well as producing a series of recordings of pianists from his own festival, Bertrand has made several in his own right. His music shows the suppleness of Pete Johnson in the treble and the beat of Ammons in the bass. But, as with all talented players, that is far from the full story, for he has carved out his own niche with an emphasis on a bouncing rocking rhythm and more melodic features of the music. Thus, "Something

Stupid" with a James Booker influence appears alongside "Death Ray Boogie" on *Sunny Boogie Jean Pierre Bertrand* (Honky Tonk Productions, HT 109; 1999). The content of this particular recording demonstrates the maturity of Bertrand's feeling for boogie-woogie and how such application can move the genre forward into new areas. Such an imaginative approach to boogie-woogie is displayed on the catchy but melancholic original "Minor Shuffle" and the several foot-tapping tunes with a Latin American beat such as "Samba Boogie" and the Ammons-inspired "In a Little Spanish Town." Axel Zwingenberger encapsulates well the unique qualities of Bertrand by comparing him to the Albert Ammons of the 1940s who retained the blues roots of the music while adding more melodious features.[8]

The third member of the French group of international-class boogie-woogie pianists, Phillipe Le Jeune (1953–) has a degree in business and uses his home city Toulouse, in southwest France, for his base. The year 1968 was formative, for it was the occasion of his attendance at a concert given by Memphis Slim. Until this time, Le Jeune had been studying classical piano and was already looking for new directions in his piano playing. Memphis Slim proved to be the explosive catalyst for change.[9] A gestation period listening to the acknowledged masters followed before he considered himself to be ready to play professionally. Appropriately, his first recording, *Dialogue in Boogie: Memphis Slim and Phillip le Jeune* (E.P.M., 157112) from 1989, was made with his mentor Memphis Slim. Le Jeune is well traveled and has made several appearances at American jazz festivals, including those in Detroit, Cincinnati, and Toledo (dedicated to Art Tatum who was born there). One of several solo recordings released in America was made in 1989 during an appearance in Houston at the Blue Moon Club and features his strongly melodic treble phrasing. Le Jeune has a wide-ranging repertoire that takes in Ellington ("C Jam Blues"), Horace Silver ("Song for My Father"), and more typical blues numbers such as "After Hours." He is a formidable player of boogie-woogie but approaches it with an open mind that searches out the nuances of expression as well as the raw, vital sound of its elementary basses.

Claude Bolling (1930–) gained his fame as the popular leader of a distinguished international big band and, more personally, as a good interpreter of boogie-woogie, which is one of his passions. His contribution in publicizing the style through radio programs as well as his incipient and recurring influence on younger European players have been inestimable. Bolling's musical career has embraced writing for film—he lived and worked in Hollywood in the 1970s—and composing "crossover" works for symphony orchestras. His early impressionable years were spent in his hometown of Cannes before moving to Paris with his Scandinavian-born father and French mother where he took piano lessons and played in the jazz clubs for a living. Early influences were the recordings of pianists Earl Hines, Willie "The Lion" Smith, and Fats Waller. His brilliant keyboard technique was soon recognized, and he was invited to work with visiting American jazzmen Sidney Bechet, Louis Armstrong, and Duke Ellington, and to record with Lionel Hampton. His command of the jazz idiom takes in boogie-woogie, which he plays with great conviction and panache, adding a twist that gives standard numbers such as "Pinetop's Boogie-Woogie" a further depth and sophistication without ever removing the elemental melodies and rhythms. Equally interesting to listen to are his versions of the timeless "No. 29," the Wesley Wallace piece, and the Leroy Garnett number "Louisiana Glide." A cross-section of his stimulating boogie-woogie playing made in 1982 can be heard on *Claude Bolling: The Original Bolling Boogie* (Mercury, 6313 370).

In Great Britain, the trend for dance bands to hold boogie-woogie arrangements in their books during the 1940s resulted in several of their pianists becoming proficient performers. Bands usually had a "rhythm" style as well as a strict tempo style for dancers, which gave some limited outlet to the jazz interests of the musicians. Many of the boogie-woogie numbers featured by their pianists became tediously formulaic, with their predictable basses and tinkling, formless trebles. Professional band pianists rarely took their interest beyond an initial competence, and it is true to say that boogie-woogie was never pursued as a serious jazz form in Britain or popularized to the same extent that we now see in Europe. Typical good examples of recordings from this period are by Yorke De Sousa, the pianist in a small combination led by Harry Parry playing on "Boogie Rides to York" from the mid-1940s and Dick Katz, a German-born pianist and founding member of the Ray Ellington Quartet, who lays down a strong beat on "Let the Good Times Roll" and an equally electrifying boogie-woogie on "Dick Katz Boogie" (Parlophone, 1949).

The one jazz-orientated pianist who studied boogie-woogie and exploited it to any depth was Billy Penrose (1925–1962), the leader of a boogie-woogie quartet for several years. He was born in Cleobury Mortimore, Shropshire, and achieved deserved recognition as an able pianist and arranger who served a number of the major bands, including Eric Winstone, Sid Phillips, Ted Heath, and Lou Praeger. It was said of him that he was the man who brought boogie-woogie to Britain. Apparently an eccentric, he reportedly entertained other band members by eating glass and razor blades. During the later stages of the Second World War, he accompanied Vera Lynn on piano at her concerts for the armed forces. His first recording of note, "Boogie in the Groove" (1945), was made as a nineteen-year-old. It is a highly original, bop-tinged piece, with a compositional form that includes breaks, complex basses, and a solid

rhythm. This was followed by "Harlem Boogie," with both numbers being released on the Parlophone label. Like Joe Sullivan, he made use of
boogie-woogie coloration in tunes other than twelve-bar blues. Two of
Penrose's boogie-woogie numbers are represented in a four-CD set, *Can't
Stop Playing That Boogie* (Jasmine Records). Penrose was forced to retire
from the music world because of ill health caused by a tropical disease.

The most powerful boogie-woogie influences for serious students of
the genre in Great Britain during the immediate post-war period were the
compositions of the second-generation players Ammons, Johnson, Mc-
Shann, Yancey, and others, aided by the reissue of many of their recordings from an earlier time. One of the earlier devotees was Cyril Schutt,
a committed boogie-woogie pianist who usually took a solo spot at jazz
concerts. The author recalls him giving a bravura performance in 1951 at
a concert featuring the Mick Mulligan jazz band and its vocalist, the late
George Melly. Schutt recorded his composition, "Steady Stomp Boogie,"
on the "88" label at about the same time; this interesting piece shows the
influence of Lewis's "Train" in the bass pattern.

Nowadays, Johnnie Parker (1929–) and Stan Greig (1930–) are recognized as being two of the best-known boogie-woogie practitioners in
Britain. Their roots are predominantly in jazz, and both have graced the
piano stool of the Humphrey Lyttelton band where Parker was featured
as pianist on the best seller "Bad Penny Blues." His career has moved between traditional jazz groups led by Mick Mulligan, Kenny Ball, and others to more limited excursions in the 1960s with the blues-based groups
of Alexis Korner's Blues Incorporated and Long John Baldry's Hoochie
Coochie Men. Parker's boogie-woogie interpretations have an individuality built around a distinctive rolling, discordant quality epitomized by
"Feline Stomp" (1954).

The pedigree of Greig is equally impressive and dates from the mid-
1950s from when he undertook either the piano or drum responsibilities
with major traditional and mainstream groups, Sandy Brown, Bruce
Turner, and Acker Bilk included. In 1957, he toured with the African-
American vocalist Brother John Sellers. Latterly, he has concentrated
on the piano and is now a well-established rhythm pianist interspersing freelance work between band engagements. He, too, has retained a
penchant for boogie-woogie, one of his first loves, and for a time led his
own boogie-woogie band. Both he and Parker used to play at least one
boogie-woogie number in their solo spots and, on occasions in the 1980s,
joined forces for a celebration of boogie-woogie at the 100 Club in Oxford
Street. The best examples of Greig's playing are available on *Stan Greig:
Boogie-Woogie* (Lake Records, LACD97), a compilation from two separate
recording dates in 1971 and 1997. One noticeable feature is his ability to
distinguish the piano styles of Ammons, Lewis, and Yancey in his work

and still avoid the accusation of being a pure copyist. Two particularly fine pieces in the Yancey style are his own compositions "Tell 'Em about Yancey" and "Last Order Blues"—the latter a haunting melody true to the emotional appeal and timing of his model. Greig's interpretations of Lewis's two train numbers, "Honky Tonk Train Blues" and "Six Wheel Chaser," are accurate renditions in both speed and atmosphere without quite capturing the richness of the chords in the originals.

In the 1960s, rhythm and blues proliferated in Great Britain, led by singer, pianist, and guitar player Alexis Korner, the "father" of this movement who worked as a solo act as well as appearing with the Rolling Stones, Spencer Davies, and other rock groups. Musicians from the rhythm-and-blues groups were themselves profoundly influenced by Jack Dupree, John Davies, and other visiting African-American musicians who shared concert billing with them. Pianists Bob Hall and George Green, though maintaining their roots in "classical" forms of boogie-woogie, are an evolutionary offshoot from this early rhythm-and-blues tradition. Hall (1942–) was born in London into a musical family and drew early inspiration from his father who was himself a fine pianist. Boogie-woogie made an initial impact when Hall heard a variety star, Winifred Atwell, playing it on the radio. There followed a period of absorbing the sound of the blues from a friend's record collection, attendance at concerts, and listening to jazz and blues from the radio station Voice of America. In parallel with this, Hall began piano lessons when he was eleven and was inevitably drawn to mastering boogie-woogie and blues during his teen years. His musical interests did not occupy all his time, however, as he studied for a law degree at the University of Durham, specializing in patent law.

Hall's first venture as a pianist in the rhythm-and-blues field was with the Groundhogs. Shortly afterward, he joined the Tramp, followed by the De Luxe Blues Band, both seminal rhythm-and-blues groups, of which he was one of the founding members. He also appeared alongside Alexis Korner and other British luminaries. Hall's keyboard abilities were soon recognized, and he became the chosen pianist to accompany visiting African-American blues artists, among whom were John Lee Hooker, Chuck Berry—who never indicated which key he was about to play in—Chester Burnett (aka Howlin' Wolf), and a legion of other famous blues stars. This work resulted in Bob Hall's appearance on over one hundred recordings in addition to several as a solo pianist. He formed and jointly led a big band, Rocket 88, with the late Ian Stewart, keyboard player with the Rolling Stones, whose members were drawn from the jazz and blues fields, all with a common interest in boogie-woogie and the blues. Other important members were the Stones' drummer Charlie Watts, Don Weller (tenor sax), and George Green (piano).

Nowadays, Bob Hall appears mainly with his partner Hilary Blythe, a singer and guitarist. They have toured Australia, Europe, and North America as a duo and regularly undertake tours in Britain. Despite this busy schedule, Hall still finds time to work as a soloist and has been a regular performer at the North Sea Jazz Festival, the San Francisco Blues Festival, and more recently, Le Rocquebrou Festival (2002). In the 1970s, Hall undertook early research into blues and boogie-woogie styles, resulting in several well-produced and informative articles appearing in the magazine *Blues Unlimited*.

Bob Hall's technical facility, from his early formal training, is evident in his near-perfect renditions of standard numbers laced with an underlying feeling for blues coloring on *Bob Hall Left Hand Roller* (Jeton, 100.33003) from 1979. His playing reminds us where the music traveled to in the hands of Pete Johnson at his most proficient, as reflected in his own composition "Erwin's Elevated Boogie." In a slower vein, "The Spider" uses a menacing, creeping bass pattern. Of the remaining sides, his adeptness is shown in recreations of Ammons's versions of "Pinetop's Boogie-Woogie," "You Are My Sunshine," and "The Sheik of Araby" as well as original numbers such as "Left Hand Roller" and "The Deker Special." A later release, *Bob Hall at the Window* (Indigo, IGOCD 2139; 1990), offers a more varied picture of Hall's boogie-woogie qualities, ranging from Taylor's "Detroit Rocks" to an appreciation of Zwingenberger's style on "Axel's Wheel." The slower, more melodic side of his work is represented on "Gone Fishing," with faint echoes of Fats Domino and a deeply felt version of the temporally demanding Jimmy Yancey number, "At the Window."

George Green (1936) hails from London, and was by occupation, until his retirement, a self-employed taxi driver. He now plays infrequently in public and reserves his music for a small group of appreciative listeners who meet from time to time at his home and at boogie-woogie parties in America. Green is a sensitive, self-taught boogie-woogie player whose skills have been inspired from listening to the works of Ammons, Merriweather, and, to a lesser extent, Yancey. His keen ear contributes to the accuracy of his interpretations, and there is a strong emotional content to his playing that is evident from his absorption at the keyboard accompanied by *sotto voce* humming. His unusually subtle touch transports the listener back in time to the original performances. One of Green's most recent "show stoppers" is his rendition of the rarely heard Romeo Nelson piece "Head Rag Hop." Unfortunately, he is a retiring character when it comes to recording, so there are few examples available of his solo piano work. Some of the best, recorded in relaxed party atmospheres, can be found on Charlie Booty's label *Rent Party Echoes, Volume 5: Dallas-Fort Worth 1978–1999* (Piano Joys, PJ009) and Volume 6 (Piano Joys, PJ010).

In 1976, Green was invited to attend the Cologne Boogie-Woogie Festival with Bob Hall after a tape of his playing had been sent to Hans Ewart, the German entrepreneur responsible for arranging the concert. Green stunned the informed audience with his own "La Paloma Boogie" and his rendition of Merriweather's "Texas Stomp." Memphis Slim invited Green to join him at the piano for a duet. Bob Hall and George Green had been playing together for some years before this event, having been brought together in Purfleet, England, by Bob Tomlinson, a devotee of boogie-woogie music. They subsequently joined forces to play many duets in Europe as members of a group, Rocket 88, in the late 1970s. One of their concerts was held in Swindon in 1978 and recorded to commemorate the fiftieth anniversary of Smith's recording of "Pinetop's Boogie-Woogie." It was issued under the title *Bob Hall and George Green Jammin' the Boogie* (Black Lion, BLP 12146). Several superlative boogie-woogie duets were made, notably "Swanee River Boogie," and a six-handed version of "Great Western Boogie," with the additional talents of the late Ian Stewart, pianist with the Rolling Stones. The honors are shared with Colin Smith (trumpet) on "Foo Woo," which owes its genesis to the influence of similar Ammons and Johnson recordings with Harry James.

Carl "Sonny" Leyland (1965–) was born in Southampton, England, and since 1988 has lived in America. Of the present generation of younger boogie-woogie piano players, Leyland is the most exciting and possesses the greatest potential as both a clever interpreter of classic boogie-woogie—delving well back into its roots—and an original performer with several compositions to his credit that compare well with the recognized standards. Coupled with his piano playing is an ability to sing the blues and other material with natural expression and conviction.

In the mid-1980s, he provided the entertainment in a south London restaurant, and it was clear then that he already possessed an abundance of talent for playing boogie-woogie in a style that captured the spirit of the Trio and of Jimmy Yancey. Since those early years, he has added other variants of the piano style and can produce rhythm and blues, rock and roll, rockabilly, and blues with equal ease and conviction. Leyland has recently begun to explore ragtime and other piano styles. Like others before him, he was first smitten by a boogie-woogie recording by the Jimmy Dorsey band, "JD's Boogie," and with his father's encouragement, discovered the work of the pioneers on records. He started learning the basses and putting tunes together. In doing so he absorbed the unique "black" tonality of the early players before joining a blues band in the south of England. A quick learner, he subsequently taught himself to read music, although his real strength has always been a well-tuned ear that picks up a tune very quickly.

Since moving to America, his reputation has grown. He initially worked in bars in New Orleans and then toured parts of the States with the Dallas-based blues band Anson Funderburgh and the Rockets and later with Big Sandy and His Flyrite Boys. He has been in demand in Europe, appearing at boogie-woogie concerts in Germany. He was one of a select band of regular performers at the highly prestigious Les Nuits de Jazz et Boogie-Woogie concerts in Paris. He has appeared at Le Rocquebrou Festival (2000) and was invited to make a third appearance at the annual Ragtime Music Festival (2004) in Orange County, California. His interests encompass film music.

Seven of the nineteen tracks on one of his 1995 recordings, *From Boogie-Woogie to Rock and Roll: Carl Sonny Leyland* (Honky Tonk), are compositions from the classic boogie era, beginning appropriately with "Pinetop's Boogie." His train piece, "Boogie Rapide," is in the spirit of Lewis's fast train pieces, whereas the slower "Night Time Is the Right Time" offers a reflective blues first recorded by Roosevelt Sykes in 1937. Leyland really stretches out in his piano playing here and in the rendition of the modern-sounding sentiments of the lyrics. Of his own compositions, "Coucous Boogie" offers particularly exciting piano playing, with "Cat and Mouse" introducing ironic lyrics to describe the perennial blues theme of failing human relationships. Leyland has made several additional recordings: one with his trio exploring the railroad as its theme offers a selection of train pieces—several are his own compositions—played in different styles, giving full rein to his talents. Titles range from "Wreck of the Old 97" through "Green Diamond Boogie" to "Streamline Train." These and a further nineteen tracks appear on *Carl Leyland Trio: Railroad Boogie* (Komodo Records). Carl Leyland is an emerging and outstandingly talented boogie-woogie pianist whose full potential has still to be realized. This recording with his trio and others can be found on Leyland's website.

Believing that opportunities for more work and a greater recognition for his talents lay in the south of England, Neville Dickie (1937–) moved from his native Durham to London in 1968 where he began entertaining in pubs and clubs. His break came when a BBC producer heard him playing and arranged for him to broadcast regularly as a solo performer and with his trio on radio. He wrote and recorded a tune, "The Robin's Return," that got into the Hit Parade of the day. Dickie's forte is stride piano, of which he is one of the finest exponents in the world, but his interests also encompass ragtime and boogie-woogie. A selection of boogie-woogie numbers from 1975 was released on *Back to Boogie Music for Pleasure* (EMI, MFP 50194). At the last count, he had made in excess of twenty recordings embracing stride, ragtime, and boogie-woogie piano. Dickie has been a regular and welcome performer at the boogie-woogie festivals in France.

He has a powerful attack at the keyboard and generates a good rhythm on such standards as "Honky Tonk Train Blues" and "Bad Penny Blues," but is equally capable of producing an empathetic, melancholic treatment for "How Long Blues." Doggett's rhythm-and-blues hit "Honky Tonk" rocks along well with a boogie-woogie treatment, as does Dickie's composition, "Back to Boogie," in a similar tempo, accompanied by a back beat from the rhythm section.

These are the significant pianists from Great Britain, many of whom have built an international reputation. Others, somewhat in their shadow, such as Jimmy Hopes, were active in the 1960s. Hopes was an enigmatic character whose early death prevented him from becoming known to a wider audience of boogie-woogie followers in Britain. Two albums were made under the pseudonym of "Precious" Clarence Turner. One entitled *Boogie-Woogie Explosions Saga* (SOC, 1041) from 1967 consists of twelve original titles. His inspiration, both in style and titles, emanates from Jimmy Yancey on "At the Graveside" and Clarence Lofton on "Lofton Diesel Train," with the latter extending the theme of Lofton's "Streamline Train." Hopes will be remembered for an early and useful article about the recordings of Albert Ammons[10] at a time when followers of the genre were short of critical, up-to-date comment about the music.

A Scottish-born pianist who is increasingly gaining recognition for his powerful and original piano work is Daniel Smith. He is seen by some as the next challenger to Jools Holland as the preeminent player in Britain. Standard boogie-woogie numbers ("Swanee River Boogie," etc.) and blues are combined with his own compositions into an entertainingly presented repertoire underscored with a dry understated wit. Smith is currently working as a soloist but is sometimes accompanied by visiting blues guitarists from the United States. He is also a very supportive rhythm pianist when playing in blues groups. Assuming he maintains his current progress, Daniel Smith will no doubt consolidate and surpass the high reputation he already holds to gain a national reputation.

Julian Phillips has emerged in recent years as a talented interpreter of boogie-woogie. He began piano playing at the age of ten and was attracted to the boogie-woogie sound in his teens. After university graduation, Phillips became a piano tuner and restorer and now combines this work with his playing. Initially, he earned his spurs in pubs and clubs both as a soloist and with his group, the Stuff, in his home county of Dorset. He has since appeared at several important festivals, notably Zwingenberger's The Long Night of Boogie-Woogie in Hamburg and more recently at Le Rocquebrou (2004). The music of Smith, Taylor, and Lofton flows effortlessly from his fingers. He is a committed, all-around performer possessing a powerful, rolling style of boogie-woogie playing that is enhanced by expressive "good time" skiffle and blues singing. Commencing in July 2005, Phillips successfully organized the annual international boogie-woogie festival in Britain at Fontmel Magna, Dorset, which drew pianists and fans from England, Germany, Holland, and Switzerland.

These American and European pianists are the best contemporary exponents of boogie-woogie music. In including them and omitting others, account has been taken of the high quality of their keyboard work and expressiveness. Additionally, they possess a talent for interpretation that captures the spirit and raw energy of the best boogie-woogie music. It is no reflection on their collective abilities to say that few outstandingly original boogie-woogie compositions have been written, since the high point of the style is the period between 1940 and 1960. The most consistently creative of them is undoubtedly Axel Zwingenberger; the most gifted in sustained attack and technique at the keyboard is Bob Seeley. Of the remainder, those showing individuality in their playing and powerful empathy with the roots of boogie-woogie music are Martin Pyrker, Carl Leyland, and Jean Pierre Bertrand, all of whom have composed high-quality, original tunes in the genre.

For the sake of completeness in any historical overview of this nature, another pathway taken by boogie-woogie music should be discussed—one that demonstrates its popularity in the broader field of commercial entertainment. Like the TOBA vaudeville tradition of an earlier age, boogie-woogie players were also an important constituent of the entertainment in American theatres, such as the Apollo, with the appearance there of Amos Milburn and others, in the immediate post-war period of the late 1940s and early 1950s. Maurice Rocco was an early talent from America who played to packed houses in British theatres, preceding the arrival of the popular Liberace who enjoyed winding up his audiences with a very fast, slick boogie-woogie technique. Then there was the "pint-sized wonder" Frankie "Sugar Chile" Robinson from Detroit who was eight years of age when he visited Britain. He could barely reach the keys and, although only attaining a height of four feet five inches as a grown man, could beat out a foot-tapping rhythm using a single-note walking bass to accompany "Numbers Boogie" and other songs in a high-pitched voice. As a child prodigy, he was well paid and eventually appeared at the London Palladium with Bob Hope in a Royal Command Performance, then in the Hollywood film *No Leave No Love* with Van Johnson, as well as providing entertainment for President Truman at the White House. Robinson retired at the age of seventeen following his final engagement at a Chicago nightclub in 1957. He was last heard of running a grocery store in Detroit, partnered by his father.

An entertainer with a more substantial international reputation was the Trinidadian Winifred Atwell (1914–1983), who became an impressive and much-loved star of theatre, radio, and, later, television in Britain. She included in her repertoire the standard boogie-woogie numbers "Hamp's Boogie-Woogie," "Yancey Special," and others that were interpreted accurately and with a solid rhythm. In her stage act, she switched between boogie-woogie and ragtime numbers played on her "other piano," a doctored upright purchased for a few pounds in a London secondhand store and fitted with a jangle sound box. Both styles can be heard on *Winifred Atwell: Five by Five* (Decca, LE 1294).

Atwell arrived in Britain in 1946 having studied classical piano in New York City and at the London School of Music. She was destined for the concert platform and did appear twice at the Royal Albert Hall performing Gershwin's *Rhapsody in Blue* and Greig's Piano Concerto with the London Philharmonic Orchestra. A successful television show that topped the ratings led to two Royal Command Performances in 1952 and 1956. Over and above her piano playing, Winifred Atwell had a pleasant, friendly personality that captivated her audiences. She was well paid and acquired all the trappings of stardom of that age: a large house in the outskirts of London with tennis courts and a private cinema. Atwell eventually moved to Australia where she continued to entertain before succumbing to a heart attack.

The closest parallel with Winifred Atwell among contemporary British entertainers is probably Jools Holland, whose rhythm-and-blues band wins high praise from television viewers and critics alike. Holland's piano background began with boogie-woogie, and he has several records to his credit in the style. A good example of his accessible music is available on *Jools Holland & His Rhythm & Blues Orchestra: Swinging the Blues, Dancing the Ska* (RADAR, 006 CD). The pounding bass and treble configurations of Ammons are captured on "You Don't Love Me," with added blues tonality underlying Holland's own vocal. "Sixth Avenue Express" is an interesting and exciting solo variant of the Ammons and Johnson piano duet, backed by precise driving section work from the band. Nowadays, Holland is recognized as an all-around entertainer, television compere, and personality as much as a pianist and leader of a well-established rhythm-and-blues band.

Fortunately, younger people are still attracted by the boogie-woogie beat in both America and Europe, and numbers continue to rise. In recent times we have had Jack Carter from England making a big impression as a fifteen-year-old at the Hotel Lutetia concert in 2001—a reputation that he has been consolidating at the annual British jazz festival in Bude and other venues; and the French boy, Vincent Gros, appearing as a nine-year-old at the Hotel Lutetia in 1997. All are helping to keep alive this strange musical aberration known as boogie-woogie.

NOTES

1. Edsel Ammons, correspondence with the author, November 19, 1985.

2. Chuck Leavell, "Radiatin' the 88's, Rock Pianos Ancestry," *Musician Magazine*, July 1990, 82.

3. Charlie Castner, correspondence with the author, June 18, 1988.

4. Michael H. Price, "The Boogie, Man It'll Get You," *Fort Worth Star Telegram*, May 19, 1994, 2.

5. Ben Conroy, "Fond Memories of Past Masters," *Mississippi Rag*, June 1991, 5. This edition also features an article about the boogie-woogie piano style by William J. Schafer, "Boogie-Woogie: Been Here and Gone," 1–4.

6. Axel Zwingenberger, *Boogie-Woogie Piano Solos* (Musikverlag GmbH Hallerstr. 72, 2000 Hamburg 13, Germany, 1986).

7. Colin Larkin, ed., *Guinness Who's Who of Jazz* (Enfield, UK: Guinness Publishing, 1992).

8. Axel Zwingenberger, liner notes, *Jean Pierre Bertrand and Trio Sunny Boogie*, Honky Tonk Records, HT 109.

9. Tad Hershorn, "Philippe LeJeune at Blue Moon, Houston," *Jazz Times*, December 1989, 1.

10. Jimmy Hopes, "Boogie-Woogie Man," *Jazz Monthly*, September/October 1971, 4–7.

Part Five

RECORDING BOOGIE-WOOGIE AND APPENDIXES

15

The National
and Independent
Record Companies

Recorded jazz music was first issued in America on the Okeh label
when a coupling of "Crazy Blues" and "It's Right Here for You" by
an African-American blues chanteuse Mamie Smith was released in 1920.
It proved so popular that the initial pressing of ten thousand records
quickly sold out. Investigation showed that the main purchasers were
African-Americans whose musical interests had largely been ignored by
record companies. Here was an untapped market. Both the major national
and a growing number of newly formed, small independent companies,
realizing this potential, began recording Bessie Smith, Ma Rainey, and
other blues singers but then diversified to cover other blues artists and
instrumentalists, many of whom were guitar and piano players. Chief
among the national companies were Columbia, the Brunswick company,
issuing under the Vocalion label, and Victor, which tailed along, showing
little initial commitment, before issuing later under its own name and the
cheaper Bluebird label. The most important of the independent companies were Paramount, Gennett, and Okeh. All of them created separate
catalogs for these musical recordings, calling them "race recordings" and
giving them a special numbered sequence. Thus Okeh ran the 8000 series
while 12000 was used by Paramount. The term *race* was first employed by
Okeh in their advertisements in an edition of the *Chicago Defender* dating
from 1922, its use then becoming universal.

Paramount and Gennett were formed in 1917. These and the other
companies continued successfully throughout the 1920s but either had
to close down or were bought out by other companies in the Depression.
Paramount managed to keep going until 1932 (John Steiner resurrected

the label); Gennett discontinued issuing under their label some two years earlier. Unlike Gennett and Okeh, Paramount did not actively seek out regional talent through field recordings but preferred to rely on the recommendations of talent scouts who invited artists to record at one of their two studios in either Chicago or Grafton, Wisconsin—the latter was taken into use in 1929 after their New York studio closed down. This recording activity left an incredibly rich legacy of piano music that we are still enjoying today. Further elaboration of the history of recording blues artists is beyond the scope of this book, but for anyone wishing to explore further, very exact research has been undertaken and documented in the book *Recording the Blues*, compiled by Dixon and Godrich.[1]

A glance at the patterns of recording blues pianists shows that many of the popular and arguably greatest masters of their craft stayed with one, or at the most, two companies, for their recording careers, or at least until such time as a company ceased trading. Thus, Leroy Carr had a prodigious output in excess of one hundred titles on the Vocalion label between 1928 and 1934, and a few on Bluebird toward the end of his career. Similarly, from 1933 until 1941, Walter Davis was under contract with Bluebird, for whom he made in excess of one hundred and thirty recordings, following a recording debut with Victor, Bluebird's parent company, which had produced twenty or so numbers. Charlie Spand remained with Paramount, visiting Grafton for most of his recordings, and only switched to Okeh in 1940 after Paramount had gone into liquidation. Apart from these major recording figures, lesser-known pianists were discovered within regions by talent scouts and their work captured mainly in situ, which has helped to identify regional features of piano styles and common musical themes. This was nowhere more so than in Texas, where minor pianists such as Bobby Cadillac, Texas Bill Day, and the better-known Alex Moore were recorded in San Antonio for Columbia. Fortunately, reissues by the Magpie, Yazoo, and Document record companies have made many of these old deleted recordings available to collectors. Often using a thematic approach to selecting particular recordings by artist, record label, or region, the selected recordings have been successfully backed up with informative liner notes. These reissues were initially available as LPs, but many have now been transferred to CD. For example, an important collection mapping the blues piano field was issued in the 1980s by Magpie as a series of twenty-one LP records, covering a remarkable range of solo pianists, regional styles, and piano accompaniments to blues singers. This was the first occasion that a collection of the Birmingham pianist Walter Roland had been made available in any great depth; likewise, a selection of important recordings by some of the more obscure Texas pianists were saved for posterity. These are found on *Piano Blues, Volume 15: Dallas 1927–1929* (Magpie, PY 4415). The quality of the recordings is exceptional, all having been taken from the original issues owned by Francis Wilford Smith. His stated intention to offer recordings retaining their original sound, without enhancement, has been admirably achieved.

An inspirational and very productive period of recording began soon after the Trio was formed and continued long after the partnership had ceased. All of their important work appeared on the major labels, notably Columbia, Decca, and Brunswick (also Vocalion), but two independent labels, Blue Note and Solo Art, also became involved. Both Alfred Lion and Dan Qualey, the respective owners of these two companies, were keen followers of boogie-woogie, and this probably helped to create the right ambience for recording the many compositions that have stood the test of time that remain outstanding examples of the genre.

The first issues on the Vocalion and Columbia labels in 1939 were the two-part "Boogie-Woogie Prayer" and the Ammons and Lewis coupling "Shout for Joy" and "Bear Cat Crawl." Johnson and Turner followed with "Roll 'Em Pete" and "Goin' Away Blues." Ammons and Johnson then made a number of recordings with the Harry James Orchestra. All these recordings were completed within one month of the opening of the Café Society, which demonstrates the interest being shown in boogie-woogie music and its commercial potential.

A further release in November 1939, on Vocalion, featured Pete Johnson and his Boys—a pick-up band drawn from the Café Society—and Joe Turner, on "Lovin' Mama Blues." The rhythm section holds together well behind Johnson's piano and there is useful lead phrasing from Lips Page on trumpet. Turner's vocal is less convincing and contains some atypical showy effects. The coupling was the heavy six-handed "Café Society Rag" by the trio, which is the least satisfying corporate effort. Exactly twelve months later, the Decca company released their first boogie-woogie album, a compilation of solo and band performances. The material had already been issued, with the exception of two new solos by Johnson entitled "Blues on the Downbeat" and "Kaycee on My Mind." The former employs a strong bass figure similar to that used by Ammons and also carries faint echoes of Jimmy Yancey's treble phrasing. The fingering is crisp, and Johnson places on record one of his musical trademarks, a chorus of single notes in the treble punctuating a rhythmical bass. "Kaycee on My Mind" is more reflective. It was said that Johnson had composed it at an after-hours session when he and Turner appeared, unsuccessfully, at the Famous Door nightspot. Out of failure was born success: His extemporizations on familiar themes produced "Kaycee." The bass has a pronounced delayed rhythm, while the treble, replete with trills and runs, is played mainly in the middle registers of the piano. His concluding choruses make use of a somber walking bass played in double time. Both numbers are good examples of the two modes favored by Johnson: one fast with a running bass; the other slow-paced and melodic.

A booklet about the artists, written by Dave Dexter, accompanied the Decca album. The pianists and tunes featured were Meade Lux Lewis ("Yancey Special"), Mary Lou Williams ("Overhand"), Cleo Brown ("Pinetop's Boogie-Woogie"), and Honey Hill ("Boogie-Woogie"). The band sides were by Albert Ammons ("Boogie-Woogie Stomp"), Andy Kirk ("Little Joe from Chicago"), Teddy Powell ("Teddy Bear Boogie"), Woody Herman ("Indian Boogie-Woogie"), and Bob Crosby ("Gin Mill Blues" and "Boogie-Woogie Maxixe"). The mixture of styles in this compilation demonstrates how the distinctions between the compositions of the acknowledged masters and commercial renderings of boogie-woogie were becoming less differentiated and more blurred. The album drew from both the "race" and "popular" files and was quite unrepresentative of boogie-woogie music. "Gin Mill Blues" was not even a standard boogie-woogie composition. Honey Hill's rendition of Pinetop's piece was played as a relaxed solo with few dynamics, whereas Cleo Brown's had more technique and less feeling than the original. The band numbers offered the listener little that was new and identified for one jaundiced reviewer the strengths and limitations of orchestrating boogie-woogie phrases.[2]

The Columbia company was less nimble than Decca in releasing its first boogie-woogie album, but it better represented the roots of the style. Issued in March 1941, the collection was for the most part a reissue of earlier material from 1939. It contained "Boo-Woo" and "Woo-Woo" by Harry James, with Ammons and Johnson, respectively; "Roll 'Em Pete" by Johnson and Turner coupled with "Boogie-Woogie" by the Count Basie Blues Five; "Boogie-Woogie Prayer" (parts 1 and 2) by the Trio; and the coupling of "Shout for Joy" and "Bear Cat Crawl" by Ammons and Lewis. An advance notice advised potential purchasers that boogie-woogie was finally being recognized as having an important place in American music.

In April 1941, Decca finally made available Lewis's version of "Honky Tonk Train Blues," first released on English Parlophone in 1935. It was included in a collection of six records entitled *Gems of Jazz, Volume One*. Other sides were by Mildred Bailey and jazz groups led by Bud Freeman and Joe Marsala. Jess Stacey provided the coupling for Lewis on the American issue with a solo rendition of "The World Is Waiting for the Sunrise." Comparisons between the first version of the "Train" issued by Paramount and later versions were inevitable. The raw power and flavor of the first were retained and to them was added lustrous treble phrasing that suggested a rolling freight train, drawn by an urgent, throttled engine intent on reaching its destination with few stops.

Decca went quickly off the mark again in November 1941 with their second boogie-woogie album, which included Lewis's "Mr. Freddie Blues," never before available on the American market (Brunswick, foreign label only). He gives the Freddie Shayne composition a somewhat agitated kind of bass and rarely moves out of the middle registers of the keyboard in extemporizing on the melody. The number moves along at a moderate tempo but is one of his less imaginative treatments. The coupling, "Celeste Blues" (1936), was already available on the Decca label. Other pieces included in the collection were "Trenches" by Turner Parrish, "Texas Stomp" (1935) by Dot Rice and Frankie Black, "Hastings Street" (1929) by Charlie Spand and Blind Blake, as well as recordings by Zurke, Lineham, and Kersey. Once again, there was an interlarding of pieces from Decca's "race" files and material by contemporary exponents of boogie-woogie.

The Blue Note releases contributed significantly to the quality of the recorded output of members of the Trio because it allowed them unrestricted time to produce their best work.[3] They were given extended rehearsal time with food and beverages at hand. Alfred Lion started the company in New York in 1939 with capital of less than one hundred dollars. He first heard jazz in 1925, played by a visiting American band, Sam Wooding and His Chocolate Dandies, in Berlin. Having fled from Nazi Germany in 1938 with his family, Lion and a longtime friend Frank Wolff, whom he met in Paris in 1934, settled in New York and began listening to jazz. Lion began to collect records and had a particular interest in blues and boogie-woogie. He was invited to attend the first Spirituals to Swing concert by John Hammond and was so enraptured by the Trio that he translated this interest into action by forming the Blue Note company with the aim of initially recording the boogie-woogie pianists solely for his own pleasure. It started out as a part-time venture with the release of sides by Lewis and Ammons, but when these recordings were favorably received, he began to devote more time to recording and invested more money in the company. Despite the relatively expensive cost of the distinctively patterned blue and white records, they sold well. He then widened the range of artists to include jazz musicians such as Sidney Bechet and Edmond Hall. This was an important decision for the development of recorded jazz, because at the time few outlets existed for high-quality jazz. The interests of the major companies were concerned, in the main, with the high-profile swing bands and popular music. Lion's success was built on two planks: an ability to recognize embryonic talent and to record artists under the best possible conditions for producing good performances. The artwork for the Blue Note record covers was in the capable hands of his partner Frank Wolff, who achieved a well-deserved reputation as a photographer capable of capturing the spirit of jazz. Many of his prints have since graced both the pages of jazz literature and record sleeves.

The first Blue Note recording session took place on January 6, 1939, and produced one hundred shellac pressings by Meade Lux Lewis. Forsaking his normal boogie-woogie style, he recorded two blues numbers, "Solitude Blues" and "Melancholy Blues." A second record released at the same time was by Albert Ammons, who made "Boogie-Woogie Stomp" and "Boogie-Woogie Blues." That sunny day in January proved to be a marathon session at which the total output of Ammons for Blue Note was recorded (nine sides) plus eight numbers by Lewis and two duets on one piano. It was only in 1983 that all of these recordings and others by Lewis were issued as a complete series on the Mosaic label, including several previously unissued titles on *The Complete Blue Note Recordings of Albert Ammons and Meade Lux Lewis* (Mosaic, MR3 103). In his search for perfection, Lion encouraged the two pianists to work out their pieces before the takes. It took some time and half a bottle of Scotch whiskey before Ammons finally dropped the waltz-time numbers he was set on playing to produce the deeply moving "Chicago in Mind." Similarly, Lewis was delving deeply into his psyche, helped by a bottle of bourbon. Lion recalled Lewis's cast-iron constitution, taking his whiskey straight with no chaser.[4]

Seven records had been issued on the Blue Note label by September 1939, including several small-group improvisations that brought together Frankie Newton, Sid Catlett, J. C. Higginbotham, and Ammons as the Port of Harlem Jazz Men; a solo recording by Earl Hines; and Lewis with Bechet, Catlett, Newton, Teddy Bunn, J. Williams, and J. C. Higginbotham in various permutations as the Port of Harlem Seven, the Sidney Bechet Quintet, and the J. C. Higginbotham Quintet. Two of the Port of Harlem tunes are available on *Albert Ammons: Boogie-Woogie Man* (Topaz, TPZ 1067).

Nearly all Blue Note recordings were issued on twelve-inch discs, the reason being that Lion was a collector first and foremost and was so absorbed by the music that he forgot to watch the length of the solos. He rationalized this later by saying the normal ten-inch discs were too constraining for good improvisation. Although some wonderful music resulted from the sessions, they were often organized in a haphazard way. In the early days of the company, Lion and Wolff attended all recording dates, provided and distributed the refreshments, and packed the records in their sleeves. On one occasion in 1944, a perfect recording by Meade Lux Lewis of a new train piece with an intriguing bass line was almost lost to posterity when it was found that the master had been spoiled. Fortunately, the sound engineer had the foresight to make a reserve master at thirty three and a third revolutions per minute, and a newly recorded train piece was born and named "Chicago Flyer."

Lewis was at his most creative on the Blue Note label. Another recording session in November 1940 produced his longest and some critics would say, best version of "Honky Tonk Train Blues," two interpretations of "Tell Your Story" (parts 1 and 2), the formidable "Six Wheel Chaser," and the pounding "Bass on Top." Reviews of the first and later recordings by Lewis and Ammons were highly favorable and supportive of the extraordinary creativity of these pianists. William Russell was to the fore with his plaudits and scholarly analysis of the "Honky Tonk Train Blues," referring favorably to Lewis's stamina and creativity, which had produced several additional and stimulating variations on the train theme.[5]

Preceding the release of these records came the four-part "Blues" improvisations—now confirmed as five parts following the discovery by the Mosaic company of the missing section. Reactions to the twenty minutes of blues music, or "forty-eight inches" as one critic preferred to call it, were universally favorable. Blue Note was given plaudits for encouraging a jazz artist to extemporize on a theme from inception to completion. These recordings were never intended to be regarded solely as an expression of the blues in their simplest form, but were more a demonstration of Lewis's sophisticated conception of blues tonality. They reveal another side of his playing in which the bass is sometimes dominant but is, more commonly, integrated with the treble extemporizations. Most critics are in agreement about his creative capacity. Martin T. Williams, in a thoughtful study of the rise and fall of Lewis, said that although the Blue Note recordings were not the equal of the "Train," they were as complex and highly developed as boogie-woogie has ever been, while still retaining sufficient contact with the folk qualities of boogie-woogie and not compromising the integrity of the genre.[6] It was evident that Lewis's brilliant technique was still allowing him to compose pieces of outstanding inventiveness containing unsurpassed textures and phrases.[7] Reactions to the recordings in the lay press were equally favorable, with the *Washington Post* suggesting that most boogie-woogie has a monotonous sameness, but Lewis's classic solos surpassed this criticism by a long way.[8]

The "Honky Tonk Train Blues" recorded for Blue Note is played at a markedly increased tempo, confirming that it had now become Lewis's show stopper, with additional choruses and more dynamics. For example, the hypnotic effect of playing the clattering cross-rhythms in the second and third choruses at a faster speed creates more excitement in the performance than before, but there is a corresponding loss of the melancholy characteristics of earlier versions. It contains sixteen choruses in all, the first seven following the original pattern faithfully with little change. New material is introduced in the eighth and subsequent choruses, and while they bring a freshness to a well-known theme, they do break the logical and satisfying progression of the train's journey.

Lewis's association with Pete Johnson can be sensed in the two-part "Tell Your Story" by his use of the bass with a rolling touch much favored by that pianist. That is as far as the similarity goes, however, with the piece, played at a medium-fast pace, carrying his own distinctive tone coloring and rhythmical complexity. Lewis's second composition drawing on a train theme for inspiration was "Six Wheel Chaser"—a reference to the coal tender behind the engine. Russell praised the basic energy of the piece and compared Lewis's effective use of his "tonal, technical and instrumental resources" favorably with those of Stravinsky in his intention to produce a similar effect in parts of his composition *Le Sacre*.[9] Using a complex chorded bass to create a persistent train rhythm like that of "Honky Tonk Train Blues," only this time played in the root position, "Six Wheel Chaser" is a powerful display of raw energy, employing fast repeated chords and short, staccato treble phrases. "Bass on Top," as its title implies, features a walking bass in different combinations while still retaining aural interest in the treble work with very rich tremolos. The harmonies and counterpoint so achieved exemplify the complex and dynamic path along which boogie-woogie music was now proceeding compared with the much simpler compositions of two of his fellow Chicagoans, Jimmy Yancey and Clarence Lofton.

Having already transferred his attention to the celeste for a brief spell as a solo instrument and later for ensemble playing, Lewis now began to explore the range of the harpsichord. The outcome is less musically satisfying than his earlier experiments with the celeste because of the harpsichord's resonant quality, which destroys the sharp contrasting tones endemic to boogie-woogie music. Four numbers were composed under the umbrella title of "Variations on a Theme" (1941). They are "Nineteen Ways of Playing a Chorus," "Self-Portrait," "School of Rhythm," and "Feelin' Tomorrow Like I Feel Today." These recordings are notable for the effects achieved on the instrument rather than for their stimulating musical qualities. There is a tendency for notes to run together on the quicker tempos, the effect of a fast keyboard action that Lewis clearly enjoyed. "Feeling Tomorrow Like I Feel Today" displays the most satisfying blend of man and instrument. They are an interesting variant of the boogie-woogie form, but four sides is too many for a repeat of his successful formula with the blues improvisations.

In his first series of Blue Note recordings, Lewis released an inventive flow of musical ideas and established new standards for boogie-woogie playing. He, like many who followed in his wake, was to be tested attempting to emulate such high-quality performances in his later recordings. Russell summarized the features that he believed contributed to Lewis's greatness: a feeling for the unique resonance of the instrument, an appreciation of tone color, independence of hands to produce such complex rhythms, and a command of form, shown in the organization of his material and its climactic intensity, to an extent that no other boogie-woogie pianist has ever exceeded Lewis's efforts.[10]

Of the nine numbers recorded by Albert Ammons, five were initially issued: "Boogie-Woogie Stomp," "Chicago in Mind," "Suitcase Blues," "Boogie-Woogie Blues," and "Bass Goin' Crazy." The four remaining pieces were released by Mosaic in 1984 (takes 13, 15, 16, and 19) and were entitled, respectively, "Untitled [sic] Ammons Original," "Backwater Blues," "Changes in Boogie-Woogie," and "Easy Rider Blues." Russell later picked up on Ammons's releases "Bass Goin' Crazy" and "Suitcase Blues" (BN-21) for review. This was at a time when the major companies had stopped issuing records owing to the Petrillo ban, and Russell led his review with a note of congratulation for Blue Note's endeavors in resuming their jazz releases at this time. He began by reminding the readers of Ammons's versatility as a pianist and then wondered why record companies and nightclubs had not capitalized on Ammons's potential as the leader of a swinging orchestra that had previously been so popular in pre-war Chicago. Furthermore, he possessed two well-developed qualities in his piano style: being able to build up to "tremendous climaxes" and a complementary technique that permitted this, both of which were apparent in the unique "Bass Goin' Crazy."[11]

Much of Ammons's treble work was embellished with ringing tremolo chords, which were set against insistent bass figures and generated a controlled rocking rhythm. Ammons's ability to play such clear tremolos was the result of his early training in copying chords from piano rolls. During their production, piano rolls were filled out by adding embellishments to the pianist's original notes, giving the phantom pianist an exceptional technique. Additionally, chords were sometimes translated on the piano roll as tremolos to give them a sustaining quality in the absence of the loud pedal, which the pianist would normally have used for the same effect. Thus it was possible to reduce the "mechanical" sound of the piano roll and to give a composition more subtlety and variation. Such complex adaptations would be unknown to Ammons when he was learning to play from piano rolls, and he would have absorbed some extremely difficult fingering techniques. He once explained how he and Lewis would place their fingers on the depressed keys of the piano player to commit the chords to memory, an arduous apprenticeship that eventually produced sufficient technique for them to play independently.[12]

The "Suitcase Blues"—probably the first piece he ever learned from Hersal Thomas—and "Chicago in Mind" are played at slower tempos with an incipient strength in the varied stride and ostinato basses. The "Suitcase Blues" captures the spirit of the Hersal Thomas original but contains fewer embellishments than Thomas brought to his playing of it. The Ammons's rendition is pared to the bone to maintain the contrast between the repeated plangent chords in the treble and a bass pattern, which sometimes resembles a tailgate trombone. Another characteristic of Ammons's piano work uses octave tremolos in an ascending and descending sequence to introduce suspense into his compositions. This was frequently done in the slower numbers "Boogie-Woogie Blues" and to a lesser extent, using fewer notes in the tremolos, in "Chicago in Mind."

On "Bass Goin' Crazy" and "Boogie-Woogie Stomp," Ammons deploys bass figures that became identifying features of many of his later boogie-woogie compositions. Both demonstrate perfectly his sustained controlled power with fast numbers. His interpretation of "Boogie-Woogie Stomp," Pinetop's classic, has never been equaled, with its stop-time breaks and forceful bass, which jumps from the deeper recesses of the keyboard to settle for a period in the middle registers before thundering on. The Blue Note release shows once again that he could build the piece into a tour de force using the minimum of notes and chords. In the unusual "Bass Goin' Crazy," the originality of the pianist is evident in the simple repeated three-chord figure in the treble, maintained throughout most of the composition, leaving the aural focus on the wild bass that begins its journey in the middle of the keyboard before cascading into an urgent chorded deeper bass. The whole has a cohesion that is achieved without reverting to the more usual pattern of playing varied choruses in the treble. "Bass Goin' Crazy" exemplifies the hypnotic feature of boogie-woogie music without losing any of its impetus from the sparse treble phrases. Although his compositions contain sharply etched treble choruses when compared to Meade Lux Lewis's pieces, Albert Ammons played them with a suppressed energy and precision, to produce a unique fluidity in his renderings that jazz critic Whitney Balliett likened to a slowly spreading stain.

It was December 1939 before Pete Johnson cut any sides for Blue Note, almost twelve months after the first session involving Ammons and Lewis. Why his debut should have been delayed for so long is not entirely clear, but the reason may have been that he was somewhat in the shadow of his two contemporaries at this point in his career. An indication of this may be gleaned from the first release on which he is accompanied by Ulysses Livingstone (guitar) and Abe Bolar (bass) in "Pete Johnson's Blues Trio"—perhaps prompting a misguided view shared by Lion and Wolff that he was less capable of high-quality solo performances. The titles arising from the session were "Vine Street Bustle," "Some Day Blues," "Barrelhouse Breakdown," and "Kansas City Farewell." However, the presence of the other musicians hinders rather than improves his impact, because his sharp and nimble basses are muffled by the heavier rhythm of the other two instruments. On "Vine Street Bustle," Johnson introduces the left- and right-hand figures from "Yancey Special." The most interesting point in the recording is achieved in the fifth and sixth choruses when the piano and guitar combine to produce an imaginative improvisation. "Some Day Blues" begins at a medium tempo with two lively opening choruses by Johnson, but then loses its initial pace by introducing some overrepetitive treble figures. Although the piano is featured less prominently in "Barrelhouse Breakdown," the trio produce a solid rhythmical number, somewhat uneven in places. The most intriguing recording from this session is the first solo performance by Johnson to appear on the Blue Note label, called "Holler Stomp." It runs to eighteen choruses, and the frantic tempo is sustained using a rapid walking bass and incisive treble choruses. The fourth and fifth choruses are notable for their adaptation of a phrase taken from Pinetop Smith's composition "Jump Steady Blues" and some fast-fingered single-note improvisations. The reverse side of the record, issued as Blue Note 12, is called "You Don't Know My Mind," a slow-paced blues in which the treble ideas are developed over a rudimentary ground rhythm. The boogie-woogie form is present, but there is little blues feeling in the sparse tone coloring. All of Pete Johnson's Blue Note recordings are included on *The Pete Johnson/Earl Hines/Teddy Bunn Blue Note Sessions* (Mosaic, MR1 119).

At this point in his career, Johnson had not had the same impact as his two associates. There were times when he sounded positively leaden and pedestrian, but there were also occasional flashes when a highly developed rhythm and a magical touch made the high treble tones ring out like so many bells, which confirmed his true ability at the keyboard. Some critics considered that he was merely the "powerhouse" of the trio who provided the background rhythm for Ammons and Lewis. One critic even relegated him to the role of a minor pianist whose overall contribution to boogie-woogie music was no more significant than primitive pianists such as Wesley Wallace, Jabo Williams, Will Ezell, and Charlie Spand.[13] Compared to Pete Johnson, these players, though important figures responsible for one or two outstanding recordings, were less capable technically. Johnson sits better in the company of Albert Ammons, for it would be inconceivable to imagine any of the pianists mentioned being capable of a partnership achieving the imaginative form and technical merit of a duet played by Ammons and Johnson. The last word on Johnson's boogie-woogie and blues interpretations is best left to jazzmen of the caliber of Duke Ellington and Count Basie, who considered him the best there was. They always went to listen to him for their own enjoyment, whenever they were in the vicinity of one of Johnson's engagements.

The other smaller independent record company of the period, Solo Art, pursued a similar policy to Blue Note of recording boogie-woogie pianists, although it did so to the exclusion of other jazz forms. In its short existence, it achieved a more representative cover of the pianists than its prestigious competitor and in a compressed period in 1939 recorded all the major pianists. The catalog contained the work of Jimmy Yancey, Cripple Clarence Lofton, and the emerging white pianist Art Hodes, as well as members of the Trio.

The owner was Dan Qualey, an Irish-American in his late twenties who resided in a small apartment on Joralemon Street in Brooklyn.[14] He had no private financial means and worked at a variety of jobs in order to pursue what started as a hobby and developed into a small business. His first venture into recording started when he was working as a bartender at the Hotel Webster in Times Square. The year was 1938, and he specialized in making recorded transcriptions of radio shows featuring jazz music. His method was to have a standing order with a transcription studio and listen for jazz music on a small radio hidden among the drinking glasses. When an interesting number was announced, he would telephone the company to record it. This often necessitated making hasty telephone calls, sometimes in the act of serving a customer. Naturally, the proprietor of the hotel could take only so much of this eccentric behavior and eventually dismissed him. Before this venture, Qualey had worked as a bank teller, movie extra, field hand in Georgia, chorus boy, waiter, and hotel clerk to feed his passion for jazz and blues music, which dated from the 1920s. His favorite musical instrument was the piano, and he enjoyed listening to most styles but, above all others, to boogie-woogie and ragtime music. He searched out recordings but soon found that there was only a limited number available representing these styles. When Meade Lux Lewis was appearing at Nick's Basement in New York in 1936, Qualey and another collector raised two hundred dollars to cover the cost of a recording session, which involved paying Lewis a fee and hiring a recording studio. Unfortunately, his partner lost his job and withdrew his share of the money, leaving Qualey without the means for fulfilling his ambition.

Another opportunity for recording boogie-woogie artists seemed to be within his grasp when the Café Society opened. Qualey was aware that boogie-woogie was undergoing an upsurge in popularity, and he believed that the folk artistry of Ammons, Lewis, and Johnson could become tainted by unwelcome commercial pressures to improve sales if the major recording companies began to vie for their talents. Initially, Qualey and a group of like-minded enthusiasts agreed to make some recordings of the trio before this possibility could occur. Qualey was again frustrated, this time by the indecision of the group who could not agree when to record the pianists, and he did not possess the technical skills to undertake the recordings. Qualey's obsession and past failures finally led him to take the initiative to record them on his own. Fortunately, this time, he managed to raise the necessary capital to start the enterprise, signaling the birth of the Solo Art company. Qualey was still thwarted in his intention to beat the major companies, however, because the early Solo Art masters were not of a sufficiently high quality to be put on the market. They overran and contained some unfortunate surface noises. Before he could recoup his losses, Columbia had stepped in and recorded the members of the trio, but this only encouraged him to search more widely for talent and to find lesser-known pianists than Ammons, Lewis, and Johnson, who did eventually record for him. Qualey's plan brought Jimmy Yancey into a recording studio for the first time.

The details of Qualey's first contact with the Yanceys show the persistence with which he hunted down his quarry. As he was unfamiliar with the South Side of Chicago, he first approached Albert Ammons at the Café Society, who gave him a detailed description of the area in which the Yanceys' apartment was situated. By knocking on doors, he eventually reached his destination by a process of elimination, to be faced by a suspicious Estelle Yancey. After explaining the purpose of his visit, he was admitted into the living room only to find that Jimmy was absent working at Comiskey Park, and was not due to return home for some hours. Qualey and Estelle passed the time discussing baseball, a common interest. When Jimmy eventually arrived home, they all talked about mutual friends before Qualey felt it was opportune to broach the subject of a recording date. Jimmy was interested but had no piano of his own, so they walked the short distance to his sister's home where he played through his repertoire for Qualey. Some of the numbers that Qualey heard for the first time were "The Fives," "Yancey Stomp," "Sweet Patootie," and the original "Yancey Special."

Qualey quickly realized that Lewis and Ammons had not exaggerated in describing the older man's talents. A date was eventually agreed for the first recording session, but Jimmy had not been playing very frequently and was out of touch, finding it necessary to practice for some weeks before he could begin to approach his best form. Even then, some of the takes were still not up to standard, and "The Fives" was attempted seven times before both men felt satisfied with the performance. The first recording was made in the summer of 1939 and issued in November. "The Fives" is played with verve and builds up to a powerful climax. "Jimmy's Stuff" is in a slower vein and employs a bass figure similar to the "Yancey Special" composition by Lewis. At this slower tempo, Yancey shows his inventive powers, both in the varied treble phrases and in the complex rhythms. The recording was welcomed in record reviews, but several reviewers noted that the absence of regular practice had affected Yancey's technique. Qualey was able to issue only these first two numbers of the series because of lack of funds, and the remaining masters were eventually sold to Rudi Blesh. All pieces have since been released on *Jazz Piano Series, Volume 1: Jimmy Yancey: In the Beginning* (Jazzology, JCE-51).

Qualey now wished to find Cripple Clarence Lofton, and Yancey advised him to visit the many clubs and dives on State Street. The Big Apple had been mentioned as a favorite haunt of Lofton, but it was almost as elusive to find as the pianist until Qualey happened to see a small card with the name printed on it stuck on the inside of a window. Entering the seedy club, Qualey approached the first person he saw and inquired after Lofton. It was Lofton himself who responded in the affirmative, and Qualey was introduced to a display of Lofton's talents at the piano, which lasted through the night with the assistance of a drum of South Side gin.

From the recording session that took place later, four of Lofton's numbers were issued on Solo Art: "Streamline Train," coupled with "Had a Dream," and "Pinetop's Boogie-Woogie" backed by "I Don't Know." The first record was released in June 1940 and was well received by the critics. "Streamline Train" was praised for its authentic joyous spirit and tone coloring, which was achieved by the pounding treble choruses played over a thunderous walking bass. Lofton always included the fifth in his walking octave basses, which gave them a full tone. The backing, "Had a Dream," is probably Lofton's finest creation, but it is not a pleasant dream in mood. It recalls the cold windswept streets and grim overcrowded tenement buildings of the South Side, poverty, hunger and squalor, unemployment, and soup-kitchen queues. The musical ideas are interpreted with unmistakable sincerity, to produce a piece of slow-tempo boogie-woogie of exceptional expressive power. The second record proved a fitting sequel to the first, with a typical Lofton romp on "I Don't Know." The number gathered its momentum from the regularly introduced piano breaks, a rumbling left hand, and a sonorous vocal. On "Pinetop's Boogie-Woogie," he makes only passing reference to the original theme, takes it apart, and then reinterprets it in a vigorous, staccato fashion. Choruses are either extended or shortened with the first three running to eleven, ten, and twelve bars, respectively, whereas the final chorus crashes through the twelve-bar barrier to its completion after fourteen-and-a-half bars. One bemused critic, remarking on the lack of shape in Lofton's work, noted that it was always employed pragmatically; another reported succinctly that Lofton had murdered Pinetop's masterpiece. Other recordings from Solo Art, including "Sixes and Sevens" and "Lofty Blues," are available on the French release *Low Down Piano, Volume 15: Clarence Lofton & Montana Taylor* (Archive of Jazz, BYG 529.065).

Although the odd criticism lingered after Lofton's first set of solo recordings, there was an air of quiet satisfaction prevalent in the reviews. It was as though his very crudity and unorthodoxy vindicated any technical shortcomings, to confirm him as a true artist playing music of an earlier era. The purity of expression that so many critics acclaimed was some-times a shroud masking a limited range of ideas, but the plaudits were nonetheless important for appreciating the genesis of boogie-woogie. This period, commencing in the mid-1930s, was one in the development of jazz and blues appreciation and criticism that marked a return to the "old" and original sounds, because it was believed that only in this music could the purity and genuine artistry of black performers be found. It was a refutation of what the purists viewed as the tainting influence of commercialism spread by radio and jukeboxes. This period witnessed the reemergence of Bunk Johnson and other old jazzmen from retirement to reproduce the sounds of their youth, some without ever completely recovering their earlier considerable flair and technique. The "back to basics" movement was conducted with considerable fervor, and present-day collectors must be grateful for the traditional music it produced.

Clarence Lofton never considered himself solely a pianist but as an entertainer who sang, danced, and also played piano. He did possess a kind of innocent virtuosity that maintained in his work the freshness and originality of an amateur player. Unfortunately, this brought in its wake conflict with the musicians' union in the shape of Mr. Petrillo, the union leader, who proclaimed Lofton to be an amateur on the grounds that he had never earned sufficient money from his playing to pay regular union dues. Lofton's stage had always been the numerous South Side clubs where he appeared, usually after the regular pianist had vacated the pi-ano stool. Following this development, he still managed a few spasmodic appearances—one of which was on Maxwell and Morgan streets with a saxophone band—but word gradually seeped through that he was not a union member and even these isolated avenues were closed to him.

One fortunate outcome of Lofton's Solo Art recordings and the atten-dant publicity given to him was the discovery that he had made record-ings in the mid-1930s as an accompanist to Red Nelson's vocal on the Decca "race" catalog—originally recorded on the Champion label. The identification was made by a jazz critic who compared two versions of "Streamline Train," one with Nelson singing the lyrics and the other Lof-ton's piano solo for Solo Art. Verification of these rare sides came when a record collector stopped off in Chicago while traveling between Los An-geles and New York to listen to Lofton playing and received confirmation from him that he had been the piano player on "Sweetest Thing Born," "When the Soldiers Get Their Bonus," and "Mother Blues." This brought the number of Lofton's known recordings to ten by 1940.

A confusing sequel to the appearance of Solo Art recordings on the market was the duplication of numbers on certain records. When Qualey was starting his company, he arranged for Meade Lux Lewis to record "Deep Fives" and "Blues De Luxe" on one record and "Closin' Hour

Blues" and "Far Ago Blues" on a second record. These were intended either as private recordings or they may have been the early spoiled recordings mentioned earlier, but they found their way to the market only to be withdrawn later because of their poor quality. The numbers given to the recordings were 12003 and 12004, which, after their withdrawal, were later designated to Lofton's "Streamline Train" and "Had a Dream" (12003) and to Pete Johnson's first Solo Art sides "Climbin' and Screamin'" backed by "How Long, How Long" (12004).

The Johnson coupling shows his adeptness in playing in more than one style, a fact largely forgotten when his boogie-woogie interpretations made their impact with white audiences. "Climbin' and Screamin'" is pure boogie-woogie, comprising a series of crisp variations high in the treble, marked by an economical selection of notes over a metronomic bass. Johnson shows his debt to Waller's influence in "How Long, How Long," with its relaxed stride bass and tenth chords. The melody of this traditional blues composition, credited to Leroy Carr, contains, to an unusual degree for Johnson, a series of florid runs and trills.

Three more recordings completed Johnson's output for Solo Art. They were "Let 'Em Jump" and "Pete's Blues," "Buss Robinson's Blues" and "B and O Blues," and "Shuffle Boogie" and "Pete's Blues No. 2." Switching to a walking bass on "Shuffle Boogie," he sounds altogether more relaxed with the tempo than on the earlier, more frantic "Holler Stomp" recorded for Blue Note; and he produces a joyous, happy tone from the keyboard. The reverse side, "Pete's Blues No. 2," continues the themes explored on the earlier released "Pete's Blues." A slow, meditative number, it catches the spirit of "Kaycee in Mind" and highlights the unique color tones and mood that Johnson was capable of producing when the chemistry was right. All these rare sides can be found on *Jumpin' with Pete Johnson* (London, AL 3549).

Albert Ammons had the distinction of being the first in the catalog with the numbers 12000 and 12001. His version of "Bass Gone Crazy," using the past tense in the title, is similar in its form to his Blue Note effort. The coupling was "Monday Struggle," and it also replicates the mood and tempo of "Boogie-Woogie Blues," another of his releases on the Lion label. The second coupling was "Boogie-Woogie" and "Mecca Flat Blues," which draws inspiration from the Jimmy Blythe composition "Lovin' Been Here and Gone to Mecca Flats."

In addition to the first aborted releases by Meade Lux Lewis, which were quickly snapped up by collectors and became rarities before they were reissued, Lewis was recorded on a cross-coupling with Ammons playing "Messin' Around" to Ammons's "St. Louis Blues." Following the pattern of his Blue Note series of blues improvisations, "Messin' Around" was in a slow tempo with thematic extemporizations in the bass supported by rhythmical chords in the treble. It was an apt choice of title for the composition. "St. Louis Blues" in the hands of Ammons was transformed into another of his powerful boogie-woogie solos that employed tremolos and the traditional Latin rhythms associated with this composition, in several choruses. This rendition, though lacking some of the usual Ammons vitality, did provide record collectors with another example of his highly individualistic piano playing. The remaining four recordings made for the company by Lewis are also in slower blues tempo and display his reflective side: "Deep Fives," "Blues De Lux," "Closin' Hour Blues," and "Far Ago Blues." A selection of these sides on Solo Art by members of the trio, including all the sides by Ammons, is available on *Giants of Boogie-Woogie* (Riverside, RLP 12-106).

Dan Qualey admired the piano above all other instruments and considered that it could reach the variety and power of a full orchestra. "Honky Tonk Train Blues" came closest to achieving this for him, and during his search for lesser-known pianists he was always looking for a composition of similar magnitude played by an unknown pianist whom he believed would have all the undiscovered talents of the top boogie-woogie players.[15] Qualey never achieved his ambition, for only one more record was cut to complete the total output of his company. Art Hodes was the pianist concerned. Dan Qualey's first contact with Hodes was at a club on Staten Island. Before inviting him to record for Solo Art, Qualey made the two-hour journey from Manhattan by subway, ferry, and bus on several occasions to absorb the Hodes piano style. Five recordings were made, but only three were released. Two different tunes were given the title of "South Side Shuffle," because Qualey decided to switch the original version with the second one. The backing was "Ross Tavern Boogie." As Art Hodes said later, "Ross Tavern Boogie" was composed as a blues with a boogie-woogie rhythm and owed its success to his deeply felt emotional commitment during the making of what was to be his first solo piano recording.[16]

The recording career of Jimmy Yancey continued with the release in May 1940 of six sides for the Victor company. It was a quite remarkable achievement for a man who less than twelve months earlier had been living in obscurity on the South Side. Although only in his early forties, Yancey was fast becoming a legend in his own lifetime as the authentic father-figure of the boogie-woogie style. This was not altogether accurate, but as his Solo Art releases had been presaged by an interview in one music magazine where he was quoted as saying that Lewis and Ammons were his two most famous pupils, it tended to exaggerate his importance as their mentor. His sudden rags-to-riches story was given additional piquancy when he appeared on the radio show *We the People* on September 17, 1940, and reported to the nation that he was the founder of the boogie-woogie style, thus adding one more name to the growing list of old-time musicians who claimed to have invented jazz music or one of its offshoots. Yancey was introduced on the program by Dizzy Dean, a gregarious baseball pitcher with the Chicago Cubs, before playing "Yancey Stomp" with a deafening accompaniment from a fourteen-piece studio band, which effectively compromised his talents for the listening public.[17]

The Victor collection, made in October 1939, included "State Street Special," "Yancey Stomp," "Five O'Clock Blues," "Mellow Blues," "Tell 'Em All about Me," and "Slow and Easy Blues." A pleasing collection of contrasting themes, these recordings are, technically, some of his best. William Russell wrote an accompanying booklet emphasizing the African rhythmical tradition of boogie-woogie music and the common heritage shared by Yancey with the Charleston rhythm. The collection was well received in reviews, led by the one in *Jazz Information* commending the artistic qualities of Yancey's music and advising those who were unable to appreciate this to remove the lead from their ears.[18] Two further sides, "Yancey Bugle Call" and "Thirty-Fifth and Dearborn," were recorded for Victor in 1941 and drew equally favorable responses from the critics. The first of the numbers was a bugle-call motif using breaks and progressively more complex variations of the simple theme. It was well received, with the jazz content of both sides being praised. All but "Five O'Clock Blues" and "Tell Em All about Me"—the oldest tune in Yancey's repertoire—are included in the four-LP set *Black & White* (RCA. PM 42395).

Yancey made several additional recordings in 1940, one of which for the Vocalion company was entitled "Old Quaker Blues" backed by "Bear Trap Blues." The first title is a fast boogie-woogie solo with a pounding left hand, which places it in the same high category of performance as "Jimmy's Stuff" and "The Fives." "Bear Trap Blues," however, is another but inferior version of "Jimmy's Stuff," the first indication that Yancey had only a few compositions in his book. Yet another recording of the period (1940) was "Death Letter Blues" and "Crying in My Sleep," both on the Bluebird label. Yancey accompanies his own vocals on both sides, but the combination of piano and voice is less effective than is his solo piano, perhaps because of the requirement to concentrate on his singing, which is not particularly noteworthy. A more satisfactory vocal version of "Death Letter Blues," this time featuring Faber Smith, with Yancey's piano accompaniment, was released at about the same time on the Vocalion label.

In the period between 1939 and 1941, several boogie-woogie pieces of exceptional and lasting quality were recorded by pianists at the peak of their creative powers. In hindsight, the importance of this recording activity becomes obvious: Authentic boogie-woogie playing was soon to be engulfed in a morass of bland commercial jingles that popularized the form in song, and watered-down piano pieces that removed the very qualities of the rawness and rhythm that had first brought the style to public attention. Out went the unpredictable dissonance and extended improvisation, leaving just an empty hulk. Fortunately, the earlier recordings remain as a high water mark long after the popular, more blander representations of boogie-woogie have been forgotten. Qualey's tenacious effort to record the Trio and others before their work became tainted by commercial interests proved not to be the disaster he had feared. In the main, it was the music and not the pianists who changed. Qualey's recordings and those of Lion and Wolff captured in perpetuity the spirit and dynamism of this elemental jazz form.

The role of specialist, independent companies has always been a significant factor in promoting the music, up to the present day. They have been active in recording new artists, re-recording new material by established pianists, and issuing previously unreleased material by these pianists, whereas the national companies, lacking commercial incentive, have tended to issue boogie-woogie collections compiled from masters held in their record archives—all previously released. The independents are, or have been, run by enthusiasts for enthusiasts.

One of the earliest ventures, in the 1940s, was the Circle Record company of jazz scholar and critic Rudy Blesh. He was author of *Shining Trumpets*—containing a considerable amount of useful comment on barrelhouse and boogie-woogie—and with Harriet Janis coauthored the seminal book *They All Played Ragtime*, which described the important pianists and social history surrounding this original American music. One of Blesh's purposes in starting the Circle company was to establish the link between African music and jazz. Blesh, like others of the period, believed passionately in causality between the two, whereas other critics sided with the view that cultural influences were equally important in shaping the music and its various offshoots. Some of his more important releases were of Morton's Library of Congress recordings from 1938 and veteran jazz musicians George Lewis (clarinet) and the Dodds brothers (clarinet and drums, respectively).

Blesh was to release rare recordings by Montana Taylor, such as the somber "Rotten Break Blues"—some were taken from his radio show *This Is Jazz* in 1947—and by Freddie Shayne in the company of Bertha Chippie Hill, Lee Collins, and others on the rugged "How Long Blues." Seven titles were recorded in Chicago by Taylor in one thirty-five-minute session, much to the amazement and delight of the studio engineers. A short time before this session, Taylor had been located working as a roof tiler. Blesh later purchased the Solo Art masters from Dan Qualey and, in turn, sold them in the 1950s to the Riverside Record Company. Some of the recordings were released before that company was sold to George Buck for issue on his Jazzology label. Buck has been true to the piano tradition established by Blesh with regular reissues of Circle material.

Other independent companies, to which earlier reference has been made, and whose owners made their own distinctive contributions to recording boogie-woogie pianists, are Milt Gabler's Commodore label and Phil Featheringill's Session label. Albert Ammons's first recordings in February 1944, after the lifting of the Petrillo recording ban, were made for Commodore and included the then unissued solo "Reveille Boogie," based on the army camp "wake-up" bugle motif, and the silky-smooth composite tune "Blues in the Groove" (two takes) with his Rhythm Kings, to which Vic Dickenson's trombone gives a forceful, driving edge. The Session releases will long be remembered for the superlative Yancey solo "At the Window" (1943). Based on the well-known theme of "Five O'Clock Blues," it progresses slowly with a deep-running emotional quality.

Karl Emil Knudsen, who died in 2003, founded the Storyville record label, which was once described as the "European Blue Note." Knudsen was a member of a group of jazz and blues enthusiasts in his native Denmark in his teen years and translated this interest into an active collection and resale of imported recordings from America and Great Britain. After giving up his engineering studies prematurely to pursue his musical interests, he diversified and started a successful concert agency that brought traditional jazz groups to Denmark from Great Britain led by Humphrey Lyttleton, Chris Barber, and others. From 1956 until the mid-1960s, he concentrated on releasing blues, and several pianists were recorded during their Danish tours. Of particular interest are recordings by Champion Jack Dupree, Memphis Slim, and Sam Price. Other pianists of note to be recorded live were Sunnyland Slim (1963), Dink Johnson, Otis Spann, Roosevelt Sykes, Speckled Red, and Eurreal Montgomery on *Little Brother Montgomery: Deep South Piano* (Storyville, SLP 228). In his search for completeness, Knudsen also identified the source of, and released, several of the more esoteric air shots and amateur recordings of boogie-woogie pianists dating from an earlier vintage. These included a number of radio broadcasts of the Trio from the Sherman Hotel in Chicago on *The Boogie-Woogie Trio: Broadcast Recordings from 1939* (Storyville, 670184) and the Yancey and Lofton recordings made for the Session label. Knudsen has made an invaluable contribution to the music in making these recordings available to the public.

The Yazoo company began issuing records in 1967 when its founder, Nick Perls (1942–1987) turned an interest in long-forgotten early blues music from the 1920s into a business. Fortunately, his financial circumstances were sound, through the family's ownership of a successful art studio, allowing him to pursue his hobby to the benefit of record collectors, although the releases on this New York based company were not money spinners. They were frequently made from old recordings, of which only one or two copies existed. On one occasion, he was said to have spent twenty thousand dollars on purchasing a collection of rare 78 rpm recordings. In later years, he included Cajun, Gaellic folk music, and Reggae in his catalog. The label was purchased by Shanachie Records in 1987, and they are attempting to keep the Yazoo recordings available in their catalog.

Perl's interest in early blues is reflected in a reissue from 1969 of an album of piano and guitar duets on which Charlie Spand and Blind Blake are included alongside Leroy Carr and Scrapper Blackwell. Another interesting issue, using rare original recordings, features the dissimilar solo talents of Lofton and Davis on *Cripple Clarence Lofton and Walter Davis* (Yazoo, L-102-5).

A more recent venture has been the cooperation between the Yazoo label and Francis Wilford Smith, who has added selected gems from his extensive record collection to their catalog. To date, releases have covered two volumes of St. Louis pianists; early recordings of Roosevelt Sykes, Lee Green, and Charlie Spand; and thematic titled releases such as *Barrelhouse Women* and *Shake Your Wicked Knee*.

It is fortunate that a few dedicated members of the fraternity of blues collectors have taken that extra step and started recording artists themselves. Those having done so have found it economically prudent to run their recording ventures alongside a mail-order side selling new and secondhand records. One such venture is the Arhoolie label started by Chris Strachwitz (1931–), who emigrated from Germany to America with his family at the end of World War II. His education was completed in America, where he eventually took up citizenship and is now living in the Santa Barbara area of California. Strachwitz has a broad interest in African-American music, of which blues is a part. From its inception in 1967, the company has released new recordings with reissued material from an earlier era. Strachwitz's interests have also widened to accommodate Mexican and zydeco music. He helped nurture the emerging talents of the young Katie Webster in the mid-1980s, and his label introduced boogie-woogie record collectors to the piano-pounding, massively voiced Big Joe Duskin whom he recorded in 1977. A later release from 1981 was vintage Albert Ammons drawing from his Mercury sides ("Baltimore Breakdown," etc.) and Solo Art ("Monday Struggle") on *Albert Ammons: The King Of* (Blues Classics, 27 1981).

Bob Koestler (1932–), possessing a similar outlook to Strachwitz, started the Delmark label in 1953—claiming with some justification to be one of the older independent labels. Born in Wichita, Kansas, Koester acquired a taste for jazz and blues from seeing and hearing the Count Basie band with vocalist Jimmy Rushing and the Lionel Hampton band. He began his venture with the release of a traditional jazz group, the Windy City Six, while living in St. Louis. His first blues recording was of Speckled Red in 1956 after that pianist had been rediscovered by policeman Charlie O'Brien. Koester settled in Chicago where he opened the Jazz Record Mart, a record store of international reputation. During this time, he purchased some of the remaining Paramount masters, probably from John Steiner, with the added attraction of being able to release some of the early recordings of blues chanteuse Ma Rainey. One of the more interesting boogie-woogie issues dating from 1998 has been of the Trio's appearance at the Hotel Sherman (1939), which also includes previously unreleased recordings of Albert Ammons and Meade Lux Lewis entertaining a group of blues experts, one of whom was Bill Russell, at the Frank Lyons studios in 1938, shortly before the first Spirituals to Swing concert (see chapter 7). These are on *Albert Ammons with Meade Lux Lewis and Pete Johnson: Boogie Woogie Stomp* (Delmark, 705).

As we have seen, Moses Asch was actively recording Meade Lux Lewis for his Asch and Stimson labels during the mid-1940s. He was another émigré who arrived in New York City from Europe with his parents in 1914. His father was recognized as one of the most influential Jewish writers. Asch's early musical interests lay in folk music, and he recorded Pete Seeger, Woody Guthrie, and Leadbelly while showing support for left-wing politics. With his death in 1985, the entire stock of his record catalog was bequeathed to the Smithsonian Institute, which had the foresight to recognize it as an important cultural legacy. Arising from this, the Folkways label came into being and continues today, having retained the most important of Asch's recordings in its catalog. Asch recorded widely from within the blues and blue-grass genres, but the talents of Mary Lou Williams and several of the boogie-woogie players, Yancey and Johnson included, appeared on an issue in 1953 called *Jazz, Volume 9: Jazz Piano Greats* (Folkways, FW 02809).

Probably the shortest-lived but one of the most aggressively independent record companies was the Riverside label that was active from 1952 until 1956. It was started in New York by two followers of traditional jazz and blues, Orin Keepnews and Bill Grauer. Originally dedicated to releasing music long in the public domain, it moved into the modern jazz field with the signing of pianists Thelonious Monk and, later, Bill Evans. In 1963, Bill Grauer was killed in a car crash and Riverside closed down, selling its stock to ABC Paramount, who resold it to Fantasy Records where it currently remains (some piano masters ended up with Jazzology). The first important releases, from the point of view of piano blues, were the very scarce Solo Art recordings of Ammons and Johnson, followed by

Yancey's Solo Art recordings released on the London label *Jimmy Yancey: A Lost Recording Date* (London, AL 3525). A two-volume set of early players was also compiled, namely, *Pioneers of Boogie-Woogie, Volumes 1 and 2* (Riverside, RLP 1009 & 1034) with numbers by Cow Cow Davenport, Jabo Williams, and Charlie Spand. All these releases were of inestimable benefit to collectors from a later age who had missed the rapid rise and fall of the Solo Art Company.

A small Chicago-based label undertaking important recordings in the blues and gospel fields is Sirens Records. It has been run since its inception in 1975 by Steven Dolins, an enthusiastic pianist and committed archivist whose aim has been to record for posterity contemporary pianists living and working in that city. The first collection dating from 1976 entitled *Heavy Timbre Chicago Boogie Piano* (Sirens, SR5002) contains performances by Willie Mabon, Sunnyland Slim, Jimmy Walker, Erwin Helfer, and Blind John Davis and was recorded while the players performed for each other at an informal studio party. The record has since been reissued with additional tracks and remains a weighty musical statement of the different sounds made by the top Chicago pianists of the day. Following this first venture, Dolins concentrated on his full-time career in a higher education institution for several years until he renewed his acquaintance with Erwin Helfer in the early 2000s. His enthusiasm rekindled, he immediately released Helfer's quirkily titled *I'm Not Hungry but I Like to Eat Blues* (Sirens, SR-5001) in 2001 and, in the same year, solos by Chuck "Barrelhouse" Goering—a younger pianist, born in 1959, who displays a promising and sincere talent for singing and playing the blues, much of it absorbed from close contacts with Little Brother Montgomery and John Davis. Goering can be heard to good effect on *Barrelhouse Chuck: Prescription for the Blues* (Sirens, SR 5004), sharing some of the pieces with Helfer.

One of the most recent releases by Sirens adds a colorful postscript to our knowledge of Chicago in the rent-party days. This is the recording of a long-forgotten interview between Doug Suggs and Erwin Helfer dating from 1956, in which references are made to Pinetop Smith and other early pianists. Two, previously unknown pieces, "Smoke Like Lightning" and "Slow and Low" by Suggs are included—the latter sounds like an amalgam of his two earlier recordings made for Helfer, in collaboration with William Russell, that were originally released on the Tone LP *Primitive Piano* in 1957 together with Speckled Red, James Robinson, and Billie Pierce. After the record rights had passed through several hands, they became the property of Dolins. All these pianists can now be heard on the reissued *Primitive Piano* (Sirens, SR 5005) dating from 2003. One can only hope that Dolins will remain an active and committed record producer and seek out more talent for his label.

In Holland, the Oldie Blues Label run by former policeman Martin van Olderon has filled an important gap for collectors, particularly during the 1970s, by releasing many previously unobtainable early recordings by Lewis, Ammons, and Johnson on vinyl. New recordings by pianists Blind John Davies and Mark Lincoln Braun were also cut. The record company that has probably made the greatest contribution to ensuring that the accepted traditions of piano blues and boogie-woogie music are not forgotten, however, is the Document label. The founder is Johnny Parth, an Austrian based in Vienna. Their recordings were initially issued on vinyl under the Flyright and Matchbox labels before the Document series commenced in the 1960s. Parth's intention has been to issue all the twenty thousand or so blues recordings spanning the early years of the twentieth century up to the 1950s, based on the discographical information contained in the aforementioned bluesman's bible *Blues and Gospel Records 1902–1943* compiled by R. M. Dixon and J. Godrich. It is a testament to Parth's commitment that he achieved this ambition before recently selling the company to business interests in the United Kingdom. Some of the early releases suffered from surface noise because they were not always the cleanest copies for recording purposes due to their rarity (c.f. "House Lady Blues" by Jabo Williams). That appears to be mainly in the past now, and recent issues have benefited from the painstaking work of sound engineers such as the late John R. T. Davies. A good example of the successful application of this technique can be experienced by the improvements made to the wire recordings of Phil Kiely and Dick Mushlitz at the apartment of Jimmy and Estelle Yancey in 1951, *The Unissued 1951 Yancey Wire Recordings* (Document, DOCD- 1007). This is one example of how rare, usually private recordings have now become available to collectors through the efforts of diligent researchers and the generosity of the owners who willingly share their treasures with others.

Until recent times, one gap in the recordings of the Trio was the period during World War II when they appeared on radio in Jubilee Shows organized for the American armed forces and on film sound tracks. Another omission was from their time at the Café Society clubs where air shots had been made but never commercially released. These are presently available on Document on *Pete Johnson: Radio broadcasts, Film Soundtracks, Alternate Takes 1939– circa 1947* (DOCD 1009) and *Rare Live Cuts: Café Society (1939) Airchecks and Milwaukee (1943)* (DOCD 1003). Now that this mammoth recording task has been completed, Document has left us with an important historical legacy covering the broad sweep of African-American blues, in all its manifestations. The new owners cite in the region of nine hundred CDs being available to the blues enthusiast.

Finally, in recognizing the contribution of independent record companies to sponsoring boogie-woogie and blues pianists, we close with an unpretentious label run by the late Charlie Booty entitled Piano Joys but unfortunately no longer issuing further recordings. The title of "unpretentious" refers only to the informal nature of the events and the tape recorders set up to capture the immediacy of pianists in full flow at the many weekend parties held in Fort Worth, Newburgh, and Evansville. The recording sessions date from the mid-1970s through the 1990s. The generic title given to the CDs is *Rent Party Echoes*. At the last count there were seven CDs, the last issue being *Rent Party Shuffle, Volume 7: Leyland, Gilman, Booty, Mason and Mushlitz, Evansville* (Piano Joys, RPE, PJO 19). The music is vital, certainly dynamic, and nearly always creative when it is played by, among others, Charlie Booty, Charlie Castner, Tom Harris, Ben Conroy, George Green, and the younger generation, represented by Carl Leyland. Since the death of Booty, the *Rent Party Echoes* series is now distributed by Puppy Jazz, a Florida-based group with most of the records available on their website.

Recording progressed to a new level with the advent of ten- and twelve-inch long-playing (LP) vinyl records, which, unlike the hazards associated with the shellac 78 revolutions per minute (rpm) records, are virtually unbreakable. A later development saw the introduction of smaller seven-inch extended players (EPs). These were, in the main, superseded by tapes—largely obsolete in 2009—compact discs (CDs), and other more sophisticated digital systems, although there has been a recent resurgence of interest in LPs with some companies recommencing their issue. The perceived advantage of the LP when it was introduced was its compatibility with extended improvisations without the need to cut off an artist's efforts after three minutes or so, which occurred with shellac recordings. The first LP was issued by Columbia in 1948, but other companies soon followed suit, leading to a wholesale change in the listening habits of music followers. Boogie-woogie benefited in several ways with the reissuing of many recordings long absent from the "race" catalogs. For example, those of Will Ezell, Cow Cow Davenport, Pinetop Smith, and others are still in circulation at auctions and secondhand record markets. Additionally, many of the earlier recordings of Lewis, Johnson, and Ammons were made available to a younger group of collectors through LP reissues. Under the late John Hammond's guidance, those shellac records from the period 1938–1941 were re-reissued by Columbia, together with numbers by Jimmy Yancey and Jack Dupree on *The Original Piano Giants: John Hammond Collection* (Columbia LP, KC 32708). A second album containing many of the important contributors to the two Spiritual to Swing concerts was initially released on two LPs, *John Hammond's "Spiritual to Swing" 1938/1939* (Vogue, VJD 550). This material, together with extra numbers from the concerts, has subsequently been released on CD.

Another technical advance, already referred to, has been the improvement of previously distorted old recordings and, at the least, the removal of the surface noise so apparent on many original shellac recordings, even when electronically recorded. Some collectors believe this to be a retrograde step, arguing that the cleaned-up versions have lost authenticity and the sharpness of the tone of the originals. There have certainly been some insensitive modifications to original recordings, particularly when the "top" has been removed from the overall tone in an effort to remove surface noise. However, in the hands of expert sound engineers such as the late Robert Parker and John R. T. Davies, the results are a definite enhancement of the original. For an example listen to the clarity of the verbal exchanges and the piano treble work on "Jump Steady Blues" by Pinetop Smith on *Jazz Classics in Digital Stereo, Chicago, Volume 2* (BBC, CD 589) and compare with the original untouched release on Vocalion from 1929. Another factor adding to the aural experience is the stereophonic effect produced by engineers, which allows individual instruments and vocalists, within an ensemble, to be heard more distinctly with greater clarity and a fuller tone

Alongside the growth of sophisticated recording techniques has been a concern for attractive packaging, giving a welcome artistic element to the design of LP album covers, which peaked in the late 1950s and 1960s. The movement began in the prewar years when Alex Steinway, a designer for the Columbia Record Company, dispensed with standard record labels and introduced more attractive covers, using original art. Mike Reid of Blue Note picked up this trend and helped define that company's distinctive jazz aura. The doyen of album art was David Stone Martin (1913–1992), who illustrated in excess of four hundred jazz albums. After training at the Chicago Art Institute, he worked as a graphic designer before becoming a freelance artist. Martin's work is much sought after, with examples on view at the Metropolitan Museum of Art in New York and the Smithsonian Institute. His gift lay in capturing the essence of jazz through hand-painted sketches of figures and shapes overlaying variously colored background washes, thus giving a vital and relevant quality to the covers. He added a sophisticated quality to many LPs and EPs, including the covers of Meade Lux Lewis's *Yancey's Last Ride* and *Cat House Piano* LPs and the more recently released Verve CD album of this music.

As a final comment, the reader should be reminded that the purpose of this chapter has been to identify the major outlets of recorded piano blues and boogie-woogie. The recordings referred to in the text are exemplars of some of the best and most important releases by these record companies. Equally, it should be observed that the recordings mentioned in this chapter and throughout the book may have initially been released on CD, exist on CD as reissued vinyl recordings, or are available only on vinyl or shellac. All types of recording are referred to in the belief that an assiduous collector will want to trace them through secondhand sales, if they are no longer in the catalogs of the record companies. Many older recordings are still available through mail order and on the Internet.

NOTES

1. R. M. W. Dixon and J. Godrich, *Recording the Blues* (London: November Books, 1970).

2. "Boogie-Woogie Music," *Jazz Information*, November 8, 1940, 23.

3. J. Lee Anderson, "The Blue Note Story," *Mississippi Rag*, October 1989, 4. For a review of significant Blue Note recordings, see Whitney Balliett, "Jazz: The Early Blue Notes," *New Yorker*, September 17, 1984, 120–21; and for comment on the Mosaic Record Companies reissues of Blue Note recordings, see Whitney Balliett, "Jazz: The Early Blue Notes (Continued)," *New Yorker*, December 24, 1984, 66–67.

4. Bill Barol, "Sounding the Blue Note," *Newsweek*, March 18, 1983.

5. William Russell, "Reviews," *Hot Record Society Rag*, November 1940, 31.

6. Martin Williams, "Meade Lux Lewis," *Record Changer*, April 1953, 3.

7. Max Harrison, "Boogie-Woogie," in *Jazz*, ed. Nat Hentoff and Albert McCarthy (London: Quartet Books, 1977), 127.

8. Russell, "Reviews," 25.

9. Russell, "Reviews," 33.

10. William Russell, "Three Boogie-Woogie Blues Pianists," in *The Art of Jazz*, ed. Martin Williams (London: Cassell, 1962), 106.

11. William Russell, "Hot Wax: Blue Note Blues," *Jazz Quarterly*, Spring 1943, 29.

12. Edward Morrow and Kyle Crichton, "Dark Magic," *Collier's Magazine*, June 24, 1939, 40, 41, 78, 79.

13. Harrison, "Boogie-Woogie," 130.

14. James Dugan, "Dan Qualey and the Solo Art Record Company," *Hot Record Society Rag*, October 1940, 2–6.

15. Dugan, "Dan Qualey," 6.

16. Art Hodes and Chadwick Hansen, *Hot Man* (Chicago: University of Illinois, 1992), 50.

17. "What's New," *Jazz Information*, September 6, 1940, 5.

18. "New Records," *Jazz Information*, July 26, 1940, 14.

Bass Patterns

This selection of basses shows the resourcefulness and versatility of pianists in producing bass rhythms for their compositions. Where an example is associated with a particular pianist it is referred to in the text.

Bibliography

All Star Boogie-Woogie: Five Piano Solos. New York: Leeds Music, RKO Building Radio City, 1942. Copyright granted to the Peter Maurice Music Co., Ltd. London: Maurice Building, 1942.

Balliett, W. *American Musicians*. New York: Oxford University Press, 1986.

Balliett, W. *Dinosaurs in the Morning*. London: Phoenix House, 1965.

Berlin, E. A. *Ragtime: A Musical and Cultural History*. Berkeley: University of California Press, 1985.

Blesh, R. *Shining Trumpets*. London: Cassell, 1949.

Blesh, R., and H. Janis. *They All Played Ragtime*. London: Sidgwick and Jackson, 1958.

Chilton, J. *Stomp Off Let's Go: The Story of Bob Crosby's Bob Cats and Big Band*. London: Image Publicity, 1983.

Collier, J. L. *The Making of Jazz*. London: Macmillan, 1978.

Collins, M. *Life of Lee Collins (Oh Didn't He Ramble)*. Chicago: Illinois University Press, 1974.

Deicher, S. *Mondrian*. London: Tescher, 1999.

Dixon, R. M. W., and J. Godrich. *Recording the Blues*. London: Studio Vista, 1970.

Duberman, M. *Paul Robeson: A Biography*. New York: New Press, 1989.

DuBois, W. E. B. *The Souls of Black Folk*. London: Longmans, 1965.

Five Boogie-Woogie Piano Solos by Pinetop Smith. New York: Leeds Music Corp, RKO Buildings, 1941. Copyright granted to The Peter Maurice Co., Ltd. London: Maurice Building, 1941.

Garland, P. *The Sound of Soul*. Chicago: Henry Regnery Publishing, 1969.

Hammond, J. *John Hammond on Record*. Harmondsworth, UK: Penguin Books, 1981.

Handy, D. A. *Black Women in American Bands and Orchestra*. Lanham, MD: Scarecrow Press, 1981.

Harris, S. *Blues Who's Who*. New York: Da Capo, 1979.

Hentoff, N., and A. McCarthey, eds. *Jazz*. London: Quartet Books, 1977.

Hodes, A., and C. Hansen. *Hot Man: The Life of Art Hodes*. Chicago: Illinois University Press, 1992.

Hodes, A., and C. Hanson, eds. *Selections from the Gutter*. Berkeley: University of California Press, 1977.

Johns, O. *Times of Our Lives*. New York: Farrar, Straus and Giroux, 1973.

Larkin, C. *Guinness Who's Who of Jazz*. Enfield, UK: Guinness Publishing, 1992.

Levine, L. W. *Black Culture and Black Consciousness*. New York: Oxford Press, 1977.

Lomax, A. *The Land Where the Blues Began*. London: Methuen, 1992.

McIlwaine, S. *Memphis Down in Dixie*. New York: Dutton, 1948.

Oakley, G. *The Devil's Music*. London: BBC Publications, 1976.

Oliver, P., ed. *The Blackwell Guide to Blues Record*. Oxford: Basil Blackwell, 1989.

Oliver, P. *Blues Fell This Morning*. London: Cassell, 1960.

Oliver, P. *Conversation with the Blues*. London: Cassell, 1967. (Second edition, London: Cambridge University Press, 1997).

Oliver, P. *The Story of the Blues*. Harmondsworth, UK: Penguin Books, 1969.

Page, C. *Boogie-Woogie Stomp, Albert Ammons and His Music*. Cleveland: Northeast Ohio Jazz Society, 1997.

Paul, E. *That Crazy (American) Music*. London: F. Mueller Press, 1957.

Plaksin, S. *Jazzwomen 1900 to the Present Day*. London: Pluto Press, 1985.

Ramsey, F., and C. Smith, eds. *Jazzmen*. New York: Harcourt Brace, 1939.

Roberts, J. S. *Black Music of Two Worlds*. New York: Praeger Publishers, 1972.

Rowe, M. *Chicago Breakdown*. London: Eddison Press, 1973.

Schainman Siegel, D. *The Glory Road: The Story of Josh White*. White Hall, VA: Shoe Tree Press, 1991.

Shapiro, N., and N. Hentoff. *Hear Me Talkin' to Ya*. New York: Rinehart, 1955.

Simon, G. T. *The Big Bands*. London: Schirmer Books, Macmillan Publishing, 1981.

Spero, S. D., and H. L. Harris. *The Black Worker*. New York: Columbia University Press, 1931.

Stearns, M. *Jazz Dance*. London: Collier Macmillan, 1968.

Stover, G. H. *The Life and Decline of the American Railroad*. New York: Oxford University Press, 1970.

Todes, C. *Labor and Lumber*. New York: International Publishers, 1931.

Traill, S., and G. Lascelles, eds. *Just Jazz*. London: Peter Davies, 1957.

Travis, D. J. *An Autobiography of Black Jazz*. Chicago: Urban Research Institute, 1983.

Wesley, C. H. *Negro Labor in the United States, 1850–1925*. New York: Vanguard Press, 1927.

Williams, C. *Boogie-Woogie Blues Folio*. New York: Clarence Williams Music Publishing, 1940.

Williams, M., ed. *The Art of Jazz*. London: Cassell, 1962.

Wright, R. *American Hunger*. London: Lowe and Bydone Printers, 1969.

zur Heide, K. G. *Deep South Piano*. London: Studio Vista, 1970.

Zwingenberger, A. *Boogie-Woogie Piano Solos*. Musikverlag GmbH, Hallerstr. 72, 1986.

A selection of magazines, newspapers, and record liner notes providing significant source material on boogie-woogie.

Anderson, J. L. "The BlueNote Story." *Mississippi Rag*, October 1989.

"As Long as They Want Me." *Time*, February 9, 1948.

Conroy, Ben. "Fond Memories of Past Masters." *Mississippi Rag*, June 1991.

Crosbie, Ian. "The Will Bradley-Ray McKinley Orchestra." *Jazz Journal International*, February 1978.

Dugan J., and J. Hammond. "An Early Black Concert from Spirituals to Swing." *Black Perspective in Music* 2 (1979).

Gelter, Doyce K. "What Is Boogie-Woogie? Two Artists Try to Tell." *Milwaukee Journal Green Sheet*, October 11, 1943.

Gleason, Ralph. "A Glance Back at a Boogie Boy." *San Francisco Sunday Chronicle*, June 14, 1964.

Hayakawa, J. "Reflections on the History of Jazz." Conference paper, March 17, 1945, source unknown.

Hill, Don, and Dave Mangurian. "Meade Lux Lewis." *Cadence Jazz Magazine*, October 1987.

"Jam for Jimmy." *Time*, October 1, 1951.

McCurdey, Jack. "Jazzman Meade Lewis Killed in Auto Crash." *Los Angeles Times*, June 8, 1964.

Murrow, Edward, and Chrichton Kyle. "Dark Magic." *Collier's Magazine*, June 24, 1939.

"Obituary of Jimmy Yancey." *New York Times*, September 19, 1951.

Pease, Sharon A. "I Saw Pinetop Spit Blood and Fall: The Life and Death of Clarence Smith, Creator of Boogie-Woogie." *Downbeat*, October 1, 1939.

Pease, Sharon A. "Will Pinetop's Sons Be Great Like Their Dad?" *Downbeat*, October 15, 1939.

Schaffer, William J. "The Art of Boogie-Woogie." *Mississippi Rag*, June 1991.

Taubman, Howard. "A Review of Negro Music, Given at Carnegie Hall." *New York Times*, December 24, 1938.

"Uptown Boogie-Woogie." *Time*, October 21, 1940.

RECORDINGS

Liner notes for the following recordings:

Albert Ammons: Boogie-Woogie Stomp, Delmark Records, CD 705.

The Barrelhouse Blues of Speckled Red, Folkways, FG 3555.

Boogie-Woogie Story, vols. 1 and 2, Milan Jazz, CD 887795 and CD 887796.

Buster Pickens, Flyright Records, FLY LP 536.

Henry Brown Blues, 77 Records, 77-LA-12-5.

Jazz Volume 10: Boogie-Woogie, Jump and Kansas City, Folkways FJ 2910.

The Magpie Piano Blues, vols. 1–21 (LP series also on CD).

Pete Johnson Radio Broadcasts, Film Soundtracks, Alternative Takes [1939–c. 1947], Document, DOCD 1007.

Robert Shaw, Arhoolie, LP 1010, distributed in the UK by Topic Records.
Rugged Piano Classics, Origin Records, OJL 15.
Sam Price and His Texas Bluesicians, Whiskey, Women Record Co., KM 704.
Uptown Boogie: The Great Unheard Performances, Catfish Records, CD KATCD 132.

MAGAZINES, PERIODICALS, AND NEWSPAPERS

The following magazines (though many are no longer in print), particularly for the period 1935–1950, are worth examining for record reviews, critiques of pianists, and their movements.

78 Quarterly
American Music
The Black Perspective in Music
Blues Unlimited
Cadence
Downbeat
Hot Record Society Rag
IARC Magazine
Jazz Information
Jazz Illustrated
Jazz Journal International
Jazz Monthly
Jazz Quarterly
Jazz Record
Jazz Report
Jazz Times USA/Canada
Le Jazz Hot
Living Blues
Memories and Jazz Report
Metronome
Mississippi Rag
Musician Magazine
New Yorker Magazine
Record Changer
Reflections on the History of Jazz
Storyville
Swing Music

Index

About the Author

Peter J. Silvester was born in Staffordshire, England. After two years spent in the Royal Air Force, he taught in secondary schools and lectured at a teacher training college. He obtained a master's degree from the University of Surrey before moving into government service. His interest in jazz and blues piano, which began in his early teens, has been maintained in adulthood as a record collector, magazine reviewer, sometime broadcaster, and enthusiastic boogie-woogie player.